THE EKPHRASTIC TURN

Inter-art Dialogues

Edited by
Asunción López-Varela Azcárate
Ananta Charan Sukla

THE EKPHRASTIC TURN

Inter-art Dialogues

Edited by
Asunción López-Varela Azcárate
Ananta Charan Sukla

COMMON GROUND PUBLISHING 2015

First published in 2015
as part of the CompLit InterArt Book Series
from the New Directions in the Humanities Book Imprint

Common Ground Publishing
2001 S. 1st St., Suite 202
University of Illinois Research Park
Champaign, IL
61821

Copyright © Asunción López-Varela Azcárate and Ananta Charan Sukla 2015

All rights reserved. Apart from fair dealing for the purposes of study, research, criticism or review as permitted under the applicable copyright legislation, no part of this book may be reproduced by any process without written permission from the publisher.

Library of Congress Cataloging-in-Publication Data

Names: López-Varela, Asunción, editor. | Sukla, Ananta Charana, 1942- editor.
Title: The Ekphrastic turn : inter-art dialogues / edited by Asunción López-Varela ; Ananta Sukla.
Description: Champaign, Illinois : Common Ground Publishing LLC, [2016] | Includes bibliographical references and index. | Description based on print version record and CIP data provided by publisher; resource not viewed.
Identifiers: LCCN 2015046510 (print) | LCCN 2015038950 (ebook) | ISBN 9781612298245 (pbk) | ISBN 9781612298252 (pdf) | ISBN 9781612298245 (pbk : alk. paper) | ISBN 9781612298252 (pdf : alk. paper)
Subjects: LCSH: Intermediality. | Ekphrasis. | Intertextuality. | Language and culture.
Classification: LCC P99.4.I58 (print) | LCC P99.4.I58 E47 2016 (ebook) | DDC 700--dc23
LC record available at http://lccn.loc.gov/2015046510

Cover Photo Credit: Mónica O'Doherty López-Varela
Logo for CompLit InterArt book series Credit: Mónica O'Doherty López-Varela

Table of Contents

Foreword   x
Introduction   xiii

Chapter 1
Intermediality of the Sanskrit Rasa-Dhvani Theory   1
    Ananta Charan Sukla

Chapter 2
Intermedializing Music   13
    Siglind Bruhn

Chapter 3
"How Do I Love Thee?" Infatuation, Passion, and Love in the Novel
and 2004 Film *The Phantom of the Opera*   39
    Deborah Fillerup Weagel

Chapter 4
Musical Patterns in William H. Gass's "A Fugue" and
The Pedersen Kid   55
    Marcin Stawiarski

Chapter 5
The Study of Accordion and Kazakh Culture: An Intermedial
Approach   78
    Zaure Smakova & Medelkhan Konysbayev

Chapter 6
The Dream Ballet: Intermedial Tensions between Music, Dance, and
Language in the Film Musical   96
    Emily Petermann

Chapter 7
Tales of Kabbarli: The Transmutation of Ancient to Modern Culture   108
   Geoffrey Sykes

Chapter 8
Alternative Insights into Comparative Literature: Interdisciplinar, Intercultural, Intersemiotic Dancing Ekphrasis and Transmedial Narrative   130
   Nicoleta Popa Blanariu

Chapter 9
Intermedial Aspects in Egyptian Fayoum Portraits   168
   Marie-Thérèse Abdelmessih

Chaper 10
Zenobia as Spectacle: Captive Queen in Arts and Literature   184
   I-Chun Wang

Chapter 11
Beijing Imaginations: Exploring the A/Effects of Tourist City Photographs   201
   Verena Laschinger

Chapter 12
Intersemiotic Translation in Wáng Wéi's Poem "Dwelling in Mountain and Autumn Twilight"   224
   Qingben Li

Chapter 13
Signs, Intermediality and Chinese Calligraphy   239
   Jinghua Guo

Chapter 14
Language, Meaning and Subjectivity   262
   Susan Petrilli

Chapter 15
Topo-Grapho-Mania: Space-Texts and Text-Spaces in Topographie Idéale pour une agression caractérisée (R. Boudjedra) and Paisajes después de la batalla (J. Goytisolo)   309
    Ilka Kressner

Chapter 16
Multimodal Satire: The Form of the Literary Substance in Japanese Writer Natsume Sōseki's First Feuilleton Novel   329
    Annette Thorsen Vilslev

Chapter 17
Literature 2.0 - Hybrid Cultural Objects in Intermedial Practice: The Case of Romania   345
    Mihaela Ursa

Chapter 18
Intermedialities in Visual Poetry: Futurist "Polyexpressivity" and Net.art   362
    Carolina Fernández Castrillo

Chapter 19
Digital Textuality and its Behaviors   382
    Leonardo Flores

Chapter 20
Cross-perceptual Metamorphosis: From Analogue Art to 3D e-Installation   404
    Asunción López-Varela Azcárate

Foreword

The *CompLit InterArt* book series, part of Humanities Collection, focuses on the importance of storytelling as a catalyst for the constitution, confirmation and modification of human experiences. As members of particular groups and communities, people understand the world as part of an organizational scheme, where individual stories interconnect, and past experiences are used in active problem solving in order to inspire social action and future improvements. Stories can be contemplated as cognitive paradigms that provide frames for meaning making processes, as people identify themselves with the protagonists seeking a better future in cooperation with others who share similar hopes and values.

In order to achieve impact, stories must show people as active agents of change and having a central role in creating solutions for their own problems. Unfortunately, in today's hyper-connected world only the most compelling stories and socio-cultural issues get noticed and shared. Traditionally, studies on storytelling came from disciplines such as history, narratology, comparative literature or semiotics, among others, all of which deal with the study of oral and written discourse. However, today digital media filter most of human experiences through computers and mobile phones. Digitalization has changed the primacy of the word, facilitating the incorporation of text, image, audio and video in a single document/story. This is one of the reasons behind the growth of heterogeneous research on intermediality, that is, the study of interactions across media formats in the same story, and transmediality, the transposition of story patterns across formats.

Since stories embody values and tangible aspects, they are important in enabling human connections in terms of relationships, emotions, and real life events, instead of abstract concepts that some people might find incomprehensible and irrelevant. Contemplating people as actors involved in their own future encourages empathy and inspires others to support collective action. Strategic storytelling helps articulate clearer goals and intentions, understand the context and set specific measurable objectives, explore audience motivations, identify interested groups and target audiences, and motivate, engage and empower people who can contribute ideas and resources to common goals.

Well-crafted stories can communicate abstract and complex ideas in ways that facilitate understanding, raise awareness, encourage people to care, and lead to action and problem solving with regards to our common cultural heritage and environment. Thus, *CompLit InterArt*, seeks to include book contributions that deal with the analysis and interpretation of stories in various media formats, including heritage archaeology, architecture, sculpture and visual media and film, dance and performance studies, or electronic literature and net-art, among others. It will explore the manifold ways in which images, discourses, communicated experiences, and stories behind them, can actually bring about change and social empowerment through specific attention to their multimodal peculiarities. While textual communication employs particular ways to tell stories, images use a different semiotic system, perhaps with a greater potential to favour communication across boundaries of language and culture. Volumes in the series will explore how people experience cultural heritage in various format forms. They will also study to what extent people's values are in line with public interpretation heritage programs, and how interpretative techniques and technologies can help foster public opinion and civic engagement in cultural patrimony.

The final goal is to illuminate theoretical and practical questions concerning the relations between art, communication formats, and new media, as well as their impact and innovation potential. In this way, the book series will involve theoretical and practical cross-fertilization over media as well as cultural borders, including interdisplinary forms of inquiry (media and communication, translation studies, semiotics, narratology, digital art etc.), and provide a historiographical background that helps to frame the evolution of art and media forms as well as the current debate on the topic of intermediality and transmediality in the context of storytelling.

The series places emphasis on the storytelling aspects of intermedial and transmedial configurations, seeking to inquire into their role of artistic practices in the construction of particular communal and cultural processes. In this sense, it can contribute to build a bridge between theoretical academic research and social practices in organizations and their missions related to art (museums, institutions, public and private enterprises, the fashion and tourist industry, and so on). The series also participates in the promotion of emerging art forms, and on their impact on storytelling and its dissemination and assimilation by broad audiences. From the technological side, it will stimulate the use of digital tools in order to integrate people's experiences into common narratives and storylines, involving paradigm changes in dramaturgy, audio-visual media, space-time digital architecture, digital archiving, memory and heritage studies.

Among the goals of the series is to contribute to thinking storytelling as a strategical tool to capture people's attention and mobilize them to take action. It will also explore technologies for new forms of digital storytelling. For example, stereoscopic and auto-stereoscopic displays, or forms of incorporating data onto intelligent clothing can be explored in order to regulate dance performances. These new environments can also be highly personalized and connected to all kinds of social and professional networks. Audio-visual sculptures can transform buildings and landscapes into ambient art, and OLED walls bring immersive three-dimensional communication into our homes, incorporating 3D landscapes that will change the atmosphere of our living rooms opening windows to world stories. 3D acquisition systems allow to compute the spatial data of objects, buildings and landscapes in order to redesign, reshape and reconstruct new worlds. All these devices allow constant connection among people and, thus, a permanent delivery of stories.

CompLit InterArt also seeks to document discussions with leading agents in areas related to art and storytelling; for example, brand and marketing strategies, business and non-profit organizations, entertainment, technology and institutions with a focus on social sciences and humanities. In this sense, contributions are welcome that pay attention to new reception and crowdfunding models, exploring the power of storytelling in networked communication, and its reach and influence for the protection of cultural heritage, environmental well-being and vulnerable situations in the world. The series seeks to enable the fruitful discussions, coming from interdisciplinary methodologies, and inspire cooperation among digital developers, multimedia-based artworks and information technologies, research institutions as well as private enterprises interested in the power of art and storytelling and content-wise forms of art.

Introduction

As a part of the book series *CompLit InterArt*, in the Humanities Collection, *The Ekphrastic Turn: InterArt Dialogues*, emerging from a special volume of the *Journal of Comparative Literature and Aesthetics* (Vol.XXXVI:2013) guest-edited by Asunción López-Varela, seeks to enhance the awareness of the materiality and mediality of cultural practices, exploring how a given medium may thematize, evoke, and sometimes imitate elements and structures of another medium. The collection of papers provides concrete examples of how narratological patterns may or may not operate, depending on the specificity of the medium, when expressed through musical, visual, gestural or electronic means. These conversions redefine the act of storytelling, showing how physical features of the art work are inseparable from the function they perform for individuals and cultures. Contributors to the collection explore various categories of intermedial and inter-art storytelling, situating their inquiry in a global context, including research from Asia, Europe, Australia and America.

Traditionally, the transposition of art (ekphrasis; from ancient Greek 'speak') across media included writing, painting, sculpture, the performing arts, music or film, and was the way by means of which artistic representations shared sense experiences. In order to incorporate sensorial aspects from human real life experiences in their works, artists have always drawn analogies with other artistic forms. An effective way to recall the sense of smell in textual formats is, for instance, by means of the visualization of food, either in the form of images, or by means of metaphorical descriptions, as in the story by Patrick Süskind, *The Perfume* (1985), all of which trigger synesthetic mechanisms in the brain.

Although transpositions of art across media have often been part of artistic practices, the explosion of visuality in the 20th-century western art was related to the impact of changing technologies for cheaper image reproduction (fundamentally photography and moving pictures or cinema). The experiments of the early avant-garde art, particularly by the Surrealists and Futurists, foregrounded the material aspects of language by focusing on graphical coding as well as the acoustic and visual aspects. They also opened the art work to their audiences, and removed partially or entirely the semantic content of discourse, anticipating many contemporary experimental digital works.

Digitalization has enabled easier, faster and cheaper interplay between texts, images, music, video, causing a renewed interest in intermedial studies since the 1990s. The term 'intermedia' was first used in 1963 by English poet-composer

Dick Higgins to describe the artistic activities of the Fluxus movement. Since then, intermedial studies have sought to unveil the composite working of various formats (image, text, audio, video), which engage various perceptual modalities in what has come to be known as multimodality. The term transmediality is more appropriate in relation to the transposition of artistic characteristic across media formats, mainly following narrative patterns, that is, storytelling. For instance, a Harry Potter novel, turned into film and, later, into a game in DVD or online format. It is important to mention that not all artistic works seek to tell a meaningful story. There are cases of concrete poetry, for instance, designed to capture the audience's attention but not to provide any particular meaning. Some of their digital counterparts, pieces of e-poetry for example, may allow active engagement (interactivity), without telling a story or providing any concrete meaning.

***

The volume opens with a chapter by the prestigious Indian professor, Ananta Charan Sukla who explores Sanskrit poetics in order to examine the concepts of *rasa*, an aesthetic experience that arises among theatrical audiences, and among the readers of literature due to a verbal potency called *dhvani*. Sukla poses an inquiry into the origins of the inter-art discussion as he examines ancient arguments in Sanskrit aesthetics to conclude that the generation of *rasa* is confined only to audio-visual and verbal arts, such as theatre and poetry, whereas *dhvani,* as a specific linguistic potency, is strictly confined to the verbal arts, not present in non-verbal arts such as dance and music.

Equally splendid is the chapter by Prof. Siglind Bruhn, one of the world's leading experts on musicology. First, she explores how works of literature and the visual arts may respond to music. Then she looks at the reverse situation. Bruhn offers an incredibly rich overview, packed with many concrete examples that illustrate how verbal or visual utterances attempt to appear as music, and also how verbal or visual utterances appear in music and musical performance.

Deborah Fillerup Weagel, an expert on adaptation and cinema, examines the interconnection of Gaston Leroux's novel *The Phantom of the Opera* and its 2004 film adaptation, showing how adaptations, whether created for stage, film, or for some other medium, can elaborate on the original source. The essay also proposes that regardless of the differences between the novel, the film, or other adaptations, the features of storytelling remain constant, as all the productions focus on the love triangle between the Phantom, Christine Daeé, and Raoul, Vicomte de Chagny.

Continuing with aesthetic intermedialities of sound, Marcin Stawiarski explores musico-literary intermediality in two works by the American novelist, short story writer, essayist, critic, and former philosophy professor William H. Gass. The chapter focuses on Gass's conception and use of language, musicality and musicalization in "A Fugue", a passage from *The Tunnel* (1995), and *The Pedersen Kid* (1961). In contrast to "A Fugue"'s overt musicalization, "The Pedersen Kid" exemplifies covert musicalization, where there seems to be a possibility of a transmedial transformation of both narrative time and sentence time (transtemporality), and which entails simultaneity, but more fundamentally, the possibility of regulating density and intensity of language zones, building up areas of tension and release around recursive and circular patterns, an intermedial texture that conveys semiotic meanings that allow an experiential (emotional) understanding of the content.

On a similar key, the chpater by Zaure Smakova and Medelkhan Konysbayev uses an interdisciplinary approach that draws on scientific works as well as on narrative sources of Kazakh oral historiography to offer integral image of the development of performance studies in *accordion* in the republic of Kazakhstan and to evaluate their significance and role in the establishment of a national musical style.

Moving towards performance, Emily Petermann considers the intermedial tensions between music, dance, and language in Hollywood film musicals. In particular, she studies the MGM Freed Unit productions of the 1940s and 1950s, characterized by a tension between the book or narrative and the musical numbers or song and dance interludes, where the numbers, far provide important commentary on the themes and actions of the film. Petermann finds that these segments are exploited in order to express emotions, fantasies and dreams that may have been censored by the characters' rational selves, and she terms this 'dream ballet'. Thus, her chapter examines the role of 'dream ballet' inquiring into the intermedial opposition of dance and speech and the way they are consigned to separate realms as serving mutually exclusive functions.

With regards to drama, the chapter by playwright and semiotician Geoffrey Sykes explores his own production *Tales of Kabbarli* which looks at the transmutation of ancient Australian rites to modern culture. His play depicts the life and thoughts of the iconic Australian figure, Daisy Bates, who in the first half of the 20th century lived with aboriginal tribes in the Australian continent. Sykes examines several stage productions in three main periods and with three different performers over several decades in order to draw attention to the remarkable inter-medial characteristics in the relationship between performers and audiences as well as the flux of intuitively conscious authorial choices in the development of the script.

Continuing with choreographic discourse, Nicoleta Popa Blanariu explores the level in which the semio-narrative categories and the Greimasian actantial model might be relevant for the understanding of dance. In particular, her study considers choreographies inspired by literary (pre)text or pre-established narrative frames. The author finds that in dance, gestural statements can be narratively semantized, caught – and thus clarified – within a story and within a constitutive aesthetics of ambiguity.

After covering the intermedial inter-artistic patterns of sound and music, performance and dance, this volume looks at artistic paintings. Looking at the "Intermedial aspects in Egyptian Fayoum portraits," Marie-Thérèse Abdel Messih, finds that these Egyptian icons from the Greco-Roman period, contest binary positions in viewing images from the past. Their execution had an aesthetic and ritual purpose, a paradoxical nature synchronizing sacred and profane, figurative and non-figurative languages, as well as intermediating Egyptian and Greek. The translation of the layers of meaning embedded in the portraits engages us in crossing and re-crossing previously set demarcations dividing temporalities, historical locations and disciplines, opening grounds for re-thinking East West dialogues.

Similarly, the chapter by I-Chun Wang explores the intermedial dialogue with historical memory, focusing on the story of the captive queen Zenobia as represented in western historical writing and visual arts. This study brings to light Zenobia's cultural identity, the symbolic meaning of the spectacle in Aurelian's triumph and Rome's disciplining system, thus unveiling the conditions of colonial encounters based on coercion, inequality and conflict. The moral duplicity present in colonial depictions both with regards to the experiences of the colonized and the colonizers, as well as the forms of transmediality used to thematize history, create a formal doubleness that impacts directly on the act of recollection, blurring the differences between historical fact and myth. Here transmediality, as defined by Werner Wolf (2011) can be seen on the level of content in myths which have become cultural scripts and have lost their relationship to an original text or medium.

Continuing with the visual arts, Verena Laschinger explores her own photographic representations of the city of Beijing as the effects of affects, in order to show how photographic narration follows the circuits of physical perception. The chapter aims to explore how city photography makes the urban environment both accessible, while simultaneously changing and creating it in its own right.

The chapter by Li Quingben also rethinks art and aesthetics from experience, proposing philosophy as a way of life, the hermeneutics of understanding the legitimacy of popular art and somaesthetics, a theory of aesthetics forwarded by Richard Shusterman, both based on the concept of non-duality which is also the basis of Li Quingben's own theory of complex cross-cultural crossings. In this paper, Li focuses on a well-known poem by Chinese writer Wang Wei, highlighting comparative translation as a mode of transcultural intermediality. It shows how translation, expressed in Saussurean terms, which operates the transfer of an instance of parole (message in Jakobson's formulation) from one langue (code) to another, is impracticable in cases of languages as distinct as Chinese and English, for instance, where elements in code are not just dependent on particular orders and rules, but on relations that are not operated under principles based on the duality between the concept (signified) and its acoustic image (signifier), as Saussure claimed. A translator from Chinese would be unable to leave content/meaning of signifiers intact, and would need to adapt it to the signified, that is, the new set of rules and ideas of the translated language which, in some cases, cultural factors may even render untranslatable.

Jinghua Guo offers insights into the intermediality of Chinse Calligraphy by showing how the soul of fine arts in China, calligraphy maintains a close rapport with Chinese cultural development. Her study aims to explore the iconic correspondences between Chinese calligraphy and their subject-matter, and develop their intermedial potential.

Continuing with topographical intermedial relations, Ilka Kressner examines the presence of Paris in two novels by exile authors Rachid Boudjedra and Juan Goytisolo. In their works Paris, the three-dimensional interlocutor of the narrations, becomes a discursive formation that revisits and subverts many images generally associated with the French capital. "Paris," is re-signified in writing. In return the material palimpsest shapes the narratives on the syntactic, semantic and narrative levels.

The chapter by Annette Thorsen Vilslev investigates *I Am a Cat* (*Wagahai ha neko de aru*, 1905), the first feuilleton novel by Japanese writer Natsume Sōseki, a study on the workings of multimodal satire and the subversion of the Aristotelian plot from the perspective of the feuilleton form, told through the eyes of a small cat. The paper focuses on the differences between western and Japanese narrative models, alongside Franco Moretti's claims in his *Conjetures*.

Sōseki's work was in many ways at the heart of Karatani's work, which Moretti mentions within the development of literature on a larger world historical scale.

In her chapter, Susan Petrilli presents the 19th century scholar of signs and language Victoria Lady Welby, a contemporary of Charles S. Peirce with whom she exchanged ideas, regularly corresponding with him during the last decade of their lives. On the background of the re-discovery of her work is the transition in sign and communication studies from so-called "decodification semiotics" to "interpretation semiotics" with respect to which Welby's work is a contribution and indicator of where sign studies lead today.

In "Literature 2.0 - Hybrid Cultural Objects in Intermedial Practice. The Case of Romania", Mihaela Ursa proposes first a theoretical and methodological framework for the intermedial study of world literature, on three levels of intermediality. She argues that, while the existing system of disciplines involved in the study of world literature is in need of an intermedial approach, there is also a new body of hybrid cultural objects that needs a frame of understanding, outside traditional disciplinary borders and outside canonical frontiers. The proposed concept of "literature 2.0" is meant to give intermedial semiotic identity to these hybrids that are no longer literature in the proper sense, but still have literary features, in spite of their digital interactivity. The concept is introduced via selected examples from present-day Romanian culture, to illustrate the challenges of intermediality as a practice of research in world literature.

In "Intermedialities in Visual Poetry: Futurist "Polyexpressivity" and net.art," Carolina Fernández Castrillo investigates the crucial role of Futurist visual poetry as starting point in the creation of an interconnected and expansive net of interdependencies between traditional artistic branches and new media in the Western world. At the beginning of the 20th-century, Filippo Tommaso Marinetti and his colleagues launched their systematic program of action as a result of the impact of new technologies on their creative process. They coined neologisms as "polyexpressivity" or "multisensoriality" to define the essence of their cultural productions based on the equivalence and the mixing of media to stimulate and implicate the participant in the construction of a total artwork.

Leonardo Flores's chapter on "Digital Textuality and its Behaviors" would seem to pose some difficulties to the conception of the total artwork, since digital textuality poses variations upon the design of writing spaces that challenge cultural expectations of how to operate the page, for instance. The chapter argues that a writer who uses a computer to design a writing and reading environment creates a space for text where the potential interactions between its elements—linguistic codes, textual appearance, behaviors, and interface—are open to the writer's expressive needs. His essay also presents and discusses a typology of textual behaviour and offers examples of electronic poetry (or e-poetry), perhaps the most concentrated use of language in digital media, as a model of the potential of digital textuality.

Because digital technologies enable a greater interplay of perceptual modes and open the way to the contemporary blending of artistic domains, the chapter by Asunción López-Varela traces the roots of analogic patterns in inter-art comparisons in Western culture, showing how the introduction of digitalization in the second half of the 20th century, and the discussion on ekphrasis has given way to a growing interest on the intermedial aspects of representation. She focuses on the possibilities open by 3D and virtual reality (VR) technologies for the preservation, dissemination and production of media art. In particular, she presents on a project called "e-Installation" which takes its name from the idea of the 'e-Book' as the electronic version of a book extrapolating this analogy to media art installations. Initiated and hosted by ZAK, the Centre for Cultural and General Studies, and the Intelligent Sensor-Actuator Systems Laboratory at Karlsruhe Institute of Technology (KIT), the project virtualizes art installations by means of advanced 3D modelling, virtual reality (VR) and telepresence technologies in order to allow the virtual re-enactment of works of media art that are no longer performable or exhibited, enabling a very high level of synesthetic immersion.

CHAPTER 1

Intermediality of the Sanskrit *Rasa-Dhvani* Theory

Ananta Charan Sukla

Rasa as a critical term is used first by a mythical sage named Bharata (4th C. B.C.– 1st C. A.D.) in his treatise on dramaturgy titled *Nāṭyaśāstra*. The term connotes a specific kind of pleasure that one experiences in perceiving a dramatic performance. Bharata borrows this term from a Vedic text titled *Taittirīyopaniṣad* (II.7) where the nature of ultimate Reality (*Brahman*) is explained in terms of gustatory delight (*ānanda*). The text reads: "That (Brahman) is certainly *Rasa* (literally, both "juice" and the act of tasting this juice); he who attains (tastes) it is delightful (*ānandī*)." Śaṅkara, the earliest commentator on this text (8th C. AD) explains this scriptural text as follows: "In common use *rasa* denotes the object(s) that tastes sweet and sour etc. Persons enjoy this *rasa* by their gustatory sense organ. But the seekers of Truth/ Ultimate Reality, indifferent of this sensory enjoyment, attain their goal by means of several methods of penance and practices and this attainment causes an extra- mundane delight (*ānanda* = beautitude) that can be compared to the sensory delight." Thus ontology is explained in terms of epistemology proposing a phenomenological approach to Truth.

Earlier, in the same text, sections four and five, Truth is explained phenomenologically because of its non-linguistic (*yato vācā nivartante*) character. It appears in the consciousness of a subject by way of an extra-ordinary (non-senseous) delight called *ānanda*. He who attains (experiences) it is fearless (of death, of all kinds of threat from natural phenomena such as fire, air and sun:section VIII). This subject attains immortality phenomenologically. Śaṅkara distinguishes between several kinds or levels of delight (happiness/pleasure) such as *moda*, *pramoda* and *ānanda* (section V). The delight caused by attainment of worldly objects is *moda* (*mud* + *ghañ*); the delight of a higher level is *pramoda* or entertainment (*pra-mud* + *ghañ*). Ānanda denotes (1) pleasure in general (*sāmānya sukha*), (2) the ultimate Reality (*param Brahman*) in its phenomenological form, the pleasure of the highest non-mundane level detached from the kind of pleasure caused by worldly relationship (such as caused by son and friends or by attainment of wealth and fame etc. i.e. absolutely unconditional), and finally (3) specific state of consciousness (*antaùkaraëavåtti viçeñah*) that is pure and devoid of all impurities due to all kinds of worldly events and associations. This absolutely unconditional *ānanda* is otherwise called *Rasa* (ultimate Reality in its phenomenological form). This is Truth (*satya*), wisdom (*jïāna*) and beautitude (*ānanda*) all in its integrated form constituting the primary or necessary signs (*svarūpa lakñaëa*) of Reality (Brahman) in its unmanifest (*asat*) form. This "unmanifest" manifests itself in the sensory form, (not by way of generation- generated or father-son relationship. This self-creation of the sensory world with its changeful phenomena is the secondary or accidental sign of Reality (*taöastha lakñaëa*); and because of this self-manifestation, the *unmanifest* is called *sukåta*. This *sukåta* is *Rasa*, and this *Rasa* is *ānanda* in its highest (purest/ unconditional / extraordinary) level.

Use of the word *rasa* in the Vedic text concerned originates in a sacrificial ritual where the juice of a creeper named *soma* was offered to the Vedic gods. Soma is the Vedic name for the Moon god famous for bestowing mental strength, lustre, happiness, and *soma rasa* is therefore considered an elixir (*amåta*) that bestows immortality. Bharata, the dramaturgist uses this word *rasa* correlating both the ritualistic and metaphysical contexts for signifying the specific delight that a theatrical audience experiences.

Bharata states that, in a dramatic performance *rasa* is generated (in the consciousness of the audience) by unification of an emotion (*bhāva*), as it is manifest in the action (*anubhāva*) of a character within necessary environment(s) (*vibhāva*). As in the context of the Vedic metaphysics *rasa* is a self-manifestation of *sukåuta*, so also in the theatrical context, *rasa* is a self-manifestation of an emotion in the action (both physical [*anubhäva*] and mental [*vyabhicārībhäva*]) of a character(s); and, more significantly, this generation of *rasa* takes place not objectively, on the stage itself, but subjectively, in the consciousness of the audience who is properly qualified. Thus *rasa* in its experiential form is a phenomenological phenomenon, never a material object. One must remember that in an empty auditorium, *rasa is not generated* by the theatrical performance on the stage. While elaborating the stage performance, Bharata takes account of music and dance as the necessary corollaries of this performance. The semiotics of the theatre therefore, consists of visual, auditory and verbal signs: dramatic dialogue, music (both vocal and instrumental) dance and the action of the actors. According to this view, mere reading of a dramatic text (poem or *kāvyam*) cannot generate *rasa*, i.e., a specific, extraordinary delight comparable (if not on par with) to the metaphysical and ritualistic *rasa*. Precisely, *rasa* is metaphorically used in the dramaturgy of Bharata.

The key concept in Bharata's theory of *rasa* is *bhāva*, literally an existence or entity in general derived from the root *bhū* meaning "to be", "to exist". In this sense *bhāva* denotes "being". But in Bharata's treatise *bhāva* means a mental entity, a state of mind, not any material object or "being", and this mental state can be comfortably translated as "emotion". Then the core point in Bharata's theory of *rasa* is that the very ontology of the theatre is the manifestation of an emotion by means of an audio-visual performance of the actors etc., and this manifestation of an emotion or *bhāva* is relished as *rasa* by the audience. The theatrical performance that manifests an emotion is designated in Sanskrit by the term *abhinaya* (*abhi-né+ac*) that means taking (an emotion) toward the audience (in its relishable form), and, as said earlier, this *rasa* does not exist materially or externally other than only as the relished emotion in the audience. Bharata therefore states that *bhāva* and *rasa* are interdependent, they manifest each other; *rasa* is nothing but an emotion *relished* by the audience – *āsvādya*: (VI, prose after 31 and 34-37) the tasted emotion. *Rasa* is not produced on the stage by the performance of the actors, but in the (perceptual) experience of the audience; not again any kind of audience, but only a properly qualified audience. This *qualified* audience is called a *sahådaya* (like-hearted / sensitive person) by Bhaṭṭa Nāýaka and Abhinavagupta (10th C. AD) the celebrated commentators, on Bharata's treatise. A *sahådaya* is a person who can share or sympathize with, or even feel in others' emotional experience.

Abhinaya, or manifestation of an emotion on the stage is constituted by three factors- (1) *vibhāva* that which externalizes permanent (*sthäyé*) emotion- such as the characters enacted by the actors and the scenic elements that stimulate this emotion; (2) *anubhāva* the physical gestures and postures that express this emotion and (3) *vyabhicäré / saïcäré bhävas*, i.e., the drifting feelings or moods associated with or accompany a permanent emotion as expressed by the facial movements. These three can be called determinants of *rasa*. The permanent emotions manifested in a performance are eight in number: love, laughter, sorrow, anger, heroism, fear, distress and wonder. They are all simultaneously present as mental states, though latently, and appear externally in accordance with their relevant stimulants. When manifested by the determinants these emotions are named eight *rasas* respectively – *Śrringära, Karuëa, Häsya, Raudra, Véra, Bhayänaka, Vébhatsa* and *Utsäha*. In these manifestations there might be several *rasas* at a time, though with a leading or dominating one as the plot and situations of a play demand. The different *rasas* are called so according to their respective emotional origins, but in essence the nature of their experience by the audience is invariably the same kind of delight, i.e. no one is more or less delightful than the other. Phenomenologically *Såigära* and *Vébhatsa* or *Karuëa* are on par. Therefore phenomenologically *rasa* is one, not many.

However, different commentators offer their different views on the process of generation of *rasa*. The major issue is the identity of the emotion that is manifested as *rasa*: is it the emotion of the characters of the play? or of the actors or of the audience? The concluding view, that of Abhinavagupta, who draws upon his predecessor Bhaṭṭa Nāyaka, is that it belongs to none of these three. Although assigned to different characters of the plays and performed by different actors at different times, the emotions are general in their forms, and it is because of their generality (*sādhāraṇya*) that they escape any individual attachment and each individual audience is capable of participating (*svātmānupraveśa*) in the performance as a whole, and enjoys thereby the emotion(s) concerned. Otherwise individual identification with the characters and their emotions would cause the respective causal efficiency affecting the audience adversely, i.e., *Śåigära* causing harmful passion, *Karuṇa* causing sorrow, *Bhayānaka* fear, so on and so forth. Precisely, one would never visit a theatrical performance for inviting such emotional adversities. Relevantly, Abhinavagupta counts seven obstacles in relishing emotion as *rasa* (Gnoli: 62-72). He also distinguishes the experience of *rasa* from any common empirical perception, from logical cognition and from the complete self-immersion (*samādhi*) of a yogin. Experience of the theatrical performance, and for that matter of all kinds of art works, involves dualism, and even when, as Abhinava observes, experience of *rasa* is the tasting of one's own consciousness which is saturated with beautitude, one must agree that this self-experience, linked with *Śaìkar's* interpretation of *rasa* in the Upanisadic context, discussed earlier, is somehow distinguished from the experience of art works in general. Therefore, I have argued earlier (2003) that *rasa* experience could not be equated with aesthetic experience in general (contra Gnoli: 72). The view that *rasa* as relishing our (spectators') own mental states (*cittavåtti*) is practically a kind of Aristotelian *catharsis* of emotions, though on a different ground. It leads virtually to a view that it is essentially an experience of pure consciousness, justifying thereby Bharata's borrowing the term from the Upaniṣadic texts and applying it to explain the nature of theatrical experience prompting finally Abhinavagupta's definition of the ontology of the theatre in terms of this experience – theatre is *rasa* (*raso nāṭyam*). Viśvanātha Kavirāja (14th C. AD) subsequently observes that *rasa* experience is only a twin of Brahma- experience (*brahmāsvāda sahodara*), never equal to, or identified with, it.

Use of the term *rasa* by Bharata for the theatrical experience is metaphorical, not literal. Abhinavagupta explains this experience by distinguishing it from other kinds of congnitions:

> This gustation (*carvaṇā* = tasting/ relishing of emotions described in terms of gustatory metaphor) is distinguished a) from perception of the ordinary sentiments (delight, etc.) aroused by the ordinary means of cognition (direct perception, inference, the revealed word, analogy, etc.);
>
> b) from cognition without active participation (*taṭastha*) of the thoughts of others which is proper to the direct perception of the yogins; c) and from the compact (*ekaghana*) experience of one's own beautitude, which is proper to yogins of higher orders (this perception is immaculate, free from all impressions [*uparāga*] deriving from external things.) (Gnoli's translation, p.82)

The semantic dimension of *rasa* in its two levels— ontological and epistemological– *rasa* as the unmanifest Reality that manifests itself (*sukåta*) and its experience as an extraordinary, non-sensory cognition, is metaphorised in explaining both the ontology and epistemology of the theatre (*nāöyam*). The manifestation of the unmanifest emotion as also its experience by the audience, both being finally identified, Abhinavagupta concludes precisely that the theatre is *rasa*, i.e., there is no theatre without *rasa* (its gestation or relish by the audience), and no *rasa* without the theatre (*rasa eva nāöyam*).

Śaṅkuka, a predecessor of Abhinavagupta, notes in his commentary on Bharata that there are two modes of communication (*avagamana*) of emotion: theatrical presentation (*abhinaya*) and verbal description (*abhidhāna/ vācana*). The first according to Bharata, has four components: *vācika* (dramatic dialogues, i.e., verbal), *āṅgika* (gestural, i.e., physical), *sāttvika* (expression of mental feelings by facial movements etc.) and *āhārya* (costume including stage decorations) (*NS*VI.23). By virtue of its semiotic scope the audiovisuality of *abhinaya* is more effective than verbal description in generation of *rasa*. Śaṅkuka exemplifies his observation by citing a dialogue from the play *Ratnāvalī* (II.2) by Harsa. Uadyana the hero of the play utters the dialogue:

> The multitude of droplets, fine rain of tears falling while she painted, produces on my body the effect of a perspiration born from the touch of her hand.

The dialogue mentions Udayana's love for *Ratnāvalī*. But the actor playing the role of Udayana does not simply read this dialogue on the stage. He enacts it by the other three components of performance- physical, mental and costumes. Śaṅkuka states: "Representation/ performance (*abhinaya*), indeed, is nothing but a power of communication (*avagamanaçakti*) - this power differing from the one of verbal expression." The statement implies that *rasa* is solely an effect of *abhinaya*, and it cannot be generated by any verbal composition of a poem.

By "poetry" Bharata refers to a narrative genre (VII: the introductory passage) and Śaṅkuka rightly explains that it refers to the verbal description of the events, characters and their emotions as they occur in the two great epics *Rāmāyaëa* and *Mahābhārata* (2nd C. B.C.). Most of the Sanskrit plays draw their plots upon these narratives, although some plays are also based on the popular legends and events of history. Bharata does not refer to the structure of a linguistic discourse by the term *kāvyam* in this context, a definition that developed much later during the 7th century and onward, a definition that Abhinava uses in his explanation of the aphorism of *rasa* in Chapter VI: "a discourse that is devoid of linguistic blemish and is constituted by tropes (*guëa* and *alaìkāra*)" that he draws upon the rhetoricians like *Bhāmaha* (7th C.), *Daṇḍī* (9th C.) and *Vāmana* (9th C.). However, Bharata's concept of poetry as a verbal narrative is clear enough to avoid any controversy. He uses the term *bhāva* in two senses- mental states that exist (*bhū*) internally and, in the opening passage of chapter VII, as externalization or perceptual manifestation of the meanings of verbal narratives by the four constituents of action/ stage performance such as physical, verbal (speeches/ dialogues), facial movements and costume. Therefore Bharata says "that which manifests (or transfigures/ embodies) audiovisually the meaning of poetry, i.e., the dramatic scripts (*kāvyārthān bhāvayantīti bhāvāh*) is *bhāva*. The difference between a reader's understanding and an audience's perceptual experience of the dialogue of Udayana quoted above is amply clarified by Śaṅkuka: a reader understands the happiness of the love-struck Udayana by way of reference; but an audience experiences the (mental) state of the hero directly by perceiving the 'illocutionany' functions of the language as performed by the actor when he touches his body and projects the state of perspiration as the signs of happiness. According to Bharata, it is this enactment of the dialogue that generates *rasa*, not its referential meaning. It is further clear that although Bharata uses the word *bhāva* in two different senses, that use is only apparent. Virtually they are correlated. When the internal *bhāva* is transformed into the external *bhāva* (perceptual form of the audiovisual kind) *rasa* is generated.

But this denial of *rasa* to poetry was challenged by a Kashmirian philosopher named Ānandavardhana (9ᵗʰ C. AD). He forwarded an intermedial theory of *rasa* by demonstrating that poetry also generates *rasa* by a specific linguistic potency called *vyañjanā*. He suggested that if *rasa*, in its Upanisadic context, is a self-manifestation of the unmanifest Reality, a *sukṛta*, then this *vyañjanā* potency of poetry also generates *rasa* by manifesting the unmanifest semantic ontology that he names *dhvani*: To be precisely clear, the linguistic potency that manifests the unmanifest is *vyañjanā*, and the manifest semantic entity (or meaning) is called *dhvani* (literally "sound"). By saying so Ānanda rejects the rhetorical theory of poetry forwarded by all his predecessors. His quest for this ontology of poetry was based on the philosophers of grammar and the Kashmirian metaphysicians named the Śaiva non-dualists. The earlier theorists based their observations on the philosophy of language preached by the realist logicians of the Nyāya School and the Vedic exegetes of the *Mīmāṁsā* school. According to them there are two semantic levels- literal or denotational (*abhidhā*) and indicative or figurative (*lakṣaṇā*). The grammarians of the Paninian school also agreed with these two schools in taking account of these two levels of meaning. The figurative use of language is necessary when the denotational level fails to express the desired meaning. For example: *Gaìgāyām ghoñah* (A hamlet in the Ganges). This expression is meaningless denotationally or referentially, because there cannot be a hamlet "in" the Ganges. Therefore, by virtue of the association of the river with its banks, one discerns the meaning of this expression as- A Hamlet on the bank of the Ganges. This secondary meaning is not simply imposed on the said expression. In fact, linguistic function as a whole is never arbitrary; it is due to its inherent potency designated in Sanskrit as *Śabda-śakti*. Therefore, meaning is a self-manifestation of this inherent potency. Not only linguistic function is due to this inherent potency, as all the philosophical schools in India agree, the creation of the whole world is also a self-manifestation of the Ultimate Reality by virtue of its inherent potency.

In addition to the two levels of linguistic potency mentioned above Ānanda suggested a third one- revelation (*vyaïjanā*). He said that when denotation and indication fail to express the desired meaning this *vyaïjanā* potency operates anchoring on either of the above two semantic levels. Taking the above expression *gaìgāyām ghoñah* as an example he suggested that the indicative potency ceases functioning after clarifying that the phrase means "a *hamlet on the bank" of* not *inside* the river Gaṅgā; but what it fails to reveal is the cool and sacredness of this hamlet because of its association with the river Gaṅgā. This desired meaning is *dhvani* and the inherent potency that reveals this *dhvani* meaning is *vyanéjanā* (from the root *vyaìj* meaning to manifest). Ānanda borrows this word *dhvani* from Patañjali (2nd C. B.C.) the celebrated commentator on the grammatical aphorisms of Pāṇini (4th C. B.C.), and infuses it with a different semantic content. Ānanda asserts that this tertiary semantic potency manifests what remains unmanifest in the first two linguistic functions, asserting further that this *dhvani* is the very "soul", the ontology of poetry, tropes being its ornamentation, and implying thereby that this *dhvani* can be compared with the *sukṛta* of the Upanisadic text mentioned above, and as such, it is *rasa* or *ānanda* (non-ordinary delight). Abhinavagupta comments that, in poetry *rasa* is the *dhvani* expression that manifests the unmanifest in the denotational and indicative functions of language (*raso vyajyah*), and following the scriptural statement mentioned above, it is clear that *dhvani* itself is *rasa* (delight) and he who relishes this meaning (*dhvani/ rasa*) also becomes delightful (*ānandé*). Precisely, just as in the case of the theatre the ontology of *rasa* is the same as its experience by the audience, so also *dhvani* as the ontology of poetry is the same as its tasting by the reader. As *nāṭya* and *rasa* are one and the same so also are *dhvani* and *rasa*. The scriptural *rasa* doctrine applied to the interpretation of the ontology and epistemology of the theatrical performance by Bharata is thus further intermedialised by Ānandavardhana to the ontology and epistemology of poetry correlating it with the *dhvani* theory of the grammarians.

Ānanda formulated his *dhvani* theory in details by a thorough analysis of its doctrinal foundations and its different categories as based on the denotational and indicative functions of language (*abhidhä-mülä* and *lakñaëä-mülä* classifications of *dhvani*). Keeping the technical perspectives aside (to avoid the length of this chapter while asking the readers for consulting the bibliography attached to it) a brief focus is shed on the three major categories of the denotational *dhvani- Vastu* (objects and events), *alaìkära* (images and tropes) and *rasa* (emotions). Ānanda observes that *rasa* is not related to any figure, it is the effect of *dhvani* only (*Dhva.A.II*). We put up the examples of the three varieties of *dhvani* mentioned above:

Vastu-dhvani

A stranger searches for a shelter in a hilly village. The sky is cloudy and evening approaches fast. A young woman standing on the threshold of a house looks at the stranger and addresses:

> O stranger, this is a hilly village. How can you get a good bed here? Looking at the *unnata payodhara*, if you want to settle anywhere, then settle.

In Sanskrit the phrase *unnata payodhara* is a paronomasia meaning both rising clouds and rising breasts. Clouds are often there in the sky of a hilly area. But the addresser (the woman) points to her own breasts and communicates the idea that if the stranger is capable of erotic enjoyment, he may spend the night with her. This communication is *dhvani* expression and what is communicated is an object (*vastu*), i.e., her breasts.

Alankāra Dhvani

Experience of an image or figure may be due to all the three cognitive processes – perception, inference and analogy. It also involves recognition implying the function of memory. Ānanda cites an example of figural *dhvani*.

> The eyes of warriors take not such joy in their ladies' saffron, - painted breasts as they take in the cranial lobes, painted with the minium of their enemies' elephants.

Here the ornamented breasts of the ladies are compared with the two frontal lobes of an elephant. But this comparison is not communicated by a straight simile – such as "lobes of the elephants are like breasts of a woman", but by a *dhvani* expression.

Rasa Dhvani

A girl waits for her lover in a lonely area on the bank of river Godavari. But the loneliness of that area is disturbed by a hermit who visits that place regularly for picking flowers. The hermit is frightened by a dog which chases him there. One day the girl said him:

> Oh hermit move on fearlessly, because the dog which chases you is killed by a lion.

Here the girl disperses the hermit by this *dhvani* communication, and what is communicated is the emotion of love of the girl who waits for her lover for erotic enjoyment. Thus what is revealed is the *Śāigāra rasa*. Abhinavagupta comments that not only the last variety of *dhvani* reveals an emotion or is an example of *rasa-dhvani* the first two varieties of *dhvani* also reveal emotions – the first one reveals the erotic desire of the addresser woman whereas the second one reveals the heroic emotion of the warriors (*véra rasa*) who prefer crushing the lobes of their enemies to squeezing the breasts of their women. Therefore the first two also aspire to the third one (*vastu-alaikāra dhvané tu rasam prati paryavasyete*). The epistemological implication of Abhinava's statement is that all our cognitive experiences are stimulated by and end in emotional responses. Further, among all our emotions love is the central one.

Whereas the *rasa* experience due to the theoretical performance is transmediated to the experience of poetic expression of *dhvani*, by the Sanskrit poeticians, this transmediation is not allowed to the experience of other arts such as painting (or the pictorial arts in general), dance and music.

Therefore, the experience of *rasa* confined to the audio-visual and verbal arts cannot be interpreted as aesthetic experience in general. Even not all the varieties of poetic expressions generate *rasa* excepting the *dhvani* expressions. Both Śaṅkuka and Abhinava agree that narrative literature in general is unable to generate *rasa* as the theatre does. (*NS*, I.107) Later treatises on painting and sculpture during the early medieval period discerned six limbs of the visual arts of three categories – three dimensional sculptures (*citra*), half-sculptures (*citrārdha*) and pictures (*citrasama*): formal distinctions (*rūpabheda*), appropriate measurements (*pramāëāni*), similitude (*Sādåçya*), proper disposition of colours (*vaṇikābhaṅga*), application of emotions (*bhāvas*) and grace (*lāvaëya*). King Bhoja (11th C. A.D) prescribes *rasadåñöi* (making eyes expressive of *rasa*) of the images. But no critic has ever accepted the view that visual arts generate *rasa* that is attributed only to the unification of *vibhāva*, *anubhāva* and *vyabhicārībhāva* in the theatrical performance and to the *dhvani* expression in poetry.

There is, however, a remote possibility for extending the *dhvani* expression to musical notes and modes of singing that might result in misunderstanding a passage in *Dhvanyāloka*.(III.33 gloss) Ānanda says: "Even those words of songs (*gītaśabdāde rasādilakñörthāvagamadarśanāt*) and non-verbal gestures (*aśabdasyāpi ceñöāde*) express *rasa*." Vinjamuri Chari comments, "This statement might seem to conflict with his basic assumption that *dhvani* is a semantic function. But of course what Ānandavardhana is saying is that suggestion also extends to non- verbal expression – which does not militate its being a function of the words too, although evidently, it does not help his argument for suggestion being a verbal function."(p.126)

The fundamental error in understanding Ānanda this way lies in two basic facts: (1) rendering *dhvani* as suggestion (or evocation) and (2) ignoring the textual context of these lines in Ānanda's treatise. The context concerned is Ānanda's analysis of the texture of poetry (*saìghaöaìā*). There may be several kinds of *dhvani/ vyaìgya* in a composition. One such is where there is no temporal sequence/ succession between the literal meaning (*abhidhā*) and *dhvani*, where both the levels of meaning are perceived even simultaneously. A poet expresses the desired *dhvani* meaning even by describing the physical gestures (of a character) without using any word. Ānanda quotes an anonymous stanza:

> Her face was bowed in shyness
> in the presence of our elders and she forced back the grief
> that gave motion to her breast. But did not the mere corner of her eye,
> lovelier than a startled deer's somehow, as it dropped a tear,
> tell me not to go? (DhvaA: III.4)

Here the gestures of the beloved *put up in words* express immediately the *dhvani* meaning (for the lover) "please stay on" by way of an ironical question. Precisely, it is an example of *abhidhāmūlā asaṁlakṣyakrama dhvani* where the reader cannot trace any temporal sequence between the literal and *dhvani* meanings. In a musical performance the words (verbal composition) of a song and the scales of its performance are so interconnected that the audience fails to determine whether he deciphers the verbal meaning before he enjoys the sounds in scales (*svarālāpa*). To conclude, Ānanda's purport is not to extend *dhvani* beyond its semantic function, to include even the semiotic functions of music and dance. They are cited only as examples for immediacy in comprehensions of two kinds of (verbal) meanings.

References

Ānandavardhana. *Dhvanyāloka* with the commentary *Locana* by Abhinavagupta (Translated with notes and commentaries by Daniel Ingalls et. al), Massachusetts: Harvard University Press, 1990.

Bharata. *Nāöyaśāstra* with the commentary *Abhinavabhāratī* by Abhinavagupta, Chaps.I, II and VI (Translated with notes and commentaries in Hindi by V.S. Siromani), Delhi: University of Delhi Press, 1960.

Chari, V.K., *Sanskrit Criticism*, Honolulu: University of Hawaii Press, 1990. *Taittirīyopanińad*, Gorakhpur: Gita Press (Any Edn.)

Gnoli, Raniero. *The Aesthetic Experience According to Abhinavagupta* (Portions from Abhinavagupta's commentaries on Bharata's *Nāöyaśāstra*, chapters-I and VI; *Dhvanyāloka*, II.4 with notes, commentaries and Introduction), Varanasi: The Chowkhamba Sanskrit Series, 1968.

Bhoja. Samarāìgaëasūtradhāra, Baroda: Gaekwad Oriental Series, 1966.

Śiàhabhūpāla. *Rasārëavasudhākara*, Trivendram, 1919.

Sukla, Ananta Charan. *The concept of Imitation in Greek and Indian Aesthetics*, Calcutta: Rupa and Co., 1977.

_____. "*Dhvani* as a Piovot in Sanskrit Literary Aesthetics" in Grazia Marchiano (Ed.), *East and West in Aesthetics*, Roma, 1996.

_____. "Emotion, Aesthetic Experience and the Contextualist Turn" in *International Yearbook of Aesthetics*, Vol.I, Lund, 1996.

_____. *Art and Representation: Contributions to Contemporary Aesthetics*, Connecticut and London: Praeger Publishers, 2001.

_____ (Ed.). Art and Experience, Connecticut and London: Praeger Publishers, 2003.

_____. "*Rasa, Dhvani and Rasa-Dhvani*: Ontology and Epistemology of Emotion in Sanskrit Literary Discourse" in Kapila Vatsyayan et al. Ed., *Aesthetic Theories and Forms in Indian Tradition*, Delhi: Indian Council of Philosophical Research, 2008.

_____. "Aesthetics as Mass Culture in Indian Antiquity: Rasa, *Śåììgāra*, and *Śåììgāra Ras*" in *Dialogue and Universalism*, Vol.VII, Warsaw.

_____. "The Poetics of Freudian Corpus: Jacques Lacan's Reading of the Sanskrit *Dhvani* Theory" in *International Journal of Humanities*, Annual Review, Illinois, 2013.

_____. *Viśvanātha Kavirāja*, Delhi: Sahitya Academi, 2011.

ABOUT THE AUTHOR

Ananta Charan Sukla was formerly professor of English at Sambalpur University (Orissa, India), visiting professor at the University of Uppsala (Sweden), founder editor of the *Journal of Comparative Literature and Aesthetics* (inception 1978), author of several books and journal articles on philosophy of religion, language and art, an authority of Sanskrit and comparative poetics, widely traveled in the Western countries lecturing at several universities, founder member of the editorial board of the *International Yearbook of Aesthetics* (1996) and editor of several projects on philosophical and literary aesthetics such as Representation (2001), Experience (2003), Essence (2003), Expression (2012) and Fiction (2015).

CHAPTER 2

Intermedializing Music

Siglind Bruhn

In the Western world, the relationship between literature and music can be traced back to the oldest poetic compositions in Greek antiquity. This relation has also been much discussed with regard to German Romantic poetry and the lyrical works of Victor Hugo in France. In our days, this category plays an increasingly important role in the numerous "verbal compositions" of contemporary poets, composers, and artists who cross the line between the two fields.[1] Literary examples range from Dadaist sound effects that eschew verbal semantics altogether to non-narrative language intended to give the listener pleasure (as music does) rather than communicating a content. While literature as music is possible in poetic, epic, and dramatic writing, it is clearly most frequently found in poetry. Painting as music may bring to mind Paul Klee's famous Zwitscher-Maschine (Twittering Machine). Similarly, Mondrian's visual representation of a "Boogie Woogie," while ostensibly referring to a specific genre, clearly tries to create music on the canvas. The Lithuanian painter-composer Mikalojus Konstantinas Čiurlionis was perhaps foremost in titling paintings with musical terms and vice versa. But also Kandinsky and several others of Mondrian and Klee's contemporaries perceived their art as primarily rhythmic. Moreover, Kandinsky, himself a proficient pianist and cellist, also strove for a visualization of "sound" in *Der gelbe Klang* (*The Yellow Sound*), a music-dramatic work that was originally to be complemented by a "green" and a "purple" sound.

---

[1] Verbal utterance as music of the recent decades includes works such as Karlheinz Stockhausen and Helmut Heißenbüttel's *Mikrophonie II*, Stockhausen's *Gesang der Jünglinge*, David Johnson's *Telefun*, György Ligeti's *Artikulation and Aventures*, Maurizio Kagel's *Anagrama*, Luciano Berio's *Ommaggio a Joyce*, Henri Pousseur's *Trois visages de Liège*, Pierre Boulez's *Poésie pour pouvoir*, John Cage's *Solo for voice I* and the texts collected in *Silence*, Gerhard Rühm's *Botschaft an die Zukunft*, Sylvano Bussotti's *Torso*, Laurie Anderson's *United States I-IV*, Dieter Schnebel's *Glossolalie*, Hans G. Helm's *Daidalos and Golem*, Hans Otte's *Modell and Alpha-Omega II*, Brazilian poet Augusto de Campos's six polychromatic poetamenos, texts based on works and ideas by Anton von Webern, etc. For in-depth discussions see Schnebel (1984) and Metzger & Riehn (1993).

Other works of art have aimed at translating compositional techniques (such as thematic development, counterpoint, canon, and leitmotif) or structural models (such as theme and variation, fugue, sonata, rondo, etc.) into the verbal or visual medium. Historically, this kind of relationship originated with the emergence of autonomous "absolute" music in the 18th century and led in extreme cases to verbal or visual utterances creating structure at the expense of conveying an actual (verbal) message. However, more often than not, such self-imposed compositional restrictions gave rise to works that are intriguing both for what they say and for how they say it. One of the particularly successful examples of such literature is by Goethe. As a fourteen-year-old, Goethe had heard the seven-year-old prodigy Mozart in a recital in Frankfurt, and the encounter influenced him deeply. During his twenty-five years as director of the Weimar theatre, Goethe staged more than 280 performances of Mozart's works (Spaethling 1987). Particularly *The Magic Flute*, which he performed 82 times, fascinated him so much that the great poet toyed with the idea of writing a sequel. While the projected composition remained a fragment, in 1773 Goethe amused himself by creating a 'Concerto dramatico' in words (Junk 1899). Steven Paul Scher lists this miniature concerto as a prime example of "verbal music" (Scher 1968: 1-12). Goethe imitates tempi and musical structures and makes every effort to compose something that would resemble music.

In his standard work for the field, *Music and Literature: A Comparison of the Arts*, Calvin S. Brown (1987) discusses cases of literary works that emulate various musical forms and techniques.[2] His examples are too many to recount here, but a short overview seems in order. According to Brown, successful examples of literary works following the variation form include Eve's morning song to Adam from Milton's Paradise Lost, where a "positive" theme is followed with a detailed "negative" variation (Milton, Paradise Lost, IV, 641-656; quoted in Brown 1987:129), Ludwig Tieck's play *Die verkehrte Welt* (*The Topsy-Turvy World*), a work with verbal overture and verbal entr'actes, the last of which is a "Menuetto con variazioni" consisting of a statement of a theme followed by three variations on it (Tieck's *Sämtliche Werke*, Vienna 1918, XIII, 5-154, discussed in Brown 1987: 129-130), and John Gould Fletcher's *Steamers* which, with its mock performance indication "(Maestoso)," underscores the designation as a musically informed poem (Fletcher 1930: 50-1). Sacheverell Sitwell in *The Cyder Feast and*

---

[2] For further discussions of these and related questions, see also Brown (1970) (1973) (1978) (1984). An extensive overview of the use of variation form, sonata, fugue, leitmotif, etc. can be found in Horst Petri (1964).

Other Poems has imitated the practice popular with many composers to take another artist's theme and write a set of variations on it.

The ABA form, one of the most basic musical molds, creates problems in literature where there is less tolerance for straightforward repetition. Possibly the only example of a poem that ignores this reservation with very satisfactory result is Theodor Storm's *Die Nachtigall* (*The Nightingale*), among whose three five-line stanzas the first and third are exactly identical. However, as soon as one abandons the notion that sections should be balanced (and the repeated section thus considerable), one finds many other poets who have written verses that more generally repeat a (shorter) beginning for a conclusion. Among such ternary poems are Keats's *Lines on the Mermaid Tavern, Bards of Passion and of Mirth*, and *La Belle Dame sans Merci*, Poe's *Dream Land*, Alfred Noyes's *The Highwayman*, etc. Brown mentions specifically the poetry of Polish writer Ujejski, whose set of eleven poems, based on compositions by Chopin, attempts to follow the musical structure. Particularly in the poem on Chopin's *Funeral March*, the poet creates an interesting variant of the musically literal [ABA] form by distinguishing the two sections through the use of different meters but avoiding verbal repetition when the initial metric structure recurs.

Among poems emulating the rondo form in the Elizabethan era Brown lists Robert Burns's *Green Grow the Rushes, O*, William Browne's *A Welcome*, and Thomas Lodge's *Phoebe's Sonnet*. Further examples include Robert Greene's *Sephestia's Lullaby*, Hebbel's *Requiem*, Nietzsche's *Der Herbst*, Thomas Hardy's *Birds at Winter Nightfall*, Austin Dobson's *In After Days*, many of the poems by Clement Marot, John McCrae's *In Flanders Fields*, and Dante Gabriel Rossetti's *Sister Helen*. Imitations of the structural devices of fugue and fugato are understandably rare given literature's linearity. However, Brown has much praise for what he considers a genuinely successful adaptation of fugal texture and structure in the section entitled "Dream Fugue" within De Quincey's *The English Mail Coach*.[3] He also mentions a fugato section in James Joyce's *Ulysses*, albeit with the reservation that it may constitute the literary equivalent to an "academic" fugue. Paul Celan in his famous poem, *Todesfuge* (*Death Fugue*), also seems to use the term not merely metaphorically. *Schwarze Milch der Frühe* (*Black milk of daybreak*), which recurs three times, functions as the fugal subject, with a development at "trinken" (drink). A counter-subject (or the second subject in a double fugue?) is given in *Ein Mann wohnt im Haus* (*A man lives in the house*).

---

[3] Thomas De Quincey, *Collected Writings*. David Masson (ed.) London 1897, XIII, 270-327. See the extensive and fascinating discussion of this literary fugue in Calvin Brown 1987: 151-159.

One can observe the introduction of new counterpoints along the way, a complicated combination of thematic material in the final stanza, modulations of several of the colors and images employed, and a brief conclusion. Moreover, recurring expressions like "abends," "mittags," and "morgens" (at evening, at midday, at morning), *Ein Grab in den Lüften* (*A grave in the air*) and *Ein Grab in den Erden* (*A grave in the ground*) serve to create a kind of space, not unlike what one finds in some of Bach's fugues.

More writers have turned to sonata form (referred to as either "sonata" or "symphony") than to any of the other forms mentioned above, though how this is to be understood is often unclear. The problem with extensive repetition as it would occur in the recapitulation is, of course, the same as in [ABA] form. Not surprisingly then, poets have found the form more unmanageable than prose writers. Gautier's famous poem *Symphonie en blanc majeur* (*Symphony in White Major*) seems to have hardly anything whatsoever to do with music—be it content or structure—beyond the title. The same holds true for Grace Hazard Conkling's *Symphony of a Mexican Garden*, despite its suggestive indications of tempo and tonality (*In A Major, Poco sostenuto, Vivace*), which seem modeled after those of the sonata movement in Beethoven's *Seventh Symphony*, and its numerous references to musical forms like aria, fugue, bourrée, and sarabande (Brown 1987: 166-167). In the *Verse symphonies* of John Gould Fletcher, the only suggestion of the musical form lies in the division into movements. The most successful application of various musical techniques to the writing of poetry occurs in the work of Conrad Aiken; these include his "symphonies" in verse as well as his many works with titles like "nocturne," "tone poem," "variation," etc.

The latter part of the 19th century brought about not only the "musicalization of literature" regularly invoked in the context of the Symbolists. The music and art historian W. Dömling maintains that one ought to speak similarly of a "musicalization of painting" (Dömling 1994: 4). Captions of works of art increasingly resonate with terms like "composition," "harmony," "rhythm," "polyphony," etc. Whistler's *Symphony in White and Nocturne in Blue and Silver*, to name just two of many, constitute parallels across interartistic space to the various poetic "symphonies." These compositions are impressionistic; they merely take the title without attempting any structural similarities with the musical genre.

In the early 19th century, two German artists were particularly successful in transferring musical techniques to their work. Philipp Otto Runge (1777-1810), when talking about his painting, *Die Lehrstunde der Nachtigall* (*The Nightingale's Lesson*), used distinctly musical terminology, declaring that for him this picture became "the same as what a fugue is in music" (Ringer 1965: 223). Visual artists have also played with counterpoint, motivic development, and other musical concepts not only in the description and titling, but in the structure of their works. Kandinsky's theoretical writings (*Concerning the Spiritual in Art*, 1912, and *Point and Line to Plane: Contribution to the Analysis of the Pictorial Elements*, 1926) contain a theory of what has been described as "the craft of counterpoint in abstract painting." But once again, Paul Klee takes the lead. As early as 1918, Klee, having begun to free his line drawings from the task of representation, had treated pictorial elements as components of musical texture. In *Drawing with a Fermata* (Klee scholar Andrew Kagan calls it a "contrapuntal scherzo"; Kagan 37), the only pictorially concrete element is the musical symbol that, insofar as it invites lingering or pausing at the performer's discretion, is itself an emblem of artistic freedom. The remainder of the work, Klee himself claimed, is organized along the principle of contrapuntal imitation: the repetition and variation of a melodic form in different registers. A little later, Klee experimented with groups of spread stacks or "decks" of flat, colored forms as the equivalent to a "fugal idea." (*Fugue in Red*, 1921). Then, having explored ways of equating the relationship between independent lines to the principles of counterpoint, Klee eventually developed a similar polyphonic theory for color. As Kagan describes it,

> He borrowed from music a dynamic conception of form. the canon (strict imitative counterpoint), in which the initial subject is repeated exactly, over and over, in different voices and registers. The continual, regular, overlapping repetitions create a very firm rhythmic and harmonic structure. Again translating the musical concept into visual terms, Klee arrived at a new paradigm of color relationships, which he called 'The Canon of Color Totality.' [...] he created a canonic structure or pattern by continually reintroducing the 'crescendo-decrescendo' color 'subjects' in different 'voices'. (Kagan 45-6)[4]

Klee himself explained this 'canonic' color relationship to his students as a "kind of three-part counterpoint." (Klee 1973: 487-491) He developed this approach further in works like *Polyphony* (1932). By contrast, he considered his most successful paintings of 1936, *Old Sound and New Harmony*, the summit of his

---

[4] For an excellent evaluation see also *Franciscono* (1985). A few other Klee titles with similar implications are *Chorale and Landscape* (1921), *Polyphonic Setting for White* (1930), *Three-part Polyphony* (1921-22), *Five-part Polyphony* (1929-30), *Polyphony* (1932).

achievements in homophony. It is important to stress that these evocative wordings are more than fancy titles; they are hints at either the interartistic problem addressed, or the acknowledged solution (or both).

Returning to literature and venturing a brief side-glance at drama, we find that what is arguably the most famous theatrical emulation of a musical structure, *La Sonate et les trois messieurs ou Comment parler musique* (*The Sonata and the Three Gentlemen; or, How to Talk Music*) was conceived by Jean Tardieu, a prolific writer of ekphrastic poetry and thus a specialist in all kinds of transmedialization (see Schwartz 1981). By far the most convincing among literary works created to follow musical designs or to emulate compositional techniques, however, are found neither in poetry nor in drama but in prose writing, particularly in novellas. Such is the case in George Sand's novella *Le Contrabandier* of 1837, which imitates in astounding detail the complex musical structure—a combination of rondo form and developed character variation—of Liszt's programmatic work, *Rondeau fantastique sur un thème espagnol* (*El Contrabandista*). Similarly, it has been argued that Anton Chekhov's novella *The Black Monk* is laid out in the form of a sonata movement in which the two contrasting themes, rather than being persons or specific conflicts, have a startling depth dimension. As Rosamund Bartlett analyzes convincingly, the two themes are motivically expressed as the polarities of life/death and reality/illusion, while being connected "harmonically" to the two male protagonists as tonic and dominant. The exposition introduces not only the relevant elements of the narrative plot, but also—musically, as it were—elements of paradox and duality. Writes Bartlett: "In its [the novella's] constant shifts in narrative tone and contrapuntal tapestry of ambiguity, modulation and inversion we may discern a deeper correlation with the language of music." The penultimate section brings the story full circle, returning to the place of the beginning and to the time ("exactly one year later"); yet "the second subject is indeed in the tonic." The story concludes with "a brief and brilliant coda" in which "the narrative pace is considerably quickened"; one is reminded of the stretto sections that conclude many classical sonata movements (see Bartlett 1998: 68). The suggestion actually goes back to a remark made by Dmitry Shostakovich in an 1894 article, in which the composer observed that he believed Chekhov's story "The Black Monk" to be constructed in sonata form "with main and secondary themes, development and so on." (Volkov 1979: 225)

The prose best suited to the adaptation of musical devices is one that emulates techniques like thematic development, leitmotif technique, or counterpoint. However, terms are often applied loosely. Albert Gier explains that "it is meaningful to speak of literary counterpoint when, for instance, a novelist highlights the same topic or theme in various strands of the action and in ever new perspectives, so that a sequence appears as a mirror image of the preceding one" (translated from Albert Gier, "Musik in der Literatur," 73) Aldous Huxley's *Point Counter Point* seems more an example of mise en abîme than of counterpoint: it plays with the idea of recursion, including that of having one of the characters an author who determines to write the book in which he appears (apart from reflecting on Beethoven's op. 132; see Kolago 1997).[5]

Beyond themes and contrapuntal entities, leitmotifs seem to offer themselves more easily for adaptation in a non-musical genre. Short, recognizable units that recur at crucial moments, have a programmatic association, and refer to something beyond the immediate content of their tones or words, occur for instance in Gabriele D'Annunzio's novel *Trionfo della Morte* (*The Triumph of Death*). In *Der Zauberberg* (*The Magic Mountain*), according to Thomas Mann's own statement, "the verbal leitmotif is no longer, as in *Buddenbrooks*, employed in the representation of form alone, but has taken on a less mechanical, more musical character and endeavors to mirror the emotion and idea." (Mann 1936: Preface vi)

Novellas such as the ones just mentioned can be appreciated (and are more commonly read) without any notion of the musical relationship. In other cases, the title of a literary work may give an indication that a relation to music is being sought. However, as Gier points out, such evidence in no way discloses whether we can expect a work of literature following musical designs or literature about music. Thus while Robert Pinget's *Passacaille* (1965) is structurally fashioned after the form musicians know as chaconne or passacaglia but does not deal at all with music in terms of its content, Alejo Carpentier's *Concierto barocco* (1974) is very much about music, without therefore being cast in any recognizable musical structure (Prieto 1993: 153-170).

This brings me to the third category in the intermediary endeavors that take music as their object: literature and painting about music. The writing on music in general or on particular musical works comes in many forms; some of them, like the program note, the textbook description, and the musical review, will be left aside here. I will also not address literary works dealing with the musician as protagonist, or works of fiction whose characters explore music as an ecstatic experience. My interest centers on those literary works that aim at transforming a musical event into something akin to its verbal equivalent—ekphrasis as "the verbal representation of a text originally composed in the musical sign system,"

---

[5] For discussions on Thomas Mann, see Basilius (1944) and Vaget (1968).

to paraphrase Claus Clüver's definition of ekphrasis as "the verbalization of real or fictitious texts composed in non-verbal sign systems." (Clüver 1997: 26)

Most poetry dealing with music in the narrower or wider sense does not deal with a specific composition. In a philosophically illuminating study on poetry about music, Albrecht Riethmüller lists literary works whose topic is music as such or what he refers to as "the awareness of music"—its sound, its rhythm, its relation to time, the emotions it evokes, etc. (Riethmüller 1996: 7)[6] Similarly, H.W. Schwab in his 1965 essay, "Das Musikgedicht als musicologische Quelle," examines only poems that speak about the external aspects of music. Poets, he holds, will either praise music as a divine art, or sing about its beneficial effects on humans. They may portray the coziness of a home in which music-making is a regular pastime or glorify a specific instrument. Occasionally, they may reminisce about a shared experience of singing, praise the power of music in communal or political activities, or applaud an individual musician. In this group fall the many 19th-century poems on composers, like Grillparzer's *Meyerbeer*, Brentano's *Beethoven poems*, Rodenberg's *Musical Sonnets* on Mendelssohn, Chopin, Schumann, and Beethoven, etc. In the poems included in both collections there are generic poetic references to melody, harmony, or rhythm, to song, dance, or musical forms (the latter are often understood symbolically), but no poetic responses to specific compositions.

In many respects, these poems are about music as it exists abstractly in the minds of authors, not about extant works created by other artists.[7] The same is true for the pictorial art. As scores of studies in recent years have explored from many perspectives (i.e. Leppert 1988), fashionable with postmodern studies, paintings in profuse numbers have dealt with music-making both as a societal emblem and as a carrier of sexual symbolism. In other cases, works of pictorial art, while dealing with a particular composer, do so in a very general way. Thus Klimt's famous Beethoven Frieze aims at representing the "essence" of the composer (and thus, presumably, his style and mode of musical expression rather than his biography), but does not transform any specific, recognizable work of art. While poets and painters thus generally seem to shy away from the task of

---

[6] The ten poems chosen for this collection include Ovid's *Syrinx*, an Anacreontic poem in praise of the lyre, Schiller's *The Dance*, Kleist's *Musical Insight*, Lenau's *Beethoven's Bust*, E.A. Poe's *The Bells*, Valéry's *Cantique des Colonnes*, Rilke's *Gong*, Benn's *Melodies*, and Bloch's *Dream*. Not one of them deals with a specific genre, much less with an individual piece of music. A lovely collection of contemporary poems about music is the one by Buchwald & Roston (1991).

[7] For a compilation of literary representations of music, musicians, or musical life, see Levith (1981).

recreating in their respective media that sister art which has often been called the most elusive of them all, there are a few examples of ekphrastic poems on musical compositions, as well as a few cases of corresponding paintings. Paul Klee's so-called "operatic paintings"—*The Bavarian Don Giovanni* (1919), *Hoffmannesque Scene* (1921), and *Battle Scene from the Comic Operatic Fantasy, The Seafarer* (1923)—fall in this category.

Especially in the case of opera, itself a combination of music with mime and visual presentation, the boundary between such "ekphrastic paintings" and mere illustrations may at first seem difficult to define. Venturing another spin-off from Claus Clüver's definition of ekphrasis as "the verbalization of real or fictitious texts composed in non-verbal sign systems," ekphrastic paintings would have to provide "a visualization of real or fictitious texts composed in non-visual sign systems." Hence depictions that can easily be identified as reproductions of the (actual or imagined) visual presentation on the theatric stage without tangible reference of the musical language do not belong in this category. The famous Edwardian illustrator Arthur Rackham's sixty-four impressions of Wagner's *Ring of the Nibelungs*, deemed among the greatest visual representations of Wagner's drama, are one example of independent illustrations that render the scene but not all of the media.[8] Similarly, set designs, even by such ingenious artists as David Hockney, by definition also do not qualify as transmedializations.

Yet a few examples of genuine transmedialization of opera into visual art do in fact exist. The artist who has me particularly convinced is the American Albert Pinkham Ryder (1847-1917), whom fellow artist (and musician, composer, curator, and writer) Tom Phillips describes as "the finest visionary master of sea and cloudscape in the [American] history of painting." (Phillips 1997: 68) Interestingly, Ryder was also fascinated by Wagner, one of the most avant-garde musicians of his day, and attempted pictorial interpretations of some of the composer's Gesamtkunstwerke, notably *The Flying Dutchman* and *The Twilight of the Gods*. In his large oil painting of 1888-91, entitled *Siegfried and the Rhine Maidens*, the figures of the three Rhine maidens in the stream who try to tease possession of the ring from Siegfried, seen approaching on horseback, provide nothing but the skeleton of the particular scene in the well-known plot.

---

[8] Analogs in visual art on literature to Rackham's Ring exist, e.g., in Edgar Allan Poe's Raven, published in Paris in 1875 "avec illustrations par Édouard Manet," and Henry Fuseli's *Prospero, Caliban, and Miranda* in Shakespeare's *The Tempest*, Act I, Scene 2 (Indiana University Art Museum). They demand that the appreciator be familiar with the literary context as a whole rather than only with the persons or events portrayed; and yet, what they depict are specific passages rather than entire works of art.

"The rest of the painting is the music," as Phillips describes it. The jagged sky in counterpoint to the undulating trees renders all the anxieties of the score in this final battle between choice and destiny. The natural forces at work, and the dark wind that twists everything into metaphor of a tumult to come, prophetically dwarf the agents of the scene. As the orchestra does in the opera, acting as a huge lens to magnify the drama, the non-thematic elements of the painting tell a grander tale than those referring more directly to the operatic action. (Ibid.)

In literature, Gabriele D'Annunzio's poem *Sopra un Adagio di J. Brahms* is a very fine example of ekphrastic poetry on music from the earlier part of the 20th century. In it the Italian poet juxtaposes the theme of desolation in the main section (pictured with ruins and a vacant throne as the center of interest) with a vision of the fallen empire's former glory in the middle section, only to return, once that vision has faded, to the original scene of despondency. Corresponding with the recurring [A] section, the poet retrieves many of the expressions used in the first section; yet the extent of change in individual words and images produces a verbal analogy to the device of musical variation employed by Brahms.

The 19th century, too, knew several poets pursuing transmedialization of one kind or another. To name just one who was known for her prolific output, Mary Alice Vialls is the author of a collection of poetry, *Music Fancies and Other Verses* (Westminster 1899). There, a sonnet on *The Tannhäuser* overture stands beside one on Chopin's Nocturne op. 37 no. 1. In the latter sonnet's octave, the poet's impressionistic treatment translates the accompanied G-minor melody that constitutes the nocturne's main theme as a questioning of pilgrims struggling along the barren track to eternal death, while her subsequent sestet depicts the E-flat-major chorale-style secondary theme as a reminder to return "to the fold and to the faith," as it were.

For intermedial responses in the reverse direction to exist, music has to be acknowledged as an art that can "speak," albeit in a symbolic rather than denotative manner. This has long been denied by many proponents of its sister arts. Yet the Western musical language has developed a highly sophisticated catalogue of signifiers that are understood, by all who are conversant in this "language," to be pointing towards non-musical objects. Among the best known are:

1. the figures of musical rhetoric developed in the 15th and 16th centuries, especially by Burmeister and his followers,[9]

---

[9] See Joachim Burmeister, *Hypomnematum musicae poeticae ... ex Isagoge ... ad chorum*

2. the "affective types" developed as an extension of the rhetorics-of-music tradition, and the influential system of categorizing the connotations of intervals, from the chromatically descending passus duriusculus expressing grief, sorrow, and anxiety to the tritone as diabolus in musica, the devil in the realm of music,[10]
3. the affective connotations linked with keys, tonalities, and modes,
4. the semantic interpretation of brief musical units as "gestures" on the basis of their kinesthetic shape,[11]
5. the tracing of a visual object (like the Cross) in the pitch outline,
6. the letter-name representation of or allusion to persons—from Bach's famous pitch signature and those of Schumann, Shostakovich,[12] Schoenberg, Berg, Webern, etc. to the acrostic bows of reverence to a patron (Schumann's Mr. Abegg, represented in his variations on A-Bb-E-G-G) or a lover (Berg's HF = Hanna Fuchs), and other cryptographic messages.[13]

When music thus acts as the subject actively responding to literature or the visual arts, a distinction is once again helpful between the various modes it may assume. A helpful way of defining what stance a composer adopts towards the work that constitutes the primary representation is a distinction between combination,

---

gubernandum cantumque componendum conscripta synopsis (1599) and *Musica autoschediastiké* (1601).

[10] Leonard Ratner, surveying the music of the 18th century, remarks that "[f]rom its contacts with worship, poetry, drama, entertainment, dance, ceremony, the military, the hunt, and the life of the lower classes, music in the early 18th century developed a thesaurus of characteristic figures, which formed a rich legacy for classic composers. Some of these figures were associated with various feelings and affections; others had a picturesque flavor." (Ratner 1980: 9)

[11] On the creation of semantic content in instrumental music through representations of the body, see Lidov (1987: 69-97). Similarly to gestures, which exploit a listener's identification with motor activity, a specific timbral quality may be linked with a particular vocal grain (what kind of feeling would be expressed if this timbre was that of a human voice?).

[12] Shostakovich based his musical monogram neither on the spelling of his name in English or French nor in his native Russian but on the German spelling established for his name, Schostakowitsch. His famous signature motif D-S-C-H [= D-Eb-C-B] is used for the first time in movements 3 and 4 of his Tenth Symphony, where, shortly after Stalin's death, it speaks for the composer's assertion of his individuality—a scandalously subversive act in Communist Russia. The Eighth Quartet of 1960 is saturated with the DSCH motto.

[13] For a set of interesting studies in this direction see the various essays by Eric Sams on the use of ciphers by Schumann (in *Musical Times* 1965: 106 and 1966: 107), and Brahms (in *Musical Times* 1971: 112).

integration, and transformation.[14] Combination relies on a coexistence or cooperation between music and a work in one of the sister arts. The complementary media are expected to add to and comment on one another but may remain basically independent of each other. Integration describes a result that is not reducible to the sum of the constituting elements, a new unit in which a verbal or pictorial element has become a part of the musical composition to such an extent that it cannot be removed without destroying the musical structure. Transformation is given when no verbal or pictorial element is combined with or integrated into the musical text as it was originally created. Instead, the composition refers to an element or a combination of elements in literary or visual texts that are not presented to the listeners' eyes or ears but given exclusively in musical language.

Two somewhat different genres of musical composition are captured in this description. Artistic collaborations of a composer with a literary or visual artist differ significantly from a composer's often solitary decision to add music to a preexisting text or visual impression. Collaborations involving music as one of the key components include the very interesting pieces *Parade L'Histoire du soldat (The Solder's Tale)*, conceived jointly by Pablo Picasso (visual), Jean Cocteau (verbal), Eric Satie (musical), and Leonide Massine (choreographic components) and L'Histoire du soldat (The Soldier's Tale) designed by Igor Stravinsky (music) and Charles-Ferdinand Ramuz (libretto), to name only two outstanding examples here. In such a joint venture, individual components complement one another but could often not stand on their own.

Music knows few cases that correspond directly to the phenomena of "emblematic writing" or the dual art work of "Doppelbegabungen." A composer like Schoenberg, who was also a gifted artist, nevertheless did not create any work in which expressions of his dual talent combine in such a way as to engender a single overarching artistic message.[15] The closest analog in recent music is probably Erik Satie. Many of his piano scores tread a fine line between musical score and artwork. Works including his own depictions or those of other visual artists (see, e.g., *Sports et Divertissements*, published as facsimile with drawings by Charles Martin) may have been intended, or so Satie scholars believe, to be looked at as much as performed. Further back in history, one composition at least seems to function as a musical analog to emblematic writing.

---

[14] The idea for this tripartite distinction goes back to a study by Hans Lund (1982) on the relation between literature and art.
[15] The only exception, involving sound and colored light, occurs in Schoenberg's *Die glückliche Hand*.

In the early 17th century, Michael Maier created a work entitled *Atalanta fugiens*. It consists of fifty musical settings in an imitative style accompanied by emblems and epigrams. (Also known as "Michael Maier's alchemical emblem book," the work is specifically intended to be appreciated "per oculis et intellectui").[16]

In addition, the field of music encompasses compositions that are manifestations of a combination of talents that is much rarer than the dual aptitude for poetry and painting, composition and painting, or music and poetry writing: synesthesia. In correspondence with some painters who claim to be putting on canvas the shades communicated to them in musical sounds, composers endowed with this gift of seeing colors when hearing pitches or chords may purport to be creating a composition consisting of sound and color. In the case of a composer like Olivier Messiaen[17] who expected his audiences to see with their inner eye the hues expressed in his chords, the visual component is, for most of us, beyond our perceptive abilities and thus beyond verification; these works thus do not literally involve two media. The composer's assertion refers to a private reality that is not easily shared by an audience and the details of which have to be taken at face value. In compositions like Alexander Scriabin's *Prometheus: Poem of Fire* by contrast, notated for *clavier à lumières* (keyboard with lights) in addition to the instruments of musical performance, the audience does enjoy a bi-medial performance. Moreover, analysis reveals that the correlations of sounds and colors are part of a complex system of spiritual symbolism (see Sabanejev 1912, Mirka 1996 [1998]:227-248)

Settings of one text in another medium, while often intriguing in themselves, also constitute a form of "music and ..." Whenever a poetic text is set as vocal music, or a dramatic text as opera, the original medium is inflected rather than transformed. Intonation—one of the many features of vocal language—is

---

[16] *Atalanta fugiens* by Michael Maier (1568-1622) is listed alternatively with the explanatory subtitle "hoc est, emblemata nova de sacretis naturae chymica" and the longer "Secretioris naturae secretorum scrutinium chymicum per oculis et intellectui: accurate accommodata, figuris cupro, emblemata, epigrammata, illustratum, opusculum ingeniis alterioribus." The work was composed in 1617 and first published in 1618. The music is for three unspecified voices; the emblems are engravings in copper.

[17] In the famous lecture he gave in the cathedral of Paris while he was composing his only opera, *Saint François d'Assise*, Messiaen expounded the relationship between the words of Thomas Aquinas he had chosen for the opera and the phenomenon of sound-color, using images like "interlocked rainbows" and "spirals of color." He finds support in Saint John whose lines "In Thy Music, we will SEE the Music, In Thy Light, we will HEAR the Light" (John 17:3) he quotes adding that "this knowledge will be a perpetual dazzlement, an eternal music of colors, and eternal color of music." (Conférence de Notre-Dame, prononcée à Notre-Dame de Paris le 4 décembre 1977, Paris: Leduc, 1978, 15). For more details see Messiaen (1986) and Hill (1998).

modified; secondary features like speech tempo, word spacing, etc. may be more or less effected, and structure may occasionally be expanded by repetitions. All other aspects of the original text, however—vocabulary and syntax, metaphors and allusions, the mode of expression and the objects spoken of—will characteristically remain completely untouched. The instrumental accompaniment may be anything from servant to partner (and, in recent times, even competitor) to the vocal part, but it is not typically entrusted with creating a self-contained musical utterance. Rather, we often speak of it as "supporting" the vocal line or "painting a backdrop" for it. The role music plays is very similar when a score is composed to accompany a slide show, video, film, etc. Such accompaniments are musical illustrations of the verbal or visual texts.

The integration of verbal and visual expressions into musical compositions includes many examples that need little reflection: neither verbal performance instructions nor the visual element of the musical notation itself would normally prompt us to think that we are dealing with a relationship between two art forms, although both instances meet the condition: musical notation would not be in existence without the medium it aims to perpetuate, and compositions would not have survived in a condition as close to their original design without the help of some means of record-keeping. Similarly, performance indications detached from the music to be performed make no sense, while music conceived with expressive nuances that cannot be specified unequivocally outside the verbal medium loses a valuable dimension when deprived of these directions. The most obvious examples of music integrating a strong visual element can be found in compositions written in graphic notation. In this system, a composer specifies or suggests performance ideas developed from the verbal directions found in earlier scores, which are now expanded and, in part or in toto, replaced by imaginative symbols that intend to activate the performer's creative participation. Known at least since the middle of the 20th century (Morton Feldman's *Projections of 1950-51*), this notational practice has moved more and more into the area of non-specific analogy of sign and intended contents. However, it is often more than doubtful that we are dealing here with a "piece of visual art" even on the simplest level of defining the term art. Notation, in all cases, is graphic in nature. And while an explicitly graphic notation of music that claims to do without any kind of "alphabet" or transliteration of clearly delineated phenomena takes the idea into often interesting territory, one hesitates to count such scores among the "integrations of music and picture."

However, genuine examples of "literature or art in music" do exist. There are cases in which visual elements that originate outside music appear integrated into a piece of music. One example occurs in scores whose visual presentation follows shapes the outlines of which suggest depicted objects. The scores of Sylvano Bussotti could be compared here with concrete poetry, in that the visual aspect of the written score conveys a message of its own. However, the combination of conventional notational components (notes on staves) with graphic elements is often rather baffling, as when the staves themselves crisscross one another in visually interesting ways that call any straightforward reading of the pitches written onto them into question. This is the case in a score entitled *Ode de Cologne*, penned by Geoffry Wharton, the concertmaster of the Cologne Philharmonic Orchestra, and depicting the front of Cologne Cathedral.[18] Much more than overtly graphic scores, such artworks trigger reflections about the signs on which we rely for musical communication.

A step further, visual representations that could possibly function as artistic objects in their own right may be declared by their authors to be intended to function as scores. Paul Moor, an American music critic who has been based in Berlin for the past decades, tells of such a "score" for a Trio, presented at Darmstadt in the early fifties by Earle Brown. As Moor recalls it, "the score at one point included a framed horizontal panel embellished with what I can only call apparently random squiggles of the Brown pen, each such panel differing individually from its two counterparts. But Nuria Nono (née Schoenberg) kindly explained to me Earle's fundamental idea: the performer (on whatever instrument) contemplating that panel should improvise whatever simultaneously just happened to come to mind. This opus became even more exacerbatedly aleatory if the three participating artistes obeyed Brown's directive to interchange parts and then go back to the top for another go-round, more or less ad libitum."[19]

Similarly, the Polish-born Israeli composer Roman Haubenstock-Ramati is said to have organized exhibitions under the title "Musikalische Graphik" (musical graphics). His exhibits included colored lithographs that bore a close resemblance to the work of artists like Kandinsky, but were ostensibly intended as scores. In other instances, a constituent part of the musical language is based on a linguistic component that would not necessarily appear independently in a poem or drama; themes shaped on the basis of letter-name allusions (B-A-C-H etc.) fall into this category. Finally, as if in combination of the implicit graphic aspect and the implicit letter names, a musical score may contain elements that graphically are both musical and verbal text. The most striking example I have

---

[18] See online at https://fbcdn-sphotos-b-a.akamaihd.net/hphotos-ak-ash3/69663_10151404138529260_1501757028_n.png.
[19] Paul Moor, electronic message to the author, 23 February 1998.

heard about is the title page of a composition for male chorus written in the Terezín ghetto by one of its inmates, the composer Pavel Haas. Besides the title itself, *Al S'fod* (*Do not Lament*), and the usual information regarding the composer, the poet—Jakov Simoni—and the scoring, Haas decorated the title page with musical notes that, while carefully placed on their staves, are actually adapted to look like Hebrew letters. As expected, the camp authorities failed to recognize this, but the ones for whom the message was intended did: it reads "Kizkeret lejon hasana harison vemuacharon begalut Terezín"—In remembrance of the first and at the same time the last anniversary of the Terezín exile (for more details, Karas 1985).

One step further, musical scores may be accompanied by verbal and visual texts in the form of epigrams and illustrations. Since epigrams are frequently quotations from extant literary works, they could, of course, stand alone and do not concern us here. Illustrations in musical manuscripts, however, form a category of their own. They were known primarily from manuscripts of late medieval and Renaissance music. An illustrative example is the famous *Chansonnier Cordiforme*, the "heart-shaped chansonnier." More fanciful than useful for music-making, it is a kind of troubadour song written into a preciously illuminated heart.[20] Similarly, the visual, verbal, and musical components appear almost inseparably integrated, and the artistic is ingeniously blended with the practical, in the manuscript pages of 15th-century canons.

Another interesting example of the integration of both visual and verbal elements into music is found in those written and painted scores that flourished in the 15th and 16th centuries and were referred to as "Augenmusik"—musical notation with a symbolic or otherwise extra-musically informative meaning that is apparent to the eye but not to the ear. Symbols include, for instance, the use of blackness in notes with many, particularly thickly drawn beams for concepts such as "darkness" and "death." The Gulliver Suite for two violins in Telemann's 1729 *Der getreue Musik-Meister* (*The Faithful Music Master*) includes a Lilliputian chaconne and a gigantic ("Brobdingnagian") gigue. The first is written in absurdly small note values (with up to six beams, hence 256th-notes in a time marked as 3/32), the other in a hilariously large time frame, whole notes grouped with 24/1 in every measure). This charming adaptation of the musical notation to

---

[20] The text of this composition by Johannes Regis (c. 1430-c.1485) begins "S'il vous plaist que vostre ie soye" (If you want that I be yours): The art work of the manuscript was done by Jean de Montchenu. (Paris: Bibliothèque Nationale, Ms. nouv. acq. fr. 2973, fol 20c-21r).

the characters thus portrayed is a case of Augenmusik since only the performers get a chance to perceive the joke.

The production of manuscripts by Baude Cordier is famous in this genre; see particularly his three-voice rondeau "Belle, bonne, sage," a love song whose staves and text together create the form of a heart. My own favorite in this genre is a four-part untexted canon by Bartolomé Ramos de Pareja (c.1440-1491), in which the single staff containing the musical sequence is bent into a circular shape and set, in golden ink, against a background of deep sky blue. Wind spirits blowing into the notes from the four sides of the page, which represent the four points of the compass, indicate the entry of the four voices, while the calligraphy fitted into the circle betrays the composer as a music theorist, who informs singers about the modes they will detect in the four-part harmony resulting from the proper execution of this canon.[21]

Opera as a genre typically relies on integrating a verbal text into the composition in such a way that both elements, lyrics and music, seem to be lacking an essential complement when represented separately. However, the degree to which the component parts of opera—the libretto on the one hand and the "pure" music on the other—are capable of also functioning independently is often considerable. Many librettos may be rather unimaginative when taken as dramatic works; but, as testified in the now established term Literaturoper, there are a number of literary works that originated as dramas and continue to stand as such, before and after they have been set to music by a composer. And as, for instance, Hindemith's symphonies *Mathis der Maler* and *Die Harmonie der Welt* prove, even the music (or part thereof) can sometimes function as a fully valid artistic testimony when taken on its own. Yet these cases are exceptions rather than the rule, and the "music alone" or "drama alone" typically differs from the corresponding component that forms a constituent part of the opera.

The third category in the field of music as the subject active on works in its sister arts focuses on works of literature or art that are "transmedialized." In such

---

[21] Ramos de Pareja's manuscript, illuminated by Gherardo and Monte da Giovanni del Fora, is today held by the Biblioteca Nationale Centrale in Florence (Ms. Banco Rari 229, Magl. XIX, 59, fol. C.111.b). Another famous example of a canon in circular notation is that by Baude Cordier, estimated to stem from the late 14th or early 15th century. Composed in the form that we know as caccia (a word that means "hunt" but, like fuga, also has implications of being chased), this canon is notated in two concentric circles. These are accompanied by four blocks of text, placed in the four corners of the page and themselves encircled by two delicately drawn concentric circles. The text block in the upper left-hand corner, containing the lyrics, is itself written on concentric circles, while the three blocks containing accompanying words (commentary, as it were) appear in normal, horizontal script.

transformations from one medium into another no verbal or pictorial element is combined with or integrated into the musical text. Instead, the musical composition refers to an element or a combination of elements in a work of literature or the visual arts that is maintained as such. While it may be reprinted in the program book, it is not presented to the listeners as part of the musical performance. Although not present before the reader's eyes, the impressions the primary work created in the composer, including any responses or associations generated in the process, reach listeners in musical language alone.

Where such transformations appear in poetry or prose on painting, they are referred to as ekphrasis. In music, such ekphrasis can take as its object a work of literature or a work of visual art. Early examples of music's responding to specific works of literature or the visual arts[22] originated in the 19th century. Modest Mussorgsky's 1874 piano composition *Pictures at an Exhibition*, in which he matches the memorial exhibition arranged in St. Petersburg for his late friend Victor Hartmann with a sounding counterpart, is probably the best-known example in this genre. Other musical responses to paintings and sculptures from the period include Liszt's 1839 piano piece on Michelangelo's *Penseroso*, one of the sculptures in the Medici Chapel in Florence, 1857 symphonic poem on Wilhelm von Kaulbach's *Battle of the Huns*, his 1862 musical reflection on six frescoes by Moritz von Schwind in the oratorio *The Legend of Saint Elizabeth*, 1862, Mahler's 1888 First Symphony with its reference to a woodcut by Schwind, as well as the various tone poems on Böcklin's famous painting *The Isle of the Dead*. Musical responses to poetry, novels, and dramas from the late 19th-century developed from overtures composed for theatrical performances that, rather than limiting themselves to their function as mere mood-preparing preludes, often allocated musical themes to dramatic personae and attempted to emulated aspects of the dramatic development. The first independent compositions responding to literary works are Berlioz's dramatic symphonies *Harold en Italie* (1834) after Lord Byron and *Roméo et Juliette* (1839) after Shakespeare as well as Liszt's symphonic poems *Tasso* (1849) after Byron, *Ce qu'on entend sur la montagne* (1850; "What one hears on the mountain," inspired by the poem *Feuilles d'automne, Autumn Leaves*), and *Mazeppa* (1851), all after Victor Hugo, *The Ideals* (1857) after Schiller, and *Hamlet* (1858) after Shakespeare. These are followed a generation later by Mahler's First Symphony *The Titan* (1888) after Jean Paul, Richard Strauss's tone poems *Macbeth* (1888) after Shakespeare, *Also*

---

[22] The qualifier "specific" refers to works that can not only be identified unequivocally by their title, but that exist in the real world and not—as do some examples in the field of program music—primarily in the composer's mind.

sprach Zarathustra (*Thus Spake Zarathustra*, 1896) after Nietzsche, and *Don Quixote* (1897) after Cervantes, and Sergei Rachmaninoff's orchestral fantasy *The Rock* (1897) on a couplet from a poem by the Russian poet Mikhail Lermontov.

Up to the end of the 19th century, however, musical responses to works from either of the sister arts were reined in by the requirements of musical genres. Composers wishing to render the details, the style, the layout, and the mood of another artist's work in musical language were only completely set free to do so with the stylistic liberation happening around the turn to the 20th century. This liberation prepared the ground for a veritable blossoming of musical transmedializations in the 20th century. A dual online database maintained at the University of Innsbruck in Austria provides a list of more than 600 composers from all over the world who have created works in response to the visual arts and almost 1000 composers referring to a literary text.[23] The majority of these composers have been or are working in the 20th and 21st centuries.

As the list of examples from literature and the visual arts responding to music given earlier and the numbers above indicate, the intermedial interest of music toward its sister arts has recently far outpaced that of the sister arts toward music. Since the number of such works is far too large to allow for a meaningful discussion of their scope and variety, this overview will end with a special case (see Bruhn 2000, 2008, 2013).

When the transformation of a work of visual art is brought onto the theatrical stage and wedded with the miming aspect of that genre, we speak of enactments. The concluding paragraphs will introduce one case of a musical enactment, using as an example the three scenes from act VI in Hindemith's opera *Mathis der Maler*.

In the first of these scenes, Hindemith's painter Mathis attempts to soothe the distraught young girl Regina with a narration of what he claims to see in a picture portraying three angels. His verbal depiction leads us to one of the second-tier panels of the *Isenheim Altarpiece*, the masterpiece of the operatic protagonist's historical model, Grünewald. At this juncture, Hindemith the librettist puts into the mouth of his character Mathis a most intriguing tripartite description and interpretation of the panel that the historical "Master Mathis" painted ten or more years prior to the year into which this fictional conversation is placed. In the way in which Mathis tells Regina about the "pious pictures," no mention is made of who created them; the narration appears guided by the idea and intention of what is portrayed rather than by an attempt to describe the visual composition in all its

---

[23] See www.musiknachbildern.at and www.klingendetexte.at

details. Mathis focuses on the spiritual aspect of this angelic concert—and so does the music in which Hindemith sets this scene.[24]

This "narrated portrayal" of the Angelic Concert is complemented in the subsequent scene by an enactment-cum-narration based on one of the two rear panels of the altarpiece, *The Temptation of Saint Antony*. The events presented on stage function on three levels here. First, in the larger context of the operatic plot, Mathis's encounter with human tempters and monstrous tormentors appears like a bad dream—or a vision, given that he perceives himself as the Egyptian hermit Antony. Second, the verbal onslaught by the seven human tempters functions as a multi-layered interpretative embodiment of what is, beyond the reference to the pictorial representation in the altar panel, both the inner story of the temptations of Saint Antony and a dramatic portrayal of the plight in which Mathis is caught. Third, the physical attack by the monsters is at the same time a tableau vivant[25] of Grünewald's depiction and its ekphrasis: the choir does not only accompany with insults and spiteful interpretations the assault by hellish monsters to which Mathis/Antony is subjected in the center of the stage, but simultaneously narrates the scene as painted by Grünewald. All images evoked in this scene also reflect a deeper spiritual meaning since they can be understood as provocations, as torments that emerge from the victim's own doubting mind. They represent his spiritual nightmares and the internal enemies that haunt his soul.

The third scene in this sequence, entitled "The Visit of Saint Antony in the Hermitage of Saint Paul" after the Grünewald panel to which it relates, limits the enactment to the visual recreation: stage design, costumes, position, and posture of the two actors. No narrative relates what we see and hear to the painting, thus allowing us to focus all the more on the symbolic significance of the scene. The older hermit Paul ("embodied" by the operatic character, Cardinal Albrecht) acts as a spiritual adviser to Antony (= Mathis). While his verbal admonitions deal unequivocally with the reality of the artist in the time of the Lutheran Uprising

---

[24] For a detailed analysis of how Hindemith's music reflects, relates to, portrays, and interprets the relevant panels of Grünewald's Isenheim Altarpiece, please refer to my extensive study on the subject, *The Temptation of Paul Hindemith: Mathis der Maler as a Spiritual Testimony* (Stuyvesant, NY: Pendragon, 1998).

[25] The term tableau vivant, "living picture," denotes a scenic reinterpretation of a pictorial work popular as a genteel pastime. Participants would choose a work of art, dress in imitations of the depicted garments, find props that matched those in the paintings, and assume the poses of the portrayed characters. For integrations or descriptions of tableaux vivants in the literatures of the 18th and 19th centuries, see the "attitudes" of Lady Hamilton and Goethe's *Wahlverwandtschaften* (Elective Affinities). More recently, the character Lily Bart in Edith Wharton's *The House of Mirth* enacts Sir Joshua Reynolds's *Portrait of Mrs. Lloyd* (painted in 1775).

and the Peasants' War, the scenic setting binds the conversation into the larger conflict of conscience that is, both literally and figuratively, through the ekphrasis of the altar panels, the subject matter of the opera. Hindemith's music adds a wealth of nuances that corroborate and enhance this interpretive layering.

> Il y a de bizarre, et même d'inquiétant, dans le fait d'une inspiration de seconde main, cherchée dans les œuvres d'autrui, et cherchée dans un art dont les buts et les moyens sont très différents de ceux qui charactérisent l'art poétique. Est-ce vraiment légitime? Est-ce vrai- ment utile et fécond? (Étienne Souriau, La poésie française et la peinture, London 1966 : 6)[26]

In his *Vorlesungen über die Ästhetik*,[27] Hegel ponders the position of the creative artist in classical art and compares it with the approach typical for the modern artist. While Hegel, when speaking of "modern," would necessarily have referred to denizens of the eighteenth century, many of his observations still ring true today when applied to the heirs of the post-classical aesthetics on which the philosopher commented more than one and a half centuries ago.

One of the points Hegel regards as focal in the distinction concerns the question why creative artists of his time were so keen to invent their own topics and contents, rather than relying on given subject matter as classical artists had customarily done. "The Greek artists," he establishes, "obtained their material from the national religion in which what was taken over from the East by the Greeks had already begun to be reshaped. Phidias took his Zeus from Homer, and even the tragedians did not invent the fundamental material which they represented. Similarly, the Christian artists too, Dante and Raphael, only gave shape to what was already present in the creeds and in religious ideas." (Hegel 1975: 439)

---

[26] There is something odd, and even disturbing, in second-hand inspiration, sought in the works of someone else, and sought in an art form of which the aims and the means are very different from those which characterize poetry. Is this really legitimate? Is this truly useful and fruitful.
[27] The title for the English translation of Georg Wilhelm Friedrich Hegel's *Vorlesungen über die Ästhetik* (first published in German posthumously in 1835; recent edition Stuttgart: Reclam, 1980) exists in two versions. I am quoting from the translation by T.M. Knox, *Hegel's Aesthetics: Lectures on Fine Arts* (Oxford: Clarendon Press, 1975). An earlier translation appeared under the title *The Philosophy of Fine Art*, trans. F.P.B. Osmaston (London: G. Bell and Sons, 1920). The chapter from which I am excerpting appears in Part II: "Development of the Ideal into the Particular Forms of Art," where it is Section II: "The Classical Form of Art."

Hegel believes that when, as in classical art, "the content is determinate and the free shape is determined by the content itself," a dual advantage is achieved: "the artist's mere caprice is excluded"; instead the artist will "concentrate himself on the task of shaping the external artistic appearance in a way congruent to such content." (Hegel 1975: 439-40) As a result, the philosopher claims,

> The artist's relation to this objectively established material is freer because he does not enter himself into the process of its generation and parturition, nor does he remain caught in a pressure to obtain genuine meanings for art; on the contrary, an absolute content for art confronts him; he adopts it and freely reproduces it out of his own resources. (Hegel 1975: 439)

These observations seem exceedingly pertinent to the question posed, by Étienne Souriau and other skeptics arguing for self-realization as the preeminent goal of the Romantic artist, about the validity of "second-hand inspiration."

In this light, the genre of ekphrasis—whether taken in the original sense with the verbal language as the sole active agent or defined more broadly and thus encompassing verbal, musical, and choreographic ekphrasis—constitutes a special case of the classical approach to artistic expression. Composers, rather than writing so-called absolute music or program music on the basis of scenarios determined by their own imagination, take the content they set out to express and shape from a pre-existing source. Instead of struggling to find what they want to express, they concentrate fully on the how of the realization.

This does not, as I have shown elsewhere in much detail, prevent the responding artist—in this case the composer—from generating and shaping meaning. In fact, every stance the composer may adopt toward the work thus creatively contemplated implies a different degree, and kind, of meaning-creating relationship between the two representations of shared contents. Especially where aspects of the composer's transmedialization seem to reflect on the poet's or painter's interpretation or on the style and details of representation, the "secondary" creation is likely to exhibit a greater complexity of statements regarding both content and aesthetics than a possible "primary" presentation of a subject matter.

Significantly though, by far the majority of the scenes and stories that inform the content underlying the intermedially engaged compositions I have examined over a period of some twenty years did not originate with the poets or painters to whose representation the composers respond. On the contrary, most of them fall, directly or indirectly, into one of the categories Hegel mentions as sources that would ideally guarantee the desired freedom from "mere caprice." Such sources include, above all, myths and legends, fairy-tales and fables, events from a shared historical or religious past, and the stories representing a nation's or region's lore or folk wisdom.

While the characteristic attitude of classical painting and poetry, as Hegel shows us, is to develop "given materials and mythological ideas [...] cheerfully in the free play of art," (Hegel 1975: 440) musical ekphrasis can be described as a further step in the same direction: as the expression of composers intent on applying their skills and imaginative powers to themes and topics they encounter in the representation of fellow artists, but which are in themselves timeless and universal.

REFERENCES

Bartlett, Rosamund. "Sonata Form in Chekhov's 'The Black Monk'," *Intersections and Transpositions: Russian Music, Literature and Society*, ed. Andrew Wachtel. Evanston, IL: Northwestern University Press, 1998, 58-72.

Basilius, Harold A. "Thomas Mann's Use of Musical Structure and Technique in 'Tonio Kröger'," *German Review* 19 (1944), 284-308

Brown, Calvin S. Music and Literature: *A Comparison of the Arts*. Hanover, NH: University Press of New England, 1987.

_____ "Musico-Literary Research in the Last Two Decades." *Yearbook of Comparative and General Literature* 19 (1970): 5-27.

_____ "The Relations Between Music and Literature as a Field of Study." *Yearbook of Comparative and General Literature* 22 (1973): 97-107.

_____ "Theme and Variations as Literary Form." *Yearbook of Comparative and General Literature* 27 (1978): 35-43

_____ "The Writing and Reading of Music: Thoughts in Some Parallels Between Two Artistic Media." *Yearbook of Comparative and General Literature* 33 (1984): 7-18.

Bruhn, Siglind. *Musical Ekphrasis: Composers Responding to Poetry and Painting*. Hillsdale, NY: Pendragon, 2000.

_____ Musical Ekphrasis in Rilke's "Marienleben". Amsterdam/Atlanta: Rodopi, 2000.

_____ (ed.) *Sonic Transformations of Literary Texts: From Program Music to Musical Ekphrasis*. Hillsdale, NY: Pendragon, 2008.

_____ *Europas klingende Bilder: Eine musikalische Reise.* Waldkirch: Gorz, 2013.

Buchwald, Emilie and Roston, Ruth (eds.) *Mixed Voices.* Minneapolis: Milkweed Editions, 1991.

Clüver, Claus. "Ekphrasis Reconsidered: On Verbal Representations of Non-Verbal Texts," in U.-B. Lagerroth, H. Lund, and E. Hedling, eds., *Interart Poetics: Essays on the Interrelations of the Arts and Media.* Amsterdam: Rodopi, 1997.

Dömling, Wolfgang. "Reuniting the Arts: Notes on the History of an Idea," *19th-Century Music XVIII/1* (Summer 1994), 3-9

Fletcher, John Gould. *Preludes and Symphonies.* New York 1930.

Franciscono, Marcel. "The Place of Music in Klee's Art: A Reconsideration," Exhibition Catalogue *Klee og musikken*, Art Center in Høvikodden, Norway (6-9/1985) and Centre Georges Pompidou, Paris (10/1985-2/1986), 272-291.

Hill, Camille Crunelle. "Saint Thomas Aquinas and the Theme of Truth in Messiaen's Saint François d'Assise." In Siglind Bruhn (ed.), *Messiaen's Language of Mystical Love.* New York, Garland, 1998, 143-166.

Junk, Victor. *Goethes Fortsetzung der Mozartschen Zauberflöte.* Berlin: A. Duncker, 1899.

Kandinsky. *Über das Geistige in der Kunst.* English edition New York: Solomon Guggenheim Foundation, 1946.

_____ *Punkt und Linie zu Fläche. Beitrag zur Analyse der malerischen Elemente.* English edition New York: Solomon Guggenheim Foundation, 1947.

Kagan, Andrew. *Paul Klee: Art and Music.* Ithaca, [N.Y.] : Cornell University Press, 1983.

Karas, Joza. *Music in Terezín 1941-1945.* New York: Beaufort Books, 1985.

Klee, Paul. "Canon of Color Totality," *The Thinking Eye: The Notebooks of Paul Klee I,* ed. J. Spiller, trans. H. Norden. London 1973, 487-491.

Kolago, Lech. *Musikalische Formen und Strukturen in der deutschsprachigen Literatur des 20. Jahrhunderts.* Anif: Müller-Speiser, 1997

Leppert, Richard. *Music and Image: Domesticity, Ideology, and Socio-Cultural Formation in Eighteenth-Century England.* Cambridge and New York: Cambridge University Press, 1988.

Levith, Murray J. (ed.) *Musical Masterpieces in Prose.* Neptune, NJ: Paganiniana Publications, 1981.

Lidov, David. "Mind and Body in Music," *Semiotica* 66/1 (1987): 69-97.

Lund, Hans. *Texten som tavla: Studier i litterär bildtrans- formation.* Lund: LiberFörlag, 1982.

Mann, Thomas. *Stories of Three Decades.* New York, A. A. Knopf: 1936.

Metzger, H.-K. and R. Riehn, (eds.). *Autoren-Musik: Sprache im Grenzbereich der Künste,* Musik-Konzepte 81; Munich: edition text + kritik, 1993.

Messiaen, Olivier. *Musique et couleurs: nouveaux entretiens avec Claude Samuel.* Paris: Belfont, 1986.

Mirka, Danuta. "Colors of a Mystic Fire: Light and Sound in Scriabin's Prometheus," in Siglind Bruhn (ed.), *Signs in Musical Hermeneutics* (*The American Journal of Semiotics* 13: 1-4, 1996 [1998]), 227-248.

Petri, Horst. *Literatur und Musik: Form- und Strukturparallelen.* Göttingen: Sachse & Pohl, 1964, 23-81.

Prieto, E. "Recherche pour un roman musical. L'exemple de Passacaille de Robert Pinget," *Poétique* 94 (1993), 153-170.

Phillips, Tom. *Music in Art.* Munich and New York: Prestel, 1997.

Ratner, Leonard G. *Classic Music: Expression, Form, and Style.* New York: Schirmer, 1980.

Riethmüller, Albrecht. *Gedichte über Musik.* Laaber: Laaber-Verlag, 1996.

Runge, Philipp Otto. *Hinterlassene Schriften.* Göttingen 1965, Vol. I, 223.

Sabanejev, Leonid. "Prometheus von Skrjabin," in Wassily Kandinsky and Franz Marc (eds), *Der Blaue Reiter.* Munich 1912.

Scher, Steven Paul. *Verbal Music in German Literature.* New Haven: Yale University Press, 1968.

Schnebel, Dieter. "Sprache als Musik in der Musik." In Steven P. Scher, ed., *Literatur und Musik: Ein Handbuch zur Theorie und Praxis eines komparatistischen Grenzgebiets.* Berlin: E. Schmidt, 1984, 209-230)

Schwab, H.W. "Das Musikgedicht als musicologische Quelle," In Walter Salmen, ed., *Beiträge zur Geschichte der Musikanschauung im 19. Jahrhundert.* Regensburg: Bosse, 1965, 127-138

Schwartz, Monika. *Musikanaloge Idee und Struktur im französischen Theater: Untersuchungen zu Jean Tardieu und Eugène Ionesco.* Munich: Fink, 1981.

Spaethling, Robert. *Music and Mozart in the Life of Goethe*. Columbia, SC: Camden House, 1987.
Vaget, Hans Rudolf. "Thomas Mann and Wagner: Zur Funktion des Leitmotivs in *Der Ring des Nibelungen* und *Buddenbrooks*," Steven Paul Scher (ed.), *Literatur und Musik: Ein Handbuch zur Theorie und Praxis eines komparatistischen Grenzgebietes*, 1968, 326-347.
Volkov, Solomon. *Testimony: The Memoirs of Dmitry Shostakovitch*. London, 1979.

ABOUT THE AUTHOR

Dr. Dr. h.c. Siglind Bruhn is a music analyst/musicologist, concert pianist, and interdisciplinary scholar. Since 1993 she has been affiliated with at the University of Michigan's Institute for the Humanities as a Life Research Associate in the fields of "Music and Modern Literatures" while also collaborating with research units in France, Denmark, Sweden, and Finland. She is the author of over twenty-five book-length monographs on 20th-century music and its relationship to literature, art, and religion. Her most recent publications in English are a study of Frank Martin's musical reflection on Death (2011), a first analytical appraisal of seminal works by Germany's most successful composer of the younger generation, Jörg Widmann (2013), and a study on Arnold Schoenberg's works from the years 1899-1914 in the context of the period's cultural upheaval (2015). In 2001 she was elected to the European Academy of Arts and Sciences; in 2008 she received an honorary doctorate from Linnaeus University, Sweden. During the years 2014-2017 she is serving as Guest Professor for Music of the 20th and 21st centuries at the Music Academies in Kraków and Katowice, Poland. For more information see http://umich.edu/~siglind.

CHAPTER 3

"How Do I Love Thee?" Infatuation, Passion, and Love in the Novel and 2004 Film *The Phantom of the Opera*

Deborah Fillerup Weagel

> Rather than viewing a film adaptation as a cultural replacement for a story or novel, it seems closer to the truth to view each work as a variation on a theme. (Stephanie Harrison, Adaptations, xviii)

The musical *The Phantom of the Opera* has captivated international audiences ever since its premiere in London in 1986. With music by Andrew Lloyd Webber, lyrics by Charles Hart, and further additions by Richard Stilgoe, it depicts a deformed and somewhat depraved man, known as the Opera Ghost or Phantom, who lives underneath the Paris Opera House in the late 1800s. Based on the French novel *Le Fantôme de l'Opéra*, by Gaston Leroux, it reveals the infatuation of Erik, the Phantom, for a gifted young singer, Christine Daaé, who does not love him but rather her childhood playmate, Vicomte Raoul de Chagny. Some of the most heart-wrenching moments of the musical occur when Erik witnesses Christine's affection and commitment to Raoul. Overcome with a sense of failure and rejection, and very much aware that his deformity has been a tremendous hindrance to him, particularly with romantic relationships, the Phantom spirals into a state of despair and seeks revenge in one way or another.

Leroux's novel has not only been adapted into this blockbuster musical, which is still being performed across the globe, but films have also been created based on the general narrative. There is, for example, the 1925 silent horror film about the Phantom, starring Lon Chaney as Erik, Mary Philbin as Christine, and Norman Kerry as Raoul. Directed by Rupert Julian and others, it became one of the most popular and successful silent movies made, and it is important historically for its contribution to the horror genre as well as to filmmaking in general. There have been other film adaptations of the novel, and two of these are based on the musical. The first is the 2004 movie directed by Joel Schumacher, which includes Gerard Butler as the Phantom, Emmy Rossum as Christine Daeé, and Patrick Wilson as Raoul. The second is a 2011 film version called The

Phantom of the Opera at the Royal Albert Hall. In honor of the 25th anniversary of the musical, elaborate performances were staged at the Royal Albert Hall in London. Ramin Karimloo starred as the Phantom, Sierra Boggess as Christine, and Hadley Fraser as Raoul, Vicomte de Chagny. The difference between the 2004 and the 2011 films is that the former was made to be a movie only, while the latter was created to be a lavish stage production that was filmed in a concert hall (that was converted into a theater for the performances). For the purposes of this essay, I examine the interconnection of the novel and the 2004 film adaptation of the musical, rather than 1925 silent film version or the filmed stage production at the Royal Albert Hall. I analyze the relationships of infatuation, passion, and love in these works and suggest that Erik exhibits only infatuation and passion for Christine, while Christine and Raoul demonstrate genuine love for one another.

Leroux's novel was first published serially in Le Gaulois from 23 September 1909 to 8 January 1910. The first complete French edition of the novel, which included revisions based on the serial version, was published in Paris by Pierre Lafitte in 1910. Today there are a variety of French editions, including some which have been abridged and even adapted for use with younger students, such as the 2005 Livre de Poche version which is part of the Ldp Policiers series. For this essay, I have chosen to use Lafitte's 1910 edition as it appears in ebooksgratuits.com. The first English translation was available in 1911, and there have been several different translations since. I will use David Coward's 2012 translation, published by Oxford University Press, which includes and introduction and notes. H. D. Kingsbury has also edited two volumes of literary adaptations of the Phantom story by other authors as can be found in Phantom Variations: Tales from the World of the Opera Ghost and Phantom Variations, Volume 2: Further Tales from the Worlds of the Opera Ghost.

Like most film adaptations of novels, there are differences between the original text and the film. This is particularly true with the 2004 movie of *The Phantom of the Opera*, because it is based on the musical which was inspired by the novel. So the film is an adaptation of an adaptation, and if we compare the movie with the novel, there are numerous changes. For example, the film begins with an auction, and there is no such event in the novel. In the movie adaptation, Joseph Buquet is hanged on stage, while in the book he is hanged early in the narrative in one of the basements of the Opera House. In the film, there is no character called the Persian, while in the original text this person has known the Phantom for years, even prior to their experiences at the opera, and he helps guide Raoul through the lower passages of the Opera House to find Erik.

The Phantom's appearance and background are also different in the movie compared to the novel. Although his face is disfigured in both mediums, in the film only one side needs to be covered with a mask because the rest is quite presentable and even attractive. His body is also of average build, and he seems to be very much a living, breathing human being. However, in the book, his head is terribly disfigured, and according the Joseph Buquet, he is

> d'une prodigieuse maigreur et son habit noir flotte sur une charpente squelettique. Ses yeux sont si profonds qu'on ne distingue pas bien les prunelles immobiles. On ne voit, en somme, que deux grands trous noirs comme aux crânes des morts. Sa peau...est tendue sur l'ossature comme une peau de tambour. (Leroux, *Fantôme*, Lafitte 16)

> tremendously thin and his coat hangs on a bag o'bones. His eyes are so deep-set you can't hardly make out the pupils which never move. In fact, all you can see is two great big black holes like sockets in a dead man's skull. The skin is stretched over the bones as tight as a drum. (Leroux, *Phantom* 13)

His skin also has a yellowish tint; he has no real nose and only a few wisps of hair. In the film, where he has no specific name and is known as the Phantom, Opera Ghost, or Angel of Music, he escapes from a freak show where he is exhibited and poorly treated, and he finds refuge in the lower areas of the opera building. In the novel, his name is Erik, and he is from the Middle East. He is given his first mask by his mother, and travels with gypsies and participates in their shows. He also creates torture chambers for royalty in the Middle East, which gives him experience in creating his own torture room in Paris. Once in France, he works as a contractor at the Opera House as it is being constructed, and this gives him access to the basement areas where he establishes his own residence.

Some other differences between the film and the book involve other characters, such as the Vicomte Philippe de Chagny (the brother of Raoul). The movie omits scenes from the novel that include him, such as when he searches in the underground basements of the Opera House, an action which results in his death by drowning. In the book the diva Carlotta is Spanish, while in the movie she is Italian. Furthermore, in the movie Raoul has direct confrontations with the Phantom, whereas in the book he never encounters Erik face to face. For additional comparisons between the 2004 film and the novel, see "What's the Difference." For a list of some other adaptations of the novel, see Ann C. Hall's

Phantom Variations: The Adaptations of Gaston Leroux's Phantom of the Opera, 1925 to the Present.

The fact that the novel has been adapted into other mediums is not surprising. Stephanie Harrison writes, "The art of storytelling has never really been as static as we like to think" (xvii). She argues that when done successfully, "adaptations extend, enhance, and elaborate on their sources" (xix). In the case of *The Phantom of the Opera*, James F. Broderick suggests that the general "story seems to cry out for dramatization for the stage or the screen" (146). He explains further:

> The plot involves wild events and exotic settings that would be at home in any grand opera libretto. The dialogue is often exaggerated and highly exclamatory. The story is melodramatic, with tears, tragedy, and tension taking their respective turns on the page. The overall impact on most readers is not, one suspects, too different from how they might feel emerging from the rarified, magical world of the opera, with its dramatic upheavals, reversals of fortune, tragically unrequited loves, and fairy tale endings. (144)

The various adaptations for the stage and film, some which include music, songs, dance, and acting, and the tremendous success of some of these renditions, have likely been inspired by performative elements in the novel.

In the book *Opera in the Novel from Balzac to Proust*, Cormac Newark points out how certain passages in *The Phantom* have dialogue that includes parenthetical sentences or phrases in italics, as though they were stage directions (149-50). For example, when Madame Giry recounts to the opera directors M. Richard and M. Moncharmin how a couple and their male friend in Box Five once caused a scene of their own during the opera, her recitation is not only dramatic but also sung. She 'performs' the story of how the husband realizes, thanks to the whisperings of a mysterious voice, that the friend is kissing his wife's arm behind his back. The account takes place during a performance of Faust at the Opera House, and Giry weaves details of the music into her narrative:

> Mame Giry tousse, assure sa voix...elle commence...on dirait qu'elle se prépare à chanter toute la partition de Gounod.
>
> "Voilà, monsieur. Il y avait, ce soir-là, au premier rang, M. Maniera et sa dame...et, derrière Mme Maniera, leur ami intime, M. Isidore Saack. Méphistophélès chantait (Mame Giry chante) : 'Vous qui faites l'endormie.'" (Leroux, *Fantôme,* Lafitte 67)

> Mme Giry coughed, cleared her throat and began. It was as if she was limbering up to sing the entire score of Gounod's opera.
>
> "Well now, sir, that night, M. Maniera and his lady wife...were in the front of the box, and their good friend M. Isidore Saack was sitting behind Mme Maniera. Mephistopheles was singing (she began to sing): 'Thou who feignist sleep.'" (Leroux, *Phantom* 48)

We see how Giry prepares to share her story almost as though she were to perform the opera. The reader knows exactly when her recitation turns into song based on the parenthetical information provided by Leroux. As Giry continues her narrative, the reader is aware of her behavior, further singing, and action:

> (Une grimace de Mame Giry.) Donc, Méphistophélès continuait sa chanson (Mame Giry chante): "Catherine que j'adore–pourquoi refuser–l'amant qui vous implore–un si doux baiser?" (Leroux, *Fantôme*, Lafitte 67)
>
> (Here Mme Giry simpers coyly.) Anyroad, Mephistopheles carries on singing (Mme Giry sings): "Catherine, whom I adore...why deny me, I implore, a sweet and tender kiss?" (Leroux, *Phantom* 48)

Once again, from the parenthetical italicized words, we know that Mme Giry is behaving coyly, and we see precisely when she begins to sing the opera libretto. She explains that a mysterious voice whispers to M. Maniera that his own wife will not deny a kiss from their friend Isidore. She says that M. Maniera

> se retourne, mais, cette fois, du côté de sa dame et d'Isidore, et qu'est-ce qu'il voit? Isidore qui avait pris par-derrière la main de sa dame et qui la couvrait de baisers dans le petit creux du gant...comme ça, mes bons messieurs. (Mame Giry couvre de baisers le coin de chair laissé à nu par son gant de filoselle.) (Leroux, *Fantôme*, Lafitte 67-68)
>
> turns sharply, this time to the left, towards his lady and Isidore, and what does he see? Isidore behind him holding his lady's hand busily kissing it through the little opening near the button of her glove...like this, your honours. (Mme Giry kisses the round place on her own hand left bare by her rough silk glove.) (Leroux, *Phantom* 49)

M. Maniera becomes upset with his friend and causes a ruckus in Box Five. We know from the italicized information that Mme Giry demonstrates the manner in which Isidore kisses Julie Maniera. Reading this particular passage is similar to reading a script for a play or for a musical, and this is one way Leroux's writing lends itself to performance.

In addition, Leroux's novel includes details and concerns with putting on a show or opera in general. This theme is one of three main types of musicals Rick Altman presents in his book *The American Film Musical*: show, folk, and fairy tale. In the show film musical, typically the plot involves preparation for a show and "the making of a romantic couple both symbolically and causally related to the success of the show" (200). Altman explains why an audience becomes so captivated with the backstage musical, one that takes the viewer behind the scenes and is not limited to the stage performance:

> The show musical gives us the illusion of seeing something which theatergoers cannot perceive: the theater audience's gaze is stopped by the stage backdrop, but the film audience can see right through that backdrop and into the wings....In other words, the show musical camera becomes an agent of voyeurism. When we go to a backstage musical we lift a veil; by pulling aside the backdrop or peeking into the wings we are able to satisfy our natural desire to look beyond, behind, and beneath. (207)

Leroux's novel fits this model in that it takes the reader behind the scenes; it enables a certain voyeurism into the private lives of the performers and those involved with the production of the opera. Altman writes further: "In the backstage musical...the film audience not only watches the theater audience watch the show, but it also observes the theater actors rehearsing the show. The show itself loses its primacy, making way for the new primary concerns of observing the show and making the show" (205). This is a significant element of the novel that makes it not only compelling to the reader but also prime material for adaptation for a musical. The novel preceded film musicals, yet the text lends itself so convincingly to performance with singers, dancers, stage hands, managers, and lovers, as though it could be a script for the stage or film. The 1986 musical which premiered in England on stage also lifted the veil and took viewers both backstage and into the private lives of the performers, as did the 2004 film.

Taking the viewer behind the scenes is one aspect of the novel and film musical; another important element deals with the love story—bringing together a couple in relation to the production of the show. Here again, Leroux's novel fits this template in a general way. In the story, the Phantom is infatuated with Christine Daeé, but she loves the Vicomte Raoul de Chagny, and Raoul in turn loves her. This complexity of relationships adds to the tension and intrigue of the novel as well as to its various adaptions for the stage and screen. Although there are a variety of differences between the novel and some of its adaptations, including the 2004 film, there is one consistent part to the story that does not change: the love triangle.

The term 'love' is often used in contemporary society in a generic and unspecific way. We speak of 'falling in love' or 'being in love,' when we are really only infatuated with someone. In his seminal book *The Art of Loving*, Erich Fromm dismisses the idea that love is a strong or passionate feeling that we have for another human being. He writes: "If two people who have been strangers, as all of us are, suddenly let the wall between them break down, and feel close, feel one, this moment of oneness is one of the most exhilarating, most exciting experiences in life. It is all the more wonderful and miraculous for persons who have been shut off, isolated, without love" (4). He explains that this intimacy often includes physical and sexual attraction and sometimes even consummation, but it is not long lasting. As the two people involved become more familiar with each other, "their intimacy loses more and more its miraculous character, until their antagonism, their disappointments, their mutual boredom kill whatever is left of the initial excitement" (4). Fromm points out that some people mistake the "intensity of the infatuation" and their "being 'crazy' about each other" as evidence of love, when in reality it is only proof "of their preceding loneliness" (4). He claims that actual love requires action and effort.

In analyzing the interaction of the Phantom and Christine Daeé, I propose that the relationship is more of infatuation and passion than genuine love. Initially there is a sense of mutual infatuation in that the Phantom becomes enamored with Christine and gives her singing lessons. Christine, on the other hand, believes the Phantom to be the Angel of Music her father spoke of before his death, so she has a certain trust and respect for him. During this time, the wall Fromm describes breaks down and they experience a certain oneness that is exhilarating. In the book *Vocal Apparitions: The Attraction of Cinema to Opera*, Michal Grover-Friedlander writes of this aspect of their relationship further. She observes that both the Phantom and Christine deal with the void of lost parents in their lives. She explains that they both experience "the wish to recover and re-create an unattainable past, a union with the parent of the opposite sex," and this "is expressed in what the prima donna and the Phantom see in each other, each through the other's voice" (24). She explains: "The prima donna follows the Phantom's voice since she believes him to be the Angel of Music, the reincarnation of her father. In turn, the Phantom's obsession with the operatic voice of the prima donna is a form of compensation. His relation to his mother was primarily through the voice, as she too could not stand his deformed facial features" (24). However, as Fromm points out, the infatuation they experience is not lasting. In getting to know the Phantom better, Christine realizes that the Angel of Music is not someone she wants to spend her life with for the long term. She becomes aware of his darker side (one who murders, who hurts or even tortures others, who imprisons others—particularly her, against her will), and she understands that he is not at all a suitable partner. Their initial intimacy loses its effect, and the Phantom who once intrigued her eventually fills her with a sense of horror.

Susan Kavaler-Adler asserts that in the 2004 film, the relationship between the Phantom and Christine can be related to the "demon lover" (150) theme found in other stories, both fictional and real. She writes, "This romance with the muse is so often, in the majority of cases I have studied in women artists and writers, turned into a tale of seduction in which the male muse transforms into a dark demon lover" (152). She discusses how the Phantom mentors and teaches Christine, who has raw talent and trusts him to help her achieve her artistic potential. However, the relationship becomes more complex as the Phantom wants not only to help his pupil but also to possess her. Kavaler-Adler explains further: "Drawn into the spell of the grandiose male father-god figure, who proclaims he can create her, (as Robert Browning's Duke creates his Duchess, and as Pygmalion creates Galatea), the young virginal woman and virginal creative singing talent allows her male master and muse to control her as a patriarchal guardian" (151-52). He does not want her to have experiences outside their relationship, and he seeks to thwart any rival, such as Christine's aristocratic suitor, Raoul. Kavaler-Adler suggests:

> The Phantom, who is both teacher and muse, molds the young heroine's voice and expression into his own image. Thus the muse turns into the archetypical demon lover. The mythic demon lover, who mirrors the sinister qualities of the narcissistic character, will always seek to mold his young female protégé's voice and expression to reflect his own idealized image. (152-53)

The Phantom's obsession with Christine, his relentless control involving both her career and her activities outside the stage, and even his living quarters which have been imbued with her presence, whether she is there or not, are evidence of his narcissism and demon lover qualities.

In her article, Kavaler-Adler recounts the actual story of Suzanne Farrell, a prima ballerina with the New York City Ballet, who turned down a marriage proposal from the famous choreographer and ballet director George Ballanchine. Farrell had become the "'princess' daughter of the male 'king' (god-daddy) ballet director" and dared "to come out of the trance" (154) of this situation which helped build her career. When she agreed to marry a younger male dancer, the aging "patriarchal director" (154) had Farrell blacklisted from companies throughout the United States and her new partner was no longer able to work at the New York City Ballet. Despite leaving her "grand choreographic director father-figure" (154), Farrell established a life with her new husband and eventually found work dancing in Maurice Bejart's Belgium Ballet company. In the end, however, she did return to Ballanchine's company, but on her own terms, married to her age-appropriate husband and having more power over her dancing roles. In comparison to *The Phantom of the Opera*, Christine succeeds in leaving her grand musician singer teacher father-figure to marry Raoul, but in the novel the Phantom dies soon after their parting. Christine, however, fulfills her promise of burying him according to his instructions. It is assumed that the gold ring on his finger, the ring he gave her for their 'engagement,' was placed there by her. So both women, who both benefitted and were haunted by demon lovers, succeeded not only in marrying men of their choosing but also eventually making peace with their obsessive mentors.

While the relationship of the Phantom and Christine is really only one of infatuation, Christine and Raoul, who knew each other as children, genuinely love one another and care for each other. Fromm claims that many people view love as "being loved" (1) rather than having the ability to love. They consider what they have to gain from the relationship instead of what they can to offer. Loving is an art that requires patience, effort, and time. Fromm writes that love requires "care, responsibility, respect, and knowledge" (24). In terms of care, "love is the active concern for the life and the growth of that which we love" (25). We go to extreme measures to protect and care for the people in our lives whom we truly love. Responsibility, according to Fromm, is not obligatory but voluntary: "It is my response to the needs, expressed or unexpressed, of another human being" (26). Respect involves viewing the person as a unique individual. It is having the attitude, "I want the loved person to grow and unfold for his [or her] own sake, and in his [or her] own ways, and not for the purpose of serving me" (26). Finally, knowledge of someone we love does not deal with the periphery; it "penetrates to the core" (27). We know the history and are aware of the deeper thoughts, desires, needs, and dreams of the person, and we interact with that person accordingly.

Raoul and Christine's relationship does not begin at the Opera House, but actually much earlier when they are children. Raoul comes from a well-established and distinguished when he is only twelve, so his elder brother Philippe who is twenty years his senior, becomes an important caretaker in his life. On the other hand, Christine is from a poor family and lives in a small town near Uppsala, Sweden. Her father is an accomplished violinist who teaches his daughter skills in music, and her mother dies when she is about five years old. Professor Valerius discovers both the father and daughter and becomes their patron and mentor. When he and his wife move to France, they take the violinist Daaé and Christine with them.

One day Christine is out singing with her angelic voice by the sea, and Raoul is with his governess. The young boy, who has been staying with his aunt, begs his governess to let him walk farther than usual so he can go toward the voice that enraptures him. When the wind blows Christine's scarf into the sea, Raoul, dressed in street clothes, goes into the water to recover it for her. In gratitude, Christine laughs gleefully and gives Raoul, the Vicomte de Chagny, a kiss. This is how the young children meet, and their relationship continues to develop during that time period. Leroux describes their activities:

> Pendant la saison, ils se revirent presque tous les jours et ils jouèrent ensemble. Sur la demande de la tante et par l'entremise du professeur Valérius, le bonhomme Daaé consentit à donner des leçons de violon au jeune vicomte. Ainsi, Raoul apprit-il à aimer les mêmes airs que ceux qui avaient enchanté l'enfance de Christine.
>
> Ils avaient à peu près la même petite âme rêveuse et calme. Ils ne se plaisaient qu'aux histoires, aux vieux contes Bretons....
>
> Mais leur grande fête était lorsqu'au crépuscule, dans la grande paix du soir, après que le soleil s'était couché dans la mer, le père Daaé venait s'asseoir à côté d'eux sur le bord de la route, et leur contait à voix basse, comme s'il craignait de faire peur aux fantômes qu'il évoquait, les belles, douces ou terribles légendes du pays du Nord. (Leroux, *Fantôme*, Lafitte 80)

> For the rest of that summer, they saw each other and played together almost every day. At his aunt's request and through the good offices of Professor Valerius, Daaé the fiddler agreed to give the young Viscount violin lessons. In this way, Raoul learned to love the melodies which had made Christine's childhood so magical.
>
> They both had similar, placid natures. What they loved best were old Briton legends.... But their greatest treat was at dusk, in the quiet of evening after the sun had set over the sea, when M. Daeé would sit next to them by the side of the road and tell them fantastic, comforting, terrifying tales of the North, whispering as if he was afraid to alarm the ghosts he raised. (Leroux, *Phantom* 56-57)

Although Christine's father eventually dies, Raoul meets him, takes violin lessons from him, hears his songs and stories, and becomes familiar with him. In this manner, both Christine and Raoul establish a relationship early in their lives and share common experiences, despite their socio-economic differences.

Thus a friendship is formed in early life that eventually develops into a long-term loving relationship. Fromm describes one aspect of love as "care" (24), a concern for the well-being and happiness of the other. Even at a young age, Raoul demonstrates a selfless concern for Christine as he plunges into the wet ocean completely clothed to get her scarf, and, indeed, she is pleased with his act. As a young man, he is also concerned for her well-being. For example, when Christine is held hostage by the Phantom towards the end of the novel, Raoul, led by the Persian and at great risk to his own life, ventures into the deep basement passages of the Opera House to rescue her. When he is finally within close proximity and is able to hear her voice, he is greatly relieved. Christine, however, understands the danger he is in, and expresses her own concern for him:

> Raoul! Raoul!...fuyez !...tout ici est mystérieux et terrible...et Érik va devenir tout à fait fou...Et vous êtes dans la chambre des supplices!...Allez-vous-en par où vous êtes venus! Cette chambre-là doit avoir des raisons pour s'appeler d'un nom pareil! (Leroux, *Fantôme*, Lafitte 346)
>
> Raoul! Raoul! You must get away!...everything here is mystery and danger!...and Erik will become completely insane!...And you, there, in the torture chamber!...Go back the way you came! There must be a good reason why the room is called by such a name!" (Leroux, *Phantom* 232).

Raoul, however, does not consider his own safety or well-being; his greatest concern is to rescue Christine, and his ultimate desire is to be with her, one way or another. He responds: "Christine!...nous sortirons d'ici ensemble ou nous mourrons ensemble! (Leroux, *Fantôme*, Lafitte 346) ["Christine!...we are going to leave this place together or we shall die together!"] (Leroux, *Phantom* 232). Here Raoul goes to extreme measures, risking his own well-being, to protect and care for the person he loves.

Fromm also suggests that genuine love involves responsibility in which a person responds to the needs, expressed or unexpressed, of another person. Initially, when Raoul meets Christine again at the Opera House after years of separation, he is strongly attracted to her but does not understand her mysterious behavior. He thinks that Christine's reference to the Phantom, or Angel of Music, is part of her vivid imagination, nurtured by the fantastic stories her father told her when she heard growing up. Leroux writes:

> La première fois que Raoul avait revu Christine à l'Opéra, il avait été charmé par la beauté de la jeune fille et par l'évocation des douces images d'autrefois, mais il avait été plutôt étonné du côté négatif de son art. Elle semblait détachée de tout. Il revint l'écouter. Il la suivait dans les coulisses. Il l'attendit derrière un portant. Il essaya d'attirer son attention. Plus d'une fois, il l'accompagna jusque vers le seuil de sa loge, mais elle ne le voyait pas. Elle semblait du reste ne voir personne. C'était l'indifférence qui passait. (*Fantôme*, Lafitte 83)

> The first time Raoul saw her at the Opera, he was struck by her beauty and basked in pleasant memories of their past. But he had been surprised by a very negative quality in her work. She seemed detached. He came back to listen to her. He followed her backstage where he lay in wait for her behind a painted flat. He tried to attract her attention. More than once he pursued her as far as the door of her dressing room, but she never saw him. Indeed she never appeared to see anyone. She was indifference itself. (*Phantom* 59).

At this point in their relationship, Raoul does not understand Christine's behavior or needs, and even when she tries to tell him about the Angel of Music for the first time, he laughs in disbelief. It is over the course of time that Raoul finally accepts the existence of the Opera Ghost, responds to the needs of Christine—particularly her need to escape Erik's hovering authority and power—and is eventually willing to risk his own life to save her from him. In the end, he marries her, assumes responsibility for her well-being, and they live a quiet life together in peace.

Fromm points out that respect is another important characteristic essential to genuine love. In a relationship with respect, a person wants the beloved to be an individual, to develop in his or her own way. Initially Raoul is attracted to Christine's angelic voice; during their first meeting as children, he is drawn to her singing. Then later at the Opera House, her extraordinary vocal performance during the gala concert strikes him like a "coup de tonnerre...les cieux déchirés, une voix d'ange se faisant entendre sur la terre pour le ravissement des hommes et la consommation de son coeur" (Leroux, *Fantôme*, Lafitte 83-84) ["lightning bolt...the heavens had opened and an angel's voice had descended on earth, captivating men's souls and capturing his heart"] (Leroux, *Phantom* 59). Despite his enormous fascination and attraction to her voice, it is not her voice alone that he loves. He cherishes her for what she is as a person and he does not insist that she sing at the Opera House. He also ignores the gossips of society who find a match between an aristocrat and a commoner like Christine to be inappropriate.

In addition, Raoul exhibits a certain knowledge of Christine, although this is something that develops over time. He has an understanding of and connection with her upbringing, and he becomes more familiar with her at the Opera House. However, as mentioned, he does not immediately understand the reality of the Phantom as both a genuine human being and his rival. Once he acknowledges and accepts the Phantom in this way, he is in a position to better know, understand, and love Christine in a more intimate way. He is ready to ask questions about her relationship with him and to empathize with her situation. Finally, she can describe some of her experiences, such as seeing Erik's underground home and interacting with him there, and Raoul listens. He also asks about her feelings towards the Phantom: "Je désirerais savoir quel sentiment il vous inspire, puisque vous ne le haïssez pas" ["If you don't hate him, tell me what feelings you do have for him."] Christine answers, "De l'horreur!" (Leroux, *Fantôme*, Lafitte 193) ["Feelings of horror!"] (Leroux, *Phantom* 134). She continues to explain:

> Comment le haïr, Raoul? Voyez Érik à mes pieds, dans la demeure du lac, sous la terre. Il s'accuse, il se maudit, il implore mon pardon!...
>
> Il avoue son imposture. Il m'aime! Il met à mes pieds un immense et tragique amour!...Il m'a volée par amour!...Il m'a enfermée avec lui, dans la terre, par amour...mais il me respecte, mais il rampe, mais il gémit, mais il pleure!...Et quand je me lève, Raoul, quand je lui dis que je ne puis que le mépriser s'il ne me rend pas sur-le-champ cette liberté,

> qu'il m'a prise, chose incroyable...il me l'offre...je n'ai qu'à partir...Il est prêt à me montrer le mystérieux chemin;...seulement...seulement il s'est levé, lui aussi, et je suis bien obligée de me souvenir que, s'il n'est ni fantôme, ni ange, ni génie, il est toujours la Voix, car il chante!...
>
> Et je l'écoute... et je reste! (Leroux, *Fantôme*, Lafitte 194)

> How could I hate him, Raoul? If only you'd seen Erik at my feet in his sanctuary by the underground lake. He blamed and cursed himself and begged me to forgive him!...
>
> He admitted he had tricked me. He loved me! He gave me his undying, tragic love!...He abducted me for the sake of that love!...He imprisoned me with him deep in the earth for the sake of love!...He respects me, but he crawled before me, he groaned and wept!...When I stood up, Raoul, when I told him I would go on despising him unless he immediately gave me back the freedom he'd taken from me, then—and this is hard to believe—he offered to let me go...I could leave whenever I liked...He was even willing to show me the secret way out...except...except that he stood up too and I was forced to remember that he is neither phantom nor angel nor genie, he is still the Voice, for he began to sing...
>
> And I listened...and I stayed! (Leroux, *Phantom* 134)

As Raoul hears about Christine's complex experience with the Phantom, his knowledge of her increases, and the couple shares an intimacy that nurtures their love for one another. This is a stark contrast to the infatuation and passion of the Phantom who abducts, imprisons, and seduces (through his singing) Christine to stay with him, at least for the moment.

Kavaler-Adler writes of Christine and her loyalties to Raoul and Erik:

> In Phantom of the Opera the young heroine is drawn both toward the white and black knights. She is drawn towards the light of day in which an embodied interpersonal love is possible, as well as towards the muse/demon lover who entrances her with the music of the night and then seeks to possess her. Both the daytime prince and the dark lethal prince of the night captivate her. Her daytime prince admires and loves her, however, not just desiring her talent. He does not seek to possess, dominate, and control her. (158)

In the end, Christine disentangles herself from the captivating voice of her mentor musician singer father phantom and marries Raoul, who genuinely loves her. He wants to share his life with her in a quiet manner, above ground and above reproach, except perhaps for those who disapprove of the disparity between rank and class. Whether a person reads the novel in its original French or in translation, sees the musical in a theater, views a film adaptation, or experiences some other rendition of the narrative, despite potential differences in detail, the one constant is the love triangle. In the end, as is seen in many film show musicals, the couple, Raoul and Christine, prevails.

REFERENCES

Altman, Rick. *The American Film Musical.* Bloomington: Indiana UP, 1987. Print.

Broderick, James F. *Now A Terrifying Motion Picture!: Twenty-five Classic Works of Horror Adapted from Book to Film.* Jefferson, NC: McFarland, 2012. Print.

Fromm, Erich. *The Art of Loving.* 1956. New York: HarperPerennial, 2006. Print.

Grover-Friedlander, Michal. *Vocal Apparitions: The Attraction of Cinema to Opera.* Princeton: Princeton UP, 2005. Print.

Hall, Ann C. *Phantom Variations: The Adaptations of Gaston Leroux's* Phantom of the Opera, *1925 to the Present.* Jefferson, NC: McFarland, 2009. Print.

Harrison, Stephanie. "Introduction." *Adaptations: From Short Story to Big Screen.* Ed. Stephanie Harrison. New York: Three Rivers, 2005. xv-xix. Print.

Kavaler-Adler, Susan. "Object Relations Perspectives on 'Phantom of the Opera' and Its Demon Lover Theme: The Modern Film." *The American Journal of Psychoanalysis* 69 (2009): 150-166. Print.

Kingsbury, H. D. *Phantom Variations: Tales from the World of the Opera Ghost.* Lulu.com, 2008. Print.

---. *Phantom Variations, Volume 2: Further Tales from the Worlds of the Opera Ghost.* Lulu.com, 2011. Print.

Leroux, Gaston. *Le Fantôme de l'Opéra.* Paris: Lafitte, 1910. ebooksgratuits. <ebooksgratuits.com/pdf/leroux_fantome_opera.pdf>. Web. 1 Jan 2014.

---. *Le Fantôme de l'Opéra.* Paris: Livre de Poche, 2005. Print.

---. *The Phantom of the Opera.* Trans. David Coward. Oxford: OUP, 2012. Print.

Newark, Cormac. *Opera in the Novel from Balzac to Proust.* Cambridge: Cambridge UP, 2011. Print.

The Phantom of the Opera. Dir. Joel Schumacher. Perf. Gerard Butler, Emmy Rossum, and Patrick Wilson. Warner, 2005. DVD.

The Phantom of the Opera at the Royal Albert Hall. Perf. Ramin Karimloo, Sierra Bogges, and Hadley Fraser. Universal, 2012. DVD.

The Phantom of the Opera: Silent Film Classic, 1925. Dir. Rupert Julian et al. Perf. Lon Chaney, Mary Philbin, and Norman Kerry. Alpha, 2002. DVD.

"What's the Difference between The Phantom of the Opera the Book and The Phantom of the Opera the Movie?" ThatWasNotInTheBook.com. Web. 28 Dec. 2013.

ABOUT THE AUTHOR

Deborah Fillerup Weagel is term teaching faculty at the University of New Mexico in Albuquerque. She is co-editor, with Feroza Jussawalla, of *Emerging South Asian Women Writers: Essays and Interviews* (forthcoming 2016) and is the author of *Words and Music: Camus, Beckett, Cage, Gould* (2010), *Women and Contemporary World Literature: Power, Fragmentation, and Metaphor* (2009) and *Interconnections: Essays on Music, Art, Literature, and Gender* (2004). Her articles have appeared in the *South Asian Review*, the *Journal of Comparative Literature and Aesthetics*, *Mosaic: A Journal for the Interdisciplinary Study of Literature*, *Western American Literature*, and a variety of other scholarly journals. She has presented her work at academic conferences worldwide.

CHAPTER 4

Musical Patterns in William H. Gass's "A Fugue" and *The Pedersen Kid*

Marcin Stawiarski

When speaking about his novella The Pedersen Kid (1961), American writer William H. Gass once declared: "I've used a fugue, literally" (Castro, "An Interview with William H. Gass" 2003: 76). But then, how literal can this inter-artistic rapprochement be in a text that does not even mention music? The reader may well be forgiven for overlooking the musical structure Gass refers to, since the text carefully bypasses any single thematization of the fugue. Intermedial reading clues are somewhat more obvious in "A Fugue" subsection of Gass's novel The Tunnel (1995). These two texts belong to two different types of musico-literary intermediality, as defined by Werner Wolf (Wolf, The Musicalization of Fiction, 1999: 35-70): on the one hand, The Pedersen Kid, implying a covert, non-thematized form of interrelation between music and literature that can only be inferred from extratextual or contextual sources; on the other hand, "A Fugue," where a slightly more overt, not thematized, but at least a more direct interrelation between the two arts is brought into life.

This article aims (a) to bring the musical influence in Gass's works to the fore by examining both "A Fugue" passage from The Tunnel and The Pedersen Kid novella in compliance with Gass's conception of language and its musicality; (b) to assess ways in which texts that do not necessarily manifest a direct link to music can be given a musical reading by focusing on intermedial time patterns; (c) and to demonstrate that the musical undertext conveys symbolic, iconic or even allegorical meanings that, in the case of Gass's The Pedersen Kid allow a better understanding of initiation and rite of passage paradigms the story draws upon.

In fact these two texts offer ample opportunity to raise questions about the interplay of temporal and symbolical contents between different media. Gass's fiction provides an example of intermedial intersections tied to a specific conception of language and thought. Intermediality thus plays a role in construing textual temporalities. Such transtemporality is conducive to a new understanding of motives and patterns in Gass's creative oeuvre.

One the most crucial aspects of Gass's writing lies in the author's stance on language and words. Linguistic formalism – motives and patterns – are a token of musical presences within the text, bringing the aesthetic side of language into the spotlight. At a public reading (Gass, "William Gass with Michael Silverblatt", 1998), Gass suggested that readers should feel language physically in their mouths. Such formal and concrete approach to language is brought to bear on the musical condition of Gass's texts.

In The Pedersen Kid, a formal structure is immediately perceivable owing to the division of the text that unfolds in three stages, each of which is further divided into three subsections. This distribution is evocative of proportional architecture. and it comes to symbolise circular movement. Furthermore, the author points to a formal, strict constraint the text is modelled upon: "I tried to formulate a set of requirements for the story as clear and rigorous as those of the sonnet" (Gass, "A Revised and Expanded Preface" 1981: xxv).

Both in his essays and in the interviews he gives, Gass makes references to the musicality of language. With varying degrees of literalness, language is thought of as a locus of a character's existence – an individual's life dependent on language or even a subject being dominated and overwhelmed by it. In "Emma Enters a Sentence of Elizabeth Bishop's" (1998), the reader will find a humoristic instance of such relationship of the character to language. In his preface to In the Heart of the Heart of the Country, by resorting to the idea of 'possession,' the author underlines the role language plays and the way in which it can become a commanding presence:

> Rhythmic, repetitious, patterned, built of simple phrases like small square blocks [...] with magical and imaginary logic [...] these stories were fond possessions which fondly possessed their possessor [...]. And the best ones were those which sounded, when you heard them for the first time, as if you had heard them many times before. (Gass "A Revised and Expanded Preface" 1981: xxii)

If words create that sense of familiar but mesmerizing effect, it is because they combine and by forming networks and interrelations, just as musical sounds do, they form full-fledged worlds and realities to be inhabited:

> [...] I knew that words were communities made by the repeated crossing of contexts the way tracks formed towns, and that sentences did not

swim indifferently through others like schools of fish of another species, but were like lengths of web within a web, despite one's sense of the stitch and knot of design inside them. (Gass "A Revised and Expanded Preface" 1981: xxxiv)

For Gass, the musical quality of a text seems to have its roots in such precedence given to language. In an interview, the author highlights the interrelationship between writing and musical composition:

When I'm practicing writing, I'm not visually oriented but auditory, so the writing of it – word by word, line by line – is done by ear, and in that sense music is the dominant art. You actually have both elements: the linear, serial problem – literature does unfold one word at a time – but the completed object has to be conceived as a whole. Those two aspects are interacting, and there's really a tension between them that can be used. (Castro, "An Interview with William Gass" 2003: 75)

Hence, the acoustic side of language plays a crucial role in the very process of writing, showing something about the genetic aspect of Gass's works – the way in which texts get written, but also the way in which Gass imagines them being read. In addition, what is at stake here is the relationship between thought and language, where language itself seems to prevail. In his essay "Finding a Form," Gass broaches his experience of writing, depicting it as a perfect fusion of language and thought: "To see the world through words means more than merely grasping it through gossipacious talk or amiable description. Language, unlike any other medium, I think, is the very instrument and organ of the mind. It is not the representation of thought, as Plato believed, and hence only an inadequate copy; but it is thought itself." (Gass, "Finding a Form" 1996: 35-36) Language is thus liberated from its subservience to thought and made coterminous with it. In another essay, "The Music of Prose," Gass examines the notion of musicality, homing in on sound patterns and rhythmical schemes in prose and drawing musical comparisons:

Yet no prose can pretend to greatness if its music is not also great; if it does not, indeed, construct a surround of sound to house its meaning [...]. For prose has a pace; it is dotted with stops and pauses, frequent rests, inflections rise and fall like a low range of hills; certain tones are prolonged; there are patterns of stress and harmonious measures; [...] alliteration will trouble the tongue, consonance ease its sound out, so that any mouth making that music will feel its performance even to the back of the teeth and to the glottal stop, [...], vowels will open and consonants close like blooming plants; repetitive schemes will act as refrains, and there will be phrases – little motifs – to return to, like the tonic; clauses will be balanced by other clauses the way a waiter carries trays; [...] clots of concepts will dissolve and then recombine, so we shall find endless variations on the same theme; a central idea, along with its many modifications, like soloist and chorus, will take their turns until, suddenly, all sing at once the same sound. (Gass "The Music of Prose" 1996: 314)

What seems especially relevant for the purpose of this paper is the fact that Gass frequently compares prose-writing to musical composition and auditory experience. The author goes as far as envisaging himself as a composer rather than a writer: "A lot of rhetorical structures are musical, with their parallelisms and so on. There is also the possibility of carrying on many voices – of polyphony. Most of my own images come, I think, from opera. I have a fondness for the catalogue aria. Often, too, I find myself talking about things in poetic forms. This stanza, I'll say to myself, is giving me trouble, instead of this paragraph. I think: this aria, this duet. (Castro "An Interview with William Gass" 2003: 76)

Several parameters combine to foster musicality of prose language: rhetorical devices, repetitive patterns, rhythmical schemes as well as sound echoes. When writing about his collection of stories, In the Heart of the Heart of the Country, Gass reflects on the musicality of language with regard to poetry: "In any case, during the actual writing, the management of monosyllables, the alternation of short and long sentences, the emotional integrity of the paragraph, the elevation of the most ordinary diction into some semblance of poetry, became my fanatical concern. (Gass "A Revised and Expanded Preface" 1981: xxvii)

What then is musicality in Gass's prose? Noticeably, there is a sort of playfulness with language his texts are deeply imbued with, springing from phenomena related to parallelisms, repetitions and rhythmical patterns. It also has something to do with Stephen P. Scher's distinction between 'word music' and 'verbal music' (Scher "Notes Toward a Theory of Verbal Music" 1970). Syntactic mirroring (hypozeuxis), for instance, singles out some structural patterns in "The Pedersen Kid." In the following excerpt, the hypozeuxis is based on {a and b} coordination (underlined) whereas verbatim repetition (italics) allows some of the words to stand out: "Hans had laid steaming towels over the kid's chest and stomach. He was rubbing snow on the kid's legs and feet. Water from the snow and water from the towels had run off the kid to the table where the dough was, and the dough was turning pasty, sticking to the kid's back and behind. (Gass The Pedersen Kid 1981: 6, my emphasis) It is noteworthy that the two elements are first exposed {(X: water → steam/towels) and (Y: water → snow)} and then interweaved {X+Y: snow and towels}.

Such musicality is far from constituting a purely harmonious aspect of prose. Quite the opposite, since in Gass's novella the narrator's voice is that of an adolescent whose language is predicated on both oral attributes and a subjective frame of consciousness, musicality is a matter of conveying a non linear, not necessarily logical, and a cyclical and repetitive linguistic temporality. The subjective consciousness is, as it were, possessed by language, overwhelmed by it, inhabiting the sentence. Consequently, the musicality of language chimes with emotional aspects. Resorting to a musical metaphor, Gass writes that "the mental representation must be flowing and a bit repetitious; the dialogue realistic but musical." (Gass "A Revised and Expanded Preface" 1981: xxvi)

Dialogues, too, are dependent on specific patterns. In the following excerpt, repetition is magnified due to epizeuxis, which provides a pattern of subsequent repetition, as well as hypozeuxis emerging in the use of both the infinitive and the negative ("neither", "not", "nothing"):

Pa don't care about the kid.

Jorge.

Well he don't. He don't care at all, and I don't care to get my head busted neither. He don't care, and I don't care to have his shit flung on me. He don't care about anybody. All he cares about is his whiskey and that dry crack in his face. Get pig-drunk – that's what he wants. He don't care about nothing else at all. Nothing. Not Pedersen's kid neither. That cock. Not the kid neither. (Gass The Pedersen Kid 1981: 6, my emphasis)

There is a ritualistic or even religious and mystical dimension to musicality, insofar as oralisation and repetition create lists and aural patterns that may remind one of litany-like, obsessive or impassioned prosody. "A ritual effect is needed" (Gass, "A Revised and Expanded Preface" 1981: xxvi), and which has something to do with the role of the body in narrative. On the one hand, the body is reflected within the narrative voice, or the necessity to find an adequate voicing for a story: "[…] few of the stories one has at the top of one's head to tell get told, because the mind does not always possess the voice for them" (Gass, "A Revised and Expanded Preface", 1981, xiii). On the other hand, the corporeity of the verb relates to what Gass describes as an "iron law of composition" that consists in "[…] the exasperatingly slow search among the words […] written for the words which were to come, and the necessity for continuous revision, so that each work would seem simply the first paragraph written, swollen with sometimes years of scrutiny around that initial verbal wound" (Gass "A Revised and Expanded Preface" 1981: xxv). Such verbal wound is the bodily engagement with the constant reprise – the author's rewriting of the text as well as its repetitive unfolding for the reader. While such corporeity suggests a textual growth/outgrowth, the author evokes an almost organic inception of his texts: "They appeared in the world obscurely, too – slow brief bit by bit, through gritted teeth and much despairing; and if any person were to suffer such a birth, we'd see the skull come out on Thursday, skin appear by week's end, liver later, jaws arrive just after eating." (Gass "A Revised and Expanded Preface" 1981: xix) Thus, textual musicality in Gass is grounded in traits related to rhetorical and prosodic devices, rhythmical and sonorous patterns, and the author's specific conception of thought and language. Written at the edges of its own mediality, building up from that swelling verbal wound, the text is formed out of derivation, extension and expansion.

Gass's technique of extension/expansion may be understood in compliance with musical structures, as is the case in one of his more overtly musicalized texts – "A Fugue" passage in The Tunnel. This excerpt may be considered a piece of evidence bringing out Gass's interest in formal musical transpositions in literature and as an interesting example of how such musicalization may be brought into being. Gass's insistence on the centrality of the material aspect of language – its musicality – finds its verification in musicalization, defined as a form of "transformation of music into literature" (Wolf The Musicalization of Fiction 1999: 51) at a structural level, so that "the verbal appears to be or become […] similar to music or to effects connected with certain compositions" (Wolf The Musicalization of Fiction 1999: 51), thus imitating music.

Musicalization here is modeled on a specific type of composition – the fugue – characterized by (a) its polyphonic texture, (b) its monothematism, (c) and its specific extension of the initial theme. It is defined as a "composition, or a compositional technique, in which imitative counterpoint involving one main theme is the most important or most characteristic device of formal extension" (Bullivant "Fugue" 1980: 9). The main point is that a fugue is not necessarily a form, but rather a type of polyphonic movement, contrapuntal technique, or simply a type of texture: "Fugue has fairly been called a procedure (or even a texture) rather than a form; and fugal treatment is found in many large works in various forms, among them ritornello and sonata" (Bullivant "Fugue" 1980: 9). What is meant by musical texture (the word itself stems from Lat. texere, meaning "to weave," thus evoking a specific type of fabric) is the nature of the combination of elements (voices) within a composition, so that, overall, one distinguishes between monophonic texture (melody without accompaniment), homophonic texture (accompanied melody) and polyphonic texture (several intermingling melodies or voices). The fugue is dominated by the latter: at least two "parts" or "voices" combine in the unfolding of the composition.

Equally important is monothematism. Even though fugues for more than one theme do exist, they are more commonly monothematic, which means that there is usually one main theme, called the subject (S) that is taken up, by dint of modifications and mirroring, by other voices. Crucial here is the process of extension and expansion of that single, initial material that will undergo variations by virtue of imitative techniques (imitation). Such extension usually abides by a rather strictly defined process, starting with an exposition, when the subject is announced by all the voices, usually at different pitches. The subject is likely to be easily recognizable, which is why its first entry is frequently unaccompanied. After the subject is announced by the first voice, comes the answer (A), which is either understood as a real answer, that is to say "a repetition of the subject in a different key" (Williams "Fugue" 1906: 16), or as a looser form of imitation of the subject. As a counterpoint to the answer, there is usually a theme which is called the counter-subject (CS) and free parts may be played by other voices (FP). The exposition comprising the statement of the subject by all the voices is the most essential part of a fugue (Boyden, An Introduction to Music 1959: 62):

		II		A		CS	FP
I		S		CS		FP	FP
			III		S		CS
					IV		A

Fugal exposition

The middle section of a fugue – made up of episodes – is freer in terms of its organization, although it commonly consists in a modulated statement of material based on the subject and the counter-subject. However, the composition remains monothematic and contrapuntal all through. It ends with a denser polyphonic part called the stretto, and, finally, a coda.

In literature, polyphonic texture remains a metaphor that can only be vaguely rendered by a text being read aloud. This impossibility has often been underlined by critics studying musicalization. Even though Gass writes that "[t]o speak of the music of prose is to speak in metaphor" (Gass "The Music of Prose" 1996: 313), his "A Fugue" can be viewed as drawing on the fugal musical technique. By overtly borrowing a musical title, the passage calls for a structural analogy with music.

But then, what elements and parameters create the effect of musical formalism? As far as musicalization is concerned, three levels should be clearly distinguished: (a) the level of concepts and ideas; (b) that of voices; (c) and that of words and their interrelations.

In terms of concepts, it could be considered that the subject matter dwells on a "refusal": [S] {not – dog}. The text is monothematic just like a fugue. The refusal is echoed by the father's order not to feed the dog at home, from which a secondary theme is derived, or a counter-subject [CS] {feed – dog – elsewhere}. The subject and the countersubject lead to yet another idea which constitutes the answer – the mother feeding or "poisoning" the dog on gin [A] {mother – feed – dog}. The three fugal elements are closely intertwined.

It should be borne in mind, however, that the assignation of any one such textual parameter in view of an analogical correspondence with fugal components, is very arduous and verges on the arbitrary. The question of a problematic identification of musico-literary analogies – should one consider a fugal subject in a text to be a narrative voice? A theme? A simple sentence? A cluster of words? – has arisen in many musicalization studies (e.g. Witen 2010), which only underlines the difficulty that structural intermediality is confronted with. Gass himself makes use of the term "fugato," suggesting a loose fugue-text relationship (Gass "William Gass with Michael Silverblatt" 1998).

As to the vocal level, the text foregrounds a narrative polyphony. Two voices combine: a first person narrator (the son) and the second, more indirect source of utterance (the father). Whereas the mother's words are reported only indirectly, the father's voice may be viewed as a quasi-autonomous narrative source, since it is set up through reported speech and free direct speech. The text thus pits one voice against the other.

As far as the linguistic level is concerned, it is possible to point out: (a) parallelisms and echoes; (b) emphatic articulation through polysyndeton (the coordinating conjunction "and" is used 16 times, "or" 7 times, and there are 8 concessive conjunctions); (c) negativity (17 negative words such as "not" or "never"); (d) word recurrences: "dog," "father," and "mother" ("dog" appears 23 times, but together with its synonyms – "pal," "spitz," and "mutt" – there are 42 occurrences).

By combining the voices (V1, for the son, and V2, for the father), the subject and the derived concepts, a clearly perceptible two-step pattern emerges as an exposition:

> [S] {V1} My dad wouldn't let me have a dog. {V2} A dog? A dog we don't need. [A] {V1} My mom made the neighbor's spitz her pal by poisoning it with the gin she sprinkled on the table scraps. [CS] {V2} Feed it somewhere else, my dad said. A dog we don't need. [S] {V1} My dad wouldn't let me have a dog. {V2} Our neighbor's spitz – that mutt – he shits in the flower beds. Dog doo we don't need. [CS] {V2} At least feed it somewhere else, my dad said. [A] {V1} My mom made the table scraps tasty for her pal, the neighbor's spitz – that mutt – by sprinkling them with gin. (Gass The Tunnel 2012: 239-240)

The pattern may be synthesized as follows, with [S] appearing twice in the two voices, followed by the derived elements [A] or [CS]:

```
I   [S] {V1} {V2}      II   [S] {V1} {V2}
    [A] {V1}                [CS] {V2}
    [CS] {V2}               [A] {V1}
```

Next comes a part that is structured through a combination of elements and then their alternation with a return to the subject and its derivatives:

> [A+S] {V2} You're poisoning Pal, my dad said, but never mind, we don't need that mutt. [A+S] {V1} My mom thought anything tasted better with a little gin to salt it up. That way my mom made the neighbor's spitz her pal, and maddened dad who wouldn't let me have a dog. [~S] {V1} He always said we didn't need one, they crapped on the carpet and put dirty paws on the pant's leg of guests and yapped at cats or anyone who came to the door. [~S] {V2} A dog? A dog we don't need. We don't need chewed shoes and dog hairs on the sofa, fleas in the rug, dirty bowls in every corner of the kitchen, dog stink on our clothes. [A] {V1} But my mom made the neighbor's spitz her pal anyway by poisoning it with the gin she sprinkled on the table scraps like she was baptising bones. [CS] {V2} At least feed it somewhere else, my dad said. [S] {V1} My dad wouldn't let me have a pal. (Gass The Tunnel 2012: 239-240)

This part may be considered as a transition leading to episodes, where the subject is re-announced, modified, as is shown the following scheme:

    III   [A+S] {V2}   IV   [~S] {V1}
          [A+S] {V1}   [~S] {V2}
                              [A] {V1}
                              [CS] {V2}

The last part seems to echo the episode section [E] in a fugue where the initial material is modulated and further transformed:

[E1→S] {V2} Who will have to walk that pal, he said. I will. And it's going to be snowing or it's going to be raining and who will be waiting by the vacant lot at the corner in the cold wet wind, waiting for the damn dog to do his business? Not you, Billy boy Christ, you can't even be counted on to bring in the garbage cans or mow the lawn. [E2→S] {V2} So no dog. A mutt we don't need, we don't need dog doo in the flower beds, chewed shoes, fleas; what we need is the yard raked, like I said this morning. No damn dog. [E3 →A+CS] {V2} No mutt for your mother either even if she tries to get around me by feeding it when my back is turned, when I'm away at work earning her gin money so the sick thing can shit in a stream on the flower seeds; at least she should feed it somewhere else; it's always hanging around; is it a light string in the hall or a cloth on the table to be always hanging around? [E1+E2→S] {V2} No. Chewed shoes, fleas, muddy paws and yappy daddle, bowser odor: a dog we don't need. Suppose it bites the postman: do you get sued? No. I am the one waiting at the corner vacant lot in the rain, the snow, the cold wet wind, waiting for the dog to do his damn business, and I get sued. You don't. Christ, you can't even be counted on to clip the hedge. You know: snicksnack. So no dog, my dad said. [E4→E1+E2+E3] {V1} Though we had a dog nevertheless. That is, my mom made the neighbor's pal her mutt, and didn't let me have him for mine, either, because it just followed her around – yip nip – wanting to lap gin and nose its grease-sogged bread. So we did have a dog in the house, even though it just visited, and it would rest its white head in my mother's lap and whimper and my father would throw down his paper and say shit! and I would walk out of the house and neglect to mow or rake the yard, or snicksnack the hedge or bring the garbage cans around. [S] {V1} My dad wouldn't let me have a dog. {V2} A dog? A dog we don't need, he said. So I was damned if I would fetch. (Gass The Tunnel 2012: 239-240)

Voices first derive elements from the subject, the counter-subject or the answer, only to go on and to combine those elements, as though the text were modelled on a denser polyphonic texture, reminiscent of the stretto part in a fugue. The end brings yet another return to the subject, followed by a coda:

V   [E1→S] {V2}   VI   [S] {V1}
     [E2→S] {V2}   {V2}
     [E3 →A+CS] {V2}
     [E1+E2→ S] {V2}
     [E4→E1+E2+E3]
     {V1}

A less linear reading of the text – provided that one imagines a simultaneous unfolding of two voices – lends itself to the following pattern:

{V1}	[S]	[A]	[S]	[A]	[A+S]	[S]	[A]	[E4→E1+E2+E3]		[S]	
{V2}		[S]	[CS]	[S]	[CS]	[A+S]	[S]	[CS]	[E1→S]	[E2→S]	[E3→A+CS]	[E1+E2→S]	[S]

What characterizes this passage is a highly structured network of patterns that take after the way in which fugal elements are exposed by means of mirroring and imitation. In music, the imitative technique is the basic operating principle of all contrapuntal works, such as fugue or canon. The musical materials undergo variations on account of mutual imitation of voices, achieved with the help of a variety of devices, some of which are enumerated below:

     augmentation   notes values are lengthened
     diminution   notes values are shortened
     inversion   the subject played upside down
     cancrizans/retrograde motion   the subject is given backwards
     per arsin et thesin   the main beat is displaced

In other words, imitation allows voices to alternate varying the initial material – or part of it – and echoing each other by exchange and mirroring.

     Similarly, in the fugal passage from The Tunnel, the first occurrence [A1] uses {(a) the neighbor's spitz (b) her pal} as (a) direct object (b) object complement; the second occurrence [A2] uses {(b) her pal} as an indirect object. While {sprinkled} in [A1] is the verb of the relative clause within the adverbial clause {by poisoning it with the gin she sprinkled on the table scraps}, it becomes a gerund in the second adverbial [A2] {by sprinkling}, whereas the adjunct {on the table scraps} in [A1] becomes the object of the main clause verb in [A2].

Other forms of variation are used in the text: displacements, like the emphatic "damn" ({the damn dog to do his business} → {the dog to do his damn business}); tense variations ({it's going to be raining} → {in the rain}, {who will be waiting} → {I'm the one waiting}); semantic variation on polysemy through antanaclasis ({lap gin} → {in my mother's lap}), through synonymy {dog → mutt → spitz}, or letter chiasmus {lap → pal}; sound variation through paronomasia ({spitz → shits, crapped → carpet, maddened → damned}), alliteration ({my mom made} or {wet wind waiting}), polyptoton ({tasty → tasted} or {yapped → yappy}), rhyme or homeoteleuton {snowing, going, raining, waiting}. The specific clipped rhythm of the text, partly due to an overwhelming majority of monosyllabic words, must also be pointed out (555 monosyllables out of 651 polysyllables – including contractions –, monosyllables thus accounting for about 85% of the words).

Only a limited number of elements forming the verbal material are used and transformed, and the text resorts to imitation, since fragments echo one another, and abundant use is made of variation and inversion. clearly, what prevails is the general impression of a polyphonic structure obtained through imitative effects.

The analysis of "A Fugue" provides crucial bearing for examining the second text under study, The Pedersen Kid. First and foremost, it must be recalled that no direct and explicit mention of music is made within this text. Therefore, if one were to venture to propound that there is a solid link between this text and musical techniques, it would be a covert and indirect form of musicalization.

The mere structure of Gass's novella is telling. Anchored in snowy scenery and showing a purely masculine universe, steeped in misogyny, sexual abuse, alcoholism and violence, the story is organized around three stages, stemming from the tripartite structure of the narrative: Gass himself points to the structure revolving around (a) discovery, (b) efforts, and (c) escape. The initial point of reference is described as "evil as a visitation – sudden, mysterious, violent, inexplicable" (Gass "A Revised and Expanded Preface" 1981: xxvi). Hence, there seems to be a structural mise en abyme articulated on a pivotal form, connoting circularity and mirroring. An intertextual intermedial bond might even be asserted between Gass's choice of theme – evil as a sudden visitation – and one of the early musicalized texts, Thomas de Quincey's "Dream Fugue" (De Quincey The English Mail Coach 1849: 1968) whose theme happens to be sudden death.

At the onset of the story, the reader is presented with the discovery of the inanimate body of a teenager, Steve Pedersen. Almost frozen, the body is found at the Sergens' farm by the farm worker, Big Hans. Once he has been revived, Steve Pedersen tells his story: he has fled his parents' farm (the Pedersens) following the appearance of a strange man, armed and clad in green mackinaw, yellow gloves, and a black hat. Big Hans, Jorge, the narrator of Gass's story, and the narrator's father, leave the Sergens' farm to go and save the Pedersens.

Beset with obstacles as their journey turns out to be, they manage to reach the Pedersens' farm, whereupon the reader is presented with a series of eerie developments, evoking dream or fancy: the owners of the farm are absent, the characters wait for the strange visitor, and then Jorge muses on a series of acts that seem to suggest he murders both Big Hans and his father. The end of the story brings us back to silence and snow: the travelers have all vanished into thin air – all but Jorge, who seems to be willing to stay at the Pedersens' farm.

The plot of the novella being very simple, the story reminds us of the monothematic nature of fugue. Gass states that "[a]ll should be subordinated to that end-" (Gass "A Revised and Expanded Preface" 1981: xxvi) but he also states that evil remains inexplicable: "The force has gone as it came" (Gass "A Revised and Expanded Preface" 1981: xxvi-xxvii). The idea of inexplicability may be associated with all forms of indeterminacy. If the source of evil remains unknown, so does the upshot of the story, so that the novella seems to end when it actually started, giving precedence to circular or spiral patterns. Inexplicability is also allied to the "covering the moral layer with a frost of epistemological doubt" (Gass "A Revised and Expanded Preface" 1981: xxvii). Perhaps the image of frost as a temporal paralysis has something to do with Rabelais's frozen images. Perhaps intermediality as well is such intangible presence, as if it were a hidden and undecipherable layer of text.

One of the readings that could be suggested for Gass's novella is attributable to its symbolical meaning as a representation of a rite of passage. The story, told from the first-person viewpoint of an adolescent narrator, Jorge, calls for a symbolical interpretation owing to its structure and the mysterious nature of the theme. The journey can then be envisaged as initiation embedded in the character's sense of heroism:

> It was like I was setting out to do something special and big – like a knight setting out – worth remembering. I dreamed coming in from the barn and finding his back to me in the kitchen and wrestling with him and pulling him down and beating the stocking cap off his head with the barrel of the gun. (Gass The Pedersen Kid 1981: 33)

The itinerary revolves around symbolic components relating to conflict, which is frequently emphasized by the lexical field of hunting and fleeing: the Pedersen kid flees his parents' farm; the Sergens are after the stranger; the Pedersens seem to have fled; finally, Jorge's father and Big Hans disappear. The text constantly refers to agonistic lexis, as in the following excerpt where the hunt for a bottle of whiskey Jorge's father has hidden is described through repetition and polyptoton encapsulating the series "hide-hunt-find":

> Ma had found one of Pa's hiding places. She'd found one [...] while big Hans and I had hunted and hunted as we always did all winter, every winter since the spring that Hans had come and I [...] found the first one. Pa had a knack for hiding. [...] She'd found it by luck most likely but she hadn't said anything and we didn't know [...] how many other ones she'd found, saying nothing. Pa was sure to find out. Sometimes he didn't seem to because he looked and didn't find anything and figured he hadn't hid one after all [...]. But he's find out about this one because we were using it [...]. If he found out ma found it – that'd be bad. He took pride in his hiding. It was all pride he had. I guess fooling Hans and me took doing. But he didn't figure ma for much. He didn't figure her at all. And if he found out – a woman had – then it'd be bad. (Gass The Pedersen Kid 1981: 8, my emphasis)

The insistence on the dichotomy fleeing/pursuing seems to recall the fugue, as though the lexis weaved an undertext, re-motivating the very etymology of the fugue. Indeed, the word itself comes from "the Latin form of the term, fuga, as well as [...] the French and Italian equivalents, chace and caccia [...]. These designations described the 'fleeing' or 'chasing' of voices characteristic of fugue – the technique of imitation [...]" (Bullivant "Fugue" 1980: 9). In other words, the lexical field begets a network of concepts related to conflict, tension and passage, as if the musical form were secretly used to provide subconscious patterns for the protagonist's initiation journey.

The rite of passage translates into an affirmation of the self through rivalry. For the young narrator, conflict is predicated on sexuality ("I was satisfied mine was bigger" [Gass The Pedersen Kid 1981: 2]; "Even if his cock was thicker... I was here and he was in the snow. I was satisfied" [Gass The Pedersen Kid 1981: 72]) as well as emancipation of the self that the ultimate disappearance/murder symbolizes. Identity is shown to build on mirroring and projection, so that, here too, the fugal principle of imitation seems to lend the text a symbolical or even allegorical value. One of the paradigms of it is the idea of blinding, smacking of oedipal undertones that cannot go unnoticed: "Pa's eyes would blink at me – as if I were the sun off the snow and burning to blind him," (Gass The Pedersen Kid 1981: 3);"As I turned my head the sun flashed from the barrel of pa's gun. [...] it flashed squarely in my eye when I turned my head just right" (Gass The Pedersen Kid 1981: 78). The initiation ends with a solemn and a quasi-religious climax, whereby the protagonist finds himself alone, proud of his achievements: "I have been the brave one and now I was free [...]. The kid and me, we'd done brave things well worth remembering. The way that fellow had come so mysteriously through the snow and done us such a glorious turn – well it made me think how I was told to feel in church." (Gass,The Pedersen Kid 1981: 79)

Furthermore, if the lexical associations predicated on fight and hunt are evocative of initiation and reminiscent of the fugue, there seems to be a correspondence between symbolic structures of the text and fugal structures on yet another level. If we follow Van Gennep's tripartite division of a rite of passage – separation, transition, and incorporation (Gennep, Les Rites de passage, 1981) – we may distinguish three clear-cut stages in Gass's novella as well as three parts in a fugue, which creates meaning through the combination and convertibility between the musical composition, mythical structures and the text.

Zones of heightened repetition and denser mirroring further signal a musical intermediality in the novella so that the text is made to operate through layers of fluctuating intensity, revealing moments of greater interweaving of elements, which brings language itself to the fore and singles out key entities, fragments and phrases.

One major device used in a fugal piece that regulates its intensity and textural layering is the stretto, from Italian "narrow" or "tight". The stretto may be defined as "the following of response to subject at a closer interval of time than first" (Corder "Stretto" 1908: 720). It is a cumulative and climaxing event in a fugue "employed towards the end of a fugue, so as to give some impression of climax" (Corder "Stretto" 1908: 720). But the device does not necessarily emerge exclusively at the end of a contrapuntal piece, and might well be used elsewhere in the composition.

In Gass's novella, there are several such zones of polyphonic densification. By tightening the textural density, the text lingers on some elements only, creating the impression of heightened speed and intensity. As a matter of fact, it does not quicken the speed of events, but provides foundation for an effect of heightened tension, as a means of zeroing in on tension itself rather than progress in narration. Stretto zones are stops – narrative silences where psychological distress is at its highest when the narrator is thrown into a panic and distress. The first zone that could bear comparison to the stretto technique appears just before the symbolic shooting, becoming a locus of uttermost tension:

> The horse had circled round in it. He hadn't known the way. He hadn't known the horse had circled round. His hands were loose upon the reins and so the horse had circled round. Everything was black and white and everything the same. There wasn't any road to go. There wasn't any track. The horse had circled round in it. He hadn't known the way. There was only snow to the horse's thighs. There was only cold to the bone and driving snow in his eyes. He hadn't known. How could he know the horse had circled round in it? How could he really ride and urge the horse with his heels when there wasn't anyplace to go and everything was black and white and all the same? Of course the horse had circled round, of course he'd come around in it. Horses have sense. That's all manure about horses. No it ain't, pa, no it ain't. They do. Hans said. They do. Hans knows. He's right. He was right about the wheat that time. He said the rust was in it and it was. He was right about the rats, they do eat shoes, they eat anything, so the horse has circled round in it. That was a long time ago. Yes, pa, but Hans was right even though that was a long time ago, and how would you know anyway, you was always drinking ... not in summer ... no, pa... not in spring or fall either ... no, pa, but in the winter, and it's winter now and you're in bed where you belong – don't speak to me, be quiet. (Gass *The Pedersen Kid* 1981: 73)

The text unfolds through a cluster of fragments and sentences. The sentences derive one from the other, as though they auto-generated themselves, as though language gave birth to more language. Repetition is enhanced: the sentences echo each other; they are repeated verbatim or with some variation; new bits are added and parts are cut off, inversed, fused, or lengthened. Like in "A Fugue," one theme is singled out {11 occurrences of horse}, a few verbs stand out {to be (15 times), to circle (7 times), to know (6 times)}, polysyndeton is used {10 times and}; negation is brought to the foreground {15 times}.

At another level, the collusion of sentences also constitutes, just like in "A Fugue," an overlap of voices, since fragments stem from previous dialogues, so that the aggregate reveals a polyphonic structure. Below are some of the echoes from earlier chapters:

They got a sense.	Horses have a sense.
(Gass The Pedersen Kid 1981: 24)	(Gass The Pedersen Kid 1981: 74)
That's a lot of manure about horses.	That's all manure about horses.
(Gass The Pedersen Kid 1981: 24)	(Gass The Pedersen Kid 1981: 74)
No it ain't. Ain't it?	Not, it ain't, pa, no it ain't.
(Gass The Pedersen Kid 1981: 28)	(Gass The Pedersen Kid 1981: 74)

This polyphonic effect is reinforced by the fact that the dialogues in the novella do not contain any specific punctuation marks related to direct speech, but unfold as though they were part of the narrative. The only mark that may suggest dialogue is the page layout, as if in a list, suggesting oral exchange.

The second textual zone that may be associated with the stretto technique is also located at a moment of acute tension at the end on the novella. The story is drawing to a close and the character's initiation is at its ultimate stage, so that the technique of the stretto becomes a means of conveying a maddened consciousness. The narrative takes after a form of ritual, and an almost religious tone, such as can be found in a litany:

> The wagon had a great big wheel. Papa had a paper sack. Mama held my hand. High horse waved his tail. Papa had a paper sack. We both ran to hide. Mama held my hand. The wagon had a great big wheel. High horse waved his tail. We both ran to hide. Papa had a paper sack. The wagon had a great big wheel. Mama held my hand. Papa had a paper sack. High horse waved his tail. The wagon had a great big wheel. We both ran to hide. High horse waved his tail. Mama held my hand. We both ran to hide. The wagon had a great big wheel. Papa had a paper sack. Mama held my hand. High horse waved his tail. Papa had a paper sack. We both ran to hide. Papa had a paper sack. We both ran to hide. (Gass The Perdersen Kid 1981: 75-76)

The narrator's consciousness seems to have worked itself up into a frenzy. There's an element of fear and emotion, marked by typographical blanks. The protagonist finding himself alone, striving to keep quiet: "All that could happened was alone with me and I was alone with it." (Gass The Perdersen Kid 1981: 75). Like a litany of consciousness, the interior monologue takes on a very emotional turn, plunging into frantic repetition.

Gass's work toys with texture as a means of regulating time effects. While it has often been pointed out that polyphonic patterns cannot be used in a literary text, there seems to be a possibility of a transmedial transformation of both narrative time and sentence time (transtemporality). In literature, polyphonic texture remains a metaphor of simultaneity, but it is, in my view, the closest one could get to musical effects in a text. What is meant by "musical effect" is the possibility of regulating density and intensity of language so that the reader stumbles on zones when the text winds back on itself, dithers, revolves around a cluster of fragments.

Sentence time, then, is closely linked to memory questions: texture effects are predicated on what repetition allows us to have retained from a given zone. By repeating and centering on selected entities, the text asserts a polyphony that is at stake not within the text itself, but at that border line between the text and the readerly activity. The stretto clearly shows that texture is not only about how many voices are used and interwoven, but that also of zones, so that parts of text clearly contrast with one another. Like the arsis and thesis dichotomy, the stretto builds up larger contrasts between tension and release at a macrostructural level. This dynamic is not only quantitative, but also qualitative, insofar as it emphasizes emotion. Hence, the stretto shows how time is handled through intersemiotic contrast.

But then, there is yet another word that comes to the fore and that the novella keeps reminding us of: the "circle" or the "round". When Gass mentions having used the structure of a fugue in his text, he adds that "it is, of course, a question of constructing a round" (Castro "An Interview with William Gass" 2003: 76). It so happens that a round is a form of canon, closely related to a "catch", also a form of canon:

> Rounds and catches, the most characteristic forms of English music, differ from canons in only being sung at the unison or octave, and also in being rhythmical in form. [...] Amongst early writers on music, the terms 'round' and 'catch' were synonymous, but at present day the latter is generally understood to be [...] that species of round, 'wherein, to humour some conceit in the words, the melody is broken, and the sense interrupted in one part, and caught again or supplied by another,' a form of humour [...]. (Squire "Round" 1908: 165)

The original title of "The Pedersen Kid" was "And Slowly Comes the Spring," which is quite reminiscent of the famous round "Sumer is Incumen In," one of the earliest canons in English. The whole fugal structure might thus have more to do with canonic rather than purely fugal patterns. Historically, and technically, the fugue is closely interlinked with the canon. The canon is characterized by its use of strict imitation, which means that parts are repeated identically. The word itself stems from Greek 'canon,' which signifies a rule or a standard, which means that the composition is "written strictly according to rule" (Ouseley "Canon" 1904: 455): "The principle of a canon is that one voice begins a melody, which melody is imitated precisely, note for note, and (generally) interval for interval, by some other voice, either at the same or a different pitch, beginning a few beats later and thus as it were running after the leader." (Ouseley, "Canon" 1904: 455)

The leading voice is usually called dux or antecedens whereas the subsequent voice will be named comes or consequens. Just like there are many different ways of using imitative techniques in a fugue, there are many different sorts of canon composition which depend on the form of imitation: canons by inversion, diminution, augmentation, or cancrizans. But three types of canon are particularly interesting here: (a) the "infinite", the "circular" or "perpetual" canons that do not come to a definite conclusion, but draw back to the beginning so that they might be executed without an end; (b) enigmatical canons that are notated cryptically rather than written in full so that the executioner must first decipher a riddle; (c) cancrizans canons or "crab" canons that are recursive, insofar as they operate "by retrogression, on account of their crab-like motion – from the Latin word cancer, a crab" (Ouseley "Cancrizans" 1904: 454).

Thanks to its tripartite structure and the indeterminacy principle, Gass's text underlines the primacy of recursive and circular patterns and temporality, instead of definite, linear and teleological structures. Rather than the final return of the tonic in a fugue, it is circularity, recursiveness and uncertainty that are given precedence in the text. This allows us to ponder to what extent Gass's novella might be a riddle canon or an enigmatic rite of passage.

It would seem that the text may be read – like some canons – upside down or from end to beginning, by reversal. The pivotal, tripartite structure allows us to fathom two parts revolving freely around the central pillar. A chiasmus found in the text highlights such reversal: "Jorge – so was I. No. I was." (Gass The Pedersen Kid 1981: 74) The exchange in The Pedersen Kid incites one to read initiation as a circular process, predicated on exchange. At the end, the protagonist declares: "we'd been exchanged, and we were both in our own new lands." (Gass The Pedersen Kid 1981: 73) The whole story may be read as an identity quest that comes back to where it started, as though through a spiral. A number of initial situations echo the ending and even some metaphors are used at both ends of the text: "I saw his head, fuzzed like a dandelion gone to seed" (Gass The Pedersen Kid 1981: 4); "where the dandelions had begun to seed" (Gass The Pedersen Kid 1981: 68). It may be stated that the text acquires two overlapping movements: (a) one, close to a palindrome or a chiasmus, based on permutation; (b) the other based on circularity and cyclicity, akin to strange loops.

The Pedersen kid seems to be replaced by the narrator. The initial snow and cold associated with the Pedersen kid turns out to have been Jorge's experience of coldness – that coldness stemming from the failed relationship with the authoritarian father – as it appears within the narrator's interior monologue: "I wanted a cat or a dog awful bad since I was a little kid. […] I'm not going to grieve. You were always after killing me, yourself, pa, oh yes you were. I was cold in your house always, pa." (Gass The Pedersen Kid 1981: 74) In this way, one could even go as far as to say that there is only one character and that – like in a monothematic fugue – all the other parts are only mirror images of the protagonist, so that the Pedersen kid might be considered as Jorge's alter-ego or a wishful self. Thus, one might envisage the text through a form of a bi-directional spiral or strange loop. If the story has anything to do with music and the fugue, it appears that it is the case, above all, thanks to its looping patterns. This is what Gass underlines himself when speaking of the Baroque style of his writing:

> Of course, you can't write a fugue except in music. But certain patterns, sets of repetitions and returns, and methods of development in the prose, are characteristic of Baroque music. My style has been called Baroque. "The Pederson Kid" is stripped, but that doesn't mean it isn't Baroque. The Baroqueness comes in its organization, its repetition, its circling around: the people lost in the snow in that story don't know where they are and circle around just as the language revolves about itself in slow loops. In that sense, the story's prose employs certain Baroque structures though the language itself is plain and simple. (Castro "Interview with William H. Gass" 1995)

To summarize, both "A Fugue" and The Pedersen Kid are structured on musical polyphonic techniques, regulating textual intensity, texture, and temporal unfolding, lending voice to transtemporality. While "A Fugue" does so in a more overt way, The Pedersen Kid is a case of covert musicalization. Since the events – and thus the meaning – of that story are uncertain, marking epistemological doubt, it seems safe to consider than just as snow is a metaphor of the inexplicable covertness, the quest of identity and the rite of passage are kept at bay, and rather than being achieved by means of a teleological pattern, they get back to the start. If Van Gennep's stages are operational here, the third one – incorporation – is only partly so, since the protagonist remains at odds with the community, as if dis-integrated. In other words, initiation does not follow a time's arrow, but folds up into a loop, and by doing so patterns itself on structures that have something to do with the fugue and the round, as though intermediality were a multiple deep-structure template.

Musicalization is not the only form on intersemiotic dimension in Gass's works. Intermediality may be more abstract in Gass and musical elements might well be related – abstractedly – to spatial, architectural or pictorial elements. Gass, makes use of an intermedial metaphor, by suggesting that his image of writing is both like an unwinding tapestry or a musical composition: "My image of a book is something created as a whole, as a complete thing, but one that can be apprehended a bit at a time. [...] a Chinese scroll you unwind; [...] a painting that you can't see all at once, [...], a piece of music." (Castro "An Interview with William Gass" 2003: 75)

It seems interesting to acknowledge the iconic tension of intermediality as Gass does, rather than question the validity of intermedial transpositions, such as musicalization. It also seems rewarding to consider multiple intermediality. In "The Pedersen Kid," each chapter contains an allusion to snakes ("[...] holding the bottle like a snake at the length of his arm" [Gass The Pedersen Kid 1981: 7]; "[...] like he was trying to kill a snake." [Gass The Pedersen Kid 1981: 58]; "[...] I thought suddenly of snakes." [Gass The Pedersen Kid 1981: 66]), and given the importance of the three male characters, I cannot help thinking about the Laocoon sculpture and Gotthold E. Lessing's essay. It might be that Gass's novella is a covert reassessment of intermedial thought, a suggestion of a larger transmedial subtext (Wolf "(Inter)mediality and the Study of Literature" 2011: 4).

REFERENCES

Boyden, David D. 1959. *An Introduction to Music*. London: Faber and Faber.
Bullivant, Roger. 1980. "Fugue." *The New Grove Dictionary of Music and Musicians*. Vol.1. Ed. Stanley Sadie. New York/London: Macmillan.
Castro, Jan Garden. 2003, "An Interview with William H. Gass." *Conversations with William H. Gass*. Ed. Ammon, Theodore G. Jackson: UP of Mississippi, 71-80.
Castro, Jan Garden. 1995. "Interview with William H. Gass." *Bomb Magazine* 51 http://bombsite.com/issues/51/articles/1862 (accessed 15 January 2014).
Corder, Frederick. 1908. "Stretto." *Grove's Dictionary of Music and Musicians*. Vol.4. Ed. Maitland, J. A. Fuller. New York/London: Macmillan.
Gass, William H. 1981."A Revised and Expanded Preface." *In the Heart of the Heart of the Country*. Boston: Nonpareil Books, xiii-xlvi.

Gass, William H. 1981 [1961]. "The Pedersen Kid." *In the Heart of the Heart of the Country*. Boston: Nonpareil Books, 1-79.

Gass, William H. 2012 [1995] *The Tunnel*. Champaign: Dalkey Archive Press.

Gass, William H. 1996."Finding a Form."*Finding a Form*. New York: Cornell UP, 31-52.

Gass, William H. 1996. "The Music of Prose."*Finding a Form*. New York: Cornell UP, 313-326.

Gass, William H. 1998. "Emma Enters a Sentence of Elizabeth Bishop's." *Cartesian Sonata and Other Novellas*. New York: Basic Books, 144-191.

Gass, William H. 1998. "William Gass with Michael Silverblatt." *Lannan*, 5 http://www.readinggass.org/audio-video. (accessed 15 January 2014).

Gennep, Arnold Van. 1981. *Les rites de passage*. Paris: Picard.

Ouseley, Frederick A. Gore. 1904. "Cancrizans." *Grove's Dictionary of Music and Musicians* Vol.1. Ed. Maitland, J. A. Fuller. London/New York: Macmillan.

Ouseley, Frederick A. Gore. 1904. "Canon." *Grove's Dictionary of Music and Musicians*. Vol.1. Ed. Maitland, J. A. Fuller. London/New York: Macmillan.

Thomas De Quincey, 1968. "Dream Fugue."*The English Mail Coach and Other Essays. Collected Writings of Thomas De Quincey*. NewYork. AMS, 270-330.

Scher, Stephen P. 1970. "Notes Toward a Theory of Verbal Music." *Comparative Literature* 22 : 147-156.

Squire, William Barclay. 1908. "Round." *Grove's Dictionary of Music and Musicians*. Vol.4 Ed. Maitland, J. A. Fuller. London/New York: Macmillan.

Williams, Ralph Vaughan. 1906. "Fugue." *Grove's Dictionary of Music and Musicians*. Vol.2 Ed. Maitland, J. A. Fuller. New York/London: Macmillan.

Witen, Michelle. 2010. "The Mystery of the Fuga per Canonem Reopened?" *Genetic Joyce Studi*es, 10. http://www.geneticjoycestudies.org/GJS10/GJS10_MichelleWiten.htm (accessed 15 January 2014).

Wolf, Werner. The Musicalization of Fiction: A Study in the Theory and History of Intermediality. Amsterdam/Atlanta: Rodopi Press, 1999.

Wolf, Werner. 2011 "(Inter)mediality and the Study of Literature." Tötösy de Zepetnek, Steven, López-Varela Azcárate, Asunción, Saussy, Haun, and Mieszkowski, Jan, eds. *New Perspectives on Material Culture and Intermedial Practice.*CLCWeb: Comparative Literature and Culture, 13.3 http://docs.lib.purdue.edu/clcweb/vol13/iss3/ (accessed 15 January 2014).

About the Author

Dr. Marcin Stawiarski teaches at the University of Caen, in France. He completed his Ph.D. thesis, entitled "Temporal Aspects of Music in the 20th-Century Novel: Conrad Aiken, Anthony Burgess and Gabriel Josipovici" at the University of Poitiers in 2007. His research focuses on the intersections of music and literature as well as representation of time in fiction.

CHAPTER 5

The Study of Accordion and Kazakh Culture: An Intermedial Approach

Zaure Smakova & Medelkhan Konysbayev

It should be noted that the study of accordion playing and of peculiarities of the use of this instrument in Kazakhstan remain at an initial stage. Issues of comparative analysis for tonal and rhythmic tuning system, and modal and compositional structures in repertoire for an accordion have yet to be raised. Aspects of the development of performance and the instrument use need to be explored. This paper uses various descriptions of Kazakh performances and of the use accordion in the period between the 19th and the 20th-centuries. The final aim is will offer an idea of the key processes that affected the development of Kazakh accordion art in general and of its national peculiarities in performance. Appearance and disappearance of many of the various ancient wind, string, and percussion instruments used by Kazakh people has occurred in different periods of time, not always proportionally to the rather vast territory of the republic. However, it can be noticed that their distribution and disappearance occurred at similar times in Kazakhstan as it did in neighbouring nations. Eventually, active and wide-spread distribution of new instruments among people significantly affected whole or partial disappearance of kobyz, sybyzga, shankobyz, and other instruments that had been used before. Dombra became a definite leader in the instrumental music (kyuis) in XIX century. In the case of accordion, Truvor Karlovitch. Sheibler indicates that its widespread assimilation across many nations after mid 19th-century became the main reason for the disappearance of Kabardian musical instruments used before (Soviet Music Magazin 1955: page 73-79) Similar tendencies can be noticed on the example of Tatar, Bashkir, Chuvash, Kumyk, Lezghin, Chechen, Ingush, and other nations.

The analysis of a larger number of sources -literature, folk material, expedition information on journeys and expeditions, and so on- has enable the authors to come to the conclusion that the historical development of Kazakh instruments has been greatly affected by the following fundamental factors: 1) the economic level and spiritual culture of the nation; 2) the development of folk instruments in neighbouring states; 3) established peculiarities of development of instruments, folk music, and performance traditions; and 4) the distribution of new musical instruments.

In the second half of the XIX century, *dombra* was the main instrument and an object of worship for akyns (extemporizer or improvising poets, and singers, that is, who perform without prior preparation or practices) typical in the *Kazakh* and Kyrgyz cultures. Almost at the same time, however, from about the mid-XIX century, accordion began to be mentioned in their works more and more frequently. Its penetration in Kazakhstan occurred as a result of continuous interaction between Kazakh and Russian musical cultures, as well as with the ones of other nations located close to the Kazakhs and who had mastered the accordion before them.

The appearance and rather intensive development of industrial manufacture (mining, coal, oil, chemical, tobacco, etc.) intensified the migration of Kazakh young people to the cities in search for jobs. Russian immigrants were an important part of this urban population as Kazakh cities and large settlements did not support the tsarist regime, a situation that also enabled a constantly developing trade, economic, and cultural relations between Russians and Kazakhs. Immigrants brought many different musical instruments with them. Accordions, mandolins, guitars and balalaikas could be heard in cities and villages, and Kazakh folk songs were heard as well as Russian and Ukrainian romances. The accordion was one of the first instruments that brought to Kazakhstan the most outstanding samples of world classics, thus providing a steady communicative relation between different national cultures.

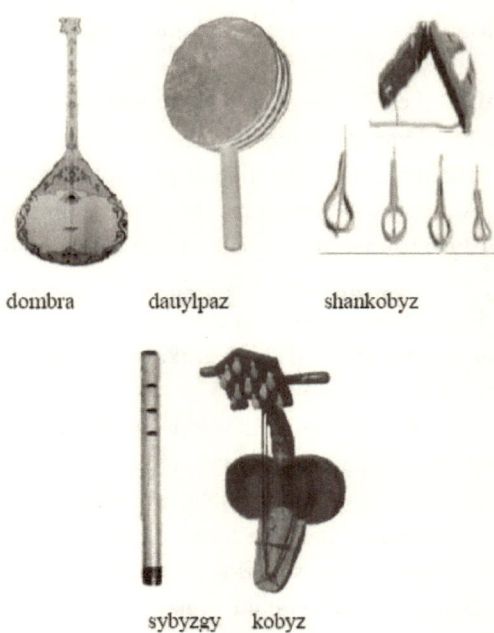

dombra   dauylpaz   shankobyz

sybyzgy kobyz

The main factors that contributed to the spread of accordion in Kazakhstan in mid 19th-century were 1) the penetration of Russian capital, 2) oriental trade fairs and sales, 3) the appearance of Tatar accordion among Kazakh nobility, 4) mass migration of Russian and Ukrainian peasants when Kazakhstan became part of Russia, and 5) the development of manufacture, mining industry with the involvement of Russian proletariat. Thus, wide-spread accordion performance was connected with historical and economic development as well as with the changing aesthetic and cultural tastes of the people. According to famous scientist Chokan Valikhanov, the merry and sad melodies from the accordion-syrnai were heard from the mid 19th-century in the Kazakh steppe (Valikhanov 1986: 205) Folk akyn singers could play several instruments, but they mastered accordion first. The instrument was given the name of '*syrnai*', a term of Turkic origin. After appearing in musical daily life, the *syrnai* became a means of singing and instrumental performance in Kazakh musical culture.

The rapid spread and stable adaptation of the accordion in the everyday life of Kazakh people, as well as its widespread appreciation, might be explained by the following factors. First, the instrument's sounds are similar to modal composition of Kazakh songs whose structure follows a diatonic tone row.

Second, accordion held an accompanying function along with a solo instrument, and had bass and accord accompaniment on the left-hand keyboard. Third, unlike dombra, accordion had fewer requirements for storage, and needed no tuning for decades, a crucial factor in Kazakhs' nomadic way of life. And forth, the accordion has a larger dynamic compass that attracted musicians from the steppe. One could play the accordion while sitting or while riding a horse. A popular legend tells of a famous akyn accordionist named Shashubai who was able to play the accordion while standing on the horseback at full gallop. Other factors that affected the rapid spread of accordion were as follows: it was cheaper and required simple construction, it was easy to play, and it was portable due to its small size and weight. For example, it one could put it in a *korzhyn* – a kind of suitcase or valise - and carry it by foot, or on top of the horse. Thus, the accordion-syrnai became very popular and used in different genres of Kazakh musical folk art for a long time.

Economic factors always affect the cultural development of any nation. Trade relations between Kazakhstan and Russia grew significantly after Kazakhstan joined Russia. Penetration of Russian capital forwarded it, as the richest sources of raw materials began to be exploited. With the expanding of market outlets, the local stock-raising and milling sectors became more closely related to Russian markets and to the ones in Central Asia and Western Europe. Large trade locations appeared in the steppe. They were trade fairs where elements of spiritual culture started penetrating along with industrial and food products from neighbouring nations as well as from far away countries. In the second half of 19th and early 20th-centuries, the largest were Koyadino-Botovskaya in Karkaralinsky district, Tainshikulskaya in Petropavlovsky, Konstantinovskaya in Akmolinsky, Petrovskaya in Atbassarsky, Karkarinskaya in Vernensky districts. Their turnover reached significant amounts (Dauir, 1993: 416). There you could buy anything, from matches to machinery. Approved manufacture based on differentiation of labour led to cheaper prices in accordions and made possible their widespread use. Due to the fact that the instruments were cheap, Russian merchants imported accordions in good supply and sold them on the trade fairs and markets.

At that time, the oriental trade fairs were in fact amazing centres of action with their entertainments. Karkarinskaya, for instance, was graphically described in the famous story 'Likhaya Godina' (Hard Times) by Mukhtae Auezov. Activities in those open-air trade centres were not limited to buying and selling. Fighters-paluans, musicians, dancers, as well as strolling actors and *akyns* performed on the fairgrounds (Auezov 1966: 328). There you could buy different musical instruments previously unknown in the steppe such as the piano, accordions, violins, and others. Having a good natural ear for music, steppe people could quickly learn anything new for them, the richest ones were happy to buy the instruments they liked from the richest musical assortment of European people.

It is interesting to cite some itineraries by ethnographer Michail Ivanin dated from 1864, "The trade fair where Kirghiz people (Kazakhs – Z.S.) buy anything they need and sell cattle, skins, wool, etc. means a pleasure time for them at the same time. The taverns open on the fairground, and then musicians and singers come to Orda. The melody 'Vanka Loved Tanka' is often heard in Orda." (Ivanin 1864: 48) The fairground was a place where they could show off their performance or virtuosic skills playing the instruments as well as sharing their repertoire, techniques, and methods of playing. Such open-air contests were like today's concerts, encouraged by the crowd.

Colonial policy of tsarist Russia and mass immigration of Russian peasants from late 18th-century resulted in the destruction of some of the traditional foundations of Kazakh society, and on the appearance of unconventional cultural forms. Violins, mandolins, balalaikas, and guitars could be bought on the fairgrounds. But such instruments were not in demand in *auls* (a type of fortified village found mainly near the mountains). Instruments were bought by workers, craftsmen from settlements and cities, and they comprised just a really small part of the total local population. Chokan Valikhanov has described the interest of people in buying an accordion in the 1850s. When travelling, he saw Russian and Tatar merchants selling accordions and music boxes, and local people readily bought them. The period of accordion spread and use by Kazakh people, stated by Valikhanov, coincides with the information from ethnographers of that period. According to itineraries by ethnographer Ivanin (1864) in his article 'Inner and Bukey Kirghiz Horde', "accordions are bought a lot and people like playing them" (cited in Izmailova & Mukhambetova 1982: 112).

The bazaar and the accordion become inseparable from each other in Kazakh national memory. In the cartoon *Mudrost i bogatstvo* (*Wisdom and Wealth*) the image of a famous steppe bazaar is characterized by the music by composer Nurgisa Tlendiyev as "witty, merry, full of accordion melodies" (Izmailova & Mukhambetova 1982: 112). The film *An Qanatyngda* (On the Song's Wing) by Shaken Aimanov, starts with the scene of an Asian bazaar where merchants are selling different household goods including an accordion. During the film songs are sung accompanied by dombra and accordion.

Many Kazakh *akyns*, singers, *kyuishi*s, and actors started their way to national recognition from performance on Koyandinskaya trade fair, near Semipalatinsk (Semey) a city in the northeastern province of East Kazakhstan, near the border with Siberia. The construction of the Turkestan-Siberia Railway added to the city's importance, making it a major point of transit between Central Asia and Siberia. Michail Ivanin and Bukey Kirghiz Horde explain that "Outstanding actor Kalibek Kuanyshbayev was a wonderful comic narrator. With his amazing serious humour but without buffooning for fun, he delivers stories from everyday life he has made up with great imitation of different voices." (The History of the Soviet Drama Theatre 1966: 328). In *The History of Accordion and Button Accordion*, Alfred Mirek indicates that other famous figures such as fighter Khadzhimukan Munaitpassov, magicians and acrobats Zarubai Kulpeitov and Zhynd Omar, as well as singer Amre Kashaubayev and poet Issa Baizakov performed at the fair (Mirek 1967: 278).

According to the descriptions given in ethnographic works, an accordion was so popular in Kazakhstan in the second half of XIX century that even common people could play it, not only professional players. The 'Notes' by merchant Zharkov from Saratov who visited Urda (currently, Ural region) in the early 1850s, provide the following facts about local women who played the accordion: "Women musicians appeared to vary pleasures. Several common Kirghiz (Kazakh) girls appeared at kibitka door and started playing the balalaika (dombra), the verganzhik (shankobyz), and some of them played the wooden accordion." (Zatayevich 1931: 278).

Along with historical and cultural prerequisites for assimilation of an accordion in national life of Kazakh people we can mark aesthetic prerequisites such as the tuning system, a tone row, timbre and the tonal features of the instrument. The modal structure of one row in Russian accordion, established under the influence of folk song art, is diatonic. In the basis of melodic structure of Kazakh music there are also diatonic modes. It seems to be crucial to use a melodic tone row in different types of accordion as a basis and Mixolydian mode, typical for Kazakh melos (Zhubanov 2002).

Until recently, the ancient wind folk instrument *syrnai* existed in some areas in the south region of Kazakhstan. For example, according to information from famous professionals in folk music Kurmanbek Zhandarbekov, Zhappas Kalambayev, and others, single bore and double bore *syrnais* could be seen among citizens of South Kazakhstan region.

Bolat Shamgalievitch Sarybayev wrote that during an expedition in the settlement of Zhagabaily in Sairam region in South Kazakhstan, they met a 70-

year-old folk singer Uzhibek Sadybekov who used to play *syrnai* well when he was young. He sang some songs from his repertoire and *kyui* called '*Syrnai*'. In spite of his age, he sang his songs in an expert manner imitating *syrnai* sound with his voice. According to information from the senior research assistant at the folklore office of Kurmangazy, in Almaty Conservatory of Music, Alma Serikbayeva and other people, such syrnai players could be met in Shuisky, Merkensky, and Lugovskoy areas of Zhambyl region (a district of Almaty Province).

Famous *dombra* player Kali Zhantleuov from the Western Kazakhstan saw a *syrnai* made of cane when he was a child and heard from local elders about previously existed *syrnais* made of cow horn (*muiz syrnai*). Another witness, Orynbek Trabayev from Nikitinka settlement in Mensky area in the East Kazakhstan, informs that in 1945 an elderly *syrnai* player lived in their aul (fortified community), and he played with the *syrnai* made of horn (*muiz syrnai*) his plangent lyrical melodies. According to *kobyz* player Sarsenbai Dosmuratov, popular *syrnai* players used to live in Tamdinsky area of Bukhar region in central Kazakhstan. Among them, Otegen Kurbanbayev was notable for his performance gift, and his repertoire consisted of his own works and other folk songs.

Accordion appeared in the second half of the 19th-century in the same region. Used to the ancient *syrnai*, the local people called the new instrument *kagaz syrnai* (literally: paper syrnai; 'klagaz' means 'paper or cardboard in Kazakh). Accordion bellows were made of cardboard, a fact that determined the name for the instrument in that area. In other regions of Kazakhstan (except for Aktyubinsk, Kyzylorda, and Karaganda regions) the accordion was also known as harmonica. The mouth harmonica in the Tamdinsky area was called *auyz syrnai* (Sarybayev Bolat 1978: 75).

Traditionally, instrumental music for *kobyz* was best presented in the south of Kazakhstan. 'In some areas the term '*kobyz*' was meant for an accordion (*kagaz kobyz*). The term *kobyz* for violin appeared in the 19th-century. In the Bugunsky and Kazyrgutsky areas of the South, an accordion was known as '*til kobyz*'. The word 'til' shows a similarity with the lateral keys of an accordion and the shape of the human tongue. (Sarybayev Bolat 1978: 156)

The instrument's name is usually passed from one to another in connection with some similarities of sounding or play methods. Thus, the plangent sound of the accordion is similar to the ancient *syrnai*, and a mouth harmonica is also similar to a *syrnai*. In the terminology, we can see the genetic code of the Kazakh term for accordion which became widespread due to the specific features of the instrument and also the emotional and aesthetic taste of people.

According to famous *dombra* player Uali Bekenov, a *syrnai* was used among Kazakh people of Xinjiang province of the People's Republic of China (this *kyuishi* came from the said province). He saw a *syrnai* that consisted of several pipes put together. According to its description, such type of instrument is the most ancient prototype of the accordion. 'A Guide for Accordions' by Alfred Mirek states that "all musical instruments can be called an accordion if their sound is made by a metal freely-skipped reed (voice) vibrating due to the air stream" (Alferd Mirek 1968: 5). This principle of sound making was known in ancient times, in the second and third millennia BCE. In those days, musical instruments of the accordion family consisted on '*ken*', '*shen*', that is, a system of cane or bamboo pipes with a metal plate in the bottom with a cut reed in the middle, and started appearing in many ancient countries of South-East Asia on the territory of current Burma, China and Japan. The sound in such instruments was made by blowing air in or out. According to description, it was soft, melodious, and lower than modern accordions (Mirek 1968: 9-10)

Thus, established traditions of use and function of the accordion and its varieties were formed in Kazakhstan by the late 19th and early 20th-centuries. The instrument and its later varieties received names such as *syrnai, harmon, kagaz kobyz, til kobyz, zhel syrnai* (Sabyrova 2009: 5-6). This is how the playing of the accordion and its types penetrated the everyday life and culture of Kazakh people becoming part of the historical, emotional and graphical, modal, tonal, and hearing of the national experience.

As mentioned above, another prerequisite for the appearance of the accordion in Kazakhstan was the influence of the neighbouring Turkic nations. Tatar and Bashkir people mastered the accordion in their musical use. It is known that a lot of representatives of Kazakh noble people, with khans, sultans, biis, and later Kazakh intellectuals among them, had close relations with Tatar people. For example, the second wife, Fatima, of one of the last khans of Bukey Horde Zhangir Bokeiuly's (1801-1845), also known as Tatar Mukhamedzhan Kussainov's daughter, was a mufti from Orenburg, known to be a learned person. In those days, Tatars considered an accordion to be an instrument just for women and was a part of their dowry. Apparently, these historical facts from the life of rich habitants of steppe were in the basis of statements by Yakov Zharkov who visited Bukey Horde in 1854 and stated that accordions were "a fun just for small children... and even adults, even the first ministers, even the khan himself." (Zharkov 1854: 231) . It is no coincidence that the most frequently encountered type of accordion is the Tatar one.

As the playing of the *kobyz* and the *sybyzgy* was of local character, the accordion became the second most popular instrument after the *dombra*. The accordion quickly became widespread in everyday music-making of Kazakh people, and found its full expression in higher forms of musical and poetic art. *Anshis, aqyns, zhyraus* became the major popularizers of this universal instrument as they enjoyed a high reputation among the people.

Folk masters who had devoted themselves to professional art were able to play several musical instruments and this was a sign of their artistic talent, image, as well as a feature of their creative thinking. Almost all Kazakh *akyns* could play the accordion. Most public performances in trade fairs and celebrations were accompanied of accordion. The whole series of *akyns* and accordion players established folk and song schools accompanied with a *syrnai*.

Among the most famous singers and accordion players we can mention Maira Shamsutdinova; among akyns – Shashubai Koshkarbayev; among zhyraus – Narta Bekezhanov. In a series of well-known *akyns* and singers of 19th and 20th-centuries, who could play the *syrna*i, we can include the following names: Zhayau Mussa, Asset Naimabayev, Yestai Berkimbayev, Taizhan Kalmagambetov, Kenen Azerbayev, Issa Baizakov, Amre Kashaubayev, Kamshibai Taubayev, Balkhashbai Zhussupov, Kubysh-akyn, Zhanak-akyn, Bolat Sybanov, Arzulla Molzhigitov, Mukhamedzhan Rustemov, Kurmanbek Bekpeissov, and many others.

Witnesses' evidences written down by Akhmet Zhubanov in his two books *Solovi stoletii* (*The Nightingales of the Centuries*) and *Struny stoletii* (*The Strings of the Centuries*) confirm dominance of vocal and instrumental practice of accordion music-making in Kazakh environment. Accordion was perceived as a new and creative phenomenon, an innovation in musical life. The musician's clothes traditionally corresponded to their unconventional image when they played the accordion. Zhubanov indicates that popular Kazakh musician singer Mussa Baizhanov had the following appearance, "Mussa plays virtuously Kazakh folk songs and kyuis as well as he first presents some samples of Russian music to his listeners. His appearance has also great impression on steppe habitants as well as his urban clothes, new manners, his playing the accordion and violin, his translations and retelling of the works by Russian poets." (Zhubanov 2002: 146-147). In another place of the same historical essay, Akhmet Zhubanov directly points out the different ethnic origin of Mussa Baizhanov's accordion: "Coming back from home from Omsk, Mussa saddled up his favourite horse, visited different auls, told people of the things he had read in newspapers, magazines, books, sang new songs, amused people with his playing the dombra, violin, and accordion." (Zhubanov 2002: 147).

The relations between Kazakhstan and Russia which originated in the 15th century pointed to the musicality of the Kazakh people and to Russian bilingualism as a result of the expansion of the instrument's use. According to Zhubanov, however, Zhayau Mussa's accordion playing remained a national composer. "His Russian language skills, knowing the musical culture of Russian nation enriched Mussa's musical vocabulary. And the fact that he accompanied his songs with the play of the violin and accordion, a recourse to originally instrumental accompaniment to non-verbal musical specification, expanded the possibilities of life description by means of sound and did not distort 'the spirit' of Kazakh music; it only enriched and garnished Zhayau Mussa's art. Zhayau Mussa was a really national composer, a significant, a diverse musical man." (Zhubanov 2002:176)

According to witnesses' evidences written down by Zhubanov, when the Kazakh accordion penetrated the steppe from the second half of the 19th-century, it was a rather large instrument, a kind of '*talyanka*' (a single-row button accordion) with small bells. Such descriptions are connected with performances of many *akyns* who participated in musical and poetic contests, and professional singers who were called *sal* and *sere*.

Alexander Viktorovich Zatayevich, an ethnographer and a collector of Kazakh musical folklore described the physical appearance of the accordion owned by popular singer of 19thcentury Maira Shamsutdinova in the following way:

> No sooner had the largest passenger steamship 'Leningrad', where I was going up the Irtysh river from Omsk to Semipalatinsk, pulled off from Pavlodar pier, that I heard the sounds of beautiful chesty and noble contralto from the windows below of third class cabins. The voice of an invisible owner was singing Kazakh songs under an unexpected accompaniment [...] a large accordion! For sure, I was downstairs a minute later and I saw a dark-haired woman in her thirties, beautiful and slim, with a serious long face and blush on her hollow cheeks. She had long oriental earrings in her ears and several rows of different necklaces on her breast. (Zhubanov 2002:245)

There is an important piece of data in Alexander Viktorovich Zatayevich's memoirs that confirms the widespread use of accordion, first in polyethnic urban environments and later everywhere else in the country. According to the ethnographer's notes, accordion playing in the east, centre and west of Kazakhstan was connected with spoken and professional singing or *akyn* traditions. In the south, it was connected with epic art. He writes that "Maira acquired early a taste for singing and music. She especially liked playing the accordion. In the cities as well as in the Kazakh steppe, the accordion with small bells, '*talyankas*' as they were called, was widespread in those years. Uali (Maira's father) bought one of such '*talyankas*' for his daughter. Maira learned to play herself and soon she became a good accordion player." (Zhubanov 2002: 247)

In Zhubanov's essay about the art of Kazakh composer and singer from the 19th-century Ibrai Sandybayev, an outstanding representative of Arkinsk (Central Kazakhstan) singing tradition, there is a vivid description of women's playing the instrument. The scientist first noticed a single-row position of accordion buttons. The slightest detail of performing communication is highlighted in the essay, including 'bravura melody' accompanied by an accordion between the verses, and a flowing 'cascade of sounds' of its tuning system, as well as a wide compass of a singing cantilena, requiring the singer to be able to perform sounding lengthiness appropriate for the features of accordion sound-making, deep breath and strength.

> The eighties of the previous century. The visitors were sitting in a semicircle at home. A young beautiful girl was sitting on the large wooden bed; it was seventeen-year-old Kakima. She had a single-row accordion in her hands. Blowing greatly the bellows, the girl was playing something bravura, and the visitors were listening to her admiringly. All of a sudden, Kakima started singing. Against the background of muted sounds of an accordion, her sonorous pleasant voice seemed especially fascinating. As a singing warm-up, Kakima had chosen a sonorous frolicsome 'Akhau-Semey'. She blew the bellows famously between the verses of the song, fingered quickly and craftily, and this cascade of sounds that had fallen down to the listeners resembled a wild horse galloping along the steppe. The visitors started moving unknowingly. When the girl was dwelling some high note, they were looking at the ceiling with their necks stretched as if they were watching a bird flying high in the sky. After that, Kakima started singing a sentimental plangent 'Gaukhar Kyz' by Zhayau Mussa. Completed one verse, she told the visitors the short story of origin of this song, and they nodded approvingly and rolled their eyes. (Zhubanov 2002: 188-189)

Ibrai Sandybaiuly dedicated his famous song 'Gakku' to this girl, the accordion player and singer Kakima. The patterned melody of this song reflects the roulades and sounding waves of development typical for the accordion playing. Besides, Ibrai Sandybayev himself is a typical representative of that new formation of musicians that appeared at the turn of the 19th-century and succeeded in mastering the tradition of multi-instrumentalism being able to expertly play several musical instruments. It is known that along with the *dombra*, Ibrai could also play the *syrnai*. This fact is confirmed by the poem of outstanding Kazakh poet of 20th-century Saken Seifullin:

> 'His 'Gakku' song is melodious and tender
> It seems to be a swan song
> His 'Kidygai' and 'Manmanger' are even better,
> But they require an accordion'.

The tradition of singing vocal and instrumental performance with an accordion was established in the central, eastern, and northern parts of Kazakhstan. A musical and poetic contest called *aitys* in Kazakh tradition required a separate type of performance with instrumental use. Some *akyns* participated in the contest accompanying their songs with accordion. Many akyns-accordion players were composers from Central Kazakhstan. Ibrai Sandybaiuly, for instance, who contested with Doskei, Essimbet, Kudaibergen; Akyn Nartai from the South of Kazakhstan, who competed with Nurlybek; and composer Kenen Azerbayev from Semirechye, who won poetess Khalima. Other contests of outstanding akyns of the 19th-century, such as Asset and Ryszhan, Asset and Kempirbai, Ibrai and Kakima, were accompanied all by an accordion.

In early 20th-century, *aitys* and collective performances of different singers in a dialogical manner became part of a very popular 'live' tradition that attracted much attention and were frequently accompanied with an accordion. Zhubanov describes the joint concert of Amre Kashaubayev and Maira Shamsutdinova as follows:

> He came back from Paris as an expert singer. Here, in Semipalatinsk, two song magicians met – Amre and Maira. In those days, the city lived with their songs. An inspired young singer and an experienced woman singer sang solo, played the dombra and accordion, and then they played and sang together. This meeting encouraged and mutually enriched

> them. Joint performance of these singers became a celebration for Semipalatinsk citizens. (Zhubanov 2002: 324)

An identical contest of singers, supported by many cheers from the audience, took place in Semipalatinsk between Amre Kashaubayev and Kali Baizhanov in the 1930s.

> Maira came from Pavlodar, Amre came from Semipalatinsk, Kali Baizhanov – from Karakarlinsk. The singers appeared one by one, but after thorough selection the best ones were allowed to participate in the final round – Amre and Kali. It was an unforgettable event. First, the singers sang different songs, and then they sang the same songs in turn without leaving the stage, playing the dombra and accordion in turn. Hardly waiting for the end of the song, the second singer immediately picked it up and sang it in his own way. The audience reacted vividly to each song and cheered the singers. When Kali was singing, he was encouraged by cheers of his townsmen, spectators from Karakaralinsk, Pavlodar, Bayanaul. Semipalatinsk citizens got behind their singers Amre. It was hard to prefer just one singer, and the jury made a decision to give the first and second prizes to both singers in equal parts (Zhubanov 2002: 330)

> Amazing Kazakh dancer Shara Zhienkulova looks back at her first Kazakhstan concert tour when the greatest singer Amre Kashaubayev sang and played the accordion. Then Amre with an accordion and Issa Baizakov with a dombra accompanied Kazakh, Tatar, and Uyghur dances of Shara. During the performance of an athlete, a famous fighter Kazhymukan Munaitpassov, Amre was playing the accordion and Kazhymukan showed his muscles of his mighty body in time with the melody. (Shara Zhiyenkulova 1983: 32-33)

Accordion spread through Tatar missioners who preached Islam among singers and *akyns* from Western, Central, Northern, and Eastern Kazakhstan. Its development was further encouraged in the southern part of the country through *akyn* Taizhan. For instance, Nartai Bekezhanov was an outstanding representative of the traditions of Kyzylorda region, who first used the accordion in the epic tradition. Melodic pattern of his *terme* (a chant with hortatory and didactic content) harmonically agrees with the shimmering sounds of the accordion. Thus, the melody depends on harmonization, or, in other words, on the performance technique of playing this instrument.

According to Zhubanov, Nartai had a single-row button accordion the same as in Central Kazakhstan. This instrument, previously unknown to Kazakh listeners, became popular through Nartai and heard on *tois* and celebrations.

> The life of a farm hand pressed Nartai. He made up his mind to take up art seriously, to become a professional singer. On his Uncle Mansur and mother Bakhytgul's advice, the young singer started his way. This was the destiny of any singer, akyn, musician of pre-revolutionary Kazakhstan. In order to gain recognition, show his skills, learn, enrich his repertoire, a singer, an akyn had to wander along the auls, cities, use the slightest chances for performance. Nartai bought an accordion with a single-row buttons (my spacing Z.S), a dombra and went to auls near Syr Darya. Quickly, he became famous. Neither toi, nor celebration occurred without Nartai. (Zhubanov 2002: 296)

The voice part depended on the plangent, ornamental sound of the accordion, originally relying of air-driven basis for sound making of and the deep breath capacity of singers as well as their individual styles. Melodic modulations, plangent and soft melodic flow are typical of Nartai's style, as well as pentatonic system of modal base, "Nartai played the accordion and sang plangently and widely. He was in his fifties then, but his voice remained strong, beautiful, and delicate. Akyns sang songs about life and working success of the Soviet people in the rear, about the victory over Hitler's invaders." (Zhubanov 2002: 299)

Written down according to the witnesses' words, historical facts about the musicians' life confirmed that the northern, eastern, and central regions of Kazakhstan, where the accordion art originated from, followed *dombra* vocal instrumental performance in the singing monody, and that there was of a single, local nature in the use of an accordion. At the same time, by early 20th-century, accordion accompaniment of singing in south-west Kazakhstan spread at a high professional level and represented as a feature of the regional *akyn* tradition of Kazakh people, demonstrated also in government concerts outside the republic. Let us address Zhubanov's essay about Nartai Bekezhanov again where he states that Nartai took part in the terms of Kazakh literature and art holding in Moscow in 1936 and 1949. Zhubanov indicates that Nartai's singing accompanied with the accordion amazed Moscow spectators. With particular skill and inspiration, he performed 'Nartai's Song' and 'Tolkyn' (A Wave).

> Let Nartai take his accordion in hand,
> Let him reach the sky with his voice,
> Let his song fly away and away,
> Let the wind carry it to Moscow way.'

'Tolkyn' differed greatly from many chanting and declamation songs of the composer. 'Tolkyn' as well as 'Nartai's Song' was made up for wide strong voice. Its music is spacious, gleefully sprawling, and pathetic' (Zhubanov 2002:.301). In 1934, Nartai Bekezhanov took part in the first republican forum of national talents. In 1939 he performed at the All-Soviet Union Agricultural Exhibition in Moscow with other participants of the amateur talent group of Kazakhstan. His talent was described by Vladimir Gorodinsky in the newspaper of 'Pravda' dated 28 August, 1939, as follows:

> The most interesting among the performances was one of akyn Nartai Bekezhanov's. He sang a long song (more exactly, the whole singing suite) 'Homeland's Celebration' playing the accordion (of so-called, Oriental or Asian type) rather than the traditional akyns' instrument dombra. Bekezhanov really charmed Muscovites with his fine skills and elaborate performance. There are no signs of any external virtuosity. Bekezhanov's singing is distinguished with rare noble manner, an actual artistry. Bekezhanov's voice is very pleasant by its timbre, tone; it is irreproachably precise. (Ozderding Biler Nartaimyn 1987: 100)

To conclude this paper, we can state the following points that bring to the fore the intermedial and intercultural aspects of accordion playing in Kazakh culture.

- That accordion playing acts as a subject of intercultural mediation during the period under study and instrument spread in Kazakhstan took place by means of inter-ethnic relations with Russian immigrants as well as with Muslim Tatars who preached Islam in the western, central, eastern, and northern parts of the republic.
- That each region of Kazakhstan was marked with its own local features of playing the instrument (in Arkinsk school -the centre, east, and north of Kazakhstan- solo spoken and professional singing and akyn traditions were marked; in Syr Darya -in the south-west of Kazakhstan- epos singing accompanied the accordion)

- That descriptions of performance practice of the period showed that accordion accompaniment was also part of the intonation of voiced songs under the influence of 'wind' plangent, overtones of the accordion.

REFERENCES

Atlas of Musical Instruments of the USSR Nations. [Атлас музыкальных инструментов народов СССР] Moscow: State Music Publishing house. 1963, pages 400

Bassurmanov, Arkady. Accordionist's Guide. [Справочник баяниста] Moscow: Soviet composer, 1982, pages 362

Gaissin, Gennady. Accordion and its Types in Kazakh Musical Culture [Гармоника и ее

разновидности в музыкальной культуре Казахстана] (To the Issue of Interaction of National Cultures). Synopsis of thesis in Art. Leningrad, 1986, pages 17

Gizatov, Bisengali. Kazakh Kurmangazy Orchestra.[Казахский оркестр имени Курмангазы] Almaty: Zhalyn, 1994, pages 166-205

Ivanin, Michael. Inner and Bukey Kirghiz Horde [Внутренняя или Букеевская киргизская орда] 12. Saint Petersburg: Epoch, 1864, pages 33

Izmailova, Lutzia, and Mukhambetova, Asiya. "Maturity of Talent." Composers of Kazakhstan 2. [Зрелость таланта в книге «Композиторы Казахстана»]Almaty: Oner, 1982, pages 112-144

Mirek, Alfred. From the History of Accordion and Button Accordion. [Из истории аккордеона и баяна] Moscow: Science, 1967

Mirek, Alfred. A Guide for Accordions. [Справочник по гармоникам] Moscow: Science, 1968, pages 534.

Mustafin, Bolat and Smakova, Zaure. Syrnai-Accordion Initial Learning Course. [Сырнай-баян үйренудің бастапқы курсы] Almaty: Zennye bumagi Securities, 2003, pages 3-202

Mustafin, Bolat. Syrnai Accordion in Kazakh Traditional Musical Being and Art of Folk Singers and Composers (anshi-akyns) [Сырнай (гармоника) в казахском традиционном музыкальном быту и в творчестве народных певцов–композиторов (анши-акынов)] Almaty: Securities, 1990.

Notes by Merchant Zharkov. Library for Reading. [Библиотека для чтения] 126, Sib, 1854, page 231

Ozderding Biler Nartaimyn. Nartai's Songs. [Песни Нартая] Disk Record. Melody, 1987.

Sabyrova, Aliya. 2009. "Anniversary of Outstanding Professional Zaure Smakova." In the World of Music 23 (33) [В мире музыки], pages 5-32, Almaty: Scientific-methods, pedagogical Magazine. Baspa LLP

Sarybayev, Bolat. Kazakh Musical Instruments. [Журнал Жалын Казахские музыкальные инструменты] Almaty: Zhalyn, 1978, pages 173

Sheibler, Truvor. "Kabardian Folklore." Soviet Music 6, [Журнал Советская музыка], pages 25-79, Moscow: Composer, 1955.

Smakova, Zaure. The Album of an Accordionist. [Альбом Баяниста] Almaty: Securities, 2003, pages 3-119

Smakova, Zaure. "The Role of Accordion in Musical Folk Art in Kazakhstan." Conferenceon the 80th Anniversary of B. Sarybayev. [Роль баяна в музыкальном фольклоре Казахстана Материалы международной научно-практической конференции «Б.Сарыбаеву – 80 лет], Pages 3-4, Almaty: LEM, 2008, pages 31-86

Smakova, Zaure. "Assimilation of Accordion in Traditional Kazakh Culture." Conference on the 100 Anniversary of P.V. Aravin. [Об ассимиляции гармоники в традиционную культуру Казахстана Материалы международной научно-практической конференции, посвященной 100-летию со дня рождения П.В.Аравина] Almaty, 2008, pages 61-128

Smakova, Zaure. "Accordion in the Musical Culture of Kazakhstan." Khabarshy 4.59 [«Хабаршы», серия историческая, №4 (59)] (2010): pages 97-171, Almaty: Kazakh National University Al-Farabi.

Smakova, Zaure. "Historical Development of Syrnai Accordion." World of Education. 2 (2011) [В мире образования. № 2]: pages 25-48 Almaty: Taugul-Print.

Smakova, Zaure. and Konysbayev Medelkhan, Anthology of Kazakh Accordion Literature. Part 2. [Антология казахстанской баянной литературы. Часть 2.] Almaty: Securities, 2013, pages 3-477

The History of Kazakhstan from the Ancient Times to the Present Days. [История Казахстана с древнейших времен до наших дней (очерк)]. Almaty: Dauir, 1993, pages 416

The History of the Soviet Drama Theatre in 6 volumes. [История советского драматического театра в 6-ти томах] Moscow: Science, 1966-1971.

Tuyakbayev, Dosmukhamed and Smakova, Zaure. Textbook for Orchestration of Kazakh Kyuis for Accordion. [Пособие по аранжировке казахских кюев для баяна] Almaty: Kanagat KC, 1999, pages 6-122

Valikhanov, Chokan. Selected Works. [Избранные произведения] Moscow: Science. 1986, pages 414

Zatayevich, Alexandr. 500 Kazakh Songs and Kyuis. [500 казахских песен и кюев] Alma-Ata: Narkompros. 1931, pages 308

Zhiyenkulova, Shara. Omirim Mening - Onerim (Art is My Life) [Өмірім менің – өнерім (Искусство – моя жизнь)]. Almaty: Zhazushy. 1983, pages 216

Zhubanov, Akhmet. The Nightingales of the Centuries. [Соловьи столетий] Almaty: Dyke Press, 2002, pages 457

Zhubanov, Akhmet. The Strings of the Centuries. [Струны столетий] Almaty: Dyke Press, 2002, pages 280

About the Authors

Zaure Smakova is Associate Professor and Chair of kobyz and an accordion of the Kazakh National Conservatory of Kurmangazy, is "The cultural figure of the Republic of Kazakhstan" having graduated with honors in Almaty in 1984 and pursuing a phD. in Leningrad conservatory in 1988. After 30 years of pedagogical work, Smakova has trained over 60 experts, including 20 winners of the international and national competitions, and publishing fundamental textbooks, repertoire collections, research articles, and CDs.

Medelkhan Konysbayev holds a Kazakh State Conservatory Degree of Kurmangazy in Almaty, and worked at Central music school in Shymkent City between 1964 and 1967, and since then as Professor of musical and national instruments at Kazakh State Woman's Teacher Training at the University in Almaty. He was also Director of the Republican library for blind and visually impaired citizens of Kazakhstan in Almaty between 1992 and 2004. He holds several certificates of honor for her service from Kazakhstan Ministry of Culture.

CHAPTER 6

The Dream Ballet: Intermedial Tensions between Music, Dance, and Language in the Film Musical

Emily Petermann

The breadth of available theories on relationships between, across, and within diverse media may at times seem overwhelming. Should we speak of interarts relations, intermedial relations, remediation, adaptation, multimediality, transmedial storytelling, convergence culture,[1] or intertextuality? Without going into all of these different vantage points here or distinguishing between them – an undertaking that fully deserves a monograph, rather than a single article – I wish to explore a particular case of intermedial relations (as I will be calling them, drawing upon intermedial theories by Werner Wolf [1999] and Irina Rajewsky [2002; 2004; 2005], as well as previous work of my own [Petermann 2014]) as they arise within a multimedial work. As in opera, non-musical film, and many other complex media forms, multiple media conjoin in the signification of the musical film. Like the opera, the musical tells a story partly through the interaction of words and music, though the precise terms of that interaction differ. Opera, for its part, possesses a distinction between the aria and the recitative, which is related to but not identical with that between the number and the book in the musical. As this paper will show, the more marked distinction between the

---

[1] The terms "transmedia storytelling" and "convergence culture" were coined by Henry Jenkins. He defines them as follows: "A transmedia story unfolds across multiple media platforms, with each new text making a distinctive and valuable contribution to the whole. In the ideal form of transmedia storytelling, each medium does what it does best—so that a story might be introduced in a film, expanded through television, novels, and comics; its world might be explored through game play or experienced as an amusement park attraction. Each franchise entry needs to be self-contained so you don't need to have seen the film to enjoy the game, and vice versa. Any given product is a point of entry into the franchise as a whole" (Jenkins, *Convergence Culture*, 95–96). Though convergence culture has become much more widespread since the advent of digital media, this concept is also relevant in the context of mid-20th-century musicals because the genre frequently transverses various media, such as when a musical begins on Broadway – often already an adaptation from a non-musical play or prose text – and is later known to fans from various stage and screen incarnations. This is the case, for example, with both Rodgers and Hammerstein musicals discussed here, *Oklahoma!* and *Carousel*.

presence or absence of diegetic music heightens the contrast between such sections and establishes different possible worlds within the musical that are characterized by song vs. speech. Both opera and the musical also employ visual arts – for example, in the form of often elaborate sets and costumes – and the musical in particular shares with the ballet, more so than with the opera, the use of dance as well. Since I will be specifically considering the musical film rather than its stage incarnation, the medial specificity of film (cinematography, lighting and filters, editing, sound mixing, etc.) also plays a role in the complex multimedial interaction of the musical's composite media. This paper aims to elucidate some of these interactions – specifically between language, music, and dance in the context of those numbers known as dream ballets – as a case study of the way intermedial relations may create different possible worlds within a multimedial work.

The paper is structured as follows: first, I briefly define the dream ballet, using its paradigmatic exemplar, "Laurey Makes Up Her Mind" from *Oklahoma!* (Broadway 1943, Fox 1955; choreography by Agnes de Mille) to illustrate the form's prototypical characteristics and functions. I then go on to sketch out several other examples from the 1940s to the late 20th century, particularly *The Pirate* (1948), *Singin' in the Rain* (1952), *An American in Paris* (1951), *Carousel* (1956), and *Labyrinth* (1986), briefly discussing the ways they have both built upon the *Oklahoma!* model and diverged from it. I then concentrate on the beach ballet in *Carousel* as an important if ambiguous example of the form in order to argue for the dream ballet as an extreme case of all musical numbers' characteristic tendency to use the different media involved – most often speech vs. song, but in the dream ballet especially dance – in order to set off distinct realms of experience. I find Possible Worlds Theory, as elucidated by Marie-Laure Ryan [1992] and others, to be very useful in this context, as the numbers can be said to open up possible worlds that are at odds with the textual actual world of the film's main diegesis. This opposition will generally be resolved in the film's conclusion, as the exploratory space of the dream-like numbers allows characters to try out emotions and even possible courses of action that may then be extended to their waking lives.[2] As I will show, numbers in general and dream

---

[2] On numbers as possible worlds, see Petermann [Forthcoming 2015]. On the way characters try out different roles in song, see Altman's concept of the "personality dissolve," [1987] 80-86. Jane Feuer has also remarked on the function of such dreamlike numbers to point up the distinction between reality and fantasy that is also involved in audience's experience of watching a film: "An analogy is created among the primary diegesis of the musical, waking life in psychoanalysis, and the life of the spectator when the lights come up after the film. Similarly, an analogy is created between the dream ballet,

ballets in particular are marked by a high degree of unreality, or, to put it another way, are marked by their removal from the more realistic world of the book as an ideal space of dreams, fantasy, heightened emotion, or even hypnosis and hallucination. Finally, this leads me to the conclusion that musicals frequently see their composite media within a framework that ranks them from most realistic (speech) to most aestheticized or ideal (dance), with music serving as a bridge between the other media and between these realms.

Agnes de Mille's dream ballet in *Oklahoma!*, "Laurey Makes Up Her Mind," is the prototype of the dream ballet, a game-changer that revolutionized the role of dance in the Broadway (and later film) musical. Liza Gennaro defines the Golden Age of dance in the musical as starting with de Mille's choreography for this Rodgers and Hammerstein book musical in 1943 (and extending through Jerome Robbins's work as choreographer-director of *Fiddler on the Roof* in 1964; Gennaro [2011] 45). Choreographers like de Mille and Robbins asserted dance's place in the integrated musical "as an essential narrative tool" and "as a conduit for emotions and ideas" (Gennaro [2011] 45, 51).[3]

The *Oklahoma!* dream ballet is a number in which a character's dream is acted out in dance – literally balletic in its movement lexicon – and separated both aesthetically and ontologically from the rest of the film. Laurey is asleep, literally dreaming, and her dream differs in numerous ways from her waking life, from the use of a dream double (the dancer Bambi Linn takes over from Shirley Jones) and ballet in contrast to movements more reminiscent of folk dances to minimalistic sets and the complete absence of language, whether in dialog or song lyrics. It is thus both literally a dream and literally ballet. Many related inset scenes in other musicals, however, resemble this number in various ways and yet are not literally "dream" "ballets." For example, in *Carousel* the corresponding scene is marked by the use of ballet, reduced sets, and minimal language (though not its total absence), but it is not actually a dream. (The nevertheless "unreal" quality of this number will thus be an important point to consider, below.) Others mark the sequence as belonging to the realm of dreams or reverie but do not use a dance vocabulary drawn from ballet. Ballet is a natural choice for such dream sequences due to its heightened narrative capabilities in contrast to many other varieties of dance. For this reason, as Jane Feuer has pointed out, "Although not every dream sequence uses ballet in the strict choreographic sense, it's natural to

---

actual dreams, and the experience of the film itself. The spectator 'wakes up' after each. The dream ballet within the film represents the relationship of the spectator *to* the film." (Feuer [1993] 76)

[3] On Robbins's use of dance as narrative tool, see also McMillin on the opening scene of *West Side Story* ([2006] 140-5).

refer to such interludes as dream ballets, since most of them do employ a narrative style of dance" (73). For example, "As the World Falls Down" from *Labyrinth* (1986) is a fantasy triggered by Sarah (Jennifer Connolly) eating the peach given her by the Goblin King Jareth (David Bowie), meant to make her "forg[e]t everything."[4] It is clearly a hallucination, and yet the variety of dance involved is not ballet but the mere suggestion of ballroom dance. Because these characters do not dance in any of the other numbers, any dance at all is enough to separate the possible world of this dream/fantasy/hallucination from the film's textual actual world, without the specific form of ballet being a necessary condition.[5] The sequence "By the Sea" from *Sweeney Todd: The Demon Barber of Fleet Street* (2007) also gestures towards the dream ballet – the depiction of a fantasy as distinct from reality primarily through a change in lighting and costume – without in this case involving any actual dance at all. Though I would hesitate to call this number a dream ballet, along with many others set in an imaginary realm but without the use of narrative dance, it demonstrates that the dream ballet's removal from the textual actual world of the film, from the "reality" of the main storyworld, can be seen as a heightened version of the numbers' general tendency to approach the ideal in opposition to the real (see Petermann [Forthcoming 2015]).

Many dream-ballet-like sequences are in fact much less narrative than the prototype from *Oklahoma!*. The dream ballet in *Singin' in the Rain*, set within the number "Broadway Melody," has qualities of reverie (as do the dream ballets in

---

[4] At the opening of the battle for the Goblin City a goblin guard rushes into the room of the castle where Jareth, the Goblin King, is sitting with Sarah's baby brother, and shouts, "Your Highness, the girl! The girl who ate the peach and forgot everything! She's here with the monster and Sir Didymus and the dwarf who works for you!"

[5] Of course, ballroom dance alone does not set this number apart from the rest of the film, but the way the sequence is clearly framed as a fantasy. After eating the peach, Sarah seems intoxicated or drugged, saying "everything's dancing" and holding onto a tree for support in her dizziness. She then looks into a bubble blown by Jareth and sees her music box with a princess in fancy dress and transitions to herself being that princess at a masquerade ball, where she dances with Jareth to the song "As the World Falls Down." The scene concludes when she breaks away from him – reminded by a glimpse of the clock with its thirteen numbers that she had been searching for something – and uses a chair to smash the convex walls of the bubble in which this masquerade had been enclosed. The use of dance is thus merely one minor factor contributing to this scene's removal from the ordinary diegesis of the film – which of course is itself already set apart by story, costumes, sets, and other devices from the framing scenes of Sarah in her New England home with her parents. The latter separation (between reality and fantasy, responsibility and childhood), however, is presented as less absolute, particularly by the conclusion in which her "imaginary" friends from the labyrinth join her in a party in her bedroom, since "every now and then in my life, for no reason at all," she still "need[s]" them.

The Pirate and *An American in Paris*), but contains only the hint of a narrative – an encounter between the "young hoofer" (Gene Kelly) who has come to New York in the performance number and a mysterious and seductive dancer (Cyd Charisse) leads him to fantasize about her in romantic terms. The number is characterized by lilac and pink sets and lighting, a change of costume that involves long, flowing, somewhat bridal white drapery, the use of wind to suggest that they are "swept away" by emotion, a change of orchestral music away from the ballroom variation on "Broadway Rhythm" playing at the party where she appears and towards a more modern style of art music that only very subtly gestures toward the previous song's melody, and, most significantly, the switch from tap, jazz, and ballroom dance to ballet movements. Yet the narrative is restricted to this brief idea of the two figures (who lack any individualization such as names or backstories) coming together in romantic fashion, as realized in their *pas de deux*, though only within the dream itself.

Dream ballets, as Feuer has noted, tend to take the form either of the dreamer's wish or desire, as in the three Gene Kelly examples I have mentioned,[6] or "a tentative working out of the problems of the primary narrative [...] foreshadow[ing] in symbolic form the eventual outcome of the plot" (Feuer [1993] 74). In contrast to the "wish ballets," Laurey's dream involves a much more extensive narrative development: this includes the dramatization of her imagined wedding with Curly, including the participation and support of the community, the dramatic reversal in which not Curly, but Jud lifts her wedding veil and she finds herself in a saloon surrounded by strangely mechanical burlesque dancers (the "Postcard Girls"; see Gennaro [2011] 50-51), both sexualized and eerily inanimate. The ballet expresses her fear of an advancing Jud, and she even imagines Jud killing Curly and carrying her off.

The dream ballet in *Singin' in the Rain* is unusual in that it is presented as a performance, a show-within-the-show, as opposed to a possible world created solely by imagining or dreaming (it is in fact at a two-fold remove from the film's main diegesis). Still, in many respects it is typical of the Gene Kelly-style dream ballet as it also occurs in *The Pirate* and *An American in Paris*. While primarily illustrating the (day-) dreaming character's desire or longing –Manuela's (Judy Garland) fantasy of Serafin (Gene Kelly) as the wild and sensual pirate Macoco in *The Pirate*, Jerry's (Gene Kelly) romantic feelings toward Lise (Leslie Caron),

---

[6] Confusingly, Feuer categorizes the *American in Paris* dream ballet – like those in *Yolanda and the Thief* and *On the Town* – as having a problem-solving function, although, as she acknowledges, the "resolution always takes place in the primary diegesis, the 'real' world" ([1993] 75).

whom he believes has just left him to marry another man in *An American in Paris* – these numbers also provide the "show" that is such a large portion of the musical's appeal. We speak of numbers as "stopping the show," but as Geoffrey Block has pointed out, "in fact these glorious extraneous moments *are* the show" ([2011] 101). For example, we don't watch a Gene Kelly musical primarily for the story, for the book, but for the spectacular choreography of his playful dance numbers.

In virtually all cases dream ballet-like sequences use a different style of dance to mark the removal from the "real world"/textual actual world of the film's diegesis. In the case of *The Pirate*'s dream ballet it is quite clear that we are seeing this erotic dance with its flames and whirling swords through Manuela's fascinated eyes, as she imagines herself in the place of the horse around which Serafin dances. *An American in Paris* actually has two sequences that could be likened to dream ballets. The longer, more traditional dream ballet at the end of the film mentioned earlier is introduced by Jerry's musing on a sketch of Paris he has just made and ripped. As the two pieces fall to the ground together, he imagines himself within the Parisian cityscape of his drawing, with its stylized color scheme and minimalistic sets.[7] Once within this drawing, he encounters Lise and dances out his love for her, which prefigures her return to him when the ballet comes to an end.[8]

Earlier in the same film, there is a sequence in which Henri (Lise's fiancé; played by Georges Guétary) tells Adam (Oscar Levant) about Lise, whom the latter has not met, and she illustrates in dance the roles they imagine for her. This is clearly removed from reality: not only is this an imagined view of her, rather than an authentic portrayal, but it is twice mediated as Henri speaks with a lover's enthusiasm and Adam then translates his words into even more exaggerated images.[9] The imagination sequence's removal from the reality of the textual

---

[7] This is reminiscent of the way Mary, Burt, and the Banks children climb into the chalk drawing in *Mary Poppins*. Indeed, the visual arts are frequently used as a tool for setting off a space within musical films that is less real and more aestheticized than the textual actual world of the film, with picture frames, crystal balls, and other visual devices used as a gateway into another space. In many cases, this also allows a change of perspective as we share the viewpoint of one of the characters – we see a character seeing and then see what they see or imagine.

[8] In addition to Jerry's own sketch, the entire ballet is inspired by the work of various French painters, including Raoul Dufy, Pierre-Auguste Renoir, Henri de Toulouse Lautrec, and others. For an analysis of the dream ballet with relation to various art-historical models, see Vache Espagnole.

[9] It is ironic that Adam is presented as thinking in visual terms, since he is not a painter but a musician – he will in fact experience something like a "dream concert" later in the film. This corresponds, however, to the film's larger interest in painting as an aesthetic lens

actual world is first marked by a literal picture frame – like the drawing that introduces the later ballet sequence – around the set in which Caron dances. This sense of artificiality continues in the exaggerated contrasts in her costumes and style as they discuss different facets of her personality: she is "an exciting girl," she is "sweet and shy," she is "vivacious and modern," she "reads incessantly," she is "the gayest girl in the world." The use of ballet, as well as stark monochrome sets, the framing device, etc., all serve to indicate that this is Adam's imagination of what Lise is like (based on but clearly not equivalent to Henri's image of her), and certainly not a realistic portrayal of her.

The prototypical dream ballet can thus be defined as a number that is ontologically removed from the textual actual world as a dream or reverie rather than actual events; it is aesthetically distinct from the book and other numbers because of the use of more abstract or minimalistic sets, a change in lighting, and often a different style of music (which corresponds to a changed style of dance)[10]; it prominently foregrounds dance, often ballet, of a style that sets it apart from the other numbers to the (near) exclusion of spoken or sung language; and through this shift in prominence from language to dance, dance takes on a more narrative role than is the case in most other numbers. Though not all of these features may be present in every case, this description takes the most influential example of the form as a prototype and sees other examples as approaching it in some but not all characteristics.

While many dream-ballet-like sequences differ from the *Oklahoma!* prototype primarily in their simplification of the latter's narrative complexity, *Carousel* provides a rather different example. Instead of being more strongly separated from the book – less narrative, more "decorative" – this sequence is more closely integrated with it even than Laurey's dream. Indeed, it is almost problematic to refer to this sequence as a dream ballet, since it appears to take place within the textual actual world of the film rather than in a literal dream. As Billy, who has died and returns to Earth after fifteen years for one day in an

---

through which to view Paris.

[10] The status of the music in dream ballets is quite interesting. Rick Altman has discussed the way music in the musical film shifts between non-diegetic (as in non-musical film soundtracks) and diegetic (when sung by characters in the film's storyworld), and "supra-diegetic" in the way it bridges these domains at the beginning and end of each number in what Altman terms an "audio dissolve." In the case of the dream ballet, music could be considered semi-diegetic, since it is not experienced by all characters, only the one dreaming, yet it is clearly part of the story world on an internal level. The music – and indeed, the entire content of the dream ballet – is thus similar to film voice-overs that represent characters' thoughts but are not actually spoken aloud for other characters to hear. On supra-diegetic music and the "audio dissolve," see Altman 66-70.

attempt to redeem himself, watches his teenage daughter dancing on the beach, the ontological status of the dance is initially unclear. Is this a fantasy of his, is it a premonition of what may happen but has not yet been realized? Yet after the dance has concluded and Louise returns to her house, she tells Enoch Snow that she will become an actress, that the "advance man" will set her up in show business, such that the previous *pas de deux* must be retroactively interpreted as symbolizing a budding relationship and conversation that was expressed not in literal words but in ballet movements. The lyrical nature of the beach ballet can be connected to its different "order of time," as McMillin [2006] terms it (6-7). Though Billy is only on earth for one day, this sequence provides several insights into Louise's life and relationship with other children in the village in such a way that it seems to encapsulate her teenage experience in a way that one literal day could not. The ballet thus partakes of elements of the montage, doing in dance what more realistic films often do through editing.

The sequence is full of parallels to her parents' experiences. This becomes most explicit at the ballet's conclusion, when Billy states that he knows what she's going through and his guide from the stars responds, "Something like what happened to you when you was a kid, ain't it?" As with Billy and Julie, the young lovers meet at a carnival, to the music of the "Carousel Waltz," where he is an entertainer (a carousel barker) and with character traits that are reminiscent of Billy's, including both his charming manner as a performer and his imperious behavior towards one of the dancers that echoes Billy's treatment of the carousel owner, Mrs. Mullin. Most significantly, the song to which Louise and her partner dance most intimately is an orchestral reprise of her parents' powerful duet "If I Loved You." Instead of the spoken conversation between Julie and Billy, in which she decides to risk losing her job in order to be with him,[11] Louise's romance takes place in an absence of language, where movement replaces all dialog and music is a bridge that connects these two sequences. Yet the limitations of language are also evident in the lyrics to that duet:

> Time and again I would try to say
> All I'd want you to know
> If I loved you
> Words wouldn't come in an easy way
> Round in circles I'd go

---

[11] There is also a suggestion of language being elided from Julie's and Billy's initial meeting as well, as they can be seen talking and laughing on the carousel, but their actual words are drowned out by the music of the "Carousel Waltz."

> Longin' to tell you but afraid and shy
> I'd let my golden chances pass me by.   (*Carousel*, "If I Loved You")

This lyric picks up the carousel metaphor that permeates the musical – characters in this film are trapped on a merry-go-round, unable to break out of established patterns and to stop going in circles and make progress, apparently even across generations. At the same time, in the order of time opened up by the number, the characters are able to achieve insights that their speaking, or book, selves cannot (see McMillin [2006], esp. 6-10, 42-43): Julie senses the direction her relationship with Billy will take, their inability to truly reach one another, while Billy expresses deep thoughts on the meaning of life and the insignificance of human problems (as in the lyric "and two little people, you and I, we don't count at all"). None of this knowledge is accessible to them in their "real" lives in the book, as McMillin observes in relation to Billy's aria "Soliloquy":

> There is a difference between the character of the singing Billy Bigelow who makes recognitions and the foolish Billy Bigelow who is killed in the robbery attempt, and this difference is not the deepening of a psychological entity but change of mode in the characterization itself. There are two Billys, only one of them capable of hitting the high G [...], and the startling, enlivening fact is that they are projected by the same performer, adept in both orders of time, the book and the number. ([2006] 43)

The beach ballet takes the inadequacy of language thematized in the duet a step further, replacing it with orchestral music and nonverbal communication in the form of dance, with only brief spoken interludes in Louise's exchanges with the Snow children (interestingly, the Broadway version of the musical used recitative for the language in this sequence, though the film uses dialog instead).[12]

One could read the beach ballet as an echo of the *Oklahoma!* dream ballet despite its changed context outside of a literal dream, as a pragmatic choice to

---

[12] There are two brief verbal exchanges within the beach ballet, both involving Louise's confrontation with the social respectability represented by the Snow children. In the first case, the oldest of the Snow girls brags to Louise that "my father bought me my pretty dress." When Louise responds, "My father would have bought me a pretty dress too. He was a barker on a carousel" the girl retorts provocatively that he was a thief, prompting Louise to strike out and steal the girl's bonnet. At the end of the ballet sequence the Snow children chant "shame on you, shame on you, shame on you...", to which Louise responds first with a gesture of physical violence, though she does not actually strike anyone, but instead sobs "I hate you, I hate all of you."

employ a structural feature that was very well received in the earlier musical for effect, although it may be less logical within *Carousel*'s own structure. One could also argue that ballet need not be restricted to dream sequences but that de Mille is here experimenting with ballet's narrative potential in a way that causes us to re-assess the musical's book-number division as the genre approaches the aestheticization of ballet. While both of these assessments have merit, I argue that the ambiguity between the real, textual actual world and the aestheticized reverie/dream/premonition in "Louise's Ballet" is primarily connected to *Carousel*'s larger interest in interrogating reality. Billy is most in his element as a carnival barker, in a clearly demarcated space of entertainment, pleasure, and freedom from responsibility, and then struggles and fails when he leaves this environment to marry Julie. His inability even to look for a job illustrates how he has always been unable to adapt himself to the "real" world of responsibility and adulthood. By attempting to live his life as if he were constantly on a carousel, an entertainer in the spotlight with no consequences to his actions, he has ruined his and Julie's lives. He must now learn to accept reality and renounce the carnival in order to prevent his daughter from making his own mistakes, and to finally break this pattern, symbolized in the finale's message of hope and companionship: "Walk on, walk on with hope in your heart and you'll never walk alone."

The close examination of dream ballets, particularly in contrast with book segments and non-dance numbers, reveals an interesting hierarchy of the arts involved in the multimedial art form that is the musical film. It becomes clear that music is the intermediate form, situated between the (relative) rationality of language and the aestheticized or "more stylized" removal from reality indicated by dance (Feuer [1993] 74). We can discern a continuum in the musical between strictly spoken scenes of the book, diegetic numbers that are "actually happening," and numbers that are possible rather than actual, i.e., dreams. Dream ballets tend to be located very close to the latter end of the spectrum, with dance supplanting language entirely. Those rare cases in which dream ballets do depict scenes that can be said to be real and actually happening within the story (as in *Carousel*, but also in Jerome Robbins's highly lyric choreography of *West Side Story*), are striking in the way they aestheticize the textual actual world of the film, which links them to (nearly) through-composed musicals such as *Sweeney Todd* or indeed to opera, as a medium that creates an aesthetic distance even for scenes of dialog and other speech (i.e., recitative vs. speech).

While in my previous research I have focused on intermedial relations within a mono-medial work, the novel that imitates musical structures (see Petermann [2014]), the film musical, as itself multimedial, offers an exciting case of intermedial interactions within a multimedial context. The film uses its composite media for different purposes and in different constellations. Where the medium of language is foregrounded to the exclusion of dance and diegetic music, we find ourselves in the world of the book, in the textual actual world of the film. Where music gains in prominence in the numbers, characters explore emotions and dreams not accessible to their rational selves. The foregrounding of dance in the dream ballet takes this a step further, aestheticizing as well as fantasizing, leaving the prosaic diegesis for the lyrical world of dreams.

REFERENCES

Altman, Rick. *The American Film Musical.* Bloomington, IN: Indiana UP, 1987.
An American in Paris. Dir. Gene Kelly. MGM, 1951.
Block, Geoffrey. "Integration." Knapp, Morris, and Wolf 97-110.
Carousel. Dir. Henry King. Fox, 1956.
Feuer, Jane. *The Hollywood Musical.* 2nd ed. Bloomington/Indianapolis, IN: Indiana UP, 1993.
Gennaro, Liza. "Evolution of Dance in the Golden Age of the American 'Book Musical.'" Knapp, Morris, and Wolf 45-61.
Jenkins, Henry. *Convergence Culture: Where Old and New Media Collide.* New York: New York UP, 2006.
Knapp, Raymond, Mitchell Morris, and Stacy Wolf, (eds.). *The Oxford Handbook of the American Musical.* Oxford/New York: Oxford UP, 2011
Labyrinth. Dir. Jim Henson. Lucasfilm, 1986.
McMillin, Scott. *The Musical as Drama,* Princeton/Oxford: Princeton UP, 2006.
Oklahoma!. Dir. Fred Zinneman. 20th Century Fox, 1955.
Petermann, Emily. *The Musical Novel: Imitation of Musical Structure, Performance, and Reception in Contemporary Fiction.* Rochester, NY: Camden House, 2014.
———. "The Hollywood Musical as a Subject for Word and Music Studies." *Essays on Silence, Absence, and Ellipsis and on Surveying the Field.* Ed. Walter Bernhart and David Francis Urrows. Word and Music Studies 15. Amsterdam: Rodopi, Forthcoming 2015.
Rajewsky, Irina O. *Intermedialität.* Tübingen: Francke, 2002.
———."Intermedialität 'light'?: Intermediale Bezüge und die 'bloße Thematisierung' des Altermedialen." In *Intermedium Literatur: Beträge*

zu einer Medientheorie der Literaturwissenschaft, edited by Roger Lüdeke and Erika Greber, 27–77. Göttingen: Wallstein, 2004.

———. "Intermediality, Intertextuality, and Remediation: A Literary Perspective on Intermediality." *Intermedialités = Intermedialities* 6 (2005): 43–64.

The Pirate. Dir. Vincente Minnelli. MGM, 1948.

Ryan, Marie-Laure. "Possible Worlds in Recent Literary Theory". *Style* 26.4 (1992): 528-533.

Singin' in the Rain. Dir. Stanley Donen and Gene Kelly. MGM, 1952.

Sweeney Todd: The Demon Barber of Fleet Street. Dir. Tim Burton. Warner, 2007.

Vache Espagnole. "Anatomy of a Ballet: Part 13, Finale and Recap." *Reel Travel: Where Travel and Classic Movies Meet*. Accessed March 17, 2014. <http://vacheespagnole.wordpress.com/>

West Side Story. Dir. Robert Wise and Jerome Robbins. Mirisch, 1961.

Wolf, Werner. *The Musicalization of Fiction: A Study in the Theory and History of Intermediality*. Amsterdam: Rodopi, 1999.

About the Author

Emily Petermann is a post-doctoral researcher in American Studies and junior faculty member of the Literature department at the University of Konstanz. Her research interests include word and music studies, the film musical, and literary nonsense. She is a founding member of the Word and Music Association Forum (since 2009), a board member of the International Association of Word and Music Studies, and co-editor of the volume *Time and Space in Words and Music* (2012). Her publications have consistently focused on intermedial relations, as in articles on the Bildgedicht in Margaret Atwood's poetry, on the relationship between music, fiction, and history in Michael Ondaatje's *Coming through Slaughter*, on the aesthetics espoused by Lucy Snowe in Charlotte Brontë's *Villette*, and on jazz novels' imitation of improvisation and live performance. Her monograph, *The Musical Novel: Imitation of Musical Structure, Performance, and Reception*, was published with Camden House in 2014.

CHAPTER 7

Tales of Kabbarli: The Transmutation of Ancient to Modern Culture

Geoffrey Sykes

The singular character of Daisy Bates in the theatrical work *Tales of Kabbarli* is selected as a vehicle of what in Australia has been termed 'reconciliation' between its traditional indigenous and its contemporary, especially white, population. As much as the character has firsthand contact with tribes emerging from desert traditional life, her connections with white society, her journalistic background and memory, enable a unique, highly articulate, and quite privileged, white perspective which integrates in direct personal experience aspects of national history that, while not forgotten, are largely passed by with social and political changes. The character voices these changes in the following intermedial way:

> I must look after these,
> they're worth more than I am.
> Native chants, signs, poems, legends, linguistic scraps and grammatical pieces.
> Must do something, with all these stories.
> Of course they are no substitute for the life, and colours, and music, and dance, I have known, but there is nothing I can do, except tell stories. (Sykes 2012: 6)

Bates, who lives between two cultures and epochs, sees herself as a mediator. The performance embodies history as the firsthand experience of a character who surprisingly engages the audience as the historical persona. The stage setting or space becomes a liminal receptacle of stored memories and narratives:

> Uncover your eyes, forget the trance. Awake in the darkness.
> Or at least make a prayer for your forgotten friends. (Sykes 2012: 4)

Literature and writings are enacted, as they are articulated, through firsthand knowledge. As a self-appointed pioneering anthropologist of the dreamtime legends of arguably the oldest and seminal culture in the world, the stories, memories, regrets and hopes of Bates assume a universal significance.

Before elaborating on the script and play in itself, and their distinct intermedial characteristics, I wish to raise yet a further textual and indeed intertextual analysis that is pertinent in this work, in as much as this paper is written by its author. This work, even if theory laden, is not necessarily theory driven. It involves a peculiar type of empirical inquiry, with a close relationship between researcher and evidence that might seem unusual in any other field. For in this case the researcher is also the author or creative writer of the empirical material, which exists in the form of a creative or theatrical work (script and production).

Although there might be many precedents for artist-written research and critiques of creative work, this article is a novel departure for myself, as I have resisted for two decades any theorization of some 20 scripts and productions undertaken in that time. Whatever personal reason exists for this separation of theory and art practice, the reluctance of a playwright to write or even to be able to write extended theory about their own work is not uncommon – indeed in view of the form of conceptual and stylistic skills required for critical writing or literary scholarship, the lack of "double-up writing" by playwrights is understandable, as is any desire to anticipate critical or audience opinion.

I seek to outline a process of textual archaeology dependent upon the writer's autobiography to stress a feature of literary work that is usually hidden from the reader, scholar or audience, and that is a process of rewriting that always occurs in the development of a script or text. The Derridean injunction that anything said is an iteration of something previously said is seen as more pervasive when revisions of one text are taken into account. A form of layering of one version within another occurs, which is not usually articulated or even remembered, however much authorial comment might be provided. The focus is on the polished version that is published or produced, and not on the patchwork of parts that it comprises. The sedimentation of textual forms in the history of a text is often buried under the received "completed" surface viewed or received by an audience. It is one privilege of authorial commentary on a work that hermeneutics can extend beyond what is known in one published version of a text.

Intertextuality can be studied within one text, not only between texts. Allusion and adaptation are observed in the process of creating, not only in the final outcome. One can label this process one of textual archaeology, and unless the author has kept meticulous files of versions – which in the digital age is increasingly unlikely - the author has a privileged role as text archaeologist. Text archaeology stresses process as much as product or publication, semiosis as much as analysis of whole text, textual intermediation rather than textual definition.

On the other hand, many opportunities seem to exist in a new found synchrony, or intermediality, of art production and theory, in particular semiotic theory, with regard to this particular work. The author has an intimate knowledge of the sources, and of the inclusion of various literary and anthropological sources. The author is creatively close to the dramatic self-consciousness, word play and text interactions of the character on stage, who become a form of authorial alter ego. The author can vouch for conscious selection of heightened literary quality and compressed intertextual references. The author as director can assist in understanding how a theatrical persona provides a rich subject field of sign gesture and language systems. The author as director has anticipated the double-role that will be assumed by the author as scholar of his own work. The author as director is familiar with bringing a detached dispassionate view of his own script that does not prevent praise of its virtue to actors as well as possible critique of its challenges. Both roles – author as director and as scholar – are made possible by their separation from the process of writing. In the case of direction, some proofing and line edits might occur, but unless it is in the workshop nature of a production, writing should be finished before the rehearsal period commences. It is disorienting for actors otherwise. The demarcation of writing from 'writing up' of a show should be categorical: it would seem disingenuous for a writer as scholar to be changing the original script to suit the needs of its critique. In the case of *Kabbarli* demarcation of the writer's roles corresponds to traditional markers of the scripts' completion. One is a prospective (August-September 2014) season in a main Sydney season; the other is a first publication of the text (November 2012). The prospective season seems a firm, definitive outcome for the long simmering of this work: its anticipation seems to be a signal to allow a discrete unusual act of textual gestation by the author. There might be other roles for textual commentary by playwrights – hopefully this one is very much timed, in production terms, with a sense of retrospection afforded by imminent completion.

This script and its production has had several versions, which provide and illustrate an archaeology of inter-medial and inter-textual literary and cultural fertilisation that the author is best and well equipped to re-capitulate. Reflection on the development of a script can include the author's relevant biography – how a script embodies not only ideas but growth and maturing of its writer and his/her engagement with lived experience and nation identity. The author can be conscious of the possibility of stage work not only representing social reality but foreshadowing emergent social change, and providing a domain of energy and intensive ideas for future social change. Finally, the author as theoretician can foresee the general opportunity for art work and art production to act as a priority and pertinent subject for semiotic study generally. This includes the opportunity to explain, with semiotic theory, dramatic performance and justify it in terms of media and everyday discourse. With regard to theory, it is more than fortuitous that my own intensive preparatory studies in semiotic theory (up to doctoral level) can be availed now in literary and theatre contexts.

What cannot be explained fully, finally, theoretically or even experientially, is the creative process itself - how the germane fragmented first encounters with a project can lead much later on in cases such as this to a work that seems seamless, final, fulfilled. This is perhaps an additional reason for the separation of theory and practice: many artists see that work as a craft, a complex practice that cannot be fully explained theoretically or in any other discourse. There might be a deep truth in this. How does an artist come to foresee or trust materials that retrospectively seem so random and informal? To speak of Peirce's sense of intuition goes some way – how formal logic and clarity need to be embedded in the vagueness of hypothetical abductive thinking – at least in theory to addressing a phenomenon that is experienced by creative artists but often ignored in theory and scholarly writing about creative works. I will not pretend in this one essay to fully address this topic fully, but to raise it serves at least one purpose.

I can say that the rich quality of verbal sources – some aboriginal, some of Bates herself (Bates 2011) is something that must have struck me as a very young writer. While this project is one of a number of "developing" or continuing works with which I have been preoccupied, this particular work has perhaps been the most enduring and given most attention. Indeed the first draft, and as I vaguely remember first one night performance, happened over 30 years ago, and dialogue in the current version has in the main been derived from that source. That first version was perhaps my second script, and first freelance or independent production (the first script received my first production experience, a sponsored two week workshop of my very first script at the Australian National Playwrights' conference in Canberra Australia - a remarkable breakthrough for a young writer). The first version was revived 15 years later in several seasons, including at the established inner city theatre of La Mama, Melbourne, where, like all the performances of the show, received very positive audience feedback and reviews.

Having raised general claims about the potential significance of *Tales of Kabbarli*, a disclaimer is necessary. The show, over one hour in length, is a one hander. Despite the use of a dancer and a musician (cello) in various productions, 80% or more of the performance is by the character of Daisy Bates. In an earlier version, she was addressing an audience in Adelaide, later in her life, about the experiences of her encounters with tribal aboriginals encountering white culture for the first time, at the transcontinental railway depot in the Nullarbor at Ooldea, South Australia. She lived in isolation from white society for two decades – with summer heat often in the mid 40'sC.

Figure 1

During the speech she shares stories, some first hand and some derived, with selected dialect, from material she had transcribed (Bates 2011). Bates is recognized as a pioneering anthropologist. If she had been a man that work would have been more appreciated, along with recognition and support for her self-appointed role as a caretaker of central desert tribal people. Her desert residence was not only on the site of a railway depot – that depot had been built adjacent to an ancient meeting place for various desert tribes. The railway and the tribes shared the same source of water from an underground soak, until the railways emptied the waters in a very short time.

> In 1922 two things happened at Ooldea.
> Two new bores were put down in the Ooldea soak.
> There was an out gush of salt water.
> It was the beginning of the end for magical Yuldil-gabbi.
> Water that had not failed for hundreds or thousands of generations failed after a few years of white presence. (Sykes 2012: 16)

There is no doubt about the extraordinary enigma, drama, production of Bates's life in the desert. Her presence in Adelaide later in life was larger than life. In her writings and presence, she seemed a conduit or mediator of desert culture to a white audience – the play repeats yet varies a familiar role of Bates, a role that is subliminally familiar to or remembered by many Australians. While this paper will recognize the literary or poetic qualities in the script, which are given dramatic realism through the journalistic background of Bates, it is one of the pleasures of theatre that ideas can be embodied – that erudition is heard instead of being read.

In 2001 the script underwent a further revision that paralleled its re-casting. It is hard to know or remember what came first. Was it the change of setting and script into a more nuanced, dramatic personalized meeting with Bates that now was set at night next to the Murray River in Victoria? Was it the opportunity afforded by the casting of Robina Beard, an eminent talented Australian theatrical entertainer, that resulted in a more nuanced script? Despite the advantage of authorial comment and recollection one might never know. The intuitive and concentrated process of script writing and production might be heightened in its consciousness, and excitingly so, yet often no traces or memories remain, even after a short time. There is no doubt that the latest and most recent revision of the script – in 2012 – did respond to the undoubted skills of its performer. There is a journey of the script and production – and writer and performer – that parallels the narrative story of the main character. Both journeys are away from a public setting and style, towards a more intimate, humorous, reflective encounter that remains a litmus test for themes and realization that resonates with the universal. There is a paradox in the historical and literary journey of this work – and that is an unexpected intersection of the personal and impersonal, of the personal and the significant.

Figure 2

This paradoxical sense of levels of signification is facilitated although not fully explained by the remarkable commitment of Robina Beard to the indigenous arts. She taught dance at the National Academy of Aboriginal and Torres Straight Dance in Sydney, and directed several dramatic productions. This background is not immediately apparent in the popular charm of her lithesome mix of dance, comic and dramatic skills – yet is fortuitous and helps explains Robina's robust, indeed inspired, commitment to this piece. The work has received continually strong reviews – in all of its seasons.

TALES OF KABBARLI REVIEW: ROBINA BEARD'S LUMINOUS TAKE ON DAISY BATES. RAFFERTY'S THEATRE.

Daisy Bates lived many lives rolled into one. She was Irish and Australian, bigamist and journalist, wife of Breaker Morant and welfare worker, activist, linguist and enraptured student of Australia's indigenous people. To the many editions of Daisy Bates, another must now be added: Robina Beard. Beard's performance as Bates in Geoffrey Sykes' one-woman play is so feather light that she barely seems to be acting. She creates a character as soft as early morning light and just as luminous. The music of her lilting Irish accent effortlessly entwines with the poeticism of Sykes's script, which draws extensively on Bates's own writings. Sykes has also directed (and designed) the production, and somehow the very smallness of the action amplifies the scale of the life Bates led.

Part of her charm is her self-deprecation, while championing the spirit, stories and causes of the indigenous people whose languages she partially documented during her last 40 years. She is alive to the wonder of dwelling in the home of the "first great human culture", develops a kindred affinity for the land, and tells us that watching their ceremonies "is as close to ecstasy as I might ever hope to come" (Bates 2011). In her photo album, she sees Morant and recalls their turbulent marriage (which ended with no divorce), and their "fighting the government and each other in turn" (Bates 2011). To sustain his little play Sykes has created dialogues not just between Bates' present and her past, or between her struggle to survive and her warming friendships with the Aboriginals, but also between her spoken lines and the lonely song of Ilir Merxhushi's cello. The two are in perfect accord." (Shand 2014)

Robina's casting was not guessed at in the early years of this work, and reminds one how, whether it is after three months or three decades, a work in progress is in a constant intermediary process – involving unexpected, unplanned and often complex interplay of pragmatic, artistic, personal, production and review/audience components, often without surety of the success or sense of a final outcome or resolution.

There have been four seasons and 27 performances, in the last twelve years, and all have featured an unusual setting in the bush at night next to a flowing River. It might not seem the best suited setting to stimulate thoughts of desert life. Yet the set resonates well with the emotive quality of Bates. She is in retirement; she wears informal clothes instead of the formal English clothes she wore almost as a uniform in the desert. She lives in a tent – she has done so for decades and old habits die hard. She is solitary and on a sort of fitful half delusionary quest for travelling nomads. She speaks dialect almost incanting a world that once was:

> Warri wan-gan-ye,
> Koogunarri wanji-wanji,
> Arri wan-gan-ye.
> My country, my country, where is it, where is it?(Sykes 2012: 20)

There is a mix of pathos and admirable determination in a 75 year old, of failing health, still pursuing a vision of justice for the peoples whom she called her own. Like her 'native' friends she is displaced, voluntarily and necessarily, from western settlement- she has become a nomadic creature of habit, in transition, intermediate, between one place and next. The river site becomes intermediate, not only between her own past and frail present, but between the past, present and her continued hopes for justice and reconciliation in the future. The river and bush resonate as emotive emblems of her inner quest and outer memory – one that also engages and intrigues audiences in ways that deserve ongoing explanation:

> A light wind loiters in the river reeds.
> Otherwise quiet as sleeping breath in the tree tops.
> The ageing moon will die with the dawn. (Sykes 2012: 4)

Space is often omitted from semiotic theory, just as it can be from a theory of language or linguistics generally. Literary texts do not have three dimensions, and words can be poor descriptors of the palpable spatial realities. Theatre theory often focuses on the actor – where gesture and expression can be studied conceptually, the setting of theatre can be a more secondary or background feature, often fulfilling a mainly functional, proximal role of setting parameters of actions, even while offering some aesthetic or emotionally resonant qualities. In *Kabbarli* the setting is quite indeterminate, defined more in relation to what it is not, or as a transition between past and future – a transitional mobile quality captured in the passage of the adjacent river. Night disguises specificity – it reinforces the isolation already present in what would be the bush setting in the day.

> I've always had to cook. For myself. For unseen guests.
> Fill a vessel with water
> carry it a hundred steps apiece;
> collect sticks and scratch twigs
> from gullies in stony ground;
> pour into a saucepan of can
> find supplies that lie in drums outside the tent;
> These little rituals of sustenance, in the big outside world.
> It's always been the same.
> Ah, supper's spread! (Sykes 2012: 20-21)

The function of fireplace, chair and tables, or belongings such as books and suitcase, assume some semblance of archetypes, generalizable objects capable of significance and symbolic association beyond their immediate dramatic role. The past is represented, not only by the few belongings, but in occasional archival still-projections; otherwise the place on stage is like a dark unconscious, a landscape of subliminal consciousness.

Several conceptualizations of the set are possible. One is its subjectification – that the dark place is one of the age and mind of its performer, that all aspects of surrounding trees, dim projected images, soundscape, shadows, as well as the oversized hanging of the stylised tent and pole – these are dimensions of the inner landscape of cognition, memory and feeling of one person. There is undoubted truth in such interpretation of stage design - and this expressionist setting goes someway to explaining the audience's engagement in a design that contravenes what might be expected. The lighting is subdued and relatively static, a long way from the bright mobile dynamic production style.

The theme of subjectified space should be of great interest to someone like Gilles Deleuze who in his later books developed themes of psychoanalysis and schizophrenia through the externalization of mind and consciousness in enriched understanding of complexified material space. In *Cinema* I, the author conceived how the perceptual and material images of cinematography provided a field of signifiers in which qualities of intensity, intentionality and consciousness could be observed and projected externally to a psychology of mind (see also Sykes 2009). Adopting Charles S. Peirce's semiotics, the author changed the key term 'sign' to that of 'image' in order to distinguish his inquiry into non verbal signification from the linguistic focus that he felt characterized semiotic traditions. Gilles Deleuze's work is helpful in showing how an abstract indeterminate setting, such as the stage production of *Kabbarli,* can assume complexity and become a field of signifying associations that facilitate a polysemy of meanings and actions in the performance. Expressions of character can resonate and be constructed in space; yet space is more than a subjective world. Space is a subliminal liminal world of in between-ness. In its Peircean vagueness, space offers actor-characters and audiences the opportunity of seeing, in some way, ancient mythical and ritualized expressions. The camp site is a meeting place and dreaming site, an enchanted aboriginal/Irish (according to both ethnic experiences of the main character), a sacred place of strange visitations and transformations.

> Who's there? (GETS UP, LOOKS AROUND)
> Is there someone there?
> There was.
> Standing in front of me.
> As close as my hand.

> An old man
> No name, no clothes, not a rag, nothing.
> Right there - he traced the shape of my foot in the ground,
> Looked at the lobe of my ear, fingered the webs of my finger. (Sykes 2012: 7)

The actor continually uses gestural language to explore, map, as it were. She seeks coordinates of her place relative to past and possible locations. The space is a mnemonic of the past. The richness of the space flows through in its gestural markings – "firsts in seconds" to use Peirce's terms.

Space is also a state – a stage within a stage. The campsite, with its random papers, piled books, typewriter, notebooks and albums, is a study, a place for Bates' expression and discourse. Although apparently solitary, the main character continually reaches out for an audience. Her main frustration, it seems, is to be denied an actual audience. Instead she seeks a virtual one – memories of events and meetings in the desert, a possible prospective audience in Adelaide, even, with some irony, the wildlife and flora at her camp.

> Who are you hiding Daisy? You won't be going to Adelaide too soon.
> Not when you have the wildlife and trees right here as your audience.
> Who else do you need? Listen. (Sykes 2012: 17)

As well as gesturing towards the natural space of the bush or desert, she constantly, directly and indirectly, addresses her ideas and language to various audiences – "Ah, my dear audience, what a wonder it is for us all to live on this continent, the place of first human culture." (Sykes 2012: 23) The sense of audience allows a humorous rhetoric of addressing self ... with some irony (who else is listening) she frequently "talks to herself." "Who are you, Daisy Bates?" she says, more than once." (Sykes 2012: 17) Such moments of self-consciousness are highly rational and anything but disturbed – they are framed by so many other moments of public rhetoric and speech making.

This busy process of interpersonal deixis spills out and continually, if indirectly, includes the theatre audience as recipients of her discursive expression. It is a theatrical style aided by Robina's background in dance – there is a grace and superfluity of gestural language within stories, within activities at the campsite, and in writerly interactions with notebooks, and in various forms of address, that make the whole diversified, busy sequence of the play into a seamless, persuasive and entertaining experience for the audience. In addition to any other boundary-mediated journey, in the show there is the historically true Irish sense of poverty, justice and also Celtic tribalism, legend and ritual. The dots in the well documented life of Bates – that she was a poor Irish woman when young – had not been articulated, to my knowledge, before the 2012 production. The focus was on Bates as an Englishwoman – sometimes she could be judged accordingly. Yet her lifelong attachment to aboriginal culture is partly explained by a deeper empathy for their legends and imaginary world, and also for their exploitation and suffering. The play explains what has for so long been seen as the enigma of the latter: of the spectre of an Englishwoman living amidst tribes at her tent.

One answer is that she is not English at all, and the intimacy, humor, poetry and storytelling of the dialogue rings even more true when regarded as an unusual and creative mediation of Irish and aboriginal heritage. The gentle rhythms and cadences of Irish also allow further compression and nuance of sentiment, ideas and allusion: she darts deftly from story to joke to wisdom to regret to memory, always conversing with the audience and never declaiming – except when rehearsing with ironic distance the rhetoric of a possible speech to be given in Adelaide, a speech that is finally discarded in favor of the audience of flora in the bush. The Irish lilt is soft on the audience's ears – the accent facilitates the compressed, deft switching between references, moments, form of address and recollection. The accent is a crucial component of multi dimensioned meditational qualities. Any over stress of the voice on any part would draw attention that would impede the flow and agility of style. As it is, the audience is constantly caught up in a light, woven conversational style: the character, almost as in Bakhtinian dialogue (Petrilli 2014: 33), includes them as virtual respondents: she anticipates an audience response, answers her own questions on their behalf, and apologizes to an absent but present audience for her mannerism. In the pattern of discourse many reflections on political responsibility and reconciliation are quickly elaborated.

The result sees the play exemplify an argument involving many dimensions of Peircean 'Thirdness', a meandering yet coherent pattern of signs that mediates many forms of address and engagement among present and past environments and persons, including the audience as virtual visitors to her camping spot. 'Thirdness' thus includes complex systems of gestures and pointing (Peirce's 'Secondness') and the qualities of place, signs and sounds in themselves, with a signifying potential that imports emotion, meaning, politics and significance and memory (Petrilli 2014: 31).

After one performance, a young audience member (a theatre student) commended the existential absurdist qualities of *Tales of Kabbarli*. These he saw as its main strength. Such a reading is possible, especially if a listener is not attuned to many of the historical or literary references. The play supports, at one immediate impression, the image of an older character lost in time and space, without bearing or clear purpose, stirred to insomnia in the middle of the night. The script offers cues to the dark night of the character's soul.

> What's that noise? Lord spare me. An endless song it seemed.
> The fire is getting cold. Soon there'll be no measure of life than the sleeping timeless heart of an aging soul.
> Ah, the bush at this hour. There's nothing to be done. I'll be catching a chill I can ill afford now I'm up. Must stir that fire. (Sykes 2012: 3)

These lines are soon undercut and embellished by other references and significances from the character. However, rather than seeing the young person's interpretation as misguided or even limited, it can be taken as a response to possible universal meanings in the play. A show about one person, at a particular time of her life, involved in recollection amidst particular indigenous tribes isolated from urban society, can be seen to resonate with wider trans-cultural and universal associations.

There were approximately 500 traditional tribal homelands or nations on the Australian continent, each with remarkable cultural, kinship, mythological, geographical and linguistic autonomy. Each tribal grouping possessed what can be regarded as a separate language: there were approximately as many languages as there were peoples, and differences in territory and culture were strictly maintained. It is remarkable that such a diverse spectrum of societies could co-exist with relative peace and without conquest or growth of empire for over 40,000 years. There are many explanations for this early, and arguably most successful, enduring of a human civilization. One relevant to this production has been the special roles of meeting places like Ooldea, in the desert where Bates lived, not within tribes but among tribes.

Once again, at its deepest resonance, the theme of space recurs – for the location of Bates at Ooldea was at the ancient site of corroboree, a meeting place of desert tribes that endured for time immemorial – 20,000 or more years – at the waterhole and springs that had always sprung from the deep artesian basin at that place near the great ocean gulf in south Australia. And this was the key to the deep significance of the image of Bates in the desert – she was a mediator, an intermedial subject, as needed between one tribe and the other, and especially between individual and collective tribes in encounters with white railway workers, travellers and government officials. She was, as it were, the chair of a great assemblage; her role 'intra' tribe mediator became necessary when the effects of drink and cultural corrosion, brought about through contact with the whites, degraded the millennium of successful meetings that had always taken place.

> Tracks made by hand
> wander the heavens
> with footprints in dust
> the crests of cockatoo feathers of curious colours
> traded by travellers in temporary truce ..
> magic totems, eaglehawk, bandicoot, kangaroo, emu,
> a score more of legendary heroic emblems ...
> came together ... along all the old tribal tracks
> to find out their ancient watering hole ...
> their meeting ground, camping place ...
> this central place of ancient civilization. (Sykes 2012: 13)

Basically Bates saw herself in her role of ambassadorial mediator among tribes (when the need arose, especially due to pressure of contact with whites) and among assembled tribes in general and white society. The latter extended to English royalty, whom she petitioned and who visited her. She argued for an aboriginal homeland under English rule, separate from the Commonwealth of Australia.

> "Ah, ' ...a realm, under the Crown.' A homeland for my people. A charter or treaty.
> Maybe I should have done that. Instead of writing to the Prime Minister all the time.
> (SHE CHANGES INTO FORMAL ATTIRE)

> Leave the desert when I could. Set up tent outside the Parliament! Why not! I could sit in my attire, like a sole representative of the aboriginal people, right there on the lawns of Parliament in Canberra. What a grand idea. Who'd have thought? Ah, such flaring hopes. My Irish "know how contrariwise", "agin the government", "agin all odds". O you were such a dreamer, old girl, in your time." (Sykes 2012: 15)

At its best, Ooldea was a forum, an ancient equivalent no less of an UN (but perhaps with more enduring success and equilibrium between members) where trading, goodwill, ceremonies were exchanged on peaceful terms. The representation of a campsite beside the Murray repeats the trope of such grand occasions, one this time indirectly inclusive of the audience. The irony and potential pathos of her diminished circumstances at the riverside as opposed to desert location, were not lost on Bates, but included as fodder for increased self consciousness and scrutiny. At no stage are her faculties diminished - verbal wit is proof of that: "I continue to light these few blank pages. The sacrament of words in solitude. It's always been your sanctuary. There's still a spark. The body might be like tortured eucalypts along the river bed, but the mind is timeless, continues to flower and bless, whatever the season." (Sykes 2012: 5)

While she celebrates her role as an international mediator for a forthcoming public talk, and finally eulogizes the bush creatures, it is the theatre audience who share, albeit virtually, a sense of occasion of the dignified forum of significance reconvened in the bush that alludes explicitly to the modern world of black and white. Bates' presentation is never merely self parody or irony. She retains a cultivated sense that the need for such a place of meeting and assemblage among peoples and nations (black and white) is as much a hope as it is a memory.

So many themes and events – of racial reconciliation, of aboriginal tribal life, of Australian history, of Bates' own life, are represented in the play, to the extent that it becomes, in many ways, a docu-drama in style, representing realities and facts that can be known in any number of other forms – stills, archival, books, places. Yet the ever-present transformation of the theatre audience and space, at the campfire, is more immediate than any representation of significance. In some diffuse, proximate way, the audience shares in a forum of significance and assemblage, through the mediation of the main character, akin to, in a latter day sense, the ancient assemblage of desert peoples. This dramatic event remains quintessentially imaginary and theatrical in nature.

The notion of assemblage is finally something more than a modern day Olympics or UN – although it might have had something in common with the ancient Olympics. Ooldea was a place for dreaming, a mytho-cartography where human and animal dreamtime creatures met in elaborate communal rituals. A play – one might say all good plays and theatre generally – works like film within a very compressed form. One or two hours is no substitute for a full book on the subject. A playwright, like a film maker, is expert in selecting, layering and fine tuning materials that could deserve much more expansive treatment. It is relatively common for thematic ambiguity or polysemy to result in multiple, complementing or competing themes that coexist in one compact experience of a play. This result can entrance or frustrate an audience. In *Kabbarli*, the theme or experience of public assemblage, and the consequent transformation of the theatrical audience into participants, engaged in a deep universal human event, points to something explicit and implicit in script and performance; yet in dimensions that might not be directly recognized by audiences in any one night, or even by the author through countless rewrites and numerous performances.

A show like *Kabbarli* is more than a representation of reality, and more than the expression of a character's subjectivity, enacted by a performer; or even more than the representation of the past, inferred from, and projected on, present political or public events. All of these aspects are there and occur within the parameters set at the climax of the show; yet there is one dimension of the climax that sets or supports all aspects leading up to and concurrent with it: this is the ritual. In its unique nightly performance of the show, there is the distinct recurrence, in modern times, of the civilized ancient sacred ceremonies that were the hallmark of human cultural experience in Australia. As Bates speaks towards the end, there is a distinct change of tense from past to present. She not only tells of corroboree events, but invokes and enacts them, in alteration from their traditional codes, afresh. There is a conjunction of words, sounds, dialect, action and soundscape, as she almost chants the following:

> from hollows upon hills that surround my camp
> come sweet accents, throaty warbles of a human melody
> picking up the chorus of the natural world
> to tell of its own destiny where,
> with every small preening or slight gargle
> spirits of ancestors above the ground
> along with those unborn beneath breathe."
> N-yinna gabbi gabbi, bur ma lee!
> N-yinna bur ma lee!
> N-yinna gabbi gabbi ...
> Sit down, water, on the stones in the shade
> Sit down on the stones in the shade
> Sit down water. (Sykes 2012: 22)

The audience is very much with her in the present, in the dust of the rivercamp becoming the desert. Indeed, we sit down with her as well as with her subliminal dark skinned neighbours. We are virtual tribes, gathered, purified, and united, in a peace that reaches to the full extent of the known earth and its peoples. The spell is cast. The ekphrastic potential of the setting fulfilled. The audience can seem mesmerized, as if spellbound, as the actress revels in her consummate control of a full vocal and gestural range.

Figure 3

Theatrical iteration of a past ceremony in an immersive present presents unspecified possibilities for the future. The audience carries out from the theatre more than what is embodied, represented or depicted; what is enacted. Possibilities inspired and authenticated from past rituals are reborn, transformed into unspecified possibilities for future action. This is the deepest sense of ritual, the embodied truth of history becoming.

> To me it is as near to ecstasy as I might ever hope to come.
> I can still sense them, those special ceremonial occasions,
> I am still sometimes able to see the shape of an Emu Man
> by light of camp fire, as he strides out of eternity with relentless brilliance
> while Yirbaik prattles her excited twitter into every crevice. (Sykes 2012: 23)

In this sense the full potential of intermediation is also fulfilled: the mixing of literary and theatrical forms, past and present, black and white culture, types of language and signs. The theatricalization of the audience and the mythopoeic lifting of the fourth wall resonates within and after the performance.

> Ah, my dear audience, what a wonder it is for us all to live on this continent, the place of first human culture.
> What magic is there, which transforms its empty landscape into a forum for intense, eternal significance? (Sykes 2012: 23)

This hyper theatrical realism explains the sense of heightened alertness that the best performances of plays, including this show on some occasions, can manage.

The last part of this paper by the author who theorizes on his *Tales of Kabbarli* uses the post Saussurian reflections developed by Nicoleta Popa Blanariu[1] on the re-schematization of ritual within contemporary performance. What she argues as elements of a mimic code (*schemata*) and conventional, "symbolical" movements of traditional ceremony, are certainly present in *Kabbarli*. The movement of stretching hands of the Emu Man are generically religious and gestural: Bates on stage does not attempt to replicate corroboree dances. However, the lithe bodily rhythms of the performer, and also of the character, instil a gestural homage that positions itself between contemporary expression and traditional ritualized expression (Alexandrov 2015: 143). This way of 'abstracting' from the body's movement potential allow certain elements to invest in and mediate a form of modern ritualized semantic. Thus, the potential of theatre to realize myths and archetypes, even at an unconscious level, can be attested to in the deceptively simple and quiet element of its style. Indeed it is precisely through the restraint and exclusion of modern theatrical style that the work is able to gesture, in poetic nuance and gestural implicature, to the mental landscape of Carl Jung (Alexandrov 2015: 143). The performance might not have the theatrical expression of Grotowski's work, but in a deceptive and subtle way approaches similar goals about the consciousness of an audience, the defamiliarized and expressionist nature of staging, and the complex performativity of the actor (Grotowski 2002).

While Robina is a lithe ex dancer, her movement never assumes merely graceful or self regarding qualities of technical virtuosity or dramatic force that

---

[1] See also her contribution to this volume.

characterize modern dance. What *Kabbarli* enables is an intensification of the choreographic language, until the show's climax produces a re-semantization of ritual, a possible retrieving of the initial kinesic signification (Blanariu 2013). This heightened consciousness of the audience, that allows re-iteration or realization of ancient ritual on a modern stage, can also be explained through the subtle, yet concurrent, sense of linguistic intermediality, from ancient to modern, poetic and vernacular, gestural and verbal, English and aboriginal dialect. Peirce's understanding of semiotics assists us for, as Petrilli reminds, he assumes a continuing interpretive relationship between dissimilar language systems (Petrilli 2014: 29).[2]

Thus, the heightened consciousness that facilitates the intermedial realization of ancient culture on a modern stage, is further explained through the use of additional language forms such as music and projected imagery. In the case of this performance, recorded music was used in some stage productions; in other words, a collage of selected short pieces was played live by a cellist on stage, providing transitions between segments of the show and sometimes underscored dialogue. Archival imagery of the character, along with impressions of aboriginal dance and the bush setting, were often included in an irregular, gentle layering of visual projection throughout the play. With the membrane of a quiescent style, the show adopted the benefits of multiform expression, by which interpretation between differing sign systems is extended beyond the parameters or elements normally associated with theatre or drama, into explicit multiform performance styles (Sykes 2014: 13-24). To attempt a micro analysis of the rich interplay of layered multiple languages of the show is beyond the scope of this paper: yet it is through such play, and the interpretive response required in an audience response, that the ekphrastic potential of the setting, the *mise-en-scène* of the performance, and its potential to mediate an ancient culture, is achieved.

This is arguably a remarkable achievement: not to replicate the traditional codes as if immutable (to do so for Bates would be almost disrespectful, especially as a woman), but to achieve mobility within and in-between cultural contexts; even more remarkable given the highly constant, millennia-long traditions. In this play, Bates as character provides a complementing (and complimentary) alteration, and a shift in the world's most enduring culture and its semiotic relations. This is born out of the demise of that same culture, something Bates could not have done living in the desert. It is also something done with profound respect, in Saussurian terms, with regard to the fidelity to the past.

---

[2] See also Petrilli's paper in this volume.

This re-semantization of ritual within contemporary theatrical form, conjoined with theoretical inquiry, can lead to one additional question. We have seen how the journey of this play, both in its whole current form and in its development over many years and seasons, can be understood to involve many types of sign and language systems. We have seen how the three sign categories of Peirce co-join and intermediate interdependently throughout the progress of the work. The complexity of the work can well be clarified using suitable interdependent semiotic terms – for example, for space, gesture and discourse. We have seen how these sign aspects move to a climax of ritualized meaning that can enable universal association for the play's import. One can ask if some fundamental issue of re-theorization is at play – this inquiry on this play is neither theory driven or led, but involves and invites a reworking of theory as a whole.

Ancient Greece and traditional religions would assume that the study of signs and language was based upon ritual and religious practice. While this assumption is mainly lost in our secular contemporary age, the possibility of the re-semantization of ritual in theatre invites the inauguration of semiotic theory within parameters other than those typically set for semiotic study in the past 100 years. Does such re-theorization, based on entirely performative and imaginary subject matter, also benefit perhaps essentially from the same process of 'writing up' of one's own creative output – probably in this regard of one or more other works – as commenced in this paper? The possibility seems intriguing, at least to myself.

To conclude, the process of 'writing up' one's own work has been a journey in itself, or rather the completion of a journey which, as suggested, has endured discontinuously for some three decades – not a long time in terms of worlds's history but long enough in terms of the lifetime of an individual writer. This paper has come at the end of a production cycle – with a season of the show marked for a major Sydney theatre later in 2014, it seems appropriate to reflect outside of vicissitudes of writing and production. To say this is to underscore the separation of writing and theory that this writer at least has always observed. One can write theory at the end of the intuitive crafted businesslike process of script and production development; one seeks supplementary goals – illumination of theory, as well as illumination of aspects of the play.

Of course it can be said that, vicariously, the journey involved and represented by *Kabbarli* has endured a great deal longer than three decades or even three centuries. Much more enduring than the longevity of anyone involved in the production, or the character of the piece, or even the black and white people that she meets at Ooldea, was the genealogy of aboriginal peoples, that preceded those who met Bates at the camping ground near the railway. This genealogy is intermediated by the play, as if the lines of script embodied lines of poeticized DNA. In Deleuze's view, the past is perceived as an endless process of becoming; its landscapes demarcated by sites (*plateaus*) of intensification and potentiality, just as the mythologized landscapes of Ooldea and the Murray riverbank will continue to be performed and embodied by future generations.

REFERENCES

Alexandrov, Ivaylo. "Archetypal Reflection of Mise-en-Scène – The Signifying Nature of the Theatrical Performance as a Process of Communication and Representation." *Southern Semiotic Review*, Volume 5, (2015): 141-150

Bates, Daisy. *The Passing of the Aborigines: A Lifetime Spent Among the Natives of Australia*. Calgary: Theophania Publishing, 2011

Blanariu, Nicoleta Popa. "Theatricalization of the Ritualistic Gesture and Dancing." *Southern Semiotic Review*, Volume 2, (2013)

Deleuze, Gilles. *Cinema 1. The Movement-Image*. Trans. H. Tomlinson & B. Habberjam. Minneapolis: University of Minnesota Press, 1986

Fischer-Lichte, Erika. *The Semiotics of Theater*. Trans. Jeremy Gaines and Doris L Jones. Bloomington and Indianapolis: Indiana University Press, 1992

Grotowski, Jerzy. *Towards a Poor Theatre*. London: Routledge, 2002

Petrilli, Susan. Sign Studies and Semioethics: Communication, Translation and Value. Berlin: De Gruyter, 2014

Shand, John. Tales of Kabbarli review: Robina Beard's luminous take on Daisy Bates. http://www.smh.com.au/entertainment/stage/tales-of-kabbarli-review-robina-beards-luminous-take-on-daisy-bates-20140822-1073i4.html#ixzz3kuIg7s4K

Sykes, Geoffrey. "The Images of Film and the Categories of Signs: Peirce and Deleuze on Media." *Semiotica: Journal of the International Association for Semiotic Studies*, Volume 176, (2009): 65-81

Sykes, Geoffrey. *Tales of Kabbarli*. Adelaide: Moore Books, 2014-8-22

Sykes, Geoffrey. "Towards a Theory of Multiform Expression." *Studii Si Cercetari Stiintifice*, Volume 32, (2014):13-24. https://sites.google.com/site/studiisicercetari/nr-17-2007/Home/31-2014/32-2014

ABOUT THE AUTHOR

Geoffrey Sykes has taught communication and media studies at the University of Western Sydney, University of Wollongong, and Notre Dame University Sydney. He completed a doctorate in Peircean studies. His doctorate was on the work of Charles Peirce, with applications in legal and media domains. It was examined by Gérard Deledalle and Vincent Colapietro. He has guest lectured at the Humanities Institute at SUNY-Stony Brook, Groupe d'Etues sur le Pragmatisme, Paris, Buenos Aires University, the State University and Humanities Institute, Moscow, and most recently the University of Bari, Italy, and the University "Vasile Alecsandri", Bacau, Romania, He has given papers to the Semiotic Society of America conferences, the Nordic Association of Semiotic Studies, ISI Summer seminars and the IASS Congress, and ICA and ANZCA conferences. He is editor of Southern Semiotic Review. Sykes has had numerous papers on semiotics and media published. In 2010 he edited an anthology called "Courting the Media". In addition to academic work Geoffrey is an established playwright and video producer. He has had over 20 professional theatre productions, and his video works have screened on national television. Geoffrey has devoted time in recent years to freelance arts, yet also wishes to continue a long standing commitment to semiotics. He is interested in the applied use of semiotics in arts, law, media, religion and education.

CHAPTER 8

Alternative Insights into Comparative Literature: Interdisciplinary, Intercultural, Intersemiotic Dancing Ekphrasis and Transmedial Narrative

Nicoleta Popa Blanariu

COMPARATIVE RESEARCH DIRECTIONS: PURISTS AND REFORMISTS

As general principles and working methods, a comparatist is nowadays free to choose, on the one hand, a traditional, "purist" approach, so to say (we shall see why) and, on the other hand, a somehow newer and epistemologically more tolerant view, even more comprehensive and maybe even more appropriate for this moment. The latter does not cancel the former, but completes and supports it in defining literature and its "science" within a wider social and intellectual context. Faced with a crisis, self-proclaimed several decades ago (Étiemble 1963: 9- 23), a deadlock of epistemological identity – of "scientific" legitimizing of its object and methods of approach -, the science of literature and, within it, the comparatist process, is now equally (if not) challenged by a problem that is no longer that of comparatists and their specific *know how*, but of the humanities in general and of the public's interest in them. In such a context, the second option upon which we shall further elaborate, has the advantage of extracting literature and its "science" from a self-centred, intra-literary approach, replacing it with an interdisciplinary one. The latter is beneficial both for the professionals (to the extent in which it provides them with new perspectives of situating and interpreting literature) and for the wide public, thus guided towards receiving literature in a way closer to the mixture of domains, expression forms and environments, with which people are often faced in social, professional, cultural life or *entertainment*.

According to the first option mentioned, the domain of comparativism would include the study of exclusively literary relationships, namely that of the "connections" and "influences" manifested through direct, positively demonstrable contacts between literatures. With the good (and less good) brought by this alternative – the possible undermining of the classic disciplinary rigour –

the "reformists" (in this context, the term appears at Adrian Marino also, in 1998: 7) are, nevertheless, widening the domain of literary comparativism to the point of assimilating it with the "study of the relationships between literature, on the one hand, and other areas of knowledge and creation", such as "arts, philosophy, history and social sciences, exact sciences, religion, etc.", on the other hand (Remak 1961 quoted. In Grigorescu 1997: 31). Thus, comparative literature may aim today both at "comparing one literature with another or other literatures" and at "comparing literature with other spheres of human expression." (Remak 1961; see also Saussi 2006; Damrosch 2006; Villanueva 2013; Tötosy and Mukherjee 2013) Without aiming to recall to attention the model, now difficult to transpose into practice, of a *uomo universale* in the Renaissance fashion, such a comparatist alternative continues the ancient cosmopolite ideal – "intercultural', *avant la letter*, to a certain extent – of the Enlightened, namely that of a "Republic of Letters" that crosses geographical and social barriers and from which, through Goethe and his predecessors, there would be born the idea of a *Weltliteratur*. To the Enlightenment desideratum, the comparatist alternative now adds one of recovered fellowship of the humanities, even their interdisciplinary collaboration with the arts and "exact" sciences (see also Schmidt 2013; Schlumpf 2013; Wolf 2013; Schroter 2013).

Such an initiative responds to the habits and expectations of the contemporary audience, for whom the aesthetic experience, particularly that of reading, has changed along with the world in which they live. Relevant in this respect is, at the level of literary creation, the actual transdisciplinary approach – not just multi or inter – of Vintilă Horia, the 1960 prize winner of «Goncourt», for the novel Dieu est né en exil. Thus, in Persécutez Boèce! (1987), Vintilă Horia applies the paradigm of the gnostic-alchemic imaginary and, intertwined with this, that of quantum Physics to the interpretation of immediately post-war, social and ideological phenomena, symptomatic, at that time, for Eastern Europe and, especially, for the Romanian space (Popa Blanariu 2014d).

THE INVARIANT, A "KEY CONCEPT" IN COMPARATIVE LITERATURE AND INTERCULTURAL STUDIES

The beginnings of anthropology rely on two correlated and controversial ideas, originating in the 18th century (Geană 2005: 30-31): "human nature" (J.F. Blumenbach) and the "psychic unity of mankind" (Adolf Bastian), founded on the hypothesis of the existence of some "elementary ideas", from which there springs precisely the cultural unity of mankind, manifested across a very wide temporal and spatial area. Against this background of preceding theses, during the 19th – 20th centuries, there will be documented the existence of some "universal categories of culture", or "universal patterns of culture" (Wissler 1965: 47-98; Geană 2005: 120-137). Such a conclusion will be reached as a result of a vast investigation conducted by the community of anthropologists, from Notes and Queries on Anthropology (1874, 1st edition) – collective work, elaborated by the Royal Anthropological Institute of Great Britain – to Man and Culture by Clark Wissler (1923), Outline of World Cultures (1963, 3rd edition) by George P. Murdock and Outline of Cultural Materials, a project coordinated by the same Murdock (1971, 5th edition). Gheorghiță Geană (2005: 138) has rightfully highlighted the relevance of the concept of "universal pattern of culture" – a "synoptic concept" (2005: 135) – for the substantiation and development of "intercultural studies". Postulating the presence of some "invariants" of the imaginary and literary discourse – which would confirm previous hypotheses related to the existence of literary "constants" (Munteano 1967; Marino 1998) and, in his opinion, would explain certain striking similarities between European Pre-Romanticism and the Chinese poets of the Pre-Christian era and the Song period – René Étiemble seems to confirm, in the middle of the 20th century, precisely these founding principles of anthropology. His disciple, Adrian Marino (1982; 1988 ; 1998), and Basil Munteano (1967), one of the eminent scholars of Romanian post-war exile, would reinforce and elaborate, in a predominantly theoretical line, Étiemble's observations (Marino 1998 ; Ursa 2014).

As a type of approach practiced within the science of literature, comparativism integrates, as it is well-known, into a wider field of research – compared epistemology – with which other disciplines also interfere, for example the history of religions and mythology, the history of ideas (Nakamura1964; Nakamura 1997), philosophy (Masson-Oursel 1923), cultural anthropology (Benedict 1959), comparative mythology (Dumézil) etc. The "comparatist method", being "indispensable to the construction of anthropological theory", has, as one of its stakes, "to decide whether two cultural elements or ensembles of cultural elements are universal or not. It was thus proven, through *cross-cultural comparisons*, the universality of the incestuous taboo, of the family, of the grammaticality of language etc." (Geană 2005: 119). From a semiotic perspective, Algirdas-Julien Greimas and Joseph Courtès (1979: 49) see comparativism as a "set of cognitive procedures, with the role of establishing certain correlations in relation to form," between two or several terms having the status of "semiotic objects". The aspiration to formalize the *pur et dur* comparativism were accomplished if, by applying some appropriate "cognitive procedures", there would be achieved a true "typological model", made of "invariants" (Greimas & Courtès 1979: 49). In relation to such a formal model, the compared terms are "variables", particular hypostases of general, typical functions. A notable attempt in this respect was undertaken by Adrian Marino (1988; 1998) who elaborated upon the observations of his French mentor René Étiemble (1958; 1963), in the direction of an envisaged "comparative poetics".

Despite such processes of formalization – fully promising and meritorious, but rather isolated, not assumed as a priority research programme by the community of comparatist scholars –, the identification and exploitation of a rigorous comparatist "methodology", based on a coherent theory, "is still to be expected" (Greimas & Courtès 1979: 49). Nevertheless, the concept of *intertextuality* could be one of the solutions to breaking the deadlock of literary comparativism – as the two semioticians suggest, also signalling, like Marino (1988; 1998), the limitations of this alternative. The respective concept may support the "methodological relaunching of the theory of «influences», on which comparative literature research essentially relies (see also Juvan 2005; D'Haen 2007). However, the inaccuracy of this concept has led to various extrapolations, sometimes to the point of discovering a certain intertextuality right in the middle of the same text (given the content transformations that arise) and, at other times, dressing old «influences» in renewed vocabulary (for example, when studying quotes, highlighted or not by inverted commas)" (Greimas and Courtès 1979 :194). As is well known, quotations, hints or plagiarism, as "co-presence" phenomena – of effective presence of a text within another text, signalled or not by inverted commas – constitutes, in Genettes's taxonomy (1982), actual forms of intertextuality, in a more restricted and accurate acceptation than that previously given to the term by Kristeva (1969) or Rifaterre (1979; 1981) and, moreover, well distinguished from what Genette (1982) had designated by *hypertextuality*, as another category of *transtextuality*. The latter constitutes – or rather integrates into – the object of poetics (Genette 1982) that, by placing Genette's conclusion within a comparatist approach, recommends it also like a component of the object of a "yet expected" (Greimas şi Courtès 1979) "comparative poetics" – a "cross-cultural poetics" (Marino 1998: 22), already prefigured by, among others, Étiemble (1958; 1963), Munteano (1967), Marino (1988).

René Étiemble (1958; 1963) and later Adrian Marino (1988; 1998) have identified, at the level of the invariant, as noted above, a(nother) "key concept of theoretical comparativism" (Marino 1998), with a meaning imposed by Étiemble and insistently theorized, aspiring towards a taxonomic system and a well-defined methodology, by his Romanian disciple, Marino. The definition – in the semiotic (meta)language – given to the invariant by Greimas and Courtès in their *Dictionary* meets, to a certain extent, the meaning given by Étiemble and Marino. According to Greimas and Courtès, a "term shall be called *invariant* if its presence is the condition for the presence of another term with which it is in relation and which is called *variable*. We are here dealing with the reformulation of the concept of assumption: the invariant is the assumed term in the assumption relation" (Greimas & Courtès 1979 :195). Continuing some remarks from the inaugural lecture delivered at Sorbonne in 1957, resumed one year later in *Hygiène des lettres,* Étiemble formulates a somehow surprising statement: "If I can explain all the themes of 18th-century European Pre-Romanticism by resorting to the Chinese poetry before Christianity and from the first twelve centuries of the Christian era, then it means that, indeed, there are forms, genres, invariants, briefly, there is man, literature." "There is (...) literature", meaning – in a possible interpretation of Étiemble's conclusion – a universal corpus of texts, that may be analysed by resorting to a set of shared and perennial criteria and features, which may be called "invariants". These may be thematic (content-related, so to say) or morphostructural (such as the actantial structure of the epic and dramatic or the formalization of narrative action, *cf.* Propp 1970; Tesnière 1959; Greimas 1973; Greimas 1986; Todorov 1975; Souriau 1950).

Reporting the invariant as a universal and transhistorical (arche)type has somehow undermined the authority that the *historical* principle of the genesis of forms had held until then (according to which a certain discursive or thematic structure is the product, *par excellence* – and sometimes, the monopoly or symptomatic result – of some cultural-historical circumstances) and, respectively, the principle of "*actual relations*" (of direct contacts between literatures, which means that a certain literature, work or author "influences", at a given moment, another literature, work or author) (Marino 1998). As long as there occur similarities and "coincidences" between literary phenomena that never came into contact or never had "connections", we cannot speak of "influences" explainable in a positive way, on the basis of some "actual relations" (Étiemble 1958; Étiemble 1963; Marino 1998). A plausible hypothesis would be, in this case, the existence of a "constant" (Munteano 1967) of literary discourse and imagination, in other words, the existence of different types of invariants (Étiemble 1963; Marino 1998: 63-66). Hence, in a time when the comparatist approach to literatures was dominated by Historicism, Étiemble proposed, as an alternative, the "study of similarities independent from direct contacts". The test of the pertinence of the concept of invariant – of its appropriateness in relation to the specific of literary phenomena – is, according to Étiemble and Marino, the very existence of these "literary coincidences, similarities, meetings and correspondences in time and space", namely of some "elements shared by a group of phenomena" (works, trends, creative lines and tendencies, or whole literatures), in the absence of actual relationships that may justify them (Marino 1998: 63-64).

Consequently, Adrian Marino defines the invariant like a "constant", both temporal and geo-cultural, a "universal element of literature", a "common feature of literary discourse or literary thought" (1998: 63-66). Thus, by its very nature, the invariant works like a "factor of stability, permanence" and like a "key element of theoretical comparativism" (Marino 1998: 66). Despite historical and geographical distances between particular works and the resulting differences, taking invariants into consideration enables the systematic and comparative study of literatures, on the basis of the relation between the invariant and the variable, between a formal and stable nucleus and a series of particular, contextually dependent elements, associated with it. The distance between the terms of this dichotomy corresponds to that between the essentially theoretical approach and the historical one, in other words, between comparatist poetics and traditional comparatism. The latter approaches, from a particularizing perspective, the singular, empirical "connections", the very "coincidences". The former aims, as much as possible, at the general principles that lead to and/ or explain, beyond the possible "actual relations", the respective "coincidences" or "similarities" (Marino 1998).

Exploiting the concept of invariant allows, to a certain extent, the reconciliation of two types of comparatist initiative: *historical* (concerned with the phenomenal, meaning the immediate and the concrete) and, respectively, *theoretical* (concerned with the essence that is manifested in history, but transgresses it, rising to the generality of transhistorical principles) (Marino 1998). With its double nature – historical and theoretical –, the invariant signalled by Étiemble and theorized by Marino approaches what Viktor Shklovsky called "*topi*" (Gr. *topos*) or "shared places": these "repeat themselves precisely because the motif expresses a certain essence", although "by repetition, it changes its essence" (Shklovsky 1974: 48). In fact, the essence does not "change", does not alter but is performed, updated through particular, historical aspects of the literary matter. The "essence" – a theoretical, transhistorical and invariable abstraction – gains the concrete and tangible body of literary phenomena (work or group of works), deployed in space and time. The essence, the general is coloured with the particular flavour of a place, epoch, creative personality. Hence, we can now better understand why Étiemble sees in the literary invariants the "conditions without which there is no beautiful form anywhere, anytime" (Étiemble 1958:

166-167). Marino distinguishes between several classes of invariants: anthropological, theoretical-ideological, theoretical-literary and, eventually, literary. From these, we shall particularly look at the last category, that of the literary invariants that prove the existence of universal human experiences, expressed in similar ways in different literatures.

Following Étiemble, Marino (1988; 1998) illustrates this category through several similarities between European literature and that of the Far East. Such similarities are difficult, if not impossible to explain on the basis of certain "connections" and "actual relations" that would make the exercising of some "influences" probable, in one direction or another. Thus, Chinese poetry from the Song era ($10^{th} - 13^{th}$ centuries) and European (Pre-)Romanticism share a common inventory of themes and motifs, well-known as marks of the Romantic imaginary: the landscape as "mood" – echo of the feelings of the poetic self –, love, the prevalence of sensitivity as *faculté maîtresse*, the passing of time, the ruins (Étiemble 1958). To the initial observation of Étiemble we have just mentioned, Marino (1988; 1998: 87) adds some similarities between the poetry of the T'ang era ($8^{th} - 9^{th}$ centuries) and the English Baroque poetry of the 17th century, the Chinese and European elegy, the themes of Chinese and European novels. Marino rightfully signals these similarities, however without arguing for them in detail – as long as his intention is to identify a general type, a pattern and not to analyse their particular, contextually dependent manifestations (*token*).

Therefore, on the basis of the references to a literary corpus demanded by our very demonstration, we shall further argue for the existence of such parallelisms between T'ang poetry ($7^{th} - 9^{th}$ centuries) – represented particularly by Li Tai Pe, Van Vei, Du Fu – and the European Baroque poetry of the 17th century. Thus, there is in T'ang poetry, the European Baroque sensitivity to time, the premonition of the end that threatens everything and the implacable fragility of life, manifested through the same poetic motifs: *memento mori, fugit irreparabile tempus, vanitas vanitatum,* and sometimes, in response to the very impermanence of life, the consolation of *carpe diem*. In fact, widening the sphere of parallelism beyond the geo-literary borders traced by Marino, but continuing and supporting his idea, the same motifs already constitute nuclei of the reflection upon the human condition in the second part of the *Epic of Gilgamesh*. Elaborated between the end of the third millennium and the beginning of the second, it was therefore written long before T'ang and European Baroque poetry; moreover, as a mythological and sapiential-narrative synthesis of the cultural traditions co-existing in the space of ancient Mesopotamia, it is deeply relevant to a *Weltanschauung* characteristic of the ancient Near East (Antonescu & Cizek

1971: 18-19). The traces of this *Weltanschauung* are yet detectable in the Judeo-Christian tradition and the literature it has inspired, this time in the virtue of explainable cultural contacts, in other words, of some "actual relations" occurred in the "intercultural" melting pot of ancient Mesopotamia, among the plurality of peoples and "stylistic matrices" (Blaga 1969 [1935]: 8-115) that have met there throughout a millenary history. Without proposing to elaborate upon this aspect here, we shall nevertheless highlight the fact that it enables a closeness, even a convergence, between the theory of invariants, formulated by Étiemble and Marino and, respectively, the philosophy of style, in the meaning given by Lucian Blaga. Specifically, we may find that outside any actual relations, the constitutive factors of the "stylistic matrix" – be they "primary" (the "spatial and temporal horizon of the unconscious", the "axiological accent", the "anabasic, catabasic attitude", namely "neutral", and the "formal aspiration") or "secondary" (Blaga 1969: 105-115) – may lead to similar forms of cultural expression, reducible to the category of "invariants", be they "anthropological" or of some other nature, according to Marino's taxonomy (1988; 1998). Thus, "Chinese art is similar to the art of French Impressionism, by its love for nuances and the ineffable" – as Blaga (1969: 105) completes the painting of the parallelisms between the Far East and Europe, independent from the direct cultural connections and possibly explainable on the basis of the correlated concepts of "invariant" (Étiemble 1958; Étiemble 1963; Marino 1988; Marino 1998) and "stylistic matrix" (Blaga 1969 [1935]).

Returning to literary parallelism proper, we find that both in the Sumero-Babylonian epic, at Van Vei and, much later, at John Donne and the English "metaphysical poets", there occurs a shared idea, formulated outside any possible "influence" between the respective literatures: the idea of man's only allowed retaliation against time and death, one that is possible only at the level of the spirit and that of creation; it is an idea that, in the 1st century BC, Horace would express through a formula that has now become classical, "*non omnis moriar*", "*exegi monumentum aere perennius*", and Malraux, many centuries later, will somehow resume it, discovering in art an "anti-destiny". Sprung from the same feeling of ephemerality, a "constant" of human nature, these poems, outside any datable positivistic "influences", similarly express – which validates the thesis of "invariants" – a fundamental human situation, that of becoming aware of one's mortal condition and the poetic exorcism of the anguish this may create. The *Epic of Gilgamesh* and European poetry being more popular to readers from the "old" continent, given the structure of undergraduate or pre-university programmes of world literature, we shall further illustrate the already mentioned common motifs (*memento mori, fugit irreparabile tempus, vanitas vanitatum, carpe diem*) by referring particularly to the poetry of the 'Tang era: for example, Li Tai-pe's *Poem on the Brevity of Life (in* Li Tai-pe *et alii*: 36-37) or Du Fu's *Ballad of the Ill Cypress (in* Li Tai-pe *et alii*: 95-96). Similarly, Du Fu's *Hawk* (*in* Li Tai-pe *et alii*: 98-99) somehow reminds of Baudelaire's *The Albatross*; like the latter's "The terrible fate/ of the ill hawk!/ Derision lurks / everywhere:/ (...) the hero of the sky is gone/ downcast/ killed/ from life without a fight" (our translation).

In the manner of more than six centuries of European humanism, there transpires, in Van Vei's verse, the proud assertion of human thought. To a certain extent, like in John Donne's panpsychic poetry and in that of the English "metaphysical poets", like in Shakespeare's sonnets, Van Vei praises the force of the spirit through which man may redeem the weakness of his body (Van Vei, *Scorching Heat, in* Li Tai-pe *et alii*: 59-60). In fact, Van Vei, together with his generation fellows, Li Tai-pe and Du Fu, prefaces, in the 8th century, a "turning point in the Chinese Middle Eve", the "beginning of a Renaissance, substantially similar to that occurring later in Europe. Just like here, it constituted a huge change of perspective, under the sign of humanism, just like here it was understood as a return to antiquity and just like here it was divined by a great poet. Whereas in Italy, its ambassador was Dante, in China his name was Li Tai-pe (Li Bo)" (Covaci 1980: 5). In our opinion, such a similarity in the parallel evolution of the two literatures, Chinese and European, could illustrate, beyond any suspicion of "influence", the existence of what Marino (1988; 1998) considers to be other two distinct types of invariants, namely "ideological" ("force-ideas", *topoi*" shared by different collective views upon the world and life) and, respectively, "theoretical-ideological", identifiable at the level of the "theoretical reflection of and upon literature", as a basis for a possible "world rhetoric (implicit or explicit) of literature", as well as of a putative "universal aesthetics" (Marino 1998: 75-76).

Examples may, of course, continue. Of the many that could be further provided, we shall mention only two. Throughout the history of culture, in various places, such as India and Greece, patterns of ritual expression have gradually been secularized; numerous forms of artistic expression detach from the syncretic set of the rite; and a multitude of literary form(ula)s derive, all over the world, from ancient, "sacred «histories» (myths, supernatural genealogies, initiation scenarios, hymns of divine glorification)" (Marino 1973: 564). Thus, the Greek tragedy has arisen, according to the most circulated, but not sole hypotheses, from the cult of Dionysus (archaic god of vegetation, as it is well known, the god of theatre, metamorphosis and dramatic illusion during the Greek classical era) (Rachet 1980). Similarly, Indian classic dance represents today the sacred story of traditional gods, and the scenic transposition of Sanskrit drama was, like Greek tragedy at its beginnings, inseparable from dance (Vatsyayan 1974). (The Greek dances that accompanied the performance of the tragedy were called *emmelia* and *hyporchem*, *cf.* Urseanu *et alii*, 1967). One further proof of the cult origin of Indian classic dance is that, before the British interdiction from the 19th century, it had been performed in temples (Vatsyayan 1974). Epic poetry covers, to a good measure, the same process, from myth to "desecrated history", from "archetype to particularized epic scheme" (Marino 1973: 565). Therefore, the transition from the sacred to the profane – from *ludus sacer* (religious game) to *ludus aestheticus* (aesthetic game) – is yet another invariant, a universal *topos*, identifiable, in the secular decanting of the means of expression characteristic of the different codes and artistic "languages": dramatic, literary, musical, choreographic etc.

There are also invariants of the epic poem, elements that define it "essentially": themes – necessarily heroic, a telling of some "extraordinary facts", famous, adventurous subjects, in the style of "traditional heroic mythology" (Marino 1973: 567) – and idealized typology, so that the epic hero usually appears like an accumulation of the virtues appreciated by the community that assumes him. *Personarum illustrium, illustres actiones* – as the European Renaissance synthesises the particularities of the heroic poem, like a species regarded as illustrative, at that time, for the epic genre (Scaliger, *Poetica*, 1561, *apud* Marino 1973: 567). There are, on the one hand, some invariants of the novel that lead, outside any "actual relations", precisely to these similarities between the Far East novel and the European realist one, highlighted by Marino, who resumes on Étiemble.

In the footsteps of Propp (1970), the semiotics of the narrative and that of drama have attempted to formalize, in this or that way, the epic or dramatic characters, thus identifying a sum of their invariants (Tesnière 1959; Greimas 1973; Greimas 1986; Todorov 1975; Souriau 1950). Without resuming in detail these semiotic, sufficiently known models, let us nevertheless remark that Todorov's scheme of Boccaccio's "archi-story" (Todorov 1975) may be applied, in our opinion, also to other epic works, possibly from other literatures and eras of creation. For example, the Milesian novella, like a narrative structure included in the ancient Latin novel – such as the episode "The Widow of Ephesus" or "The Boy of Pergamum" (in Petronius, *The Satyricon*) or the miller's story and the story about Filesiterus, Barbarus, Areta (from Apuleius, *The Golden Ass*). The Milesian ancient novella and Boccaccio's Renaissance one – the latter formalized by Todorov (1975) through a generative model that he calls "archi-story" – have, in fact, beyond the constitutive invariants of the "archi-story", several other shared features: themes (observation of morals – realist, without idealization tendencies); the narrator's attitude (critical, so that these novellas constitute fragments from a fresco of morals, evoking the Greek-Latin antiquity in a succulent-satirical manner and, respectively, Renaissance Italy); humour (popular, rude, not once bawdy). Although they come from different historical cultures and eras, the two types of novella may be described on the basis of the same narrative categories – semio-narratologic invariants, eventually – identified by Todorov. Therefore, these are reducible, in our opinion, to the same narrative scheme, the same typological model. Such a finding may be reached through the analysis of narrative (action) "verbs", "proper names" (agents) and "adjectives" (states, properties, statutes) that are involved, according to Todorov (1975), in the verbal-action manifestation of the respective narrative "agents".

Relations of Dependence[1] or Influence[2]. Translation, Adaptation, Intersemiotic Transposition

For didactic reasons and provided that such a schematization would not exhaust the complexity of the analysed facts, Dan Grigorescu (1997: 196 – 197) systematizes thus the main phenomena that are the object of comparative research: "elementary" borrowings (quotations, pastiches); translations; adaptations; imitations – "serious" (including stylizations) or humoristic, critical (parodies); influences ("fact reports"); parallels suggesting the existence of an influence; synchronic parallels (within a determined cultural area); historical analogies, including typological appropriations (inside or outside a shared cultural area); ahistorical analogies (systemic) based on literary constants or anthropological constants; ahistorical analogies or non-systematic – in literature ("rhetorical", stylistic) or crossing the boundaries of literature (established between various arts).

The relations of "dependency" or "influence" are "binary relations" (Claudon & Haddad-Wotling 1997: 23): a work (or a group of works) influences the elaboration of an(other) work(s). A particular case of these binary relations is represented by translations and adaptations. Baudelaire's translations from Poe,

---

[1] The term is found at F. Baldensperger, in "Littérature comparée: le mot et la chose", *Revue de littérature comparée*, no. 1, Paris, 1921.
[2] René Wellek uses the term of "influence" in his polemics with the French comparatists (cf. *Théorie de la littérature*, Seuil, 1971, p. 67, the 1st English edition, New York, 1942).

those of Rilke from Valéry or of Stefan George from Baudelaire are famous. Paradoxically, the best "translations" are not servile, *mot-à-mot* transpositions of the original, but at the same time, the expression of the translator's personality. The latter may allow or suppress, in the process of translation, the manifestation of virtualities from the initial text, by means of selected equivalences, semantic traits of the original. For example, a famous sonnet by Ronsard – "When you will be very old" ("Quand vous serez bien vieille", from *Sonnets pour Hélène, Amours d'Hélène* 1578), translated by Yeats, in *The Rose*, with the title *When you are old and grey and full of sleep* (see Claudon & Haddad-Wotling 1997: 22-23). A known Italian pun has thus been confirmed: *traduttore, traditore*. But, it is precisely this "treason" that turns the translator into a creator. In other words, the translation enjoys a relative aesthetic and semantic autonomy.

Because poetry, in its essence, is "untranslatable", Roman Jakobson (1963: 86) believes that the only possibility is "creative transposition". This may be transposition inside the same language – from one poetic form into another –, a transposition from one language into another and, finally, "intersemiotic transposition" (Jakobson 1963: 86). The latter means conversion from one system of signs (or expressive means) into another. For example, literature is transposed into music, dance, cinematography, painting. The intersemiotic relations may constitute the object of comparatism in the broad sense: "where there is no relationship established between man and text, work and receiver, land and traveller, there is the end of the domain of comparative literature" (Guyard 1978: 5).

Particularly, Charles Gounod (1818 – 1893) is the author of a romantic *Faust* (1859) – opera in five acts on a libretto by Michel Carré and Jules Barbier, after Goethe's version of the myth of Faust. The construction of the musical discourse follows, quite suggestively, at least in some parts, the narrative theme from Goethe's version. For example, the beginning of the latter is musically "transposed" by Gounod through tumultuous sonorities, bells' sound (a reference to the bells of Ascension that prevent Faust from committing suicide), *adagio*. This term is found not only in the meta-language of music, but also in that of ballet, where it designates the duet sequences. In Gounod's transposition, *adagio*, as accompaniment of pair dance evokes the Faust – Margareta episode that, in Goethe's version, is a combination between the Faustian theme and the myth of Don Juan.

At this point, it shoud be highlighted that resurfacing the "intersemiotic" relations between literature and arts, Jakobson (1963) foreshadowed, in such a way, today's multi- and intermedial studies, even the latter's crossing with the wide domain of comparative literature.

INTERMEDIAL, TRANSMEDIAL, *EKPHRASIS*

The concept of *intermediality* "covers any kind of relation between different media" (Grishakova & Ryan 2010: 3), with two types of "storytelling media": the artistic (words, sound, and images used by writers, composers and visual artists) and the technological (channels of communication such as cinema, television, print, electronic books) (Elleström 2010; Grishakova & Ryan 2010: 3-4; Kafalenos 2012: 115). Marina Grishakova and Marie-Laure Ryan distinguish many types of relations between these media: "intermedial reference (texts that thematize, quote, or describe other media), intermedial transposition (adaptation), transmediality, multimodality (the combination of more than one medium in a given work: e.g., opera, comics, or the words and gestures of oral discourse)", and "a generalized form of ekphrasis" (Grishakova & Ryan 2010: 4), "perhaps better known as remediation, in which a work in one medium is re-represented in another medium" (Kafalenos 2012: 115). Similar to "transmediality" is the "framing borders" concept, already theorized by Werner Wolf (2006). This is related to phenomena, including narrative, which can be represented in more than one medium. Depending on the author as sign-maker, the form of modal resources may vary. Gunther Kress (2003) argues that there are cases of transformations within a medial mode, and cases of transduction across modes, with ekphrasis (description of a work of art by a verbal text) being a form of transduction:

> A new theory of meaning cannot do without the concept of transformation; it explains how the modal resources provide users of the resource with the ability to reshape the (form of the) resources at all times in relation to the needs of the interests of the sign-maker. Transformation needs to be complemented by the concept of transduction. While transformation operates on the forms and structures within a mode, transduction accounts for the shift of 'semiotic material', for want of a better word, across modes. (Kress 2003: 36)

In this sense, ekphrasis may be encountered in Virgil's *Aeneid*, when he describes what Aeneas sees engraved on the doors of temple of Juno, in Carthage, or in Homer's *Iliad*, Book 18 when the description of the shield of Achilles is simultaneous with its fabrication by Hephaestus, by request of the goddesse

Tethys. (As Lessing remarked, in his *Laocoon*, this is a dynamic description, which does not depict the manufactured object, but its spectaculous making process.) By means of a semantic extension, ekphrasis becomes a rhetorical device in which one artistic medium relates to another medium: a painting may represent a sculpture, or a musical composition may evoke some *Pictures at an Exhibition* (the Moussorgski's cycle of piano pieces "describing" – as a "remediation" – paintings in sound). Similarly – a form of reverse ekphrasis –, a piece of music or a dance re(-)presents a literary text: *Don Giovanni* by Mozart, *Romeo and Juliet* ballet by Prokofiev, *Don Quixote*, originally choreographed by Marius Petipa to the music of Ludwig Minkus; *Esmeralda*, inspired by Hugo's Romantic Novel, *Notre-Dame de Paris*, originally choreographed by Jules Perrot, with music by Cesare Pugni; *Faus*t and Ionesco's *Les Chaises* choreographed by Maurice Béjart, etc. (Popa Blanariu 2008).

A very interesting example of complex intermedial relation – multimodality, transmediality and reverse ekphrasis (or "re-mediation") – is Nijinski' s *Afternoon of a Faun*; both the music by Debussy and the ballet were inspired by a symbolist poem by Stéphane Mallarmé, *L'Après-midi d'un faune*. The costumes and sets were designed by the painter Léon Bakst. Rejecting classical formalism, it is one of the first modern ballets, inspired by ancient Greek artwork and Egyptian and Assyrian frescoes. (Nijinsky wanted to evoke the image of a satyr shown on Greek vases). Bakst had collaborated with a remarkable theatre director, actor and theatrical producer, Vsevolod Meyerhold, whose experiments were focused on two-dimensionality, stylized postures, narrow stage, pauses and pacing to point up the most important moments of his productions. Meyerhold's theatrical attempts were assimilated to Nijinski's choreographic idiom in *Afternoon of a Faun*, whose most important features were the angular, flattened body expression, emulating the poses on the Greek vases, and where stasis often replaced movement. Bakst recommended the two-dimensional staging to Nijinsky "as a way to solve the problem of recreating in three-dimensional space the rhythms of the flat, painted figures found on the sides of Greek vases" (Mayer 1977: 139). "This method of stylization signaled a radical departure from Isadora's and Fokine's renderings of ancient Greek dance in its move away from the free 'hellenistic' movement Nijinsky's predecessors represented as Greek (what Levinson called the 'simplified and vulgarized hellenism' of our day." (Scholl 1994: 70)

A transmedial relation between poems, dancing and drawings is established by Gigi Căciuleanu, Romanian dancer, choreographer and artistic director of The Chilean National Ballet. The genesis of his compositions is based upon the "dependency between the understanding of visual images, textuality and narrativity" (López-Varela 2011: 7) as a transmedial relation and construction of meaning:

> *- I saw in your choreography notebook a lot of poems and drawings. Is this another way of doing it?*
>
> *- These poems are really just texts from which I started and towards which I'm going. The texts are just like the drawings that help me memorize the idea. A line or a word helps me memorize a movement or a mood that generates a movement more than writing it down word by word would help me. That's why a poem is, to my mind, an essence, it is a text. A few words, a few lines scribbled on paper talk to me. They are there only for me. They are my tools.* Take for instance Japanese calligraphy: you decipher it in a second, because you don't just get the written word, but the philosophical concept, too... They are hieroglyphs. […] the public will be carried towards some symbols that often unfold on more than one level, in different energy registers. (Căciuleanu 2002: 244).

In *Gilles Deleuze por Vera Mantero*, the Portuguese choreographer uses intermedially the recorded voice of the philosopher as a soundtrack of her movement which follows both the rhythm and some affective and also conceptual contents of philosopher's verbal discourse. Thus, the verbal flow is "remediated" into/ by the kinesic shape.

REMEDIAL WRITING. FROM TEXT TO BODY SCORE (CASE STUDY: *SIGNALS OF THE REAL*)

In its October 2014 version, performed at the "Bacovia" Theatre from Bacău, in Romania, within Contemporary Dance Festival, *Signals of the Real* was directed by Geoffrey Sykes – the author of the script –, choreographed by Alysha Firbank, who also performed, together with Galina Bobeicu and Cristian Osoloş, accompanied by the soprano Brânduşa Moţoc, Liviu Mera playing the cello, and Cornelia Erhan the piano.

In *Signals of the Real*, it's remarkable the playright's power to build atmosphere, move the spectator somewhere else – within an imprecise and apparently exotic space, one which "who knows", we "have all already seen in our dreams", as the text says. Here, even sadness becomes luminous and anguish is healed through the power of the imagination, inner freedom that enables us to regain control of our lives and ourselves. Geoffrey Sykes did not want a show of contemporary dance properly, but a multimodal construction – a "multi-shape creation", as he claims – where poetry, painting, music and dance combine and answer each other, where gesture dances with the light, the words uttered on stage with live music, silence with the video projections and performers with the spectators' look. Galina Bobeicu, Cristian Osoloş and Alysha Firbank play three refugee artists from a "lost civilization", turned into a "big mistake". The sombre themes of the story (the war, Big Brother, the control of the individual and the instrumentalization of creativity, the freedom of conscience as a fraud by defrauding the Establishment, the alienation and the drift of the contemporary world) are all resolved in the luminous utopia of a (yet?) possible "revolution of conscience".

Geoffrey Sykes devised his show like a poem of psychoanalytically decrypted elements, as in the creation of his mentor, James Gleeson. (For example, the sea evokes the dark depths of the unconscious). In this cathartic "fable" of all sorts of elements – exorcism of the fear smouldering in the unconscious, shielded into the heart of civilization – Alysha dances with the gentle, calm energy of the earth; Galina and Cristian, with the histrionic, changing, playful energy of the air, or with the fluid, unsubmissive energy of water. An interesting solo is that of Alysha Firbank – playing the Dancer – at the "Mohenjo-Daroo coffee shop" (an enclave of freedom through creativity, which subversively avoids the "North regime"), as soon as the press announces the failure of the expected revolution. Alysha dances in a crouching posture, with wringing and alarming moves, with balance broken near the platform – like a creature of the sea, suddenly helpless, wrecked on an arid shore, which hinders her movements like a fisherman's net. The solo is a sequence of failures and recoveries, a hesitation between resistance and resignation. The dancer passes from the straight, proud, statuary posture to one of lament and full abandonment – lowering the eyes and arms, bending and squatting – the surrender of the body along with exhaustion of the will. From ascending, confident, almost proud movements, to desolate gestures, searching for the ground with fatigue and renunciation.

While the Dancer is performing her solo, the other two characters, the Philosopher and the Painter, withdraw anxiously into closed, defensive or reluctant postures, with their arms folded around their bodies – like in a gesture of defence or only concentration – with their heads bowed and eyes lost into the ground. There is in this sequence – without being the only one – a synergy of gestures, an interactional and emotional synchrony of the three characters – in fact, predictable and highlighted well by the choreographic design. The three characters thus externalize – amplifying through synergy – confusion, concern, deadlock, deception, vulnerability in front of a mechanism of social control, whose aggression is difficult to avert. Visual contact is suspended, none of the three looks at the others, each of them being engrossed in their own thoughts and fears. Then, Alysha, the Dancer, lies on the platform, with her arms stretched aside and her face upwards, in a posture of crucifixion; she detaches herself from the ground, with lateral spinning movements of the body, which amplify a lament movement of the head that moans woefully to the right and to the left. In virtue of a kinesic polysemantism, which associates – like in poetry – a multitude of meanings connoted to the same structure of expression, the respective sequence overlaps, at the same time, the evocation of a movement of ambush and watch, described on the horizontal level, like in the ancient warrior dances (in the Greek "*pyrrhic*", for example). Some other times, Alysha slides in a crouching posture, almost wiping the soil, with a furtive creeping of haunted creature, trying to get lost somewhere, in the hollows of the ground.

In another sequence, after the ultimatum visit of the Inspector, the Dancer naps and the Philosopher and Painter dance with slow, almost hypnotic movements, as if floating in weightlessness – a drowsy dive into an "elementary music", a quasi-vegetative regime of existence, pre-conceptual and pre-reflexive; the conscience of individuality is dissolved. Suddenly, "imagination is no longer forbidden"; newspapers announce that "a revolution took place" overnight. The hallo of Neptunian sonority is replaced by the passionate inflections of the tango – a music of life, feelings, of the fully alive creature who assumes itself with open eyes. Finally, the Inspector's voice is uselessly threatening, powerless in front of the assault of imagination, which seems to be a key to freedom – inner freedom, in any case, which all the three characters are searching.

Signals of the Real is a parable on a possible road towards inner freedom. The story is not new, but it is necessary to be, now and then, reminded. In order to be able to believe that in the life of each of us there is still place for ourselves, beyond the habitual "to do lists", "*comme il faut*", "as required". This road begins with a step, and the three characters take it by dancing, eventually becoming immune to what could wither their joy of living and saps of creativity. Borrowing (ironically?) the voice of the director Geoffrey Sykes, the Inspector – who subjects the refugee artists to a harsh indictment, filling the background with his face oversized through video projections – seems to be a lookalike of Big Brother, prophetically imagined, in 1984, by Orwell, in one of his dystopias,

1984. To the spectator's comfort, Geoffrey Sykes does not hesitate to rehabilitate utopia. It feels good to go to the theatre and find out that not everything is lost. That joy and hope have not gone out of fashion and, even if it were otherwise, they may yet be restored to stage, in the applauses of the audience (Popa Blanariu 2014d).

TRANSMEDIAL RHETORIC: SPACE AND VISUAL METAPHOR IN CONTEMPORAY DANCE (CASE STUDY: *IF I HAD...*)

Some rhetorical figures are essentially transmedial, able to manifest themselves both by verbal and non verbal – particularly visual – tools. All kinds of dance are based upon a rhetoric of space, which could join the evocative value of music, nature sounds (rain, spring, sea, birds, rustle of leaves, wind soughing etc.) or body (breath, beat of hearth), even silent. As previously said (Popa Blanariu 2014b), the body is the crossroad of the biological and cultural – representational – experience of human being. It has a basic rhetoric potential, which is exploited, in various cultures, through both verbal and non-verbal communication. As a proof, Lakoff's and Johnson's concept of orientation metaphor, able to transpose certain concepts into space, as well as Fontanier's metonymies of the physical, or Greimas' metonymic actors identified in the bodily segments and acting each in the name of an actant (Greimas 1973; Greimas 1987). Therefore, the body is an expressive space (Merleau-Ponty 1945), the symbolic value of its segments being deeply involved in choreographic significations. We largely talked about this elsewhere (Popa Blanariu 2008; 2013b; 2014b; 2014c; 2015a). So here, we only aim to illustrate the visual metaphor in contemporary dance, by means of Giovanni Zazzera's piece *If I had...* (performed at the "George Apostu" Cultural Centre from Bacău, in Romania, within October 2014 Contemporary Dance Festival).

If Geoffrey Sykes catches the "signals of the real" (which, of course, may be understood in so many different ways), Giovanni Zazzera (*If I had...*) struggles to make his way among them, through the mess of arrows that have invaded the stage – possible vectors of the options from which life is slowly knitted, but bewildering by their imperative agglomeration, even paralysing through the dose of risk, unknown, unpredictability, the inevitable bet implied by every choice. Visual metaphor of the idea of show, the arrows emerge from almost everywhere, from the background wall, the platform, the choreographer's hand. As a way of correlating the idea with the choreographic expression, Giovanni Zazzera's show is characterized by the systematic exploitation of the rhetoric of space, at the interface between the physical place in which the dancer evolves, and its evocative or symbolic connotations. Thus, the show manages, as a thematic dominant, the spatialization of a deadlock, a dilemma, a process of deliberate-rational or intuitive choice; briefly, the representation of a dubitative existence regime ("If I had..."), which is, eventually, our daily given, although we may not always be aware of it.

The figures of space are diverse and meaningful in the show's thematic context: line, circle of idle spin, intersection or overlapping of meanings and directions (possible visual transposition of a chaotic agglomeration of hypotheses and possibilities of existence). Sufficiently varied are also the ways of covering the stage space: step of marking time, walking in a line (following the path indicated by the rows of arrows), spinning in a circle – a circle of divergent arrows (as a figure of deadlock, difficult progress, captivity here and now, of a suspended or difficult to foresee future, beyond the undefined prolonged present of an *embarras du choix*). There is a remarkable posture repeated in the show: that of suspended walk, of a step stopped in the air, between start and finish, like a doubt or an alternative arrived too late, when another way, maybe better, is yet imaginable, but already impossible to materialize; the posture evokes, to a certain extent, the state that invades you when you see the train leaving the station, with your seat vacant, although you have your ticket in your pocket.

There are also many spatial and kinesic figures of hesitation in this performance: the hesitation before taking a road that opens in front of us, with all its temptations and uncertainties; "pass!" and step for marking time – maddening hesitation transposed, for example, in the progressive intensification of the rhythm, reaching a movement raced to the maximum, but in the same spot, like the engine of an airship before taking off. Somehow surprised by his own posture and choice, focused on an endless calculus – as if negotiating with chance – the dancer throws himself head first, no matter what, like in a roulette game ; he takes an unexpectedly wide jump, as wide as the road from the project to its materialization, from start to finish. The decision has been made, the dice cast, it is a one-breath jump, like swallowing bitter medicine without chewing it. Surrounded by the many possibilities, tendencies and temptations, Giovanni Zazzera struggles to find in himself the spring for a valid choice and the path to follow. The only red arrow from the platform, with which Giovanni Zazzera dances, points, at a certain moment, upwards, above the fret from the stage and above the heads of the spectators – a proof, probably, of the option for a certain mode of living (Popa Blanariu 2014d).

NARRATIVITY AS TRANSMEDIALITY. DANCING LITERATURE, A REVERSE *EKPHRASIS*

Verbal expression does not exhaust the resources of narrativity, which is in fact, transverbal and transmedial. Narrative structures influence meaning creation also in oniric 'language', figurative painting, and in choreographic composition. The story line is sometimes thin, without necessarily disappearing, as in the case of confessional, lyric dance. From a historical, typological and functional point of view, a distinction may be drawn between ritualistic, archaic dance, integrated in magical-religious practices and, respectively, "aesthetic" dance, partially derived from the first one. In aesthetic dance, the desecration of the ritualistic expression (kinesic transposition of the mythical, original narration) has entailed the "desemantization" or, rather, the demotivation of gestual statements (Greimas 1970, 1983). However, these are not left dissimilar, but can be narratively semantized, caught – and thus clarified – within a story and within the constitutive ambiguity of the aesthetic. Even acrobatic numbers carry narrative syntagms comparable to those originating in folk tales, as in the shows of the company Cirque du Soleil (see Greimas 1970, 1983). In other words, aesthetic gestuality may specify its meanings by integration into a (semio) narrative structure, which is manifested kinesically. The actantial model of narrative discourse comes from extrapolating a syntactic structure (formalized by Lucien Tesnière 1959) from the phrase to the transphrastic level. Thus, Étienne Souriau (1950) demonstrated the validity of the actantial scheme for the dramatic genre, Vladimir Propp (1970) built his formal model starting from epic texts, and Eero Tarasti (1996) applied the semiotic and narrative theory to a musical corpus. Tarasti supports his own approach with the Greimasian concept of "generalized narrativity". Maintaining that human language has an immanent narrativity, Solomon Marcus (1989) traced the interdependence between lyric and narrative as two types of behaviour and discourse and, as he remarqued, human language has an "immanent narrativity", and "converting the lyric into language" means, at the same time, "narrativizing the lyric" (Marcus 1989: 94-95). Similarly, Galen Strawson (2004) studied the episodic and diachronic narrative styles as two distinct views on the existential process and project related to its temporal aspects (430). Strawson's conclusion is that "Narrativity, it is in the sphere of ethics more of an affliction or a bad habit than a prerequisite of a good life. It risks a strange commodification of life and time – of soul, understood in a strictly secular sense. It misses the point. 'We live', as the great short story writer V.S. Pritchett observes, 'beyond any tale that we happen to enact'." (Strawson 2004: 450)

This paper proposes an analysis on the measure in which the semio-narrative categories and the Greimasian actantial model are relevant for the understanding of choreographic discourse as reverse ekphrasis. In particular, the study considers choreographies inspired by literary (pre)text or pre-established narrative frames. It is necessary, according to Algirdas J. Greimas, to draw a fundamental distinction between two levels of representation ad interpretation: a) an 'apparent' level of the narrative, where its various manifestations are subjected to exigencies characteristic of linguistic or non-linguistic (particularly choreographic) manifestation substances; b) an 'immanent' level, which may constitute a structural core, where narrativity is situated and organized before its manifestations. Therefore, there is a semiotic level shared by all narrativities, distinct from the linguistic level, which it precedes (Greimas 1970, 1983, 1973; Greimas & Courtès 1979). The semantic level is configured by the projection of the narrative syntax. The semio-narrative categories organize the explicit, canonical forms of narrativity – epic literature or colloquial, quotidian narrativity –, but also narrativity dissimulated in seemingly non-narrative discourses, such as the political or the scientific discourse. Non-epic does not necessarily imply non-narrative. The "semio-narrative competence" refers to the fundamental grammar of the enunciation/ discourse, which precedes the enunciation and is implied by the latter (Greimas & Courtès 1979: 104); whereas "discursive competence" is constituted in the course of the enunciation and governs the enunciated discursive forms. (Greimas & Courtès 1979: 104) Narrative grammar is independent from the discursive manifestations, (Greimas 1973: 162) even if it is actualized by means of the latter. Narrative structures are general archetypes of the imaginary, whereas discursive (thematic or figurative) configurations are, to a much greater extent, dependent upon the culture in which they are manifested. Particularly the choreographic discourse is the syncretic – transmedial and multimodal – result of the general narrative structures and of the particular discursive configurations (bodily, rhythmic, spatial). There is, however, the other side of the shield: the excessive extension of the concept of narrativity presents the risk of its becoming brittle and inefficient. "If almost any discourse is narrative (Greimas 1983; Greimas & Courtès 1979), then the category of narrativity loses the ability of seizing a specific difference, distinct in the vast ensemble of discursive formations in Foucault's sense"

The distinction between actants and actors enables the separation of two "autonomous levels" of reflection upon narrativity (Greimas 1973: 161). Actants are related to a narrative syntax, whereas the actors "may be recognized in the particular discourses in which they occur". An actant may be manifested through several actors, as well as one actor may manifest several actants (Greimas 1973: 161). The actantial scheme proposed by Greimas implies certain dissociations: subject vs. object, sender vs. receiver, adjuvant vs. opponent. It is supported by the formalizations of Propp (for the Russian fairy-tale) and Souriau (for the dramatic genre). The following lines focus on narrative coherence in dance, tracing a brief historic revision of choreographic expression in the West, from Romantic ballet d'action to modern (psycho)drama.

The so-called Italian and French ballets from the 16th and 17th-centuries were mosaic performances which interwove vocal and instrumental music, recitative and stage movement sequences. Although such an ensemble had a certain narrative organization, the dance – performed especially through mimic gestures – contributed but little to the unfolding of the action. In time, the dancing technique improved; the ballet sequences were included into composite shows without any other role but that of highlighting the mastery of the performer.

The imperative of subjecting the choreographic movement to a coherent narrative technique is clearly stated by Jean Georges Noverre (see *Lettres sur les arts imitateurs en général et sur la danse en particulier*, 1760), the reformer of Western ballet in the 18th-century. A "ballet d'action" should consist of an "exposition", a "climax" and a "dénouement", divided into acts and scenes, each containing an introductory part, a middle development and an ending. Noverre's project is reflected in the great Romantic ballets from the first half of the 19th-century. Even before the dissemination of Noverre's programmatic text, Franz Hilferding van Wewen, an Austrian dancer, had staged the play *Britannicus* by Racine, at Vienna, in 1740. His choreography had a clear narrative unity, anticipating the Romantic "ballet d'action". At the turn of the century and by 1914, the increasing relevance given to virtuosity, at the expense of expressivity, determined Mikhail Fokine, choreographer of many performances at Diaghilev's company, to resume the ideas-strengths of the reforming programme that Noverre had proposed, and among these, the principle of integrating each choreographic element into the logic of "dramatic action" (a narrative law). Dancing and mimetic gestures have no meaning in ballet, Fokine warns, unless they contribute to rendering dramatic action; they should not be used as mere entertainment or fun, unrelated to the plan of the entire ballet (see Fokine Estate archive)

The promoters of modern dance in America and Europe believed that ballet cannot express inner life, due to its artificial technique, depthless fantasy and narrative plot. However, a pioneer in modern dance, Martha Graham, has elaborated her choreographic language so that it may support her in expressing dramatic content. She has often appreciated her compositions as dramas. Besides the sociopolitical meaning, Pina Baush's creations have an element of psychodrama, manifested as the exteriorization as kinesic projection of a succession of inner events: the becoming of the ego, meaning, lato sensu, narrative coherence. Nevertheless, ballet is, according to George Balanchine (1988), such a rich form of art that it should not be merely an 'illustration' not even of the most significant literary sources, and should speak for the self and about the self. Thus, in early modern dance, certain choreographers have tried to exploit procedures already tested in literature, showing how narrative is not the monopoly of literature. Fragmentary narrative, flashback or temporal dislocation, are among the techniques employed by Martha Graham in *Clytemnestra* (1958). Moreover, the semio-narrative categories transgress the verbal, and can be expressed choreographically, as I will show in the following lines.

Choreographic movement is, according to Rudolf Laban, the result of a certain "mood" or "quest" for a certain object of desire regarded as "valuable" (Laban 1994: 20). Even when dance renders an inner (psycho-emotional) path, it may be analyzed with the tools of the semiotics of narrativity, since narrativity may be understood, lato sensu, as an expression of processuality and of becoming, par excellence. Greimas formalizes the "absolute interior dramatization" as a "subjective actorial structure" (1973: 168). The narrative structure is not equally clear in all dance genres. Laban distinguishes between pure dance, on the one hand, and forms of stage dance such as ballet, mime and dramatic art (Laban 1994: 125). Narrative organization is pronounced in the ballet d'action and in the other forms of "theatrical" dance (Laban 1994: 125). Nevertheless, pure dance has no traceable story; even its movement may be described, it is often impossible to render its content through words (Laban 1994: 22). Artistic symbols are polysemic, connotative, programatically "ambiguous" (a term that Jakobson uses to establish the specificity of aesthetic semiosis). "Non-sequential" (continuous), the emotional substance should, however, mould itself onto the "sequential" (discretization) capacities of (verbal or non-verbal) language, in order to achieve a representable shape: "The transition from lyric behaviour to lyric expression represents a real tour de force, because the emotional, by its non-sequential nature, should adapt to the sequential structure of language." (Marcus 1989: 94) Hence, the relevance of the co(n)text in establishing significations.

From the point of view of the followers of the classical tri-partition of genres (lyric, epic, dramatic), the 'interference' between the lyric and the narrative could be amended. Solomon Marcus argues, however, for the presence of a dialectic relation between the lyric and the narrative, as types of behaviour and discursive genres. Since human language has an "immanent" narrativity, "converting the lyric into language means 'narrativizing the lyric'," "[...] emotional content should metamorphose into a discrete structure" which could be, in particular, an organization of choreographic kinemorphemes. (Marcus 1989: 94-95) Thus, the tendency of the lyric to become imbued with a narrative structure is essential and unavoidable. Narrative is "referential" unlike the lyric, defined by its "pronounced hermeneutic nature." (Marcus 1989: 96) This observation seizes, in a generalizing statement, an aspect which Jakobson had restricted to epic and verbal narrativity. Epic poetry, centred on the third person, engages the referential ("cognitive," "denotative") function, whereas lyric poetry, oriented towards the first person, resorts particularly to the "emotive" or "expressive" function (Jakobson 1963: 219). In Solomon Marcus' view, the principle of "interference" of the lyric and the dramatic is inspired by the dynamic logic of the contradiction (see also Lupasco 1935). It may be regarded as a confirmation of the complementarity of linguistic functions (Jakobson) or of the complementarity of the "cognitive" and "emotive" aspects (see Stevenson, Ethics and Language 1944) in the operation of poetic signs.

Thus, the structure of the message is not restricted to any of the language functions, but is a result of all of them. Among them, one comes into prominence, varying according to the communication situation, as the "dominant" function (Jakobson 1963: 214). Concerned with the metaphorical expression, Charles Stevenson observes that the descriptive (referential) and emotive significations do not exist in isolation, but as distinct aspects of a "complete" situation. Emotive signification depends upon a descriptive signification, and also an emotive signification which depends upon a 'vague' situation. For Umberto Eco (1989), the difference between the referential and the emotive does not concerns so much the structure of the expression, as it does its use and, hence, the context in which it is pronounced. According to Marcus, "the interference of the lyric and the narrative should be related to the general process of interference of the non-sequential and sequential activities [...] Hence, there occurs a natural tendency for balance between the lyric and the narrative [...] The lyric and the narrative tend towards each other as well as take their distance from each other." (1989: 95 – 96) From this "dynamic logic" of opposites, the lyric may be "narrativized" by means of kinemorphemes (rhythmic and choreographic discrete symbols) and by the joint mobilization of the "referential" and the "emotive", that projects the substance of interiority towards the exterior. Thus, the following lines look into the actantial structure of the musical and/or kinesic discourse.

According to Eero Tarasti, even "absolute" music, the opposite of "program music" and, unlike the latter, cleansed of all epic referentiality and intrigue (meaning that it does not attempt to 'tell' anything in its own language), has a narrative structure. In fact, a question he poses is "how can narrativity which is hidden in absolute music be disclosed?" (Tarasti 1996: 47). Tarasti supports his own approach with the Greimasian concept of "generalized narrativity". For example, in the opera show – a syncretic ensemble, an "intertextual and polidiscursive" totality– music reflects the protagonists' actions, meaning that the "musical themes function like actants." (Tarasti 1996: 58) Based on this criterion, we may distinguish between "subject-themes, object-themes, adjuvant-themes, opponent-themes" in the opera music, (Tarasti 1996: 64). For Tarasti, these actantial categories reveal the "dramatic" dimension of the opera music. Subsumed under the same general theory, a semiotics of choreographic expression may be usefully connected to musical semiotics. Manifested autonomously or complementarily in the musical and/or (only) in the kinesic substance, the choreographic signification may be constituted on the basis of the same narrative-actantial structures.

For example, in *La Esmeralda*, a ballet in 3 acts, 5 scenes, inspired by *Notre Dame de Paris* by Victor Hugo, choreographed by Jules Perrot, with music by Cesare Pugni, presented for the first time at the Ballet of her Majesty's Theatre, London on March 9, 1844, (and in 1994, by a Ballet and Symphonic Orchestra Moussorgsky from St. Petersburg), a series of musical tones mark the character of the protagonists and the scenes. It is, for instance, deep, grave and sombre, as a background for the scene in which Frollo and Quasimodo plan the kidnapping; suave, graceful and tonic in the following scene as a background for the heroine, as well as in the previous one which illustrates the saving of the poet at the Court of Miracles; rhythmic, parade-like for the occurrence of the soldier (Phoebus), changes abruptly when Phoebus sees Esmeralda lying on the ground; and discreet and spiralling when anticipating the idyll. Thus, musical-kinesic syncretism manifests the actantial roles of subjects and objects, protagonists and opponents. The musical actors (the sonorous marks of the protagonists) and the choreographic actors (with their kinesic-postural marks) cover various positions within the actantial scheme.

In agreement with the stage action that they imagine, the musical preferences of the choreographers, are not once eclectic, going, as Maurice Béjart does, as far as the shocking mixture of certain stylistic extremes, usually regarded as incompatible: "Let's say today I do a ballet on music by Beethoven, then by Pink Floyd, then on Indian music, on music by Bach, but I mix Bach with Argentinean tangos – as I did in Faustus." (Béjart interviewed by Silvia Ciurescu 2002: 190) Why this mixture? A seemingly gratuitous extravagance, a diagnosis which dance-chronicles have repeatedly applied to Béjart, mixing Bach with Argentine tango is, actually, an ingenious musical transposition of the skill of full knowledge, as a mark of Faustian personality. It is a way of suggesting, by the musical themes selected, the extremes which define it: the evil and the angelic, experiencing fall and ascent, sensual passion and spiritualized abnegation. Between Argentine tango and Bach, the history of *Homo fausticus*, tormented with deep descents and great impetus, is inscribed on a musical scale. Tango evokes passion, sensuality; at the other extreme, Bach's music connotes spiritualization, the satisfactions of contemplative serenity. We believe that by choosing this surprising combination, Béjart concentrates the duality of the Faustian being (in search of himself between Heaven and Earth, between redemption and fall, or even "beyond Good and Evil") in an intentionally heterogeneous musical discourse. Bizarre, seemingly random and gratuitously eclectic, the music of the show supports, in reality, the logic of its actantial organization. The subject confronts the anti-subject within the space of individuality of the same 'actor' (the Faustian hero). The musical themes of Béjart's show, those of the subject and the anti-subject (Greimas 1973: 162-63, 166-67), reflect the assumption of this actantial scheme. In a sequence from another of Béjart's shows, *Ballet for life*, the same relation between subject and anti-subject – confrontation in the space of the same actor – is achieved through musical-visual syncretism (or multimodality). The dominating semantism of associating music with image results from intersecting the semantic axes of the two "discourses". The soundtrack – the song "I want to break free", from Queen's album *The Works* – meaningfully repeats the statements: "I'm falling in love, / God knows what I'm falling in love. / (...) I want to be free, / I want to break free. / God knows how I want to break free." With this soundtrack, in the sequences which serves as background, Jorge Donne, the famous dancer, appears as a crucified clown, laughing, while nails are driven into his palms, and returning with a diabolical mask on his face. At the figurative level of discourse, the postures, mimics, accessories unfold two thematic symbols reunited in the potentiality of the same individual. This reconciliation probably means the gaining of the coveted freedom; Christ and Lucifer, meaning Love and Rebellion. The tragic clown reunites both valences: the subject and the anti-subject, meeting and clashing in the inner forum of the same actor, in the Greimasian, narratological meaning of the term.

The semio-linguistic reinterpretation of the traditional concept of "dramatis personae" is relevant for the actantial organization of choreographic discourse. The actantial roles may be assumed by different dancers or by the same dancer. In an actantial relation, the body is distributed to the metonymic actors, that is, the different segments of the body involved in the discursive performance (on this see Greimas 1983). Even a 'solo' dance may manifest an actantial, polemic structure or, on the contrary, a contractual structure, corresponding to the moods or emotions expressed. The duality of emotions may be represented by two different dancers or by a single one; thus, the inner tensions of the same individuality are being projected (Laban 1994: 22).

The game of actantial functions is a "mobile constellation" (see Groupe µ 1972) which refers to two aspects. First, although the discourse reduces the story-telling to one single point, each character may occupy the privileged position and orient the other functions differently. Structurally speaking, the actantial constellation is invariable. In terms of performance, through the distribution of concrete characters on the standardized actantial positions, it is variable. Secondly, the other type of narrative 'mobility' introduces process in the analysis upon the actantial relations. For each participant, the game of relations may change; an opponent may provide help, and a friend may turn into a rival. For example, the ballet *La Bayadère* (The Temple Dancer), staged in four acts and seven tableaux by French choreographer Marius Petipa to the music of Ludwig Minkus, in the last show produced by Rudolf Nureev and staged at Paris National Opera (the ballet was first performed at the Imperial Bolshoi Kamenny Theatre in St. Petersburg, Russia, on 4 February 1877). The High Brahmin oscillates here between the hypostasis of opponent and that of adjuvant, and these actantial roles are actualized by choreographic predicates, manifested, in their turn, through kinesic figures. As opponent, the Brahmin performs a sign similar to the one which means 'death' in the French gestural code of the deaf-mute. As adjuvant, he also assumes the prerogatives of the 'referee who attributes good', according to the actantial typology of Souriau (1950). Nikyia, the Bayadère, performs a detour of the stage with arms wide open. By means of mimics and posture, the attendance signals unavailability: the body or face towards the public or backstage, the eyes fixed offstage. The High Brahmin's circular movement disapproves hostility towards the heroine. His gesture redraws the protective circle of mages and alchemists: with the arm and the palm stretched forward, a sign of interdiction and/or imposing distance. Several actantial functions may merge in the same character; in this case, those of the opponent and adjuvant. Functional syncretism finds appropriate ways of expression, in non-verbal (kinesic or proxemic) codes. To manifest the actantial isotopies, each choreographic text/discourse selects its own means of expression (see Popa Blanariu 2008). These may be integrated into a restrictive system, such as the code of classic ballet, or, on the contrary, may be open, like modern dance.

As mentioned, the globality of discourse (verbal or non-verbal) is constituted like a network of actants and predicates. The concepts of actant and actor enable the establishment of two classes of discursive isotopies: predicative and figurative, thematic, affective isotopies etc. The former ensure the identity of the actants, whereas the latter that of the actors. We may distinguish between two situations: a) the same actant corresponds to an entire class of predicates, which he assumes throughout the discourse; b) each predicate may manifest several actants (Fontanille 1998: 142). The same kinesic "figure" may manifest, in the discourse, different predicates, by means of which distinct actants are performed. An illustration can be provided with a sequence from *Cartea lui Prospero* (UNATC, 1994), Sergiu Anghel's choreography of Shakespeare's *The Tempest*. In this case, raising one's arms is an act distributed both in the discourse of the adjuvant – the ethereal spirits, loyal to Prospero, as well as in that of the opponent, Caliban, the beastly spirit (Fluchère 1960). The opponent raises his arms to beg for mercy, to announce his surrender, while the adjuvant raises his arms as a sign of threatening power. The mimics and the emblematic objects constitute, in this case, distinct elements. The presence/absence of thyrsi – a sign of punitive authority – marks the gesture of raising one's arms: (threat, victory) in the case of the adjuvant, (defeat/ surrender) in the case of the opponent. The homokinesis (which we have named in this way by analogy with verbal homonymy) may be solved only contextually. The same (semiologic) figure is distributed to several distinct semantic units (predicates and actants). The opposition of the signs euphoria/dysphoria corresponds, in this case, to predicative (sememic) oppositions: to succeed/ to fail, to conquer/to be defeated. Taking into account the semantic level, the predicative and actantial isotopies may be identified only in context.

The predicative value of a figure may be established only within discourse. Critics of Shakespeare's *The Tempest* believe that its fundamental theme is the victory of spirit over matter, of *melos* over *chaos*, of man over himself. Prospero, who enslaves the beastly and ethereal spirit, finds no rest until he accomplishes the regeneration of his enemies. It is the ultimate victory, the victory of spirit over matter, of love over hate (on this see Fluchère 1960). In Anghel's choreographic adaptation, these major thematic isotopies from Shakespeare's text enable the subsuming of the kinesic figures under two predicative isotopies by means of these, two distinct actantial categories, the adjuvant and the opponent, are manifested. By 'cosmotic predicates' I designate those predicates which are achieved through ascending, rhythmic, synchronized figures. They correspond to the thematic isotopy melos – harmony and order, imposed by the power of the demiurgic spirit. The chaotic predicates are those which are manifested through descending, arrhythmic figures. They are subsumed under the thematic isotopy chaos: crude, instinctual nature. The class of cosmotic predicates generates the adjuvant; that of chaotic predicates, the opponent. Cosmotic predicates are achieved through figures such as: jumps, wielding thyrsi, as well as through the consistently straight posture of the head, neck, back (in ancient ritualistic dances, the displaying of weapons had an apotropaic function, protecting against forces which threatened the order of the world). The chaotic predicates are rendered through figures of decline: steps staggering sideways and backwards, heavy balance, shaking, walking/crawling on all fours, collapsing.

The Tempest - choreography and dramaturgy: Sergiu Anghel (Anghel's youtube channel)

In the scene of Caliban's surrender, kneeling is, apparently, an act through which the adjuvant, as well as the opponent, is manifested. However, verbal polysemy may constitute a source of confusion. Despite designation by means of the same (verbal) term, there are two distinct kinesic figures, which manifest their own predicate and, correlatively, their own actant. It is an obvious distinction between the way in which Caliban kneels humbly and the way in which the spirits loyal to Prospero kneel threateningly and victoriously. Caliban, the beastly spirit, collapses heavily on his fours, like a wild defeated animal: with his hands and both of his knees on the ground, and his head lowered. The good spirits place one knee only on the ground, keeping their backs straight and heads upwards. How one supports oneself (on one or both legs) constitutes, in this scene, a distinct postural trait which serves for actantial individualization. Adjuvant – winner, in a posture which compensates (by the ascending posture of the back and head) the downward meaning of kneeling. Opponent – defeated, bending his entire body towards the ground. Kinesic figures verbalized through the same term ("to kneel") correspond, on the semantic level, to different predicates (to conquer/ to be defeated) and different actants. The semantic (predicative) value of the two figures is established in the co(n)text.

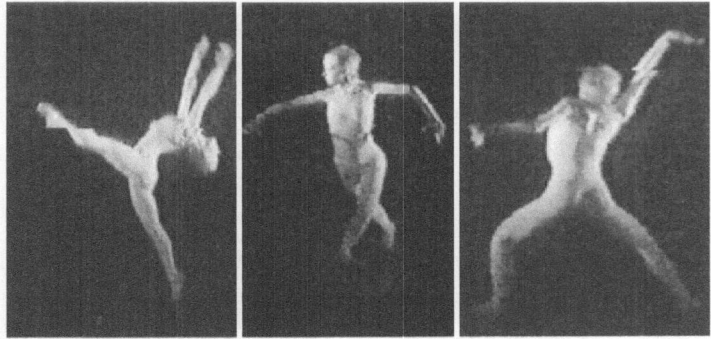

Ariel, the ethereal spirit: ascending movements

Caliban, the beastly spirit. Low movements

To conclude, even when dance renders an inner (psycho-emotional) path, it may be analyzed by means of semiotic tools as applied to narrative, since narrativity is an expression of process. By means of choreographic kinemorphemes and the joint mobilization of the referential and the emotive, the inner substance of moods, feelings, affective events can be projected towards the exterior, shaped and rendered by dancing.

CONCLUSION

The evolution of comparative literature has been revealing, for more than a century, a sinuous process of self-definition: as of the beginning of the 20 th century, it has been emerging like a diverse set of research, with studies covering "international literary relations", from a historical perspective in line with the established tradition of founders and eventually building a comparative poetics, whose necessity and legitimacy are nowadays acknowledged. As far as its specific field is a "tertium comparationis, that does not belong to any of the studied texts" – or, we may add, to none of the domains to which it is associated in an interdisciplinary way – but "maintains relations with each of these", general and comparative literature is being mistaken for a "methodological utopia" (Pageaux 20 0: 35). This (also) involves a relatively unrestrictive delimitation of the object and working methods (Wellek 1965: 282-295; Étiemble 1963), with all the positive connotations or the opposite ones associated with this state of fact. At the "crossroads of certain sets", each with its particularities, comparative literature beneficially feeds on these very "interferences", "meetings, exchanges" (Pageaux 2000: 34 – 35) between literatures and between domains of study. However, its very flexibility – available for constant assimilation and adaptation – determines the problem of a rigorous comparatist "methodology", founded on a coherent theory (Greimas & Courtès 1979: 49), to remain yet unsolved. The contributions of Étiemble (1958; 1963), Munteano (1967) or Marino (1988; 1998), among others, built around the concepts of "invariant" and literary "constant" have thus shaped, as of the middle of the 20 th century, a completely up-to-date research programme – yet unfinished – able to associate literary and intercultural studies, comparative literature and (inter)cultural anthropology. Resurfacing, at about the same time, the "intersemiotic" relations between literature and arts, Jakobson (1963) foreshadowed, in turn, today's multi- and intermedial studies, even the latter's crossing with the wide domain of comparative literature, as it is now globally understood: like an eminently interdisciplinary and – how else if not – intercultural domain. As a form of reverse ekphrasis, a piece of music or a dance may re(-)present, particularly, a literary text. Morover, the semio-narrative categories and the Greimasian actantial model are relevant for the understanding of choreographic discourse as reverse ekphrasis. In dance, gestural statements can be narratively semantized, caught – and thus clarified – within a story and within a constitutive aesthetics of ambiguity.

REFERENCES

Antonescu, Venera, Alexandru Cizek. Istoria literaturii universale și comparate. Antichitate orientală și clasică (History of World and Comparative Literature. Oriental and Classical Antiquity), București: Universitatea București, 1971

Balanchine, George. *Ballet Master,* New York: Random House, 1988.

Baldensperger, Fernand. „Littérature comparée: le mot et la chose", in Revue de littérature comparée, no. 1, Paris, 1921.

Béjart, Maurice. *Interview by Silvia Ciurescu, in Plural*, Bucharest: The Romanian Cultural Foundation, 3-4 (15-16) 2002: 187 – 92

Benedict, Ruth. *Patterns of culture, with a new preface by Margaret Mead*, Boston: Houghton Mifflin, 1959.

Blaga, Lucian. "Orizont și stil," in *Trilogia culturii, fwd. Dumitru Ghișe*, București: ELU, 1969 [1935].

Claudon, Francis, Karen Haddad-Wotling. *Précis de littérature comparée*, Paris: Nathan, 1992.

Claudon, Francis, Karen Haddad-Wotling. *Compendiu de literatură comparată*, trans. Ioan Lascu, București: Cartea Românească, 1997.

Căciuleanu, Gigi. *Interview by Silvia Ciurescu, in Plural*, Bucharest: The Romanian Cultural Foundation, 3-4 (15-16) 2002: 241 – 46

Chabrol, Claude, ed. *Sémiotique narrative et textuelle*, Paris: Larousse, 1973.

Covaci, Ion. "Cuvânt înainte" (Foreword), in *Li Tai-pe, Van Vei, Du Fu, Trei poeți din Tang* (Three Poets of the Tang), trans. and fwd. Ion Covaci, București: Univers, 1980.

D'Haen, Theo, "Antique Lands, New Worlds? Comparative Literature, Intertextuality, Translation," in Forum for Modern Language Studies, Published by Oxford University Press for Court of University of St. Andrews. doi:10.1093/fmls/cqm003

Damrosch, David. "World Literature in a Postcanonical Hypercanonical Age." In Saussy, Haun (Ed)., *Comparative Literature in an Age of Globalization*, Baltimore: Johns Hopkins U.P., 2006, 43-53.

Dospinescu, Liviu. «Les "querelles" interculturelles au Théâtre du Soleil: politique et représentation dans "Le Dernier Caravansérail", in Studii și cercetări științifice – seria filologie, 27.1 (2012). <https://sites.google.com/site/studiisicercetari>.

Fokine, Michel. Fokine Estate Archive. http://www.michelfokine.com/ (accessed 15 January 2014).
Eco, Umberto. *The Open Work,* trans. Anna Cancogni, Cambridge: Harvard University Press, 1989.
Étiemble, René. *Hygiène des lettres*, Paris: Gallimard, I, II, III, 1952/ 1955/ 1958
Étiemble, René. Comparaison n'est pas raison. La crise de la littérature comparée, Paris: Gallimard, 1963.
Elleström, Lars. *Media Borders: Multimodality and Intermediality.* Palgrave Macmillan, 2010.
Fluchère, Henry. Shakespeare, trans. Guy Hamilton, foreward by T.S. Eliot, London: Longmans, 1960.
Fontanier, Pierre. *Les Figures du discours, fwd. Gérard Genette*, Paris: Flammarion, 1977.
Fontanille, Jacques. *Sémiotique du discours,* Limoges: PULIM, 1998.
Foucault, Michel. *L'Archéologie du savoir,* Paris: Gallimard, 1969.
Geană, Gheorghiță. *Antropologia culturală* (Cultural Anthropology), București: Criterion Publishing, 2005.
Genette, Gérard. *Palimpsestes*. La Littérature au second degré, Paris: Seuil.
Greimas, Algirdas Julien, *Du Sens,* Paris: Seuil, 1982.
Greimas, Algirdas Julien."Les Actants, les acteurs et les figures", in Claude Chabrol (Ed.), Sémiotique narrative et textuelle, Paris: Larousse, 1973.
Greimas, Algirdas Julien, and Joseph Courtès. *Sémiotique. Dictionnaire raisonné de la théorie du langage*, Paris: Hachette, 1979.
Greimas, Algirdas Julien. *Du Sens, II*, Paris: Seuil, 1983.
Greimas, Algirdas-Julien. *Sémantique structurale,* Paris: PUF, 1986.
Grigorescu, Dan. *Introducere în literatura comparată* (Introduction to Comparative Literature), București: UNIVERSAL DALSI & Editura Semne, 1997.
Grishakova, Marina & Ryan, Marie-Laure, eds. *Intermediality and Storytelling. Narratologia Contributions to Narrative Theory.* Berlin: de Gruyter, 2010.
Groupe µ. *Rhétorique générale*, Paris: Larousse, 1972.
Guyard, Marius-François. La littérature comparée, Paris: PUF, 1978.
Horia, Vintilă. *Persécutez Boèce!,* Lausanne: Editions L'Âge d'Homme, 1987.
Kress, Gunther. *Literacy in the New Media Age*, London: Routledge, 2003.
Jakobson, Roman. *Essais de linguistique générale,* Paris: Minuit, 1963.

Juvan, Marko, "Generic Identity and Intertextuality", in *CLCWeb: Comparative Literature and Culture* 7.1 (2005): <http://dx.doi.org/10.7771/1481-4374.1255>

Kristeva, Julia. *Séméiotikè. Recherches pour une sémanalyse,* Paris: Seuil, 1969.

Laban, Rudolf. *La Maîtrise du mouvement,* trans. Jacqueline Challet-Haas et Marion Hansen, Paris: Actes Sud, 1994.

Lakoff, George P., Mark Johnson. *Les Métaphores dans la vie quotidienne* [Metaphors we live by], trans. Michel de Fornel, Paris: Minuit, 1986.

Levițchi, Leon. "Comentarii" (Commentaries on The Tempeste), in *William Shakespeare, Opere complete,* 8, trans. Leon Levițchi, București: Univers, 1990.

Li Tai-pe, Van Vei, Du F, *Trei poeți din Tang* (Three Poets of the Tang), trans. and fwd. Ion Covaci, București: Univers, 1980.

López-Varela Azcárate, Asunción. "Intertextuality and Intermediality as Cross-cultural Comunication Tools: A Critical Inquiry." *Cultura. International Journal of Philosophy of Culture and Axiology* 8.2 (2011): 7–22.

López Varela, Asunción. "Introduction to Intermedial Aesthetics and World Literatures", in *Journal of Comparative Literature and Aesthetics* (special issue: On Intermedial Aesthetics and World Literatures). Guest Editor, Asunción López Varela. Vishvanatha Keviraja Institute, Orissa, India, Vol. XXXVI, nr. 1-2, 2013, 5-30.

Lupasco, Stéphane. *Du devenir logique et de l'affectivité,* vol. 1: *Le dualisme antagoniste,* vol. 2: *Essai d'une nouvelle théorie de la connaissance,* Paris : Vrin, 1935.

Marcus, Solomon. "Liric și narativ: de la comportament la text" (Lyric and narrative: from behaviour to text), *in Invenție și descoperire* [Invention and discovery], București: Cartea Românească, 1989.

Marino, Adrian. *Étiemble ou le comparatisme militant,* Paris: Gallimard, 1982.

Marino, Adrian. "Epic," in *Dicționar de idei literare* (Dictionary of Literary Ideas), I, București: Eminescu, 1973.

Marino, Adrian. *Comparatisme et théorie de la littérature,* Paris: Presses Universitaires de France, 1988.

Marino, Adrian. *Comparatism și teoria literaturii,* trans. Mihai Ungurean, Iași: Polirom, 1998.

Masson-Oursel, Paul. *La* philosophie comparée, Paris: Alcan, 1923.

Mayer, Charles S. "The Influence of Leon Bakst on Choreography", *Dance Chronicle* 1 (1977):127- 42.

Merleau-Ponty, Maurice. *Phénoménologie de la perception*, Paris: Gallimard, 1945.

Munteano, Basil. *Constants dialectiques en littératures et en histoire: problèmes, recherches et perspectives*, Paris: Didier, 1967.

Nakamura, Hajime. *The Ways of Thinking of Eastern Peoples: India-China-Tibet-Japon*, University of Hawaii Press, 1964.

Nakamura, Hajime. *Orient şi Occident. O istorie comparată a ideilor*, trans. D. Luca, Bucureşti: Humanitas, 1997.

Nicolescu, Basarab. *La Transdisciplinarité. Manifeste,* Paris: Editions du Rocher, 1996.

Noverre, Jean Georges. *Letters On Dancing and Ballets,* Princeton Book Co Pub, 2004.

Noverre, Jean Georges. *Lettres sur la danse et sur les ballets,* seconde édition, Gale ECCO, Print Editions, 2012.

Pageaux, Daniel-Henri. *La Littérature générale et comparée*, Paris : Armand Colin, 1994.

Pageaux, Daniel-Henri. *Literatura generală şi comparată,* trans Lidia Bodea, fwd. Paul Cornea, Iaşi: Polirom, 2000.

Popa Blanariu, Nicoleta. *Când gestul rupe tăcerea. Dansul şi paradigmele comunicării* (When the Gesture Breaks the Silence: Dancing and the Paradigms of Communication), Iaşi: Fides, 2008.

Popa Blanariu, Nicoleta. "Utopie et pragmatisme: le projet interculturel, in Studii şi cercetări ştiinţifice, seria filologie, 24.2 (2010), 11-18. <https://sites.google.com/site/studiisicercetari>

Popa Blanariu, Nicoleta. "Narrativity as Transmediality. Dancing Literature: a Reverse Ekphrasis". In *Journal of Comparative Literature and Aesthetics* (special issue: On Intermedial Aesthetics and World Literatures). Guest Editor, Asunción López Varela. Vishvanatha Keviraja Institute, Orissa, India, Vol. XXXVI, no. 1-2, 2013, 129 – 141

Popa Blanariu, Nicoleta. "Towards a Framework of a Semiotics of Dance", in CLCweb: Comparative Literature and Culture, 15.1 (2013). <http://dx.doi.org/10.7771/1481-4374.2183>

Popa Blanariu, Nicoleta. "Literatura generală şi comparată: teme, concepte, modalităţi de abordare." In *General and Comparative Literature:*

themes, concepts, approaches, Bacău: "Alma Mater" Publishing House of Vasile Alecsandri University, 2014.

Popa Blanariu, Nicoleta. "Semiotic and Rhetorical Patterns in Dance and Gestural Languages", in *Southern Semiotic Review*, 4, 2014b. <http://www.southernsemioticreview.net/>

Popa Blanariu, Nicoleta. "À partir de Greimas. Semiotic and Communication Patterns in Dance", in *Southern Semiotic Review*, 3, 2014c <http://www.southernsemioticreview.net/>

Popa Blanariu, Nicoleta. "The interdisciplinary research group LOGOS, associated partner of the «E-motional festival», october 2014 (the EU Culture programme, 2007-2013)", în *Studii şi cercetări ştiinţifice, seria filologie*, 32.2 (2014d), 25-31.

Popa Blanariu, Nicoleta,. "Communication Paradigms in Dance and Performance Studies", in *CLCweb: Comparative Literature and Culture*, 17. 2, 2015a.

Popa Blanariu, Nicoleta. "Frontiere (inter)disciplinare şi alternative metodologice în literatura comparată: interculturalitate şi «transpunere intersemiotică»" (Interdisciplinary borders and methodological alternatives in Comparative Literature: intercultural and intersemiotic transposition), in Journal of Romanian Literary Studies, 6, 2015b, 581-595. <http://www.upm.ro/jrls/?pag=JRLS-06/vol06-Rls>

Popa Blanariu, Nicoleta. "Bacău dance connection", in Ateneu, 550, 16, 2015c <http://ateneu.info/wp-content/uploads/at2015_06_NET.pdf>

Popa Blanariu, Nicoleta. "Vintila Horia: o lectura intertextuala", in *Studii si cercetari stiintifice, seria filologie*, 33.1 (2015d):

Propp, Vladimir. *Morphologie du conte*, Paris: Seuil, 1970.

Rachet, Guy. *La tragédie grecque*. Paris: Payot, 1973.

Rachet, Guy. *Tragedia greacă*, trans. Cristian Unteanu, Bucureşti: Univers, 1980.

Rifaterre, Michael. *La production du texte*, Paris: Seuil, 1979.

Scholl, Tim. *From Petipa to Balanchine: Classical Revival and the Modernization of Ballet*, New York: Routledge, 1994.

Shklovsky, Viktor. "Romanul grec şi locurile sale comune", in *Despre proză*, I, Bucureşti: Univers, 1974.

Souriau, Étienne. *Les Deux Cent Mille Situations dramatiques*, Paris: Flammarion, 1950

Stevenson, Charles. *Ethics and Language*, Yale University Press, 1944.

Shakespeare, William. The Works of William Shakespeare Gathered into One Volume, New York: Oxford University Press, 1938.

Saussy, Haun ed. *Comparative Literature in an Age of Globalization,* Baltimore: Johns Hopkins U.P., 2006.

Sykes, Geoffrey. "Toward a Theory of Multiform Expression", in Studii şi cercetări ştiinţifice – seria filologie, 32.2 (2014). <https://sites.google.com/site/studiisicercetari>

Tarasti, Eero. *Sémiotique musicale,* Limoges: PULIM, 1996.

Tesnière, Lucien. *Éléments de syntaxe structurale,* Paris: Klincksieck, 1959.

Tötösy de Zepetnek, Steven, "The New Humanities: the Intercultural, the Comparative, and the Interdisciplinary". Global Society, 1.2 (2007), pp. 45-68.) , <http://dx.doi.org/10.2979/GSO.2007.1.2.45>.

Tötösy de Zepetnek, Steven, Comparative Literature. Amsterdam – Atlanta, GA: Rodopi, 1998

Tötösy de Zepetnek, Steven, and Mukherjee, Tutun (Eds.) Companion to ComparativeLiterature, World Literatures, and Comparative Cultural Studies. New Delhi: Cambridge University Press India Pvt. Ltd, 2013.

Ursa, Mihaela. "Universality as Invariability in Comparative Literature: Towards an Integrative Theory of Cultural Contact", in Primerjalna književnost , 37.3 (2014): 149-161

Urseanu, Tilde, Ion Ianegic. *Liviu Ionescu. Istoria baletului,* Bucureşti: Editura muzicală, 1967.

Vatsyayan, Kapila. *Indian Classical Dance,* New Delhi: Ministry of Information and Broadcasting, 1974.

Wellek, René. *Théorie de la littérature, Paris*: Seuil, 1942.

Wellek, René, Austin Warren, *Teoria literaturii,* trans. Rodica Tiniş, notes and pref. Sorin Alexandrescu, Bucureşti: ELU, 1967.

Wissler, Clark. *Man and Culture,* New York: Johnson Reprint Corporation, 1965 [1923].

Wolf, Werner and Bernhart, Walter, *Framing Borders in Literature and Other Media*, Amsterdam: Rodopi, 2006.

Wolf, Werner. "(Inter)mediality and the Study of Literature". In Tötösy de Zepetnek, Steven (Ed.), *Digital Humanities and the Study of Intermediality in Comparative Cultural studies*, Purdue Scholarly Publishing Services, 2013, 19-31.

ABOUT THE AUTHOR

Nicoleta Popa Blanariu teaches comparative literature at the University "Vasile Alecsandri", since 1999, and holds a PhD in Philology at the University "Alexandru Ioan Cuza" in 2004. Her interests in research include literary anthropology, comparative intercultural studies, intermediality, visual semiotics, and performance studies. She published articles in Romanian, French and English, the translation of Patrice Pavis's *Dictionnaire du théâtre* as *Dictionar de teatru* (with Florinela Floria, 2012) and two single-authored books: *Când gestul rupe tăcerea. Dansul și paradigmele comunicării* (*When the Gesture Breaks the Silence: Dancing and the Paradigms of Communication*) (2008); *Literatura generală și comparată: teme, concepte, modalități de abordare (General and Comparative Literature: themes, concepts, approaches* 2014). Among her most recent works: "Communication Paradigms in Performance and Dance Studies", in *CLCweb: Comparative Literature and Culture*, 17. 2 (2015); "De la Weltschmerz la kakia valentiniană. Personaje eminesciene în structura actanțială a miturilor dualist-gnostice" (From Weltschmerz to Valentinian Kakia. Eminescu's Romantic Characters in the Actantial Structure of the Dualistic-Gnostic Myths), in *Studii eminescologice* (2015); "Towards a Framework of a Semiotics of Dance", in *CLCWeb: Comparative Literature and Culture* 15.1 (2013); "Narrativity as Transmediality. Dancing Literature: a Reverse Ekphrasis", in *On Intermedial Aesthetics and World Literatures (Journal of Comparative Literature and Aesthetics*) (special issue ed. by Asunción López Varela, 2013); "Performativity and Ritualistic Interaction", in *Perspectives on Interaction*, Cambridge Scholars Publishing (ed. by E. Bonta, 2013) ; "Towards a Poetics of Performance: Embodiment and Verfremdungseffekt as Fuzzy Aspects of Acting", in *The International Journal of the Humanities: Annual Review,* vol. 10 (ed. by Asunción López Varela, 2013).

CHAPTER 9

Intermedial Aspects in Egyptian Fayoum Portraits

Marie-Thérèse Abdelmessih

The national and international image of Egypt is always 'past' without present; silenced pasts, and de-voiced present. Its multiple pasts have encouraged archaeologists, anthropologists, art historians, and philosophers, at home and abroad to lay authoritative claims on its visual and literary texts. Their attempts resulted in strict classifications, and misreading continuities and discontinuities, misrepresenting Egypt's cultural identity, which has already suffered from the politics of exclusion, along a history of subjectification by different repressive powers. Although the histories of Egyptology, Greco-Roman studies, Coptology and Islamic art should be studied in continuum, they have always been considered as separate disciplines. Until this day, Greco-Roman and Coptic eras are not given much interest, and most Europeans do not acknowledge the Greco-Roman debt to ancient Egypt. The glorification of the Pharaonic era was part of the imperial politics to slight Muslims and Christian Copts, explicitly or implicitly denying modern Egypt's relations to its pasts. In a Western imagination implemented by nineteenth century Egyptology, Egypt is a glorious past divorced from a degenerate present (Reid, *Whose Pharaohs* 2001; Colla, *Conflicting Antiquities* 2008), an image lately fostered by the Egyptomania pervading the West. In response, nativist religious revivalism motivated by a politics of exclusion has developed to counter the image constructed by the West.

Furthermore, the reformist nationalist response to colonial misrepresentations has also marginalised large sectors under the pretext of forming a unified national identity. The reformist's claims are based on a transcendental history and determinate concepts of reality, to foster their power through knowledge. The alternative, in such a case, is to deconstruct 'realities' constructed by Western liberalism, or nationalist essentialism through a postcolonial translation; "all forms of cultural meaning are open to translation" because they resist totalization (Homi Bhabha, *Nation* 1990: 314). The translator's choice is determined by a historical crisis in the present, ensuing from rupture with the past that may be mitigated through a translation process negotiating difference. In this paper I attempt a postcolonial translation of the Fayoum portraits (1ˢᵗ–5ᵗʰ C. CE), Egyptian icons from the Greco-Roman period, executed at a transitional period in Egypt's history, and therefore, subject to misreadings de-voicing them. They are representations of silence, executed in anticipation of death, and translating them may help in intermediating cultures, or – according to the portraits – traversing death. In this respect, my practice will be speculative and interventionist as it will attempt the translation of ritual icons into a profane language. As such, a postcolonial translation of the portraits may become a resistance against colonial and nationalistic discourses to re-locate them in a broader cultural context that safeguards them against death by a politics of exclusion.

Worldwide emerging interest taken in the Fayoum portraits in Egypt (1999 Exhibition) urges a reconsideration of image viewing methods, to reassess the historical location of Egypt, as a site of intervention. Historically and stylistically the portraits belong to a period of transition between the Pharaonic masque and the highly stylised Coptic icon. In the ritual context, the portraits express the religious syncretism prevalent in an open society whose natives intermarried with immigrants from east and west. The portraits challenge essentialist notions of identity by representing identity 'under erasure', or rethinking identity as operating in a different paradigm (Stuart Hall, "Who Needs" 1). The portraits deconstruct the idea of a stable Egyptian identity recurring throughout a changing history, by representing a process of becoming, intermediating elements from multiple cultures.

The portraits are visual representations intermediating Egyptian theology, Stoicism, Neoplatonism and Asiatic learning. They are the first visual representations of the plural singular/individual in the history of Egyptian art, and raise questions around the One and All, a discourse that re-emerged in Western thought intermittently until the nineteenth century, under different 'isms' (Martin Bernal, *Black Ahtena*, 1987). The translation of the layers of meaning embedded in the visual language of the portraits dislocates them from their ritual context, to relocate them in the profane world. Being dead and alive, and belonging to the past and the present, they are representations that go beyond representation. The translation of their visual context should proceed through a chain of transformations, engaging us in crossing and re-crossing previously set demarcations, intermediating temporalities, historical locations and disciplines.

The silent/silenced portraits communicate through competing languages that call for a postcolonial translation (Tejaswini Niranjana, *Siting Translation*), intermediating different language codes. This differs from traditional translation used since the Renaissance considered as a transfer between linguistic texts. It is now agreed upon that translation as an activity mediating two code systems is not restricted to the linguistic level (Andre Lefevere, "Composing" 75), but moves beyond the source/target dichotomy to found a third dimension where original and translation become donors and receivers (Viera, "Poetics" 97). In that context, a postcolonial translation of the portraits' competing languages is an intervention in cultural and political systems, intermediating national and international to promote a cosmopolitan language.

The Fayoum portraits, Greco-Egyptian artifacts of Roman times are not icons of worship, but still retain their hold on us as viewers. During the reign of Tiberius (ad 14-37), the three dimensional Egyptian funeral mask was replaced by painted portraits fitted on to the mummies. This came along with other aspects of synchronizing Greek and Egyptian religions. As signs intermediating Egyptian and Greek art there is something in them beyond mimetic representations of the dead. By doubling the funerary art of Egypt and Greece they interrupt both traditions: the Egyptian abstract tradition and the mimetic, taking after the Alexandrian school based on Apelles' naturalistic tradition. They are 'Egyreek' creations that egyptianized the Greek and grecized the Egyptian. Arch-shaped gilt stucco frames forming garlands interrupted the illusion of depth. Unlike the Roman imperial portraits, the Egyptian portraits concentrated on the face. The Pompian portrait is a social representation addressed to a social group. The Fayoum portraits are surrogates to people living, or remembered alive, and who appear to exchange glances with the living, because in some way they are still alive. Their wide-opened eyes inspired by an Egyptian iconography replete with eyes – the eyes being the windows of the soul – adapted maximum expressiveness in minimal space. The alternation of their silent eyes between the fixed gaze and the silent glances has incited many to speak for them.

By being ripped off their mummies, the context of death, these portraits have not lost their aura, nor has their gaze lost its energy. Conversely, they have pluralised, since reading them needs a constant temporal and spatial movement. These portraits do not simply intermediate two traditions, but also engage in past and present temporalities. They intermediate points of junction and disjunction; by doubling two traditions they rupture both. As such, visualising the portraits needs going beyond the mimetic or symbolic interpretation; they are aesthetic and non-aesthetic. The mimetic Greco-Roman tradition suggests a backward movement since it refers to a past temporality, a farewell, and a closure. The Egyptian funerary iconography refers to an inevitable rupture with the past, its abstract style a sign of non-closure, a passage to the beyond. As we read traces of Greek, in the portraits, the Egyptian is erased, and as we preserve the Egyptian, the Greek is transgressed. The translation of the portraits should be quadruple because of the paradoxical nature of their visualization. They are Greco-Roman and Egyptian; they belong to the past and the present. Although they are meant to have a performative function in the ritual context, we are also interested in their extra-contextual performance at present.

Now that the portraits are desacralized, secularized, by being excavated from the underworld, there are several possibilities for translating them. Visualizing them needs a constant shift from the figurative/visible to non-figurative/invisible dimension within two cultures, along past and present temporalities. The backward forward movement pluralizes the portraits, negotiating otherness by transgressing its fixation. They give room for the boundless experience of difference, and as such, their representation of death problematizes their historical meaning, and East/West historical location. A re-translation of the Fayoum portraits may re-evaluate the long held idea of the incompatibility of Egyptian and Greek/East and West.

With Walter Benjamin's postulation in *Reflections* that: "(e)very expression of human mental life can be understood as a kind of language" (314), divisions between verbal and non-verbal language have been eclipsed by major questions waged by the indeterminacy of the visible and invisible. This would apply to the translation of the hieroglyph and the portraits. The hieroglyph, the Egyptian script, as visual/verbal representation cannot be expressed in any fixed sequence of words, and the message it conveys, may only be reproduced via a process of enactment (Eric Iverson, *The Myth* 11). Although the portraits are considered a rupture in Egyptian iconography, they bear several characteristics suturing the abstract and the mimetic. I borrow the term 'suturing' from W.J.T. Mitchell who takes after Lacan's definition of the term as the "junction of the imaginary and the symbolic", the process by which the subject (the 'I') is constituted both as a division and a unity (Mitchell, *Picture Theory* 91 -2).

However, at the time the portraits were executed, the hieroglyph was in decline with the conquest of the last pharaohs. Henceforth, it became the secret language of priests, who bred false conceptions of its symbolic significance, rendering it obsolete, and stultifying its dynamic cultural role (Peter Daniels and William Bright, *The World's Writing* 73). Consequently, its reception in the Greek philosophic circles induced recurrent debates. Through Plotinus (204-270 CE) hieroglyphic studies were enmeshed with Neo-Platonism until the eighteenth century. (Iversen, *The Myth* 45; Bernal, *Black Athena* 163). Hieroglyphs were used by the Neo-Platonists to explain the allegorical nature of things, as they illustrated the relation between sign and meaning. This generated the notion of a symbolic system of writing expressing the abstract by means of concrete images or material objects. (Iversen, *The Myth* 49). Eventually, the predominance of alphabetical writing set a word image divide for several centuries which according to Mitchell's *Iconology: Image, Text and ideology,* reflects the Western spirit body divide.

At a time when sacerdotal fanaticism reduced the hieroglyph to the condition of 'logos', the portraits may have filled a gap the newly acquired alphabetical language has created (Daniels and Bright, *The World's* 73 - 8), by its linearity, by its effacement of the visual incorporated in the hieroglyph. The visual language of the Fayoum portraits supplements the hieroglyph by representing the visible and invisible. Therefore, understanding the portraits' language needs a translation founded on what Benjamin propounds as a "continuum of transformations" (*Reflections* 325) that can trace the "material community of things in their communication" (*Reflections* 330). A proper reading of the portraits requires their visualization as intermedial sites of accordance and discordance with the hieroglyph, before its decline. The hieroglyph proper bears semiotic elements, representing the world as an indivisible whole. Free from any message, it is the language of the secret knowledge, engaging the reader in reading what has never been written. Similarly, the portraits mediate a double sense: a material sense translatable into verbal language, and an immaterial, "a non-sensuous similarity", unfolding mental meanings (*Reflections* 335), incommunicable in verbal language.

The portraits are not confined to the static mimetic, but become a space for mobility. The viewer entering the site of the image engages in the dialectic of the inexpressible expressed, re-enacting 're-presentation', or generation of meaning in the image. In Jacques Derrida's terms it becomes "a supplementary return toward a greater naturalness" (*Of Grammatology* 239) whose muteness brings it closer to death. The hieroglyph and the portraits are events, flowing over the borders of their limits, anticipating the after-life, and awaiting an encounter with death, inscribed in images. The excavation of the solemn parade of portraits in the Fayoum district brings traces of the fable of eternal life inscribed in images of death. The mummies to which the portraits were attached were kept at home with their families for a generation or two until they passed out of memory. They were eventually sent to the cemetery when their memory ceased to have ties among the living. Still, the excavation and exhibition of the portraits in the present transforms them into a site of re-enactment that transgresses death as closure.

When buried, the portraits become mere figures of repetition, remains of the past. After being placed in the cemetery, the portraits are separated from their temporal environment, and their excavation augments their dislocation. As traces/images from the past, the act of seeing them in the present is inscribed in recollection. Thus the figure of repetition escapes sameness or identification to become a point of departure. In another context, Maurice Blanchot propounds that "seeing the image, presupposes a distance, a separation that becomes an encounter" (*The Space* 32). The portraits intrigue us urging us to draw back only to recollect the remains of the past, which have left their traces in the present. Such an act of recollection resists the museumification of the portraits that would bring them to a standstill, as a mere act of repetition. Conversely, their excavation becomes an event mobilizing a resistance to previous concepts of selfhood and history. The importance does not lie in the portraits or what they stand for but in their potential for translation.

The portraits represent those awaiting the unveiled secret and therefore abide in silence. They "touch the limits of truth", as Derrida would have it. The portraits become a "hieroglyph of a biography," an "allegory of the subject," for they hold a past life, an existence and at the moment of being painted they become "a fugitive crossing the line, all lines" (*Truth* 179). In that sense, they are present and absent, a paradox already embedded in the mummies to which the portraits were attached. The mimetic features in the portraits simulate the presence of an absent, and mark the growing importance to the function of absence. Absence raises the possibility for the portrait to become the sign of an unspoken word, "the silence of a voice" as Jean-Christophe Bailly suggests (*L'apostrophe Muette* 80). Ancient Egyptians gave less concern to memory since death was an anticipation, a sojourn to the future; it, therefore, brought peace and resignation. For the Greeks, death meant residing in the darkness of Hades. The portraits mediate both concepts, at the point where the Egyptian vision of death picks up the thread that – out of despair – has already slipped off the Greek's hands.

The portraits are sited an in-between location, intermediating Egypt and Greece, past and present, life and death. Their intermediality is represented in the *Three Figure Shroud* (Moscow, Pushkin Museum) portraying the deceased, dressed in a Greek white tunic, assuming a Greek posture, his weight on one foot signifying a forward step to the other world. While Osiris's mummy is represented in a frontal position, on the figure's left, Anubis receives him from a side posture, on the right. The three figures stand in a boat; that has landed at the threshold of a new world, marking the end/beginning of his journey. The shroud represents the Greek secular world within a sacred Egyptian context, a chain linking existent and non-existent/visible and invisible. As such it fosters the silent language of the hieroglyph often abstracting what is beyond representation. The Egyptian gods are never visible to the living, and therefore represented in animal form, a sign of their difference; the animal form represents the visible part of the invisible. The unity of separate entities in the realm of the existent in Egyptian belief involves a duality. Egypt is the two lands, or 'Upper and Lower Egypt', and in the Moscow shroud, previously referred to, Osiris wears the crowns of both sites. In Egyptian ontology the nonexistent/invisible is not simply transformed into the existent/visible, and thus erased; both coexist together. By analogy, death and life, sun and moon, day and night co-exist, an expanse which makes it possible for Egypt and Greece to co-exist as well. The deceased is participating in the death ritual, while the viewer who exchanges asymmetrical glances with the deceased is also at the frontier, where in the act of re-reading the shroud, the viewer translates the encounters between time present and past, thus stepping into the future, the time beyond.

The Moscow shroud, as well as the portraits, reveals something beyond representation, making it difficult for the beholder to translate. The portraits intermediate archaeological, aesthetic and symbolic demarcations. They are in this world, and in the other, joining both and participating in each. Their paradoxical nature needs a different expanse that transgresses surface viewing, in order to capture the evasive relation between visible and invisible. Only then can the viewer break away from fixed modes of seeing, determined by the principles of art history or archeology, in order to modify ways of visualizing conceptual and pictorial images. At the time of their execution, the portraits were not simply meant for aesthetic effects, but had a ritual performative function. At present, an appropriate reading needs to subvert customary modes of viewing by dislocating and relocating them to syncretise sacred and profane spheres. This requires a translation that synchronizes the figurative and the non-figurative, in order to raise possibilities for re-presentation or making present.

By suturing sacred and profane, past and present the reading of the portraits cannot remain speculative. They require an intermedial strategy that reads them as ritually effective *ikons* at their time, as well as inexhaustible images with possibilities of representation or making present, such that a postcolonial translation of their quadruple dimension becomes the enactment of an event in our present history. This calls for re-reading the significance of death as passage in Egyptian ontology. In Egyptian ontology life and death are not determinate opposites but ambivalent experiences: "You sleep that you may wake; you die that you may live" (*Pyramid Text* 1975b, Eric Hornung, *Conceptions* 155). This suggests the wholeness of living, as practice, opening up potentialities for transformations and the transfer of centrality. Upon such terms, the process of life becomes an enactment of change, an alternation of the centres of activity, rather than triumph and conquest in a game of power. Aging is not a loss but a retreat from activity for the rejuvenation of the life energy. By analogy, the sun god retreats from his rule, leaving the space to the moon god Toth. For order to be established there must be an exchange of roles. According to Hornung, a papyrus dating from the New Kingdom attributes to gods and kings a limited stretch of time, whereby the throne alternates from one to the other (*Conceptions* 155). Later, in the New Kingdom, not only kings become gods after death, but all men, as well, emphasizing role exchanges, flux, and death becoming a passage towards a future journey. Re-creation is not an elimination of the negative elements, but their incorporation within life.

The Fayoum portraits intermediate life and death by abstracting the life span captured at the instance of death, the time in-between, the present that articulates past and future, the threshold to the other life. As early as the Coffin Texts, the present is felt to be an evil time and a time full of promise, in Egyptian culture (Hornung, *Conceptions* 154), a concept embedded in the Moscow shroud, as well. The shroud represents Osiris - whose death is archetypal - mummified, sunken in the past. His son Horus takes over his role as the sun god signifying 'tomorrow', and is represented by a sun disc on Anubis's dog head. Anubis, the supervisor of mummification, who hosts the deceased in the world of death, holds also Ankh - the key for the future – in his hand. The sun's rebirth in the morning is renewal, a repeated renewal occasioned at the beginning of creation. The beginning of the world cannot have happened without the existence of death; birth corresponds to death. The sun's daily death and rebirth is a promise that the blessed will pass via death into a new life. By negotiating past and present, death and rebirth, repetition and renewal, the shroud becomes an intermediate site reconciling distant realms and changing temporalities.

The notion of renewal in time has been gradually altered in the Nineteenth Dynasty Turin Canon of Kings. Time became fixed, thus grounding the notion of eternal recurrence in history rather than myth. Since then, the god Toth, the archivist assigns a fixed life span to all creations (Hornung, *Conceptions* 155). This concept is represented in the Moscow shroud, where the deceased holds a scroll in his hand, probably an archive of his doings in his assigned life span, his passport to the other life. Life is not an unchanging endlessness, a repetition, but a renewal. Meanwhile, the written scroll of life shows that the deceased does not master historical knowledge, and is estranged to his own existence. He has lived not knowing what is to come, and by death his past life belongs to him no more. It becomes a writing traced in a scroll for others to decipher. In a related context, Derrida remarks that Toth mediates writing and death (*Dissemination* 96 - 107). In the after-life – the other life – that life will acquire another meaning, which remains invisible. Derrida's postulation generates the idea of death and writing involving process and stasis, the timed and timelessness.

Death occurs in time, but for rejuvenation one must step – somehow – outside time. The deceased represented in the portraits sees her/himself at a time beyond the temporal. The coexistence of the temporal and atemporal corresponds to the visible/invisible duality. The moment of death is the juncture at which the deceased will envision the other, when s/he takes the challenge to embark on the journey. The deceased's gaze of anticipation and challenge is the unspoken word that carries the viewer to the threshold of death as passage, rather than exclusion. It is the starting point for the viewer to transmute a static presentness long remaining identical with itself into an outward experience. Exchanging gazes with the portrait arouses an enigmatic experience that involves subjectivity and estrangement, rationalisation and divination. At the threshold, the deceased's anticipation arouses the viewer's enthusiasm, as s/he stands at an intermedial space raising a latent historical problem between self and other/East and West. Hence, the portraits become a virtual space where the ability to die becomes a "pre-requisite of history", in order to revive the memory of what has been long forgotten (Mario Perniola, *Enigmas* 71). The mutual exchanges between viewer and viewed in the world of the living and the dead, past and present translates into a transfer of centres of activity, and a dislocation of the fixed gaze. It is not only the deceased represented in the portrait who is undergoing transformation, but the viewer as well. A postcolonial translation of the past involves an acceptance of difference opening up a dialogue with the other, guiding the viewer along her/his venture across the threshold, and opening up to a local/global culture.

The deceased represented in portraits are in anticipation of the event of dying, of seeing the invisible. Their proximity to death is an anticipation of the future life. Meanwhile, these portraits are images painted during a past life time, and kept as an inscription helping the spirit to identify the deceased before embarking on the voyage to the future life. Being is doubled, as that which is known in life and the unknown, the-would-be in death. The unknown is part of the nonexistent, which may be considered as the unconscious or the unarticulated unlimited, the limitless expanse in space and time that envelops creation. The encounter with the other self, the nonexistent, means accepting the challenge of death. Most of the panels have 'Good Luck' written on them, as an amulet providing the moral support needed on such a hazardous voyage. Negation of existence is not only basic for rejuvenation, but for existence as a whole. Nonexistence is the complementary other of existence. Death alone reveals the ambivalence of the nonexistent.

The negative aspect of death is only experienced by the damned whose existence is extinguished after death. Negative elements in existence are a hostile challenge of constant duration. The damned, representing evil are expelled from existence but not eliminated; the existent cannot be totally released from imperfection. Transcendence is inconceivable, since it aims at total unity, an undifferentiated oneness, which in the Egyptian concept would be the condition of the world before creation. The creation of life means the birth of duality, a concept that accepts difference as complementarity. The starting point for the creator is generating the existence/nonexistence duality in order to diversify into a multiplicity. The Egyptian ontology is not founded on an abstract intellectual system, but generates concepts concurrent with everyday challenges. It is pragmatic in so far as it admits disorder, allows for reciprocal response between human and divine; the hieroglyph is the language that represents this system of thought. The silence of the hieroglyph in its incompleteness instigates an intermedial dialogue, an exchange with the other that re-starts as long as it is re-read.

Such an exchange is also present in the Moscow shroud. It represents the deceased and the gods on equal par, their partnership engaging them in the maintenance of their existence. As such life/death, man/god is dependent for a living order that opens a space for diversified creative acts. Likewise, the other portraits represent the deceased's equality with the gods, in terms of preserving their singularity. The unfixed gaze expresses their mutability, an anticipation of a-would-be role in the afterlife. Though the portraits, in some sense, keep up the hieroglyph being aniconic or non-figurative, by touching the spiritual, their gaze speaks of a consciousness that is singular. Singularity as an aspect of solitude is unknown in the Egyptian tradition founded on the idea that individuality springs from an originally united nature (Hornung, *Conceptions* 171). The one is incorporated in the All. At this point, the portraits deviate from the hieroglyph, by becoming more expressive of their *divine* individuality, and man's *singularity* becomes an attribute for his immortality. The portraits combine the moment of anticipation of the self as would be divine, with enlightened consciousness that already claims deity. Hence the portraits advance another challenge that contains the other by confirming its presence, not by transgressing it. As such, the portraits are considered an event in the visualization of the self with regard to deity and deification.

By preserving the self as 'singular', the portraits advance the concept of the 'chosen' that complies with the idea of 'transcendence', a later outcome of the cosmotheistic turn of the post-Amarna theology, that matured in Late Antiquity with related movements in Stoicism and Hermetism (Jan Assmann, "Mono-Pan"

142-44). The pre-Amarna traditional Egyptian religion does not provide texts defining absolute conceptual borders between high and low, true and false, believer and non-believer. Religious texts are concerned with ritual, what to recite not what to believe. They do not condemn other religions, nor censor deviations from accepted rites (Assmann, "Mono-Pan" 131). It was Akhanyati who founded a new religion in the middle of the 14th century based on the idea of divine unity, praising the sun as the source of light and time. However the concept of the One, according to Akhanyati had a physical meaning; it was a cosmological discovery.

This concept gradually grows into an open monotheism as revealed in the *Corpus Hermeticum*. It refers to the divine as that which has: "authority over the cosmos of mortals and unreasoning animals," and that he displayed "to lower nature the fair form of god" (*Hermetica* 1). God gives birth to a man like himself and wants "a person who is mindful to recognize himself" (*Hermetica* 5), in order to reach up to god. Hence god is transcendent, and to reach him one has to transcend "the material body" to rejoice the presence of the father," for "(t)his is the final good for those who have received knowledge to be made god" (*Hermetica,* 6). Death for the chosen is another form of transcendence, and the anticipation of death is reaching the edge of transcendence. The earlier notion of the duality of existence and reciprocal exchanges within vital elements becomes at this stage an aspiration for identification with supreme power. Life's challenge that has once been for difference and rejuvenation is transformed into a need for sameness and repetition.

The portrait belongs partly to the hieroglyphic, partly to the mimetic. The face portrayed may be a hieroglyph of an existence, not a narrative biography. Nevertheless, the mimetic aspect in the portraits incorporates a polarity that forms a rupture in the aesthetics of the hieroglyph. The portraits represent a self that remains the other: the other that sees the face witnesses the unknown side of the self. In that context, I quote Benjamin Andrew: "The seer is seen while he sees, and thus there is vision in things... painting you... I who am speaking, but also I am the one to whom one isat looks speaking, and someone about whom one is speaking ("Philosophy and Painting" 188). Both painter/viewer and painted/viewed see, but remain mute, incapable of voicing what the other misses. Their silence involves a paradox: The reversibility of what is visible with what sees may either lead to a polytheistic experience or a monotheistic vision. The portraits are polytheistic to the extent that they intermediate different traditions. Conversely, the mutual identification of seer and seen/self-and other lifts consciousness to a point of unification, transcendence, concurring with a monotheistic vision. Awareness of the other as identity is in a sense, a negation of difference. Added to that, seeing the invisible as the singular individual entails isolation. As against the hieroglyph – the sign designed for re-composition, for re-integration – the portrait is a rupture signaling the violent act of isolation. At this point, the portraits and the hieroglyph intersect.

The Egyptian masque or hieroglyph abstracted characteristic traits intermediating organic and inorganic in a combinatory system where places in life and the afterlife exchange and merge. This system has procured exchangeable locations enhancing the notion of co-existence. Conversely, the Fayoum portraits witness a dislocation in place causing anxiety. An Egyptian ontology that has previously integrated soul and body, high and low, life and death is threatened to become a threshold to a divisive world dislocating the body and prioritizing soul. "The body mortal" can only soar when "the senses are restrained" (*Hermetica*, 3). The portraits are material, and their very materiality reveals the soul, and the soul of the *great* gods is consciousness. The ongoing discourse that gradually overtakes restricts consciousness to a chosen few, whose mind can "contain so great a bounty... so the human mind shines with the light of consciousness... (and) never obstructed by darkness" (*Hermetica*, 77). The growth of such a divisive discourse places the One above the all, and breaks with an earlier Egyptian conception of the gods' nature as limited in time, space, power and knowledge, and concomitant with the more general phenomenon of their diversity. This tenet fostering the notion that one is part of all, while difference is an attribute of the same, does not confer on the gods absolute qualities or absolute existence. Nonetheless, the portraits and the hieroglyph overlap in so far as they merge visible and invisible. Self-consciousness in the portraits is assertive, but their fixed gaze seems to be interrupted by some furtive glances exchanged with the viewer. By partaking in two realms, they are conjunctive and disjunctive sacred and profane. They are the gods that are scared of becoming, and by being apprehensive of the future, the beyond, they remain subject to an unpredictable present.

In the earlier Egyptian tradition, the hieroglyph remains anonymous, and the mask seeks a state of anonymity through the abstraction of singular features. The hieroglyph and the mask have an existence not situated in a fixed time, but an open time of endless choices. The viewer recognizes her/himself in the hieroglyph as the actor, as s/he takes part in completing that which remains unfinished in existence. This does not imply the impersonality or the dissolution of the self, but reveals the inexhaustibility of primal matter – or the non-existent – the life challenge germinating creativity. In fact, the incompleteness of the hieroglyph is derived from that same notion of the incompleteness of existence that calls for remodeling. The renewal continuum is not a repetitive procedure leading to a status quo, but a revolutionary process of rebirth. The notion of death as finality pertains to the nonexistent; what exists is always in motion. (Hornung, *Conceptions* 182-3). The portrait has made use of the invisible language of the hieroglyph to gain access to the invisible parts of the self, only to the extent that it retains the subject silent. Unlike the hieroglyph, the interpretation of the portrait's silence may either induce the polarization or plurality of meanings.

In this respect, the Fayoum portraits represent the tempestuous collapse in an ambivalent present, or what Mario Perniola defines as the "Egyptian enigma", a condition resulting from a confusing encounter between past and future (*Enigmas* viii). It is the point where two apparently inverse visualizations of life and death hybridize while opening up to different horizons. The portraits are positioned at a point of intersection, where the singular self becomes a site of contradiction; difference may be a privilege conferred upon the chosen, but the privilege of singularity risks the mutability and the unpredictability of history. The portrait unveils a joy and fear of death; death may be anonymity or oblivion. The portraits' eyes shift between the ecstatic gaze and enthusiastic glances, such that the moment of death becomes the true moment of life. Eyes silently transfuse an existence in time, trodden paths leading to the final passage that should be traversed. There is an awareness that death is not a given but must be attained. If a decision regarding death must be taken, this entails a possibility of death, a resolution that needs consciousness. Such a resolution gives man the power of a maker, and death becomes a possibility for transcendence. Hence the avoidance of death as repetition is not by rebirth – as in the former Egyptian ontology - but by the singular/individual *power* to begin. Consciousness of singularity, transcendence and power concur with the apprehension of death, and with the awakening of responsibility (Derrida, *The Gift* 40 – 1). Responsibility comes along with the consciousness of difference, the necessity to draw borderlines in concession to the Law, a submission to an absolute transcendent. Whether this transcendent force is transfigured as epistemology or divination, its language will replace the hieroglyph by the logos, eventually leading to Babel.

In order to resume reading the other, a postcolonial translation should be re-invested with the strategies enabling it to read the invisible in language, hence reviving the hieroglyph. By operating a system of "transversal taxonomies" this may intermediate points of disjunction. Perniola opines that this system is capable of uncovering affinities between apparently discordant aspects, while tracing oppositions among seemingly similar aspects. The inventory involves a conceptual and organizational activity that throws new light on the past (*Enigmas* 73). The Egyptian Greek/East West binary may be reassessed in the light of a new reading of the past image, a conceptual reassessment that may in turn remodel our standardized organizational activity that has inherited an imperial construction of the world. A postcolonial translation of the portraits shows possibilities of change beyond closed societies or globalism. It develops modes of intermediality through translatability, an understanding of difference, and an ability to trace intermedial relations between the One and the All within a historical context. Such a dialogue may overpower the discourse of essentialism/modernity with its exclusive/imperial tendencies to naturalize power, a discourse that has effaced large sections of local/global history. The translation of the open-eyed portraits may transform them into intermediate channels, passages to sail through, away from the gaping abyss of the void, towards future possibilities.

ACKNOWLEDGEMENTS

This article is a modified version of "Translating Silence/Traversing Death", previously published in *Ephemera: critical dialogues on organization* 3 1 (2003): 7-25. I wish to thank Prof. Steffen Bohm, University of Essex, who was, then, editor for giving me permission to re-publish it.

REFERENCES

Anonymous. *Hermetica: The Greek Corpus Hermetica and the Latin Asclepius*. Trans. Brian Copenhaver. Cambridge: Cambridge UP., 1995

Benjamin, Andre. "Philosophy and Painting in the Age of their Experimentation: Contribution to an Idea of Postmodernity". *The Lyotard Reader*. Oxford: Basil Blackwell, 1989

Assmann, Jan. "Mono-, Pan and Cosmotheism: Thinking the 'One" in Egyptian Theology'. *Orient* XXXIII, 1998, 130 – 43.

Bailly, Jean-Christophe. *L'apostrophe Muette: Essai sur les portraits du Fayoum*. Paris : Hazan, 1997.

Benjamin, Walter. *Reflections*. Trans. Edmund Jepchoh. New York: Harcourt Brace Jovanovich, 1978.

Blanchot, Maurice. *The Space of Literature*. Trans. Ann Smock. Linclon: Nebraska UP., 1989.

Bernal, Martin. *Black Athena: The Afroasiatic Roots of Classical Civilization*. London: Free Association Books, 2 Vols, 1987.

Bhabha, Homi, ed. "DissemiNation: time, narrative and the margins of the modern nation." *Nation and Narration.* London: Routledge, 1990, 139-70.

Cardinal, Roger. *Figures of Reality: A Perspective on Poetic Imagination.* London: Croom Helm, 1981.

Colla, Eliott. *Conflicting Antiquities: Egyptology, Egyptomania, Egyptian Modernity.* Duke UP., 2008.

Daniels, Peter & William Bright, eds. *The World's Writing Systems.* New York: Oxford UP., 1996.

Derrida, Jacques. *Of Grammatology.* Trans. Gayatri Chakravorty Spivak. Baltimore: The Johns Hopkins UP., 1974.

Derrida, Jacques. *Dissemination.* Trans. Barbara Johnson. Chicago: Chicago UP., 1981.

Derrida, Jacques. "Sending: On Representation". *Social Research* Vol. 49. No.2 (1982): 294-326.

Derrida, Jacques. *Truth in Painting.* Trans. Geoff Bennington & Ian McLeod. Chicago: Chicago UP., 1987.

Derrida, Jacques. *The Gift of Death.* Trans. David Wills. Chicago : Chicago UP., 1995.

Doxiadis, Euphrosyne. *Portraits du Fayoum: Visages de l'Egypte ancienne.* Trans. Dennis Collins. Paris: Gallimard, 1995.

Fayoum Portraits Exhibition. Mohammad Mahmoud Said Museum, Giza, Cairo, 1999

Hall, Stuart. "Who Needs Identity." Stuart Hall & Paul Du Gay, eds. *Questions of Cultural Identity.* London: Sage Publications, 1996, 15-30.

Hornung, Erik. *Conceptions of God in Ancient Egypt: The One and the Many.* Trans. John Baines. New York: Cornell UP., 1982.

Iverson, Erik. *The Myth of Egypt and its Hieroglyphs.* New Jersey: Princeton UP., 1993.

Lefevere, Andre. "Composing the Other". Susan Bassnett & Harish Trivedi, eds. *Post-colonial Translation: Theory & Practice.* London: Routledge, 1999, 75-94.

Mitchell, W.J.T. *Iconology, Text, Ideology.* Chicago: Chicago UP., 1987.

Mitchell, W.J.T. *Picture Theory.* Chicago: Chicago UP., 1994.

Niranjana, Tejaswini.. *Siting Translation: History, Post-Structuralism, and the Colonial Context.* Berkley: California UP., 1998.

Reid, Donald M. *Whose Pharaohs? Archaeology, Museums, and Egyptian National Identity from Napoleon to World War I*. Berkeley: California UP., 2001.

Perniola, Mario. *Enigmas: The Egyptian Moment in History*. Trans. Christopher Woodall. London: Verso, 1995.

Viera, Else Ribiero Pires. "Liberating Calibans: readings of *Antropofagia* and Haroldo de Campos' Poetics of transcreation." Susan Bassnett & Harish Trivedi, eds. *Post-colonial Translation: Theory & Practice*. London: Routledge, 1999, 95-113.

ILLUSTRATIONS

Three Figure Shroud, c. 125 – 150. Tempera on linen, 185 X 125 cm. Moscow, Pushkin Museum, n 5749. Purchased by V. S. Golenishchev in Cairo, 1889; acquired 1911.
https://s-media-cache-ak0.pinimg.com/736x/d1/75/74/d17574f06 7af9fdb9ffa4e73bcb24ed5.jpg. Accessed 13/09/2015.

ABOUT THE AUTHOR

Marie-Thérèse Abdelmessih. Professor, English & Comparative Literature, Cairo University. Director, MA Program in Comparative Literary & Cultural Studies, Kuwait University, Faculty of Arts. Publications in Arabic: *Transcultural Reading of Literature* (1997; 2004); *Visual and Verbal Cultural Representations* (2001); *National Culture: Global or International Options* (2006; 2009). Member, Egyptian Writer's Union; Advisory Board of the Egyptian National Centre for Translation; International Advisory Board & Associate Editors, CLCWeb; International Prize of Arabic Fiction (IPAF); American Comparative Literature Association (ACLA); European Network of Comparative Literary Studies (ENCL); the International Comparative Literature Association (ICLA); British Comparative Literature Association (BCLA). Modern Language Association (MLA).

CHAPTER 10

Zenobia as Spectacle: Captive Queen in Arts and Literature

I-Chun Wang

Topics related to the Roman Empire are omnipresent in European imaginary at this time of national construction and imperial expansion, particularly in Britain. Retold in the form of medieval romances, history witnesses the Roman Empire expanding its frontiers, reaching a territory that included northern Europe, the Middle East, and North Africa (Nicolet 1991: 1). Revolts within the empire were frequent, and "no dates identifies the moment when Rome ceased to rule her subjects through coercion" (Ando 2000: 19).

Embodying the nation, attention was directed to representative females such as the beautiful queens from the pagan world: Bernice of Cilicia (28-?), Cleopatra of Egypt (69-30 BC), Mavia, Queen of the Saracens (364-378 C.E.), Boadicea of the Inceni, or Zenobia of Palmyra (240-c.275). Many of them were paradoxically portrayed as potentially subversive, dominating and destructive. Although she charmed the most powerful men at her time, the incomparable Cleopatra suffered oppression and miscegenation when Caesar launched his conquest over her land. Queen Mavia's experience as a slave placed her in the epicentre of the political and military encounters with the violent Roman troops and other invaders such as the Goths. The image of Berenice, the client queen of Roman province of Judaea, was often reduced to her love affair with the future emperor of Rome, Titus Flavius Vespasianus, who eventually left her. During the Jewish revolt, Berenice went to Jerusalem to request Gessius Florus, the procurator of the Judaea Province to spare the lives of Jews. Boadicea of the Incenic and Zenobia of Palmyra were both client queens of Rome, and warrior queens who thrust themselves in military campaigns against Rome when their subjects were ill treated and humiliated by imperial powers. If Boadicea represents a tribal queen fighting for the Roman oppressor in Britain, Zenobia is her counterpart in Palmyra, the oasis located on the route from the Syrian coast to Mesopotamia.

Unlike the Incenic warrior (see Wang 2012), Zenobia attracted less attention from artists, writers, biographers and playwrights. In this paper, I shall provide an outline of her importance in the arts and in European cultural memory. When Zenobia was captured she was brought to Aurelian in Rome fully decorated with beautiful clothes and in gold chains for display in a triumphant and spectacular parade (De Pauw 1998: 77).

This paper explores in particular the image of the chained queen, shamed and disciplined, as it has passed on the collective imaginary of Western visual arts and literature. The story of this warrior queen involves a space that Mary Louise Pratt has defined for colonial encounters, where "people geographically and historically separated come into contact with each other and establish ongoing relations, usually involving conditions of coercion, radical inequality and intractable conflict" (2008: 8). The discussion of the interactions between sculpture, pictoric and literary representations brings to light the symbolic meaning of the historical figure of Zenobia as a spectacle of power dynamics. Alexandra Warwick and Dani Cavallaro have argued that

> In the pre-seventeenth century, the exertion of power on the individual is accomplished through spectacle: An individual looks upon various displays of state power such as pageantry or royal processions, where the body of the monarch is its locus, and the surplus of that real body's power constitute the body politic. By contrast, the subject, who, often simultaneous, sees public exhibition of torture and execution along the pageantry...The state has the right to his or her body in terms of pain and violence. (2002: 72)

Septimia Zenobia was a queen of the Palmyrene Empire in Roman Syria, which was annexed to Rome around 64 BC when Pompey (Gnaeus Pompeius Magnus106-48 BC) conquered Levant. As an oasis in the Syrian desert, and at the crossroads between East, West and Africa, Palmyra was enriched by various cultures. Its key-position on the route of Silk Road and traffic lines to Damascus, Babylonia, linking Persia, India and China, allowed the city to develop into a trade and mercantile centre. Emperor Hadrian visited the city in 129 AD and annexed it to Rome, granting it a free status. Eventually, Palmyra became a part of the Roman Province of Syria.

When her husband, King Septimius Odaenathus, was assassinated in 267, Zenobia was left as a regent mother to the one-year-old heir. Zenobia claimed to be a descendant of Dido, Queen of Carthage, and the Ptolemaic Greek Queen Cleopatra VII of Egypt. Though there is no concrete evidence of this, she had knowledge of the ancient Egyptian language and showed a predisposition towards Egyptian culture. Under her leadership her realm expanded and she conquered Egypt, then under Roman's rule. In 269, she declared her land independent of

Rome (Kidder 2010:76). The Roman emperor Aurelian (Lucius Domitius Aurelianus 214-215) sent new legions to oppose Zenobia's forces (Pollard 2000: 24-8). She led her revolt against Rome for five years and was finally captured by Aurelian in 274, finishing up her reign as Queen of Egypt and Palmyra (Southern 2009: 115-21).

Significant discussions on Zenobia include Richard Stoneman's historical exploration on *Palmyra and Its Empire*, Jennifer Tobin's historical lecture series *The Grandeur that was Rome: the Roman Art and Archeology*, and Donelle Ruwe's "Zenobia, Queen of Palmyra," a comparative study on 18th-century pedagogical novels. Zenobia's story can be found in Boccaccio, Chaucer, Christen de Pizan, Juan Luis Vives, Ben Jonson, Thomas Heywood (Wayne 1987: 50). Giovanni Boccaccio (1313-1375), in *On Famous Women,* expressed his idea that women with masculine qualities were valuable. Literary critics believe that a large portion of Geoffrey Chaucer's (1343-1400) the "Monk's Tale," which may have been written before the rest of the *Canterbury Tales*, likely dated for a first-edition 1370s of the text, was published shortly after Chaucer returned from a trip to Italy where he was exposed to Boccaccio's *Concerning the Falls of Illustrious Men* and *Decameron*. The book is a collection of seventeen short stories or exempla with the tragic endings of historical figures such as Zenobia. Her matchless beauty, military skills and perseverance in confronting the powerful Roman ruler are praised in the tale: "with gilte chaines on her neck hanging / crowned she was, after her degree, and full of pierrie charged her clothing" (Chaucer 1860: 89).

> Aurelian, when that the governance
> Of Rome came into his handes tway,
> He shope upon this queen to do vengeance; prepared
> And with his legions he took his way
> Toward Zenobie, and, shortly for to say,
> He made her flee, and at the last her hent, took
> And fetter'd her, and eke her children tway,
> And won the land, and home to Rome he went.
> ("Prologue, The Monk's Tale" 88)

Keiko Hamaguchi draws attention to Zenobia's description in Chaucer, her attire representing a pagan woman of the Orient, allied with other pagan figures such as Delilah, Deianira and Judith (Hamaguchi 2005: 184). However, following the traditions of representing female virtues, both Christine de Pizan (1364-1430) in

Book of the City of Ladies, and Ben Jonson (1572-1637) in *Masque of Queens* stressed that Zenobia embodied the qualities of good and virtuous females.

In his canonical text, *The History of the Decline and Fall of the Roman Empire* (1879), Edward Gibbon describes Zenobia sumptuously dressed in imperial purple,

> Confined by fetters of gold; a slave supported the gold chain which encircled her neck, and she almost fainted under the intolerable weight of jewels. She preceded on foot the magnificent chariot, in which she once hoped to enter the gates of Rome. It was followed by two other chariots, still more sumptuous, of Odenathus and of the Persian monarch. The triumphal car of Aurelian (it had formerly been used by a Gothic king) was drawn, on this memorable occasion, either by four stags or by four elephants. The most illustrious of the senate, the people, and the army closed the solemn procession. Unfeigned joy, wonder, and gratitude, swelled the acclamations of the multitude. (Gibbon 1879: 359)

The Roman Empire is notorious for its tradition to lavishly exercise public spectacular entertainments, including animal displays, gladiatorial shows, public executions, circuses, and pompous processions with hundreds of captives, defeated generals, the royal families of the conquered kings, and wagonloads of plundered treasures. The displays functioned to stage publicly the powers of the empire. The emperors were also part of the show, which served their self-interests and popularity (Beacham 1999: 5-20). Richard Beacham names Pompey as one of the most acclaimed and triumphant conquerors among the Roman emperors. According to this scholar, Pompey celebrated his forty-fifth birthday with a spectacle that lasted two days, with "hundreds of captives representing the fourteenth nations and the nine hundred cities that Pompey had defeated" (Beacham 1999: 50). Titus also displayed seven hundred captives from the Jewish war, celebrating the glory of his father Vespasian and himself (Joshel 2010: 67-8). Plutarch recorded the Roman citizens who put on their best gowns and the streets that were decorated with flowers at the triumph of Aemilius Paulus where displayed armours, treasures, and four hundred gold crowns sent from cities to honour him (Joshel 2010: 278). In the case of Aurelian, the magnificent triumph included twenty elephants, four royal tigers, rare animals, followed by ambassadors, sixteen hundred gladiators, a long train of captives and gifts from different parts of the world as well (Gibbon 1879: 359). Besides its glorious achievements in the arts and in literature, a part of the core of Roman culture rested on the values of a warrior society that showed courage on the battlefield, and impressed its rivals with professionally disciplined troops.

Exemplified in the Roman spectacle, the gaze coveys the separation between observers and observed within a dynamics of power relations. For Jacques Lacan, the observed subject "loses a degree of autonomy upon realizing that he or she is a visible object" (1988: 127). In post-colonial discourse, gazing at the colonial subjects can connote a sense of control, with the gazer also dominating discourse ability to judge. Public denigration, according to Foucault (1975, 11) serves to reinforce the power of the punisher, greater if the captive is admired for her nobility and fortitude. According to Ida Ostenberg, the parade in Rome was always an ostentatious performance where "by rights of war, Rome took up the peoples and places that were led and carried before the triumphator as possessions of the *res public* and offerings to gods" (Ostenberg 2009: 272-4). This culture of spectacle would confirm the Romans as victors, debase the identity of the defeated, and at the same time legitimate their military power. Harriet I. Flower also contends that this spectacle was "one of the most typical features of life in the city of Rome" and served as performance of the achievements for the political class (Flower 2004: 323). The captive kings and queens under the gaze of the Roman citizens not only demonstrated Rome's military prowess but also reinforced the subjugation of the foreign others. This subjugation is apparent in many of the visual representations of Zenobia, as well as in some of the historical records and literary works.

An early painting by Nicholas Colombel (1664-1717) depicted Zenobia with a heavy black chain on her wrists and a dark shroud over her head, led by a Roman soldier and surrounded by many others.

Nicholas Colombel (1664-1717) oil on canvas
http://commons.wikimedia.org/wiki/File:Colombel_-
_Zenobia,_Queen_of_Palmyra.jpg

Edward Gibbon's description of Zenobia, using Aurelian' voice, suggests that the emperor admired her beauty, bravery and eloquence: "The Roman people speak with contempt of the war which I am waging against a woman. They are ignorant both of the character and of the power of Zenobia. [...] Yet still I trust in the protecting deities of Rome, who have hitherto been favourable to all my undertakings" (Gibbon Vol. 2, 24). Yet the humiliation spectacle is used as punishment for this rebel queen:

> Her fortitude, however, did not last. The soldiers, with angry clamour, demanded her immediate execution, and the unhappy queen, losing for the first time the courage which had so long sustained her, gave way to terror, and declared that her resistance was not due to herself, but had arisen from the counsels of Longinus and her other advisers. It was the one base act in the woman's life. She had purchased a brief period of existence at the expense of honour and fame. Aurelian, a fierce soldier, to whom the learning of Longinus made no appeal, at once ordered his execution. The scholar died like a philosopher. (Gibbon 1879: 357)

Gibbon seems to be critical here with the figure of Zenobia. Her secretary and chief counsellor, a prominent Roman philosopher and rhetorician Cassius Longinus (c. 213- 273 AD), may have encouraged Zenobia to regain independence from the Roman rule. After falling into the hands of the Romans, Cassius Longinus was executed and Zenobia was imprisoned.

The painting by the Venetian Giovanni Battista Tiepolo (1696-1770), "Zenobia in the Triumph of Aurelius", highlighted the conqueror standing in his chariot and chained Zenobia walking in front with downcast eyes. In a contemporary production, "Zenobia in the Triumph of Aurelius" (in *The Story of the Greatest Nations* Vol. III, Rome, Ellis 1901: 438), the focus is set on the rich decorations and chains on her neck and body. The flowers on the street form a sharp contrast between the supposedly celebrating atmosphere and Zenobia's emotionless face. Behind her are the shadows of Roman soldiers on horses, implying Zenobia's status as a captive to be enslaved by tyrannical power of Rome.

190 The Ekphrastic Turn

"The Triumph of Marcus Aurelius" (AD 121-180) - Galleria Sabauda, Turin, Italy -
Tiepolo, Giandomenico (Giovanni Domenico) (1727-1804)
Visual Art Encyclopaedia Visual Art Encyclopaedia http://www.wikiart.org/en/giovanni-battista-tiepolo#supersized-rococo-241020/

Zenobia in the Triumph of Aurelius
Collected by Historical Heritage: http://www.heritage-history.com/books/horne/rome/zpage438.gif

In his Gibbon description of the spectacle of the rebel queen through the streets Rome:

> Unfeigned joy, wonder and gratitude swelled the acclamations of the multitude [...] in the treatment of his unfortunate rivals, Aurelian might indulge his pride, he behaved towards them with a generous clemency which was seldom exercised by the ancient conquerors. Princes who, without success, had defended their throne or freedom were frequently strangled in prison, as soon as the triumphal pomp ascended the capital. These usurpers, whom their defeat had convicted of the crime of treason, were permitted to spend their lives in affluence and honourable repose. (Gibbons 1879: 359)

In "Queen Zenobia Addressing Her Soldiers" (1725-1730) also by Tiepolo, Zenobia, wearing a helmet with white plums and a red colourful mantle and armour in the upper body, has a commanding manner that shows her as a leader to her soldiers and comrades.

Giovanni Battista Tiepolo, "Queen Zenobia Addressing Her Soldiers", 1725/1730, oil on canvas,
National Gallery of Art, Washington D.C, Samuel H. Kress Collection

Another two pictures by Tiepolo, "Queen Zenobia before Emperor Aurelianus," represents the queen in woman's attire, grasped by a stout Roman soldier. She stands before the young emperor with a young boy clinging to her clothes. On the right side of this Rococo history painting, a dead or wounded body lying on the ground while several women captives are standing behind.

"Queen Zenobia before Emperor Aurelianus"- Galleria Sabauda, Turin, Italy - Tiepolo, Giandomenico (Giovanni Domenico) (1727-1804)
Visual Art Encyclopaedia http://www.wikipaintings.org/en/giovanni-battista-tiepolo/

Gibbons wrote that:

> To Zenobia the victor behaved with a generous clemency such as the conquering emperors of Rome rarely indulged in. He presented her with an elegant villa at Tibur, or Tivoli, about twenty miles from the imperial city; and here, surrounded by luxury, she who had played so imperial a role in history sank into the humbler state of a Roman matron. Her daughters married into noble families, and the descendants of the once Queen of the East were still known in Rome in the fifth century of the Christian era. (359)

In contrast to Gibbon, Irish writer Adelaide O'Keefe (1776-1865) was interested in the interaction between Rome and its client kingdoms. Daughter of John O'Keefe (1747-1833), a famous Irish actor and playwright of farces and musical dramas, she adapted the legendary story into a first-person narrative, telling how Zenobia constructs her kingdom, extending her territory to Egypt, from Euphrates to the Proontis, and from Mount Taurus to the southern limits of Ethiopia. In a soft tone, the author reveals Zenobia's relationship with her cultural tradition, the tension before the final battle, the fear of her people and her motherly feeling towards her soldiers. The paragraphs that drew the readers' tears include

Zenobia's speech and final hours at her cell when betrayed by Aurelian. The emperor had promised to preserve the people of her land, but "Palmyra was taken, sacked and all the inhabitants of both sexes, of every rank and age, were put to death, and the buildings set on fire" (O'Keefe 1814: 302). Furthermore, O'Keefe condemns the ways that the Romans treated their enemies, and the fact that Aurelian could not restrain his troops from violence because of the cultural discrepancies between the East and the West. Even earlier in this historical narrative, Zenobia swears that "if the Roman eagle attacks the Syrian palm, heaven will fight in the cause of innocence, and Aurelian learn that the eastern empire yields not to the western" (O'Keefe 1814: 16). O'Keefe also pays a lot of attention to the psychological factors that drag the city-state down by describing how inhabitants reacted when they heard Aurelian's troops had conquered Phrygia, Galatia, Cappadocia, marching toward Antioch she stands in front of her people swearing that she would never give Palmyra to Rome. Through the voice of the Roman general Marcellus, the Irish writer conveys the wish of the imperial troops: "The loss the freedom; she must live to adorn the triumph of Aurelian" (O'Keefe 1814: 270), and in the last paragraphs of the narrative, the witness describes Zenobia's tragic ending: "Zenobia, her feet and hands loaded with golden chains...mounted in the same chariot, built by Firmius to carry her triumphantly through Rome, was led in triumph by her conqueror, who well knew she never had willingly done thus had she but known the events that had taken place since her departure from Asia" (O'Keefe 1814: 297) O'Keefe's Zenobia lives the rest of her life in a distant room of a mansion in imperial room, being deprived of freedom and energy: with her limbs still confined by chains, weighty robes, massive with gold and invaluable jewels, bracelets, ornaments, leaving her reclined upon a couch, leaving behind her Palmyra, which "now remains stupendous and magnificent ruins" (O'Keefe 1814: 303).

William Ware's (1792-1853) *Zenobia, or the Fall of Palmyra* hit a record of publications in 1834, with eight different editions. It is categorized as a historical romance in epistolary form, and the letters describe the visit of Lucius Manlus Piso to Palmyra in a series of letters sent to Marcus Curtius. William Ware's description of the procession of Aurelian's triumph is reported through the eyes of a friendly Piso. Once more, the rich spectacle and display of Romans' power begin with a long train of elephants clothed in gold and scarlet, and on whose back sit natives from Asia and Africa in the rich costumes of their countries. Lions, tigers, leopards and animals from every part of the world, more than two thousand gladiators, gilded wagons bearing treasures of art, rich clothes, embroideries, and gold sculptures and jewellery, an innumerable train of captives with downcast eyes, and among them women warriors from the shores of Danube

(1838: 278). However, in this fictionalized narrative, Piso looks into the response from the multitude and describes Zenobia as one of the elements in the spectacle: "She is on foot, and exposed to the rude gaze of the Roman populace...toiling beneath of rays of a hot sun and the weight of jewels and chains of gold on her neck and arms which were borne up by attendant slaves" (1838: 279). Touched by Zenobia's grief, Piso describes Zenobia's vacant gaze fixed on the ground. Having known Zenobia in his visits to Palmyra, Piso empathizes with the suffering of the captive queen.

Most historians and biographers drew information on Zenobia's story from Gibbon and Ware. Some, like William Wright claimed that "In all the annals of perverted patriotism and abused power there is no more brutal spectacle than the triumph of great and imperial Rome over that humbled and helpless Queen." (1895: 167) Others, like Frank Boott Goodrich in *Women of Beauty and Heroism* (1858), described Zenobia as adopting "an inconstant and ambiguous policy." She sought to rule the Greeks by love, the barbarians by fear...She exacted from her subjects that species of worship which the Persians paid to the successors of Cyrus" and toleration was used for all cults (1858: 62). For Goodrich, Aurelian was smart in dealing with Zenobia and offered advantageous surrender to her and her subjects (Goodrich 1858: 69).

"Zenobia's Last Look upon Palmyra" by Herbert Gustave Schmalz (1858-1935), a member of the Pre-Raphaelites, is one of the popular paintings on Zenobia. As an artist particularly interested in representing Oriental cities and figures, Schmalz represents his canvas as a mixture of grey, dark blue and purple, with Zenobia wearing a headdress, waist belt and chains on both wrists, clothed by a dark mantle and looking into the distance at the blurred buildings. Her "noble melancholy suffuses her brow as the sun goes down behind the wheeling desert birds" and a Roman soldier in the lower part of this painting seems to be ready to lead her away (Stoneman 1994: 200).

Zenobia as Spectacle

Herbert Gustave Schmalz, "Zenobia's Last Look upon Palmyra" (1988) Art Gallery of South Australia, Adelaide., http://en.wikipedia.org/wiki/File:Herbert_Schmalz-Zenobia.jpg

"Zenobia Captive" (1878) oil on canvas. Copyright Peter Nahum Ltd, London
https://commons.wikimedia.org/wiki/File:Sir_Edward_Poynter,_Zenobia_Captive_1878.jpg

A contemporary of Schmalz, Sir Edward John Poynter (1836-1919), painted "Zenobia Captive" (1878). Poynter was president of the Royal Academy and director of the National Gallery. He was fascinated by classical and legendary motifs and the representation of the East and the Near East (See Raymond

Schwab, *The Oriental Renaissance: Europe's Rediscovery of India and the East, 1680–1880*, 33). In this painting, the captive queen is represented as a beautiful woman standing by the side of the window wearing a huge Oriental headdress decorated with gold and turquoise; pearl and gold necklaces are seen on her neck and wrists while her body was exuberantly decorated with jewels and laden with encircling chains.

A rare poem by Myron Mason (see *Graham's Illustrated Magazine of Literature, Romance, Art, and Fashion* 1848: 185-90) is again focused on the topic of the Aurelian's triumph and the shame brought to Zenobia's land.

> 'T was holiday in Rome
> Her sevenfold hills were trembling with the tread of multitudes
> Who thronged her streets...
> The sire, the son, the matron and the maid,
> Joined in bestowing on their emperor
> The joyous benedictions of the state.
> Alas! About the day's magnificence
> Was spread a web of shame... (1848: 185)

Mason then points out the victory and triumph constructed by Emperor Aurelian is actually stained with cowardice and cruelty, while his dazzling fame is tarnished by insult to the captive queen, forced to bow to Rome. Mason's tyrant/oppressor is described as an invisible power with "wide-extended hands" to "plunder the prostate nations," "under the golden eagles of the empire" (185). In shifting images from the battlefield to the process of triumph, Mason depicts the spectacle of music, banners, and trumpets, as well as the immense spoils and the victims of victory, exposing the tyranny imposed by the Romans.

Many of the visual artworks and historical writings described present the captive queen Zenobia in her dignified surrender to the empire. Her bodily rhetoric reveals a discourse of pain in which as sovereign and warrior she masters her emotions: "She could not weep; the evil was too great for tears... there being no other way in which to give vent to the grief that wrung her soul in every feeling and affection" (Ware 1838: 170). The theme of Zenobia in chains, narrated or represented by literary and artistic works, reveals punishment and degradation as part of the disciplining system in the Roman Empire. However, Zenobia was freed by the emperor, who granted her an elegant villa in Tibur (modern Tivoli, Italy) where she dedicated herself to pursuing the philosophical interests she had learnt from her preceptor Cassius Longinus.

Unlike other Zenobia figures, surrounded by people gazing at her, Harriet Hosmer's (1830-1908) marble sculpture stands alone, embodying the queen's majesty, dignity and stoicism. Hosmer was chiefly drawn to female characters whose stories could be viewed as allegories for her strongly held feminist beliefs. Hosmer's Zenobia was based on William Ware's romance described above (see Waller 1983: 22). While most male writers showed Zenobia "decked with jewels and golden chains" so that "courageous though she was, halted very frequently, saying that she could not endure the weight of her gems" (Waller 1983: 23), Hosmer diminishes the chains to wrist manacles and reduces all ornaments to only those necessary, not only to convey her royalty but also avoid traditional portrayal of women as objectified jewellery. The Queen recreated by Hosmer does not appear frustrated but clutches her chains, embodying strength and authority instead of victimhood.

Zenobia in Chains by Harriet Hosmer, https://goo.gl/8qmIsN
https://commons.wikimedia.org/wiki/File:Zenobia_SLAM_4067.jpg#/media/File:Zenobia_SLAM_4067.jpg; http://www.victorianweb.org/sculpture/nudes/moore3.html

This paper has focused on different depictions of queen Zenobia of Palmyra both in the visual arts and in historical and fictionalized accounts. It has shown how the literary and the iconographic canons are defined together, and how works by writers and visual artists are made into intermedial artefacts of recollection, imitation and emulation that encouraged audience participation.

Zenobia was one of the most popular queens in Arabian-speaking countries. Egyptian poet Ahmad Zaki Abû Shâdy (1892-1955) wrote Al-Zabbâ or Zenobia, Queen of T*admor*, a historical operetta in four acts. Salim al-Bustani (1846-1884) and Jurji Zaydan (1861-1914) published respectively two historical novels entitled *Zanûbyâ Malikat Tadmur* (1871) and *Zenobia*. According to Elin Sand (2001) Zenobia's story reflects a trend of searching for an autonomous Syrian identity in the Arabian tradition. But this is another story.

REFERENCES

Ando, Clifford. Imperial Ideology and Provincial Loyalty in the Roman Empire. Berkeley: U of California P, 2000.

Beacham, Richard C. Spectacle Entertainments of Early Imperial Rome. New Haven: Yale UP, 1999.

Bolzoni, Lina The Gallery of Memory: Literary and Iconographic Models in the Age of the Printing Press. Trans. Jeremy Parzen. Toronto: U of Toronto P, 2001.

Chaucer, Geoffrey. The Canterbury Tales. With an Introduction by George Gilfillan. Edinburgh: Battantane, 1860.

Chouein, Youssef M. Arab Historiography and Nation State. London: Routledge, 2003.

De Pauw, Linda Grant. Battle Cries and Lullabies: Women in War from Prehistory to the Present. Norman: U of Oklahoma P, 1998.

Ellis, Edward S. and Charles Horne. The Story of the Greatest Nations. Volume III (Rome). New York: Francis R. Niglutsch, 1901

Flower, Harriet I. The Cambridge Companion to the Roman Republic. Cambridge: Cambridge UP, 2004.

Foucault, Michel. Discipline and Punish. New York: Penguin, 1975.

Gibbon, Edward. The History of the Decline and Fall of the Roman Empire. Vol. 1. New York: Harper, 1879.

Goodrich, Frank Boott. Women of Beauty and Heroism: From Semiramis to Eugenie, a Portrait Gallery. New York: Derby and Jackson, 1858.

Joshel, Sandra. Slavery in the Roman World. Cambridge: Cambridge UP, 2010.

Hamaguchi, Keiko. "Transgressing the Borderline of Gender: Zenobia in the Monk's Tale." The Chaucer Review 40.2 (2005): 183-205.

Kidder, David S, and Noah D. Oppenheim. The Intellectual Devotional Biographies. New York: Rodale, 2010.

Lacan, Jacques. Seminar One: Freud's Papers On Technique. Cambridge: Cambridge UP, 1988.

Mason, Myron L. "Zenobia." Graham's Illustrated Magazine of Literature, Romance, Art, and Fashion. 33 (1848): 185-90.
Nicolet, Claude. Space, Geography, and Politics in the Early Roman Empire. Ann Arbor: U of Michigan P, 1991.
Ostenberg, Ida. Staging the World: Spoils, Captives and Representation in the Roman Triumphal Procession. Oxford: Oxford UP, 2009.
O'Keefe, Adelaide. Zenobia, Queen of Palmyra: A Narrative, Founded on History. London: Rivington, 1814.
Plutarchus, Lucius Mestrius. Plutarch's Lives. Trans. John Dryden. Vol. 2. London: J. and R. Tonson, 1911.
Pollard, Nigel. Soldiers, Cities and Civilians in Roman Syria. Ann Arbor: U of Michigan P, 2000.
Pratt, Mary Louise. Imperial Eyes: Travel Writing and Transculturation. New York: Routledge, 2008.
Sand, Elin. Woman Ruler. Lincoln, NE: iUniverse, 2001.
Schwab, Raymond. The Oriental Renaissance: Europe's Rediscovery of India and the East, 1680-1880. Columbia: Columbia UP, 1987.
Southern, Pat. Empress Zenobia: Palmyra's Rebel Queen. New York: Continuun, 2009.
Stoneman, Richard. Palmyra and Its Empire: Zenobia's Revolt Against Rome. Ann Arbor: U of Michigan P, 1994.
Waller, Susan. "The Artist, the Writer, and the Queen: Hosmer, Jameson, and Zenobia." Woman's Art Journal 4.1 (1983): 21-28.
Wang, I-Chun. "The Semiosis of Imperialism: Boadicea or the 17th-Century Iconography of a Barbarous Queen." Cultura: International Journal of Philosophy of Culture and Axiology 9(2)/2012: 227–236
Ware, William. Zenobia, or the Fall of Palmyra. 9th Edition. Vol. 1. New York and Boston: Crosby, 1838.
Warwick, Alexandra and Dani Cavallaro. Fashioning the Frame: Boundaries, Dress and the Body. New York: I.B. Tauris, 2002.
Wayne, Valerie. "Zenobia in Medieval and Renaissance Literature." Ambiguous Realities: Women in the Middle Ages and Renaissance. Eds. Carole Levine and Jaenie Watson. Detroit: Wayne State UP, 1987. 48-65.
Wright, William. An Account of Palmyra and Zenobia with Travels and Adventures in Bashan and the Desert. London: Thomas Nelson, 1895.

ABOUT THE AUTHOR

I-Chun Wang is Chair Professor of English at the Center for Languages and Culture and Dean of the College of Humanities and Social Sciences at Kaohsiung Medical University. Since 2014, she holds a joint appointment at National Sun Yat-sen University where she was formerly Dean of College of Liberal Arts and taught English Renaissance drama and from 2006 through 2013 directed the Center for the Humanities. Her research interests include comparative literature, and English Renaissance drama. She edited and co-edited books and special issues for *Canadian Review of Comparative Literature*, *CLCWEB*, and *Cultura*. Her publications have appeared in *Journal of Comparative Literature and Aesthetics*, *East Asian Cultural and Historical Perspectives*, *and Identity Politics, Cityscapes: World Cities and Their Cultural Industries* ect. Her full-length studies include *Disciplining Women: the Punishment of Female Transgressors in English Renaissance Drama* (1997) and *Empire and Ethnicity: Empire and Ethnic Imagination in Early Modern English Drama* (2011).

CHAPTER 11

Beijing Imaginations: Exploring the A/Effects of Tourist City Photographs

Verena Laschinger

THE TRAJECTORY OF CONSCIOUSNESS[1]

In the following I am going to reflect upon selected photographs of Beijing taken on two trips to the Chinese capital in 2010 and 2011. Beginning with the first shot taken upon arrival, where I knew practically nothing about the place, I am going to offer interpretations of Beijing tourist photographs, each of which results from "a complex, ongoing, spontaneous interaction of observation, understanding, imagination, and intention" (Shore 2007: 132). I do not attempt to solve the mystery of each photographic decision (which is impossible) nor do I aim to retrace the exact route of my journey through the city. Taking one or two digital images at a time, I will summarize my reflections in accompanying texts that function both as captions and critical interpretations on what it means to have taken tourist photographs in Beijing. I hereby follow Walter Benjamin who, predicting that captions would become essential components of images, demands the photographer read her own work (Benjamin 1980: 215). By describing perception and representation in my photographs, I recount a trajectory of consciousness about the Chinese metropolis, which goes from physically experiencing Beijing, to responding to this experience by photographing the urban environment, to finally re-viewing the material within the discursive frames of photography theory and Chinese socio-politics. Using aspects of phenomenological philosophy by Gaston Bachelard and Mark Johnson as a conceptual framework, I aim to relay my ruminations by way of Yi-Fu Tuan's narrative-descriptive procedure, which to some might seem "less analytically

---

[1] I wish to thank Vivian Blaxell for suggesting this phrase and for her editorial remarks on earlier versions of this text. I am also grateful to William A. Callahan for taking me on a tour through Beijing, to Beate Hampe for alerting me to the work of Mark Johnson, to Ilka Saal, whose many forms of support included mentioning Jill Bennett's work, and to Charlton Payne for his thoughtful remarks and editorial diligence.

penetrating," but really "has the merit of being more inclusive and faithful to the complexities of actual experience" (Tuan 1991: 695). As an exercise in self-reflection, the paper will be consciously personal in tone.

While it is true that a similar self-reflexive investigation of tourist photography's a/effective relationship with place could have taken another city as its example, my choice of Beijing is not accidental. And it is my argument that none of the Beijing photographs is either. As the following image-texts show, each of my tourist photographs of Beijing is the result of a complex set of a/effective responses to the specificities of an urban space and culture, which were at the time unfamiliar to me. Trying to explore some of the manual actions as well as the mental steps on the way to a more comprehensive take of this unknown terrain reveals not only how my Beijing photographs are both the specific products of actions and reflections as well as productive of actions and reflections. More importantly this trajectory of consciousness makes clear how the communicative properties of city photographs not only make accessible, but in fact create and modify the urban environment, how the pictures repeat conventions, only to suddenly offer genuinely personal views of Beijing, how they generate a perpetual exchange between the photographer, the viewer and their respective environments both current and represented. The interest here is on the creative faculties of tourist city photography, the most widely practiced of all amateur photographic genres, as cultural practice, and hence assessing photographic quality is not the issue here.[2] Instead, I want to make a case for the "dynamic, self-modifying process" of picture making (and viewing), which American photographer Steven Shore calls a "feedback loop" (Shore 2007: 132). Assuming the twin role as photographer and (re-)viewer, I will reflect upon the affective resonances the Beijing snapshots spin off by retracing my experience of the city while taking these pictures. Bound to the photographer's physical experience of place, they can make the observer's affective impulses ricochet, too.

As research on the body as primary locus of imagination shows, one could claim that the city photographer *feels* her environment before she processes and

---

[2] In the heated debate about photography's relevance as an independent art form, which preoccupied artists and critics during the first half of the twentieth century, Clement Greenberg highlighted the literariness of photographs. In "Four Photographers" he asserts that "photography is literary art before it is anything else" (Greenberg 1964: 183). While today a photograph's literariness is an agreed upon fact, it is less taken as an indicator of its artistic quality, encoding social distinction in an aesthetic alphabet, but more as a sign of photography's potential to create social cohesion. Especially amateur photography has become the topic of much research due to the fact that it is widely practiced across race, class, and gender boundaries.

conceptualizes it. Likewise, the observer's affective responses to the place represented in the picture "are not born of emotional identification or sympathy", but one could argue that they "emerge from a direct engagement with sensation as it is registered in the work" (Bennett 2005:7). While the observer's affective responses are potentially unrestricted, open to all sorts of creative interpretation, they are not random, but can be triggered by the spatial arrangement represented by the picture, which itself is a result of the photographer's response to the encountered spatiality, that is to say, to embodied experience of place. Whatever meaning an observing third party draws from a city snapshot is simultaneously imbued with her memories of other places, and guided by the photographer's embodied experience of this place. In both instances cognition follows affect. Given that such affective responses are perfectly able to "work as a catalyst for critical inquiry" (Deleuze cit. in Bennett 2005: 7), the principal concern of this case study is thus to explore and exemplify how Beijing as a place triggers this process both in general and in very specific ways, how narration follows affection, how meaning in tourist city photography is ultimately the effect of affects.

Already in his seminal phenomenological study *The Poetics of Space,* Bachelard explained how in young children the experience of primal architectural space frames the perception of any other space in the future, intimate or foreign. He undertakes a "systematic psychological study of the sites of our intimate lives," a "topoanalysis" of the house from top to bottom (Bachelard 1968: 8). He explores the house's vertical layout from the attic as safe haven to the cellar's murky darkness, as well as the intimacy of nooks and corridors. Like nests, drawers, and corners, they shape our archetypal notion of space. He proceeds to show how from then on "a flicker of the soul is all that is needed" to recall these notions at all times (Bachelard 1968, xxii-xix). The imagination can best be triggered by poetic images, which account for nurturing human experiences of place, and which allow readers of poetry to recall primal spaces over and over, and long after they have moved away from the house, where the experience was initially made. The poetic image activates the reader's body memory, while appealing to her "creative consciousness" (Bachelard 1968: xxii-xix). Having evoked memory and imagination in tandem, the poetic image spins off reverberations, an extraordinary capacity, which Bachelard refers to as "oneiric" in his own lyrical writing (Bachelard 1968: 152).[3]

Probably the most famous proponent of practiced oneirism was Roland Barthes, who in *Camera Lucida* "borrowed something from phenomenology's

---

[3] *oneiros* = Greek for dream. For a profound analysis of the relation between imagination and memory encapsulated in Bachelard's concept of oneirism see Trigg 2012.

project", thus casting Bachelard's argument about the poetic image wider to include photographs (Barthes 2000: 20).[4] Feeling that certain photographs resonated with his soul, Barthes read them as if they were poems, exploring them "not as a question (a theme) but as a wound: I see, I feel, hence I notice, I observe, and I think" (Barthes 2000: 21). Animated by a photographic detail (the equivalent of Bachelard's poetic image), which disturbs and distresses him, his memories and imagination are set off, and a sense of intimacy is triggered. Pricked by "a *punctum*" (Barthes 2000: 47), he gave himself over to what Bachelard calls "*direct revery*" (*sic*) (Bachelard 1968: 169). From both Bachelard and Barthes we can infer that poetic images can be employed in literary texts, photographs, as well as in other visual media.[5] Permeated with oneiric depth, a photograph's poetic faculties make it highly suggestive. By way of miniaturizing inhabited space, the photograph becomes "a nucleus, a spore, a dynamized center" (Bachelard 1968: 157). Born from imagination, containing large in small, a photograph may serve the viewer as a familiar entry into another world. Whether it does, however, depends on the reader/viewer's attitude. In order not to have its "oneirism reduced to dust," Bachelard claims, "an image that dreams, [...] must be taken as an invitation to continue the daydream that created it," and it must be approached with "an oneiric attitude" (Bachelard 1968: 152). This is not a trite demand. Admitting to having been affected is a highly personal matter and risky, as *Camera Lucida* shows. It requires giving up a certain intellectualism, which like a suit of armor is frequently used to keep emotions at bay. "The image, in its simplicity, has no need of scholarship. It is the property of

---

[4] True to Bachelard's claim that it was the poets first and then the philosophers, who bestowed such daydreaming with dignity (Bachelard 1958: 160), writers such as Susan Sontag, John Berger, and Roland Barthes indulged in such imaginative activity, thus spearheading the burgeoning scholarly interest in photographs in the 1970s and 80s. In their philosophizing on photographs they exercised fluency in two languages, "one expressive, the other critical" (Barthes 2000: 8). Popular proponents of such bilingualism, such as Alain de Botton, followed suit, catering with his philosophical picture books to the general reader.
[5] Photography, film, let alone the Internet, were not on Bachelard's scholarly radar in the 1950s. Since then much work of great poetic quality has been produced by these technologies. Apparently, poetic images or *puncti* can be found in literary and visual work independent of genres, as long as it is endowed with oneiric depth and approached with oneiric attitude. One might claim that even depictions of gruesome war scenes have the potential to set off the viewer's imagination as Timothy O'Sullivan and Alexander Gardner's lyrical Civil War photograph *Harvest of Death* shows. However, there is a limit to our imaginative capacities, Susan Sontag argues. Discussing the oxymoronic title of Jeff Wall's photograph "Dead Troops Talk", Sontag concludes in "Looking at War": We, who have never been in the line of fire "can't imagine how dreadful, how terrifying war is" (Sontag 2002: 98).

a naïve consciousness," and one that "comes before thought" (Bachelard 1968: xix-xx).

Yet, drawing on Mark Johnson helps to understand imagination to be hard-wired in the human body. While for most people the term imagination "connotes artistic creativity, fantasy, scientific discovery, invention, and novelty", as a result of nineteenth-century Romanticism, the American philosopher considers it the conceptual node connecting philosophy with literature, and neuroscience (Johnson 1987: 139). Consisting of five main components, which he identifies as categorization, schemata, metaphorical projections, metonymy, and narrative structure, imagination is part of what is shared when we understand each other and communicate in a community. Incorporating neuroscience to highlight the *bodily* basis of meaning, imagination, and reason, Johnson finally disavows the Kantian body-mind dichotomy (Johnson 2005:17). Which visual experience we find meaningful, and how we reason about it, depends upon "structures of imagination that make our experience what it is" (Johnson 1987: 171). Taking the cue from Maurice Merleau-Ponty, whose phenomenological philosophy emphasizes the body as the primary site of cognition, Johnson puts it this way: "[…] the world as we *know* it contains *no* primary qualities […], because the qualities of things as we can experience and comprehend them depend crucially on our neural makeup, our bodily interactions with them, and our purposes and interests. For real human beings, the only realism is an embodied realism" (Lakoff and Johnson 1999: 26). Ultimately, and despite their differences in method, scope, and discourse, Johnson and Bachelard come to a similar conclusion: that we understand places by way of our imagination, which is shaped by affects, which are themselves effected by body-space relations.

A/EFFECTING THE URBAN ENVIRONMENT

Like many tourists these days, I caught the first glimpse of Beijing from a plane. The establishing shot onto the Beijing municipality reduces the urban high-rise settlement to the size of a miniature. Aerial photography has long been criticized for exerting scopic power, for using the bird's-eye perspective as a position of superiority, in order to first shrink and then control the object in the finder. From above, any place seems available and legible, easily built, quick to destroy like some child's Lego brick arrangement.

Aerial view of the greater Beijing municipality

"Distance creates miniatures," turning monumental objects isolated on the horizon into "homelands for the eyes" (Bachelard 1968: 162). Yet, the aerial image is just "a semblance of appropriation" (Sontag 1977: 24). Upon arrival perspectives switch. Confronted with the spatial immensity of the city from an eye-level perspective, the process of shrink and control so easily exercised from the air is inverted. Clueless of how Beijing is organized, incapable of comprehending Chinese characters, and stunned by the sensory impact of moving masses, smells, climate, sounds, and traffic, the foreign spectator feels reduced to the size of a shrimp and proceeds humbled by the metropolitan experience. Clearly space "is not something we are inserted into, as though it has existed all along and awaits the subject's arrival" (Trigg 2012: 4), but is relational. According to the phenomenological axiom of *being-in-the-world*, we can only experience the world by relating our subjective selves to space at all times. The experience of place is neither "reducible to a set of objective properties," nor depending "wholly on a sociopolitical context," but instead "fundamentally affective" (Trigg 2012: 4-5). Ultimately we understand places by way of our imagination, which itself is shaped by affects, which are effected by body-space relations.

Reading the photograph with Johnson's linguistic theory of imagination excavates specific image schema operative as meaning making capacities, "structuring particular experiences schematically, so as to give order and connectedness to our perceptions and conceptions" (Johnson 1987: 75). Johnson defines image schemas - such as, most prominently, horizon, front, back, left, right, center-periphery, compulsion, attraction, and blockage of action - as "recurring patterns of our sensory-motor experience by means of which we can make sense of that experience and reason about it, and that can also be recruited to structure abstract concepts" (Johnson 2005: 18-20). My photograph of Beijing's high-rise buildings takes its key meaning from a verticality schema. It allows for conceptualizing a relational arrangement of some*body* being *above* somebody else. While for the airborne passenger about to arrive in Beijing, one of the world's largest metropolises, the Google Earth view facilitates a feeling of being in control, hence helping to manage anxiety as well as stimulate anticipation of arriving in a city unknown, the tourist photograph also already carries a place specific meaning. From the verticality schema, inferences can be drawn about the relationship of buildings and people in the People's Republic, about architecture that speaks of social hierarchy and class distinctions. The simple shot taken from an airplane window provides a view of conflicts and change in communist-capitalist China. The aerial image documents massive urban development. It tells a story of the state's project of transforming Beijing from a low city to one augmented by the monumental, of members from a growing middle-class pushing to the periphery to live in compounds, interspersing with drops of color a surrounding otherwise dominated by shades of grey and pale yellow owing to the smog in the air and the sand blown in by winds from the Gobi Desert. What seems like a generic, treeless dystopia to the uninformed visitor, signals social benefits to the local in the lower circuits of backstreet Beijing. To them upper floor habitation expresses social mobility.

A familiar word written on the side of a Beijing bus sets off the imagination

While taking photographs involves decisions about focus, angle, frame, etc., from a neuroscientist perspective most such decisions are made unconsciously. And while it might be true that "all we see or seem, is but a dream within a dream," as Edgar Allan Poe once put it, it is equally correct to say that what a photograph shows and how we understand it is never arbitrary (Poe 2007: 326). Each photograph is the idiosyncratic result of the photographer's physical experience of a specific space and situation, which turns the picture into "a nexus of living meanings," ultimately making its expression "indistinguishable from the thing expressed" (Johnson 1987: 175). Floating through an unintelligible urban and linguistic environment as a newly arrived tourist city photographer, I was seeking for familiar signs on the streets of Beijing. Finding the word 'love' written on the side of a public bus, I took the picture above. Spotting the sign from a street cab, where I sat capturing details, bits and pieces of people, signs and vehicles streaming through the city, did at the time anchor me. Struggling to gain comprehension and orientation, it made me attribute a positive sense to Beijing. Within a second the city seemed less alien and, just as I promptly drew inferences, the Chinese-illiterate viewer of the photograph presumably does so as well.

The English term 'love' juxtaposed with a series of Chinese characters dominates semantics. Reading love in conjunction with red, commonly understood as color code for love, sustains a positive feeling resonating from the image. The poetic atmosphere is further sustained by the perception of rain glistening on the street (though it was in fact awash with water from the soapy liquids sprayed by a street cleaning vehicle), together with the stretch of dark evoking and collapsing all at once bittersweet memories of kissing on the street, and moments of tenderness on a dark and rainy day. Like a neon sign, it advertises Beijing as a place of love. "[T]he fiery pool reflecting it in the asphalt," makes the sign "superior to criticism" (Benjamin 2004: 476), because processes of simplification and identification are operative in the ways we experience the world and reason about it. Or to phrase it with Johnson and Lakoff, we conceptualize the world according to "color concepts, basic-level concepts, spatial-relation concepts, and aspectual (event-structuring) concepts" (Lakoff and Johnson 1999: 16), and apply these structures of imagination both to familiar and unfamiliar places. The same imaginative patterns hence instigate both the act of taking a picture and its subsequent interpretation.

Various instances of drifting on the streets of Beijing

For the tourist cruising through the city in a taxi, there's hardly more to get than a quick impression of the city framed by the side window of the car and thus perceived as if it was a motion picture. One snapshot follows another in short succession. In 1931 Walter Benjamin announced that soon the day would come, "when there will be more illustrated periodicals for photographers than game and poultry shops" (Benjamin 1980: 212), thus criticizing snapshots for approaching the accidental with little ingenuity, and reproducing hollow shelled, flat surface views. Forged by processes of technological reproduction, snapshots bear witness to an equalizing "sense of similarity in the world," which Benjamin perceived as potentially dangerous (Benjamin 2008: 10). Vision becomes accidental in the realm of interchangeable images of places – or images of interchangeable places. While such criticism certainly has a point, it is also true that a lot of duck is still being sold in Beijing. Hence the question remains whether snapshots of Beijing necessarily miss the point?

Yingjin Zhang celebrates drifting as an ideal mode by which to visually render the city, because "in its conceptual indeterminacy and sensory immediacy, drifting facilitates boundary crossing (local/global), class commingling (rich/poor), and cultural mixing (Chinese/foreign)" (Zhang 2008:225). As a visual practice, drifting makes a supportive statement on the lived experience of drifters, "the people of *liu*" - migrants, homeless people, outcasts," who, as Michael Dutton explains, "bear the mark of cultural difference and are all stigmatized as criminals for the same reason: floating and thus producing chaos" (Dutton 1999: 81). Their mobility – be it social or spatial – poses the ultimate threat to a system obsessed with homogeneity and fixity. As a mode of living, drifting is considered subversive in Chinese culture, which traditionally attributes a crucial role to place and stability. As a visual mode, drifting is integrative, and thus a potent mode by which to visualize Beijing from the position of the tourist (according to Tom Scocca the majority of tourists, who visit and picture Beijing, are Chinese), who is also an outsider to the city and its social order, yet does not have to bear the burden of stigma (Scocca 2011: 5). Drifting through Beijing in a cab, the tourist (Western or non-Western) is lost in comprehension. Adhering to the particular properties of street photography such as "instantaneity and multiplicity" she documents in the "purposely open-ended, unbalanced pictures" that result from her snapshooting the state of not-belonging as a logical outcome of increased mobility (Westerbeck and Meyerowitz 1994: 34). The pictures represent a mobile existence, which for an increasing number of people in Beijing has become less an exception than the norm be it due to more varied modes of transportation, the Chinese Government opening the country for more tourism from abroad as well as to increased intra-national tourist activities of the Chinese themselves, or be it due to an increasing exchange of goods and information in the rapidly changing and globalizing country.

The futuristic shell of the Beijing National Center for Performing Arts

This is how the complaint commonly goes: Tourist shots are boring, because the tourist photographer is prone to follow only the beaten tracks and to shooting well-known sights in the city, while ignoring the rest. Like her itinerary, her gaze is "socially organised and systematised" (Urry 2002: 1). Consequently, tourist city photographs of Beijing tend to reiterate the dominant discourse of capitalist modernization, which "has in recent years become the hegemonic paradigm for thinking and writing modern Chinese history" (Wang 2004: 2). Long thought to be entrapped in a "hermeneutic circle" (Urry 2002: 129), tourist photographs were deemed productive of generic views before recent studies, including the updated versions of Urry's *The Tourist Gaze*, highlighted their performative and creative potentials.[6] While they do not physically bring places into existence, they

---

[6] *The Tourist Gaze* has been stirring a lot of debate since it was first published in 1990. Urry, who takes tourism and everyday life to be mutually exclusive, contrasts the tourist

"can direct attention, organize insignificant entities into significant composite wholes, and in so doing, make things formerly overlooked – and hence invisible and unreal – visible and real" (Tuan 1991: 685). Tourist city photographs are not only responsive to but also productive of so-called place-myths (Shields 1991: 61). They feed into the urban imaginary of the city, which they depict.[7] As speech acts they have communicative impact. They structure experience and make meaning by way of composition, choice of subject, point of view, color and format. And sometimes, acting as interferences, they might even direct the debate into spheres not fully explored or purposely silenced.

Exploring urban Beijing, I, too, am sightseeing the buildings millions of other tourists visit each year. Stopping in on landmarks praised in guidebooks, such as the Beijing National Center for Performing Arts (*Egg*) or the Olympic Stadium (*Bird's Nest*), I doggedly follow the routes along which the Chinese Government has strategically spectacularized the city. Winning the Olympics bid in 2001, a radical makeover of the urban design was initiated with the strategic efforts to brand Beijing as global city. Starchitecture was promoted along with the Olympic Games mega-event. An urban geography of promise helped to trade in the "[p]reviously prevailing imaginaries of Beijing as a traditional walled city and a sacrosanct site of China's imperial power and socialist enterprises" (Zhang 2008: 221). Today, all over town magnificent landmarks sport their avantgarde aesthetics. As "prime orientation clues," they help clarify "the order of cities" (Jacobs 1992: 384, 390), simultaneously signaling the city's diversity and unity

---

gaze with regular, day to day to experiences of the visual world. Others, refusing to consider the tourist gaze as a deviance, have contested Urry's notion by pointing out the ubiquitous nature of tourism and hence of the tourist gaze. Jonas Larsen criticizes Urry for ignoring the performative aspects of tourism and tourist photography. Larsen also worked on the impact of mobile subjects and objects on the gaze. Pointing at the creative aspects of tourist photography, Dean MacCannell argues in *The Tourist* that photography produces rather than consumes tourist attractions. While it is true that many tourist photographs are taken in a habitual fashion, many scholars agree that these are nonetheless potentially creative and non-predictable. While MacCannell introduces the notion of the second gaze, Gillespie investigates the reverse gaze of the self-reflexive tourist. Furthermore, recent research on tourism and tourist photography has shown that aspects of physicality factor into the process of meaning making in complex and creative ways, and not just in terms of how travel routes choreograph tourist streams. Judith Adler, Soile Veijola, Eeva Jokinen, and later Urry himself highlight the corporeal nature of tourist experiences such as physical proximity and co-presence at live events, bodily arousal in adventure tourism, spa travel and sex tourism.

[7] As early as 1974 Jonathan Raban claimed in *Soft City* that the city "as we imagine it, the soft city of illusion, myth, aspiration, and nightmare, is as real, maybe more real than the hard city one can locate on maps, in statistics, in monographs on urban sociology and demography and architecture" (Raban 1974: 2).

Thirty years later Andreas Huyssen concludes that urban imaginaries are "part of any city's reality, rather than being only figments of the imagination" (Huyssen 2008: 3).

that knits its bits and pieces together. Behemoths like the Olympic Stadium, which is the product of international creative collaboration, are constructed with the objective to affirm integration with the global economy as Beijing's new order, both to its residents and the rest of the world. But the locals promptly pet named the landmark *Bird's Nest*, allegedly associating the woven geometric structure of the stadium with a culinary specialty in Chinese cuisine, which goes by the same name, bird's nest soup.

Taking pictures of Beijing's trophy buildings, I consume the iconic visual order of a city creating for itself the coveted identity as global. But does the cityscape like landscape in nineteenth-century paintings really inevitably become an "object of fetishistic practices involving the limitless repetition of identical photographs taken on identical spots by tourists with interchangeable emotions" (Mitchell 2002: 15). Which emotion do tourists supposedly share regardless of individual traits, backgrounds and mental models? Which is the emotion that my photograph is bound to resonate like every other? The futuristic eggshell of the Beijing National Center for Performing Arts visually announces China's promising future. Capturing the landmark seems to reinforce the building's principal symbolic message. But while the picture is clear in terms of composition, highlighting the building's magnificence, its somber mood contradicts the optimistic narrative. And does the woman in front not bend her head in a silent gesture of protest? The picture is at least ambivalent. Intuitively, it seems, the tourist city photographer gets the drift of why Beijing residents might call these buildings nest and egg, both of which are "primal images," giving "evidence of a cosmic situation" (Bachelard 1968: 91, 94).[8] As metaphors they describe states of mind, unhappy ones, that is, because, in order to "make so gentle a comparison between house and nest, one must have lost the house that stood for happiness" (Bachelard 1968: 100). Or to phrase it with Ai Weiwei, artistic consultant to the construction of the *Bird's Nest*, who refuses to ignore the social injustice and political oppression the Chinese Government wishes to hide behind glitzy facades: "Beijing is a nightmare. A constant nightmare" (Weiwei 2011: n.p.).

---

[8] Clearly, the argument bears the mark of Western philosophy, and it might seem presumptuous to read buildings in Beijing with the works of a French philosopher. After all, urban planning in the Chinese capital has been following specific and complex cosmological principles for more than 3000 years. But if the house is a "psychic state," if it is indeed "the deepest dream image to express our happiness" (Bachelard 1968: 72), aspects of house symbolism apply across cultures. Even more so in the case of these buildings, which were constructed in a joint venture of international cooperation partners.

Giant digital screen on Tiananmen Square

As Wu Hung states in his study on the political history of monuments in Beijing, "gates and walls were two principal features of a capital in traditional China" (Hung 1991: 86). While walls formed enclosures, each boxed into another, gates opened access to one at a time without concealing the center, "the emperor – the embodiment of the imperial order – who could maintain his power because he was invisible from the public space" (Hung 1991: 87). With Mao appearing above Tiananmen on October 1, 1949, however, the "old architectural symbolism collapsed" (Hung 1991: 88). Having erased the boundary between in- and outside, one could say that the city's rigid architectural "container schema logic" was eschewed, or rather that it was modified, since it no longer needed to be "physically instantiated" (Lakoff and Johnson 1999: 32). With Jack out of the box, it continued to exist only as a conceptual schema, distinguishing Chinese people/party members from Capitalist outsiders. From then on, the square took a new meaning and was used to expose power rather than conceal it. Like no other public space in China, Tiananmen Square was brutally and strategically re-designed for the spectacle of power in the following decades.

When I photographed Tiananmen Square the day after the National Day festivities in 2011, it was still dressed up with enormous flowerbeds. In the back of the Monument to the People's Heroes a huge digital screen facing the portrait of Mao displayed lofty images of clouds above a luminous azure sky, apparently alluding to the vast spaciousness of the universe. The metaphor is as common as the meaning that is made from it. Inviting anyone looking to imagine themselves floating above the ground, the visual symbolism is directly linked to the physical experience of flying and appeals to people's desire to sever their earthbound ties. Clear like a blue sky, the promise of freedom emanates from the digital screen.

Speaking of China's global aspirations and the promise they hold for the people, Tiananmen Square, this time, was used to convey politics poetically. Overwhelmed by the monumentality of the square and the wide blue screen, the imaginative process happened instantaneously.

Even a perfunctory glance at the picture makes the blue pull me in. Before I notice, I am infused with some immense longing. Obviously the spectator (of both the screen and the photograph) is seduced by these state-sponsored visuals (at once imperial, socialist and recently globalized). The screen contains and freezes a sanitized version of the real, which is proclaimed official, preferred, or to phrase it in the terminology of Chinese State officials, harmonious. The supersize screen on Tiananmen Square transmits an image campaign of globalizing China expanding like the blue sky and hiding human cost underneath the canopy of official state doctrine. The lived experience of globalization, singularized into billions of individual people and their stories about success, struggle, or failure, injustice, and progress, remains out of sight. Digitally transmitting the message of power on a screen continues old tradition in modern ways. Once again, that which is most important in China stands enclosed in a box on Tiananmen Square. Providing "a locus of coalescence for political expression, collective memory, identity, and history," as Hung states in his reading of Tiananmen's architectural history, the square "has been and will continue to be a prime visual means of political rhetoric in modern China" (Hung 1991: 85). It so happens that even a rigorously cropped tourist city photograph of Tiananmen Square conveys this message.

Hazy view of the moat, which surrounds the Forbidden City

Shortly before this picture was taken, I rested to follow the line of trees along the reconstructed moat that has been surrounding the Forbidden City for almost 600 years. I thought I was feeling the aura of the historical place, that "strange web of time and space: the unique appearance of a distance, however close at hand" (Benjamin 1980: 219). I remember looking at the scene with a romantic or "semi-spiritual" attitude characteristic of much modern tourism (Urry 2002: 11). Spiritual search for the auratic or not - at the time I felt physically exhausted after sightseeing the Forbidden City and mentally exhilarated, which admittedly the photograph does not capture. It is at best reminiscent of other landscape images. Conventionality prevails in terms of perspective and vantage point. But its sullen, melancholic atmosphere still pulls me in and affects me in spite of my awareness that the haze that makes it look vaguely impressionist is in fact the infamous Beijing smog, less a romantic blur than an indicator of the city's impending ecological collapse. The aesthetics of manmade destruction cause confusion in the photographer and the spectator, who gets arrested in an apprehensive dilemma. Finding the horrific beautiful seems inconceivable, a profound confusion of established categories.

How do we, then, caption the photograph, given that an image accompanied by the right phrase may mysteriously amplify its magic - which is hardly news in China? After all, to the Chinese artist "calligraphy, poetry, and painting are all part of one venture, the purpose of which is to evoke – or, to put it more strongly, to conjure or create – the personality and mood of a landscape" (Tuan 1991: 691). An ecology-conscious phrase seems apt given the "deep, mythic resonance" China's pollution problem has in the consciousness of the Western tourist, reminding us after all "that our Western standard of health and prosperity relied on the existence of places that were sickened and poor" (Scocca 2011: 11). And yet, the picture speaks to me in an altogether different way. In this picture air pollution does give a nice tint to the Beijing cityscape, because for me it will always be framed by my memory of physical exhaustion paired with a semi-spiritual exhilaration.

"Trauma takes two forms in modern China," Ban Wang explains in his study on trauma, memory, and history in modern China, "one is the latent memory of past catastrophes of imperialism and colonialism as well as atrocities of the authoritarian political order. The other is the ongoing shock of the damaged lifeworlds under the impact of transnational capital and the massive commodification of social relations" (Wang 2004: 8). Employing the memory-history distinction of French historian Pierre Nora, Wan shows examples of Chinese cultural production that are steeped in intimate and local memory work, nostalgia, and myth. The trend to "reenchant quotidian life and human relations",

Wang claims, corresponds with a change in societal formation from local, traditional, mundane, and communal to global, impersonal, and rational (Wang 2004: 12). While the former is represented by the idiosyncratic milieu of the traditional *hutongs*, the latter finds its spatial expression in Beijing's *starchitecture* and, of course, Qianmen Street. Here international retailers, expensive teahouses and Peking Roast Duck restaurants attract the tourist hordes pouring down from the Forbidden City via Tiananmen Square to Qianmen Street, Beijing's 560 year old market area on Beijing's famous midline, which was renovated for the 2008 Olympic Games.

Buildings on both sides of the pedestrian street, which look like postmodern pastiches simulating Qing Dynasty architecture, front a façade of transnational capitalist consumer culture. Transmitting civic lessons of progressive conduct, like department stores did in turn-of-the century American metropolises, the Qianmen Street-spectacle has a pedagogical function. Staging shophouses, mixing local products with transnational consumer articles, Qianmen Street instructs on globalized economy of the Chinese sort. Zoned off from the notoriously aggressive traffic in the Chinese capital, Qianmen Street was created in the mode of Nanjing Road in Shanghai following the European concept of *Fussgaengerzone*. Safe from speeding vehicles, the view into shop windows unobstructed by parking or passing cars, flaneuring pedestrians orderly navigate an area, where communist Beijing musealizes capitalism, which is to be looked at, experienced and practiced on the go. What used to symbolize the central bloodline for eternal energy flows is now re-dedicated to cash flows. Next door from the shopping street are some remaining *hutongs*, where life is bustling at least for the time being in a less sanitized, presumably traditional way. With bulldozers waiting in the wings to demolish derelict buildings along with beautiful courtyards, some *hutong* residents grab their own share of Beijing's global marketability by selling nick-nack, souvenirs, and Chairman Mao memorabilia. Here, too, a sense of loss has been unleashed, creating in return the unique selling point that many in the city try to benefit from. Where capitalism reigns, selling out what once was and never will be again, tourists are allowed to enter; the rest, where poverty, desperation, and dislocation rule, is closed off.

Advertisements and photographs of historical buildings placed next to each other on Qianmen Street

Qianmen Street is a model site specifically designed to exhibit China's globalizing economy. Being a memorial space or *lieu de mémoire* (Nora cit. in Wang 2004: 12) it simulates spatial as well as temporal and cultural continuity.[9] On this reconstructed section of Beijing's famous North-South axis life is no ongoing process, but presented as history completed. Chosen because of its symbolic resonances, the one kilometer long strip had to be at least partially ruptured from its past, its old buildings deconstructed, the steady flow of organic living disrupted, to make it now reference globalized economy. The violence imposed on the place and the people by this act of resignification is glossed over by the brand new look. Photographs of the buildings before renovation are exhibited on the renovated walls as if to attest to their authenticity. Almost indistinguishable from the advertisements surrounding them, the nostalgic views of the historic shophouses become another commodity, enforcing rather than countering the homogenizing effects that result from globalization. Meant to narrate a tale of legitimate urban development, the photographs of the original frontispieces perform the opposite. Displaying history, bearing witness not on objects but on time, they increase the sense of artificiality, which oozes from the place. Seemingly minor decorative details and disparagingly strewn all over the place, the photographs on Qianmen Street memorialize economic globalization as national trauma, while showcasing it.

---

[9] Pierre Nora's distinguishes *lieux* and *milieux de mémoire*, memorial spaces and places of memory, which allows for conceptualizing the rift in urban design captured in my pictures of Qianmen Street.

People on a Beijing sidewalk waiting to cross the street

This last photograph is one of the few I took of people in Beijing. It is focused on the man with the flag making him stand out from the other people in the picture, who are apparently waiting for a signal to cross the street. With their movements arrested, the picture freezes the moment of waiting. Everybody has their heads turned into a different direction. Some seem a bit lost, as if searching for clues, others eager to take in more visual input, while the rest passes time by vacantly staring into space. Clearly, these people inhabit the same space, but disparate worlds of thought. What the picture does not show but announces, is the moment, in which the traffic-guide in the center will summon everybody's attention by waving his flag and thus precipitate them to re-join as an army of walkers on their orchestrated march on Beijing sidewalks.

Portraying an ordinary street scene, the picture speaks of a control regime, which directs and organizes the flows of people in public space. And it speaks of individuals submitting themselves to an authoritarian power, which ushers them into staying on track. But this is only one part of the narrative. Another exists between the little Chinese girl in the yellow jacket and the tall Caucasian man on the left, both of whom are almost completely turning away from the viewer. If we follow the direction of their gazes we are drawn to the triangular blue section cutting into the picture on the left top, and next, into a world beyond the frame of the picture. Their views expand the narrow constraints of the image and the scene of silent obedience it represents. The connecting line (invisible though) between the girl and the guy structures the picture in such a way that an alternative meaning is suggested. Looking into a different direction from anybody else, the

Asian youth and the Western tourist bring the blue segment at the top into focus, turning it into a visual and symbolic juxtaposition to the man with the flag in the center. As dominant visual elements, the sky and the man with the flag now speak to each other, representing freedom and state authority respectively. Building up tension between two opposing forces, the picture represents more than an ordinary street scene. Here a greater moment and a greater decision are at stake. This tourist city photograph can be read metaphorically as suggesting that standing out from the crowd makes all the difference. With connected views literally opening up an escape route, the girl and the guy cooperate in creating a moment of resistance. It can also be read as a metaphor for the act of imagination *per se*. All it takes for a new way of seeing to open up is a small movement of the body.

Pushing places into meaning in similar ways as "our ancestors have sung the world into existence" in their epics, photographs can take on a foundational quality (Tuan 1991: 687). Some photographs even become "sacred images for a secular society", like the iconic 'tankman' shot of a solitary man forming a human bulwark against an approaching tank on Tiananmen Square in 1989 (Hariman and Lucaites 2007: 2). Whether we caption the image as the perfect visualization of China's rising democratic movement, or of the restraint and kindness of the Peoples' Liberation Army, as Communist Party loyalists do, ultimately and regardless of ideological preferences, we all understand the picture along our space-body concepts: as an encounter of unequal forces, a symbol of strong meeting weak.[10] While the image of a citizen stopping a tank "could be taken – and has been taken – anywhere in the world", Tiananmen Square, with its awe-inspiring, dwindling expanses, provides the perfect setting in which to stage such an archetypal encounter of small versus large (Hariman and Lucaites 2007: 224).

Certainly, the tourist city photographs discussed in this case study do not go near assuming such impact. However, by illustrating the tourist photographer's geographical (and thus conceptual) trajectory through the city, by calling forth imaginative powers, they, too, construct meaning about Beijing. Albeit new to the city, the tourist photographer physically familiarizes herself with the unfamiliar urban environment, thrusting herself into this new space as a transposition of the space experienced as first model. With all perceptual and cognitive faculties operating, in order to adjust primary templates of space with the unfamiliar spatiality of the city, the photographer connects past and present experiences of space. While illustrating the photographer's geographical trajectory, her *way* of

---

[10] See the re-interpretation of the Tiananmen Square 'Massacre' by Bill, the Butcher, "The Tiananmen Square 'Massacre': A New Look," *Subversify* (January 15, 2010), n.p.

seeing Beijing, each snapshot testifies to her idiosyncratic merging of different temporalities and spatialities. This is basically performed in ongoing creative bouts as an act of perpetuated imaginative activity.

While each snapshot speaks as much of the photographer's embodied experience (space adjusted to her mental model) as it speaks of the city's materiality, it literally keeps both parties alive by establishing a relation between subject and space at any given moment. Gesturing to Barthes, who made the readers of *Camera Lucida* aware that personal photographs, made to keep memories alive, always carry the death of the photographic object with them, I would like to point out the invigorating effects the very *act* of picture making has on the photographer and the place. Connected by a multitude of affects each *act*ivates the other. The snapshots discussed in this paper continue to create more and other Beijing imaginations, both for me and certainly for other viewers. The meanings such tourist photographs convey of the city are related to various somatic experiences of then and now. Meaning is made in a continuing process facilitated by affects, which are "revealed to flow *through* bodies and spaces" (Bennett 2005: 13). Hence the readers of this paper might find themselves conjuring up mental images of the Chinese capital, whether or not they have already been there. Beijing imaginations will arise in their minds, visions choreographed by their affective responses to encountered signs reverberated by the photographs discussed in this paper. Performing what Tuan calls a sort of maintenance work, even pictures by an amateur photographer unfamiliar with the city are involved in the process of place making, because if naming is "the creative power to call something into being" (Tuan 1991: 688), picturing is the creative faculty to keep it alive.

REFERENCES

Adler, Judith. "Origins of Sightseeing." *Annals of Tourism Research* 16 (1989): 7-29. Print.

Bachelard, Gaston. *The Poetics of Space*. 1958. Boston: Beacon, 1968. Print.

Barthes, Roland. *Camera Lucida*. 1980. London: Vintage Books, 2000. Print.

Benjamin, Walter. "A Short History of Photography." 1931. In *Classic Essays on Photography*. Edited by Alan Trachtenberg. 199-216. New Haven, Conn.: Leete's Island Books, 1980. Print.

---. "One-Way Street." In *Walter Benjamin: Selected Writings 1*. 455-76. Boston: Harvard UP, 2004. Print.

---. *The Work of Art in the Age of Mechanical Reproduction*. 1936. Translated by J.A. Underwood. London, New York, et. al.: Penguin, 2008. Print.

Bennett, Jill. *Empathic Vision. Affect, Trauma, and Contemporary Art*. Stanford, California: Stanford UP, 2005. Print.

Berger, John. *Ways of Seeing*. London et. al: British Broadcasting Corporation and Penguin Books, 1972.

Bill the Butcher. "The Tiananmen Square 'Massacre': A New Look." *Subversify* January 15, 2010. Web. <http://subversify.com/2010/01/15/the-tiananmen-square-massacre-a-new-look>

Dutton, Michael. "Street Scenes of Subalternity: China, Globalization, and Rights." *Social Text* Issue: Globalization? 60 (Autumn 1999): 63-86. Print.

Gillespie, Alex. "Tourist Photography and the Reverse Gaze." *ETHOS* 34.3 (2006): 343-66. Web. <http://ebookbrowse.com/gillespie-tourist-photography-and-the-reverse-gaze-pdf-d324828304>.

Greenberg, Clement. "Four Photographers: Review of *A Vision of Paris* by Eugene-Auguste Atget; *A Life in Photography* by Edward Steichen; *The World Through My Eyes* by Andreas Feininger; and *Photographs by Cartier-Bresson*." *New York Review of Books* January 23, 1964. Web. <www.nybooks.com/articles/archives/1964/jan/23/four-photographers/>.

Hampe, Beate, ed. *From Perception to Meaning. Image Schemas in Cognitive Linguistics*. Berlin, New York: Mouton de Gruyter, 2005. Print.

Hariman, Robert, and Lucaites, John Louis. *No Caption Needed. Iconic Photographs, Public Culture, and Liberal Democracy*. Chicago, London: University of Chicago Press, 2007. Print.

Hung, Wu. "Tiananmen Square: A Political History of Monuments." *Representations* 35 (Summer 1991): 84-117. Print.

Huyssen, Andreas, ed. *Other Cities, Other Worlds*: *Urban Imaginaries in a Globalizing Age*. Durham, London: Duke UP, 2008. Print.

---. "Introduction: World Cultures, World Cities." In *Other Cities, Other Worlds*: *Urban Imaginaries in a Globalizing Age*. Edited by Andreas Huyssen, 1-23. Durham, London: Duke UP, 2008. Print.

Jacobs, Jane. *The Death and Life of Great American Cities*. 1961. New York: Vintage Books, 1992. Print.

Jenkins, Olivia. "Photography and Travel Brochures: The Circle of Representation." *Tourism Geographies* 5.3 (2003): 305-28. Web. <www.tandfonline.com/doi/pdf/10.1080/14616680309715 >.

Johnson, Mark. *The Body in the Mind. The Bodily Basis of Meaning, Imagination, and Reason.* Chicago and London: The University of Chicago Press, 1987. Print.

---. "The Philosophical Significance of Image Schemas." In *From Perception to Meaning. Image Schemas in Cognitive Linguistics.* Edited by Beate Hampe. 15-33. Berlin, New York: Mouton de Gruyter, 2005. Print.

Lakoff, George, and Johnson, Mark. *Philosophy in the Flesh. The Embodied Mind and Its Challenge to Western Thought.* New York, NY: Basic Books, 1999. Print.

Larsen, Jonas. "Families Seen Sightseeing: Performativity of Tourist Photography." *Space and Culture* 8.4 (2005): 416-34. Web. < http://sac.sagepub.com/content/8/4/416.full.pdf>

MacCannell, Dean. *The Tourist.* 1976. New York: Schocken, 1999.

---. "Tourist Agency." *Tourist Studies* 1.1 (2001): 23-37. Web. <http://tou.sagepub.com/content/ 1/1/23.refs>.

Merleau-Ponty, Maurice. *Phenomenology of Perception.* 1945. Translated by Colin Smith. London, New York: Routledge, 2002. Print.

Mitchell, William J. T., "Imperial Landscape." In *Landscape and Power.* Edited by W. J. T. Mitchell, 5-34. Chicago, London: University of Chicago Press, 1994, 2002. Print.

Nora, Pierre. "Between Memory and History: Les Lieux de Mémoire." Translated by Mark Roudebush. *Representations* 26 (Spring 1989): 7-24. Print.

Poe, Edgar Allan. "A Dream Within a Dream." 1849. In *Great Tales and Poems of Edgar Allan Poe.* 326. New York: Simon & Schuster, 2007. Print.

Raban, Jonathan. *Soft City.* London: Picador, 1974. Print.

Scocca, Tom. *Beijing Welcomes You. Unveiling the Capital City of the Future.* New York: Riverhead, 2011. Print.

Shields, Rob. *Places on the Margin: Alternative Geographies of Modernity.* London: Routledge, 1991. Print.

Shore, Steven. *The Nature of Photographs.* London, New York: Phaidon, 2007. Print.

Sontag, Susan. *On Photography.* London, New York, et al: Penguin, 1977. Print.

---. "Looking at War. Photography's View Of Devastation and Death." *The New Yorker* (December 9, 2002): 82-99. Web. <http://www.newyorker.com/archive/2002/12/09/021209crat_atlarge>.

Trigg, Dylan. *The Memory of Place. A Phenomenology of the Uncanny*. Athens, Ohio: Ohio UP, 2012. Print.

Tuan, Yi-Fu. "Language and the Making of Place: A Narrative-Descriptive Approach." *Annals of the Association of American Geographers*. 81.4 (Dec. 1991): 684-96. Print.

Urry, John. *The Tourist Gaze*. 1990. London, Thousand Oaks, New Delhi: Sage Publications, 2002. Print.

Veijola, Soile, and Jokinen. Eeva. "The Body in Tourism." *Theory, Culture and Society* 11 (1994): 125-51. Print.

Wang, Ban. *Illuminations from the Past: Trauma, Memory, and History in Modern China*. Stanford, California: Standford UP, 2004. Print.

Weiwei, Ai. "The City: Beijing." *Newsweek* August 28, 2011. Web. <www.thedailybeast.com/ newsweek/2011/08/28/ai-weiwei-on-beijing-snightmare-city.html>. Accessed August 31, 2011.

Westerbeck, Colin, and Meyerowitz, Joel. *Bystander. A History of Street Photography*. Boston, et. al: Little Brown and Company, 1994. Print.

Zhang, Yingjin. "Remapping Beijing: Polylocality, Globalization, Cinema." In *Other Cities, Other Worlds*: *Urban Imaginaries in a Globalizing Age*. Edited by Andreas Huyssen, 219-41. Durham, London: Duke UP, 2008. Print.

All photographs are taken by the author, © Verena Laschinger.

ABOUT THE AUTHOR

Verena Laschinger teaches at Erfurt University, Germany. From 2005 to 2010 she was employed as an Assistant Professor of American Literature and Culture at Fatih University Istanbul, Turkey. She holds a Ph.D. frcm Ludwig-Maximilians-University Munich, Germany. Her research interests include Turkish-American Literature and American photography. She also is a founding member of the European Study Group of Nineteenth-Century American Literature.

CHAPTER 12

Intersemiotic Translation in Wáng Wéi's Poem "Dwelling in Mountain and Autumn Twilight"

Qingben Li

Along with Li Bai (701-762) and Du Fu (712-770), Wáng Wéi (699-761) is one of the greatest Chinese poets of the Tang dynasty, a period when Chinese poetry is thought to have reached a zenith. In Chinese literary history, Li Bai is often regarded as shixian (诗仙), that is, a Daoist of poetry, while Du Fu is shisheng(诗圣), a Confucionist of poetry. Wáng Wéi is seen as shifo (诗佛), that is, a Buddhist of poetry. Wáng Wéi served most of his life at the Tang court, but Buddhism was very important to him so that he was able to combine civil and religious life, a fact also reflected in his pen name Mo-jie (摩诘). Preceded by Wéi (维), the syllables produce Wéi-mo-jie (维摩诘) is the Chinese translation for Vimalakirti, a central figure of the Buddhist sutra. A layman and a sage, Vimalakirti, a contemporary of Gautama Buddha (6th to 5th century BCE), was the perfect model for Wáng Wéi's dual role of civil servant and contemplative recluse.

Zen Buddhism (Chán) is a school of Mahayana Buddhism that originated in China during the 6th-century. Traditionally the origin of Chán in China is credited to the monk Bodhidharma who is recorded as having come from India during the time of Southern and Northern Dynasties. The word Zen derived from the Sanskrit word dhyāna, meaning "absorption" or "meditation" (pronounced in modern Mandarin: Chán). Zen was initially adapted from the Indian texts to the Chinese culture, exposed to Confucianism and Taoism. Various sects struggled to attain an understanding of the Indian texts. The Tathāgatagarbha Sutras (如来藏经) and the idea of the Buddha-nature were endorsed because of the perceived similarities with Taoism. The idea that the ultimate reality is present in the daily world of relative reality fitted into Chinese culture, which emphasized the mundane world and society. Seeing self-nature is considered as the primary path to reach the buddhahood or nirvana, the transcendence of body and mind, by means of sudden (a feature of the Southern School led by Shenhui) or gradual enlightenment (Northern School led by Yuquan Shenxiu) into true nature,

224

followed by purification of intentions. Buddha-nature made of wisdom (prajna), and emptiness/ form (sunyata) (the Prajnaparamita Sutras and Madhyamaka emphasized the non-duality of form and emptiness). The short text Two Entrances and Four Acts, written by T'an-lín (曇林; 506–574), contains teachings which are attributed to Bodhidharma. Attributed to Hui Neng 慧能 (638-713) there is The Platform Sūtra of the Sixth Patriarch (see online translation by McRae, John 2008). An anecdote dating back to a passage from the Lankavatara Sutra (楞伽经) and the Surangama Sutra (楞严经) warn about the dangers of taking Zen writings literally. Vimalakirtinirdeua (佛说维摩诘经) is another of the most popular Buddhist sutras in medieval China was first translated into Chinese from Sanskrit by Zhiqian in the Wu Kingdom in south China between 222 and 229 CE.

A translation and commentary on the Vimalakîrti-nirdeùa was written by Seng Zhao (384-414) describing conversations and debates between the Buddha and his disciples, the bodhisattvas, and among them, Bodhisattva Manjusri and Sage Vimalakirti, and between Uakyamuni's disciple Uariputra and Vimalakirti's servant maiden, who is commonly known as tiannu, or the Daughter of Heaven. The debate between Vimalakirti and Manjusri, used as the central motif in most visual representations of the sutra (see Ning Qiang 2004), focuses on the emptiness, bitterness, and illusory nature of human life. Taking himself as an example, Vimalakirti pretends to be ill and uses his illness as a metaphor to help his audience understand his philosophy on the bitterness and unreality of human life. Seng zhao's Zhaolun (Treatises of [Seng]zhao) is perhaps the most significant text for the study of the early Mādhyamika school (549-623 CE), a philosophical development that arose within Mahāyāna Buddhism in India during the first few centuries CE, and its relationship to the indigenous Daoist and Confucian traditions. Mahāyāna concentrates on distinguishing between concepts and ideas as necessary but insubstantial tools for functioning within the world of conventional reality and the false sense of duality between subject and object that they often engender. According to the tradition, Buddha explained that the Dharma-nature cannot be realized until form and emptiness are apprehended together.

> It is like a man pointing a finger at the moon to show it to others who should follow the direction of the finger to look at the moon. If they look at the finger and mistake it for the moon, they lose (sight of) both the moon and the finger. Why? Because the bright moon is actually pointed at; they both lose sight of the finger and fail to distinguish between (the

states of) brightness and darkness. In doing so, they mistake the finger for the bright moon and are not clear about brightness and darkness. (Luk n/p)

This paragraph puts forth an interpretation of signs (in this case gesture) as mediator, a similar conceptualization as the ones presented by Charles Sanders Peirce and his Harvard School of Pragmatism and Semiotics. Furthermore, According to Tao-yüan, Bodhidharma did not make a display of verbal expressions [pu-shih yü-yen], and did not establish words and letters [pu-li wen-tzu]." Yang also indicates that Bodhidharma did not establish words and letters [pu-li wen-tzu] as directly pointing to the source of mind [ch'ih-chih shin-yüan], nor engaging in gradual methods [pu-chien chieh-ti] to attain Buddhahood immediately [ching-teng fo-ti] (Welter 2000: 93)

In Zen there is a close relationship between sensing, dynamism and perception, which along with conscious cognition and communicative performance are necessary in order to recognize self-nature. "When a false thought appears, correct it with rightness. When you are lost in self-nature, clear yourself by recognizing it. When a delusion is coming, replace it with wisdom. When doing evil, stop it by doing good." (Hui Neng 慧能, 2002: 163) This means that unreflective habits must be brought into critical reflection both in an objective and subjective way (see also Shusterman 2009: 133-5).

Vimalakirtinirdeu's translator, Seng Zhao (僧肇 384-414), recognized the significance of movement and stillness in giving birth to Yin and Yang. Movement contributes to separation, while stillness engenders combination (for a translation of Sengzhao's works see Liebenthal 1968). Self-awareness in Zen results from the alternation of these two principles. Zhao lun (肇论) explains "It is necessary to find stillness in the movement of things because, despite their movement, things reside in a constant state of stillness." (Seng Zhao, 1999.1; 5) Seng Zhao provided another few examples to explain the concepts of movement and static, and their relations with the natural world, since early Zen practitioners found refuge in forests and mountains. Examples of constant static are for Seng Zhao the hurricane blowing down the high mountains, or the river urging without torrent ceaselessly, and dusts floating everywhere without moving at all, or the sun and the moon, who follow each other in rotation. In terms of ontology, Seng Zhao understood nature as a motion that never ends beneath whose surface lies stillness. He explains that past events only exist in the past, and present things only exist in the present, so there is no connection between past and present and hence no change or movement. Seng Zhao also explained that meditation required and emptiness of mind that can only be achieved in a tranquil place in nature so that mind and body is aware of all senses, thoughts and delusions as well as good and evil.

The theme of emptiness and Wáng Wéi's Zen Buddhist approach to nature is fully represented in his famous octave with five characters, lv-shi (律诗) also known as "Dwelling in Mountain and Autumn Twilight" (山居秋暝). Firstly, let's gloss the Chinese characters of this poem as follows:

> 空山新雨后，
> Empty Mountain newly rain after
> 天气晚来秋。
> Sky Qi evening come autumn
> 明月松间照，
> Bright moon pines between shine
> 清泉石上流。
> Clear brook stone over flow
> 竹喧归浣女，
> Bamboos clatter (go) home washing girl
> 莲动下渔舟。
> Lotus shift (go) down fish boat
> 随意春芳歇，
> As (one) please spring fragrance wither
> 王孙自可留。
> Prince's descendants willingly can stay

This poem wu-lv (五律) has eight lines with five characters on each line. A single rhyme has to be used throughout the poem on the even line. As a tonal language, Chinese characters can be classified as "level" or "deflected", where certain tone patterns are imposed. The most important requirement is such that the second line of couplet needs to be a tonal reciprocal of the first, which emphasizes tonal counterpoint and syntactic parallelism. This also stands for the ying-yang parallelism of traditional Chinese thought. This poem follows a penta-syllabic scheme of tonal alternation between level and deflected tones which start with a level tone. There are many well-known translations of this poem:

Version 1: "On an Autumn Evening in the Mountain" (Trans. Chang and Walmsley, 1958:113)

>After newly-fallen rain in this vast mountains,
>When evening descends the air has the feel of fall.
>The limpid moon sparkles through the pine needles,
>The crystal stream glides glistening over the rocks.
>Babbling from the bamboo grove heralds the return of the washing girls,
>Lotus leaves sway as the fisherman pushes along his sampan...
>Although the fragrance of spring flowers has faded
>My good friend, you should still stay on for the beauty of autumn.

Version 2: "Autumn Dusk at a Mountain Lodge" (Trans. Yip, 1972:25)

>Empty Mountain after fresh rains:
>It is evening. Autumn air rises.
>Bright moon shines through pines,
>Clear spring flows over stones.
>Voices among bamboos: washing girls return;
>Lotus-leave move: down glide fishermen's boats.
>Here and there, fragrant grass withers,
>O prince, you do not have to go.
>(Allusion to two lines in the Ch'u Tz'u, Songs of South, "Summoning the Recluse": "O prince, return! In the mountain, you should not tarry.")

Version 3: "In the Hills at Nightfall in Autumn" (Trans. Robinson, 1973:75)

>In the empty hills just after rain,
>The Evening air is autumn now.
>Bright moon shining between pines,
>Clear stream flowing over stones.
>Bamboos clatter- the washer women goes home
>Lotuses shift- the fisherman's boat floats down.
>Of course spring scents must fail
>But you, my friend, you must stay.

Version 4: "Living in the Mountain on Autumn Night" (Trans. Barnstone, Barnstone, and Xu, 1991:7)

> After fresh rain on the empty mountain,
> Comes evening and the cold of autumn.
> The full moon burns through the pines,
> A brook transparent over the stones.
> Bamboo trees crackle as washerwomen go home,
> and lotus flowers sway as fisherman's boat slips downriver.
> Though the fresh smell of grass is gone,
> a prince is happy in these hills.

Version 5: "Autumn Twilight, Dwelling among Mountains" (Trans. Hinton, 2006:76)

> In Empty mountains after new rain,
> It's late. Sky-ch'I has brought autumn-
> Bright moon incandescent in the pine,
> Crystalline stream slipping across rocks.
> Bamboo rustles: homeward washer women,
> Lotuses waver: a boat gone downstream.
> Spring blossoms wither away by design,
> But a distant recluse can stay on and on.

Translations from Chinese into English are generally difficult. Besides, poetry might not have an ultimate translation. In the following lines I will focus on some of the words and features in this poem that make it impressive and therefore a piece of 'world literature'. I will also return to comment upon the translations above.

One of the most striking terms is the first character/word in the first line, kong (empty). Somehow, it can also be regarded as a synthetic form of the central theme of the poem. But what does the Kong mean? Why did the author call the mountain with the word kong-shan (Empty Mountain)? Is it referring to nobody, no sounds? In the following line of the poem, there are references to movement, bodies and sounds, such as the moon shining between the pines, or the flow of the brook, the crackle of bamboos, swaying lotuses, girls going home, and finally the gliding boat. Kong, in fact, refers to a spiritual space, which symbolizes the Zen concepts of body and mind transcendence. This theme is further emphasized by the following three characters/words xing yu hou (新雨后), literary 'after new rain'. The expression means that the mountain will be renewed with the rain, just like the body and mind of human beings. This is the first step in order to enter the Zen Buddhist field of emptiness. The line also dissolves the duality subject/object, in accordance with traditional Chinese Zen Buddhism, where humans are part of the whole natural order.

This brings to mind another well-known story from the Vimalakirti Sutra. It records that in answer to a group of bodhisattvas who had asked him to explain the concept of non-duality, Vimalakirti kept silence and did not say a word. Just like the "pointing finger" mentioned earlier, his silence was the only way to explain the "thunderous silence", the "great lion's roar of profound silence". In his analysis of this Wáng Wéi's poem, Willis Barnstone argues that the contrast between silence and movement intensifies the inner tension beneath the superficial stillness. In his view, Wáng Wéi's "Dwelling in mountain and autumn twilight" provides "another example where the stillness of sound and movement is conveyed paradoxically by its opposite, by noise and activity". (Barstone, Barstone, and Xu, 1991:xx)

In response to my idea about the multi-dimensional model of cross-cultural research focusing on literary adaptations (see Cultura: Journal of Philosophy of Culture and Axiology, Dec. 2012) professor Yi Chen analyzed "Bird Song Dale" (Niao Ming Jian) another of Wáng Wéi's important poems. In her paper "Semiosis of Translation in Wáng Wéi's and Paul Celan's Hermetic Poetry", Chen points out:

> According to Vimalakirti, the enlightened lay scholar and chief exponent of the Vimalakirti Sutra, the distinctions of all beings are in fact caused by "names," and in this sense, they are not real; only emptiness is real. Yet, emptiness itself is also a name, thus, is empty. By pointing to "silence," which symbolizes the highest wisdom, and which is contrasted with a mere indication (or gesture) of speechlessness, the Vimalakirti Sutra demonstrates an authentic approach to the truth of "emptiness", i.e. the possibility of non-dualistic thinking. (Chen, 2012: 90)

I must admit that her description "emptiness itself is also a name, thus is empty", is incisive and penetrating, and really grasps the motif of the Zen Buddhism. However, it does not mean that names or language are of no use, otherwise, we would not need much time to analyze Wáng Wéi's poem. What it signifies is that the distinctions among beings, caused by name and language, should be abandoned and endowed with non-dualistic thinking.

For the last twenty years or so, American scholar Richard Shusterman has been seeking to bring into his research the immediate dimension of somatic experience in relation to the outside world and nature in particular. For Shusterman, the fact that humans cannot see a connection between immediate somatic experience and their own lives indicates that their philosophical conceptions about the world are dominated by idealistic paradigms, hostile to the body. Shusterman's theory of somaesthetics seeks to define art experiences as a crucial background condition that can help widen "the realm of art by challenging the rigid division between art and action that is supported by definitions that define art as mimesis, poiesis, or the narrow practice defined by the institutional art world" (Shusterman, 2002: 29.)

Like other contemporary scholars (most popularly Judith Butler in Bodies that Matter). Shusterman advocates a definition of art as performance and dramatization, thus supplementing the idea of the illuminating nature of art (for the Asian roots of this conception, see Ghosh "Art as Dramatization and the Indian Tradition." 2003). Shusterman's definition involves the harmonization of two frames: the formal institutional frame and the experiential content (see Shusterman, "Art as Dramatization," in Surface and Depth), characterizing historicism and naturalism respectively. Thus, his account of interpretation is constructed with regards to the two opposites, analytic aesthetics and deconstruction. The fist attempts to construct an objective meaning identified with the artist's intention and built into the formal features of the work (Shusterman, Surface and Depth, 67). On the other hand, deconstruction emphasizes the systematic play of differences and the fact that every re-reading is an approximation or a "misreading" of the original.

According to Shusterman contemporary aesthetic ideals of body remain enslaved by shallow and oppressive stereotypes that serve more to increase profits for the cosmetics industries. He thinks that despite the renewed interest on the body, there is no conceptual framework that allows cooperation between the natural sciences and aesthetics. According to him, Western philosophy, from Kant through Hegel, Schopenhauer, and even 20th-century existentialism, has emphasized contemplation (see "Somaesthetics and the Revival of Aesthetics"). Shusterman defines somaesthetics as "the critical, meliorative study of the experience and the use of one's body as a locus sensory-aesthetic appreciation (aesthesis) and creative self-fashioning [...], devoted [also] to the knowledge, discourses and disciplines that structure such somatic care or can improve it." (Shusterman, "Somaesthetics and Care of the Self: The Case of Foucault", 532-

533). The term 'soma' emphasizes both the cultural and biological dimensions of corporeality, and signifies, as in Zen, a static/dynamic unity 'body-mind'.

Turning back to the poem by Wáng Wéi, "Dwelling in mountain and autumn twilight", the second line starting from the second line "tian qi wan lai qiu (天气晚来秋)" is very difficult to understand even for Chinese people. Particularly, the last three characters "wan lai qiu (晚来秋)" seem unreasonable. This sentence had been amended by the author in order to make the first word tian qi keep parallelism with the first words kong-shan in the first line, using the method of anastrophe (word order inversion). The correct syntactic order should be wan lai tian qi qiu (晚来天气秋), meaning the evening comes and the weather gets cooler in the autumn. Here the noun qiu (秋) means both autumn and cool, and has been used as a verb, referring to the process of season changes. So versions 1, 2, and 3 of the translations above may be correct. I noticed that Mr. Barnstone translated qiu with the word "cold of autumn", as shown in the translation which I labeled as version 4. This choice extends out of my understanding, because the word "cold" is not consistent with the leisure mode which this poem expresses from the perspective of Zen Buddhism. The word "cool" may be more appropriate for the translation of qiu. I also think wan (晚) for "late" in version 5 is not appropriate, Wan just means evening.

The following four lines could be regarded as the wealthiest poetic images in this poem. Each line could be illuminated as a painting. In fact, Wáng Wéi was famous for both his poetry and his paintings. Su Shi (苏轼) (1037–1101) one of the major poets of the Song Dynasty, claimed that Wáng Wéi's poems held a painting within them, and that in viewing his paintings one could envision poetry.

Regarding the translation of these four sentences, I think all of the five versions above are wonderful, although the translators use different words to translate them. What I would like to stress is that the movements between these lines show how silence is understood from the perspective of Zen Buddhism, just as pointed out above. In the third line, the reader is invited to look up and see the bright moon shining between the pines. In the fourth line the reader is asked to look down and find the clear spring flowing over stones. The two actions can be explained by the Chinese traditional aesthetic pattern and proverb, "yang guan fu cha (仰观俯察)", which represents the unity between sky and human beings (for more information see my paper "Zhou Yi and Ecological Aesthetics"). The non-duality perspective, present both in Zen Buddhism and Shusterman's Somaesthetics is even more obvious in lines 5-6 of the poem. Here I would like to emphasize two points: one the one hand, the interchangeability between human and natural beings, and at the same time, the cancellation of the cause/effect opposition. The second character/word xuan (喧) in line 5 points to the bamboos and the washing girls simultaneously. This character is really difficult to translate; in the dictionary one can find it meaning "noisy" but it can also express much subtler connotations of this word, in which the sound is not unpleasant at all. It might help to visualize a group of washing girls walking home in the twilight, their laughs sounding like bamboo shoots beaten by the wind. The metaphor is not just only an analogy. It seeks to provide the sensation of simultaneity, of both images happening at the same time.

None of the five translation above can do this, express these two both meanings simultaneously. It is almost as if language (any language) is not enough to convey a sensation that needs both body and mind to be felt and understood. A similar situation occurs in line 6. The second character/word dong (动) means 'move', and refers both to the lotuses and the boat. The identification between human and natural beings and the interchangeability between cause and effect is also present in these images is present in all these examples. It is not clear that the cracking sound of bamboos originates from the girls' washing, nor the rocking of the boat is the cause of the lotuses' swinging. Wáng Wéi's use of the Chinese characters indicates that it may also be the other way around. In terms of Zen Buddhism, this means that it not the lotuses or the boat that move, it is our hearts. In other words, when our heart is still and at peace, everything around us is also peaceful; nothing in the world, no external or mundane power, such as the sight of beautiful women in the poem, may cause it to stir. The poem expresses the pleasure and peace that this realization provides, and it does so particularly in its last two lines. Sui-yi (随意) in line 7 and Wáng-sun (王孙) in line 8 are again very difficult to translate, hence the many misunderstandings in the translations above. In this poemm sui-yi means "feel free to" not "by design", as in version 5. The most appropriate translation of line 7 should be "let spring blossoms feel free to wither", which is works as an anaphor to "autumn come" in line 1, and to the expression "stay" in the last line again.

Wáng-sun, is a literary quotation from Ch'u Tz'u (an anthology of The Songs of the South and Ancient Chinese), as Wai-lim Yip pointed out (Yip, 1972:25). Here it refers to both you and me, meaning "everybody will be happy to stay here". In contrast to the depicting scenery of the previous six lines, these last two express ideas and emotions, as part of the sudden enlightenment that Zen Buddhism provides. Likewise, the realization embodies Richard Shusterman's conception of somaesthetics. Shusterman speaks of analytical somaesthetics (descriptive and theoretical devoted to description and explanation), pragmatic somaesthetics (normative and prescriptive; proposes methods of somatic improvement and engages in their comparison, explanation, and critique) and practical somaesthetics (programs of disciplined, reflective, corporeal practice aimed at somatic self-improvement". (Shusterman, "Somaesthetics and The Second Sex: A Pragmatist Reading of a Feminist Classic", 112-114). The inspiration of readings such as Wáng Wéi's poems might be useful to practical programs of somatic self-improvement. The artistic fields are particularly apt to enabling the flow of emotions and empathic connections required to shape body and mind. The 5th Zen patriarch HongRen's (601-675) describes the connection in the following way: "The mind is not inside, outside, nor in the middle; it is not contemplated in terms of suchness and thusness, gradual or progressive. The motion of the mind is like a stream forever flowing [...] not thought in terms of arising and perishing that would only yield reversal and cessation. Finally, the flowing thoughts would be self-extinct in stillness." (Hong Ren 弘仁, n/p) Similarly, Zen master Lianchi (1535-1615) was enlightened while watching a crowd of monks taking a shower together, an episode that he described in "Ode to bathing", with the metaphor of the flow of water to illustrate the relationship between body and mind. (Lian Chi, 1999:590).

In my paper "Rethinking the Relationship between China and the West: A Multi-Dimensional Model of Cross-Cultural Research focusing on Literary Adaptations" I argued that the complexity of cross-cultural exchanges needs to be explained across space as well as time, situating cultural development within a much wider historical field, rather than in East/West or North/South dichotomies. With the example of Ji Junxiang's The Orphan of Zhao, a play adapted by Voltaire in L'Orphelin de la Chine, and re-adapted by Lin Zhaohua in 2003, including Voltaire's misreadings, and the analysis of Wang Guowei's theories on drama, in turned influenced by Schopenhauer's views on tragedy in The World as Will and Representation, I argued for the complexity of cross-cultural adaptations, mis-adaptations and critical interpretations that contribute to keep works in circulation turning them, as David Damrosch has argued, into world literature. A similar case can be made of Wáng-Wéi's poetry. American scholar Ernest Francisco Fenollosa, who spent a long time in Japan as professor of philosophy in Tokyo Imperial University, and whose art collections provided inspiration to many America poets, also when after his death in 1908, his unpublished notes on Chinese poetry and Japanese drama were entrusted by his widow to Ezra Pound, thus influencing Pound's ideogramic poetics as well as the early imagistic experimentations of authors such as T. E. Hulme and Amy Lowell, Wallace Steven's, or William Carlos William's. There is also an increasing penetration of Chinese aesthetics in the Black Mountain poetry of

Denise Levertov, work by James Wright and Robert Bly, in the Beat Poetry of Jack Kerouac, Allen Ginsberg and Gary Snyder, and most recently in poets like Sam Hamill and Robert Hass (see Barstone, Barstone, Xu, Lost in the Mountains: Poems of Wáng Wéi : xxiv-xxv; see also Wai-lim Yip's analysis of Wáng Wéi's influence upon Gary Snyder's poetry, 1972: viii)

Despite the interest of studies such as these, I am weary about understanding the circulation of influences in such simple terms. The main point that I try to make in this paper is precisely that translation can contribute to cross-cultural communication, but that there are many layers of meaning beneath the words of a poem, which sometimes a translation into another language cannot capture. I sympathize with Shusterman's idea of textual meaning inspired by Wittgenstein's later works. His notion of language games as a correlate to understanding in terms of shared and interpersonal abilities "to handle or respond to [something] in certain accepted ways" (Shusterman, Pragmatist Aesthetics 2000; 90), implies that interpretation is not the discovery of the inherent meaning of the text (or artwork), but a re-construction. Interpretation is always relative to certain rules given within the game. Since these rules change across cultures and over history, and some even disappear from use, we can speak of a plurality of correct interpretations of the same text both in synchronic and diachronic dimensions (Shusterman, "Logics of Interpretation: The Persistence of Pluralism", in Surface and Depth, 49). This is the reason why we can explain Wáng Wéi's poem from a comparative perspective between Zen Buddhism and Somaesthetics, a dialogue that hopes to bring East and West one step closer together.

REFERENCES

Abe, Masao & Heine, Steven. *Zen and Comparative Studies*, Univ of Hawaii Press 1996

Barnstone, Tony; Barnstone, Willis, and Xu, Haixin *Laughing Lost in the Mountains: Poems of Wáng Wéi*, Hanover, N.H.: University Press of New England 1991

Chappell, David W. "Hermeneutical Phases in Chinese Buddhism." In Donald S. Lopez, Jr. (Ed.), *Buddhist Hermeneutics*, Honolulu: University of Hawaii Press, 1988, 175-205.

Chang, Yin-nan and Walmsley, Lewis C. *Poems by Wáng Wéi,* Rutlant, Vermont: Charles E. Tuttle Company, Inc. 1958.

Chen, Yi. "Semiosis of Translation in Wáng Wéi's and Paul Celan's Hermetic Poetry." In López-Varela, Asunción (Ed.) *Semiotics of World Cultures.*

Thematic Issue Cultura. International Journal of Philosophy of Culture and Axiology 9(2)/2012: 87–102

Damrosch, David. *What Is World Literature?* Princeton: Princeton UP, 2003

Dumoulin, Heinrich. *Zen Buddhism: A History. Volume 1 & 2: India, China, Japan* World Wisdom Books. 2000-2005

Ghosh, Ranjan.K. & and Shusterman, Richard "Art as Dramatization and the Indian Tradition." *The Journal of Aesthetics and Art Criticism* 61.3 (2003): 293–298

Hinton, David. *The Selected Poems of Wáng Wéi*, New York: New Directions Books 2005

Hong Ren 弘忍 , *on the supreme vehicle* 最上乘论. <http://wenku.baidu.com/view/156b3d1aa300a6c30c229f0c.html>

Huineng 慧能, 2002 , *Tan jing* 坛经 Xi'an: San qin Press.

Li, Qingben "*Zhou Yi* and Ecological Aesthetics", *Journal of Central-South University for Nationalities*, 6 (2010): 23-28.

Li, Qingben and Guo Jinghua "Rethinking the Relationship between China and the West: A Multi-Dimensional Model of Cross-Cultural Research focusing on Literary Adaptations." In López-Varela, Asunción (Ed.) *Semiotics of World Cultures. Thematic Issue Cultura: International Journal of Philosophy of Culture and Axiology.* 9(2)/2012: 45-61

Lian Chi 莲池 Yunxi Lianchihong Dashi Yulu 云栖莲池宏大师语录 *Classic essence in Zen* 禅宗经典精华 Vol 13, Beijing: Religious culture Press 1999

Liebenthal, Walter. *Chao lun; the treatises of Sengzhao. A translation with introduction, notes, and appendices, 2nd edition.* Hong Kong: Hong Kong University Press & Oxford University Press 1968

Luk, Charles. (translator) (Year unknown), *The Surangama Sutra*, Buddha Dharma Education Association Inc.

McCauley, Charles. *Zen and the Art of Wholeness*, iUniverse 2005

McRae, John. "The Platform Sutra of the 6th Patriarch." Translated from the Chinese of Zongbao. *Taishō* 48. 2008 <http://www.thezensite.com/ZenTeachings/Translations/PlatformSutra_McRaeTranslation.pdf>

McMahan, David L. *The Making of Buddhist Modernism*. Oxford: Oxford University Press 2008

Meng-Tat Chia, Jack. "A Review of Enlightenment in Dispute: The Reinvention of Chan Buddhism in 17th-century China," *Journal of Buddhist Ethics.* 18, 2011 <http://blogs.dickinson.edu/buddhistethics/files/2011/06/JBE-Chia.pdf>

Nadeau, Randall L. *The Wiley-Blackwell Companion to Chinese Religions*, John Wiley & Sons 2012

Ning, Qiang. *Art, Religion, and Politics in Medieval China: The Dunhuang Cave of the Zhai Family.* University of Hawai'i Press 2004.

Oh, Kang-nam. "The Taoist Influence on Hua-yen Buddhism: A Case of the Scinicization of Buddhism in China," *Chung-Hwa Buddhist Journal,* 13, 2000
<http://www.thezensite.com/ZenEssays/HistoricalZen/Taoist_Influence_on_Hua-Yen_Buddhism.html>

Robinson, G. W. *Wáng Wéi: poems,* Harmondsworth: Penguin Group 1973

Seng Zhao *Zhao lun* 肇论, Dazhi Yuanzheng Sheng sengzhao Fashi Lun 大智园正圣僧肇法师论 *Classic essence in Zen* 禅宗经典精华 Vol 1, Beijing: Religious culture Press 1999

Shusterman, Richard "Somaesthetics and Care of the Self: The Case of Foucault", *Monist,* 83 (2000): 530-551.

Shusterman, Richard "Pragmatism and Criticism: A Response to three critics of Pragmatist Aesthetics" *Journal of Speculative Philosophy,* 16.1 (2002):26-38.

Shusterman, Richard. *Surface and Depth. Dialectics of Criticism and Culture*, Ithaca: Cornell University Press 2002

Shusterman, Richard "Pragmatism and East-Asian Thought", *Metaphilosophy*, 35, 2004

Shusterman, Richard "Pragmatist Aesthetics and East-Asian Philosophy", *Naked Punch* May 2006 <http://www.nakedpunch.com/shustermanchina.htm>

Shusterman, Richard "Somaesthetics and the Revival of Aesthetics", *Filozofski Vestnik*, 28. 2, 2007

Shusterman, Richard "Somaesthetics and The Second Sex: A Pragmatist Reading of a Feminist Classic", *Hypatia* 18 (4):106 - 136.

Shusterman, Richard "Body Consciousness and Performance: Somaesthetics East and West". *The Journal of Aesthetics and Art Criticism* 67:2 (2009):133-145

Welter, Albert. "Mahakasyapa's smile. Silent Transmission and the Kung-an (Koan) Tradition." In Steven Heine and Dale S. Wright (Eds) *The Koan. Texts and Contexts in Zen Buddhism*, Oxford: Oxford University Press 2000

Yip, Wai-lim. *Hiding the Universe: poems by Wáng Wéi*, New York: Grossman Publishers 1972.

ABOUT THE AUTHOR

Dr. Qingben Li is professor and director of the Institute for Comparative Literature and Cultural Studies in Beijing Language and Culture University. His current research is most especially concerned with the cross-cultural studies on comparative literature and culture.

CHAPTER 13

Signs, Intermediality and Chinese Calligraphy

Jinghua Guo

Chinese uses Chinese characters known as hanzi. These are symbols, based on ancient iconic ideograms, and do not comprise an alphabet. This writing system, in which each character generally represents either a complete one-syllable word or a single-syllable part of a word, is called logo-syllabic. Each character has its own pronunciation. Being literate in Chinese requires memorizing about 4,000 characters.

Because many commonly used Chinese characters have 10 to 30 strokes, certain stroke orders have been recommended to ensure speed, accuracy and legibility in composition. So, when learning a character, one has to learn the order in which it is written, and the sequence has general rules, such as: top to bottom, left to right, horizontal before vertical, middle before sides, left-falling before right-falling, outside before inside, inside before enclosing strokes.

The strokes in Chinese characters fall into eight main categories: horizontal (一), vertical (丨), left-falling (丿), right-falling (丶), rising (╱), dot (丶), hook (亅) and turning (⁻, ㄴ, 乙, etc.). Correct stroke order, proper balance and rhythm of characters are all essential of Chinese calligraphy. The "Eight Principles of Yong" is an outline of how to write these strokes. They can all be found in the character for "yǒng" (永, which translates as "forever" or "permanence"). In many cases, a calligrapher will practice writing the Chinese character "永" many times in order to perfect the eight basic essential strokes contained within the letter. It was believed that the practice of these principles would ensure beauty in one's writing calligraphy.

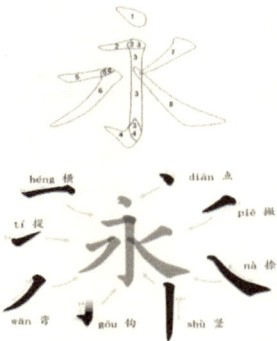

Image from< http://en.wikipedia.org/wiki/Eight_Principles_of_Yong>

The expression "Four treasures of the study" refers to the brush, ink, paper and ink stone used in Chinese and other East Asian calligraphic traditions. The head of the brush can be made of the hair (or feather) of a variety of animals, including wolf, rabbit, deer, chicken, duck, goat, pig and tiger, and sometimes even a newborn child, who would preserve this as a souvenir. The artist usually completes their work of calligraphy by adding their seal at the very end, in red ink. The seal serves as a signature and is usually done in an old style.

Many East Asian scripts (such as Chinese, Japanese and Korean) can be written horizontally or vertically, because they consist mainly of disconnected syllabic units, each conforming to an imaginary square frame. Traditional Chinese is written in vertical columns from top to bottom; the first column is on the right side of the page, with the text starting on the right. In modern times, using a Western layout of horizontal rows running from left to right and being read from top to bottom has become more popular.

In Chinese calligraphy, Chinese characters can be written in five major styles. These styles are intrinsic to the history of Chinese script. The oldest style is 'seal script' which continues to be widely practiced, although most people today cannot read it.

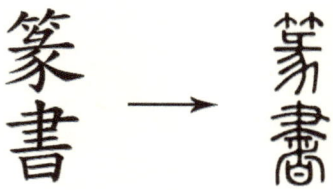

http://en.wikipedia.org/wiki/File:Seal_Eg.png

In clerical script, characters are generally "flat" in appearance, and wider than in seal script and modern script, both of which tend to be taller than wider. Some versions of clerical are square and rectilinear.

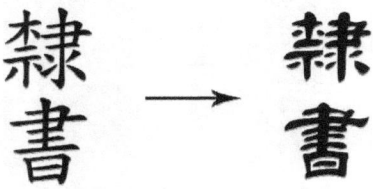

http://en.wikipedia.org/wiki/File:Clerical_Eg.png

The semi-cursive script approximates normal handwriting, in which strokes and sometimes characters are allowed to run into one another. Here, the brush leaves the paper less often than with the regular script and characters appear less angular.

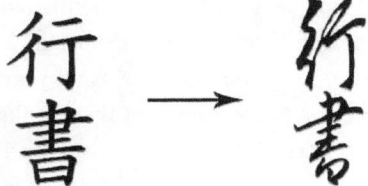

http://en.wikipedia.org/wiki/File:Semi-Cur_Eg.png

The cursive script is a fully cursive, with large simplifications and ligatures. It requires specialized knowledge to be read. Entire characters may be written without lifting the brush from the paper at all, and characters frequently flow into one another, being highly rounded and soft in appearance, with a noticeable lack of angular lines.

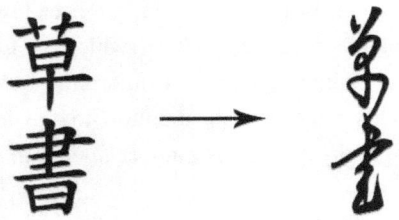

http://en.wikipedia.org/wiki/File:Cur_eg.svg

The regular script developed from a semi-cursive form of clerical script. As the name suggests, this script is "regular," with each stroke written slowly and carefully, the brush being lifted from the paper and all strokes distinct from each other.

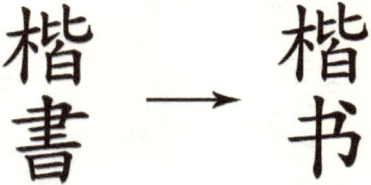

http://en.wikipedia.org/wiki/File:Regular_Eg.png

In the ancient Chinese tradition, artists extracted the primary principle for artistic creation from real life: "Both ancient Chinese characters and mixed-seal characters are imitations of objects." (SuoJing, 2007: 19 cited in Peng & Geng 127) WeiHeng (?-291), a great Chinese calligrapher, argued that "Seal characters designed in the forms of birds and young frogs are pictographic scripts, which are created by imitating appearance of objects." (SuoJing, 2007:14 cited in Peng & Geng 127) With a history of over six thousand years, Chinese calligraphy, occurred initially in the New Stone Age, and then in the graphics sculptured in bronze during Shang and early Zhou Dynasty, the bird-pest calligraphy in the 'Spring and Autumn Period', the seal script calligraphy in Qin and Han Dynasties, and the Song typeface in Song Yuan Ming and Qing Dynasties. All of these used materials as varied as bronze weapons, seals, pennant, bricks, tiles, paper-cut, cloth-embroidery, prints, and so on, a clear sign of its intermedial potential. (Li mingjun, 1996: 3)

Furthermore, Marge Landsberg (1980) has noted that there are many languages, like Chinese, that contain elements which are not just symbolic and arbitrary. As mentioned in Charles S. Peirce's classification of signs, they also include iconic and imitative forms. According to Peirce (1839-1914), an icon is a non-arbitrary intentional sign, a designation which is to a significant degree representational and has some degree of isomorphism and resemblance to the object it designates. This paper draws attention to the iconic correspondences between Chinese calligraphy and their subject-matter in order to point out its intermedial qualities.

For Charles Sanders Peirce and the Harvard School of Pragmatism, a sign is an object standing for that an experience of the former affords knowledge of the latter in some respect or capacity. This includes sounds, images, gestures, scents, tastes, textures, words and so on. The sign creates in the mind a more developed sign, a mental effect or thought that Peirce calls 'interpretant' and which gives the sign significance or meaning, becoming in turn a sign in a dynamic process ad infinitum. In Peirce's conception, signs can be divided into icons, indices and symbols. Symbols are arbitrary and unmotivated, reliant on conventional usage to determine meaning. Symbolic signs are agreed upon for given purposes and they can be found in most alphabets. Indices always point, reference, or suggest something else by means of Peirce outlined three types: tracks, symptoms, and designations. Tracks often have a physical, cause & effect relationship, but are not simultaneous with their object (i.e. foot or paw prints). Symptoms are simultaneous with their object, and distinguishing between symptom and object may be impossible (i.e. fever is a symptom of infection; smoke is a symptom of fire). Lastly, designations point or signify while being distinct from their object (i.e. proper names, a pointed finger, and the word 'this'). Finally, icons are signs that resemble what they stand for. Originally called "likenesses" by Peirce, icons have a "topological similarity" to their object (i.e. figurative painting -not surrealist or modern- and photographs). Peirce creates three subcategories of icon: image, metaphor and diagram. The relations of resemblance between 'images' and objects are relatively simple, their attributes based on sensory qualities. Diagrams and their objects share structural relations even if they may have a degree of arbitrariness (i.e. maps and equations). Metaphors "represent the representative character of an object by representing a parallelism in something else" (Johansen 2002, 40; also Burks "Icon, Index, and Symbol", 1949: 675). Though technically conveyed through the non-iconic symbols of language, this includes literary metaphors. Peirce's definition, however, remains much broader, with signs occupying several categories simultaneously (i.e. a thermometer is an index but also a metaphoric icon).

In Chinese artistic calligraphy, every character is a kind of creative decorative form designed by the artist who takes inspiration from nature. Chinese characters fall within six categories: self-explanatory characters, pictographs, pictophonetic characters, associative compounds, mutually explanatory characters and phonetic loan characters. Among them, pictographs were used as the earliest form of writing and a basic way of words building, undoubtedly linked to drawing, and thus "describing objects as they are" (XieHe, 1997: 55; see also 479-502). XuShe also emphasized that hieroglyphic characters are learnt "from outside and made into words through painting." (XuShe, 2010: 4) Resemblance is an integral part of Chinese writing, no matter how simplified or abstracted. This fact conforms to Peirce's ideas where icons represent relations of direct imitation between signifier and signified on the basis of external peculiarities. (Peirce, 1885: 181) Thus, his theories have had a particular impact on the logic of imaging, graphic and intermedial signification (Michael Leja, "Peirce, Visuality, and Art", 2000: 26). In another section of the article on Archaic Chinese Graphology, Jiang LiangFu claims that

> The overall spirit of the Chinese characters started with human life, or rather, from the entire body of human being's. The presence of all LIFE IS perceived by the senses of seeing, hearing, touching, smelling, tasting, and especially the sense of seeing is the most important. This has created the characters 牛, 羊, 虎 (ox, sheep, tiger) characterizing their heads. These parts are easily be recognized by people, and to create characters like 龙, 凤 (Chinese dragon, Chinese phoenix) which the luckiest signs and universally worshiped by Chinese. (1984: 66)

The characters like 日, 月, 水, 雨, 山 (sun, moon, water, rain and mountain) are also very typical examples of form imitation. By stylized drawings, they represent the appearance of the objects. 水 (shuǐ, "Water") represents the lines of a flowing river. 山(shān, "Mountain") presents the undulating peaks of mountains. 雨(yǔ, "Rain") resembles the appearance of the rain coming from sky. The character 牛 and 羊 are easily recognized by imitating ox' and sheep' heads; while (马, "horse") (鸟, "bird") and (龟, "tortoise") are the stylized drawings of the entire forms of their corresponding animals. The objects and their corresponding Chinese pictographic characters are shown in the table below.

objects	Regular Script (Simplified)	Pinyin	Meaning
⊖	日	ri	Sun
☽	月	yuè	Moon
⋈	山	shān	Mountain
水	水	shuǐ	Water
⋒	雨	yǔ	Rain
Ψ	牛	niú	Cow

Signs, Intermediality and Chinese Calligraphy

✦	羊	yáng	Goat
✦	马	mǎ	Horse
✦	鸟	niǎo	Bird
✦	龟	guī	Tortoise

http://en.wikipedia.org/wiki/Chinese_character_classification

There are also some types of calligraphy that are more imaginative. For example, Dragon's Claw Calligraphy, Tassel Calligraphy, Bird-pest Calligraphy or Tadpole Calligraphy, where additional imaginative details are added to the writing.

The origin of Tassel Calligraphy dates back to the mythology of Yan Emperor Shen-nung (神农) 5000 years ago. Known as the Emperor of the Five Grains and the patron of agriculture in ancient China, Shen-nung taught ancient Chinese practices of agriculture and use of herbal drugs. After testing and tasting hundreds of plants, he finally discovered the tassel plant. He created one text for record and celebration, where the bottoms of character strokes look like tassels. Today, Chinese regard him and Yellow Emperor (XuanYuan Shi, 轩辕氏) as father of the nation and branch ceremonies to worship every year. Shen-nung's tassel calligraphy created eight characters "日月盈晨、辰宿列张", which are so beautiful and elegant that they have become the wonders of world's writings. They reflect Shen-nung's great joy for the golden harvest.

Images from
http://blog.163.com/shz6763814@126/blog/static/58093441201043110 5249685

As another typical example, Tadpole Calligraphy is named for the strokes based on its appearance. It is written using a tadpole-like stroke with thick heads but thin tails. Tadpole calligraphy has been regarded as one of the eight original texts or symbols of China that are mysterious and would need further analysis.

http://baike.baidu.com/link?url=Qyiopdoy3o9qFsHHZX8UpGHE0mS66WL72aiCeXa-QcX0lSVlR06FRGb-2OogdgM8

Bird-pest Calligraphy prevailed from the later Spring and Autumn Period to the Warring States Period in the south of ancient China. This calligraphy reflects vividly the ancient culture of these areas. The images of birds, insects and fish are added to the strokes and combined with Chinese characters. This kind of style often takes the form of golden gilding and looks noble and gorgeous. Hence, Bird-pest Calligraphy adorns many ancient Chinese weapons, containers and sacrificial vessels. The inscription on King Goujian's sword (King Goujian was King of Yue, famous for his perseverance in time of hardship) illustrates this point well. The attachment of images not only provides a decorative effect, but also adds to the complexity of the strokes, making the calligraphy unpredictable and quite difficult to identify. Therefore, sometimes Bird-pest Calligraphy was also used to inscribe flags to convey commands because it was difficult to decipher and falsify. After the Han dynasty this style was used primarily in seals and it evolved into a kind of art font.

Modern Chinese scholar, Guo Moruo (郭沫若, 1892-1978), commented that images of birds and pests were added to the calligraphy under aesthetic consciousness, and that it also emphasized their utility as decorative patterns on cloth. This was the origin of the first ancient Chinese references to calligraphy as arts work.

Images from http://baike.baidu.com/view/328118.htm

With time, the strokes added to the characters in Chinese calligraphy incorporated the patterns taken from the natural world combined with abstractions. For example, a particular type of Chinese calligraphy known as Flying White Calligraphy came from cursive characters drawn with seals, and evolved into a novel style of calligraphy characterized by its hollow strokes done with a half-dry brush. Huang BoSi (1079—1118) who lived in Earlier Song Dynasty explained that "It takes that part same like silky hair to stand for white, cites its kinetic potential to fly as flying" (Huang BoSi. "Dongguan Yulun, Flying white", 2010: 83) Created by Cai Yong (133-192) in the Han Dynasty, the story tells that he was inspired by the artisans painting the walls of the Royal Library with a broom dipped in lime. This type of calligraphy came to be executed with bamboo rather than a brush. Because of the special brush technique applied, ribbon-like wide lines are left behind, giving an impression of jumping or leaping on the paper surface without losing contact with it, all executed in one stroke. Owing to this, Flying White becomes more of an aesthetic brush technique than a style, and it also has found favour in neighbouring countries, such as Japan. Kuukai (空海, 774–835) was a Buddhist monk, scholar and also possibly the greatest calligrapher of all time in Japan; in his work he brilliantly merged Flying White with semi-cursive script (行書).

"To flutter" (翻), calligraphy by Kuukai (空海), flying white style, early Heian period, 9th century C.E.

Images from http://www.beyondcalligraphy.com/flying_white_script.html

In the Tang dynasty of ancient China, symbol painting was interwoven with Flying White, such as dragons, birds, or other motifs. The work of Empress Wu (武则天, 624 - 705), the only empress in Chinese history, exemplified and illustrated this point well. She managed to develop her own style of Flying White decorated with bird drawings. Her work was like her character; strong, expressive and bold.

Fragment of the top part of a tablet attributed to Empress Wu Zetian (武则天), character "仙" (immortal), flying white style, Tang dynasty, 699 C.E.

http://www.beyondcalligraphy.com/flying_white_script.html

Flower-Bird-Dragon-Phoenix Calligraphy (花鸟龙凤字) is also tremendously popular. It is a free cursive style with an auspicious and joyful meaning and a great visual appeal, where words and drawing are fused together. This kind of pictographic calligraphy originated during Han dynasty and thrived in Tang dynasty and now has become one of the popular categories of folk art in China. One of the reasons for its popularity is that a pictograph of a pair of Flower-Bird-Dragon-Phoenix can be finished very quickly, only in 3 to 5 minutes. The brushes for it are not ordinary ones and made from special materials. Once painted on the paper, it will appear as different colours. When observing an example, one is amazed by its interesting, vivid appearance and folk craftsmen's creativity. The patterns look like flowers, forests, ships or butterflies, but in fact the texts are people's names or encouraging phrases for wishes. Flower-Bird-Dragon-Phoenix Calligraphy incorporates characters and patterns effectively to show happiness and good luck. It embodies both traditional painting's clearness and western painting's colourfulness. Because of all these unique characteristics, Flower-Bird-Dragon-Phoenix Calligraphy lives up to its name as a rarity in China's history of culture.

(家和万事兴, meaning Harmonious family makes everything prosperous)
Images from <http://www.culture-sh.com/en/craft/CraftItem.aspx?ID=11>

Chinese characters evolve from pictures and signs, and the art of calligraphy develop naturally from this special writing system. The Ancient Chinese use calligraphy to communicate by using strokes companied with painting to pursue the beauty of nature and man's spirit. Luxun (鲁迅, 1881-1936) said that calligraphy is painting. Chinese calligraphy maintains the beauty factor in nature and has exactly the same origin as painting.

Eave tiles use characters, suns, moons, and stars; Graph-Text uses carriages and horses; Floral Currency employs turtles and cranes; JiaQing porcelain shows characters organized by pines, and so on. Eave tiles are small accessories in classical Chinese architecture fixed at the end of rafters for decoration and for shielding the eaves from wind and rain. They emerged as a culture in their own light during the Zhou (c.11th century-771 B.C.) and reached their zenith during the Qin and Han (221 B.C.-220 A.D.). In the interring years, Eave tiles underwent the transition from a half-round design to a cylindrical design, and from plain surface to decorative patterns, from intaglio to bas-relief carvings, from lifelike imagery to abstraction, and from patterns to inscriptions, until they became an art that involved many intermedial aspects, including language, literature, aesthetics, calligraphy, carving, decoration and architecture, with themes that ran the gamut from nature and ecology to mythology, totems, history, palaces, yamens, mausoleums, place names, auspicious phrases, folklore, and family names. Together the eaves tiles form a history book that reflects vividly the natural scenery, humanities, political science and economics.

http://www.chinaculture.org/classics/2008-05/06/content_132864_2.htm

In addition, some calligraphy styles scenes are taken from popular myths, folklore, and historical figures. The iconicity of these themes is always fused with the creator's ideographic thinking, for instance Monk Tang's "Pilgrimage to the West".

Based on the changeable shape of Chinese characters, Shenzhi Poetry (神智诗) was formed in ancient China and characteristic of its witty literary style. These poems would not be written directly on paper, but expressed by poets through presenting characters' abnormal formation appearance, including the size, thickness, length, order density, the amount of strokes, missing strokes, the height etc methods . People need to read these poems not only as a visual experience but also in their guessing ability, like playing word games. Only in this way, readers can comprehend the ingenious design of the poems and the hidden wisdom of poets. Su Shi, a literary figure from the Song Dynasty, was believed to be the creator of this kind of poetry. His works are regarded as the most classical Shenzhi examples of poetry in ancient Chinese calligraphy history.

Signs, Intermediality and Chinese Calligraphy

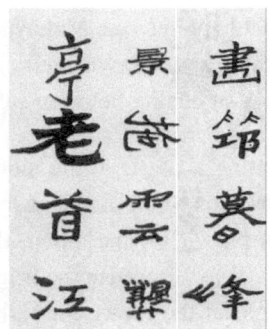

长亭短景无人画，老大横拖瘦竹筇。回首断云斜日暮，曲江倒蘸侧山峰。《晚眺》
苏轼

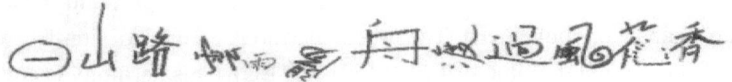

In Chinese thought the secular and the sacred are contemplated as opposites interlinked in harmonious proportions. While the secular world is reflected in the liveliness of natural depictions, the sense of holiness and timelessness also permeates these images. Much of the sacred timelessness is inspired in Zen (Chán meaning "absorption" or "meditation"), a school of Mahayana Buddhism that originated in China during the 6th-century. Traditionally the origin of Chán in China is credited to the monk Bodhidharma, recorded as having come from India during the time of Southern and Northern Dynasties. The idea that the ultimate reality is present in the daily world of relative reality fitted into Chinese culture, which emphasized the mundane world and society.

Seng Zhao's Zhaolun (Treatises of Seng zhao) is perhaps the most significant text for the study of the early Mādhyamika School (549-623 CE), a philosophical development that arose within Mahāyāna Buddhism in India during the first few centuries CE, and its relationship to the indigenous Daoist and Confucian traditions. As Qingben Li (2013) points out, Mahāyāna concentrates on showing how signs, representing concepts and ideas as well as real objects, should not be contemplated with a false sense of duality between subject and object.

> It is like a man pointing a finger at the moon to show it to others who should follow the direction of the finger to look at the moon. If they look at the finger and mistake it for the moon, they lose (sight of) both the moon and the finger. Why? Because the bright moon is actually pointed at; they both lose sight of the finger and fail to distinguish between (the states of) brightness and darkness. In doing so, they mistake the finger for the bright moon and are not clear about brightness and darkness. (Luk n/p cited in Qingben Li 2013, 38)

Seng Zhao (僧肇 384-414) recognized the significance of movement and stillness in giving birth to Yin and Yang. Movement contributes to separation, while stillness engenders combination. Self-awareness in Zen results from the alternation of these two principles: "It is necessary to find stillness in the movement of things because, despite their movement, things reside in a constant state of stillness." (Seng Zhao, 1999, cited in Qingben Li 39) Seng Zhao understood nature as a motion that never ends, beneath whose surface lies stillness. He explains that past events only exist in the past, and present things only exist in the present, so there is no connection between past and present and hence no change or movement. The word 'harmony' came to signify 'without conflict' from around the time of LaoZi (571-471BC). This harmony is embodied in the abstract symbol 'He', which means 'and' in Chinese, coming to describe the unity of non-identical things (see Zhang Dainian. Key Concepts in Chinese Philosophy, 2005: 270)

The metaphor of a celestial wheel is used by Zhuang Zhou (369-286BC) to explain how "all things belong to their own species, their births and deaths coming again and again manifested in different situations. The beginning and the end of this alternate progress is just like a great wheel rotating without stop. Nobody is able to find the sequence in which things have happened" (Zhuang zhou, 2009: 171) This view is present in Tao, "the connection between Yin and Yang" (Confucius.2010: 290), an "opening and closing named 'change'" (Confucius.2010: 298) Yang is the power of creation, while Yin nourishes life. Both interact and produce innumerable variations, seasonal patterns, plant renewing, fading, decay and death, new birth, etc. Owning to this central idea, Chinese calligraphy is articulated in an intermedial harmonious equilibrium that puts together the popular and the divine, as well as sound and image, writing and painting.

For example, the popular decorative character 寿 shou (longevity) is used to express abundance of blessings, and visually the amount of strokes conveys this idea, while the stretching and undulating forms transmit the meaning of immortality. 寿 is sometimes drawn in a composition with ancient coins in order to convey the progress of longevity. In ancient Chinese culture, coins also are named for 泉 (quan) which sounds like 全 (quan, meaning together/ fullness). The Chinese pronunciation of a bat sounds 蝙蝠 (bianfu); while the pronunciation of the character 蝠' is identical to the character 福 (fu, meaning Happiness). The following picture (Figure1) with images of the bat, the ancient coin and the character 寿, conveys good wishes and a deep meaning that happiness and longevity will last forever. The plant presented in the picture is Ganoderma lingzi (灵芝), regarded as fairy plant and a symbol of happiness in ancient China.

<http://image.baidu.com/i?tn=baiduimage&ipn=r&ct=201326592&cl=2&jm=index&lm=-1&st=-1&sf=2&fmq=&pv=&ic=0&nc=1&z=&fb=0&istype=2&ie=utf-8&word=%E5%AF%BF%E5%AD%97%E5%9B%BE%E7%89%87&f=3&oq=%E5%AF%BF%E5%AD%97%E5%9B%BE&rsp=0>

Besides, the creation of Chinese character Biáng also can serve as a good example. Premier Li Si in the Qin Dynasty is traditionally credited with the invention of the Biáng character, but in a popular version, it was a poor scholar in Xian city who, inspired by the sound of dough being drummed 'Biang Biang', created the character. 'Biang' is a complex character made of 58 strokes of various types. Xian and Shanxi providence residents describe the graphic patterns in 'Biang' using the following visual song:

> A point rises up to heaven, and the yellow river has two bends. The character "eight" (八) opens its mouth, and the character "speak" (言) walks in. You make a twist, I make a twist, (幺 'tiny') you grow, I grow (長), and we add a horse (馬) king in between. The character "heart" (心) forms the base, the character "moon" (月) stands at the side, a hook (刂 'knife') at the right to hang sesame candies, and we ride a carriage to tour (radical: 辶 'walk') the streets of Xianyang.

< http://en.wikipedia.org/wiki/File:Bi%C3%A1ng_%28regular_script%29.svg >

'Biang' conveys the idea of simultaneity, being here and there, present and past, earthly and heavenly, popular and sacred. But it also conveys the intermedial multiplicity of Chinese calligraphy. 'Biang' is sound, image, and cultural metaphor at the same time.

The Chinese character feng (the wind) is created when a pictograph for aninsect (chong; originally hui, a type of snake (Figure1), is placed inside the character fan, which means the origin (Figure2). The resulting character (Figure3) is explained in an ancient Chinese text as; "when the wind blows, insects are born." This meaning of feng has evolved due a multitude of cultural influences and beliefs; the belief that wind" lives" in caves before rushes out into the world; that all kinds of insects live in caves; that both wind and insects are a cause of destruction for man. These all led to the "when the wind blows, insects are born" interpretation. The wind is also viewed as a "pernicious influence," that windy weather can cause disease, again a perciveved distructive force. The simplified version (Figure 4) keeps the meaning of movement of the air in the Eastern and Western cultures. (Subhuti Dharmananda, http://www.itmonline.org/articles/feng/feng.htm)

Chong or Hui Fan   Feng Feng (traditional)

Another type of folk calligraphy is a palindrome, which conveys the principles of non-duality and Zen, offering the visual metaphor of a cyclic and dynamic view of space-time.

A palindrome may be written in different forms, either as short couplet or a traditional poem, it is a word, phrase, number or other sequence of units that has the property being read in either direction. A Chinese word is not composed of letters or syllables, but a character. Chinese palindromes have to be phrases or sentences and are much easier to construct than in languages written with an alphabet. The adjustment of punctuation and spaces between words is generally permitted (for several examples see Peng and Geng 2013).

> "可以清心", "以清心可", "清心可以", "心可以清"

> May make a heart pure, being pure make a heart, a pure heart can be permitted, a heart can be made pure

> "月是故乡明", "是故乡明月", "故乡明月是," "乡明月是故", "明月是故乡"

> The moon is bright in hometown; is the hometown bright moon; the hometown bright moon is it; hometown is bright for the moon; the bright moon is hometown.

Su Hui (苏蕙, 357-？) was a Chinese poet from the Pre-Qing period. She was well known for renovating the genre and producing the most visually and structurally impressive palindrome masterpiece to date. Using multicolored silks, she wove the poem onto brocade. Her poem consists of 841 characters and is in the form of a twenty-nine by twenty-nine character grid. This example can be read in any directions, forward, backwards, vertically, horizontally, diagonally. It may even be read within its color-coded grids. Su Hui's works is regarded as one of miracles of Chinese literary history.

http://image.baidu.com/

Some Chinese expressions employ metaphorical images to convey meaning. For instance, the expression of love can take the form of two butterflies, two swallows, fish or lotus.

http://image.baidu.com/i?tn=baiduimage&ipn=r&ct=201326592&cl=2&lm=-

LiuXie (465-520) explained that the feelings hide beyond words and that forms only partially show their meaning (2007: 226), with much meaning remaining 'hidden' in 'empty spaces' through which the readers would be able to create interpretations based on their own feelings, thoughts OR experiences, as in Qingben Li (2013) shows in the example of Wáng Wéi's poem "Dwelling in

Mountain and Autumn Twilight". This means that Chinese characters embody a dynamic quality which is much related to Zen principles. Finally, the Tao symbol of Yin and Yang itself represents heaven as a circle and earth as a square (a sphere and a cube in tri-dimensional representation):

> Utmost Yang is solemn, somber; utmost Yin is brilliant, shinning. The solemn and somber comes from heaven; the brilliant and shinning comes from earth. The two intermingle, interpenetrate, perfect harmony and so things are generated from them."(Confucius.2010: 314)

When Yin and Yang are connected to spirit and matter, ideas and their representations (signs); reunited creation takes place; separated death occurs. As shown, Chinese calligraphy captures this complex dynamics and correlation between the visual, the sonic, reality and imagination.

The culture of the ancient Chinese calligraphy texts, also gives new charm in the modern life. The official logo and pictograms designed for Beijing Olympic Games can serve as perfect examples to this. The inspiration for creating these pictograms originates mainly from Chinese characters. The logo for Beijing Olympic Games entitled "Dancing Beijing" features a stylized calligraphic character 京 (jīng, meaning capital) thus referring to the host city.

As for pictograms, in ancient China they were made of strokes of seal characters as basic forms and integrated the pictographic charm of inscriptions on bones and bronze objects, becoming the simplified embodiment of modern graphics. The pictograms for Beijing Olympics are praised as the beauty of seal characters. They showcase the appealing and flowing beauty of seal characters fully. For instance, the pictogram for swimming is made up of two parts. The top element is the brief symbol for a person; the bottom element is the symbol for water.

As illustrated above, water is written as ')' in the seal character. Therefore, based on the source, several curved strokes are applied to express the flowing of water in the pictogram for swimming.

A second good example is from the pictograms for athletics and football. Both of them originate from the seal character (舞) in order to show the visual effect of running actions. By using lines, these two pictograms not only express the attractiveness of sport spirit but also are aesthetically pleasing

The pictograms for Beijing Olympics illustrate well the effects of sharp contrast between the black and white colours, just as used in the traditional Chinese artistic form of rubbings.

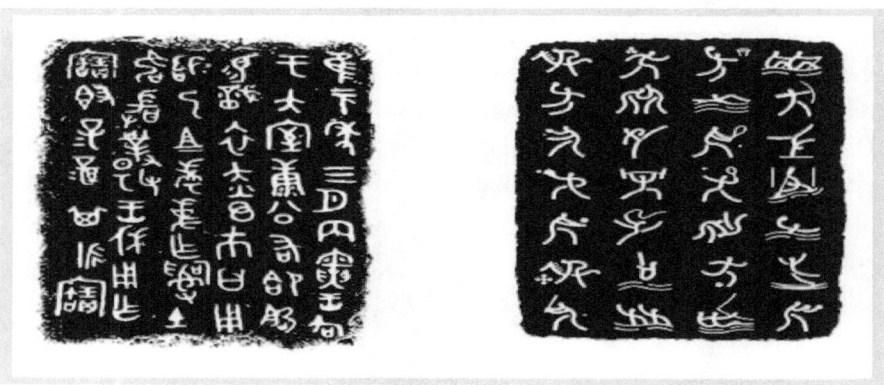

http://creativerepository.com/2010/01/14/evolution-of-olympic-pictograms-1964-to-2012/

The pictograms of the Beijing Olympics display a distinct character of motion, a graceful aesthetic perception of movement and rich cultural connotations, thus arriving at the harmony and unity of form with conception.

To conclude, Chinese characters are complex signs that rely on hybrid combinations of different types of signs, as distinguished by Harvard pragmatist Charles S. Peirce. The paper has shown the intermedial qualities of Chinese calligraphy and the influence of Zen Buddhism upon traditional Chinese writing in general. Signs are shown as complex structures that mediate between reality and human interpretation, tinted with cultural and ideological significances.

Note: Research for the article above is funded by 《中华文化的跨文化阐释与对外传播研究》 Key Projects of Philosophy and Social Science Research by the Ministry of Education, P.R. of China (13JZD032), 《跨文化阐释视阈下中西文化比较模式的建构与研究》 Research Program of Science and Technology at Universities of the Inner Mongolia Autonomous Region, P.R. of China (NJSY14074) and 《内蒙古地区大学英语多模态教学模式下学生多元文化认知能力培养的研究》 Research Project by Inner Mongolia Academy of Social Science (2015). Copyrights release to the author.

REFERENCES

Burks, Arthur W. "Icon, Index, and Symbol", *Philosophy and Phenomenological Research*, Vol. 9, 1949.
Confucius (孔子). Xici xia 系辞下) *ZhouYi* （周易）. Trans. Guo Yu （郭彧）. Beijing: Zhonghua book company, 2010.
Huang BoSi（黄伯思). "Dongguan Yulun, Flying white" （东观余论）, *Selected Writings of Previous Dynasties' Calligraphy* (历代书法论文选续编). Shanghai: Shanghai Calligraphy and Painting Press, 2010.
Jiang LiangFu (姜亮夫). *Archaic Chinese Graphology* (古文字学). Hang Zhou: The People Press of Zhejiang, 1984.
Johansen, Jorgen Dines. *Signs in Use: An Introduction to Semiotics*, New York: Routledge, 2002.
Landsberg, Marge E. "The Icon in Semiotic Theory". *Current Anthropology*, 21, 1980.
Li Qingben (李庆本). "Intersemiotic Translation: Zen and Somaesthetics in Wáng Wéi's poem 'Dwelling in Mountain and Autumn Twilight'" Vishvanatha Kaviraja Institute, Orissa, India, *Journal of Comparative Literature and Aesthetics*, 36 (2013): 37-46.
Li Mingjun (李明君). *An Illustrated history of Artistic Calligraphy in China* (中国美术字图史说). Beijing: The People and Art Press, 1996.
LiuXie (刘勰). "Being hidden and shown" （隐秀）. *The Outline of Chinese Aesthetic History* (中国美学史大纲).Ye Lang （叶朗）. Shanghai: The People Press of Shanghai, 2007.
Liu Rong. "Amazing ChineseEavesTiles". <http://www.chinaculture.org/classics/2008-05/06/content_132864_2.htm>
Luk, Charles. (translator) (Year unknown), *The Surangama Sutra*, Buddha Dharma Education Association Inc.

Peirce, Charles Sanders. "On the Algebra of Logic: A Contribution to the Philosophy of Notation". *American Journal of Mathematics*, Vol. 7, Johns Hopkins University Press, 1885.

Peirce, Charles Sanders. *Peirce on Signs. Writings on Semiotics*. Chapel Hill: University of North Carolina Press, 1991.

Peirce（皮尔斯）, "Logic as Semiotic: The Theory of Signs"（作为指号学的逻辑：指号论）. *Selected Writings of Charles Sanders Peirce*（皮尔斯文选）. Trans.Tu Jiliang（涂纪亮）. Beijing: Social Sciences Academic Press, 2006.

Peng Lingling, Yang Geng "Cultural Semiosis in Artistic Chinese Calligraphy." *Cultura. International Journal of Philosophy of Culture and Axiology*, 10.2 (2013): 127-140.

Seng Zhao *Zhao lun* (肇论), Great Treatise on the Perfection of Wisdom 大智园正圣僧肇法师论, *Classic essence in Zen (*禅宗经典精华), Vol. 1, Beijing: Religious culture Press, 1999.

SuoJing（索靖）. "The Tendency Of Cursive"（草书势）. *Selected Writings of Previous Dynasties' Calligraphy*（历代书法论文选）. Shanghai: Shanghai Calligraphy and Painting Press, 2010.

Subhuti Dharmananda. "FENG: The Meaning of Wind in Chinese Medicine with special attention to acupoint fengchi (GB-20)". http://www.itmonline.org/articles/feng/feng.htm.

WeiHeng（卫恒）. "Siti Shushi"（四体书势）. *Selected Writings of Previous Dynasties' Calligraphy*（历代书法论文选）. Shanghai: Shanghai Calligraphy and Painting Press, 2010.

XieHe（谢赫）. *"Explanations of Ancient Paintings"*（古画品录）. Shanghai Chinese Classics Publishing House,1991.

XuShe（许慎）. Shuo Wen Jie Zi Xu（说文解字序）. *Selected Writings of Previous Dynasties' Calligraphy*（历代书法论文选续编）. Shanghai: Shanghai Calligraphy and Painting Press, 2010.

Zhang Dainian. *Key Concepts in Chinese Philosophy*. Beijing: Foreign Languages Press, 2005.

Zhuang Zhou(庄周). *Zhuang Zi* (庄子). Beijing: Public Literature and Art Press, 2009.

ABOUT THE AUTHOR

Jinghua Guo(郭景华) teaches English at Inner Mongolia University of Technology and is working towards her Ph.D. in comparative literature at Beijing Language and Culture University. Her fields of interests in research include cross-cultural studies and cross-media studies. Guo's recent publications include "Translation, Cross-cultural Interpretation, and World Literatures," *CLCWeb: Comparative Literature and Culture* (with Qingben Li, 15.6 2013) and "Rethinking the Relationship between China and the West: A Multi-Dimensional Model of Cross-Cultural Research focusing on Literary Adaptations", *Cultura. International Journal of Philosophy of Culture and Axiology* (with Qingben Li, Vol.IX(2).2012:45-60).

CHAPTER 14

Language, Meaning and Subjectivity

Susan Petrilli

TOWARD "INTERPRETATION SEMIOTICS"

The mid 1970s onward were decisive years in studies on signs, language and signifying processes considering developments in general sign theory as well as the diversified specific semiotics which also flourished at the time. These are the years marked by a transition from so-called "decodification semiotics", which was influenced either directly or indirectly by Saussurean linguistics, through "signification semiotics" to "interpretation semiotics", largely a derivation of the Peircean-Morrisian tradition. In fact, two major reference points for anybody wishing to understand the transition on the scene of sign studies during the twentieth century include Ferdinand Saussure and subsequent interpretations (or perhaps better, misinterpretations) of his sign theory, on the one hand, and Charles S. Peirce and his writings, on the other. Limiting our attention to studies in the USA after Peirce, Charles Morris is another significant exponent of interpretation semiotics and continuator of Peirce's work under certain aspects, followed by his alumnus Thomas Sebeok, inventor of "global semiotics" (Sebeok 2001).

However, the present text has a focus on another rather extraordinary figure on the scene of studies on signs and language, the 19th century English philosopher Victoria Lady Welby (1837-1911). Welby was a contemporary to Peirce and though they never met they were in dialogue and theorized together, Peirce in the U.S.A., Welby in the U.K., leaving us with a fascinating corpus of letter exchanges. A partial edition containing Peirce's letters to Welby appeared in 1954, instead a complete edition proposing the full correspondence was presented in 1977 thanks to initiative by Charles Hardwick. Welby introduced "significs" toward the end of the 19th century, a term she coined for her special approach to signs and meaning to underline the connection in live communication with sense and value. Her work raised interest among a large community of intellectuals in her day, as in the case of Charles K. Ogden as a young university student and admirer of significs, and inspired the significs movement in the

Netherlands which in fact involved intellectuals from different countries and different disciplinary fields, reflecting the interdisciplinary and international nature characteristic of her approach. Nonetheless during the course of the 20th century Welby's work largely went unnoticed until relatively recent times, though she was never completely forgotten thanks especially to the important correspondence with Peirce. Today Welby's significs is at last coming to the fore with reeditions of her works, collections in Italian translation, and research dedicated to her, all of which has contributed to drawing attention to her as a scholar in her right (see Welby 1983, 1985b; Petrilli 2009, 2015a; Nuessel, Colapietro, Petrilli 2013).

Ferment in critical thought and theory in specific countries cannot be viewed separately from the context of intellectual developments globally and in relation to different disciplines and fields of study. Transnational and transdisciplinary interconnections have led to the flourishing of such a great multiplicity of semiotic methodologies, theories, and practices that to speak of the "adventures" of the sign is undoubtedly appropriate (Ponzio 1990). Furthermore, semiotic studies have developed interdependently through encounters between research and researchers on the vertical axis of historiographical reconstruction – numerous contributions trace developments in the life of signs, verbal and nonverbal, and the sciences that study them, from ancient times across the medieval and through to the modern era – and on the horizontal axis with the flourishing of numerous "special semiotics", as Umberto Eco tagged them in his book of 1984, *Semiotics and Philosophy of Language*.

An important issue taken into consideration by Eco in his 1984 book is the relation between general semiotics and philosophy of language. As he clarifies in his introduction: "I believe that semiotics is philosophical in nature given that it does not study a particular system but proposes general categories in the light of which different systems may be compared. And for general semiotics philosophical discourse is neither advisable nor urgent: it is simply constitutive" (Eco 1984: xii). Besides signaling a connection between general semiotics and philosophy, the title of Eco's book also underlines the fact that semiotics and philosophy of language, a field not easily distinguished from general semiotics, do not converge. For a fuller understanding of the specificity of semiotic discourse, it is important to look at semiotics through the eyes of philosophy, and particularly the philosophy of language (nor is reference here exclusively to verbal language). Philosophy of language, in fact, can be described as exploring external margins and excesses with respect to the "semiotic field", or science – or "theory" (Morris) or "doctrine" (Sebeok) – of signs (cf. Ponzio 2011). Recalling the expression "metalinguistics" as used by the great Russian philosopher Mikhail M. Bakhtin to characterize his reflections on language insofar as he transcends the limits of linguistics (specifically in Bakhtin 1963; Ponzio 2008b), we propose to characterize the philosophy of language in terms of "metasemiotics" as an indication of the attempt to overcome the limits of philosophy of language when practiced in terms of the analytical tradition.

On the other hand, in Eco's opinion, all special semiotics can be considered as grammars of specific sign systems and need not carry out philosophical reflection on the categories upon which these systems are grounded – which of course does not mean to deny their philosophical foundations. Eco makes this statement in reply to Emilio Garroni (see Garroni 1977, and his polemic response to Eco in Mincu 1982), who instead takes the opposite stand. Garroni maintains that as much as the special semiotics may privilege empirical research, they must be fully aware of the categories through which they operate. Cesare Segre (in Marrone 1986: 153-163) also believed that so-called "specific semiotics" must deal directly with problems of a philosophical order, given that they work within a specific theoretical framework and at some stage they too must inevitably deal with general problems of semiosis.

The practitioners of semiotics work in a great variety of different fields including aesthetics, the arts, psychology, psychoanalysis, ideology, translation theory, information theory, literary theory, philology, mathematics, biology and the life sciences generally, anthropology, architecture, cultural studies, marketing, media studies, communication studies, and much more, in addition to philosophy and linguistics of course. Semiotic theory has benefited from the contribution of theories and methods imported from different fields and domains which, in their turn, are enriched by their use of semiotic instruments, methodologies and perspectives.

As anticipated above, semiotics today may be described as transcending the phase designated as "decodification semiotics" (or, if we prefer, "code", or "equal exchange semiotics") – subdivided into "communication semiotics" (Saussure, Buyssens, Prieto) and "signification semiotics" (Barthes) – and as working in the direction of so-called "interpretation semiotics" (Peirce, Morris, Bakhtin, Sebeok, Barthes, etc.). In this framework we now propose the following study on Victoria Welby as a contribution in this direction and indicator of where sign studies can lead us today (Petrilli 2014a, 2015a).

On Signifying and Understanding

The English philosopher Victoria Welby (1837–1912) introduced the term "significs" for her special approach to the study of sign and meaning towards the end of the 19th century. Significs transcends pure descriptivism and presents itself as a method for the analysis of signs beyond logico-gnoseological boundaries and thematizes their relation to values – ethical, aesthetic and pragmatic. Significs investigates the ethical-pragmatic and axiological dimension of signification. With her significs Welby was committed to interrogating sense. Beyond the study of meaning and language understood in strictly gnoseological terms, in fact, significs is concerned with the problem of significance, with the import of meaning and meaning producing processes for human behaviour. Other expressions used by Welby to qualify her significs include "philosophy of interpretation", "philosophy of translation" and "philosophy of significance" (Welby 1983 [1903]: 89, 161; Petrilli 2009: 273–275).

Welby took her distance from the traditional terms of philological-historical semantics as developed, for example, by Michel Bréal (Petrilli 2009: 253–300). Nor did she limit her attention to what is generally known as speech act theory or text linguistics. Instead, she focused on the generative nature of signifying processes and on their capacity for development and transformation as a condition of human experiential, cognitive and expressive capacities. Even more characteristically, she thematized the development of values as a structural aspect in the development of signifying processes. The "significal method" actually arises from the association of the study of signs and meaning to the study of values. The conjunction between signs and values is not only the object of study of significs, but also provides its perspective. As such, significs is applicable to everyday life as much as to the intellectual, to the ethical and emotional spheres of sign activity, therefore to problems of meaning, language, communication and value in the broadest sense possible.

Welby analyses meaning according to three different levels or classes of expression value: "sense", "meaning" and "significance" which are co-present and interact to varying degrees in the live processes of signification and interpretation among speakers. She developed her meaning triad from different points of view with corresponding terminology: to the triad "sense", "meaning", "significance" there corresponds the distinction between "signification", "intention" and "ideal value". Moreover, the reference of sense is "sensal" or "instinctive"; the reference of meaning is "volitional"; and the reference of "significance" is "moral". Other triads include the distinction between "instinct", "perception" and "conception" for different levels in human psychic process;

"planetary", "solar" and "cosmical" for different types of experience, knowledge and consciousness (Petrilli 2009: 20–24; see the dictionary entry "Significs", by Welby, Stout and Baldwin, now in Petrilli 2009: 195–196, andWelby 1983 [1903]: 46–47, now in Petrilli 2009: 265–266).

The meaning of the term "sense" is ambivalent. It is also used to indicate the overall import of an expression, its signifying value. But as one of the three apexes in her meaning triad, "sense" denotes the most primitive level of pre-rational life, the level of initial stages of perception, of immediate response to the environment and practical use of signs. As such it indicates a necessary condition for all experience. "Meaning" concerns rational life, the intentional, volitional aspects of signification. "Significance" implies "sense" in the restricted sense, though not necessarily meaning, and is also indicated with the term "sense" understood broadly. "Significance" concerns the sign's import and ultimate value, its overall bearing, relevance and import for each one of us. It denotes expression value in terms of the condition of being significant, of signifying implication, of participative involvement, which ultimately also involves the question of responsibility.

Welby continues to specify her triadic model for the analysis of meaning throughout her writings through to her 1911 encyclopaedia entry, "Significs", where she further gives the following definitions: "Sense" refers to "the organic response to environment" and "essentially expressive element in all experience"; "Meaning" is purposive and refers to the specific sense which a word "is *intended to convey*"; "Significance", which includes sense and meaning and transcends them, refers to "the far-reaching consequence, implication, ultimate result or outcome of some event or experience" (in Hardwick 1977[1911]): 169; now in Petrilli 2009: 345–350). Triadism is a pivotal characteristic of Welby's thinking (see her unpublished essay of 1886, "Threefold Laws", now in Petrilli 2009: 331–340; for a more complete picture of triadic correspondences in Welby's writings on significs, see the table of triads presented by H. Walter Schmitz in his 1985 volume, *Significs and Language*, now in Petrilli 2009: 948–949).

According to Charles S. Peirce, Welby's meaning triad coincides with his own tripartition of the interpretant into "immediate interpretant", "dynamical interpretant" and "final interpretant". In his own words from a letter to her of 14 March 1909:

> Let us see how well we do agree. The greatest discrepancy appears to lie in my Dynamical Interpretant as compared with your "Meaning". If I understand the latter, it consists in the effect upon the mind of the

Interpreter that the utterer (whether vocally or by writing) of the sign intends to produce. My Dynamical Interpretant consists in direct effect actually produced by a Sign upon an Interpreter of it. They agree in being effects of the Sign upon an individual mind, I think, or upon a number of actual individual minds by independent action upon each. My Final Interpretant is, I believe, exactly the same as your Significance; namely, the effect the Sign *would* produce upon any mind upon which circumstances should permit it to work out its full effect. My Immediate Interpretant is, I think, very nearly, if not quite, the same as your "sense"; for I understand the former to be the total unanalyzed effect that the Sign is calculated to produce; and I have been accustomed to identify this with the effect the sign first produces or may produce upon a mind, without any reflection upon it. I am not aware that you have ever attempted to define your term "sense"; but I gather from reading over what you say that it is the first effect that a sign would have upon a mind well-qualified to comprehend it. Since you say that it is Sensal and has no Volitional element, I suppose it is of the nature of an "impression". It is thus, as far as I can see, exactly my Immediate Interpretant. (Hardwick 1977: 109–110)

As we understand from Peirce's observations above, his "immediate interpretant" concerns meaning as it is ordinarily and customarily used by the interpreter and as such it more or less corresponds to Welby's "sense", the interpreter's immediate response to signs. A discrepancy is identified between Peirce's "dynamical interpretant" and Welby's "meaning". The "dynamical interpretant" concerns meaning in a given context, specifically the effect of the sign on the interpreter. From this point of view, Peirce's "dynamical interpretant" can be correlated with Welby's "meaning". But while Peirce refers to the *actual* effect produced by the sign, Welby, instead, underlines the *intended* effect, which is the effect the utterer intends to produce, but which is not necessarily the effect achieved. However, Peirce's "final interpretant" and Welby's "significance" are described as corresponding exactly insofar as they both indicate interpretive potential at the highest degrees of significance and understanding (Petrilli 2009: 288–294). Moreover, Peirce considered such convergences between his own triad and Welby's as an indication of their validity.

Welby studies the nature of significance in all its forms and relations evidencing the close relation between the generation of signifying processes in human experience and the *production* of values. From this point of view, the notion of significance can be associated with Charles Morris's conception of "significance" as developed in his 1964 monograph, *Signification and Significance*. Furthermore, Welby thematizes the interpretive function as the condition for signifying processes, hence for communication, expression and understanding. The connection between signs and values enhances the human capacity to establish relations with the world, the self and others.

This connection also orients translation processes from one sphere of knowledge into another and from one sphere of action into another, from one pragmatic interpretant to another, which is inevitably an ethical-pragmatic interpretant or, if we prefer, a semioethical interpretant. Sense, meaning and significance are enhanced through ongoing translation processes.

Welby's theory of sign and meaning conceptualizes ongoing translative processes beyond limits and boundaries as ultimately imposed by identity logic and official discourse. In this sense her translational theory of meaning can be described as a theory of the "transcendent". In this connection, another interesting definition of "significs" is that formulated by Welby in *Significs and Language* (1911), which reads as follows: "the study of the nature of significance in all its forms and relations, and thus of its working in every possible sphere of human interest and purpose" (Welby 1985a [1911]: vii). Welby was concerned with the practical bearing of sense, meaning and significance "not only on language but on every possible form of human expression in action, invention, and creation (Welby 1985a [1911]: ix). Furthermore, as she had already specified in *What Is Meaning?*, as the "philosophy of Significance" significs involves the "philosophy of Interpretation, of Translation, and thereby of a mode of synthesis accepted and worked with by science and philosophy alike" (Welby 1983 [1903: 161).

The problem of sign and meaning provides a unifying perspective on the kaleidoscopic plurality of experience and communication. This means to study the processes through which signs and meaning are produced. To study such processes involves analysing the conditions of possibility that enable their articulations and transformations. Such processes unfold on a synchronic and diachronic axis, and relate to verbal and nonverbal sign activity, to linguistic and non-linguistic semiosis in general.

This is the perspective adopted by Welby and her significs. She researched the signifying processes of ordinary life and ordinary language, of the sciences, of the human potential for interpretation and expression, and of the manifold expressions of human sign activity at large. Perception, experience and cognition are mediated by signs, such that the relation between speaking subjects and their world is indirect and approximate insofar as it is a sign-mediated relation in ongoing interpretive processes. Further, given that our relation to so-called "objective" reality is a sign-mediated relation in which are generated the signifying processes of expression, interpretation, communication, all of us – everyday humans and intellectuals – are potential "significians". Together we produce signifying processes and, in turn, we evolve in signifying processes that go to form the anthroposemiotic sign network.

After investigating problems of interpretation relatively to the Sacred Scriptures, Welby's interest in ethical-theological discourse focused more closely on linguistic-philosophical problems and found expression in a series of essays published towards the end of the nineteenth century. These include "Meaning and Metaphor" (published in *The Monist*, 1893) and "Sense, Meaning, and Interpretation" (published in two parts in the journal *Mind*, 1896), a book of reflections, *Grains of Sense* (1897), and her monographs, *What Is Meaning? Studies in the Development of Significance* (1903) and *Significs and Language. The Articulate Form of Our Expressive and Interpretative Resources* (1911). Editorial events that have contributed to the revival of significs today include republication of these works. *What Is Meaning?* was reproposed in 1983 and the volume *Significs and Language,* containing Welby's 1911 monograph together with a significant selection from her other writings, published and unpublished, in 1985. In those same years an anthology of writings by Welby appeared in Italian translation, *Significato, metafora, interpretazione* (Welby 1985), followed by another two, *Senso, significazione, significatività* (2007) and *Interpretare, comprendere, comunicare* (Welby 2010). The first monograph ever on Welby appeared in 1998, *Su Victoria Welby. Significs e filosofia del linguaggio*, by S. Petrilli.

Recently, a large collection of papers by Welby has now been made available in the volume *Signifying and Understanding. Reading the Works of Victoria Welby and the Signific Movement* (1,048 pp., see Petrilli 2009). This volume presents papers from the Welby Collection at the York University Archives (Toronto, Canada), together with a selection of texts published during her lifetime. However, a significant part of Welby's work is still hosted yet unpublished in the archives. A large corpus of other printed matter by Welby or relating to her is available in the Welby library housed in the London University Library, London (UK). In addition to writings by Welby and her correspondence with preeminent figures of the time, *Signifying and Understanding* also includes a complete description of the materials available at the Welby Archives in York and three updated bibliographies listing all her writings as well as writings on Welby, her significs, as well as on the Signific Movement in the Netherlands and its developments. This movement was originally inspired by Welby through mediation of the Dutch poet and psychiatrist F. van Eeden (1860-1932), and flourished across the first half of the twentieth century (cf. Schmitz 1990; Heijerman-Schmitz 1991). *Signifying and Understanding* also features an anthology of writings by first generation significians like Frederik van Eeden, Gerrit Mannoury, L. E. J. Brouwer, and David Vuysje.

The most recent large-scale editorial initiative for the promotion of Welby's research and writing and of the movement it inspired is publication of the collective volume, *On and Beyond Significs. Centennial Issue for Victoria Welby*, as a special issue of the international journal for semiotic studies, *Semiotica*, edited by Frank Nuessel, Vincent Colapietro, and myself, in 2013.

After her death, more than as an intellectual in her own right, Welby's name continued circulating among the international community of researchers thanks above all to her correspondence with Charles S. Peirce (see Hardwick 1977). She was in the habit of discussing her ideas and to this end entertained epistolary exchanges with numerous personalities of the day. In addition to Peirce, these included names like Bertrand Russell, James M. Baldwin, Henry Spencer, Thomas A. Huxley, Herbert G. Wells, Max Müller, Benjamin Jowett, Frederik Pollock, George F. Stout, Ferdinand C.S. Schiller, Charles K. Ogden, Henry and William James, Mary Everest Boole, Julia Wedgwood, Michel Bréal, André Lalande, Henri Bergson, Henri Poincaré, Rudolph Carnap, Otto Neurath, Harald Höffding, Ferdinand Tönnies, Frederick van Eeden, Giovanni Vailati, Mario Calderoni and many others. Part of this correspondence was edited and published by Welby's daughter Mrs. Henry (Nina) Cust, in two volumes, *Echoes of Larger Life*, 1929, which collects letters written between 1879 to 1891, whilst *Other Dimensions*, 1931, covers the years from 1898 to 1911. Other selections with various interlocutors have also been made available in *Signifying and Understanding*. We could claim that developments on significs are not necessarily attached to any individual name, but one who deserves special mention is Charles K. Ogden who discovered Welby and her significs as a young university student at Cambridge, and whose research was significantly influenced by her, even though he mentions her but briefly in his epochal book with Ivor A. Richards, *The Meaning of Meaning*, 1923. Ogden promoted significs as a university student during the years 1910-1911, had met Welby personally at that time and was dedicated to spreading her ideas.

Welby was concerned with the entire signifying universe, with a special interest in signifying processes in the human world, particularly in verbal expression, but without falling into the trap of anthropocentric oversimplification.

She in fact was focused on verbal expression, the language of the "man of the street" as well as of the intellectual, but with reference to the larger context, what we may also call the great "biosemiosphere", in which language is engendered. However, she knew that to deal with her special interest area adequately, it was necessary to understand its connections to the larger context: consequently, she extended her gaze to ever larger totalities, beyond the verbal to the nonverbal, beyond the human to the nonhuman, beyond the organic to the inorganic. From this point of view, Welby may be considered as prefiguring contemporary global semiotics and developments in the direction of biosemiotics as conceived by Thomas Sebeok who enquires into the connection between semiosis and life and asks the question, "Semiosis and Semiotics: What Lies in Their Future?" (in Sebeok 1991: 97–99). Moreover, given its special focus on *significance* in human behaviour, Welby's significs may be read as proposing a *new form of humanism*, by contrast with semiotic analyses conducted exclusively in abstact gnoseological terms.

With its focus on the relation between sign, value and behaviour, in particular the sign's ultimate value, or significance, on the connection therefore between sign and value in all its aspects – pragmatic, social, ethic, aesthetic, etc., significs is particularly concerned with the effects and implications of the conjuction between signs and values for human behaviour.

The special slant in Welby's studies on signs and meaning in the direction of the relation to values and the broad scope of her special perspective enables us to read "significs" as a prefiguration of "semioethics". This expression was introduced by myself with Augusto Ponzio as the title of our monograph of 2003, in Italian, *Semioetica* (now forthcoming in English translation), and as the title of an essay commissioned to us by Paul Cobley for *The Routledge Dictionary of Semiotics*, 2010.

And insofar as it is focused on the pragmatical-ethical implications of human signifying processes, significs is a major source of inspiration at the origin of "semioethics" with which it overlaps. As emerges from Welby's own words as reported above, attention on the interpretive-translational dimension of sign activity and the connection with values is programmatic for significs from its very inception.

"Semioethics" is a neologism which has its origins in the early 1980s with "ethosemiotics" and subsequently "tel(e)osemiotics" to name an approach or attitude we deem necessary today more than ever before in the context of globalization and global communication. Semioethics is not intended as a discipline in its own right, but as a perspective, an orientation in the study of signs. By "semioethics" we understand the propensity in studies on signs, semiotics, to recover the ancient vocation of the latter as "semeiotics" (or symptomatology), which focuses on symptoms. A major issue for semioethics is "care for life" in a global perspective (see Sebeok 2001) according to which semiosis and life converge (see Ponzio and Petrilli 2005: 562). This global perspective is made ever more urgent by growing interference in planetary communication between the historical-social and biological spheres, between the cultural and natural spheres, between the semiosphere (Lotman) and the biosphere.

SIGNIFICS, LANGUAGE AND CONSCIOUSNESS

To carry out research on language adequately, verbal language, the main working instrument at our disposal must be in good working order. Consequently, for Welby the problem of reflecting on language and meaning in general immediately takes on a dual orientation. It concerns not only the object of research, but also the very possibility of articulating discourse. Welby was faced with the problem of constructing a vocabulary in which to formulate her ideas adequately. She soon realized that a fundamental problem in reflection on language and meaning concerns language itself, the medium through which reflection takes place. She described the linguistic apparatus at her disposal as antiquated and rhetorical, subject to those same limits she wished to overcome and to those same defects she aimed to correct.

In her effort to invent a new terminological apparatus Welby offered alternatives to terms sanctioned by use. She introduced the term "sensal" to underline the expression value of words, by contrast with "verbal" for reference to the specifically linguistic or verbal aspect of signs, whether graphic and phonic. The term "interpretation" appears in the title of her 1896 essay, "Sense, Meaning and Interpretation" (in Petrilli 2009: 430–449) and was initially proposed to designate a particular phase in the signifying process. Subsequently, on realizing that it designated an activity present throughout all phases of signifying processes, the term "interpretation" was replaced with "significance"; this is an example of how Welby's terminological quest was motivated by concrete problems of expression. Unlike "semantics", "semasiology" and "semiotics", the word "significs" was completely free from technical associations. As such, it appeared suitable to Welby as the name of a new science that intended to focus on the connection between sign and sense, meaning and value (pragmatic, social, aesthetic and ethical), as she explained in a letter to the German philosopher and sociologist Ferdinand Tönnies, winner of the "Welby Prize" of 1896 for the best essay on significal questions (Petrilli 2009: 192–194, 235–248).

Other neologisms related to "significs" include the noun "significian" for the person who practices significs and the adjective "significal". The verb "to signify" indicates the generation of meaning at maximum degrees of signifying value and "to signalize" more specifically the act of investing a sign with a given meaning. In her 1896 essay Welby had also proposed the terms "sensifics" with the corresponding verb "to sensify". These were subsequently abandoned as being too closely related to the world of the senses. But even when Welby used terms that were readily available, including those forming her meaning triad, "sense", "meaning" and "significance" (1983 [1903]: 5–6), she did so in the context of an impressively articulate theoretical apparatus that clarified the sense of her special use of these terms.

Welby introduces images from the organic world to denounce the "maladies of language" and "linguistic pathology", largely caused by the use of verbal expression that is inadequate or antiquated, featuring metaphors and analogies that are outdated and simply incorrect. On the level of logical procedure, the poor use of language and expression is inseparable from the engendering of false problems, misunderstanding, and confused reasoning (Ponzio 2006). The human understanding of differences and commonalities among signs, senses and meanings also requires to be improved. In Welby's view, this state of affairs calls for the development of a "critical linguistic consciousness" and appropriate "linguistic therapy". But a correct diagnosis of "linguistic pathology" requires an adequate theory of signs and meaning (Petrilli 2009: Ch. 4). Significs takes on the dual task of theoretical analysis and therapeutic remedy, as it attempts to offer practical suggestions for the solution to problems of signification.

As part of her commitment to logical, expressive, behavioural, ethical and aesthetic regeneration, she advocated the need to develop a "linguistic conscience" against a "bad use of language" which inevitably involved poor reasoning, bad use of logic and incoherent argumentation. The very need to coin the term "significs" – a term difficult to translate into other languages, as discussed in her correspondence, for example, with Michel Bréal or André Lalande regarding French and Giovanni Vailati for Italian (Petrilli 2009: 302–310, 407–418) – was a clear indication in itself of the existence of terminological obstacles to development in philosophical-linguistic analysis. Welby's condition was typical of a thinker living in a revolutionary era characterized by the transformation and innovation of knowledge: she was faced with the task of communicating new ideas which involved renewing the language through which she was communicating.

Welby was sensitive to problems of everyday language and in proposing the term "signifies" kept account of the everyday expression "What does it signify?" with its focus on ultimate value and significance beyond semantic meaning. But Welby's commitment to the term "signifies" risked appearing as the expression of a whimsical desire for novelty, given that such terms as "semiotics" and "semantics" were already available. Charles S. Peirce and Giovanni Vailati were among those who did not initially understand her proposal, maintaining that the introduction of a new term could be avoided. Yet she quickly converted them to her view by demonstrating that terminological availability was in fact only apparent, for none of the words in use adequately accounted for her own special approach to signs and meaning. Though she proposed a neologism for the study of language, Welby did not fall into the trap of technicalism, just as, despite her constant efforts to render expression as precise as possible, her aim was not to (fallaciously) eliminate the ambiguity of words. Ambiguity understood in the sense of polysemy plays a fundamental role in language and communication, which is something Welby recognized and thematized distinguishing ambiguity from confusion and bad language usage. She aimed to describe aspects of the problem of language, expression and signifying processes at large which had not yet been contemplated or which had been mostly left aside by traditional approaches. More precisely, she proposed to reconsider the same problems in a completely different light, from a different perspective: the significal.

Significs is also described by Welby as "a method of mental training" which concentrates intellectual activities on "meaning", the main value and condition for all forms of study and knowledge (Welby 1983 [1903: 83]). Again, significs is "a method of observation, a mode of experiment" which "includes the inductive and deductive methods in one process" (Welby 1983 [1903: 161]). This is what Vailati baptized the "hypothetical-deductive method" and Peirce the "abductive" or "retroductive method". The scope and reference of significs is universal. From this point of view it emerges as a *transdisciplinary* method and not as a "supplanting system". Most significantly: "The principle involved forms a natural self-acting critique of every system in turn, including the common-sense ideal" (Welby 1983 [1903: 162]), therefore significs is also *metadisciplinary*.

THE PROBLEM OF POLYSEMY AND DEFINITION

Welby distinguishes between two types of ambiguity: (1) ambiguity in the sense of polysemy constitutive of the word, a positive attribute connected to a multiform and dialogic view of reality and, as such, a necessary condition for expressivity and understanding; (2) ambiguity as obscurity, expressive inadequacy which is the cause of confusion and equivocation and provokes "paralysis of thought". She denounces such negative effects with innumerable examples throughout her writings (Welby 1985a [1911]: XIII, 37–38). Her characteristic recourse to organic analogies to talk about language serve to evidence such characteristics as "plasticity", "expressive ambiguity" and "adaptability" as distinctive features of verbal expression. For example, Welby establishes an analogy between context and environment and consequently between the mutually adaptive mechanism that regulates the relationship between word and context, on the one hand, and between organism and environment, on the other: "If we enthrone one queen-word instead of another in the midst of a hive of working context-words, these will behave very differently. They will expel or kill or naturalize it" (Welby 1983: 40, & note). The word, like the organism, adapts to its surroundings which it modifies and, conversely, the context influences and somehow modifies these.

In "Meaning and Metaphor" (1893), Welby criticizes the concept of "plain meaning" from a pedagogic and theoretical perspective, underlining the need to recognize the symbolic character of language, the widespread (though often unconscious) use of analogies and metaphors and the relationship between symbolic systems and what they symbolize, the pervasiveness of imagery in so-called "literal" or "actual" language which she uses as an argument against the fallacious tendency to establish a net distinction between literal language and metaphorical language:

> ... we might begin by learning better what part symbolism plays in the rituals of expression, and ask ourselves what else is language itself but symbolism, and what it symbolizes. We should then examine anew the relations of the "symbolic" to the "real"; of image, figure, metaphor, to what we call literal or actual. For this concerns us all. Imagery runs in and out, so to speak, from the symbolic to the real world and back again. (Welby 1893, in Petrilli 2009: 422)

The infinite possibilities of expression and signification are actualized by signs as their meanings are gradually specified in live communicative contexts. And though not necessarily in the same terms as Peirce, ideator of the renown triad that distinguishes between symbol, index and icon, Welby recognizes symbolicity, indexicality and iconicity as interacting dimensions constitutive of signifying processes to varying degrees.

Welby elaborates a dynamical, structural and generative theory of signs and meaning, where polyvalency, changeability and vagueness are thematized as their distinctive features. She criticizes the myth of "plain meaning", common-sense, clear and obvious meaning, of language described in terms of invariability, uniformity, univocality, of words and locutions defined as though they were numbers, tags, or symbols enjoying unanimous consent. The text must be freed from the prejudice of interpretation reduced to decodification. It is important to specify meaning and thereby evidence the overall significance, import, and ultimate value of a given utterance, as when we ask the question, "What do we really mean?"; but, to specify and clarify does not imply to accept the concept of "plain meaning", which Welby considers a mere fallacy when it involves reductionism and oversimplification. As an example, she indicates the widespread belief that a text can evolve into a single reading, into an absolute and definitive interpretant valid for all times (Welby 1893, in Petrilli 2009: 22–23, 423; Welby 1983: 143). Broadly, the point addressed by Welby with her concept of "plain meaning" can be compared to the critique elaborated by Antonio Gramsci in relation to the concept of "common sense".

Welby appreciates the "plurivocal" and "polylogic" capacity of language and at once signals reductive interpretations of the concept of ambiguity. Plasticity and ambiguity are qualities that render the sign adaptive to new contexts, to changing habits of behaviour. Such qualities are a condition for progress in knowledge, for the development of verbal and nonverbal expression, for signifying processes at large and their potential for allusive reference (Welby 1985a: ccxli and ccliv). Ambiguity is an essential aspect of interpersonal relationships where successful communication emerges from interaction between the codified aspects of language and creative, responsive understanding which cannot be reduced to the processes of decodification (Petrilli 2012). Welby shared her appreciation of ambiguity and polysemy with her contemporary, Giovanni Vailati. Subsequently, other authors who were to work along similar lines include Ferruccio Rossi-Landi, Adam Schaff, Mikhail Bakhtin.

"Clear" and "convincing" discourse often implies oversimplification which, paradoxically, engenders obscure and "perverse" discourse. The use or, rather, the misuse of such concepts as "plain meaning", "common sense" and "common place" are examples. When applied under the mask of "simplification" and "clearness", the foregoing terms tend to reduce the potential polylogism of language and expression to the condition of monologism. This occurs with metaphors when the stratification of sense deposited in them is exchanged for univocal, literal meaning. Mystifications of this sort often ensue from a lack of awareness of the "semiotic materiality" of the sign, of its vocation for otherness, its socio-historical consistency (see Petrilli 2010: Chs. 2, 5). The importance of the role of the enthymeme, of the unsaid, the implicit in discourse is often neglected; the fact that words and signs in general are impregnated with senses engendered in a signifying history of their own. Understanding and communication rest on the unsaid, the unspoken, implicit meaning, on that which is understood.

On a diachronic axis, the meanings and values of words and utterances, whether implicit or explicit, may accumulate, overlap, change, disappear even, or develop. On a synchronic axis, the unique experience of the single speaker influences the modality of perception and interpretation. Different factors are at work to condition meaning value in a structure that is never identical to itself. These factors include the specific historical-social-cultural context, communicative context, linguistic usage, inferential procedure, psychological and emotional factors, memory, attention, intention, psychological and emotional factors, attention, intention, the capacity for making associations, allusions, and assumptions, enthymemes, memory, circumstance, linguistic usage, the tendency to symbolize or picture, the a-priori conditions of language, etc. Welby thematized dialectic complementarity and interdependency between the forces of indeterminacy and determinacy, vagueness and exactitude, plurivocality and monologicality, between the centrifugal forces and the centripetal forces operative in language, ultimately, in our own terminology, between the logic of alterity and the logic of identity. The genetically and structurally dynamical character of language, its inherent potential for creativity and innovation, and the action of such variables as those just listed – all these aspects invalidate recourse to definition as an absolute and definitive remedy for the mystifications of language.

Welby focuses on a series of specifically linguistic issues such as the role of definition in the determination of meaning, the relationship between literal meaning and metaphorical meaning, the role of metaphor, analogy, and homology in the enhancement of expressive potential. Expressive precision can be attained by exploiting different linguistic resources; for example, by distinguishing between the different meanings of words that seem to be similar but in fact are not, and by identifying similarity among words that seem to have different meanings but do not. However, Welby claims that to be a significian does not mean to be a "precisionist" in the sense of working for the "mechanical exactitude in language" (see the Welby files entitled "Significs (1903–1910)" and "Mother-Sense (1904–1910)", now in Petrilli 2009, in particular pages 249, 270, 336, 576,

705, 808). On the contrary, meaning is inherently ambiguous and to neglect this particular quality can lead to monological signifying practices that lay the conditions for the tyranny of dogma and orthodoxy. At a metadiscursive level, though ready to propose new terms for the study of language and meaning Welby kept her distances from the temptations of technicalism. And while she was critical of the fallacy of eliminating ambiguity, polysemy from the utterance, she was committed at once to making her expressions as precise as possible. The following passage on the meaning of the words "fact" and "idea" is an interesting example:

> Taking both words in the generally accepted English sense what in the last resort is the difference between Fact and Idea? What is that essential meaning of both which, if changed, will necessitate a new word to express what we are losing? Surely there can be no doubt of the answer. If we can say of any supposed fact that it is false: unreal from one point of view, untrue from another (these again never to be confounded), it ceases to be fact. No fact can be either unreal or untrue, only our idea of it. Otherwise we may as well say at once that the real may be the delusive, or the true may be the deceptive. Of course the "real" tends to become illusory to us, and the true deceptive, owing to the inadequacy of our inferences, which is again due to our little-developed interpretive power. But this must become more adequate when we have learnt to make sense, meaning, and significance our central concern, and have developed our sensifying and signifying faculties. (Welby 1983: 40–41)

"Linguistic consciousness" implies development of the critical and interpretive capacity and rejection of such tendencies as dogmatism, pedantry and anarchy in linguistic usage, logical inference, and sign behaviour in general.

Liberation of language from the so-called "linguistic traps" that obstacle its development and articulation, as Wittgenstein too observes, is a condition for mastery over one's surroundings. In this framework, Welby recognized the usefulness of definition, but not in an absolute sense. Definition serves limited, but specific purposes. What is most worth expressing and interpreting often escapes definition (Welby 1983: 10) whose effective usefulness is restricted to special interests. Definition does not account for the ambiguity of language understood as a condition for successful communication. And when resorting to definition to solve problems of meaning and expression, the greatest good arises in the process of working toward that definition rather than in its actual formulation, as the English philosopher Henry Sidgwick observes in his epistolary exchanges with Welby (their correspondence is preserved in the Welby Collection, York University Achives, Box 14, see Petrilli 2009: Appendix 3).

Welby distinguished between "rigid definition" and "plastic primary definition" (1985a, b, 2010). The former is always secondary because of its tendency to freeze meaning and render it static in the orientation toward a single, univocal meaning. By contrast, "plastic primary definition" keeps account of the live character of language and therefore of its capacity for adaptation to new signifying contexts. Welby discusses the problem of definition in her correspondence with Giovanni Vailati who took a similar view. Rather than limit definition to single words, he underlined its usefulness in determining the meaning of propositions. The meaning of single words is often only determined in relation to other words, in the linguistic context, in the context of the proposition itself. To exemplify his view, Vailati indicated such terms as "to be", "to act", "to produce", "to represent", "to manifest", etc. The meaning of the linguistic context itself is also determined in its relation to the single words forming that context (Vailati/Welby, 12 July 1898, in Vailati 1971: 140–142; Welby/Vailati, 27 February 1907, in Petrilli 2009: 415). Only in a correct theoretical framework can definition be implemented, though never as a remedy to the problems of linguistic equivocation. Without denying its value for technical language, definition tends to eliminate the expressive plasticity of words, responding inappropriately to their inherent liveliness with lifelessness and inertia (Welby 1983: 2; Petrilli 2009: 4.5.).

To solve problems of language, rather than resort to definition we need an adequate theory of sign and meaning. We know that Welby thematizes a tripartite division of meaning into "sense", "meaning" and "significance"; other important distinctions include that between "plain", "actual" or "literal", "direct" meaning, on one side, and "figurative", "indirect" or "reflective" meaning, on the other. Signifying processes do not respond to the binary view which distinguishes between the two poles of "metaphorical, indirect or reflective meaning", on one hand, and "literal, direct or actual meaning", on the other. Indeed, the term "literal" is considered by Welby to be more figurative and more ambiguous than the term "metaphorical" itself (1893, in Petrilli 2009: 422). Instead, she hypothesizes a third region of meaning constitutive of signifying practices, a "third value" of meaning – neither entirely literal nor entirely figurative – in which the "metaphorical" and the "literal" combine to varying degrees (Welby 1983: 139, 292; a similar approach is elaborated by Ferruccio Rossi-Landi, though independently of Welby, see Rossi-Landi 1985: 115–120). The "third value" or "third region" of meaning hypothesizes a contact zone where boundaries are not defined and interpretive processes are generated in the interaction among signs. Metaphorical meaning cannot be reduced to ornamentality, nor is it exclusive to the language of literature or to the artistic vision in general. On the contrary, metaphorical procedure is structural to the development of knowledge and to signifying processes at large. This indeterminate, third value, or third region of meaning runs through the whole of language, including ordinary language, where the actual and the symbolic, the real and the ideal, the direct and the reflective intermingle, as in a painting. The same utterance can translate across different regions of meaning – actual and direct, symbolical, figurative, or some combination of such elements, thereby revealing its ambiguous nature and capacity for adaptation and transformation as requested by the live processes of communication.

The influence of metaphorical meaning is active even when we are not aware of it. The processes of metaphorization and symbolization neither have systemic nor typological boundaries. On the contrary, they permeate the sign network in its complexity where there exist metaphorical signifying paths which are already traced and which are so deeply rooted in the language and consciousness of utterers and interpreters that their meaning seems simple, fixed, definite, like "plain meaning". But there are also metaphorical signifying paths that are immediately recognizable as such owing to their inventiveness, creativity, and capacity for innovation. These are engendered by relating interpretants in the sign network that may even be distant from each other, thereby producing signifying processes which are completely new, unexpected, unpredictable, even surprising. Though we may choose programmatically between the "literal" and the "metaphorical", in reality this is no more than a pseudo-choice, one which habours the danger of ensuing in artificial exaggeration in one sense or in the other (Petrilli 2012: Ch. 7).

Analogy and metaphor operate implicitly and unconsciously in everyday language as well as in scientifical-philosophical language. For this reason, Welby believes that the study of such meaning production devices must be systematically introduced into educational programmes, with continuous testing on a practical level, according to the criteria of effectiveness on interlocutors in communication. A "significal education", the acquisition of a "significal method", is required from the very first years of schooling, as she writes to Charles K. Ogden in a letter dated 24 March 1911 (the main part of their correspondence is now available in Petrilli 2009):

The work wanted must begin in the nursery and elementary school; the instinct of clarity in speech now burdened beneath a load of mere helpless convention perpetually defeating expression must be fostered and stimulated. When the generation now represented by my grandchildren marry their children must have their racial sense brought out and worked upon – with significal discrimination! While the elements of reading and writing are taught as now but not as obeying the same rigid (not logical) laws. Then the first school will appeal to this: their desire to express as to know and infer will always be stimulated and ordered: they gradually their anarchic or dogmatic tendencies will be raised into interpretive ones. I think it ought not to be difficult to awaken us. We are even now always being startled by what turns out to be the too-too of a tin-trumpet. But to be able to say what we ought to mean and to act upon our true conception of a subject – that is the aim. (Welby/Ogden, in Petrilli 2009: 774)

To this end both Welby and Vailati (who fully subscribed to the orientation of her studies) insisted on the need for *critique of imagery* and analogy and on the need to create habits of analysis, classification, and verification of expressive devices in general, particularly when a question of verbal signs (the sign *par excellence*). Such habits, she argues, should be instilled from infancy. As a defense against linguistic anarchy, Vailati, too, underlined the need for critical reflection on language to begin in childhood. He advocated developing the habit of reflecting on *"questioni di parole"* or, as Welby says, "verbal questions", in their radical interconnection with the processes of argumentation and knowledge acquisition. Vailati says as much in a letter to Welby dated 12 July 1898:

I believe the exposition and classification of verbal fallacies and, above all, their *caricatures* (in *jeux de mots*), to be one of most effectual pedagogic contrivances for creating the habit of perceiving the ambiguities of language. It is a remedy somewhat analogous to that resorted to by Lacedaemons, who, in order to keep alive in their sons the horror to intoxication, compelled them to assist to the *dégoutants* deeds and sayings of the ebrious Ilots. (Vailati 1971: 141)

Vailati, like Welby, advocates the need for a "critique of language", for awareness of the complex nature of the meaning of words, the unconscious use of which often gives rise to misunderstanding and linguistic traps. At the same time, he turns his attention, again like Welby, to the expressive potential and practical functioning of ordinary language. For Vailati, rather than focus on the construction of an artificial language in the effort to solve problems of ambiguity and misunderstanding, the task of language analysis and philosophical speculation is to enhance and renew common language, revitalising its connection with life in all its aspects and at all levels, from everyday ordinary language to the higher spheres of artistic, scientific and professional language.

Welby analyzes verbal expression not only in order to describe it, but to explain it, with the ultimate aim of transforming, regenerating and subjecting it to conscious and critical implementation in signifying practice. Given its natural inclination for investigation and enquiry, its curiosity and capacity for questioning, the child is the supreme critic and a model. Welby contrasts the provocation of questions to the monologizing constriction of the order of discourse, emphasizing the importance of confrontation and comparison among different points of view, the condition of dialogic interrelatedness.

Language and logic, linguistic signs and inferential processes are interconnected by relations of mutual interdependency, such that the bad use of language involves the bad use of logic. On promoting the need for "language study", Welby underlines the inevitable connection between language, thought, action and values. Faulty conceptualization, false problems – e.g. the fallacious contrast between "free will" and "determinism", "freedom" and "necessity" – are largely the result of language problems and bad linguistic usage.

Vailati (who was one of Welby's most devoted readers) shares the aims of her research, as he illustrates in a letter to her dated 19 March 1903. He lists three points on which they agree strongly:

1. Your insisting on the need for a critique of imagery, for a testing of analogies and metaphors (especially when "unconsciously" or "semiunconsciously" used, as it is always the case in the *current* and *vulgar* ones).
2. Your warning against the tendency of pedantry and school-learning to discourage the development of linguistic resources, by the inhibitions of those spontaneous variations that are the necessary condition of organic growth.
3. Your valuation of the practical and speculative importance of raising language from the irrational and instinctive to the rational and volitional plane; in which it is considered as a means or contrivance for the performance of determined functions (representative, inferential,

communicational, etc.) and for the attainment of given ends. (Vailati 1971: 144)

As Welby recognizes in a letter dated 27 February 1907 (in Vailati 1971), Vailati shared a common interest in the relation between language and thought, in problems specifically related to the human capacity for linguistic expressivity, meaning and argumentation. His article of 1905, "I tropi della logica", centres on the problem of the use of metaphors taken from the physical world, and is directly inspired by Welby's 1903 monograph, *What Is Meaning?* In "Alcune osservazioni" on the role of analogy and confrontation in the development of knowledge, first published in 1899 (now in Vailati 1987), Vailati deals with questions similar to those proposed by Welby in her 1896 essay, "Sense, Meaning and Interpretation". He theorizes the method of comparison and confrontation among different sign systems, the sciences that study them and their respective languages. Such a method is fundamental to highlight convergences and divergences among different disciplines, areas of knowledge and culture. In another essay of 1905 (now in Vailati 1987), "La ricerca dell'impossibile", Vailati compares the formulas of moral discourse with those of geometry and in an essay of 1908 (in Vailati 1987), "La grammatica dell'algebra", he compares verbal language and the language of algebra. The method developed by Vailati (1967) is comparable to Welby's interpretive-translative method and fits in well with the project for significs. They both thematize the need to bring the unconscious use of logical-linguistic mechanisms to consciousness in the effort to overcome the inadequacies of our inferences and interpretive capacity. The "sensifying and signifying faculties" must be improved by bettering our understanding of the problems of meaning, as Welby never tired of repeating.

COMMON SPEECH AND COMMON SENSE

Welby criticizes attempts at overcoming obstacles to mutual understanding by neutralizing linguistic diversity through recourse to a universal language. Whether this involves imposing the primacy of one natural language over another, or constructing an artificial language, this solution to the problems of language and communication is nothing less than delusory. She recognizes that the great variety of languages, dialects, jargons, slangs, etc. favours the development of our linguistic-cognitive resources. Examples are provided by popular culture and the popular instinct of the "man in the street", described as unconsciously philosophical and a model to apply in the study of language related issues. Welby underlines the "significal" import of popular idiom, especially as it finds expression in everyday language and in folklore: "...both slang and popular talk, if intelligently regarded and appraised, are reservoirs from which valuable new currents might be drawn into the main stream of language — rather armouries from which its existing powers could be continuously re-equipped and reinforced" (Welby 1985a [1911]: 38–39). Distinction and diversity among languages enhances signifying, interpretive, and communicative practice. In contrast, the imposition of an artificial universal language leads to levelling the multiplicity of our cultural, linguistic and psychological patrimony, of possible worldviews and logics. According to Welby difference (linguistic and non-linguistic) is not the cause of division and silence, but, on the contrary, favours the possibility of interconnection and signifying continuity. Differences engender other differences as part of a detotalizing totality in continuous evolution (1983 [1903]: 212).

In Welby's terminology, "common meaning" is an expression that contains both the idea of universal validity and of the specificity of signifying processes. Like Rossi-Landi (1961) and his concept of "common speech" (*parlare comune*), for Welby too such expressions as "common language", "common speech", "common meaning" and "common sense" are not limited to "ordinary language" or "everyday language" in the terms theorized by the English analytical philosophers. "Everday language" is just one aspect of linguistic expression. Taken globally, considering the different languages that make a historical-natural language and the multiplicity of historical-natural languages over the globe, difference in linguistic expression overall is subtended by a universal patrimony specific to humanity indicated with such expressions as those listed above. In Welby's theory of language and meaning these expressions indicate, precisely, common signifying material operative in the great multiplicity of languages and jargons forming a single natural language, as much as across the great variety of different non-verbal languages and cultures populating the sign universe. Such material constitutes the "foundation of all sectorial differences of speech", of "mere technical or secondary meanings", as Welby says in a letter to Thomas H. Huxley dating back approximately to the years 1882–1885 (in Cust 1929: 102).

The expressions "common meaning", "common sense" and "common speech" denote a sort of *a priori* in a Kantian sense, a level of reference common to all languages – a set of operations that constitute the repeatable and constant material forming the conditions for human expressivity. To such common material may be traced analogical and homological similarities in human biological and social structures that interconnect different human communities beyond historical-cultural differences. This common patrimony of communicative techniques allows for translation from one universe of discourse to another, indeed is a condition for translational processes across different languages, whether internal or external. As Rossi-Landi argues, we must focus on underlying processes and identify the universal empirical procedures operated by speakers in all languages (when translating interlinguistcally for example, but also when teaching, learning, or simply conversing in the same language) (Rossi-Landi 1961: 204ff.).

The expressions above, "common speech", "common language", "common meaning" and "common sense", do not neglect the great multiplicity of different languages forming the cultural patrimony of humanity; they do not eliminate plurilingualism and polylogism by tracing them back monologically to a mythical original language, an *Ursprache*, to the universal linguistic structures of some *Logos*, or to biological laws that govern and unify all human languages. To recognize commonality or an underlying unity does not imply reconducting difference to identity. On the contrary, Welby, as Rossi-Landi after her, recognized the plurilinguistic and pluridiscursive value of language and distanced herself from monologizing temptations. These are inherent, for example, in Noam Chomsky's linguistic theory, which fails to explain the communicative function of language or its social and intersubjective dimensions. The notion of common speech, as clarified by Rossi-Landi, does not contradict plurilingualism and plurivocality, i.e. the simultaneous presence of multiple languages and multiple voices (Rossi-Landi 1992: 134–136). On the contrary, it alludes to the similarity in functions carried out by different languages which, in their diversity, satisfy similar needs of expression and communication. Therefore, common speech serves to explain difference, variability and multiplicity among languages in terms of the needs of different traditions of experience and expressivity, which develop different means, solutions, and resources to satisfy expressive and communicative demands common to all human societies.

Antonio Gramsci is another noteworthy figure who gave special attention to the question of what he too denominated "common sense". Most significantly, the syntagm "common sense" is present in the opening pages of his *Quaderno* 1 (Gramsci 1975a), included in the list of "main topics", dated 8 February 1929. Like Welby, Gramsci too has a dual attitude toward "common sense": he both criticizes the concept, but also recovers it and renews it (Sobrero 1976). He criticizes common sense when it implies imprecise and incoherent beliefs and outdated worldviews that have sedimented in languages and cultural systems. But there also exists a "broad region" of "common sense" (*senso comune*), of "good sense" (*buon senso*) which subtends our conception of life and morals and involves all social classes; "common sense" thus understood refers to the ideas, senses and values commonly accepted by all social strata, unwaringly and uncritically (Gramsci 1975a, *Quaderno* 1: 65, 75–76). This is a recurrent theme in Gramsci's 1949 monograph, *Gli intellettuali e l'organizzazione della cultura* (Gramsci 1971a). Such "philosophy without philosophers", what Gramsci also calls "low philosophy", an "inconsequent, incoherent, disruptive philosophy" (1975a, *Quaderno* 8: 173) is the form in which "high philosophy" – which responds to the interests of the ruling class – variously circulates among the masses (an important contribution on this point is Gramsci's monograph, *Il materialismo storico e la filosofia di Benedetto Croce*, first published in 1948, see Gramsci 1975b):

> Every social stratum has its own "common sense" which is at the bottom of the most widespread conception of life and morals. Every philosophical trend leaves a sedimentation of "common sense": this is the document of its historical effectiveness. Common sense is not something rigid and static; rather, it changes continuously, enriched by new scientific notions and philosophical opinions which have entered into common usage.
>
> "Common sense" is the folklore of "philosophy" and stands midway between "folkore" proper (that is, as it is understood) and the philosophy, the science, the economy of the scientists. "Common sense" creates the folklore of the future, that is, a more or less stiffened phase of a given time and place. (Gramsci 1975a, Q 1, 65: 76)

In order to create a new political and cultural hegemony, a task Gramsci assigns to the party ("The Modern Prince", *Note sul Machiavelli*, 1971), common sense among the masses must necessarily be replaced with an organic conception of the world (cf. Boothman 2008). To this end, the production of hegemony is not only a question of demystifying backward beliefs upheld by common sense, but also of *identifying any spontaneous, progressive tendencies in it*. Gramsci holds that in order to affect common sense it will be necessary to place oneself "in the sphere itself of common sense", "detaching onself sufficiently to allow for a mocking smile, but not contempt or haughty superiority". Taken *in toto* common sense is not an "enemy to defeat"; instead, a "dialectical" relation – in my terminology, a "dialogical" relation – should be established with it (cf. Gramsci 1975a, Q 1: 65, 75-76).

Although Gramsci did not distinguish often between "common sense" and "good sense" (he recurrently says "common sense", that is, "good sense"), all the same he sometimes speaks of "good sense" in terms of protection against the excesses of inane intellectualism and also as the reasonable part of common sense. Gramsci observes that Manzoni, in his *Promessi Sposi* (Ch. XXXII), distinguishes between "common sense" and "good sense" *à propos* the deadly plague of 1576 and the plague-spreaders. As Gramsci observes:

> Speaking about the fact that there were indeed people who did not believe in plague-spreaders, but that could not support their opinion against widespread popular opinion, Manzoni adds: "There must have been a secret outlet of the truth, a domestic confidence: good sense was there; but it remained hidden, for fear of common sense". (1975a, Q 10 II: 48)

To critique and surmount deep-rooted "common sense", exploiting its "good sense" as well, is the necessary condition for dissemination among the masses of a new, more unitary and coherent conception of the world, of a new common sense (Gramsci 1988: 188). This involves organizing the system of superstitious and folkloristic philosophical conceptions typical of the masses into a new national popular philosophy, to the end of spreading a new culture, one that is organic and in keeping with the ideology of a new "social block", shared therefore by all strata of society. Common sense in Gramsci is closely connected with the problem of ideology.

Rossi-Landi refers to Gramsci in several passages throughout his writings. One particularly important passage relevant to our present discourse is from his 1978 monograph *Ideologia*, in a chapter titled "Ideology and social practice". After dedicating the first three paragraphs to the introduction of ideology into the problematic of social reproduction", to social reproduction as the *arché* or beginnning of all things, and to the articulations of social reproduction, Rossi-Landi dedicates the fourth paragraph to the question of sign systems, ideologies and production of consensus, and he refers to Gramsci. He observes that Gramsci, even if in "pre-semiotic" terms, had already identified the role carried out by sign systems in the social reproduction system and, precisely, in the relation between co-called "structure" and "superstructure" (Rossi-Landi 1978: 111). This paragraph concludes with the statement that in Gramsci's view, the most important goal for the "New Prince" (reference here is to the Machiavellian-Gramscian conception of the "Prince": the "New Prince" is the party) is *to reorganize verbal and nonverbal sign systems* for the sake of revolutionizing social teleology. Let me add that this means to reorganize "common sense", with its "common places" and its "good sense", *as a function of new social planning*.

According to Rossi-Landi, Gramsci knew that to develop and impose a new ideology and, consequently, to permeate the dominant mode of production with new ideological values, to permeate culture with new ideological values was only possibile through sign systems. These are described as the *mediating* level between the two levels of modes of production and ideological institutions.

ENTER PRAGMATISM

Technical terminology to be considered scientifically adequate should begin, according to both Welby and Peirce, with a critical reading of common experience, common sense, and common speech – here now understood in the reductive sense of everyday language and meaning – given their pervasive and often unconscious presence in technical language itself; for example, in the expressions of temporal-spatial relations (see Peirce's letter to Welby dated 16 December 1904, in Hardwick 1977: 48). Any kind of research, including the philosophical, must elaborate a "technical nomenclature" whose every term has a single definite meaning that is universally accepted among the experts of the subject. According to Peirce's "ethics of terminology (*CP* 2.219–2.226), a scientificallly valid nomenclature, which breaks with individual habits and preferences and satisfies the requisite of unanimity among specialists, must be supported by moral principles and inspire a sense of decency, of respect. The introduction of a new conception in philosophy calls for the invention of appropriate terms to express it. These should always be used by the scientific community according to their original meanings, whereas new technical terms that denote the same things and are considered in the same relations should not need be introduced. Peirce expresses himself clearly on this point, as in his 1905 article "What Pragmatism Is" (*CP* 5.411–5.437; the first of three on pragmatism published in *The Monist*) and particularly in the paragraph "Philosophical nomenclature" (*CP* 5.413).

By comparison with the other sciences, philosophy is a rather peculiar case, insofar as it presents the need for *popular words* in *popular senses*, not as part of its own terminological apparatus, but as its objects of study. Philosophical language, therefore, requires special terminology — think of that supplied by Aristotle, the scholastics, or Kant — which takes its distance from the "common speech" of everyday language and is distinct from it. "It is good economy for philosophy", as Peirce says,

> to provide itself with a vocabulary so outlandish that loose thinkers shall not be tempted to borrow its words. [...] The first rule of good taste in

writing is to use words whose meanings will not be misunderstood; and if a reader does not know the meaning of the words, it is infinitely better that he should know that he does not know it. This is particularly true in logic, which wholly consists, one might almost say, in exactitude of thought. (*CP* 2.223)

In Peirce's view, Kant, a "confused pragmaticist", made the mistake of not using the adjectives "objective" and "subjective" in a sufficiently specialized sense, thus causing them to lose their usefulness in philosophy altogether. On the basis of such premises, Peirce, in his paper on "The Ethics of Terminology", lists seven rules for the formation of a desirable philosophical terminology and system of logical symbols (*CP* 2.223–226).

According to Peirce's critical common-sensism,[2] no person is endowed with an infallible introspective power, not even when it comes to the secrets of one's own heart, no flawless means of knowing just what one believes or doubts. But he also maintains that there exist indubitable beliefs that are more or less constant. Such beliefs partake of the nature of instincts, intended in a broad sense. They concern matters that come within the reach of primitive mankind and are very vague (e.g. fire burns). A philosopher should regard an important proposition as indubitable only after having systematically endeavoured to attain doubts about it, remembering that genuine doubt does not ensue from a mere effort of the will, but must be the expression of experience. An indubitable proposition can be false, but insofar as we do not doubt a proposition, we must regard it as perfectly true, perfectly certain. While recognizing that there exist propositions that are each individually perfectly certain, we must also admit the possibility that one or more of them may be false (*CP* 5.498). In any case, doubt as theorized by the critical common-sensist is not doubt as envisaged by the Oxonian intellectual, i.e. doubt for its own sake, for the sheer pleasure of argumentation. The clever pragmaticist does not love the illusory power of brute force, but rather the creative power of reasonableness, which subdues all other forms of power and rules over them in the name of knowledge and love. As a supporter of *reasonableness*, the pragmaticist invests doubt, understood as the power of critical interrogation, though not amiable, with high moral value.

Aspects of critical common sensism are relevant to the pragmaticist insofar as they evidence the conditional character of belief, "that the substance of what he thinks lies in a conditional resolve", and the need for the quest for truth as the only way to satisfy the wishes of the heart (*CP* 5.499). The pragmaticist is open-minded and free of prejudice and, as such, is the most open to conviction and the most careful to distinguish beween truth and falsity, probability and improbability. The pragmaticist enquires into the relationship between inferences and the facts from which they derive and establishes a relation of affinity between thought and action in general. Beginning with the assumption that action in general is guided mostly by instinct, pragmaticism establishes that belief, too, is a question of instinct and desire (*CP* 5.499). And while it is true that, with the evolution of the species, instincts are constrained by the various degrees of self-control, they are not dominated completely. Therefore, given the familiarity and quasi-invariability of irresistable and instinctual desire, the inevitable interconnection between pragmaticism and critical common sensism should not be doubted.

SIGNS, SENSE, AND SUBJECTIVITY

Working in a pragmatic framework with reference to subjectivity, to self considered as a set of actions, practices, habits, Peirce identified "power" as opposed to "force" as a fundamental characteristic. Self is a centre oriented towards an end, an agent devoted to a more or less integrated set of "purposes". The latter can be related to Welby's "purport" or "ultimate value", the third element of her meaning triad or "significance". Power is not "brute force" but the "creative power of reasonableness", which by virtue of its agapastic orientation rules over all other forms of power (see *CP* 5.520). Power or the ideal of reasonableness is the capacity to respond to attraction exerted on self by the other; power and reasonableness are related to the capacity for response to the other and the modality of such response is dialogue. Semiotics understood as semioethics must account for the "reason of things". However, the *reason* of things cannot be separated from the capacity for *reasonableness* which is other-oriented. The issue at stake is the following: given the risks inherent in social reproduction today for life, *human beings must at their very earliest transform from rational animals into reasonable animals*.

Welby's significs and Peirce's semiotics contribute importantly to a better understanding of individual identity and the interpersonal relation. Welby describes the single individual in terms of the relation between "Ident" and "self" (Petrilli 2009: Chp. 6). The Ident is a generative centre of multiple *selves* and at once a multiplicity inhabiting each one of our selves. Thus described the Ident is a dialectical and open unit with respect to the sum total of its parts, its multiple selves. With respect to the self, the Ident represents an overflow, an excess value, a gift (Welby 1907, in Petrilli 2009: 645). The human being is a community of parts, distinct but not separate. Far from excluding each other, these parts, or selves, are interconnected by dialogic relations of mutual dependence. They are founded in the logic of otherness and non-indifference among differences. This approach excludes the possibility of undifferentiated confusion among parts, of homologating the other onto self. And to the extent that it represents an excess, an overflow with respect to the sum of its parts, the I or Ident is not the "individual" but the "unique". What Welby understood by "unique" – which has no relation to Max Stirner's (1844) conception of the unique, of singularity and its monadic separatism – can be translated with the concept of "non relative otherness" and "significance" (Levinas 1961; Ponzio 2009b).

The relation between the self's humility, fragility and vulnerability and the risks implied in its readiness to venture *towards* the other had are portrayed by Plato in his myth about Eros (in the *Symposium*), a sort of intermediate divinity, or demon, generated by Penia (poverty, need) and Poros (the God of ingenuity), who finds his way even when it is hidden. Welby described the connection between self-enrichment and risky opening *towards* the other as a condition for evolution. On the basis of this connection we can develop a critique of the condition of "being satisfied", therefore, an orientation towards "transcendence" with respect to reality, that is, to the world-as-it-is, to ontological being, given and determined once and for all. "Dissatisfaction" is an essential component in the concept of "mother-sense". It signals the need to recover the critical instance of the human intellect, the capacity for otherness, creativity and innovation, for shifting and displacing sense. Thanks especially to the procedures of abductive logic, this critical instance allows for prevision and "translation" understood in a broad sense, that is, beyond the limits of interlingual translation, translation as interpretation and verification of verbal and nonverbal signs alike. Scientific rigour in reasoning is possible on the basis of mother-sense or primal sense, as conceived by Welby, and agapastic logical procedure, as described by Peirce. This implies the courage to admit to the structural necessity of reasonableness by contrast with reason for the evolution of sign, subject and consciousness, which means to recognize the logic of otherness, intercorporeity, dialogue, love, inexactitude, instability and crisis.

A semiotic approach to the self allows for a more global perspective – biological and cosmical – than any historical-cultural contextualization can offer. Rereading Peirce, "chance", "love" and "necessity" regulate three modes of evolutionary development in the cosmos. In relation to the semiotic self, "love" or "agapasm" provides a significant framework to discuss problems at the heart of Welby's own research and precisely in relation to Peirce's. Moreover, Peirce's logic of vagueness highlights abduction as the main protagonist in the development of the "thought-sign" (Petrilli and Ponzio 2005: 473–477).

VAGUENESS AND MISUNDERSTANDING

The only important alternative to pragmaticism, at least the version criticized by Peirce, is traditional logic. The latter contends that thought has no meaning except itself and that substance is a category, an irregular pluralism of functions (*CP* 5.500). Logicians have elaborated a great many different categories, but they all agree that those concepts which *are* categories are all simple, and that they are the only simple concepts. The fact that something may be true of one category that is not true of another does not imply that these differences constitute the identifiable specificity of that concept: "Each is other than each of the rest but this difference is unspecifiable and thus indefinite. At the same time there is nothing indefinite in the concepts themselves" (*CP* 5.501). Peirce proceeds to establish a relation of affinity between differences connected to concepts and different qualities of feeling. The differences are perceived, just as we perceive different fragrances of different flowers, but the different qualities which may be predicated of each fragrance do not at all constitute the fragrance; they are not part of the fragrances themselves. As to their relations, nothing can be predicated except that each one is other than every other. Therefore, those relations are indefinite; but there is no indefiniteness about the feelings involved. On Peirce's account, concepts as analyzed by the logicians are no more than another kind of quality of feeling. Though the logician would never admit this on the grounds that concepts are general while feelings are not, s/he cannot demonstrate this position. Instead, Peirce maintains the following:

> [Concepts and feelings] are different no doubt; but the difference is altogether indefinite. It is precisely like the difference between smells and colours. It must be so, because at the very outset they defined concepts as qualities of feeling, not in these very words of course, but in the very meaning of these words when they said that concepts possess, as immediate objects, all the characters that they possess at all, each in itself, regardless of anything else. (*CP* 5.501)

Proponents of individualism would agree, Peirce argues, that reality and existence are coextensive; in other words, that reality and existence are either alike true or alike false with regard to every subject; they have the same meaning, or *Inhalt*. Many logicians would refuse such a position as a *reductio ad absurdum* of individualism, the two meanings to their mind clearly not being the same: "*reality* means a certain kind of non-dependence upon thought, and so is a cognitionary character, while *existence* means reaction with the environment, and so is a dynamic character" (*CP* 5.503). A misunderstanding characteristic of individualists is their belief that all other human beings are individualists as well, including the scholastic realists whom they thought believed that "universals exist". In reality, many great thinkers of the past did not believe that "generals" exist, but regarded them as "modes of determination of individuals" and such modes were recognized as being of the nature of thought. According to Peirce, the metaphysical side of pragmaticism attempts to solve the problem by accepting the existence of "real generals" and by seeking to answer the question: "In what way can a general be unaffected by any thought about it?" (*CP* 5. 503).

Another misapprehension clarified by Peirce is this: for the pragmaticist, the import, or adequate, ultimate interpretant – Peirce says exactly the "ultimate interpretation" – of a concept is contained in a "habit of conduct" or "general moral determination of whatever procedure there *may come to be*" (*CP* 5.504, italics in original). The import of any word (except perhaps a pronoun) is not limited to what is in the utterer's mind *actualiter*, that is, at the moment; but, on the contrary, it is "what is in the mind, perhaps not even *habitualiter*, but simply *virtualiter,* which constitutes the import" *(CP* 5.504*).* Every animal has habits and thus has innate ones. Insofar as an animal has cognitive powers, it must also have "*in posse* innate cognitive habits", this being Peirce's interpretation of innate ideas. Pragmaticists share these positions with a critical philosophy of common sense and they should not be considered as individualists, neither of the metaphysical nor of the epistemological type.

In line with critical common sense, Peirce maintains that all beliefs are *vague.* He even goes so far as to claim that the more they are indubitable, the vaguer they are. He goes on to discuss the misunderstood importance of *vagueness,* even in mathematical thought. Vagueness is no less than constitutive of belief, inherent to it and to the propositions that express it. It is the "antithetical analogue of generality":

> A sign is objectively *general*, in so far as, leaving its effective interpretation indeterminate, it surrenders to the interpreter the right of completing the determination for himself. "Man is mortal". "What man?", "Any man you like". A sign is objectively *vague,* in so far as, leaving its interpretation more or less indeterminate, it reserves for some other possible sign or experience the function of completing the

determination. "This month", says the almanac-oracle, "a great event is to happen". "What event?" "Oh, we shall see. The almanac doesn't tell that". The *general* might be defined as that to which the principle of excluded middle does not apply. A triange in general is not isosceles nor equilateral; nor is a triangle in general scalene. The *vague might be defined as that to which the principle of contradiction does not apply.* For it is false neither that an animal (in a vague sense) is male, nor that an animal is female. (*CP* 5.505)

Generality and vagueness do not coincide. Indeed, they oppose each other, though on a formal level they are seen to be on a par. A sign cannot be at once vague and general in the same respect, as Peirce says, "since insofar as the right of determination is not distinctly extended to the interpreter it remains the right of the utterer" (*CP* 5.506). Furthermore, only if a sign is not indeterminate can it avoid being vague or general; but "no sign can ever be absolutely and completely indeterminate" (*CP* 5.506).

In the light of his logic of relations, no proposition has a single subject, but rather has different levels of reference. On this aspect, Peirce refers to an article by himself published in *The Open Court* in 1892, "The Reader is introduced to Relatives" (*CP* 3.415–3.424). Even if only implicitly, all propositions necessarily refer to the truth, "the universe of all universes". Therefore they refer to the same determinately singular subject, understood both by the utterer and the interpreter, and assumed by all to be real. At a more restricted immediate level, all propositions refer to a non general subject.

In his paper "Consequences of critical common-sensism" (*CP* 5.502–537), Peirce reflects further on the role of vagueness. Communication among interlocutors is never completely definite, never completely non-vague, for where the possibility of variation exists absolute precision is impossible. Beyond expressing his hope that qualities of feeling among different persons may one day be compared by physiologists and thereby no longer represent a source of *misunderstanding*(!), Peirce identifies a cause of misunderstanding in the intention itself of intellectual precision and in the very commitment to explanation and specification, on the one hand, and in the diversity of experience among different persons, which is as calling for an uneliminable situation of dialogue both with others and with self on the other. From this point of view misunderstanding is inevitable, indeed, we might add, the very condition for understanding. Communication is necessarily vague because no man's interpretation of words is based on exactly the same experience as any other man's. Even in our most intellectual conceptions, the more we strive to be precise, the more unattainable precision seems. It should never be forgotten that our own thinking is carried on as a dialogue, and though mostly in a lesser degree is subject to almost every imperfection of language". (*CP* 5.506)

Therefore, just as when we look closely at the detail of a painting we lose sight of its overall sense, the more we attempt to be precise, the more unattainable precision seems, even when we are dealing with intellectual conceptions.

Vagueness is the common matter that subtends communication and constitutes a condition of possibility of communication itself; it is an *a priori* condition for the formulation of the propositions to be communicated. Such vagueness is strictly dependent upon reference to the different experiences of each one of us, from organic-instinctual life to intellectual life. Thus understood, more than postulating vagueness as the cause of *misunderstanding*, Peirce like Welby recognizes it as the condition of possibility of communication, thanks to which it is possible to formulate or actualize the propositions that form our communicative exchanges. Moreover, communication is achieved in terms of dialogue, whether interior dialogue or dialogue with other interlocutors external to oneself. Variability in the experience of the individual implies variability at the level of explicit interpretation and also at the level of implicit understanding. Therefore dialogue and understanding, as negotiated in communication, are strictly dependent upon vagueness, variability, the implicit and the unsaid. Understanding is possible thanks to the understood, and as such is always vague. The risk is that the more we attempt to be precise, the less we understand each other. To explicate the indeterminate and render it comprehensible means to undertake new interpretive/translative courses, new signifying paths, and thus to introduce new implications, new variables, and hence a new degree of vagueness. Ultimately, communication is dialogic investigation and approximation by interlocutors with respect to the referent of discourse—both the general referent, truth, and the immediate, special referent. Speaking, saying, explication, determination, understanding—all these stand firmly rooted in the understood, the unspoken, the unsaid, in implied meaning (Petrilli 1998a: 95–105; 2013: 186–88).

Expression and communication are achieved thanks to the relation among signs, or, better, among interpretants. And given the close association of interpretation to translation (as evidenced in particular by Roman Jakobson 1959), to the point that under certain aspects these terms overlap and may be considered synonymous, the relation among interpretants is a translational relation (see also Petrilli 2014a: Chs. 10, 11, 15). Meaning is achieved through processes of transferral and transvaluation in the interaction, to varying degrees of dialogic responsiveness, among signs. And as we have also aimed to evidence in this chapter, indeterminacy, ambiguity and vagueness are necessary conditions for continuity of such interpretive/translative processes in human semiosis.

MOTHER-SENSE, MODELING, LANGUAGE

In a series of unpublished manuscripts from the early twentieth century (now in Petrilli 2009: Chp. 6), Welby proposes the original concept of *mother-sense* which plays a central role in her description of the self and signifying processes, of the human capacity for the construction / interpretation of worldviews. Mother-sense is closely connected to gift logic. Synonyms include "primal sense", "primary sense", "native sense", "original sense", "racial sense", "racial motherhood", "matrix". Welby distinguishes between "sense", therefore "mother-sense" and "intellect", therefore "father-reason". With this distinction she intended to indicate the general difference – which cuts across sexual difference – between two fundamental modalities in modelling sense, therefore in the generation / interpretation of signs. Mother-sense and father-sense can be isolated at the level of abstract theory, but in material reality and in terms of sense producing practice (where "sense" includes "meaning" and "significance"), they are strictly interrelated. There is never either the one or the other because there's always both the one and the other in relations of reciprocal complementarity: neither the logic of reason nor the sense of logic (Deleuze), nor any well-reasoned logic nor logical sensing, but reason-becoming and sense-becoming, both of which are beyond bivalent logic. Sexual identity is always ambiguous which is consonant with Peirce's "logic of vagueness" (see Hardwick 1977; Petrilli 2014a: Chp. 8.6).

Mother-sense is the originating source of sense and critique; it is implied by the logic of otherness and corresponds to the capacity for knowing in a broad and creative sense through feeling, perceiving, intuiting, beyond cognitive leaps. From this point of view it is commonly described as "intuition", "judgement", "wisdom"; evoking Peirce, it allows for the idea to be intuited before it is possessed or before it possesses us. As the capacity for knowledge, which may also be understood in the Peircean sense of *agapic or sympathetic comprehension-recognition,* or *à la* Bakhtin in terms of *responsive understanding,* mother-sense is an endowment of the "human race" in its totality. In fact, another name for mother-sense is "racial sense", described as "an inheritance common to humanity" without boundaries in terms of sexual gender, the female, even though from a socio-historical perspective the woman easily emerges as its main guardian and disseminator.

In constrast to mother-sense, the intellect according to Welby translates into a capacity for acquiring knowledge largely oriented by the logic of identity, that is, where the logic of univocal identity dominates in the balance with otherness logic. Associated with rational inference, the intellect alludes to the acquisition of knowledge through the processes of asserting, generalizing and reasoning about data as they are observed and experimented with the cognitive instruments of logic and science. Its limit lies in the tendency to allow for the tyranny of data we wish to possess, but which end up possessing us. The reign of knowledge covered by the intellect is fundamentally entrusted to the jurisdiction of the male, but this is mainly due to socio-cultural reasons and not because of some special natural propensity for rational reasoning exclusive to the male. Welby maintains that the intellect derives from mother-sense and must not be separated from it: the penalty, otherwise, is loss of sense and significance, therefore homologation and leveling onto identity understood as monological, univocal, closed identity achieved by excluding the other. Mother-sense can be understood in the double sense of the Latin verb *sapere* which means both "to know" and "to taste of" (in Latin *scio* and *sapio*): what the intellect must exert itself to reach and to know, mother-sense – with its special capacity for acquiring knowledge and at once for transcending cognitive limits – already perceives in the double sense of this verb.

In terms of logic, to the expression "intellect" is associated the capacity for inferential processes of the inductive and deductive type, where the logic of identity dominates over the logic of alterity. On the other hand, to "mother-sense" are associated signifying processes dominated by alterity, in semiotic terms by the iconic dimension of signs; "mother-sense" alludes to the creative and generative force of sense resulting from the capacity of connecting things that seem distant from each other, but that in reality are attracted to each other; on the level of argumentation, "mother-sense" implies logical procedure of the abductive type regulated by the logic of otherness, creativity, dialogism, freedom and desire. Peirce explicitly established a relation between desire and meaning: both belong to the sphere of signs and values, where meaning value is connected with desirability. For the full development of cognitive and expressive potential, logic and reason, scientific research must be grounded in mother-sense. Furthermore, "mother-sense" includes "father-reason" (even if latently), while the contrary is not true. For this reason, both mother-sense and the intellect must be recovered in their original condition of dialectic and dialogic interrelation on both the phylogenetic and ontogenetic levels. In logic as understood by Welby, the broader and generative dimension of sense, mother-sense, interweaves with rational, intellectual life, father-reason in a relation of dialectic interdependency and reciprocal enrichment and empowering.

Significs aims to recover the relationship of reciprocal interpretation between the constant *données* of mother-sense and the continuous constructions of the intellect. Mother-sense supplies the material of immediate, unconscious and interpretative intuition; from an evolutionary viewpoint, it constitutes a further stage in the development of value with respect to animal instinct. Therefore, "mother-sense" is together "primordial and universal, at all stages of human development; though varying greatly in the part which it plays in the thought-life of human beings at such stages. And as Mother-sense is the Mother of sense, it is still occasionally found in women. Hence the peculiar authority accorded in all times to 'wise women' […]" ("Mother-Sense and Significs", 15 April 1907, in Petrilli 2009: 704). As such mother-sense is the condition for significance before and after signification. It concerns the real insofar as it is part of human practice; and the ideal insofar as it is the condition by virtue of which humanity aspires to continuity and ongoing development in the generation of actual and possible worlds and of signifying processes at large.

Furthermore, mother-sense converges with knowledge that is instinctively religious, intending by "religious", recalling the etymology from *religare* (to unite, to relate, to link), our feeling consciousness of the solar relationship; a universal sense of *dependency*, particularly developed in women, upon something greater than the human; therefore, a universal tendency towards religion where "religion" is understood as interconnection with a world that is other, vaster, more elevated, a world made of other origins and other relationships beyond the merely planetary, a world at the highest degrees of otherness and creativity, which involves the capacity for translation/interpretation, for association (Welby, 29 October 1906, *Ibid.*: 809–11). Mother-sense is a transcendent sense, that is, it converges with the capacity to transcend the limits of sense itself. It tells of the true sense and value of the properly human. Mother-sense does not simply imply "anthropomorphism", but more broadly "organicomorphism" and "cosmomorphism". From this viewpoint too Welby's approach can be associated with Peirce's, in particular his synechism.

Important implications connected with the concept of "mother-sense" described as the generative motor of signs and sense emerge in light of the concept of "language" or "modeling device" (Sebeok 1986, 1994). Like language understood as writing *ante litteram*, writing before the letter (Petrilli and Ponzio

2005: 377–428), mother-sense is an a priori which precedes knowledge and communication, a necessary condition for the acquisition of knowledge through different sign systems, verbal and nonverbal (cf. Petrilli 2014a: Ch. 2). Secondary or derived forms of signifying behaviour, including that connected to intellectual work, proceed from a primary modeling source of sense, as its expressive possibilities, as possible and actual constructions of the world. As a modeling procedure, mother-sense is the condition of possibility for the development of sense and significance before and after the production of intentional meaning, of inferential procedure, in particular the abductive, and for translation into a potentially infinite number of different worldviews.

"Mother-sense" is transcendent with respect to gender as much as it may be sexually differentiated in patriarchal capitalist society. All the same though it is a transgender concept it does tend to be more alive in women for the daily practices they carry out, for example, in their role as mother or wife. Such practices are oriented by the logic of self-donation, gift-giving and responsibility for the other, responsiveness towards the other, care for the other. Most importantly Welby also underlines the woman's role as the main repository of mother-sense in the development of language, which means to say in the construction of the symbolic order. She claims that the history of the evolution of humankind is the history of deviations in the signifying social network, in the capacity for discernment and critique which is the most serious deviation of all insofar as it leads human beings to be satisfied with existence as it is. This attitude contrasts with the condition of eternal dissatisfaction necessary for the development of experience, awareness and the expressive capacity generally. In her papers on eugenics, Welby claims that "We are all, men and women, apt to be satisfied now [...] with things as they are. But that is just what we all came into the world to be dissatisfied with" (in Petrilli 2009: 727). The concept of "mother-sense" signals the need to recover the human capacity for gift logic implicated in inferential procedure, the capacity for otherness, dialogism and unprejudiced thinking. It accounts for the critical instance of the intellectual capacity, for open-mindedness. This involves the capacity for shift and dislocation in sense producing processes beyond the order of discourse, for prevision and anticipation, for translation (understood in a broad sense) across time and space, across the different orders of signs systems and value systems related to them, across different languages and cultures.

Recovery of the relation of rational intellect to mother-sense, of reason to reasonableness, reason oriented by the logic of otherness, is a condition for developing a radically critical social consciousness capable of transcending the constraints of convention, while criticizing the threat of vague and void abstractions. Welby thematizes the need to safeguard mother-sense for the sake of future generations and their development. Like Peirce who introduces the concept of agapasm (creative love) and maintains that the evolutionary results it generates are directed towards something concrete, Welby too (independently from Peirce) describes the logic of mother-sense as oriented towards one's concrete neighbour, that is, one's neighbour by affinity and similarity, though distant in time and space. Human behaviour oriented by "creative love" involves inferential procedure of the abductive order, ruled by the logic of otherness. The self is structured and articulated in the relation with the other, turned to the other in close "proximity" (Levinas), the other understood as a "concrete abstraction" (Marx), in its "sign materiality" which alludes to the self's incarnation in a body and its signs.

The sense of symbolic pertinence (particularly alive in the child) can be recovered by reasserting the connection between mother-sense and rational behaviour. Considering that critical work is largely mediated by language understood as verbal language, Welby thematized the need for a "critique of language" and focused on the relation of language to consciousness, thought, to the self, which is grounded in mother-sense (Petrilli 2009: 379–84). She thematized the need for "critical linguistic consciousness", for linguistic practices free from prejudice and ignorance, which otherwise obstacle the full development of the human understanding, expression and interpretation.

As to inferential procedure, abduction is characterized by high degrees of otherness, creativity, even eccentricity. In contrast to induction and deduction governed by the logic of identity, the relationship between interpreted and interpretant in abductive argumentation is not guaranteed by codes, but emerges in terms of risky hypothesis, where the parts are related by similarity, attraction and reciprocal autonomy. Abductive inferential procedure is founded in the logic of otherness and is substantially dialogic; it is characterized by otherness, dialogism, and creativity. It proceeds on the basis of fortuitous attraction among signs in relations dominated by iconicity. Abductive inferential procedure is risky, it advances arguments that are mainly tentative and hypothetical, leaving a minimal margin to convention (symbolicity) and to mechanical necessity (indexicality). To the extent that it transcends the logic of identity and equal exchange, abduction belongs to the sphere of excess, exile, *dépense*, of giving without a counterpart, without returns, of desire (Bataille 1970, 2001; Mauss 1923–4). Insofar as it is regulated by the law of creative love, it is articulated in the dialogic relation among interpretants and develops in terms of the "interesting". Obviously, the concepts of agapasm, abduction and desire are closely interrelated. The end of agapastic development is the evolutionary process itself (cosmos, language, thought, self), continuity in signifying processes and semiosis in general. Creative development articulated through hypotheses, discoveries and qualitative leaps is achieved thanks to the combined effect of agapasm, the relation of attraction among interpretants, and of synechism, so that no datum, idea or individual exists in isolation.

SIGNIFICS, SEMIOTICS, SEMIOETHICS

Reading the works of scholars of the sign like Welby and Peirce provides us with theoretical instruments for a more adequate understanding of social symptoms and critique of the world today, of the world-as-it-is. This world (our own), the world as it is shaped and connoted in the era of globalization and global communication, is oriented by the logic of identity and characterized by the representation of difference based on this type of logic. "Identity" is understood here as *closed and egocentric identity* and difference based on identity logic thus understood is *identity-difference* (Petrilli 2013: 190-195). Difference orientated by the logic of closed identity leads to the construction of worlds and worldviews based on separation and dominion among identity-differences – whether these concern gender, ethnic group, ideology, religion, etc. Identity logic thus described subtends "the globalization of indifference" and inevitably results in the need to defend the interests of identities, to the point even of accepting the logic of war.

Instead, from the perspective of *significs* or *semioethics* (Petrilli and Ponzio 2003, 2005, 2010), difference is thematized in terms of otherness logic and dialogism and emerges as *otherness-difference*. Such logic involves the capacity for unity on the basis of intercorporeal dialogue and co-participation, even when encounter involves discord. Global hospitality, peace and freedom call for the relation of involvement with the other which cannot be achieved on the basis of closed identities, barriers and alibis. Instead, what is required is the relation of responsibility for the other, dialogic responsiveness towards the other, to echo Mikhail Bakhtin, across boundaries and relative alibis. In this framework, commitment to human rights means commitment to the rights of the other.

Significs is the name of that discipline or theoretical orientation in the study of signs and language that encourages one to ask questions like: "What does it signify?", "What does it mean?", "In what sense?" It is not surprising that the expression "significs" should have been introduced (in 1894 circa) by a woman – Victoria Welby precisely. Nor is it surprising that she never entered the Pantheon or genealogical tree of the "Fathers" of the language and sign sciences, despite her connections with scholars like Charles S. Peirce, Bertrand Russell, Charles K.

Ogden, George F. Stout, John M. Baldwin, Ferdinand S. Schiller, Ferdinand Tönnies, Frederik van Eeden, and many more.

"What does it signify?", "In what sense?", "Why?" are questions Welby induces one to ask in the face of any form of expression, verbal and nonverbal, piece of human behaviour or social practice. "The most wonderful of all words is the 'Why'. It is ours wherewith to press into and probe, to conquer and govern the very centres of mental life" (Welby, 23 August 1911, now in Petrilli 2009a: 514). As a significian, she focused on the relation of signs to values, ultimately on the relation of signs to life. She thematized the need for critical awareness and interpretation to enhance the value of the single individual, the potential for significance, and to safeguard human dignity under all aspects (Petrilli and Ponzio 2005: Chp. 2; Petrilli 2009: Chp. 4).

The logic of significs is associated with a new form of humanism, the "humanism of otherness" (Levinas 1961, 1972) by contrast with the "humanism of identity". It is also associated with "dialogism", "intercorporeal dialogism" (Bakhtin 1981). In this framework, responsibility is connected with the other, with the capacity for responsiveness which, in turn, is connected with gift-giving logic, the capacity for creative love, care for the other, and construction of new worlds. Welby's special approach to signs and language favours reflection upon issues relating to human rights, responsibility, freedom, hospitality and listening. Welby predicates love and care for the other, compassion, justice, and patience – all guiding values for healthy social practice. She identifies gift logic as a constitutive component in the relation among signs, in the generation of signifying practices, in the construction of subjectivity. Otherness and excess, overflow and transcendence with respect to identity logic are determining factors in the dynamics of interpretive processes and expressive systems, including the verbal, which is all one with the dynamics of the development of subjectivity, interpersonal relations and experience of the world.

REFERENCES

Bachtin e il suo circolo. *Opere 1919-1930*, ed., trans. and commented by Augusto Ponzio, a bilingual Russian / Italian edition, in collab. with Luciano Ponzio for the translation from Russian, intro. by A. Ponzio, pp. vii-xlviii, Milan, Bompiani [= "Il Pensiero Occidentale"]. 2014.

Bakhtin, Mikhail. *Problemy tvorčestva Dostoevskogo*, Leningrad, Priboj; It. trans. and ed. by M. De Michiel, *Problemi dell'opera di Dostoevskij*, intro. A. Ponzio, Bari, Edizioni dal Sud, 1997 (the result of comparing the first and second edition); new It. trans. and Russian original in Bachtin e il suo circolo, 2014, 1053-1423.

---. *Problemy poetiki Dostoevskogo*, Mosca, Sovetskij pisatel', 2a revised and enlarged edition of Bakhtin 1929; Eng. trans. by *Problems of Dostoevsky's Poetics*, ed. by C. Emerson, Intro. by W. C. Booth, Manchester, Manchester University Press, 1984.

---. *The Dialogic Imagination*, Austin, Texas University Press, 1981.

Boothman, Derek. "Hegemony: Political and Linguistic Sources for Gramsci's Concept of Hegemony". In Richard Howson & Kylie Smith (eds.), *Hegemony. Studies in Consensus and Coercion*, 33–50, New York, Routledge, 2008.

Cobley, Paul. *The Routledge Companion to Semiotics*, Intro. 3-12, London, Routledge, 2010.

Cust, Mrs. Henry (Elizabeth) (Ed. & Intro.) *Echoes of Larger Life: A Selection from the Early Correspondence of Victoria Lady Welby*, London, Jonathan Cape, 1929.

---. (Ed.) *Other Dimensions: A Selection from the Later Correspondence of Victoria Lady Welby*, Intro. by L. P. Jacks, London, Jonathan Cape, 1931.

Eco, Umberto. *Semiotica e filosofia del linguaggio*, Turin, Bompiani. Eng. trans. *Semiotics and Philosophy of Language*, Bloomington, Indiana University Press, 1984.

Garroni, Emilio. *Progetto di semiotica. Messaggi artistici e linguaggi non-verbali*, Rome-Bari, Laterza, 1973.

---. *Ricognizioni della semiotica*, Rome, Officina, 1977.

Gramsci, Antonio. *Gli intellettuali e l'organizzazione della cultura*, Rome, Editori Riuniti. 1971a

---. *Letteratura e vita nazionale*, Rome, Editori Riuniti. 1971b.

---. *Note su Machiavelli*, Roma, Editori Riuniti. 1971c.

---. *Quaderni dal carcere*, ed. by V. Gerratana, 4 vols. Turin, Einaudi, new ed. 2001, 1975a

---. *Il materialismo storico e la filosofia di Benedetto Croce*, Intro. by L. Gruppi, Rome, Editori Riuniti, 1975b

---. *Lettere dal carcere*, vol. 1, Rome, Editrice l'Unità, 1988.

Hardwick, Charles. (Ed. with the assistance of J. Cook). *Semiotic and Significs. The Correspondence between Charles S. Peirce and Victoria Lady*

Welby, Pref., ix–xiv, Intro., xv–xxxiv, by C. S. Hardwick, Bloomington-London, Indiana University Press. 1977.

Heijerman, Eric; Schmitz, Walter H. (Eds.) *Signifies, Mathematics and Semiotics. The Signific Movement in the Netherlands*. Proceedings of the International Conference, Bonn, 19-21 November 1986, Münster, Nodus Publikationen. 1991.

Jakobson, Roman. "On Linguistic Aspects of Translation", in R. Jakobson, *Selected Writings*, Vol. II: 260-266. The Hague: Mouton, 1971 [1959].

Levinas, Emmanuel. *Totalité et infini*, The Hague, Martinus Nijhoff; Eng. trans. by A. Lingis, *Totality and Infinity*, Intro. by J. Wild, Pittsburgh, Duquesne University Press, 1969 [1961].

---.*Humanisme de l'autre home*, Montpellier, Fata Morgana; Eng. trans. by N. Poller, *Humanism of the Other*, Urbana: University of Illinois Press, 2003 [1972]

Marrone, Gianfranco. (Ed.) *Dove va la semiotica? Quaderni del circolo semiologico siciliano* 24, 1986.

---. Ed. *Materiali semiotici. Quaderni del circolo semiologico siciliano* 30.

Mincu, M. Ed. *La semiotica letteraria italiana*, Milan, Feltrinelli, 1982.

Nuessel, Frank; Colapietro, Vincent and Susan Petrilli. (Eds.) *On and Beyond Signifies. Centennial Issue for Victoria Welby. Semiotica*, Intro. by Frank Nuessel and Vincent Colapietro, Special Issue 196, 1/4, 2013

Peirce, Charles S. *Collected Papers of Charles Sanders Peirce* (i 1866-1913), Vols. I-VI, ed. by C. Hartshorne & P. Weiss, 1931–1935, Vols. VII-VIII, ed. by A. W. Burks, 1958, Cambridge (Mass.), The Belknap Press, Harvard University Press. [In the text referred to as *CP* followed by volume and paragraph number]. 1931–1958.

Petrilli, Susan. *Teoria dei segni e del linguaggio*, Bari, Graphis, 1998a..

---. *Su Victoria Welby. Signifies e filosofia del linguaggio*, Naples, Edizioni Scientifiche Italiane, 1998b.

---. "Meaning, metaphor and interpretation: Modelling new worlds", *Perspectives on Metaphor. Semiotica* 161(1/4), 75–119, Special Issue, Guest ed. Frank Nuessel, 2006.

---. *Signifying and Understanding. Reading the Works of Victoria Welby and the Signific Movement*, Foreword by P. Cobley, xvii–x [= Semiotics, Communication and Cognition 2, Editor: Paul Cobley], Berlin, Boston, De Gruyter Mouton, 2009.

---. *Sign Crossroads in Global Perspective. Semioethics and Responsibility*, Preface, vii–ix, Intro., xi–xiii, by John Deely, New Brunswick (U.S.A.) and London (U.K.), Transaction Publishers, 2010.
---. *Expression and Interpretation in Language*, Pref. by Vincent Colapietro, New Brunswick (U.S.A.) & London (U.K.), Transaction Publishers, 2012a.
---. *Un mondo di segni. L'avere senso e il significare qualcosa*, Bari, Laterza, 2012b.
---. *The Self as a Sign, the World and the Other*, Pref. by Augusto Ponzio, New Brunswick (U.S.A.) & London (U.K.), Transaction Publishers, 2013.
---. *Sign Studies and Semioethics. Communication, Translation and Values*, [= Semiotics, Communication and Cognition 13, Editor Paul Cobley], Berlin, Boston, De Gruyter Mouton, 2014a.
---. *Riflessioni sulla teoria dl linguaggio e dei segni*, Milano, Mimesis, 2014b.
---. *Victoria Welby and the Science of Sign. Significs, Semiotics, Philosophy of Language*, New Brunswick (U.S.A.) and London (U.K.), Transaction Publishers, 2015a.
---. *Nella vita dei segni. Percorsi della semiotica*, Milan, Mimesis, 2015b.
Petrilli, Susan and Augusto Ponzio. *Semioetica*, Rome, Meltemi, 2003.
---. *Semiotics Unbounded. Interpretive Routes in the Open Network of Signs*, Toronto, Toronto University Press, 2005.
---. *Semioetica e comunciazione globale* [= Athanor XXIV, 17], ed. by S. Petrilli, Milan, Mimesis, 2013-14.
Ponzio, Augusto. 1990. *Man as a Sign*, ed., trans. intro., and appendixes by S. Petrilli. Berlin, New York, Mouton.
---. "Metaphor and poetic logic in Vico." *Perspectives on Metaphor. Semiotica*, 161-1/4, pp. 231-249. Special Issue, Guest ed. Frank Nuessel, 2006.
---. *A mente. Processi cognitivi e apprendimento linguistico*, Perugia, Guerra, 2007.
---. *Linguaggio, lavoro e mercato globale. Rileggendo Rossi-Landi*, Milan, Mimesis, 2008a.
---. *A revolusão bakhtiniana*, San Paolo (Brazil), Contexto, 2008b.
---. *Da dove verso dove. La parola altra nella comunicazione globale*, Perugia, Edizioni Guerra, 2009a.
---. *Emmanuel Levinas, Globalisation, and Preventive Peace*, Ottawa, Legas, 2009b.
---. *Rencontres de paroles*, Paris, Alain Baudry & Cie., 2010.

---. *La filosofia del linguaggio*, Bari, Edizioni Laterza, 2011.

Rossi-Landi, Ferruccio.. *Significato, comunicazione e parlare comune*, Padua, Marsilio, 1980. [New ed. by A. Ponzio, 2006.]

---. *Ideologia*. Milan: ISEDI. New expanded edition, Milan, Mondadori, 1982. New edition by A. Ponzio. Rome, Meltemi, 2005; Eng. trans. from the 1982 ed. by R. Griffin, *Marxism and Ideology*, Oxford, Clarendon Press, 1978.

---. "Wittgenstein, Old and New", *Ars Semeiotica* IV, 1, 29–51; Now in Rossi-Landi 1992°, Ch. 4, 1981[1979].

---. *Metodica filosofica e scienza dei segni*, Milan, Bompiani. New edition by A. Ponzio, 2006.

---. *Between Signs and Non-signs*, ed. and Intro. by S. Petrilli, ix–xxix, Amsterdam, John Benjamins, 1992.

Schmitz, Walter H. 1985. "Victoria Lady Welby's Significs: The Origin of the Signific Movement", in Welby 1985a, ix-ccxxxv.

---. (Ed.) *Essays on Significs. Papers Presented on the Occasion of the 150th Anniversary of the Birth of Victoria Lady Welby*, Pref. by H. W. Schmitz, i-ix, Amsterdam, John Benjamins, 1990a.

Sebeok, Thomas A. *A Sign Is Just a Sign*, Bloomington-Indianapolis, Indiana University Press, 1991.

---. *Global Semiotics*, Bloomington, Indiana University Press, 2001.

Sobrero, Alberto."Folklore e senso comune in Gramsci", *Etnologia e antropologia culturale* 1, 1976.

Vailati, Giovanni. *Il metodo della filosofia. Scritti scelti*, ed. and Intro. by F. Rossi-Landi, new ed. by A. Ponzio, Bari, Adriatica, 2000.

---. E*pistolario 1891–1909*, ed. by G. Lanaro, Intro. by M. Dal Pra, Turin, Einaudi, 1971.

---. *Scritti*, 3 Vols, ed. by M. Quaranta, Bologna, Forni, 1987.

Welby, Victoria. "Meaning and Metaphor", *The Monist* 3.4 (1893): 510–525. Now in S. Petrilli 2009a, 421–430.

---. "Sense, Meaning and Interpretation", *Mind* N.S, 5.17(1896): 24–37, 5.18 (1896): 186–202. Now in S. Petrilli 2009a, 430–449.

---. *Grains of Sense*. London: J. M. Dent & Co. 1897. [A selection of passages is included in S. Petrilli 2009a.]

---. *What Is Meaning? Studies in the Development of Significance*, London, Macmillan. 1903.

---. *Significs and Language. The Articulate Form of Our Expressive and Interpretative Resources*, London, Macmillan & Co. 1911a. Now in Welby 1985a.

---. Significs. In *The Encyclopedia Britannica*. 11 ed., Vol. XXV, 1911b, 78–81, Cambridge, The University Press, in C. Hardwick 1977, 167–175; and in Petrilli 2009, 345–350.

---. *What Is Meaning? Studies in the Development of Significance*, ed. and Preface by A. Eschbach, ix–xxxii, Intro. by G. Mannoury, xxxiv–xlii [= Foundations of Semiotics 2], Amsterdam/Philadelphia, John Benjamins, 1983 [1903].

---. *Significs and Language*, ed. and Intro. by H. W. Schmitz [= Foundations of Semiotics 5], Amsterdam-Philadelphia, John Benjamins, 1985a. [Includes Welby's monograph of 1911, *Significs and Laguage* and a selectionof other writings by her].

---. *Significato, metafora, interpretazione*, It. trans., ed., and Intro. by S. Petrilli, Bari, Adriatica, 1985b.

---. *Senso, significato, significatività*, It. trans., Intro. "Il senso e il valore del significare," vii–lx, and ed. by S. Petrilli, Bari, Graphis, 2007.

---. *Signifying and Understanding. Reading the Works of Victoria Welby and the Signific Movement*, Pref. by P. Cobley, Berlin, Mouton, 2009. [This monograph by S. Petrilli includes a vast selection of published and unpublished writings by Victoria Welby].

---. *Interpretare, comprendere, comunicare*, It. trans. ,ed. and Intro., 11–96, by S. Petrilli, Rome, Carocci, 2010.

Welby Collection in the York University Archives and Special Collections, Scott Library, York University, Downsview, Toronto, Ontario, Canada. The *Welby Collection* presents 42 boxes divided into two main sections: Box 1-21: *Correspondence* 1861-1912; Box 22-42: *Subject files*.

About the Author

Susan Petrilli is Professor of Philosophy and Theory of Languages at the University of Bari Aldo Moro, Department of Lettere, Lingue e Arti, Italianistica e Culture comparate, where she teaches. She is Director of the PhD program in Theory of Language and Science of Signs at the same University. Her most recent monographs include: *Sign Crossroads in Global Perspective. Essays by Susan Petrilli, 7th SSA Sebeok Fellow. The American Journal of Semiotics*, Volume 24.4

(2008), *Signifying and Understanding. Reading the Works of Victoria Welby and the Signific Movement* (2009), *Sign Crossroads in Global Perspective. Semioethics and Responsibilities* (2010), *Parlando di segni con maestri di segni* (2011), *Expression and Interpretation in Language* (2012), *The Self as a Sign, the World and the Other* (2013), *Un mondo di segni. L'avere senso e il significare qualcosa* (2012), *Riflessioni sulla teoria del linguaggio e dei segni* (2014), *Sign Studies and Semioethics. Communication, Translation and Values* (2014), *Nella vita dei segni* (2015), *Victoria Welby and the Science of Signs. Significs, Semiotics, Philosophy of Language* (2015). With Augusto Ponzio she co-directs the following book series: *Nel segno* (Bari Laterza); *Gli Strumenti, serie gialla* (Bari, Graphis); *Di-segno-in-segno* (Lecce, Manni); *Segni-di-segni* (Lecce, Pensa). In 2008 she was nominated *7th Thomas A. Sebeok Fellow of the Semiotic Society of America*. In 2012 she was nominated Academic adviser of the Institute of Semiotics and Media Studies (ISMS), Sichuan University, Chengdu, China. She is currently Visiting Research Professor at The University of Adelaide, South Australia.

CHAPTER 15

Topo-Grapho-Mania: Space-Texts and Text-Spaces in Topographie idéale pour une agression caractérisée (R. Boudjedra) and Paisajes después de la batalla (J. Goytisolo)

Ilka Kressner

This essay proposes an analysis of the intermedial relations and cross-fertilizations between literature and space. It examines the presence of Paris as a discursive formation, material reality, and three-dimensional interlocutor in two novels: *Topographie idéale pour une agression caractérisée* (1975) by Algerian writer Rachid Boudjedra and *Paisajes después de la batalla* (1982) by Spanish author Juan Goytisolo. Boudjedra's and Goytisolo's textualized topoi transcend the notion of space as a metaphor or as inspiration of a literary work. Instead, "Paris" becomes an unfolding discourse (hence the quotation marks), a configuration that oscillates between the space and the page, an energetic field that connects the city and the text (Bal 1991).

The criticism of the intermedial relations between word and image, and the vindication of the visual as a medium in its own right, have seen thought-provoking discussions during the last decades (W.J.T. Mitchell 1986, Culler 1981, Bal 2001, Hirsch 1997). In comparison, the study of the relation between word and architecture as two equal, mutually motivating modalities of enunciation has only received partial critical analysis. While the criticism on art forms that unfold in time and space, most notably theatre, pantomime and dance, is vibrant and growing (Biringshaw 2001, Leabhart 1989, *Music, Space and Place* 2004), space is seldom analyzed as an actant and active force that affects other media. This essay will focus on examples of the less studied intermedial relation between writing and space illustrated in two novels. I will argue that Boudjedra's and Goytisolo's texts propose readings of space as a modality of expression. The novels are cases in point of a cross-participation of space in writing and of writing in space, where the materials of both media are combined rather than merely juxtaposed or cited. In *Topographie idéale pour une agression caractérisée* (henceforth: *Topographie*) and *Paisajes después de la batalla* (henceforth:

Paisajes) words and signs do not merely refer to, represent, or interpret space from a neutral perspective. Instead, they shape and re-signify a particular "Paris," as much as they are shaped and re-signified by it. The peculiar spatial experience in both novels affects the material of writing on the most basic morphological and syntactical levels, from the choice of words (and inclusion of words from other languages and alphabets) to the crafting of sentences, paragraphs, punctuation marks or lack thereof. Moreover, space shapes the novels on the semantic and narrative levels, too: human reactions to the three-dimensional, such as claustrophobia, the feeling of getting lost in space, or solitude amidst the masses are re-created via fragmented discourses, narrative repetitions and alternations between detailed descriptions and vague allusions to scenes that need to be interpreted on the intradiegetic level by the characters and extradiegetically by the readers.

Boudjedra and Goytisolo create narrative counter-spaces, which aim at transgressing a discourse of Paris as a cultural cliché and gravitational center of Western dominance. On the metanarrative level, these text-spaces also propose alternative aesthetics of the novel. Beyond any naïve realist description, theirs is a creative and personal interpretation of space in and as writing. *Topographie* captures this mutual entwinement of space and script in the equation "l'espace – c'est à dire, la feuille de papier" (173, "Space, that is to say, the piece of paper," my trans.). This quote forms part of an inner monologue of the disoriented protagonist, who tries to find his way through the subway system and make sense of the metro plan. The readers might sympathize with his disorientation; like him, they are confronted with unstable narrative perspectives and space-times that may change within a single paragraph or even sentence.

How does the intermedial relation take shape in the case of writing and architecture? Intermedial's etymology might give a first – spatial – hint, apropos the interaction of the two media: the term "medium" derives from the Greek "meson;" it defines an element between two distant objects, a common area or public way ("medium" *OED Online*). In both novels, "Paris" is such a site of encounter between a work of art and a three-dimensional space. The experience of space modifies the text, which becomes a field of potential connections. Such a narrative, albeit bound to the written page, appeals to different senses. *Topographie* and *Paisajes* circumscribe the French capital less as an architectonic given, and more as a vector and area of interactions, among human beings, thoughts, things, senses and not last, as a realm of semantic experiments. Henri Lefebvre's *La production de l'espace* is one of the main conceptual bases of my approach. Lefebvre's description of space not as a given, but as a medium, an intermediary and acting entity (337), informs my conception of space in *Topographie* and *Paisajes*.

Both Boudjedra and Goytisolo wrote their novels in Paris while in exile. Boudjedra had fought for the National Liberation Front (FLN) during the Algerian War of Independence from 1959-62. He studied in Paris from 1969-72, where he earned his Ph.D in philosophy from the Sorbonne, with a thesis on Louis Ferdinand Céline. Shortly after returning to Algeria, he was forced to emigrate to Morocco as the result of his open political criticism. He taught in Morocco from 1972-75, before returning to his native Algeria in 1975. *Topographie* was written in France and Morocco. Goytisolo had immigrated to France in 1956 to escape Francoism. *Paisajes* was the fifth novel he wrote in the French exile, after the trilogy *Señas de identidad* (1966), *Reivindicación del Conde don Julián* (1970), *Juan sin tierra* (1975) and *Makbara* (1980). All his creative and critical writings were censored in Spain during Francisco Franco's dictatorship.

The narrative "Parises" in both books run counter to most of the images generally associated with the French capital. Boudjedra's setting is entirely under ground: the protagonist, an illegal and illiterate immigrant, travels the Parisian metro. The novel describes his day-long and ultimately tragic odyssey through the functionalist setting, from the railway station Gare d'Austerlitz using the metro lines 5, 1, 12, 13 and 13bis (those numbers are the titles of the five chapters of the text), until the moment he arrives at his aim, the station stop Porte de Clichy. When he emerges from below ground, he is attacked by a group of fascists. He dies shortly afterward as a result of their beating. His blood on the pavement makes a pattern of lines that are similar to those of the metro plan he had attempted to decipher, yet to no avail, during his travel.

Goytisolo's bizarre scribe surreptitiously marks different bourgeois neighborhoods – among those, his own, the Sentier – by stealthily rewriting street signs, names of cafés, cinemas and shops with Arabic and Turkish letters. He works toward a radical re-signification of the city, where the xenophobe Europeans will become colonialized analphabets of a newly lettered city. He engages in dubious journalistic activities and erotic correspondences; he tinkers with the idea of joining a radical guerrilla movement, yet is discovered by a terror commando and forced to write down a list of his sins (which is, at least in part, the text of *Paisajes*). As the result of the detected lack of honesty in his avowal, he is killed by a bomb, which had been attached to his body while he was writing his confessions. Postmortem, the dismembered writer ("escritor"), who equates himself with his writing ("escritura") disperses into a limitless space, which is rendered in the text as a string of words with few punctuation marks that evokes a breathless discourse: "Desmembrado y hecho trizas como tu propio relato alcanzas al fin de el don de la ubicuidad... puedes callejear escribir extraviarte en el doble espacio de la cives y el libro inventar trayectos laberínticos desorientar desorientarte: esparcir la materia narrada al azar" (*Obras completas III* 1045, "dismembered, torn to bits like your own story you finally attain the gift of ubiquity... you may stroll through the streets write lose your way in the double space of the city and the book invent labyrinthine itineraries to disorient to disorient yourself: scatter the material of the story to the four winds," *Landscapes after the Battle* 156-7). The written landscapes after the battle have become textual spaces in motion.

The setting in both novels is a place of long literary tradition (Stierle 1998). "Among all cities, none has been linked closer to the book than Paris... For centuries, the bare Seine-quays have been covered with ivy made of scholarly pages: Paris is a great library, flowed through by the Seine" (Benjamin 1982, 356, trans. mine). Walter Benjamin's declaration of love to the city has itself become another ivy leaf of it. Boudjedra's and Goytisolo's novels are drafted on the palimpsest of this rich tradition of the writing about "Paris," yet theirs are highly idiosyncratic readings of the French capital.

One of the narrative techniques employed to measure up to the magnitude of the city has traditionally been to select a metonymical center. Examples of this method are for instance Victor Hugo's descriptions of the cathedral of Notre Dame in *Notre Dame de Paris* (1831), Emile Zola's focus on the market halls in *Le ventre de Paris* (1873), and Roland Barthes's semiotic study of the Eiffel Tower as the pars pro toto of the city in *La Tour Eiffel* (1964). These approaches are based on the premise of a readability of the city. The ability to determine a center presupposes a distant, often elevated, point of view.

Opposed to this strategy of the localization of a center is a decentering of the vision, as proposed in another literary tradition, that of the 'tableau.' This genre shows more commonalities with the idiosyncratic creations by Boudjedra and especially Goytisolo. Among its first examples, even before the French Revolution, was Louis Sébastien Mercier's *Tableau de Paris* (1782-88). Mercier described Paris from the perspective of a marginalized intellectual in the form of a series of selective observations on the physiognomy of the city. His style is sketchy and personal. The narrative point of view is immersed in the city; it renounces the center. For Mercier's multiple narrators, space is both stimulating and confusing to the eye. The 19th century saw a continuation of the tableau in the 'physionomies' a genre dedicated to short descriptions of city life and different milieus, often written by various authors and printed in the literary supplements of journals. *Le diable à Paris* (1845), a best seller of the period, is a series of 'physionomies,' set in an ironic tone. According to the framing narrative of the collection, the devil has come to Paris. He is bored and is then entertained by different storytellers, who describe scenes of daily life that range from a visit in a public swimming school to a shopping spree in one of the new department stores. The volume also portrays different types of inhabitants of the city, among them, a character that becomes central to the writing of Paris in the second half of the 19th and beginning 20th centuries – the flâneur. With his *Tableaux parisiens* (1857) and *Petits poèms en prose* (posthumous 1869), Charles Baudelaire proposes a reading of Paris as an allegory of the city-stroller's own subjectivity. Paris is an active character of the scenes of modern life: it hurls in the background when the lyrical voice observes a passer-by ("A une passante"), it dreams the dream of its own evasion ("Les sept vieillards") and becomes anthropomorphized with its deepening wrinkles ("Les petites vieilles"). Most notably, the city has become the locale of the subject's perpetual inspiration, combined with a growing awareness of lack of communication and solitude amidst the crowds. The *Petits poèmes en prose* sum up this experience with the lapidary "multitude – solitude: termes égaux et convertibles pour le poète actif et fécond" ("Les foules," *Œuvres complètes I* 291, "Multitude – solitude: equal and interchangeable terms for the active and fertile poet," *The Parisian Prowler* 21). Paris remains a central source of inspiration in literary texts of the beginning 20th century, now in a much more ludic sense. The Surrealists are engaged in their city with all their senses. In *La liberté ou l'amour!* (1927), Robert Desnos takes the semantics of names of spaces, monuments and signs on billboards as his source of fabulistic creation. His city is inhabited by mythical creatures. In Benjamin Péret's "Il était une boulangère" (1925), the protagonist, Pope Pius VII, chases condors on the rooftop of Notre Dame cathedral and fights snakes on the Boulevard Raspail. In *Le paysan de Paris* (1926) Louis Aragon evokes a metaphysics of space. Paris is perceived as a living body, where the passers-by morph into blood cells in the arteries of its boulevards. Those transport not goods or labor, but dreams and yearnings. The city, according to the Parisian peasant, can only be apprehended in motion. Aragon's novel includes a city plan. The map, however, is void:

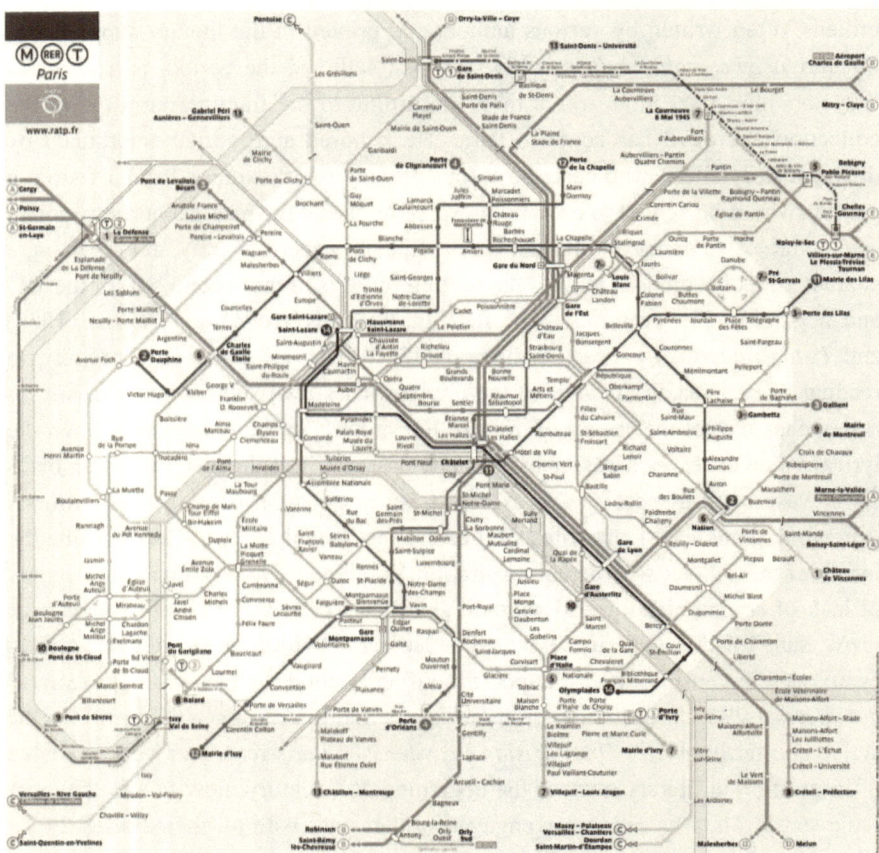

The white rectangle can be read as an invitation for the readers to play and draw a mental map of a discursive "Paris" of their own. More likely, it may visualize the impossibility to reduce their city to a set of lines and words on a piece of paper. The walking through and reflecting on space are both movements; likewise, for the Parisian peasant, space itself is changing and in motion.

Topographie and *Paisajes* are written on the palimpsests of these variegated city-fictions that portray, if not directly the city, the reactions, perceptions, and world (or city) views of its inhabitants. The two novels present fragmented, immersed and limited perspectives, similar to those of the 'tableaux.' They conjure up the fantastic within the daily grind through the power of fiction and atmosphere, and suggest the existence of an elusive space as spectacle and inspiration for the literary creation, comparable to Surrealist city-fictions. In the words of Goytisolo's writer-protagonist-roamer: "la complejidad del ámbito urbano – ese territorio denso y cambiante, irreductible a la lógica y programación

–, invita a cada paso a trayectos versátiles, que tejen y destejen, lienzo de Penélope, una misteriosa lección de topografía" (*Obras completas III* 973, "The complexity of the urban environment – that dense and ever-changing territory irreducible to logic and to programming – invites him on every hand to ever-shifting itineraries that weave and unweave themselves, a Penelope tapestry, a mysterious lesson in topography," *Landscapes* 86). The mysterious topographic lesson is woven into the fabric of the text, which itself has been "invited" by the experience of space. In reference to the Odyssey, that paradigm of a wandering made text, the novel gestures toward the production of space in writing.

Boudjedra proposes a reading of Paris under ground, but not in the tradition describing the dirty sewers that serve as a romantic counterpart of conspiracy in Victor Hugo's *Les misérables* (1862) or the devilish underworld of Gaston Leroux' *Fantôme de l'opéra* (1910). The topography of the Algerian author's novel is the functional metro system. The uniform surroundings and the seclusion of the system set free the protagonist's associations and memories; he mentally replaces the objective space-time with a subjective space-time-discourse. In these confined surroundings, time is relative, moldable and expansive. As a result of the close physical interaction with other passengers, bodies are not always perceived as entities, but as fleeting and blurred images. For example, the protagonist does not observe the silhouettes or complete bodies of other passengers, but their shoes: "les centaines de pieds de pointures différentes et chaussées diversement avançant... l'un après l'autre... ou glissant, ou se hâtant dans un mouvement syncopé" (88, "...the hundreds of feet of numerous sizes and shapes moved forward... one after the other... or slid or advanced hastily in a syncopated movement"). In the first sentence of the novel, which continues over three pages, the protagonist is only indirectly described via parts of his body (his hand) or the objects he is carrying (a piece of paper with his destination's address and a bulky suitcase). The human body has no priority over the objects, and time is no structuring device of the narration.

This narrative shows many similarities with works by French 'nouveau romanciers.' In an analogous way, Alain Robbe-Grillet's *Instantanés* (1963) also zoom in on fragmented elements of the bustle in a metro station and allude to the passengers' spatial disquiet. The literary inspiration was probably not one-sided: one year after the publication of *Topographie*, Robbe-Grillet published *Topologie d'une cité fantôme* which, in addition to its title, bears many spatial similarities to Boudjedra's work. In *Topographie*, as in many 'nouveau romans,' the city is portrayed as a possible crime scene. Detective fiction is one of the literary genres most intensely engaged in reading space, and particularly that of the modern megalopolis, with a scrutinizing eye for evidence. One of the narrators of Boudjedra's text is a detective in charge of investigating the protagonist's assassination. His advice to his staff, which is repeated on several occasions in the novel, highlights the necessity to study space and its two-dimensional representations in order to understand the crime: "je compte sur vous un conseil: lisez attentivement la carte du métro" (28, "here's my advice to you: read the plan of the metro with utmost attention"). The crime is never solved; the only glimpses of the course of events are embedded in the fragmented and at times contradictory accounts by the protagonist and by an evasive voice in free indirect style that describes his body in space after his death.

Topographie and *Paisajes* further reference writings of the city by another group of artists, of immigrant authors of the second half of the 20th century, who broach the issue of urban sign systems that are exclusivist and potentially dangerous for the non-initiated. In his fictions that take place in the metro, Argentinean author Julio Cortázar evokes visual fragments of sudden nearness, and refers to the potential threat of place: some station stops seem to engulf their users ("Texto en una libreta" *Queremos tanto a Glenda*, 1980). In "El perseguidor" (*Las armas secretas*, 1959) the Parisian metro elicits passivity and self-abandonment to visual stimulations. It is a dream-space of subjective time beyond the clocked surface. Bodies are perceived as fragmented, possessions are forgotten amidst the crowds, words and signs serve not to explain and orient, but to perplex and estrange. Boudjedra and Goytisolo, too, develop the themes of spatial disquiet, corporeal fragmentation and semantic disorientation. In their narratives, space is a deceiving and estranging instance and marker of power structures, particularly for its illiterate users. Both novels explore the impact of signs in space and point toward the dogmatic consequences of a civilization obsessed with a certain order of things. In his introduction to Goytisolo's novel, published by Espasa Calpe, Andrés Sánchez Robayna reads *Paisajes* as "una serie de 'valores culturales' puestos en solfa. El personaje [está] situado en los 'márgenes' de una cultura o de una civilización absurda, que ha dado lugar a una generalizada hipocresía social" (18, "a series of 'cultural values' that are ridiculed. The character is situated at the 'margins' of a culture or an absurd civilization that has led to an overall social hypocrisy," trans. mine). While the character in *Topographie* is at the mercy of repressive and exclusivist signs, the protagonist of *Paisajes* highlights a more autonomous interaction with signs in space, as he is able to challenge established codes and redetermine his (written) life world.

Herbert Marcuse, Marc Augé, and Barbara Lang have highlighted the specificity of the closed system of transportation with its peculiar sets of rules. For Lang, the sudden nearness to other passengers creates a strange kind of momentary community, yet never of trust (*Unter Grund* 18). According to Marcuse, in such a space of technological rationality, "a comfortable, smooth, reasonable, democratic unfreedom prevails" (*One Dimensional Man* xv). Passengers have to obey a set of procedures that temporarily transform them from individuals to synchronized entities. Augé describes the moment one enters the closed metro system as the coming into effect of a contract between the human being and the surroundings: "le voyage dans le métro, s'il se définit en général comme individuel, est simultanément et éminemment contractuel" (*Un ethnologue dans le métro* 77, "Now, travel in the metro, if defined in general as individual, is simultaneously and consistently contractual" (*In the Metro* 43). Boudjedra's illiterate user is ignorant of that contract. His presence in the highly regulated space of the metro is described as an "intrusion" (8). When he tries to escape the underworld by jumping over the barrier, he is filmed by surveillance cameras and sent back by members of the supervisory staff.

The protagonist in *Paisajes*, in contrast, is aware of the codes and order of things of the functional transit space. He knows how to decipher and moreover rewrite signs in a variety of languages. For this lonely misanthrope, the metro is a counter-space to the abhorred monuments of pompous Paris and a source of spatial potentialities. In an exuberant enumeration, he exemplifies his alternative interpretation of space: "El metro de París... es vasto y rico en posibilidades: ramificaciones, encrucijadas, pasajes, trayectos de dirección única, desvíos, parábolas, medias vueltas, elipses, cuppos di sacco. Examinar el plano del metro es ceder al recuerdo, evasión, desvarío; abrirse a la utopía, la ficción y la fábula" (974, "The Paris métro... is vast and rich in possibilities: ramifications, intersections, connecting points, one-way journeys, roundabout itineraries, parabolas, half circles, ellipses, dead ends. To examine the map of the métro system is to yield to memory, to escape, to delirium; to accept utopia, fiction, fable," *Landscapes* 87). The fluidity of space, which is rendered in a similarly fluid discourse, is by no means disquieting for the narrator. He enjoys drifting through the veins of the city in its incessant bustle. Yet, unlike Boudjedra's passenger, he does have a private space of his own, where he can retire to draft plans of erotic excesses, write instruction manuals for the creation of insurrectional cells and new invasions of the city. However, in a sardonic twist, Goytisolo has his misanthropist being raped in this innermost place of bourgeois privacy, his apartment in the Rue Poissonnière. It is only post mortem, in the chapter titled "La ciudad de los muertos" ("The City of the Dead") that he reaches a true space of freedom and the gift of ubiquity.

A central ideological subtext of *Topographie* is the growing racism in France during the 1970s. *Paisajes* refers to acts of terrorism by separatist Spanish groups from the late 1970s to early 1980s. Both racism and terrorism radicalize the idea of a territory defined as one's own, against a perceived spatial and ideological threat from an outside (or an infiltrated outsider). The French Front National Party was founded in 1972, it soon radicalized its position from a populist-nationalist toward an openly right-wing party with anti-Semitic undertones (Buzzi 15, 22). After the transition to democracy in 1975, Spain suffered a wave of terrorist acts, most violently by the Basque nationalist terror organization ETA. The separatist groups rejected the autonomous communities that had been established by the constitution of 1979, and fought toward independent republics. Especially the Basque Country saw acts of terrorism against the status quo of the autonomous community: The party 'Herri Batasuna,' the second-strongest party in the Basque government and political arm of the terrorist association ETA, proclaimed in 1979 that they would fight for an independent Basque Republic and not shun acts of extreme violence (Berneckerm 249).

Both *Topographies* and *Paisajes* are evident responses to those contemporary events, even though the respective forms of racism and terrorism are only indirectly described in the case of *Topographie* and are hyperbolized in that of *Paisajes*. The stranger in Boudjedra's novel is either unaware of the xenophobic gestures of the passengers around him or interprets them incorrectly. The text specifies that, besides being illiterate of French, he does not even speak the language "de son pays[,] il baragouine un dialecte montagnard" (46, "...of his own country, he only smatters a rural dialect from the mountains..."). *Topographie* does not criticize racism on the discursive level, but instead presents limited perspectives or elusive points of view that allude to situations of restriction and abuse. By doing so, it precludes any quick judgment or sentimentalism. Instead, it emulates the described situations for the reader to experience them in the act of reading. Even the final episode of the racist beating of the stranger, which is described on several occasions and in different versions in the form of prolepses, is not rendered in an accusative or suffering tone. Instead, the victim depicts the attacks from a neutral and detached perspective. His dying is portrayed in ekphrastic terms, again with reference to the plan of the metro. He is "tachant le pavé d'un liquide douteux... y dessinant comme un graphisme non sans rapport avec ceux qui l'avaient fasciné pendant son séjour sous terre" (129, "...staining the cobblestones with a doubtful liquid... and drawing some kind of graph not unlike those that had fascinated him during his sojourn underground"). The protagonist, who had failed to decipher the signs on the city walls and billboards, inscribes himself onto space. The victim of the racist attack writes with the symbol of life, as he bleeds to death. The tragedy of this scene is even intensified by the reference to a group of street sweepers from the Maghreb, who had just cleaned the pavement shortly before the attack and will discover the dead body soon afterward. Similarly to the protagonist, although to a lesser degree, they suffer from racism and are exploited to maintain the status quo. In the novel, the political critique is rendered indirectly through a fragmented language, dramatic repetitions, harrowing images and disquieting spatial perspectives.

Paisajes on the other hand directly references the racist discourse and hyperbolizes it with biting sarcasm. For example the fragment "¡Atención morenos!" ("Watch your Steps, Swarthy-Faces!") is a note of caution for suntanned Parisians returning from their holidays to not take the metro: as a result of their darker skin complexion, they might be taken for illegal immigrants and suffer harassment by police officers patrolling under ground. The language and images of many fragments in the novel are reminiscent of news broadcasts. The first chapter, "Hecatombe" ("The Hecatomb"), sets the stage for the sequence of narrative snapshots of violence the protagonist observes, suffers from, performs or yearns for. For instance, when he is contemplating the Palais Royal and the Louvre, he confesses his "deseo vehemente de dinamitar el lugar" (938, "a violent desire to dynamite the place," *Landscapes* 52). Another chapter describes the neighborhood under siege by an ominous authoritarian regime. The protagonist is forced to fill out a questionnaire and is subsequently led to a truck that will transport him to a distant place. A loudspeaker yells at him to "ser útil y obedecer sin rechistar a las órdenes y decretos de mis salvadores!" (1003, "to be useful and obey without a word the orders and decrees of my saviors!" *Landscapes* 115). The chapter "Interpreten correctamente a Marcuse" ("Read Marcuse Correctly") describes in a taunting manner the protagonist's ideation of a revolution to overcome what he, mimicking Marcuse, calls the current state of alienation toward a better world that will be ruled, of all things, by Walt Disney figures, such as Donald Duck, Pluto, Mickey Mouse and the Hundred and One Dalmatians. "Refugiado en su antro, a salvo de bombardeos e incendios, el perspicaz gurú de la imparable revolución de los ochenta consulta los astros para determinar el momento más favorable a la realización del ideal disneyista: los idus de mayo" (967, "Holed up in his den, safe from arson and bombardment, the perspicacious guru of the inevitable revolution of the eighties consults the stars in order to determine the most favorable moment for the realization of the Disneyite ideal: the ides of May," *Landscapes* 80). His manic plans for a spatio-ideological occupation, however, will be foiled by an even more drastic act of terrorism, that of an intrusion by members of an ominous guerilla group into the utmost space of privacy and realm of collected thoughts: the apartment is searched and the folders with the protagonist's writings are ultimately destroyed, just before he becomes the victim of an attack by a terror commando of no clear mission.

Both novels denounce the violent claim of territorial misappropriation via the characters' interaction with space. Despite their limited (in the case of *Topographie*) and derisive (in the case of *Paisajes*) perspectives, the protagonists have an acute awareness of the fragility of their surroundings. The stranger in Boudjedra's text is described to be "étouffé... par l'étroitesse des lieux alors qu'il [est] habitué... au grand large" (144, "...suffocated.. by the narrowness of the surroundings, he, who is used to the large expanse"). The normalized and aseptic sites of the metro system, "le traumatisent profondément au point qu'il va buter à nouveau contre le parois du piège comme une souris prise" (115, "...traumatize him so deeply that he bangs yet again into the inside walls of his trap, like a mouse in a cage"). Like a laboratory mouse, the protagonist is put to the test but, unlike the mouse, cannot adapt to the formalist spaces that surround him.

The spaces that the nameless traveler encounters are the antipodes of anthropological dwellings that allow for inscription or even molding, which would "bear the impression of its occupant" (Benjamin, *The Arcades Project* 220). The sites in *Topographie* mostly display man-made materials, such as glass, steel and metal. They reflect the passenger's image back upon himself and, thus, increase his feeling of being at the mercy of the surroundings. The underground system of transportation is for him a disconcerting series of repetitions. Some of these repetitions are spatial (descriptions of tracks, gangways, escalators), others are graphic (signs, slogans, titles of posters and geographic plans) or discursive (repetitions, at times verbatim, at times in variation, of textual passages in different contexts). In the narrative world of *Topographie*, the visual sense is misleading. In a sequence, when the protagonist is on an escalator, he observes that

> les... affiches.. se réverbérant sur l'inox recouvrant les escaliers roulants, multipliant ainsi les structures, faussant les topographies et créant artificiellement des semblables d'espaces... qui ne sont quand même pas de vrais miroirs... mais la tentation reste grande de... savoir quel est leur rapport avec l'espace réel, hachuré, strié, sectionné, et

désarticulé comme un mille-pattes qui ne saurait plus démêler sa tête de sa queue. (16-17, "...the... posters... were reverberated on the stainless steel of the escalators, thus they multiplied the structures, and created misleading topographies and artificially similar spaces... that are nevertheless no real mirrors... but the temptation remains to find out about their relation to the real, hachured, striated, sectioned and disarticulated space, like a millipede that cannot distinguish its head from its tail any more.)

Advertising has adapted the strategies of warfare (Haubl 13). It visually overwhelms and disorients its vis-à-vis. All attempts of the protagonist to make sense of the two-dimensional images and texts, and integrate them into his three-dimensional surroundings fail. The quoted passage renders this disorientation with a string of gerunds. This verb form portrays the actions performed by space as being invariable and unfolding in a time of no clear end. Instead of a rational understanding of "real" space, the foreigner's reaction to his surroundings is that of fright: "à cause de l'affiche publicitaire il croit qu'il s'est trompé et panique" (195, "because of the poster he thinks that he made a mistake and panics"). It is certainly no coincidence that the advertisement that has the power to morph and dissect space and mislead the character would convey a nationalist message, which invites the onlookers in capital letters to "RÉVEILLE[R] VOS INSTINCTS DE GAULOIS" (61, "AWAKEN YOUR INSTINCTS AS A GAUL"). Language has become a tool of exclusion, and this, not only on the intratextual level: Unlike the illiterate protagonist, who observes the signs in the metro system, the readers of Boudjedra's novel do understand the slogans and perceive the tragic irony.

Goytisolo plays a similar linguistic-spatial game; yet in his case, the gazers of incomprehensible signs are the readers of *Paisajes*, who are unfamiliar with Turkish and Arabic: The description of the main character's rewriting of the street signs is followed by the inclusion of some of those words in the text of the novel. For instance, when a disoriented Frenchman looks for the logo of the newspaper *L'Humanité*, he finds that "su enseña roja, orientada al bulevar...: ¡ahora se llamaba انسانية!" (890, "its red sign, turned toward the boulevard...: it was now called انسانية!" *Landscapes* 6). The word is not translated; it is simply included in the Spanish text as a sign. The readers who do not understand Arabic might guess that انسانية is a translation of the word humanity, but the main valence of the sign in the sentence is its interruptive visual power, and not semantic reference. Written language gains a materiality on paper. The single word displays a sensuous and dynamic quality. This is especially relevant in the case of the word being Arabic. Hédi A. Jaouad notes, when referring to works written by authors from the Maghreb (among them Boudjedra, however, the observations are also relevant in the context of *Paisajes*): "[their] texts reflect a preoccupation with writing as a creative trace and its concretization. Concretism in literature, especially in poetry, is neither new nor original. One may argue, nonetheless, that the Islamic tradition... has advanced the dynamics of the graph" (67). The insertion of Arabic words in the Spanish text in *Paisajes* highlights this material and dynamic quality of the word, and thus transforms the literary text into a field of dynamic graphic interactions.

Goytisolo's technique, which pays back the urban "semiocracy" (Baudrillard *L'échange symbolique* 121, *Symbolic Exchange* 78) in its own coin, – through new signs that interrupt and redefine the space of the city, – was much en vogue during the time he wrote his novel. In *Crimes of Style – Urban Graffiti and the Politics of Criminality,* Jeff Ferrell defines graffiti as an unregulated cultural practice, "emerging out of the Black neighborhood and street gang cultures in New York City" (6) in the late 1970s. This act of political provocation places the emphasis not on signals of political significance, but on signs that resist immediate interpretation, at least by most of their onlookers. Jean Baudrillard proposes an example of the use of graffiti of a striking similarity to the activities described in *Paisajes*: "les graffiti recouvrant tous les plans de métro de New York comme les Tchèques changeant les noms des rues de Prague pour dérouter les Russes: même guérilla" (*L'échange symbolique* 124, "graffiti covers every subway map in New York, just as the Czechs changed the names of the streets in Prague, to disconcert the Russians: guerrilla action," *Symbolic Exchange* 81). Goytisolo's graphs inserted in the established order of signs, however, cannot all be interpreted as semantically void, as Baudrillard proposes in the context of his study of graffiti. For the protagonist of *Paisajes*, the signs on the walls of the public spaces are "invitaciones a quien quiera o sepa leerlos: mítines, reuniones, veladas, mesas redondas" (*Paisajes* 915, "invitations to anyone who wishes and knows how to read them: meetings, gatherings, evenings, round tables," *Landscapes* 29). What marks the distinction between Goytisolo's and Baudrillard's more pessimistic approach in the quote above is probably the verb "querer." Indeed, the juggler of words in *Paisajes* (as well as the protagonist of *Topographie*, despite his constant failure) is an avid decipherer of signs. Words are riddles, semiotic challenges that might acquire meaning in the process of attentive reading. The protagonist does not shy away from any effort to make sense of them. Even in a moment of utmost danger, with the explosive charge tied to his chest, he cannot resist the temptation to copy a set of mysterious signs into his notebook. Sitting on the body of a ruined car, "procura[s] descifrar su [de los ideogramas] enigmática significación. Una pasión voraz de aprender, de asimilar los símbolos, creencias, lenguaje[s]...absorbe por completo tu atención" (1040, "try to decipher their [of the ideograms] enigmatic meaning. A devouring passion to learn, to assimilate the symbols, the beliefs, the languages... absorbs all of your attention," *Landscapes* 153). Beyond its preposterousness, this scene of the obsessive transcriber of signs in a city-landscape after a battle may also be interpreted as a gesture of resistance to violence. If space is not only a medium of communication, but also a creator of meaning, the multilingual signs that cover the ruins may be cues to understand and, thus, actively participate in the discursive creation and meaning of space. According to this interpretation, the very process of interpreting signs in space becomes a deeply democratic endeavor. In his study of Goytisolo's novel, Carlos Fuentes stresses the egalitarian impulse of the otherwise egocentric character. The act of patiently deciphering unfamiliar signs is in Fuentes's view an emblem of the democratic undertaking itself: "la democracia es... un esfuerzo de educación exigente" (71, "democracy is a demanding effort of learning," trans. mine). The foreign figures on the walls "parodia[n] el lenguaje abstracto de la sanidad occidental y [lo] obliga[n] a revelarse como lugar común, morralla (y muralla) política; incitación comercial...para remitirnos al lenguaje del otro" (86, "parody the abstract language of Western sanity and force it to reveal itself as a stereotype, as chump change (as a political wall) [Fuentes plays with the phonetic contiguity of the Spanish words morralla (cheap money) and muralla (wall)] a commercial incitation... to lead us to the language of the other," trans. mine). The endeavor to decode the language of the other is a means of establishing a critical distance from one's own systems of reference, among them, those of conventional perceptions of space.

The characters in both novels are fascinated with maps. Yet their maps are not the results of clearly traceable processes of abstraction from space to paper. They do not literally cover the space they represent, as explored in Jorge Luis Borges's much cited fable "Del rigor en la ciencia" (*Ficciones*, 1944), or cover the mere void of postmodern hyperreality according to Baudrillard (*Simulacres et simulation*). In Boudjedra's and Gotyisolo's novels, maps are objects of play and visual invitations to confabulate. A geographical plan triggers subjective associations, in the vein of free interpretations of inkblots in a Rorschach test. Space is less defined via fixed points, and much more as an itinerary and sequence of routes. For Goytisolo's scribe, the map of Spain resembles a hide of a goat, hung upside down to dry, with its snout pointing to the African continent (*Paisajes* 1025; *Landscapes* 137). While many of the associations of the protagonist of *Paisajes* are metaphorical, Boudjedra's foreigner associates mostly in a metonymical fashion. He finds fragments of the lines of the plan on the wrinkled faces of passengers (155) and sees similarities between the metro lines and the lines of sweat that have tainted the piece of paper with the destination address that he holds in his hand. He realizes that the lines of the plan have entered his inner body: "les lignes du plan... imprègnent son crâne" (227, "the lines of the plan pervade his cranium"). The character's associations based on contiguity, open up new mental spaces in addition to the three-dimensional network system of the Parisian metro. For the traveler underground, the "topographie de l'espace et celle de la mémoire [se] mélange[]nt" (*Topographie* 19, 110, 141, 143, 226, this passage is repeated several times in variations, "the topography of space and that of memory intermingle"). Trauma changes common language; it marks and estranges it from itself, forces the narrative voice to conjure disturbing images and repeat them in different contexts. The spatial trauma of the protagonist's Parisian odyssey is re-created via the materiality of the text that takes the form of a disconcerting maze of shifting perspectives. With its at times page-long sentences, made of strings of parentheses, the novel is an analogous text-space to the topographic spaces of the underground and the merging sites of memory. The discourse of a frantic search is explored in its etymological sense as a "running to and fro" (*OED*, etymology "discourse") and a process of becoming sign via the act of moving through space.

The non-chronological discourse, with its repetitions of several key images at different instances, is multidirectional: *Topographie* can be entered/read at any point of the narration. It shares this characteristic with *Paisajes,* which has been described as a "novela.. fragmento... mosaico... de imágenes fuertemente dislocadas o dispersas" (Sánchez Robayna 15-16, "novel... fragment... mosaic... made of images that greatly dislocate and disperse," my trans.). The telling title of the last chapter of Goytisolo's novel, "El orden de los factores no altera el producto" ("The Order of the Factors Does Not Change the Product") invites divergent readings. In addition to a roaming in criss-cross, the text may also be read linearly, starting with the last chapter and ending with the first one, according to the direction in which Arabic is read. Finally, *Paisajes* can be read as a cluster of beginnings that take place in each of its chapters. Randolph Pope proposes a numeric interpretation of the novel composed of 77 chapters: "The sacred number seven, associated with creation and the pillars of wisdom can be read as an indication of the creation in second degree or the imitation of creation, and therefore, a disturbing dispersion, which the novel describes" (133). *Paisajes* is in fact no chaotic dissemination, but a clearly marked construct and account of disseminations, a discourse that presents processes of ideologization and performs deconstructive readings of them. As in the case of *Topographie*, Goyisolo's text changes; it includes slogans and signs found in space, and stages as well as rearticulates them in the new text-zone of the novel.

Toward the end of his text, Goytisolo changes from justified text to a typeset reminiscent of a poetic text. The word at the end of the traditional setting is "libro" ("book"). In a book about the metanarrative changes of writing as a result of alternative experiences and projections of space, the word "book" initiates a visual breakup of the established format (and punctuation) as well as the roles of writing, narrating and reading:

> tú yo mi texto el libro
> yo: el escritor
> yo: lo escrito
> lección sobre cosas territorios e historia
> fábula sin ninguna moralidad
> simple geografía del exilio (*Paisajes* 1046)

> You I my text the book
> I: the writer
> I: the written
> lesson on things territory [h]istory
> story without a moral
> elementary geography of exile (*Landscapes* 157)

The enumeration "tú yo mi texto el libro" highlights the changeability of narrative instances. The enunciating "I" is in one line the writer, in the next one, the written text. The three indented final lines allude to the traditional moral at the end of a narration, but again are written against this expectation. The readers are told that *Paisajes* is a lesson, a story, and finally a 'geo-graphy' (space-writing) of exile.

Topographie and *Paisajes* portray, each in its own way, novel readings of the relation between the discursive two-dimensionality and architectonic three-dimensionality of the city. Theirs are writings about spaces, which concretize in analogous text-spaces. Boudjedra and Goytisolo stage their secondary "Paris" discourses, shift positions, and present erring narrative perspectives. Both novels highlight the progressions and continuous oscillations between literature and space. Instead of focusing on the two extremes, they measure the interactions and grapho-spatial cross-fertilizations of both media.

REFERENCES

Aragon, Louis. *Le paysan de Paris.* Paris: Folio, 1996.

Augé, Marc. *In the Metro.* Trans. and intro.: Tom Conley. Minneapolis: University of Minnesota Press, 2002.

---. *Un ethnologe dans le métro.* Paris: Hachette, 1986.

Bal, Mieke. *Reading "Rembrandt." Beyond the World-Image Opposition.* New York: Cambridge University Press, 1991.

---. *Looking in: The Art of* Viewing. Amsterdam: G and B Arts International Imprint, 2001.

Baudelaire, Charles. *Œuvres complètes I.* Paris: Bibliothèque de la Pléiade, 1975.

---. *The Parisian Prowler.* Trans. Edward Kaplan. Athens: University of Georgia Press, 1989.

Baudrillard, Jean. *L'échange symbolique et la mort.* Paris: Gallimard, 1976.

---. *Simulacres et simulation.* Paris: Galilée, 1981.

---. *Symbolic Exchange and Death.* Trans. Hamilton Grant. London: Sage, 1993.

Benjamin, Walter: "Paris: Die Stadt im Spiegel." *Gesammelte Schriften.* Ed. Rolf Tiedemann. Vol.4.1. Frankfurt a.M.: 1982. 356-359.

---. *The Arcades Project.* Trans. Howard Eiland and Kevin McLaughlin. Cambridge, MA: The Belknap Press at Harvard University, 1999.

Bernecker, Walther L. *Spaniens Geschichte seit dem Bürgerkrieg.* Munich: Beck, 1997.

Borges, Jorge Luis. *Ficciones.* Barcelona: Destinos, 2009.

Boudjedra, Rachid. *Topographie idéale pour une aggression caractérisée.* Paris: Folio, 1996.

Briginshaw, Valerie. *Dance, Space, and Subjectivity.* New York: Palgrave, 2001.

Buzzi, Paul. "Le Front National: Entre national-populisme et idéologie d'extrême droite." *Le discours politique en France – Evolutions des idées partisanes.* Ed. Paul Bréchon. Paris, 1994. 15-22.

Cortázar, Julio. *Queremos tanto a Glenda.* In *Cuentos completos III.* Mexico D.F.: Punto de Lectura, 2013.

---. *Las armas secretas.* In *Cuentos completes I.* Mexico D.F.: Punto de Lectura, 2013.

Culler, Jonathan. *The Pursuit of Signs: Semiotics, Literature, Deconstruction.* Ithaca: Cornell University Press, 1981.
"Discourse, n." *OED Online.* December 2013. Oxford University Press. 10 Feb 2014
 <http://www.oed.com/view/Entry/53985?rskey=xmFgoq&result=1>.
Ferrell, Jeff. *Crimes of Style – Urban Graffiti and the Politics of* Criminality. New York: Northeastern University Press, 1996.
Fuentes, Carlos. *Geografía de la novela.* Madrid: Alfaguara, 1993.
Goytisolo, Juan. *Landscapes after the Battle.* Trans. Helen Lane. New York: Seaver Books, 1987.
---. *Obras completas III. Novelas (1966-1982).* Barcelona: Gutenberg, 2005.
Haubl, Rolf. "Früher oder später kriegen wir euch." In *Bilderflut und Sprachmagie – Fallstudien zur Kultur der Werbung.* Ed. Hans Hartmann and Rold Haubl. Opladen: Verlag für Sozialwissenschaften, 1992. 9-32.
Hirsch, Marianne. *Family Frames: Photography, Narrative, and Postmemory.* Cambridge, Mass.: Harvard University Press, 1997.
Jaouad, Hédi A. "The Dialectics of the Archaic and the Postmodern." *Studies in 20th Century Literature.* Vol. 15.1 (Winter 1991): 59-76.
Lang, Barbara. *Unter Grund. Ehtnographische Erkundungen in der Berliner U-Bahn.* Tübingen: Tübinger Vereinigung für Volkskunde, 1994.
Leabhart, Thomas: *Modern and Post-Modern Mime.* Hampshire: Macmillan, 1989.
Lefebve, Henri. *La production de l'espace.* Paris: Anthropos, 1974.
Marcuse, Herbert. *One Dimensional Man; Studies in the Ideology of Advanced Industrial Society.* Boston: Beacom Press, 1964.
"medium, n. and adj.". *OED Online.* December 2013. Oxford University Press. 14 February 2014.
 <http://www.oed.com/view/Entry/115772?redirectedFrom=medium>.
Mitchell, W.J.T. *Iconology: Image, Text, Ideology.* Chicago: Chicago University Press, 1986.
---. *Picture Theory.* Chicago: Chicago University Press, 1986.
Music, Space and Place: Popular Music and Cultural Identity. Ed. Andy Bennett, Stan Hawkins and Sheila Whiteley. Burlington, VT: Ashgate 2004.
Pope, Randolph. *Understanding Juan Goytisolo.* Columbia, SC: University of South Carolina Press, 1995.
Robbe-Grillet, Alain. *Instantanés.* Paris: Les Éditions de Minuit, 1963.

Sánchez Robayna, Andrés. "Introducción." *Paisajes después de la batalla.* Madrid: Espasa Calpe, 1982. 15-29.

Stierle, Karlheinz. *Der Mythos von Paris – Zeichen und Bewusstsein einer Stadt.* Munich: Deutscher Taschenbuch Verlag, 1998.

About the Author

Ilka Kressner (Ph.D. University of Virginia). Focusing on 20th century to contemporary Spanish American literature and film, her research interests include intermediality (text, image, sound), conceptions of space in the text (encompassing the related topics of vertigo, free fall, and velocity) and most recently ecocritical studies. Her scholarship and teaching examine Spanish American literatures, film and art from a variety of cultural and national contexts, often from a comparative perspective. Her articles have appeared in the *Bulletin of Hispanic Studies, Iberoamericana, Hispanic Journal, Revista Chilena de Literatura*, and *Hispanófila*. Her monograph *Sites of Disquiet: The Non-Space in Spanish American Short Narratives and their Cinematic Transformations* was published with Purdue UP (2013). She has co-edited *Walter Benjamin Unbound* (2015), a special issue of the journal *Annals of Scholarship*; and is currently working on a book project on Latin American travel photography and writings from the 1950s to 70s.

CHAPTER 16

Multimodal Satire: The Form of the Literary Substance in Japanese Writer Natsume Sōseki's First Feuilleton Novel

Annette Thorsen Vilslev

Many agree that the novel is a hybrid genre. Whether the novel (as genre) is the same around the world is a question that has spurred discussion in comparative studies. An oft-quoted essay on the subject is Franco Moretti's "Conjectures of World literature", which in 2000 was the outset of a renewed discussion of the concept World Literature, the term used by Johann Wolfgang von Goethe when referring to a particular Chinese novel in a conversation with his assistant Johann Peter Eckermann in 1827. Moretti's text is a discussion of the evolution of the novel, and his conclusion (or one of them) is that in the larger world perspective, the Western novel is rather the exception than the rule. The hypothesis that Moretti sets out to investigate is what he has called "Jameson's law", with reference to Frederic Jameson's introduction to Karatani Kōjin's *Origins of Modern Japanese Literature*. Jameson "noticed that in the take-off of the modern Japanese novel, 'the raw material of Japanese social experience and the abstract formal patterns of Western novel construction cannot always be welded together seamlessly'" (Moretti 2000: 58). Moretti *conjecture*s that "the modern novel first arises not as an autonomous development but as a compromise between a Western formal influence (usually French or English) and local materials" (Moretti 2000: 58).

Moretti compared and found striking similarities between Karatani's account of the history of the modern Japanese novel and Roberto Schwarz's essay "The Importing of the Novel to Brazil". He then wanted to put this to test against descriptions of the novel in other places. Karatani's work was originally published in Japanese, then translated and published with a preface by Jameson in 1993. It begins with Karatani analyzing the writing style of Japanese writer Natsume Sōseki (1867-1916). Jameson also wrote an essay on "Sōseki and Western Modernism", but Moretti, insisting on distant reading, does not mention Sōseki. Jokingly, he even tries to avoid mentioning particular authors that he did in fact read (he cannot, however, in a footnote but help mentioning some writers,

Futabatei Shimei, for example, who is often said to be the first modern Japanese novelist).

Since Sōseki's work was in many ways at the heart of Karatani's work, which Jameson (and then Moretti) compares with the development of literature on a larger world historical scale, I find it interesting to look into how the first novel Sōseki wrote, *I Am a Cat* (*Wagahai wa neko de aru*, 1905), actually negotiated the relation between form and substance in a world literary context. Luckily, it is not that hard to theorize about, since Sōseki, who was also a theorist of literature, already did so himself in his *Theory of Literature* (*Bungakuron*, 1907). The publication of his theory followed *I Am a Cat*, but the actual notes for the work were written during the years Sōseki spend studying English literature in London from 1900-2.

This article, as indicated by its title, concentrates on analyzing Sōseki's first feuilleton novel as a form of intermediality, and in relation to the discussion of the novel in world literature. Sōseki's first novel is not only a satire of Japanese society at the time. It does, of course, make fun of the *noveau riche* (like the Kaneda-family, the "money-fields"), and of the new intellectuals graduating in high-browed theories, as well as of the artists, writers and painters in Japan. The characters are often self-parodies of Sōseki and the friends attending his famous Thursday meetings, *mokuyōkai*. Apart from the local setting, it is, however, also mocking the West, satirizing religion, and the idea of the universality of English literature. Karatani writes about Sōseki that "[h]is real concern was to point out that universality was not a priori, but historical" (1998, 12), and he shows how that is the case linguistically when Sōseki is resisting the totalization of a standard past-tense prose (a literary third person focalized *-ta* form) that developed alongside the modern Japanese novel and with translations of Western novels to Japanese.

Also explicitly and thematically, Sōseki contests Western universality. He often does so ironically and in dialogue with not only English literature but also with literature from the rest of Europe, the US and from China. As Andō Fumihito points out in his essay "Wagahai wa 'we' de aru", in a dedication which he wrote in English in a copy of his book, which belonged to a North-American reader called Mr. Young, Sōseki satirically wished that the novel would remain utterly foreign to Westerners:

> Herein, a cat speaks in the first person plural, we. Whether royal or editorial, it is beyond the ken of the author to see. Gargantua, Ouixote, and Tristram Shandy, each has had his day. It is high time this feline

King lay in peace upon a shelf in Mr Young's library. And may all his catspaw-philosophy as well as his quaint language remain hieroglyphic in the eyes of the occidentals. (Andō 1993: 22)

Jonathan Swift, whom Sōseki was also reading, defined satire as: "a sort of glass, wherein beholders do generally discover everybody's face but their own, which is the chief reason for that kind of reception it meets in the world, and that so very few are offended with it." (Swift 2008: 104) Sōseki's first novel, which he began to write in 1905, combines different modes and aesthetic styles in satirizing not only Japanese society but also both orientalist ideas about Japan and Japan's "auto-orientalism" (to borrow an expression Said used about the internalization of orientalism in the Middle-East).

Furthermore, Sōseki wrote and theorized about the evolution and the intensified global circulation of literature in the beginning of the last century. Thus, the purpose of this article is to investigate how exactly this novel satirically negotiates the genre, and its own production and creation by incorporating a multiplicity of both local and worldwide references, other media, and other artistic genres and forms. My argument is that it does so by focusing on the role of affects, and by commenting not only on the Japanese social experience but also on the idea of universal western forms; including homely realist aesthetics of the minute and everyday life, the sublime, local and worldly customs (eastern and western) and religious practices (Buddhist and Christian alike).

Sōseki's first critical essays accompanied the first Japanese translation of Lawrence Sterne's *Tristram Shandy*, introducing and recommending the western classic to Japanese readers. The novel, as a genre in the Japanese context, is itself a sort of translation. The Japanese word for novel is *shōsetsu*, originally a Chinese word, was first used during the Meiji-period (1868-1912) by Tsubouchi Shōyō (1859-1935) as the equivalent in Japanese to the English *novel* or the French *roman*.

Since the Meiji restoration of 1868, which ended two centuries of isolationist politics of the Tokugawa shogunate, Japan increasingly imported western cultural products and translated or adapted western literature, such as the novel. Even before the import of western printing techniques, the material conditions for mass-production and consumption of literature had already been established with the development of woodblock printing techniques from China, and *en gros* with the development of movable types imported from Korea, enabling the publication of books on a wide-range of subjects, from entertainment to education. As early as 1721, there were printing guilds in the towns that developed around the castles of the samurailords (*daimyō*). Apart from poetry such as *tanka* (short Japanese poems) and *haikai renga* (collaborative popular linked verse), prose fiction, such as *gesaku* (often parodical entertainment literature), or *gebun* (satirical prose written for the educated samurai-class), developed alongside oral storytelling such as *rakugo*, comical reading by one professional storyteller, the *kabuki* theatrical performances, and the *bunraku* puppet theatre.

With new literary magazines and newspapers in the Meiji period, the literature of the day could be even more rapidly circulated to a growing literate public. In short, with a growing bourgeoisie, publishing industries and commercial centers in towns like Edo (the old name of Tokyo before the restoration) had already been buzzing for decades when Sōseki began writing. Import of foreign literature and new printing techniques speeded up distribution. In the wake of the popularity of his first novel, Sōseki became one of the first professional writers in Japan, later signing a contract with *Asahi Newspaper*. The speed of the production and the circulation of the ongoing serialization of Sōseki's first novel decide not only its form but also its content, since, as we shall see, it allows for the inclusion of extradiegetic comments. Furthermore, it allows for simultaneous translations of World Literature into Japanese – such as one we will soon be acquainted with, Hoffmann's *Kater Murr* in 1906, to interfere (intradiegetically in narratological terms) in the universe of the novel.

I will analyze how the novel, which was published as a feuilleton/serial novel (in Japanese *rensai shōsetsu*), takes advantage of new printing techniques in developing its particular form. In a world literature perspective, and in the light of his literary theory, Sōseki's modern Japanese novels can be seen as both examples of intermediality and as transculturations, mixing cultures spatio-temporally, combining aesthetic genres, early western novels and essayistic genres, with Japanese oral and dramatic genres, his prose and poetry.

In *Theory of Literature* Sōseki described the form of the literary substance as revolving around affect. To avoid simply accepting the idea that the west provides the empty form (or technique) and Japan the content (or the soul) in Sōseki's work, I analyze Sōseki's work as intercultural experimentations with different modes, styles and genres. The term intermediality has mostly been used in media studies, yet if particular ways of writing are seen as medial configurations in their own right some intermedial aspects might already be foreshadowed in comparative literary studies, which have traditionally focused on the circulation, production and reception of the text. This analysis thus focuses on investigating the feuilleton format of Soseki's first novel *I Am a Cat* as a type of intermedial negotiation of form and genre.

In her "Intermediality, Intertextuality, and Remediation: A Literary Perspective on Intermediality", Irina Rajewsky distinguishes between a narrow and a broad definition of intermediality. Broadly speaking, the *inter* prefix refers to something taking place between different media. According to Rajewsky intermedial references, however, do not just designate the juxtaposition or simultaneous use of different media in an art work but point to how concrete media refer to, define themselves in relation to, and "remedialize" other media: "the definitive intermedial aspect has to do with the reference itself which a given media product (such as a text, film, etc.) makes to an individual product, system, or subsystem of a different medium, and to its medial specificities. Hence, the media product (and its overall signification) constitutes itself in relation to the media product or system to which it refers." (Rajewsky 2005: 59) In this sense Rajewsky seems to be, at least to some extent, in agreement with the idea that all media are mixed (see Mitchell) and that they compete (see Bolter/Grusin). Jens Schröter and W. J. T. Mitchell among others have argued that intermediality or mixed media is prior to single media as such, that all media in a sense has some sort of intermedial quality per se. Also concentrating on typological questions Rajewsky, however also insists that media studies therefore must consider the diachronic aspects of media in order to be able to explain concrete medial configurations and their specific intermedial qualities: "In fact, the criterion of historicity is relevant in various ways: with regard to the historicity of the particular intermedial configuration itself, with regard to the (technical) development of the media in question, with regard to the historically changing conceptions of art and media on the part of the media's recipients and users, and finally with regard to the functionalization of intermedial strategies" (Rajewsky: 2005: 51).

In what follows, I argue that Soseki's first feuilleton novel points to the historicity of its configuration both as an intermedial and intercultural phenomenon in Japan. The specificities of its reception and production are intricately linked to the intermedial references that it strategically uses to equally enhance and ironize about its own aesthetics, as well as to challenge the possibilities and limitations of it own media specificities. Sōseki's was never supposed to be a novel. The success of the first installment of *I Am a Cat* simply seemed to have called for a continuation. It was published in *Hototogisu* (*The Cuckoo*) one of the new literary magazines of the day. This literary magazine circulated the modern haiku to the public but also published other texts. Sōseki wrote the first installment of *I Am a Cat* as a piece of prose fiction on request from one of the editors of *Hototogisu,* Takahama Kyoshi (1874-1959), who then later requested a second chapter. More installments were to follow so the story continued (with a few interruptions) from January 1905 to August 1906. The result of this serialization was Sōseki's first feuilleton novel, which, consecutively, was published in three volumes (in 1905, 1906 and 1907, respectively). Some years later, in 1911, the novel was published in one book. Sōseki had previously published shorter prose texts in *Hototogisu*; for instance, letters humorously describing his time in London. These early prose texts ironize about his own sense of cultural displacement by satirically defamiliarizing situations where his literary alter ego is walking around in London, or when he is trying to bicycle around in the countryside. Though *I Am a Cat* was meant to be a similar short story, it, nonetheless, initiated Sōseki's career as a novelist. In only ten years, he succeeded in publishing, among other things, a dozen novels, the final *Meian* (*Light and Dark*) left unfinished in 1916. The first sentences of *I Am a Cat* introduce the recollections of a stray-cat, looking back at its first experiences of the world as a little kitten:

> I am a cat but as yet I have no name.
> I haven't the faintest idea where I was born. The first thing I do remember is that I was crying "meow, meow," somewhere in a gloomy damp place. (Natsume, 1961: 1; SZ 1)
> 「吾輩は猫である。名前はまだ無い。どこで生まれたかとんと見当がつかぬ。何で薄暗いじめじめした所でニャーニャー泣いていた事だけは記憶している。」(*SZ* 1, 3)

The scene describes the cat first impressions and feelings. In his theory Sōseki describes the form of the literary substance as *impressions/ideas accompanied by emotions* (Natsume 2009: 52). The cat recalls in detail what it felt like when it saw for the first time such a creature as a human being close up. Told through the eyes of a young cat, it is as if looking through a somewhat strangely world-deforming magnifying glass. Similar to Swift's Gulliver visiting strange foreign countries, faces become strange landscapes.

> It was there that I met a human being for the first time in my life. Though I found this all out at a later date, I learned that this human being was called a Student, one of the most ferocious of the human race ... This was probably the first time I had a good look at a so-called "human being." What impressed me as being most strange still remains deeply imbedded in my mind: the face, which should have been covered with hair was a slippery thing similar to what I now know to be a teakettle. I

have since come across many other cats but none of them are such freaks. Moreover, the center of the Student's face protruded to a great extent, and from the two holes located here, he would often emit smoke. I was extremely annoyed by being choked by this. That this was what they term tobacco, I came to know only recently. (Natsume 1961: 1)

The reception of the two novels Sōseki published after *I Am a Cat* reflects its popularity. In a certain sense, Sōseki's success could probably be compared to that of Dickens' in England half a century earlier, although stylistically both authors are not really comparable. Sōseki's novels were part of a modern and commercial publishing industry in Japan. Department stores were making merchandise even before the Meredith-inspired *Gubijinsō* (Field Puppy) was in the press: "Mitsukoshi department store offered Gubijinso-Yukata (kimono for the summer), Gyokuhodo launched Gubijinso-rings, and vendors of newspapers at stations sold *Asahi Shinbun* crying 'Sōseki's *Gubijinso*.'" (from Komiya Toyotaka's biography, *Natsume Sōseki.* Iwanami Shoten, 1938: 572-573. Translated by Tohoku University Library's Sōseki Library) Mitsukoshi was the first "modern-style" department store founded in 1904. The popularity of the cute *I Am a Cat*, and maybe especially the more straightforward, though more zany, *Botchan* ("little master") undoubtedly played a role here.

http://dodjer.com/comedy/5222-Kon_Ichikawa_Wagahai_wa_neko_de_aru_aka_I_Am_A_Cat_1975.html

Inspired by his friend Masaoka Shiki (1867-1902), who modernized the haiku-genre, Sōseki used an aesthetic style called *shaseibun*. This word already indicates an intermedial aesthetics. *Shasei* means to sketch, as in drawing something, and *bun* refers to writing or style. In Japanese the three Chinese characters of *shaseibun* 写生文 (copy/life/writing) as a compound means *sketching style*, a literary style or an aesthetics of the everyday and the concrete. After Shiki's early death, the style lived on not only in modern haiku-poetry but also in short stories and novels, in Sōseki's among others. In *I Am a Cat,* Sōseki's literary alter ego, Kushami-sensei, has a go at sketching, unsuccessfully according to the cat, but his writings receive immediate success. Already in the second chapter, the cat directs attention to its newly gained fame. In chapter five, a satirical metacommentary refers to the textual form of *shaseibun*, more appropriate for a short *haiku* than a long serialized novel: "If I wrote down everything that happened during a twenty-four hour period, it would take at least twenty four hours to read it. Even an eager espouser of *Shaseibun* like me must confess that it is a feat which a cat can by no means perform." (Natsume 1961, 150, *SZ* vol. 1, chapter 5; translation by Andō Fumihito)

[「二十四時間の出来事を洩れなく書いて、洩れなく読むには少なくも二十四時間かかるだろう、いくら**写生文**を鼓吹する吾輩でもこれは到底猫の企て及ぶべからざる芸当と自白せざるを得ない。」(SZ 1, 183)]

The Japanese reception of Sōseki's work usually contrasts his grotesque realism and his later psychological realism with the Japanese naturalist school (*shizenshugi*). In "Discourse on Fiction of the Self" (*Literature of the Lost Home*, 1995), Kobayashi Hideo (1902-1983), for example, criticized *shishōsetsuka*, I-novelists, who supposedly wrote in a straight-forward autobiographical manner, as opposed to writers like Sōseki and Ōgai. The *bundan* (literary circle), to which Sōseki and his friend Masaoka Shiki belonged, tended to use detached irony, humor, and even satire within the autobiographical material, as it occurs in *I Am a Cat*. The influence from his friend Masaoka Shiki's *shaseibun*-aesthetics is most obvious in Sōseki's novel *Kusamakura* (lit. grasspillow), where an artist retreats to the mountains, and which describes itself novel as a *haikuteki shōsetsu* ("haiku-like novel"). In his aesthetic theory (*shaseiron*), Shiki, described the new haiku-poetry as a kind of picturesque realism, a sketching of impressions of the immediate surroundings, of the concretely experienced. Shiki's insistence on this immediateness has to be understood in relation to the old, and according to Shiki, stiffened *haikai renga* tradition, where poetry composition in groups relied on knowing ideal phrases from the tradition, and thus how to fill in the right words in the right place. Sometimes Sōseki uses the term *haiku shōsetsu* (like in *Kusamakura*) to refer to this specific style, which, nonetheless, seems to build on somewhat similar aesthetic principles as *shaseibun*. Historically, the words have slightly different connotations, since one refers to Japanese literary traditions and the other *shaseibun* is associated with western inspired painting and the use of a western naturalistic perspective.

Sōseki knew how to take advantage of the affective mode of this aesthetics. I would argue that he combines it with his own psychology-inspired theory about the role that feelings play in literature. Concrete ideas, impression and sensations, he concludes, are used worldwide to engage more effectively readers's emotions. The concrete, more easily than the abstract, engages emotions in the reader (e.g. Natsume 2009: 66). To convey abstract ideas, writers therefore often need to recreate sensible properties. Sōseki was, of course, not the first to come up with this technique of anthropomorphism in using the point of view of a cat to reveal the follies of society. As he points out in *Theory of Literature*, personification has been frequently used in literature around the world.

In his first novel Sōseki combines concrete impressions coming from the *enstranging* perceptions of the kitten, with media satire. The world, contemplated through the eyes of the cat towards which people might be more immediately sympathetic, is more engaging than through the eyes of a high-browed professor of English literature, overworked with theory. Thus, the satirical mode of the texts, with the help of hyperboles, personifications, essayistic, and digressive techniques, critically reflects on topics such as Japanese society and art scene, and also western aesthetics, religion, and the supposed universalism of the form of western literature.

The only universal in literature, according to Sōseki's theory, is simply the use of feelings. The form of the literary substance changes with the collective focal point of a given age, the affective structures of society and also with the media and material conditions of production and reception. *I Am a Cat* is, thus, a splendid example of how a new print culture is followed by commodification. However, it also shows how the possibilities of the serialized format and feuilleton novel are used to create a multimodal satire able to incorporate and negotiate references to World Literature.

The first pages of *I Am a Cat* present concrete perceptions, sensations and basic emotions from the moment-to-moment experience of the cat. In a similar way, Sōseki's theoretical texts describe consciousness in terms of concrete sensations before moving on to more complex emotions, finally pinpointing that literature is continuously changing with the focal point of society, noticing how increasingly interconnected it is at a global level and, thus, he includes references to literature in German, French, Spanish, Danish, Norwegian, Russian and Chinese. Rather than imitating one previous Japanese or western form, *I Am a Cat*, mixes multiple genres and styles. A humorous satire of Japanese society, the novel is also a critical transcultural appropriation of oral traditions, drama, poetry and essayistic techniques, eclectically juxtaposing different modes and genres, high and low culture, old and new styles, popular and academic, eastern and western references. As Karen Thornber has shown (in *Empire of Texts in Motion* 2009), its reception, "afterlife", effectively also form and forms part of Chinese, Korean, Taiwanese transculturations (-spatializations and -textualization) of Japanese literature in what she proposes to call "intra-empire East Asian literary contact nebulae".

Following Sōseki's own theory, and looking at the affective dimensions of literature in relation to a conception of everyday aesthetics, new media-information-serialization and the rapid translation and consequent circulation of World Literature that effectively influences both content and form in Sōseki's novel, one can try to conceive of the many-headed monster that the little kitten becomes in terms of a number of everyday aesthetic categories: "The analysis of Sōseki's narrative-flow into small numbered sections has a similar effect on perception, combining the minute with the infinite; that such an arrangement owned something to journalism and serialization is scarcely and alternative casual explanation, since the form of the newspaper ultimately loops back into the general determinations of bourgeois culture in its own right." (Jameson 2007: 300-1)

Sianne Ngai (2012) has shown that aesthetic categories such as 'cute, interesting and zany' are useful for studying aesthetic in Europe and the US. Ngai initially limits her proposal to the cultural history of Europe and US, though in the analyses she also discusses the Japanese concept of *kawaii* in works by artists like Murakami and Nara, whom she sees as having most thoroughly thematized this particular aesthetic category of 'the cute' and its ambiguity (even in terms of sound there seems to be a thin line from *kowai*, frightening in Japanese, to *kawaii*, cute). Exploiting the cuteness of the cat, Sōseki's novel combines different styles, media and cultures, and his novel might be best described by a combination of all of Ngai's three categories: the interesting relates to the novel as theory-orientated, the cat is both cute and annoying (tiny, helpless and lazy), and the writing itself, like the people visiting – money-men, artists, scientists and philosophers alike – are all a bit zany, performing or elaborating on theories. Kōjin Karatani (2008) proposed to call Sōseki's style grotesque realism. Furthermore, the satirical mode in this novel, I argue, is itself the product of a multimodal, transcultural intermedialization and circulation.

Sōseki's novels reject the coherent plot that the famous professor from Waseda University, Tsubouchi Shōyō, had recommended modern Japanese writers in 1885. They seem to explicitly express a non-plot-aesthetics. For example, *I Am a Cat* (1905) is episodic and digressive, *The Miner* (*Kōfu*, 1908) concludes stating that it is not a novel and, most explicitly, *Kusamakura* (1912) inspired by his friend Masaoka Shiki, that Sōseki describes as *haiku-shōsetsu*. As Masao Miyoshi has described, in the Meiji-period "the *shōsetsu* is published in a serialized form. Unplanned at the beginning, the progression of the narrative is coordinate of outside time." (Miyoshi: 1991: 151) Here I am also arguing that the feuilleton form of *I Am a Cat* is used to reject pre-structured coherent plots.

The structure of the novel is circularly mirrored in the movements of the cat itself. When the cat is left in a bamboo-thicket, and miaowing turns out to be of no avail, "[...] commenced to circle the water by going around to the left" (Natsume, 1961: 2) In the final instalment, the cat, now on the brim of a rain barrel with water: "[...] went aimlessly around as if taking a walk. [...] I don't know myself whether I was sleeping or walking [...] But I wasn't afraid of anything! I simply made one more step and then heard a splash: suddenly I was floating on some water. It was terribly disagreeable so I began to struggle but I could only claw at the water." (Natsume, 1961: 430) In a way, the feuilleton creates its own framing, a kind of cyclic pattern repeated throughout the novel, which in the end invoking the merciful Buddha. "namu amida butsu", a prayer used in the Buddhist Jodo (Pure land) sects, and 南無阿弥陀仏: なむあみだぶつ "namuamidabutsu", often recited at funerals. (Natsume, 1961: 431) In the middle, however, the cat had also asked the reader for permission to give its own humble views on God, now the one in the Christian Bible, and after explaining how the very diversity of human faces may have led people to believe in a creative omnipotent creator, the cat has its own view on the case: "considered from a cat's point of view, this same variety might possibly be interpreted as proof of God's incompetence." (Natsume, 1961: 156)

The episodic and simultaneously digressive narration brings to mind western classics such as Manuel de Cervantes' *Don Quixote* and Lawrence Sterne's *Tristram Shandy*, a novel "with no hero, no plot, no beginning and no end, like a sea slug whose head can't be told from his tail" (Sōseki cit. Sakuko Matsui 1975: 46), a formulation he then repeats for his own novel, "no plot, no structure; it is a writing with no beginning and no end, like a sea slug whose head can't be told from his tail" (Matsui 1975: 299). Like in *Tristram Shandy,* the style is both erudite and humorous, a mix of the early modern traditions Japanese *gebun* og *gesaku,* "a comic clash between the world of learning and that of human affairs." (Matsui 1975: 50) From the *rakugo*-genre, which Sōseki enjoyed since childhood, the novel has inherited the dialogical play on dialects:

> The main Japanese influence upon [Sōseki's] writing were, oddly enough in a man of gentle birth, those *rakugo,* comic recitations by professional storytellers, to which his childhood circle had been addicted. The *rakugo*-techniques are especially noticeable in what is known as his masterly use of dialogue. It is also worth stressing that, though his Chinese studies resulted in a style as concise as the literary language traditionally employed in the composition of *tanka* and *haiku,* much of the vitality of his prose writing derives from his skilled exploitation of colloquial Japanese speech. (Natsume 1984, "Introduction": 13)

In *rakugo* the narrator develops a one-man-show that tells the story by means of different voices, gestures, grammar and tone. In Japanese, a shift in verbs, or verbal inflexions can indicate the gender and class of the person speaking, relative both to whom they are speaking to and to the situation/context. In *I Am a Cat,* a character who often visits Kushami tries to imitate different voices, a boatman, a geisha, recounting the staging of one of the Japanese dramatist Monzaemon Chikamatsu's (1653-1725) most famous *bunraku*-play *The Love Suicide at Amijima* (1720), also performed in *kabuki*-theater, where all characters are today performed by men. The cat-narrator is not impressed by his imitation of voices: "Although Tofu tried to imitate the manner of speech of the various characters when he mentioned them, he didn't seem to know much about them himself." (Natsume 1961: 43)

Another thing that oral narrating and the feuilleton novel might have in common is the use of repetitions. In oral performance, the repetition of sounds and rhythm help enhance short-term memory; in the feuilleton, repetition of the characterization of people is useful, as when in *I Am a Cat* the reader is reminded of previous situations by phrases like "typical Meitei", used to create a coherent story universe (*diégèse*) even if the plot is not.

Between the publication of the first chapter and the second, the cat, *neko,* had become quite famous in Japan, in a similar way as it happened when Miguel de Cervantes comments on the fame of Don Quixote and Sancho Panza, in the wake of the reception of the first book (and on the impostor Alonso Fernandez de Avellaneda who meanwhile had published a false sequel). As *Don Quixote* is influenced by the reception of the first book, the setting and characters of *I Am a Cat* are already familiar by the time the sequel appears. The second book is a more domestic farce, mostly played out in the heart of Kushami's house, the 奥座敷 *okuzashiki* or living room. The second chapter begins: "During New Year's holidays, I became somewhat famous and I liked being able to feel a little proud of myself." (Natsume 1961: 16) [「吾輩は新年来多少有名になったので、猫ながら一寸鼻が高く感ぜらるゝのは有難い。」] (*SZ* vol.1, 22) The fame of the cat in 'realtime' (extradiegetic remarks) is incorporated into the univers of the novel (intradiegetically), indicating that a period of time has passed since the first chapter.

Modern print technologies, and the stepped up distribution in new literary magazines, enables *I Am a Cat* to eloquently comment on its own reception already in the second chapter. Serialization allows for self-ironical comments where the cat, like *Don Quixote,* exhibits its own pretentiousness. Exploiting, formally and satirically, the temporality of its own serialization, "real-time" actually determines the progression and thereby the content of the story. Thus, the novel only comments on the temporality of the written medium as such. While in *I Am a Cat*, the reader is often made aware of the narrator's role, Sōseki's last novel, *Light and Darkness* (*Meian* 1916) tends to minimize the presence of the narrator, experimenting with third-person narration and focalization. Though occasional authorial remarks do occur, the authorial voice in *I Am a Cat* is quite unobtrusive, having become ironically incorporated in the shape of Kushami, who has many similarities to Sōseki himself, the proud owner of a cat. The authorial position is thus itself satirized.

A romantic cat figure from world literary history is, as promised, still to appear unexpectedly in Sōseki's novel, and it is one to which Sōseki pays a special tribute, when he, like Don Quixote, is accused of being an impostor. Kater Murr is the philosopher's cat in E.T.A Hoffmann's *Lebens-Ansichten des Katers Murr* (1822) (*The Life and Opinions of the Tomcat Murr*). Published for the first time in Japanese translation in May 1906, this translation coincided with the running serialization of Sōseki's novel, supposedly causing a great deal of comments and even allegations of plagiarism (see Keene 1984: 312). Our Japanese cat narrator comments on the resemblance between the two: "The other day I happened to meet one of my own kind. His name was Kater Murr. I had never met him before, but he talked so impressively that I was somewhat amazed." (Natsume, 1961: 427) Thereby Sōseki had his cat explain that any likenesses of his cat and this distant cousin Kater Murr were strictly coincidental, since the cat denies any previous acquaintance with the German cousin Kater

Murr. The similarities might actually stem from somewhere else, that is, from the translation and circulation of World Literature that makes the two connected in ways that probably Sōseki himself had already realized, seeing Kater Murr as a distant cousin.

The works of Sterne and Swift also influenced Hoffmann in creating his Kater Murr (see Natsume, 1986), so certain family-likeness is not that surprising. Furthermore, both novels, the German and Japanese, are inspired by parodies of the confessional novel and the classical *Bildungsroman* (see Granzow 1960: 66, 157). So with the serialized tragic-comic cat coming to consciousness on the first pages, Sōseki's first feuilleton novel incorporates a number of other aesthetic genres, literary styles, and authors (Hoffmann, Shiki, Swift). Losing consciousness on the last page, the cat metaphorically disappears into the sea of World Literature when he drowns in a barrel in Kushami's backyard.

To sum up, serialization in *I Am a Cat* brings the novel close to the media specificity and material conditions for its production. Thus, production, reception and circulation determine the form of the novel. The literary form and content are constituted simultaneously within a diachronically highly intermedial field by using, not only intertextual references, but also what Irina Rajewsky terms "intermedial references," incorporating genres and media such as theatre and shorter poetic forms like the haiku. Mnemonics or gestures from oral and dramatic traditions, like *rakugo* or *kabuki*, also help structure the text. Thus the feuilleton form, exemplified in *I Am a Cat*, allows intermedial negotiations of literary form and aesthetics, using its particular spatio-temporal modality (see Elleström 2010) to equally enhance and satirize its own essayistic style, as well as its aesthetic aspirations of being able to *sketch* realistically like a haiku, the concrete everyday impressions from moment to moment.

With the incorporation of other art forms and genres in its own aesthetic expression, and with the possibility of reception interaction, the feuilleton novel constitutes a particular type of intermediality. Similar spatiotemporal medial modality might be found in more recent serialized types of art and entertainment industry, such as blogs or digital-games satirizing plots, where a certain amount of audience participation is also possible.

References

Andō, Fumihito: "Wagahai wa 'we' de aru – 'neko' ni okeru katarite to dokusha" Waseda daigaku bungakukenkyū, 29, 1993.

Cervantes, Miguel de: *El Ingenioso Hidalgo Don Quixote De La Mancha*. Nabu Press 2010
Eckermann, Johann Peter: *Gespräche mit Goethe in den letzten Jahren seines Lebens*. Insel Verlag, Frankfurt. 9. Auflage 2006
Elleström, Lars: *Media Borders*. Palgrave Macmillan 2010.
Granzow, Hermann: *Künstler und Geschellshaft im Roman der Goethe-Zeit*. Philosophische Fakultät der Rheinischen Friedric-Wilhelms Universität, 1960
Hoffmanns, E.T.A: Die *Lebensansicht des Katers Murr*. Patmos Verlag 2006.
Karatani, Kōjin: *Origins of Modern Japanese Literature*. Duke University Press, 1998.
Kōjin, Karatani (2008) 'Rethinking Sōseki's theory', Japan Forum,20:1, 9 - 15
Komiya Toyotaka: *Natsume Sōseki*. Iwanami Shoten, 1938
Jameson, Frederic: *The Modernist Papers*. Verso, 2007.
Matsui, Sakuko: *Natsume Sōseki as a Critic of English Literature*. The Center for East Asian Cultural Studies. Tokyo Press, 1975.
Miyoshi, Masao; H.D. Harootunian (ed.): *Postmodernism and Japan*. Duke University Press, 2003 (1989).
Moretti, Franco: "Conjectures on World Literature" *NLR* 1, (2000): 54-68
Natsume, Sōseki: *I am a cat*. A novel by Natsume Sōseki, transl. K. Shibata, M. Kai, Kenkyusha, 1970.
Natsume, Sōseki: *Je suis un chat*. Gallimard, 1986
Natsume, Sōseki: *I Am a Cat*, transl. Aiko Itō & Graeme Wilson. Tuttle, 2002 (1972).
Natsume, Sōseki: *Kusamakura*; translated with an introduction and notes by Meredith McKinney. Penguin Books, 2008.
Natsume, Sōseki: *Theory of Literature*, transl. Bourdaghs et al. Columbia University Press, 2009.
Ngai, Sianne: *Our Aesthetic Categories: zany, cute, interesting*. Harvard University Press, 2012.
Rajewsky, Irina O.: "Intermediality, Intertextuality, and Remediation: A Literary Perspective on Intermediality" in *Intermédialités. Histoire et théorie des arts, des lettres et des techniques* 6 (2005): 43-64.
Swift, Jonathan: *A Tale of a Tub. And Other Works*. Oxford World's Classics, 2008.

Thornber, Karen: *Empire of Texts in Motion: Chinese, Korean, and Taiwanese transculturations of Japanese literature*. Harvard 2009

Tsubouchi, Shōyō: *The Essence of the Novel*. University of Queensland 1981

ABOUT THE AUTHOR

Annette Thorsen Vilslev holds a Ph.D. in Comparative Literature from the University of Copenhagen. Following her research stay at Waseda University in Tokyo, she has worked on the novels and the literary theory of Natsume Soseki and his place in World literature. She has published several reviews and articles on the topic and is currently working on a monography on Soseki.

CHAPTER 17

Literature 2.0 - Hybrid Cultural Objects in Intermedial Practice: The Case of Romania

Mihaela Ursa

Although some similarities have been established between intermediality, intertextuality, intersubjectivity, and interdisciplinarity, as far as world literature is concerned, the question of intermediality is relevant on two different levels that need further conceptual elaboration: **1.** the level of an intermedial redefinition of the ways in which we approach literature, that is, an intermedial, theoretical and methodological treatment of traditional objects of study (literature in its classic sense) or of traditional disciplines (aesthetics, history of literature, theory of literature). Two subdivisions require special attention at this level: **1.1.** the study of world literature as an intermedial approach, able to replace the traditional nation-based literary systems, and **1.2.** the study of world literature as a transmediality-oriented practice, capable to open the traditional understanding of literature as an aesthetic object (i.e. literarity at its best) towards other media where transmedial features manifest themselves (e.g. narrative, fiction, description, etc.). Finally, level 2 presupposes creating an entirely new intermedial system and discourse for hybrid cultural objects that are impossible to fit within traditional frames of disciplinary discourse (see Schröter's concept of *synthetic intermediality*, as the fusion of several media into an *intermedium* that is more than the sum of their parts, i.e. "graphic poetry").

Since I am still developing the detailed study of each of these levels and sublevels from a theoretical point of view, I resume here to listing them as a preamble of my subsequent reading of intermediality. For the present paper I intend to discuss some examples from present-day Romania (relevant for East-Central Europe) for each of the three situations mentioned above, insisting on my proposition of understanding the hybrid forms of textual activity within a frame that I term "literature 2.0".

There is inexplicable resistance among humanities scholars to the idea that cyber-technologies can be used as cultural formative forces, on one hand, and, on the other, to the idea that the new globalized and digitized world can methodologically transform their disciplines for the better. As a result, some of them would rather fight to the death inside the besieged citadel of a traditional concept of humanities, than try to explore the technological dystopia they believe to be the result of the information culture, in order to find possible tools to revive a world of their own. While it is hardly a secret that humanities do not enjoy the most privileged status in our posthuman era (see concepts like "dehumanities" and "transhumanities", in Epstein, Emerson), as they are subjected to marginality within institutional frames of education (Tötösy de Zepetnek and Vasvári, "The Comparative" 3-5) and suffer accusations of uselessness on social ground (Ikpe, Bacon, Kernan), it is quite puzzling that some humanist scholars seem to enjoy the Romantic aura of nonconformity and isolation derived from this rather unfortunate situation. In a metaphorical way, this is the situation of too many scholars of literature studies in East-Central Europe (dealing as we speak with national histories of literatures, historiography or even comparative literature). Of course traditional scholarship made the rule in East-Central Europe even after 1990, since the same professors were – for the most part – kept in their chairs through the fall of the communist systems (Tötösy de Zepetnek and Vasvári, "The Comparative" 19, Terian, "Constructing" 78), but there are some deliberate refusals of interdisciplinary and intermedial approaches, for fear of losing the power and presumed autonomy of a discipline (Marino). Even intermediality theorists of the Western world sense that integrating literary studies as cultural studies or as media studies involves sacrificing the "need for sound disciplinarity" and scientific identity (Wolf, Schmidt, "Literary Studies" 13). However, comparatists working on world literature everywhere tend to involve at least a few (whether implicit or explicit) intermedial procedures in their study, regardless if they adhere to the polysystem theory (theorized by Even-Zohar), to the global-system theory (developed from Wallerstein), to the idea that texts should be analyzed in radial cuts along epistemes (Moretti), or to none of the above. Analyses of comparatist approaches as *tertium comparationis* enterprises (Kadir 3-9) prove that there is motion and circulation between several fields (history of ideas, ideology, mythology, sociology, literary history, text analysis, narratology, etc.) if not a proper and conscious use of intermedial devices, namely shifts between semiotic fields in case of literary adaptations to film or music, transmedial views on features such as fictionality, narrativity, description, etc. (see Wolf 22-23, for a selective list of "transmedial features" or Schröter's understanding of "formal or transmedial intermediality"). While that would encourage us to claim an aprioric intermedial nature (Schröter's primeval or "ontological intermediality") to the study of world literature, a further set of problems arises with regard to intermediality in the case of hybrid cultural objects.

This reference to hybridation should not be read in the sense Sturm-Trigonakis gives "hybrid texts" in her seminal *Comparative Cultural Studies and the New Weltliteratur*, where she refers to texts that exhibit characteristics of linguistic and cultural hybridity and/or transculturality, belonging to a "new world literature". I term "hybrid cultural objects" different forms of collaborative writing, graphic novels, blogs, i-phone novels, and an entire set of digital experiments whose intermedial character is so striking, that they are not allowed inside traditional systems (frequently, though arguably, presumed to be monomedial in nature). I have given such experiments the portmanteau title of "literature 2.0" (a work-in-progress concept, see Ursa), in order to give recognition to their intermedial and interactive character.

Due to political and social conditions imposed by communist regimes before 1989, "high culture" and especially "high literature" were the main tools for surviving, subversive forms of individual freedom. In Romania, the concept of "surviving through culture" or "resistance through culture" (Cornis-Pope "From resistance") is still revered. However, much has happened in the last two decades and the idea of protecting the status of high culture and of keeping literary studies as "pure" as possible, for the same reasons as before 1989, is impossible to support, to say the least.

In my teaching practice of comparative literature since 1998, I have heard students (entirely dedicated to their work and hoping for a cultural and social role for their subject of study) expressing doubts on the extent of the social impact of their studies, both for their own future and for the change they might have been able to make in a given field. Just recently, a student approached me asking for possible explanations of the fact that she felt faculty years and the study of comparative literature and of other literary fields were "building a bubble" around her, both protecting and debilitating her from/ to the "real world". Although anecdotic, I find this situation to be the very reason why an intermedial approach is crucial to the study of world literature, even if it means sacrificing the literary field to a larger frame of media studies (Schmidt) or of comparative cultural studies (Tötösy de Zepetnek, "From Comparative"). It could aim to shift attention from different objects (literary works, authors, tradition or contemporaneity) or different media (words, visual or other type of images) to the very connection of those objects or media to some idea of cultural change. I choose the case of East-Central Europe, insisting on the Romanian situation, to illustrate the extent of this scholarly emergency, since the problems arising from the addiction of East-

Central Europe to the idea of purity and highness of the aesthetic object as a means of political and social survival make the issue of intermediality more complicated than it already is.

At the beginning of the 20th century, Romanian studies could relate to previous comparative attempts made by B. P. Hasdeu and Lazăr Șăineanu in studies on folklore, in Titu Maiorescu's studies of aesthetics or in C. Dobrogeanu-Gherea's sociological analyses, but mostly in the programmatic effort of Hugo Meltzl de Lomnitz to derive comparative literature from Goethe's concept of *Weltliteratur*. While Hasdeu, Maiorescu or Gherea are preoccupied, first of all, to establish Romanian specifics inside the cultural and the literary realm, in order to establish a national literature, Hugo Meltzl de Lomnitz moves towards world literature when he founds, in 1877, „Acta Comparationis Litterarum Universarum", conventionally considered to be the first journal of comparative literature (Voia, Bassnett). The journal is neither the result, nor the example of a "national" tradition (Romanian, Hungarian etc.), since its project is plurilinguistic to begin with, not to mention transnational (Voia 186, Bassnet). "Acta comparationis" initially has a threefold target: a reevaluation of literary history, unjustly seen as a "servant" to philology and history, a reevaluation of translation as an art and, finally, a constant and careful support of multilinguism.

A system of national literatures cannot avoid hierarchical operations. As a consequence, comparative literature within the national literatures frame of reference is based on the idea of influence, that is, of a center of cultural power irradiating and formatting "smaller" or "minor" cultures. The project of world literature as devised by Lomnitz (Emerson, Marno, Lopez) does not accept cultural hierarchies of large/ small cultures, central/ peripheral literatures etc., maintaining that all literatures have equal chances to be represented in world literature. However, it is quite ironic for Romanian or Hungarian comparative studies (and mostly for the school of Cluj) that "Acta comparationis" had no real impact upon the development of comparative literature. The French model of comparative reasoning ruled the cultural climate of East-Europe through the 20th century (when the communist power din not reject comparatism altogether during the fifties and the sixties), empowering the very imperialist perspective that Lomnitz' multilinguism had tried to break. The possibility of reopening an East-Central European regional school of comparative studies seems to enjoy a rather bleak perspective (Bojtár).

An interesting conjunction happens in Romanian culture with regard to the national question, when "the national argument" is used as a claim to universality. One should not disregard this obsession for universality. When coming from a marginal culture, one cannot be blamed for revering foreign models that seem to have universal value (Cornis-Pope, Transnational), and Goethe is perfectly aware of this fact when he considers "the need for an intercourse with great predecessors" to be "a sure sign of a higher talent". However desirable, the same models can have a "crushing weight" (Damrosch 2003, 9), so there is no wonder that theories of value related to the national factor appear to counterbalance this weight. Even in Goethe's sense of *Weltliteratur* and of a "supernational literature", a certain dream of an all-encompassing universality is visible. In the Romanian literary studies of the sixties surges a theory that serves nationalist ideology, saying that a certain creator is "so Romanian, that he becomes universal". Especially Mihai Eminescu, still considered iconic for all kind of national ideologies, is named "the national and universal poet", his work being taught as such in secondary school and high-school curricula of today.

A seminal proposition in favor of world literature in Romania comes around 1948, when Tudor Vianu–disciple of the aesthetics professor Karl Gross of Tübingen–introduces a course of comparative literature at the Faculty of Letters and Philosophy in Bucharest, later to become a first volume of comparative studies (1960, reprinted, revised and completed in 1963). When arguing that world literature should be studied as an academic subject, Vianu is in fact promoting the very method of comparative literature. He understands world literature within the so-called "theory of peaks". Paying tribute to the super evaluation of the aesthetic and the literarity, Vianu's concept of world literature will direct comparative study towards a study of the Great Books and the literary canon, while at the same time keeping the task of explaining the life and history of human societies as a result of operations of generalization and universalization starting from this study of the literary canon.

Less explored in Romanian comparative studies is the concept of "world literature" as a "mode of circulation and of reading" (5), as devised by Damrosch. With its dependence on translation studies (quite disregarded in Romanian studies, with a few notable exceptions – Paul Cornea, Gelu Ionescu, Sorin Mărculescu, etc.), this concept of world literature projects a phenomenology of literature, rather than an ontology of literature, since works of art manifest themselves differently in their generative space and outside it. This last concept of world literature goes against the "present-ism" that "erases the past, as a serious factor, leaving at best a few nostalgic postmodern references, the historical equivalent of the local color" (Damrosch 17). To this, one can add the obvious refusal of localism that presupposes that untranslatable content is completely opaque to the foreign public. This understanding of world literature dismantles the nation-based literary system, or rather opens it to a dynamic view of the alterations of the work of literature in a heterogeneous reception.

A meaningful example in this sense are the books of Dan Lungu, a sociologist by formation and one of the best sold Romanian contemporary fiction writers. His best seller is *I am a communist biddy* (*Sunt o babă communistă*, 2007, also adapted to film in 2013), immediately translated to French, German, Italian, and appreciated abroad. It tells the story of an old nostalgic of the communist regime, who is expecting her long departed daughter, now living abroad, to come home for the holidays and the approaching elections. The story is told with a very keen eye to the details of communist life and to the cultural and ideological gap between Romanian generations, but also with humor and irony. Relevantly, the book enjoyed more public appreciation outside Romanian borders, partly because it gave expression to a repressed form of "Ostalgia" (Berger, Blum) to the considerable amount of literate Romanians living abroad, but also because it was able to translate, in understandable terms, the Ostalgia to the Western world. Meanwhile, many Romanian critics found it "guilty" of a shallow representation of Romanian communism. Studied from a national literature point of view, books like Lungu's novel are difficult to fit the frame, while an intermedial view of world literature makes it possible to stress the relation between reception expectancies and a given work circulating between receiving systems.

The novels of Marin Mălaicu-Hondrari, *The book of all intentions* (*Cartea tuturor intentiilor*, 2006), *Closeness (Apropierea, 2010)* and *The sniper* (*Lunetistul*, 2013) are good examples in support of the switch from a nation-based system of evaluation to an intermedial world literature one. They stem from the author's real life experience as a poor Romanian worker and a starving artist in recent Spain. Bearing no specificity to the "national" (even the concept of home is understood in intrinsic, intimate terms, rather than social ones), his novels are considered to resemble Roberto Bolaño's attempts to reconcile a popular culture referent (detective story, for instance), with a very high conception of fictional construct. Although new to the literary scene, Mălaicu-Hondrari gained a significant amount of Romanian and non-Romanian readers/ fans precisely because he seems to write from a transnational conscience point of view. Some critics say that he writes the same novel over and over again, only changing and constantly moving the authorial perspective.

To formulate a partial conclusion so far, the first challenge of intermedial practice within world literature is to re-write traditional disciplines and objects of study in an intermedial fashion, that is, to shed light on their ability to overflow their domain of predilection and to flood new fields, giving birth to new practices and methods. It is my contention that disciplinary discourses (such as the discourses involved in the study of national literatures) can be given conventional medial status. I find the concept of "remediation" particularly useful here, even if it was designed (Bolter and Grusin) to refer to media, and not to disciplinary approaches. Cultural studies (including the literary domain) are a "hybrid field of scholarship" (Tötösy de Zepetnek and Vasvári, "The Comparative") emerging from critical humanities and social sciences theories. As such, due to remediation, traditional disciplines move towards different places within a system of disciplines as soon as the need for new disciplines (or "indisciplines") emerges, much in the way Friedrich Kittler (cited in Schröter 38) believes new media force the media system to a new distribution. This way, "old" media rather coexist with the "new" ones, than are replaced by them. Following this train of thought, we can relate to "old disciplines" becoming defining "traces" (in the Derridean sense of the term) in the disciplinary language of "new disciplines". Cases of intertextuality or interdisciplinarity are, in this sense, former manifestations of intermedial junctures, but they have not attempted to dismantle the nation-based literary field as world literature does in its dynamic view of a generator of circulation between cultures. Intermediality acts as a reorganizer inside the system of disciplines devoted to literary studies and one of its main actions of remediation is the advance of comparative reading from a position related to national literatures studies towards a position related to world literature studies.

However, not all challenges of intermediality in the approach of world literature come from the national problem. Some arise from a very tight understanding of literature within the frames of the aesthetic convention. The case of Romania is even more interesting at this second level. Maybe the first difficulty in implementing intermedial study in Romania, besides poor dissemination of a dynamic understanding of world literature (the polysystem theory of Even-Zohar, and the consequences of Damrosch's redefinition are still poorly explored) is the traditional lack of approval, within academic and scholarly media, of both theory and method.

Inside the traditional corpus of literary studies (theory, history and criticism), Romanian literary history was and still is (with the exception of a few studies published in the 2000-s) written by authors of literary chronicles and reviews, that is, by a very particular type of literary critics. The literary chronicle enjoyed in Romania a prestige with no equal among the other East-European countries, since it was the first medium of Western cultural contact during communist years and a place where ideological censorship could be kept to a bare minimum, not to mention subverted. Rather than being condemned for its lack of scientific character, impressionistic criticism based on taste alone was used instead or as a critical method of reading and interpretation, outside theory. One can justify the situation up to one point: when theory meant ideology, Romanian intellectuals were seeking a sort of relief from communist ideological pressure by turning to non-ideological areas. Due to the subsequent conclusion that only aesthetic fiction is "real literature", non-fiction and non-fiction studies are still seeking field legitimacy inside Romanian literary studies, unlike in Hungary, Slovakia or the Czeck Republic. Since the most influential theoretical system within Romanian literary studies is still Vianu's theory of the mutation of aesthetic values, literary critics and scholars assuming his stand disregard non-fiction literature as a kind of literature that cannot fulfill the aesthetic requirements. Although massively published in Romania after 1990 in the form of diaries of previously censored authors, detention memories of communist prisons or testimonies of various kinds, non-fiction still lacks both a theoretical frame and a proper recognition with Romanian literary hierarchies and canon. Authors of non-fiction are often not considered to be "real writers" and writers who are not aesthetes (such as Norman Manea or Paul Goma, who author novels based on their own experiencing of the Gulag or the communist repression) are also contested, in spite of their Western world-acquired fame and recognition. The massive literary production born out of trauma, exile, prison, terrorism, although not written by aesthetes, acquires a growing importance both in understanding the world and in the preferences of readers. Recently, a dispute about the alleged lack of aesthetic value of Norman Manea's novels divided the Romanian literary world (see the issues of "Observator cultural" journal of February 2013). The extremely heated arguments polarized the polemicists: on one hand, advocates of the "aesthetic beauty" as unique value of literature, and on the other defenders of the idea of an "ethical aesthetic" as value of representation of human and humanity in literature.

Integrating literature studies within media and cultural studies would give recognition to one of the things that readers have always known: that literature formats behaviors and sets markers of understanding and interpretation in the inform space of reality. Seeing the idea of literature as a "social system" and literary activities as "acting roles" (Schmidt, "Why literature" 230) turns the study of literature into a rich field for media studies and into an empirical enterprise in search of new methodology. The study of literature as an alternative praxis, with aesthetic and pragmatic value, would help integrate the aesthetic view within a more comprehensive frame. The main objection to sacrificing the specific aesthetics of literature can be met within media studies, where specific forms and materialities of different media receive special semiotic attention. An intermedial approach to both fiction and non-fiction literature could find ways of inscribing both types of literature within the literary system, since Western theoretical solutions for non-fiction literature have not been adopted in Romanian studies. This way, intermediality can create coordination between terms from the aesthetic frame of value-judgment with terms from the ethical frame of value-judgment, in a way that would give non-fiction and fiction literature equal chances.

The main intermedial challenge addressed to world literature studies today is, however, one that seems ontological in nature. Just as one needs to speak of a new type of digital being, replacing more and more the good old human being, world literature scholars need to define and assess works and phenomena that no longer belong to literature *per se*, whether fiction or non-fiction. The issue in question in the discussion of the hybrid nature of new cultural objects is the digital phenomenon, in itself connected to the transformations of the global world.

In a traditional sense, literature is an analogic system, based on sequencing and linearity. Reading, just like writing, has to follow lines of words, rows of letters, which means it has to gradually complete the entire trajectory of a system of signs that become, in the process, a virtual world. Cyber-literature is, in exchange, a digital system: image-reading is a simultaneous phenomenon and both authoriality and reception become interactive. The user, ex-reader, takes active part in the creation and the completion of the world she or he "reads", and authorial control becomes relative to the point of its total absence from a product that was initiated by a random writer. As a rule, almost any kind of content can be treated either analogically, or digitally, but that treatment in itself does not make it better or worse, only better or worse suited to specific expectations and to specific evaluation criteria.

Much of the journals in Romania are accessible on electronic support, even if some of them have rudimentary sites, hardly up-to-date, and with little interactive options. An exception is *www.liternet.ro,* exclusively accessible online and allowing interaction from contributing to commenting and editing. Examples of proper digital literature are a few collaborative blogs such as *http://avestory.wordpress.com,* where content is created by multiple users: a first author has launched the first episode of the story and a few collaborative outlines. Every written new episode is created by a new reader, launching a new narrative path or action logic, to be reconfigured by the new content addition which, in its turn, would respect or antagonize the previously given course(s) of events.

The opening of new cultural portals, the massive movement of literary and cultural journals from paper to screen, the booming fashion of self-expository web pages and blogs (of writers or readers), the appearance of new literary praxes make it culturally urgent to investigate this intermedial domain where literature and digital technology mutually condition each other. New genres, such as *cyberpunk fiction* (Heim, Olsen), languages–*codework poetry* (Hayles) or traits–*ergodic literature* (Aarseth) seem to be born to make the "literary" adjective impossible, insufficient or improper to use. For East-Europe, as for most parts of the world living through the digital assault, one of the main issues of researching such cultural mutations is the extreme polarizing of reactions from reception media (readers, literary or cultural critics, internet users and fans, philosophers of cultural, monomedial specialists) facing the contact between the literary and the digital.

Literature and literariness are forced to rethink and rewrite their own definitions, theories, concepts, as well as the traditional inventory of praxes. None of these happen in harmonious consent, as one can only expect. On the contrary, they seem to be forced to defeat some kind of traditional medial resistance, by surpassing some kind of analogic-type system inertia. The magnitude of the digital turn is perceived somewhere between apocalypses of print culture (Birkerts) and discussions of new cognitive conditions and neuro-positions of the posthuman (Hayles). It was pointed out (Ryan) that the possibilities of literary fiction reading (world-projection, alternative world immersion, communication and identification or empathy between reader and literary characters) are similar to those offered by electronically created virtualities (Virtual Reality - VR, 3D or multipleD visual technologies, users interaction), but there is still work to be done on this level, especially from a comparative cultural studies point of view.

There are literary experiments in today Romania that were facilitated by their web existence and that can open the reading public to the possibilities of an intermedial view on this literature 2.0. Radu Vancu, one of the most prominent Romanian poets of the present day, has started one of his poetry volumes (*Sebastian dreaming, Sebastian în vis,* 2011) as a blog (*http://sebastianinvis.unspe.com*) where he would publish poems inspired by the birth of his son. When the amount of poems (that had gained appreciation, criticism and debate on the comments of the blog) became a book, critics have noted the rebirth of the same text through a medial turn from screen to paper, from simultaneity to progressive reading. While it gained literary coherence, the volume lost the interactive feedback of the blog readers, who altered and continued some of the poems in their own comments. The same author was involved in another web experiment testing the boundaries of intimacy-writing. Vancu started an internautic epistolary with poet Claudiu Komartin, of the same generation, publishing their letter-exchange in real time, on a cultural blog open to the public. Reactions were extremely polar: those coming from a culture of reading delighted in the possibility of seeing the old art of letter-writing revived in such a literary and erudite manner, but those coming from the popular or even punk culture (poets included) did not hesitate to criticize the same experiment for its alleged bookish artificiality. The main issue here was the clash of two monomedial visions: young artists, born in the digital culture, sanctioned as an unjust usurpation the attempts to turn web literature into literature proper, feeling the need to protect some kind of medial propriety. Although *in nomine* the web literature is welcoming for all, some forms of expression (borderline and popular) are understood as having more representative rights than others (bookish and aesthetic).

Another Romanian example of literary consecration by means of the cyberspace is the blog of Iv cel naiv (Yves-the-naïve, *http://ivcelnaiv.ro*), who publishes enjoyable short versified poems of extreme expressive concentration. Due to the popularity of his blog among the literature cyberfans, Iv cel Naiv was also published on paper and, as a result, released to the mainstream culture. Even so, he still has a secret identity and his books became somehow autonomous from their author or, to be exact, became the sole creators of their author. Finally, the most influential phenomenon in the world of Romanian literary blogs was a blog of literary commentaries, entitled "A woman-reader's bookish terrorism", still available at *http://www.terorista.ro*, although no longer active. Without being a scholar or a literary critic, the author would post her reading notes under the nickname LuciaT, daily or every other day for almost three years without interruption (for the most part, she read a book every other day). Her secret identity stirred massive rumor in the world of bloggers, especially since her blog had an average of 10.000 hits a month, but also in the world of literary and art scholars and critics. As the author declares on her last post of April 7, 2009, under pressure of being accused of serving the interests of certain publishing houses and of hidden promotion of some authors before others, but also under pressure of threats and even violent messages urging her to reveal her identity, she ceased the activity on her blog (although reemerging after a while, with much less success, as a literary commentator for an online magazine). Although it would be difficult to assess the exact influence she had upon the Romanian literary scene, I feel confident to say that her blog altered at least the language used by literary critics (most of them were reading the blog, openly or secretly), contributing to the simplification of specialized jargon and the opening of the literary commentary to a larger audience.

A Romanian pioneer of the intermedial approaches to making literature, while keeping its print form, is Simona Popescu, a writer and professor of literature. With a team of collaborators, she initiated an experiment of medial openness entitled *Rubik*, after the famous cube named after its creator, an object of passion among Romanian adolescents during communist years. Entitled "collective novel" and written by 29 authors, *Rubik* was meant to create an effect of writing, to test whether people with average writing abilities could come together and develop a writing community ethos outside the literary convention. Taking action and changing places were essential constituents of this collaborative experiment. Although published in very good conditions of distribution and visibility, *Rubik* had moderate effect in the cultural world. Critics generally saluted its exotic, unique form of literary art, and the anticipation of a future form of literature, but stayed within "festive" rather than "critical" frames of appreciation. The book made very few (but very passionate) fans within the reading public, but its impact was somehow restricted and contextual, due to its hybrid nature.

One of the ways of constructing viable intermedial channels between "the literary" and "the digital" is, in my proposition, a hypertextual integration of assumptions on the generative potential and on the methodological possibilities of virtual worlds. This way, the concept of virtuality will be treated as an interface (and a transmedial feature) between analogic forms of literature and digital ones, in order to place traditional and digital forms and phenomena inside the same intermedial system, which I name for now "literature 2.0". The term "web 2.0" (DiNucci, O'Reilly) involves a series of cumulative modifications of the way in which the web is used, that turn it into a platform for media applications. Value and knowledge are created by the users, who become generators and modifiers of certain content (ideas, text, images, video, and other applications). Both term and concept have gained global notoriety for practical reasons, by the very popularity it enjoys with web users, but also by implicit and explicit theoretical recognition of the usefulness of the model.

Following this model, the proposition of a "literature 2.0" does not argue with existent theories and methods of literary study, nor does it deny the analogic or traditional model of literature. Instead, it tests whether traditional instruments of analyzing literary phenomena are still valid and can be reused in conformity with the new imperatives of hybrid cultural objects. Tool-restructuring must take into account both the traditional author and the digital user as creators of the forms of literature 2.0, with their different levels of participation. Not only the definition and forms of literature are modified at digital impact, but, as one could expect, the very disciplines in the study of literature. As such, a new and urgent necessity emerges: the rereading and rewriting of critical approaches and their sets of instruments and systems of praxes. Their re-inscriptions in the field of media theory, instead of theory of literature and comparative literature would give more suitable tools for the reception of the growing number of hybrid cultural objects like those described above. As public expectancies move towards popular culture, requesting intelligible language, quick evaluative response, sharpness of expression, integrating genres and species formerly considered to be paraliterary, literary commentary cannot pretend not to understand the magnitude of this reception shift.

A traditionalist environment such as the Romanian one has consumed a lot of negative energy in the war between digital and analogue literature (even if, by irony of culture, not much digital literature has been produced here, and the transmedial experiments are only starting as well). The traditionalist opposition formed by professors of literature, influential literary critics and historians, still argue in favor of keeping the literary system neat and closed. Local polemics between critics and bloggers are notorious, as well as tensions between different groups of "cultural bloggers". On the other hand, some local theoretical research has been seriously done in the field and is totally worthy of attention. An important example is Ion Manolescu's analysis of the cyberpunk fiction and comics literature. A professor of literature himself, Manolescu is also a devoted fan and theorist of digital culture and especially of the comics phenomena (where he integrates comics, graphic novels, comic strips, etc.) However, even in his research, limits of the actual disciplinary frames are visible. In order to give a better recognition to the Romanian tradition of comics, but also to place it within a literary frame, Manolescu attempts the inclusion of comics within the literary canon, stressing on transmedial features such as aesthetic accomplishment, psychological depth of the characters, and pluridimensionality of narrative. While extremely important for the opening of a closed-aesthetics canon of literature, these attempts compromise on the nonliterary features of hybrid cultural objects, as long as they try to impose a literary view. In the cases of hybrid objects, the very cultural basis is different from the start. Psychological rules of the isolated self (that Manolescu finds in both literature and graphic novels) do not apply to an object-based understanding of a "communal" experience of the self (see the example of the digital creation *Loss of Grasp* in Bouchardon and López-Varela Azcárate 68). Rules of literary performativity (from reader-response theories) do not apply to the gestural performativity of digital interaction (see "scenario-control", Rheingold).

Hostility from contemporary literary criticism and theory towards intermediality, critics' resistance to the use of virtual technology are primarily due to the addiction of the written culture to the phenomenon of sign disappearance. The cherished utopia of digital technologies seems to be, from this point of view, the perfect transparence of the medium. However, to the written culture and to the literary tradition this is a sign of the disciplinary apocalypse. Signs are regarded, in the analogue culture of the written word, as the very substance of all reality. To be able to recognize their contribution to the construction of reality, signs should be as visible as possible and by all means non-transparent. In a traditionally literary world, a way of communication based on a transparent medium deprives the user of his critical faculties, resulting in semiotic blindness.

As far as the future of intermedial studies in Romania is concerned, the most important reason for hope is the significant amount of graduates of comparative literature (most of them benefitting from more than necessary stages abroad) who have defended or are about to defend MA dissertations or PhD theses on intermedial subjects of world literature touching other media, forms of art, or social praxes: comic books, graphic novels, computer games, collaborative writing, cyberpunk culture. Their existence is not only the best guarantee that intermedial studies in Romania have a future, but also a sign of an educational intermedial turn that, in spite of their personal idiosyncrasies, scholars of literature and humanities can no longer ignore or minimize.

REFERENCES

Aarseth, Espen J. Cybertext: perspectives on ergodic literature. Baltimore: JHUP, 1997.

Bacon, Wallace A. "I. A sense of being: Interpretation and the humanities". Southern Speech Communication Journal 41.2 (1976): 135-141.

Bassnett, Susan. Comparative Literature. A Critical Introduction. Oxford: Blackwell, 1993.

Berger, Peter L. "Four faces of global culture". National Interest 49 (1997): 23–30.

Birkerts, Sven. The Gutenberg Elegies: The Fate of Reading in an Electronic Age. London: Macmillan, 2006.
Blum, Martin. "Remaking the East German past: Ostalgie, identity and material culture". Journal of Popular Culture 34.3 (2000): 229–53.
Bojtár, Endre. "On the Comparative Study of the Region's Literatures". Neohelicon 29.1 (2002): 27-33.
Bolter, Jay David, and Richard Grusin. Remediation: Understanding new media. Cambridge: MIT P, 1999.
Bouchardon, Serge, and Asunción López-Varela Azcárate. "Making sense of the digital as embodied experience." CLCWeb: Comparative Literature and Culture 13.3 (2011): 7.
Cornis-Pope, Marcel. "Transnational and Inter-National Perspectives in post-1989 Comparative Literary History." Neohelicon 30.2 (2003): 71-78.
Cornis-Pope, Marcel. "From resistance to reformulation". History of the Literary Cultures of East-Central Europe: Junctures and Disjunctures in the 19th and 20th Centuries: Types and Stereotypes. Eds. Marcel Cornis-Pope and John Neubauer. Vol. 4. Amsterdam: John Benjamins, 2010. 39-50.
Damrosch, David. "Comparative Cultural Studies". The Canonical Debate Today: Crossing Disciplinary and Cultural Boundaries. Eds. Liviu Papadima and David Damrosch. Vol. 149. Amsterdam: Rodopi, 2011. 169-78.
Damrosch, David. What Is World Literature? New Jersey: Princeton UP, 2003.
DiNucci, Darcy. "Fragmented future". Print 32 (1999): 221-22.
Emerson, Caryl. "Answering for Central and Eastern Europe". Comparative Literature in an Age of Globalisation. Ed. Haun Saussy. Baltimore: JHUP, 2006. 203-211.
Epstein, Mikhail. "Transculture: A Broad Way Between Globalism and Multiculturalism". American Journal of Economics and Sociology 68.1 (2009): 327-351.
Even-Zohar, Itamar. "Polysystem theory". Poetics Today 1.1/2 (1979): 287-310.
Hayles, N. Katherine. "Print is flat, code is deep: The importance of media-specific analysis". Poetics Today 25.1 (2004): 67-90.
Heim, Michael. "The Design of Virtual Reality". Cyberspace/cyberbodies/cyberpunk: Cultures of technological embodiment. Eds. Mike Featherstone and Roger Burrows, eds. Vol. 43. New York: Sage, 1996. 65-78.

Ikpe, I. B. "Beyond Relevance: In Praise of Useless Knowledge". South African Journal of Higher Education 24.4 (2010): 525-537.
Kadir, Djelal. Memos from the Besieged City. Lifelines for Cultural Sustainability. Stanford: Stanford UP, 2011.
Kernan, Alvin. What's Happened to the Humanities? Princeton: Princeton UP, 1997.
Lopez, Alfred J. "Introduction: Comparative Literature and the Return of the Global Repressed". The Global South 1.1 (2007): 1-15.
Manolescu, Ion. "Popular Culture and the Romanian Postmodernist Canon". The Canonical Debate Today: Crossing Disciplinary and Cultural Boundaries. Eds. Liviu Papadima and David Damrosch. Vol. 149. Amsterdam: Rodopi, 2011. 247-62.
Marino, Adrian. Comparatisme et Théorie de la Littérature. Paris: PU de France, 1988.
Marno, David. "The Monstrosity of Literature: Hugo Meltzl's World Literature and Its Legacies". World Literature, World Culture: History, Theory Analysis (2008): 37-50.
Moretti, Franco. "Conjectures on world literature". New left review (2000): 54-68.
O'Reilly, T. „What Is Web 2.0". O'Reilly Media, 2004. < http://oreilly.com/web2/archive/what-is-web-20.html>
Olsen, Lance. "Cyberpunk and the Crisis of Postmodernity". Fiction 2000: cyberpunk and the future of narrative. Eds. George Edgar Slusser, and Thomas Alan Shippey. Vol. 10. U of Georgia P, 1992: 142-52.
Rheingold, Howard. Virtual Reality: Exploring the Brave New Technologies. New York: Simon & Schuster, 1991.
Ryan, Marie-Laure, "Media and Narrative". The Routledge Encyclopedia of Narrative Theory. Ed. David Herman, Manfred Jahn, and Marie-Laure Ryan. London: Routledge, 2005. 288-92.
Schmidt, Siegfried J. "Literary Studies from Hermeneutics to Media Culture Studies". Digital Humanities and the Study of Intermediality in Comparative Cultural Studies. Ed. Steven Tötösy de Zepetnek. Purdue: Purdue UP, 2013. 5-18.
Schmidt, Siegfried J. "Why literature is not enough; or, Literary studies as media studies". Emerging Visions of the Aesthetic Process: In Psychology,

Semiology, and Philosophy. Ed. Gerald Cupchik and János László. Cambridge: Cambridge UP, 1992. 227-43.
Schröter, Jens. „Discourses and Models of Intermediality". Digital Humanities and the Study of Intermediality in Comparative Cultural Studies. Ed. Steven Tötösy de Zepetnek. Purdue: Purdue UP, 2013. 32-42.
Sturm-Trigonakis, Elke. Comparative Cultural Studies and the New Weltliteratur. Purdue: Purdue UP, 2013.
Terian, Andrei. "Constructing Transnational Identities: The Spatial Turn in Contemporary Literary Historiography". Primerjalna knjizevnost 36.2 (2013): 75-84.
Tötösy de Zepetnek, Steven, and Louise O. Vasvári. "The Study of Hungarian Culture as Comparative Central European Cultural Studies". Comparative Hungarian Cultural Studies. Purdue: Purdue UP, 2011. 11-33.
Tötösy de Zepetnek, Steven, and Louise O. Vasvári. "The Comparative and Contextual Study of Literature and Culture and Globalization". The Cambridge Companion to Comparative Literature and Comparative Cultural Studies. Ed. Steven Tötösy de Zepetnek and Tutun Mukherjee. Cambridge: Cambridge UP, 2013. 3-35.
Tötösy de Zepetnek, Steven. "From Comparative Literature Today toward Comparative Cultural Studies". CLCWeb: Comparative Literature and Culture 1.3 (1999).
Ursa, Mihaela. "Literatura 2.0". Vatra Literary Journal 491.2 (2012): 29-31.
Voia, Vasile. "Programul comparatist al lui Hugo Meltzl de Lomnitz". Caietele Echinox 1 (2001): 258-261.
Wolf, Werner. "(Inter)mediality and the Study of Literature". Digital Humanities and the Study of Intermediality in Comparative Cultural Studies. Ed. Steven Tötösy de Zepetnek. Purdue: Purdue Scholarly Publishing Services, 2013. 19-31.

About the Author

Mihaela Ursa teaches comparative literature at the Babes-Bolyai University of Cluj, Romania. In addition to numerous articles in Romanian and English on cultural studies, literary theory and criticism, she published, in Romanian, books on comparatism, postmodernism, critical theory, gender studies, fictionality and erotic literature.

CHAPTER 18

Intermediaities in Visual Poetry: Futurist "Polyexpressivity" and Net.art

Carolina Fernández Castrillo

The conceptualization of intermediality is closely related to early 20th-century avant-garde movements where media borders were continuously overlapped. Among all the cultural proposals at that period, Futurism still retains an important place in the integration of traditionally separate disciplines into a single work through the use of new media and the influence of technological development.

It is not a coincidence that the inaugural act of Futurism was the publication in 1909 of the fundational manifesto in *Le Figaro*, the most popular daily newspaper at that time in Paris. Its author, Filippo Tommaso Marinetti, used mass media to spread Futurist postulates beyond Italian frontiers to reach the whole world through an unprecedented campaign that lead up to the age of globalization. He launched his antitraditional and revolutionary program from the cultural epicentre of Europe to attack the heart of high culture in order to claim the beginning of a new era inspired by 'the beauty of speed'. It was one of the first attempts to set a theoretical system to bring the impact of technology, industrialization and new means of communication, transportation and information into the cultural field.

Marinetti started the Futurist reconstruction of the universe adopting the analogical foundation of life as the main principle to state a new socio-cultural scenario aligned with the effects of modernity in the way of living. Due to his literary roots, the analogy depicted the fulcrum of an intermedial condition where interdisciplinarity became an incomparable framework for creation. From visual poetry, the Futurist leader together with some of his colleagues as Ardengo Soffici, Fortunato Depero, Paolo Buzzi, Carlo Carrà or Francesco Cangiullo outlined a roadmap that could be applied in every artistic expression from painting to cinema, from literature to photography.

By doing so, the Futurists laid the foundations for achieving the same recognition both for old artistic fields and new technical media. They understood that new media was not just a simple consequence of industrial era but a decisive achievement that would change the whole cultural and social system. For this purpose, they tried to understand the fundamental conditions of every single medium to build a complex network of interdisciplinary intersections. It was also necessary to define the aims, challenges and boundaries of such an innovative project through a new vocabulary adapted to the current circumstances. Marinetti and his companions coined neologisms such as 'polyexpressivity', 'modernolatry' or 'multisensoriality' and adopted 'dynamism', 'simultaneity', 'velocity' and 'totality' as key words to express their faith in the potential synergies between art and media.

Futurist attempts to determine intermedial traits can be related to present efforts from Comparative Media Studies to define the impact of new technologies on the creation, dissemination and reception of knowledge in the digital age. Scholars such as Henry Jenkins, Werner Wolf, Lars Ellestrôm, Marina Grishakova or Marie-Laure Ryan, among others, are exploring new options to refer to those intermedial processes resulting from media crossings. Therefore, as it happened at the beginning of last century, we are dealing with a broad variety of neologisms characterized by the use of prefixes like 'trans-', 'cross-', 'inter-', 'multi-', 'pluri-', 'meta-' and 'post-', and concepts like 'hybridization', 'interactivity', 'transition', 'convergence', 'immersion', etc.

Futurist practices on visual poetry and multisensoriality, influenced by collage paintings or film editing processes, became crucial to establish a complex system of "remediations", as stated by Jay David Bolter and Richard Grusin (1999), between traditional arts and new media. As the experience of Marinetti and his revolutionary followers demonstrates, a systemic revision of artistic changes in line with technical development becomes essential to set new aesthetic and cultural principles, an intuition that nowadays makes more sense than ever before.

Italian avant-garde was not the first to look forward to an integration of the arts through a theoretical system. Starting with the German opera composer Richard Wagner, who in 1849 introduced the concept of the *Gesamtkunstwerk*, for many decades, artists, poets, musicians and theoreticians had been seeking a medium to create a total artwork and also to express their concern with individual and social consciousness.

In the early 18th-century, numerous treatises on the limits of the arts were published. They attempted the formulation of new strategies to reflect the transition of social and cultural sphere to modernity. Those proposals generated intense debates and controversies concerning the role of intellectuals and their position in an unrestrained ontological transition.

In contrast to Ricciotto Canudo's essay "La naissance d'un sixième art. Essai sur le cinématographe" (1911) or Futurist manifestos on the relation between different media, some theorists were against the interrelationship between artistic genres, such as Gotthold Ephraim Lessing, who in 1766 claimed that "these bad influences are manifested in poetry through descriptive obsession and in painting with the allegorical habit, wanting to turn the first a speaker box [...] and the last one a mute poem" (1994: 239).

After many frustrating attempts along the end of the 19th-century, in 1909 *Fondazione e Manifesto del Futurismo* was the first set of principles to push the limits of art to its breaking point. Marinetti's desire of provocation and rupture with traditions secured him a leading position among modernist cultural tendencies, anticipating the experimental practices of the historical European avant-garde:

> We stand on the last promontory of the centuries! (...) It is from Italy that we launch through the world this violently upsetting incendiary manifesto of ours (...) The oldest of us is thirty: so we have at least a decade for finishing our work. When we are forty, other younger and stronger men will probably throw us in the wastebasket like useless manuscripts—we want it to happen! (...) Erect on the summit of the world, once again we hurl defiance to the stars! (Marinetti 1909)

Futurism, as the avant-gardes that came after it, was grounded in the traumatic loss of faith in the traditional cognitive framework and in the experience of fragmentation and disintegration. In fact, the absence of coordinates became the starting point for their action program: "Time and Space died yesterday. We already live in the absolute, because we have created eternal, omnipresent speed." (Marinetti, 1909) As Asunción López-Varela pointed out:

> At the centre of this crisis were the new technologies and methodologies of science, the epistemology of logical positivism and the relativism of functionalist thought [...] The artist as visionary would attempt to create what the culture could no longer produce: symbol and meaning in the dimension of art, brought into being through the agency of language. [...] (2011: 208-209)

Some of the most innovative Futurist contributions arose from the fundamental alterations in the perception of time and space caused by the introduction of railroads, photography and media communication. The depiction of speed and motion was meant to illustrate such technical developments through a rapid and vibrant style based on the principle of simultaneity. This term was introduced on February 1912 in the preface of the catalogue for the Futurist exhibition at the Bernheim-Jeune gallery in Paris (Boccioni, Carrà, Russolo, Balla, & Severini) and it represented the core idea of Futurist imaginary. For this reason, Umberto Boccioni reacted angrily to Robert Delaunay's appropriation of this word.

The aim of Marinetti and his colleagues was to immerse the observer in the so-called "polyexpressive" experience, an all-embracing process that would appeal to all the feelings and senses simultaneously. Instead of representing one detail or another of the reality, Futurist art seeks to realize a "complete fusion in order to reconstruct the universe making it more joyful, in other words, recreating it entirely" (Balla and Depero 1915). Hence, this creative procedure required both the fusion of all aesthetic experiences and a participative role of the viewer, only possible by virtue of an intermedial approach closely related to the cognitive concept of analogy.

In *Manifesto tecnico della letteratura futurista* (1912), Marinetti proclaimed the destruction of syntax and the abolition of the punctuation. In this way, he stated that perception by analogy would settle the basis of an innovative methodology for both literature and the visual arts: "Analogy is nothing but the immense love that connects distant, seemingly different and hostile things. It is through very vast analogies that this orchestral style, at once polychromatic, polyphonic, and polymorphous, can embrace the life of matter." (Marinetti 1912) In this text, he also mentioned the potentiality of "imagination without strings" and "words in freedom", two concepts that, one year later, he would develop in the manifesto of *Distruzione della sintassi - Immaginazione senza fili - Parole in libertà* (1913).

> The imagination without strings, and words-in-freedom, will transport us to the essence of the matter. With the discovery of new analogies between things remote and apparently contradictory, we shall value them ever more intimately. Instead of humanizing animals, vegetables, and minerals (a bygone system) we will be able to animalize, vegetize, mineralize, electrify, or liquefy our style, making it live the very life of matter. For example, to render the life of a blad of grass, we might have; 'I will be greener tomorrow.' But with words-in-freedom we might have With: Condensed metaphors-Telegraphic images-Sums of vibrations-Knots of thought-Closed or open fans of movement- Foreshortened analogies-Color Balances-The dimensions, weights, sizes, and velocities of sensations-The plunge of the essential world into the water of sensibility, without the concentric eddies produced by words-Intuition's movements of repose-Movements in two, three, four, five different rhythms-Analytical exploratory telegraph poles that sustain the cable of intuitive strings (Marinetti 1913)

Marinetti also announced the introduction of 'onomatopoeic harmonies' to render the sounds and noise of modern life; the 'typographical revolution' to emphasize the expressive force of words; 'multilinear lyricism' to allow the poet to play with "several chains of colors, sounds, odors, noises, weights, densities, analogies. One line, for example, might be olfactory, another musical, another pictorial." (Marinetti 1913) In *"Modernolatria" et "Simultaneità"*, Pär Bergman explores the multiple connections between Futurist multilineal lyrism and Wagnerian postulates on total artwork (1962: 241).

Marinetti was convinced that the separate branches of art would attain new poetic heights when put to the service of the "polyexpressive" reconstruction of the universe. He "saw the artist as a revelatory being whose task was on the one hand to penetrate reality and on the other hand to create a new reality" (Ohana 2010: 46). Marinetti developed his strategy inspired by the method of the intuition and the concepts of vitality, dynamism, instinct and pure perception, present also in Henri Bergson's theory of consciousness as flux:

> We shall give flesh and blood to the invisible, the impalpable, the imponderable, the imperceptible. We shall find abstract equivalents for all the forms and elements of the universe, then combine them together according to the whims of our inspiration in order to create plastic complexes that we will put into motion (Balla and Depero 1915)

The influence of cinematic processes was also an essential contribution to Futurist literature, poetry, painting and theatre's renewal. According to Mario Verdone, montage was the best gift that the 20th-century had given to the art world (1967: 39). One of the most representative examples of the decisive influence of cinema upon poetry and literature was *L'elisse e la Spirale. Film + Parole in Libertà*, a novel written in 1913 and published in 1915 where Paolo Buzzi tried to incorporate the logic of film editing (to obtain a better understanding of cinema's role in Futurist intermedial project, see Strauven 2006, Lista 2009 and Fernández Castrillo 2011).

Attracted by the illusion of an unmediated experience, Futurists proclaimed the death of the book and their preference toward the novelty of cinematic logic and sequence. They developed a particular approach announcing that all the artistic disciplines should be transformed by the new media. In all through Futurist manifestos, essays, speeches and artworks there is an effort to achieve the equivalence of the media as well as to mix them together in new combinations. As mentioned before, the method introduced by Italian modernist avant-garde turn out to be a pioneer contribution to Comparative Media Studies and, more specifically, to the theory of intermediality. Werner Wolf supports that, in a narrow sense, the term "intermediality" refers to the participation of more than one medium, or sensory channel, in a given work, whereas, in a broad sense, it is the media equivalent of intertextuality and it covers any kind of relation between different media (1999: 35-36).

The insistence of Futurists on work across media borders led them to explore the media-specific idiosyncrasy of each respective medium, and also to experiment with the mixing of old and new artistic disciplines. Not one single artistic branch remained untapped. Among all their proposals, visual poetry needs to be taken in consideration in order to explain the roots of Futurist hymn to the future based on the principle of intermediality. In *The Aesthetics of Visual Poetry, 1914-1928*, Willard Bohn suggests that "Combining painting and poetry, it is neither a compromise nor an evasion but a synthesis of the principles underlying each medium." (1986: 2). Unlike the so-called 'figurative poetry', 'ideograms' or 'calligrams' created at that time, Futurist poems are not just a bridge between image and text but also the conjunction of the rest of disciplines in a unique artwork. In *Distruzione della sintassi - Immaginazione senza fili - Parole in libertà*, Marinetti rejected any relation to Symbolist legacy:

> I oppose the decorative and precious aesthetic of Mallarmé and his search for the exotic word, the unique and irreplaceable, elegant, suggestive, exquisite adjective. I have no wish to suggest an idea of sensation by means of passéist graces and affectations. I want to seize them brutally and fling them in the reader's face.
>
> I also oppose Mallarmé's static ideal. The typographic revolution that I've proposed will enable me to imprint words (words already free, dynamic, torpedoing forward) every velocity of the stars, clouds, airplanes, trains, waves, explosives, drops of sea foam, molecules, and atoms (Marinetti 1913)

A new awareness of the printed page leaded Futurists to examine the spatialization and visualization of the poetic message. As Achille Bonito Oliva points out, the contemplation of these poems is founded in "the spatiotemporal" perception, similar to that of painting, of a unitary dimension not as the presence of an absence (2007: 18). The revolutionary idea of "words in freedom" was a project in progress always open to new experimentations that Giovanni Lista summarizes in two main categories: 1. The interaction between codex based on synesthetic and synoptic principles that results in multi-sensory experiments; 2. The impact of typographic innovation together with the material components of the Futurist poetry: format of the page, ink colours, typefaces, texture of the paper, book-binding technique, etc. (Lista 2009: 293)

In addition to the different types of intermedialities, from the fusion of different arts and media into new genres or the representation of one medium into another, the words started to call attention to themselves. They were no longer perceived as transparent signs, but assumed an artistic value as a result of the creative typography.

> My revolution is directed against the so-called typographical harmony of the page, which is contrary to the flux and reflux, the leaps and bursts of style that run through the page itself. For that reason we will use, in the very same page, *three or four different colors of ink,* and as many as twenty different typographical fonts if necessary, For example: *italics* for a series of swift or similar sensations, *boldface* for violent onomatopoeias, etc. The typographical revolutions and the multicoloured variety in the letters will mean that I can double the expressive force of words. [...] And so I shall realize the fourth principle contained in my *First Manifesto of Futurism* [...] "We affirm that the beauty of the world has been enriched by a new form of beauty: the beauty of speed." (Marinetti 1913)

Gabriella Belli (2007: 49) affirms that, until 1911, Futurist writings looked much more innovative than painting experiences. The icons and the letters of the alphabet became signs and shapes able to express any kind of feelings and emotions, appealing simultaneously to all the senses of the readers and the viewers. Another distinctive trait of Futurist contribution to the cultural renewal is the influence of mass media in visual poems and word-paintings, as we may observe in Carlo Carrà's *Manifestazione interventista* (*Festa patriottica-Dipinto parolibero*) (1914), a collage made of tempera and pasted newspapers clippings on cardboard inspired by Guillaume Apollinaire's first visual poem "Lettre-Océan", published in *Les Soirées de Paris* in the same year. Both authors glorify the *élan vital* and render the atmosphere of Modern life by the creation of a "polyespressive" symphony:

> The snatches of music in the poem are matched by a fragment of sheet music pasted to the collage and by assorted references to an "orchestra" and 'canzoni' ('songs'). Similarly, the sounds made by Apollinaire's new shoes ('cré cré') the phonograph's scratchiness ('zzz'), and the bus's motor ('rro oo to ro ro ro') correspond to Carrà's onomatopoeic 'crucra crucra',

'bree bree', 'cric crac', 'zzzz', and the sounds of various vehicles ('Trrrrrrrrrrrrr', 'traak tatateaak') (Bohn 1986: 13)

Focusing his analysis on the mutual admiration that existed between Apollinaire and Carrà Willard Bohn explains the similarities between the cited figurative poem and the word-painting:

> Both have the same geometrical configuration. The lines of poetry in the poem, like the phrases and painted papers in the collage, form a series of concentric circles radiating outward from a circular center, from which extend a number of symmetrical 'spokes'. The same can be said of the principal techniques employed. Both works exploit the visual properties of written language to create ideogrammatic compositions in which the formal configuration reinforces the linguistic message and vice versa. If they are essentially pictures formed of words, they are also literary works the structure and spatial relations of which are determined by the [...] physical properties of the text, by the juxtaposition of the words on the page (or canvas). Perception and conception, image and metaphor tend to emerge into one indivisible whole. In this context the compositions represent extreme examples of concrete metaphor (1986: 9, 13)

Apollinaire and Carrà comprehended that new media (as radio or cinema), the principles of advertising, magazine illustrations and the new means of transmission (as the telegraph or the telephone) were exerting a strong attraction on the population and, at the same time, they constituted innovative communicative models to emulate for their effectiveness and attractiveness.

Futurists did not hesitate to create their own newspapers and magazines as *Lacerba* (1913-1915), *La Balza futurista* (1915) or *L'Italia Futurista* (1916-1918), among others, to divulge both their visual analogies, multilinear lyrics and word-paintings. All of them, were inspired by the success of the pre-Futurist international magazine *Poesia* (1906-1909), founded by Marinetti. They also launched Edizioni futuriste di *Poesia* and Edizioni di *L'Italia Futurista* where they published their anthologies and volumes on the mentioned topic.

Marinetti incorporated Futurist literary and poetic revolution to his declamatory style and, on the other hand, he also applied the immediacy and the strength of verbal communication to his writings. As noticed by Lista (2009: 294), the first period of Futurist experimentation in visual poetry was dominated by the principle of *dynamis*, turning visual poems into a multisensorial seismograph of Modern rhythm. Together with this polyphonic reflection of urban experience, the physical value of the page (*physis*) progressively started to have a main position as a result of the Futurist typographical revolution.

Zang Tumb Tumb (1914) by Filippo Tommaso Marinetti, cover.

Marinetti tried to synthesize both perspectives in *Zang Tumb Tumb* (1912-1914), his first book of "words in freedom", that required considerable skill from the typesetter for its revolutionary typographic style. He depicted the *hinc et nunc* of a violent scene in the battlefield by an onomatopoeic recreation of the noises; using different sizes and styles of types; with the incorporation of lyric equations; through the destruction of the syntax and the presence of an agglomerate of "words in freedom" to affirm the "beauty of the speed"; and, finally, with the "multilinear lyricism" to achieve "the most complex lyric simultaneities".

In *Lo splendore geometrico e meccanico e la sensibilità numerica*, Marinetti explains the idiosyncrasy of his lyric equations:

> I create true theorems or lyrical equations, introducing numbers which I've intuitively chosen and placed within the very center of a word; with a certain quantity of + - x +, I can give the thickness, the mass, the volumes of things which words otherwise have to express. The arrangement + - + - + + x, for example, serves to render the changes and accelerations in speed of an automobile. The arrangement + + + + + serves to render the clustering of equal sensations. (E.g.: *fecal odor of dysentery + the honeyed stench of plague sweats + smell of ammonia,* and so on in "Train Full of Sick Soldiers" in my *Zang tumb tumb*) (Marinetti 1914)

Intermedialities in Visual Poetry 371

Montagne + Vallate + Strade x Joffre (1915) by Marinetti. Printed paper, 19,3 x 16 cm. From http://en.wikipedia.org/wiki/File:Marinetti-Motagne.jpg

Useful decoding instructions for some of the most popular Futurist visual poems are also found:

> Everything must be banned which doesn't contribute to expressing the evanescent and mysterious Futurist sensibility with all its new geometrical-mechanical splendour. The free-wordist Cangiullo, in *Fumatori II^a* had the felicitous idea of conveying the long monotonous reveries and self-expansion of the smoke-boredom during a long train journal by means of this *painted analogy*.
>
> TO sM**OKE**
>
> Words-in-freedom, in their continuous effort to express things with maximum force and greatest depth, naturally transform themselves into self-illustrations.
>
> By means of free, expressive orthography and typography, synoptic tables of lyrical values and designed analogies (Marinetti 1914)

It is worth emphasising the contribution of the free-wordist Ardengo Soffici who became the theorist of the "imagination without strings" and the "synoptic tables" in order to achieve the liberation of the word. It is also remarkable Angelo Rognoni's precognition of the typographic sculptures. Meanwhile, Fortunato Depero paid attention to the potentiality of abstract verbalization and as a result of his interdisciplinary research he created a new conceptual language called "onomalingua", based on the onomatopoeic sonority to communicate feelings instead of concepts. His most famous book, *Depero Futurista* (1927), also known as "Libro imbullonato", anticipated the mechanical book, whereas in *Numero Unico Futurista Campari* (1931), in *Liriche Radiofoniche* (1934) and *Fortunato Depero nella vita e nelle opere* he gradually renounced to the graphical and linguistic experimentation characteristic of his unfinished volume *New York. Film Vissuto*.

In 1916, Edizioni futuriste di *Poesia* published Francesco Cangiullo's *Piedigrotta: parole in libertà*, a masterpiece of visual poetry in which he described the orgiastic celebration of Napolitan festival. Three years later he presented the first Futurist book-object: *Caffèconcerto. Alfabeto a sorpresa* in which he represented, show by show, a variety spectacle. In 1923 with *Poesia pentagrammata*, Cangiullo explored the relations between figurative poems and music. Among some of the most interesting projects of visual poetry we find also two unpublished collections: Paolo Buzzi's *Conflagrazione* (1914-1918), an experimental handwritten diary, and Marinetti's anthology *Paroliberi* futuristi, which was announced in 1915 in the flier *Parole, consonanti, vocali, numeri in libertà* but it was never published. In 1932 the founder of Futurism finally published *Parole in libertà futuriste tattili, termiche, olfattive* an essential reference work for the European avant-garde, the highest expression of multisensorial research in Futurist poetry. The book was printed in metal sheet to render the mechanical aesthetics and to realize Marinetti's old dream of creating a book made of nickel. It also implemented the main postulates of *Il Tattilismo* (1921), a Futurist manifesto on sensory stimulation, an early form of interactive art.

In fact, the audience's attitude toward the printed page played an important role in Futurist visual poetry which anticipates the characteristic involvement of the public in performance practices and the emancipation of the user in the digital age. The reader became a participant and his interaction with the text an adventure to live. Jean-Pierre Goldenstein points out that one of visual poetry's major functions is to force the reader to investigate an infinite number of paths, preventing him from deciphering a preexisting sense (1988: 160). Willard Bohn studies in depth the reader's role in visual poetry. He explains that:

> [...] the poem cannot be reduced to a single meaning, since each reader brings something different to the text. The reading process is also complicated by the nonlinear format of much of the poetry [...] In carrying out the procedures connected with consistency building, readers are continually forced to modify their interpretations [...] The average reader doesn't have a chance of reproducing the author's thought patterns and associations (Bohn 2001: 30)

As we have seen, in their rebellion against *passéist* cultural malaise, Futurists announced the unquestionable relevance of the media experience and its unavoidable influence in the search of a whole new set of linguistic and communicative techniques, more adapted to express the complexity of Modern condition through a "polyexpressive" approach. Their original response to the epistemological crisis caused by the impact of industrialization, mass media and new technologies in their society is nowadays a grounded model extremely helpful in deciphering the intermedial idiosyncrasy of new cultural expressions in online communication.

Futurist postulates on intermedial practices could belong to our own era. Media archaeologists often compare the reception of reproductive and broadcast media in the early 20th-century to current strategies for integrating digital technology. Regarding the influence of the earlier moments of cultural and technological transition, Tom Gunning sustains that "the introduction of new technology in the modern era employs a number of rhetorical tropes and discursive practices that constitute our richest source for excavating what the newness of technology entailed." (2003: 39). This self-conscious awareness of change and conceptual uncertainty is evident nowadays. David Thorburn and Henry Jenkins claim that "there is an urgent need for a pragmatic, historically informed perspective that maps a sensible middle group between the euphoria and the panic surrounding new media" (2003: 2). In their book *Rethinking media change: the aesthetics of transition*, these authors suggest to approach media intersections as a process instead of a static completion.

> On this view, convergence can be understood as a way to bridge or join old and new technologies, formats and audiences. Such cross-media joinings and borrowings may feel disruptive if we assume that each medium has a defined range of characteristics of predetermined mission [...] A less reductive, comparative approach would recognize the complex synergies that always prevail among media systems, particularly during periods shaped by the birth of a new medium of expression (2003: 3).

Such convergences occur regularly in the history of the "information society", a term introduced by Marshall McLuhan in *Understanding Media: the extensions of man* (1964) in reference to the effect of emerging technology in data creation, distribution and manipulation in the post-industrial era. In this regard, Marinetti and his avant-garde colleagues assumed a pioneer position since, more than one century ago, they focused their artworks, performing acts and manifestos on pursuing the ways in which media interact, replace and cooperate with one another in the cultural sphere. From their initial incursions in visual poetry to the following contributions in a myriad of uncategorized genres, there are three focal points that resume their intermedial paradigm's: the principle of "simultaneity", "instantaneity" and "totality". These three main characteristics anticipate Randall Packer and Ken Jordan's definition of new media in the digital age:

> Integration: the combining of art forms and technology into a hybrid form of expression.
> Interactivity: the ability of the user to manipulate and affect her experience of media directly, and to communicate with others through media.
> Hypermedia: the linking of separate media elements to one another to create a trail of personal associations.
> Immersion: the experience of entering into the simulation or suggestion of a three-dimensional environment.
> Narrativity: aesthetic and formal strategies that derive from above concepts, which result in nonlinear story forms and presentation (2001: xxxv)

Although new applications for digital media emerge over the time, it can be stated that, at the present, the most distinctive feature of online creative procedures is the encouragement of interaction, that is, the sharing of collaboration within the artistic process itself. Digital code fulfils the old Futurist dream of achieving an interactive and 'polyespressive' artwork by the principles of 'numerical representation', 'modularity', 'automation', 'variability' and 'transcoding' (Manovich 2001). The critic Friedrick W. Block (2007), claims that, in media poetry, movement transforms into animation and processuality whereas interaction becomes participation. Futurist strategies developed in visual poetry, as the "multilinear lyricism" or "words in freedom", become embedded in the commands and interfaces of computer software as Marie-Laure Ryan sustains: "The digital revolution of the last decade has let words on the loose, not just by liberating their semantic potential, as most avant-garde movements of the past hundred years have done, but in a physical, quite literal sense as well." (1999: 1)

Along the same lines, Katalin Sándor argues that: "the artistic practices of visual print poetry, of pattern poems, calligrams, concrete poetry, lettrism, and colleages have come to function as a continually recycled 'resource' for digital poetry." (2012: 147)

As outlined above, net artworks continue the everlasting avant-garde aspiration of increasing the immersion and the aesthetic response of the observer. Loss Pequeño Glazier claims that:

> The conditions that have characterized the making of innovative poetry in the twentieth century have a powerful relevance to such works in twenty-first century media. That is, poets are making with the same attention that they did through the movements of the previous century and they are doing so with new materials — and new materials alter what constitutes writing. Through recognizing the conditions of such making and by appreciating the material qualities of new computer media we can begin to identify the new poetries of the twenty-first century. Putting such a vision together is more than a simple concatenation of strings of practice; it involves recognizing the interwoven matrices through which e-writing makes its way (2001: n/p)

Lori Emerson defines these creative processes as performative events "complete with their own set of viewer/viewed relation" (2003: 91). When we refer to the new expressions of digital culture, we should remember that the term "Internet art" or "net.art" englobes all artistic branches that use Internet as the main medium and that cannot be produced, manipulated, spread or experienced in any other way. Ryan centres the definition of net.art on the code's key role: "By net.art, I mean any work available on the World Wide Web that takes advantage of the computer, not only as a mean of production and dissemination, but also as support necessary to the performance of the text. In other words, I restrict the category net.art to works that need to be executed by code." (2012: 132).

From the beginnings of computer-based literature, at the end of the sixties, to the creation of interactive e-poems, there have been many artists and academics that have enriched avant-garde postulates on intermedial qualities of figurative texts. However, Marjorie Perloff mentions the risk of misunderstanding the role of visual poetry in the electronic age by fetishizing digital condition as something in itself remarkable, instead of appreciating the real sense of net-poetry:

> [...] poetry is an especially vexed case because, however we choose to define it, poetry is the *language art*: it is, by all accounts, language that is somehow extraordinary, that can be processed only upon rereading.

Consequently, the "new" techniques, whereby letters and words can move around the screen, break up, and reassemble, or whereby the reader/viewer can decide by a mere click to reformat the electronic text or which part of it to access, become merely tedious unless the poetry in question is, in Ezra Pound's words, "charged with meaning." (2006: 143-144)

Many terms have been suggested to describe such poetry, from "cyberpoetry", to "digital poetry", "computer poetry", "media-poetry", "interactive poetry", "net-poetry", "electronic poetry", "e-poetry", etc. Friedrich W. Block (2007) ennumerates the specific criteria to distinguish digital poetry from other literature: 1) the mechanical, algorithmic generation of texts (supporting or complete), 2) electronic linkage (in the computer, on Intranet or Internet) of fragments and files of the same or also different media types, derived from this the 3) multi- or non-linearity of both text structure and individual reading matter and if required 4) multimediality and animation of texts in the broadest sense 5) interactivity as a 'dialog' between machine (hard and software) and user as a -dependent on the programming- reversible or irreversible intervention into the display or data base text, as a telematic communication between different protagonists on the computer network; derived from this 6) the shift or even de-differentiation of traditional action roles such as author, reader, editor.

Among the numerous examples of digital poetry which follow Futurist premises, it should be pointed out *C•O•G•(I) An Interactive Kinetic Textual Composition* (2002) created by Loss Pequeño Glazier, professor of Media Studies at University of Buffalo, New York, and director of Elecronic Poetry Center (EPC). Despite a certain grade on ingenuousness, the cited artwork incarnates the Futurist "words in freedom" in the digital age, including movement, colours and a dynamic typography.

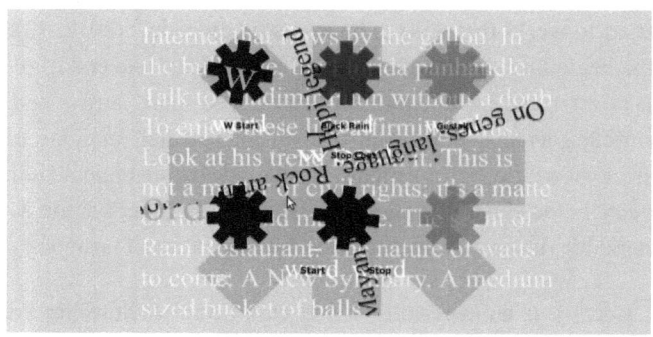

C•O•G•(I) An Interactive Kinetic Textual Composition (2002) by Loss Pequeño Glazier

Another example of the digital accomplishment of "words-in-freedom in movement" and "animated writing" is Dan Waber's *Strings* (1999), where the moment of words 'yes/maybe' recreates a 'flirt', or the growing 'haha' stands for contagious laughing, a reverberation of the "instinctive deformation of words" that "corresponds to our natural tendency to use onomatopoeia." (Marinetti 1913)

Strings (1999) by Dan Waber

Yet one more example of the achievement of "the most complex lyric simultaneities" comes from Thomas Swiss's web-based work in which he explores the relationships between sound, image and text through a collaborative strategy. Tim Berners-Lee defines "intercreativity" as "the process of making things or solving problems together" (1997). In this case, the poet establishes a network of relationships between his production and the linked images, texts and sounds others create, moving from individual to composite authorship.

These are just some examples of the first e-poems at the turn of the 20th - century. There are now many digital artists and poets who develop new strategies to accomplish avant-garde expectations by means of augmented reality, or user generated systems. María Mencía's ongoing series of generative poetics texts or Airan Kand's interactive installations, among many others; a valuable effort that would deserve more extensive study.

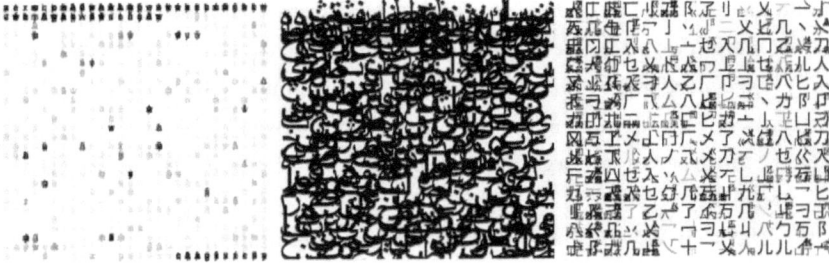

Generative poems (on going) by María Mencía. Presentation and exhibition: (PAN) Palazzo delle Arti, Naples, Italy, 2010.

To conclude this essay, I would like to point out that under the pressure of technological innovations and mass media society, Futurists made a special effort to renovate the traditional artistic expressions by exploring their intrinsic value. The rise of modern visual poetry reflects the end of the power of abstraction of the word in favour of its embodiment by the juxtaposition of divergent artistic elements in the creation of an interconnected and expansive net of interdependencies.

The multisensorial tables of "words in freedom" acted as a synthesizing crucible providing the perfect formula for the revitalization of the creative process; a method founded on the concept of intermediality which is, still nowadays, a valid reference model. In fact, the avant-garde aesthetic strategies live on in present-day hipertextualities, hibridations, collages or mash-ups in the "remix culture" (Manovich, 2007).

Nowadays, new cultural expressions as net.art, or more specifically digital poetry, demand standards of definition agreed by a global community as it happened at Futurist time, when a large number of artists congregated around programmatic texts to coin new terms to define the "polyexpressive" nature of the multimedia experience. Therefore, Futurist legacy is still nowadays an inspiring milestone to face the reception of digital technology since the inherent potential of intermediality is and will continue to be in development.

REFERENCES

Balla, Giacomo and Depero, Fortunato. *Ricostruzione futurista dell'universo.* Milan: Direzione del Movimento Futurista (pamphlet), 1915.

Belli, Gabriella. "La scrittura futurista e l'uso del manifesto". *La parola nell'arte: ricerche d'avanguardia nel '900: dal futurismo a oggi attraverso le collezioni del Mart.* VV.AA. Milan: Skira, 2007. 45-49.

Bergman, Pär. *Modernolatria"et $'imultaneità." Recherches sur deux tendances dans l'avant-garde littéraire en Italie et en France à la veille de la première guerre mondiale.* Stockholm: Bonnier, 1962.

Berners-Lee, Tim. "Realising the full potential of the web". <http://www.w3.org/1998/02/Potential.html> 1997. Accessed 14 July 2015.

Block, Friedrich W. "Digital poetics or On the evolution of experimental media poetry". *netzliteratur.net.* <http://www.netzliteratur.net/block/p0et1cs.html> 2007 Accesed 14 July 2015.

Boccioni, Umberto; Carrà, Carlo; Russolo, Luigi; Balla, Giacomo; Severini, Gino "Les exposants au public". *Les Peintres futuristes italiens, exhibition catalogue.* Galerie Berheim-Jeune & Cie: Paris, 1912. 1-14.

Bohn, Willard. *Modern visual poetry.* Newark: University of Delaware Press; London: Associated University Presses, 2001.

Bohn, Willard. *The Aesthetics of Visual Poetry, 1914-1928.* Cambridge: Cambridge University Press, 1986.

Bolter, Jay David and Grusin, Richard. *Remediation: understanding new media.* Cambridge, Massachusetts and London: MIT Press, 1999.

Bonito Oliva, Achille. "La parola totale". *La parola nell'arte: ricerche d'avanguardia nel '900: dal futurismo a oggi attraverso le collezioni del Mart.* VV.AA. Milan: Skira, 2007. 17-19.

Canudo, Ricciotto. "La naissance d'un sixième art. Essai sur le cinématographe". *Les Entretiens Idéalistes*, 25 October 1911.

Emerson, Lori. "Digital Poetry as Reflexive Embodiment". *Cybertext Yearbook (2002-2003).* Markku Eskelinen, Raine Koskimaa, Loss Pequeño Glazier and John Cayley Ed(s). Publisher: JK, 2003. 88-106.

Fernández Castrillo, Carolina. "Futurismo e attrazioni del precinema". *Il precinema oltre il cinema. Per una nuova storia del media audiovisivi.* Ed. Elio Girlanda. Roma: Dino Audino Editore, 2011. 59-69.

Glazier, Loss Pequeño. "Language as Transmission: Poetry's Electronic Presence (Excerpt)". <http://epc.buffalo.edu/authors/glazier/dp/intro1.html> 2001 Accessed 14 July 2015.

Glazier, Loss Pequeño. *C•O•G•(I) An Interactive Kinetic Textual Composition.* 2002. <http://epc.buffalo.edu/authors/glazier/e-poetry/cog/cog-about.html> Accessed 14 July 2015.

Goldenstein, Jean-Pierre. "La Lecture and défi : remarques sur quelques aspects de l'Esprit nouveau en poésie." *En hommage à Michel Décaudin.* Ed. Pierre Brunel *et al.* Paris: Minard 1986. 160

Gunning, Tom. "Re-Newing Old Technologies: Astonishement, Second Nature, and the Uncanny in Technology from the Previous Turn-of-the-Century". *Rethinking media change: the aesthetics of transition.* Ed(s). David Thorburn and Henry Jenkins. Cambridge, Massachusetts: MIT Press, 2003. 39-60.

Lessing, Gotthold Ephraim. *Laocoonte ovvero sui limiti della pittura e della poesia.* Milan: Rizzoli, 1994.

Lista, Giovanni. "Il riscaldamento dei media. Cinema e fotografia nel futurismo". *Vertigo. Il secolo di arte off-media dal Futurismo al web.* Ed(s). Germano Celant and Gianfranco Maraniello. Milan: Skira, 2009. 33-38.

Lista, Giovanni. "Dal paroliberismo al libro-oggetto". *Futurismo 1909-2009: Velocità + Arte + Azione.* Ed(s). Giovanni Lista and Ada Masoero. Milan: Skira, 2009. 293-317.

López-Varela, Asunción. "Canon and Border-Crossing in the work of Mina Loy". *Les réescritures du canon dans la littérature du langue anglaise.* Ed. Claire Bazin and Marie Claude Perrin Chenour. Paris: Université Paris Ouest Nanterre La Défense, 2011. 203-219.

Manovich, Lev. "What comes after remix?". *Lev Manovich website.* 2007. <http://www.manovich.net/articles.php> Accessed 14 July 2015.

Manovich, Lev. *The language of new media.* Cambridge, Massachusetts: MIT Press, 2001.

Marinetti, Filippo Tommaso. "Fondazione e Manifesto del Futurismo". *Poesia*, V. 1-2, February-March, 1909.

Marinetti, Filippo Tommaso. "Manifesto tecnico della letteratura futurista". *I poeti futuristi.* Milan: Edizioni futuriste di *Poesia*, 1912.

Marinetti, Filippo Tommaso. "Distruzione della sintassi – Immaginazione senza fili – Parole in libertà". *Lacerba*, I, 12 (15 June) and 22 (15 Nov): 1913.

Marinetti, Filippo Tommaso. "Lo splendore geometrico e meccanico e la sensibilitá numerica". *Lacerba*, 6, 15 March 1914.

McLuhan, Marshall. *Understanding Media: the extensions of man.* New York: McGraw-Hill, 1964.

Ohana, David. *The Futurist syndrome.* Brighton and Portland: Sussex Academic Press, 2010.

Packer, Randall and Jordan, Ken. *Multimedia: from Wagner to virtual reality.* New York-London: Norton & Company, 2001.

Perloff, Marjorie. "Screening the Page/Paging the Screen: Digital Poetics and the Differential Text". *New Media Poetics. Contexts, technotexts and theories.* Ed(s). Adelaide Morris and Thomas Swiss. Cambridge, Massachusetts and London: MIT Press, 2006. 143-162.

Rainey, Lawrence; Poggy, Christine; Wittman, Laura (Eds.) *Futurist Manifesto's. Futurism: an anthology.* New Haven: Yale University Press, 2009.

Ryan, Marie-Laure. ""Net.art: Dysfunctionality as Self-Reflexivity". *Between Page and Screen. Remaking Literature Through Cinema and*

Cyberspace. Kiene Brillenburg Wurth (Ed.). New York: Fordham University Press, 2012. 127-143.

Ryan, Marie-Laure. *Cyberspace Textuality: Computer Technology and Literary Theory.* Bloomington and Indianapolis: Indiana University Press, 1999.

Sándor, Katalin. "Moving (the) Text: From Print to Digital". *Between Page and Screen. Remaking Literature Through Cinema and Cyberspace.* Kiene Brillenburg Wurth (Ed.). New York: Fordham University Press, 2012. 144-156.

Strauven, Wanda. *Marinetti e il cinema. Tra attrazione e sperimentazione.* Pasian di Prato: Campanotto Editore, 2006.

Thorburn, David and Jenkins, Henry. "Introduction: Toward an Aesthetics of Transition". *Rethinking media change: the aesthetics of transition.* Ed(s). David Thorburn and Henry Jenkins. Cambridge, Massachusetts: MIT Press, 2003. 1-16.

Verdone, Mario. *Ginna e Corra. Cinema e letteratura del futurismo.* Edizioni Bianco e Nero: Roma, 1967.

Waber, Dan. *Strings.* <http://www.vispo.com/guests/DanWaber/haha.htm> 1999. Accessed 14 July 2015.

Weibel, Peter. "The post-media condition". *La condición postmedia.* VV.AA. Madrid: Centro Cultural Conde Duque, 2006. 90-100.

Wolf, Werner. *The musicalization of fiction: a study in the theory and history of intermediality.* Amsterdam-Atlanta, GA: Rodopi, 1999.

AUTHOR'S PROFILE

Dr. Carolina Fernández Castrillo is Associate Professor of Media Studies & Digital Culture at Madrid Open University and Guest Professor in the Master in Visual and Digital Media at IE School of Communication. She obtained her PhD with distinction at Sapienza University of Rome and Complutense University of Madrid (European Doctorate Mention, Extraordinary Doctoral Award and Best PhD Royal Complutense College at Harvard University). She has been lecturer at both universities and visiting researcher at ZKM Center of Art and Media Karlsruhe and Bayreuth University (both in Germany), Yale University (USA) and Utrecht University (Netherlands). She is the author of several publications and invited lectures in international seminars and conferences on Transmedia Storytelling, Media Archaeology and Web Culture. As invited editor, she has recently coordinated the special issue on Media Art: Art, Science and Technology of Icono14. Journal of Communication and Emergent Technologies.

CHAPTER 19

Digital Textuality and its Behaviors

Leonardo Flores

Electronic literature is a set of experimental practices that explore the capabilities of the stand-alone or networked computer as a medium for creation, production, and reception of literary works. If translated to different media, say by printing them out, they might lose the extra-textual elements that I describe as 'behavior'. These textual behaviors are programmed instructions that cause the text to be still, move, respond to user input, change, act on a schedule, or include a sound component. The elaborate terminology we can use to describe the materiality of print texts, with all their graphical, bibliographical, and linguistic codes is available and useful to apply to electronic texts displayed on a screen, but it would be incomplete without a discussion of its programmed characteristics. For example, a poet writing for print media must think about word selection (with semantic and phonetic considerations), sequence (morphological and syntactical considerations), and appearance (including graphical and bibliographical codes). A poet writing for electronic media must add interface (a mechanism for traversing the text) and behavior (what the words do and under what conditions) to all the previous considerations.

Reading is a skill; something we learn as children and become increasingly proficient at through learning and practice. Since most of the literacy training we receive is through print media—books, newspapers, magazines, journals, and so on—its conventions and technologies have become deeply ingrained in our reading practices, and we are rarely aware of them. For instance, we don't have to think consciously of turning pages, determining which word to read next, or that we are beginning a new sentence. Some print works challenge these conventions, forcing us to reexamine our reading practices, but they constitute a small portion of the works we read in print.

We are also used to reading on screens, be they movie theater, television, computer, smartphone, or tablet screens. When watching subtitled films, for instance, we are basically reading text that operates in a strict schedule: it needs to follow the pace of dialogue. In television news programs, we have screens loaded with text that is constantly changing, whether appearing or disappearing on or scrolling in the bottom of the screen. Video games tend to work more with images than language, but these images are charged with information which must be identified and interpreted (or read) by the player. Successful players are necessarily good readers of not just visual and aural information, but also of the program's responses to their actions.

Most documents that we read on a computer screen follow print conventions while adding a few of their own, such as the incorporation of links, and using hypertext for organization. These are rarely problematic, but when we encounter e-poetry or other first generation electronic objects—"a class of artifacts that have no material existence outside of computational file systems" (Kirschenbaum "Materiality" 2001)—our traditional reading skills are insufficient. Our training in reading print does not account for words that move and form new textual combinations, nor does it teach us to explore the textual surface with the mouse to reveal hidden elements, for instance. Readers are often disconcerted by a text that imposes a reading schedule, or texts that are impossible to reread because they change every time they are accessed. So how do we read the dancing signifier?

I have already suggested that when language is inscribed in programmable media such as a computer it can be described in terms of linguistics, appearance, and behavior. Since our reading skills have prepared us to see through the appearance of texts to reach a linguistic meaning, but not to deal with texts that exhibit behavior, I propose a typology that describes six behavioral characteristics: static, kinetic, responsive, mutable, scheduled, and/or aural. The ability to identify and account for the signifying strategies of these behaviors allows for more sophisticated readings of e-poetry and by consequence e-texts in general.

But before discussing the typology itself, I must pause to explain my decision to describe this textual characteristic as 'behavior', unpacking some of the connotations and denotations that load the term beyond the scope I am using. Let's take as a point of departure a dictionary definition of the term:

1) a: the manner of conducting oneself b: anything that an organism does involving action and response to stimulation c: the response of an individual, group, or species to its environment.
2) the way in which someone behaves; also: an instance of such behavior.
3) the way in which something functions or operates. (Behavior)

It becomes apparent that the term is closely associated with the actions of living organisms, and only in its third definition describes inanimate objects. This is not accidental: the term 'behaviour' has not been used to describe such objects for long, not since 1943, when Arturo Rosenblueth, Norbert Wiener and Julian Bigelow published an essay titled "Behavior, Purpose, and Teleology" where they defined it as: "any change of an entity with respect to its surroundings. This change may be largely an output from the object, the input being then minimal, remote or irrelevant; or else the change may be immediately traceable to a certain input. Accordingly, any modification of an object, detectable externally, may be denoted as behaviour." (1943: 18)

Of interest in their definition is how broad its scope is, including living organisms or inanimate objects, and how it focuses on externally detectable changes. N. Katherine Hayles points out that this approach is "relatively unconcerned with internal structure" and that it leads to "'black box' engineering, in which one assumes that the organism is a 'black box' whose contents are unknown. Producing equivalent behavior, then, counts as producing an equivalent system." (How we became posthuman 1999: 94) She argues that it is not a neutral term and that the attempts to apply it to machines have been ideologically motivated to "elide the very real differences existing between the internal structure of organisms and that of machines" (How we became posthuman 1999: 94). As part of her discussion, Hayles asserts that Richard Taylor, a philosopher who challenged Norbert Weiner's definition of behavior and purpose, "sensed that behavior had been defined so as to allow intention and desire to be imputed to machines" (How we became posthuman 1999: 97). These are all considerable problems with the term behavior, and should be addressed in order to justify its usefulness as a methodology.

First of all, do machines have intentions and desires? In a conversation with French semiotician Philippe Bootz during the E-Poetry 2001 conference, he said that animation is the symbolic presence of the author in the text, and the cursor is the symbolic presence of the reader. I see these presences as the intentions and desires that fuel the behavior of e-texts, which are encoded into the source document that is executed by a computer. The computer orchestrates all these instructions in its processes, prioritizing some and overriding others so what emerges is its behavior, which in turn responds to a whole complex matrix of intentions and desires—the writer's, reader's and everyone else's who contributed to the workings of a computer. So computers have intentions and desires encoded within them, and their external behaviors may be interpreted as expressions of those intentions.

The typology of behavior I will now discuss provides a critical vocabulary to describe this feature of electronic texts. It is a brief list of characteristics which I have observed in e-poetry, along with some basic subcategories, that should describe a wide range of behaviors programmable into electronic texts. One could think of this as a taxonomy, which can be used to tag different textual behaviors within an electronic text.

- Static texts are the default we're used to in print—they are texts that do not move or change on the screen.
- Scheduled texts may reveal themselves over time, which may be linear or looped; they may force a rate of reading by disappearing or scrolling; they may also trigger events over a programmed or random schedule.
- Kinetic texts move on the screen: this motion may be looped or linear, random, programmed, or responding to cues from the reader.
- Responsive texts take advantage of the computers' interface devices (most commonly the mouse and keyboard) to create a feedback loop between the reader and the text.
- Mutable texts involve programmed or random changes or may be generated on the fly.
- Aural texts have a sound component: verbal, musical, or simply noise.

These categories are not by themselves unique to electronic media, nor are they mutually exclusive. They are often found in combination and in some cases they are inseparable—aural and kinetic texts are always scheduled, for instance. The next few sections will provide a brief genealogy of each behavior and discuss some of their subcategories, and implications as outlined above, providing examples from a variety of e-poems.

STATIC TEXTS

When we think about words in a document, we assume that they remain still so we can read them. We also assume that they will remain the same, so we can reread them if necessary. Motion and mutability are not characteristics we ordinarily attribute to words because the materials on which they have been inscribed don't usually allow for such changes. Static texts are so ubiquitous that traditional definitions of text are based upon this behavior, or lack thereof. In Scholarly Editing in the Computer Age, Peter Shillingsburg defines text as "the actual order of words and punctuation as contained in any one physical form, such as manuscript, proof, or book" (1996: 46). This notion of text arises from a centuries old relationship between alphabetic technologies and the media in which they have been recorded. In simpler terms, documents have been produced in stone, clay, papyrus, vellum, wood, paper, and other materials that lend physical stability to the inscriptions they carry. The words etched, inked, penciled, or glued onto those surfaces are not likely to move from where they are placed, and any motion of these depend on the manipulation of the materials they are placed upon. They are also not likely to change, even though they may be interpreted differently by readers. Therefore, in any given document, the text is defined by the design and stability of the materials in which it is inscribed.

The moment words start to appear on screens, the static default becomes simply another option available for their display because we are dealing with time-based media that can display moving images. So even if the text displayed is perceived as static it is being constantly redrawn many times per second. As Hayles explains, "when a text presents itself as a constantly refreshed image rather than as a durable inscription, transformations can occur that would be unthinkable if matter or energy, rather than informational patterns, formed the primary basis for the systemic exchanges." (How we became posthuman 1999: 30)

Some of the transformations occur at the level of textual behavior, but they can also be changes in the appearance of the text, or even linguistic information of the text. More importantly, these transformations are possible because texts in digital media are informational patterns which are subject to manipulation and reconfiguration in computers. This is obvious to anyone who can use a word processing program to modify a word's font, size, color, emphasis, spacing, indentation, and many other of its visual characteristics. What isn't obvious to many users is that we are changing the word's informational pattern in ways that the computer can recognize and reconstruct and that this pattern is particular, not universal. A different piece of software or computer may not recognize the pattern in the same way or may not have the font available, and it will interpret the information as it is able, reshaping the information pattern to conform to its capabilities. Therefore, static texts in digital media are not stationary objects in repose: they are informational patterns processed and constantly inscribed on a computer screen.

Purely static texts in electronic media can be similar to texts in print, especially when there is "remediation" at work—a term coined by Jay David Bolter and Richard Grusin to describe "the representation of one medium in another" (Remediation 2000: 45) —such as the representation of print in digital media. However, since the computer is such a powerful simulation tool and can be used to create writing environments for texts to inhabit such as hypertext, three-dimensional spaces, and other designed characteristics of a digital writing environment, the texts may require elaborate navigation or manipulation to read them. For example, Jason Nelson's "Birds Still Warm From Flying" requires readers to manipulate a virtual cube to read the texts arranged on all its sides, and create new combinations of its lines.

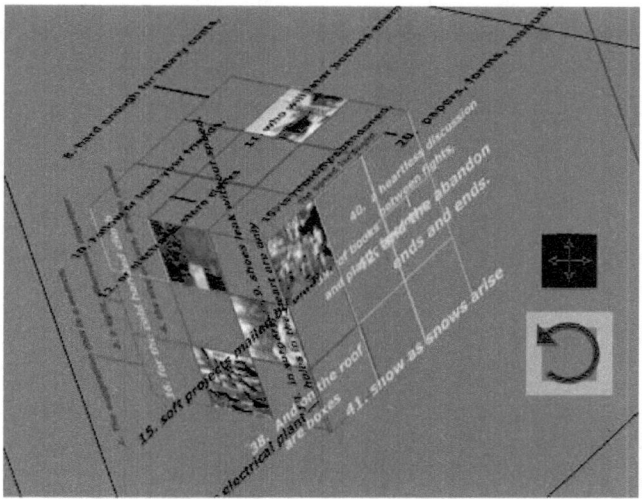

"Birds Still Warm from Flying" by Jason Nelson

Stasis is the most common text behavior in electronic media, but that doesn't make it any less of a behavior than the others. The specter of possibility haunts texts in digital media, because we cannot trust that what we see is what we get, what conditions might change over time or through interaction.

SCHEDULED TEXTS

Because computers are time-based in their operation, the texts they process have the capacity to be scheduled. Texts with this behavior are either finite or open-ended. If finite, they can be described in terms of duration—whether they are linear or looped. The events triggered in the scheduled text can be described as singular or recurrent. If recurrent, we can describe them in terms of frequency of their recurrence. A key concept here is the event—an action that changes the state of the electronic object, triggered by a preprogrammed schedule or user input. An example of a schedule-driven event is when a computer goes into sleep mode after a predetermined period of inactivity.

These subcategories become more complex in combination with other behaviors, such as mutability and responsiveness, because the scheduling can be random, variable, or affected by the user. Scheduling texts can have several implications as illustrated by three examples:

A basic feature of print texts is that the reader controls the reading rate. Scheduled texts take control of that reading rate over part or all of the work. A good example of this behavior is evident in the works produced by Young-Hae Chang's Heavy Industries which displays one phrase, word, letter, or line at a time synchronized to the musical soundtrack—resulting in a text that plays like a film and demands the reader's unflinching attention for the duration of the work. The text unfolds in a linear fashion, and cannot be stopped or reversed once activated.

**WE SWUNG
INTØ THE
PARKING LØT**

"Dakota" by Young Hae-Chang Heavy Industries

When scheduled e-texts are looped they provide the opportunity of re-reading the sequence that has occurred. Brief loops do not give the impression of scheduled operation, because they present multiple opportunities for re-reading, as is the case of the minimalist animation in Ana María Uribe's "Gimnasia 3" which alternates a cluster of letters P and R in a looped to create the ilusion of an orderly group of letters exercising by lifting and lowering a leg.

Two frames in Ana María Uribe's "Gimnasia 3"

A schedule can also offer recurring events on specific time intervals, such as the 10-second intervals between textual re-configurations in "White-Faced Bromeliads on 20 Hectares" by Loss Pequeño Glazier, or the multiple marquee delays which cause lines to appear and disappear at different rates in "Larvatus Prodeo" by Braxton Soderman and Roxanne Carter.

There is very little scholarship done on scheduling of texts, an area that merits further exploration. Some related fields that may provide fruitful information are studies on reception of oral language and recorded texts, such as audiobooks, and studies of subtitles, captioning, and other uses of language in time-based visual media, such as film and video.

KINETIC TEXTS

The moving image moves. But where does that movement come from? For a certain approach in art history, an image is a discrete, whole entity. To move from one image to another is already an immense wrench: even the analysis of a diptych is wildly complex. What then is it to speak of "a" moving image, constructed from thousands of constituent images? In what sense is it an image? Cinematic movement is a fundamental challenge to the concept of wholeness and integrity, its becoming a test of the primacy of existence. In particular, it raises the question of temporality: when is the object of cinema? When, indeed, is the moving image? (The Cinema Effect 2004: 5)

This excerpt from the introduction to Sean Cubitt's book The Cinema Effect asks a relevant and provocative question about the ontology of the moving image which I will adapt to the discussion of kinetic texts. To what extent can a word in motion be considered a single signifier? More importantly, how does the shifting position of a word in motion reconfigure its relation to other linguistic, graphical and behavioral elements in ways that affect its meaning?

The singularity of the rendered electronic image is a perceptual event, whether it is still or in motion, because it is drawn and redrawn many times per second in order for humans to achieve persistence of vision. As computer graphics, however, these electronic objects can be multiple or singular, depending upon whether they are vector or raster graphics. Any change in a raster graphic modifies its composition as a numerical object, whereas the formulas that create the vector graphic can have movement programmed into them, as is the case with Flash animation. For the sake of convenience, I will take the computer science approach of "object-oriented programming" to treat all kinetic texts as singular objects because it is more flexible towards incorporating other behaviors, even if they are composed of multiple frames.

The primary theoretical approaches towards computer animation comes from cinema—and appropriately so. In The Language of New Media, Lev Manovich uses "the theory and history of cinema as the key conceptual lens through which I look at new media." (2002: 9) His exploration goes in both directions, however, seeing also how digital media and their capabilities transform cinema, a deep study on how the history of cinema informs and helps us understand new media work. However, its focus falls more on characteristics of new media, imagery and visual narrative rather than on written language and its signifying potential when placed in motion. John Cayley sets out to rectify this need in "Bass Resonance," an essay that explores the cinematic history of words in motion, focusing on the work of Saul Bass—a man famous in film history for his animated title sequences at the beginning of films like Anatomy of a Murder (1959), North by Northwest (1959) and Goodfellas (1990). This brief essay describes some of the effects of Bass' dancing words, aligning his practice and much of the practices of e-poetries with Concrete poetics. Both studies place kinetic texts and images in digital media in historical, cultural, and cinematic contexts, yet their interest isn't with the complexities of textuality in motion and their implications for poetic practice.

An essay that takes an important step in that direction is "The Software Word: Digital Poetry as New Media-Based Language Art" by Janez Strehovec. This essay focuses on the aesthetics and cultural space that digital poetry is establishing for itself—one that moves away from the "lyrical and 'projective saying'" (2004: 143) and even beyond remediation of print poetic traditions (2004: 145). More importantly, he asserts that "words inside textscapes are words-images-virtual bodies; they are self contained signifiers which must be perceived not only considering their semantic function but also their visual appearance as well as their position and their motion in space." (2004: 149) Strehovec is accurate when discussing digital poetry and its aesthetic function, yet his discussion of kinetic texts is insufficient. Like Manovich, he argues that kinetic texts basically operate on the concept of the loop. This is a weakness in their argument because they are privileging one of several control flow statement types, roughly categorized as follows:

- continuation at a different statement (jump),
- executing a set of statements only if some condition is met (choice),
- executing a set of statements repeatedly (loop),
- executing a set of distant statements, after which the flow of control returns (subroutine),
- stopping the program, preventing any further execution (halt) (Wikipedia Contributors, "Control Flow").

These control flow statement types are what make all the textual behaviors possible and make animation in digital media so unique, since it is able to incorporate other elements discussed in this typology, such as responsiveness, mutability, and scheduled operation. Let us explore further some of the potential and implication for kinetic texts.

Time in an animation may be finite, looped, or open-ended. Finite kinetic texts have a clear beginning and ending. For the reader to re-experience the animation, they may have to reload the text and experience it again from the beginning. Brian Kim Stephans' "The Dreamlife of Letters," for example, is a long kinetic e-poem that unfolds without allowing readers to pause, "rewind," or skip through the text. Looped animation allows the reader to re-read the kinetic text when it cycles through. Sometimes the loop can blur the sense of a beginning and end for it. For example "Ah" by K. Michel and Dirk Vis creates a stream-of-consciousness effect by the moving of words at different speeds flowing from right to left on the screen.

K. Michel and Dirk Vis "Ah"

In Jim Andrews' "Seattle Drift" words are left adrift and readers have to chase after them until the screen is left blank. There is an option to stop the text from drifting, and to even 'discipline' it back into its original configuration, but the drift cannot be reversed nor repeated once it starts because it is semi-randomly determined.

Word motion can affect reading in several ways. It blurs the line between reading and looking, especially when motion serves as an obstacle to reading. The reader may see texts in motion and not have the time to recognize them, in which case, the words are perceived more as objects than as signifiers. This foregrounds the graphical aspect of the text, reducing the impact of the semantic codes in the document. In Jim Andrews' videogame poem "Arteroids," words and lines of verse move on the screen and chase the player's word ('desire' below) at increasing speeds, until the reader's interaction focuses increasingly on shooting and avoiding collision with the texts rather than reading them.

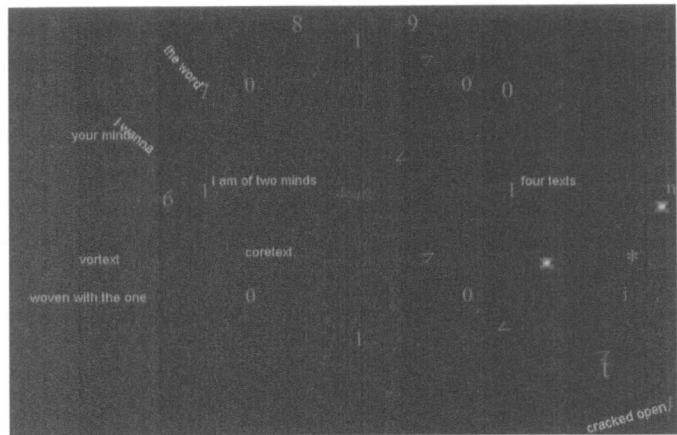

Jim Andrews' "Arteroids" (play mode level 161)

It may reconfigure the word order, producing different phrases and meanings. This is evident in a work like "Slipping Glimpse" by Stephanie Strickland, Cynthia Lawson Jaramillo, and Paul Ryan in which lines and words drift to form new textual combinations, and the potential for multiple readings, for example water movement below:

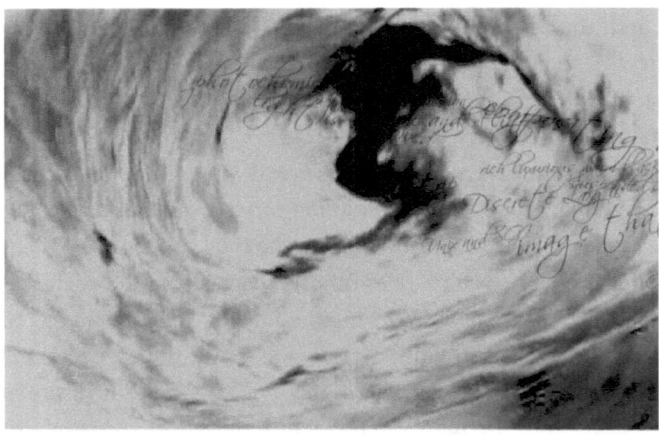

Stephanie Strickland, Cynthia Lawson Jaramillo, and Paul Ryan "Slipping Glimpse"

Works like "The Dreamlife of Letters"by Brian Kim Stefans create a grammar of motion by grouping words with the same or similar movement. For instance, in the section from "dread to drip" the words "read" and "ream" are alternated in an 11-word semicircle which moves by the stationary letter "d" to form the words "dread" and "dream," after which the solitary letter "d" drops from the center of the screen to fall by the suddenly appearing word "rip," forming the word "drip" for a brief moment. All the words in this section of the poem share the same letter "d." The visual organization of the alternated words ream and read cascading in their curve from top to bottom of the screen to form dream and dread highlight the relationship between both pairs of words: what is the relation between dreading to dream and reading a ream of paper, or perhaps reading is like reaming juice out of a fruit? What is the relation between the liquid action of dripping and the very solid action of ripping? The juxtaposition of these words is brought about through patterned motion.

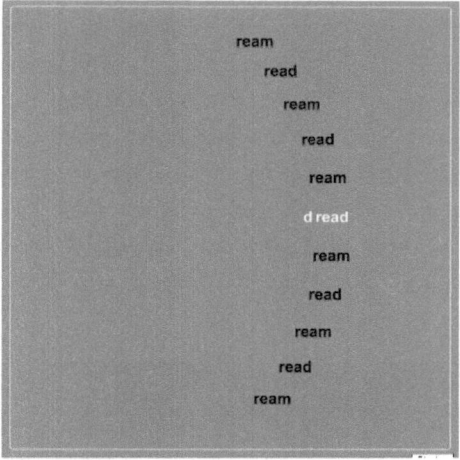

Brian Kim Stefans's "he Dreamlife of Letters"

There is much more to explore on the implications and effects of motion in texts, an endeavor undertaken by Alexandra Saemmer, who explores the "animated metaphor" in her 2007 book Matières textuelles sur support numérique and in other publications and presentations.

RESPONSIVE TEXTS

I have chosen to describe these texts as 'responsive' rather than 'interactive' because the latter term has generated some controversy in its previous uses. This arises from the fact that all texts are interactive, because to read is to interact with the graphical and semantic codes contained within a document to generate meaning. There is also interaction with the physical document in which the text resides, such as page turning and other physical manipulations, in the case of printed texts. The responsive texts I refer to, however, take advantage of the computers' interface devices to allow for input from the reader (such as mouse, keyboard, and touchscreen).

The distinctive feature for responsive electronic texts is the presence of a feedback loop that takes into account the reader's input and responds according to its programmed instructions. By 'input' here, I do not refer to the mental interaction that is always supplied by readers, as described by Wolfgang Iser's reader's response theories, but to options programmed into the text by the author for the reader to trigger. These input cues (such as links, hotspots, cursor movement, keyboard entries, or others) may be manifest or hidden, allow for voluntary or involuntary interaction, and have immediate or delayed reactions.

Manifest input cues find their clearest example in the traditional underlined link that is such a staple of hypertext. In general, manifest cues are invitations for input, be it as simple as a clicking on a link or entering text into a box. Hidden input cues are also an invitation to interaction, but of the exploratory kind. They challenge the reader to discover aspects of the text not apparent to the naked eye, by using the tools at their disposal, most commonly the mouse. The mouseover function, for instance, reveals hotspots and may trigger responses from the text, as in Andy Campbell's "Dim O'Gauble" where arrows guide navigation and hidden hotspots.

Andy Campbell's "Dim O'Gauble"

Voluntary triggering of responsiveness is the most common, and perhaps the friendliest towards the reader. The reader chooses to activate hotspots or links. Involuntary triggers, however, present interesting possibilities. For instance, to have links or hotspots activated by a mouseover, not a click of the mouse, and to have these cues hidden can create a sense of being trapped in an environment, in which any movement of the cursor can set off effects beyond his/her control.

Most of the reactions of responsive texts are immediate, creating a fairly direct correlation between action and reaction. There is a sense of discovery whenever a reader activates an input cue, particularly the first time a responsive e-text is read. Delayed responses from activated input cues blur the correlation between action and reaction. This is one of the most important devices for Philippe Bootz's e-poem "Passage" because it reinforces the 'unique-reading' experience of the poem. This poem in three movements allows for interactivity during the second one, but its input cues are hidden and its reactions postponed as the input gathered by the program during this movement is then used to generate the third, which is necessarily different every time it is read, partly due to the programming, partly because of the variations in interaction.

All texts are responsive and interactive, irrespective of the media they inhabit, because they are machines for signification. The act of reading is by definition a dynamic interaction with the document that holds the text: and different writers will place different demands upon the reader and offer different cues for such interactivity. Electronic texts externalize aspects of this interactivity by scripting the reader's function in a work, creating interfaces for the interaction to occur, and incorporating data collected through the computer's hardware devices.

It is worth noting that I use the term 'computer' in the broadest sense possible, including gaming consoles, touchscreen devices, mobile phones, and installations that include processors, programming, and any input or output devices. The crucial point is that the reader's symbolic presence and actions are read by the e-texts themselves, which as electronic objects have built in variables and responses informed by those events. And that presence can be established through GPS, accelerometers, microphones, cameras, gyroscopes, compasses, pressure sensors in shoes, touchscreens, keyboards, mice, touchpads, or any other kind of peripheral device and represented in the text.The extent to which a text can be changed by interaction can be best described in the next element of the typology: mutability.

Mutable Texts

Mutable texts incorporate deliberate variation into their design, making rereading the same text difficult, if not impossible. Mutable texts involve programmed, random, or user-defined changes in the document. Mutability is not a distinctive feature of electronic texts. Works like Cent Mille Milliards de Poemes by Raymond Queneau use the book as a machine (and the reader as engine) to create

100,000,000,000,000 possible sonnets. This is a sonnet in which each page is cut under each of its 14 lines, so the reader can open each line on any of 10 pages, thus creating 1014 possible combinations. And yet, the work as a book is present to the reader, who can make choices based on page numbers and lines. Nothing is hidden, and while the potential line combinations are enormous, the fact remains that the individual lines will not change from what they are.

Loss Pequeño Glazier's e-poem "White-Faced Bromeliads on 20 Hectares" exhibits some significant differences from Queneau's, particularly regarding issues of user access and control, as described in "Reading Notes:"

> Instructions: Allow this page to cycle for a while so you can take in some of the images and variant titles. When you are ready, press "begin". Once there, read each page slowly, even aloud, watching as each line periodically re-constitutes itself re-generating randomly selected lines with that line's variant. Eight-line poems have 256 possible versions; nine-line poems have 512 possible versions. (n/p)

While it too has a finite number of variants, their access is not user-defined, and the variables are hidden from the reader. It also operates on a schedule, changing the displayed text every 10 seconds. Thus, the reader doesn't have: 1) control over the changes, 2) the ability to reread the same text, unless it is through printing out a given version, or capturing the image of one of the displayed documents, 3) access to the variants. The mutability is very much a part of this text: it shifts during the reading, encouraging the reader to reread read backwards, start over and over, attempting to make sense of this textual moving target. My article "A Shifting Electronic Text: Close Reading 'White-Faced Bromeliads on 20 Hectares'" elaborates on the challenge of reading this text and provides strategies for approaching it.

The difference between these two works goes deeper than their relation to the user/reader: they represent the paradigm shift from floating signifiers to flickering signifiers. According to N. Katherine Hayles in "Virtual Bodies and Flickering Signifiers" (2002), the floating signifier embodies the dialectic between presence and absence, while the flickering signifier shifts to a dialectic based on pattern and randomness. Each page/line of Queneau's book/poem represents a choice for the reader: what lines become present and which lines are absent. Glazier's e-poem has built in randomness, yet it is structured enough that a pattern emerges from the flickering lines of his poem.

Espen Aarseth coined two neologisms in Cybertext which become useful for the discussion of mutable texts: scriptons and textons. Scriptons are "strings [of signs] as they appear to readers," and textons are "strings as they exist in the text"

(1997: 62). Aarseth describes Queneau's Cent mille milliards de poemes as containing 140 textons that can combine to produce 100,000,000,000,000 possible scriptons (1997: 62). Aarseth goes on to develop a typology of "modes of traversal" of cybertexts: a useful one to show the similarities between print and electronic works that require the reader to spend "non-trivial effort" in their traversal.

A similar calculation could be applied to Glazier's "White-Faced Bromeliads," with a significant difference: that the possibilities are part of the text, but the reader is presented with only a fraction of these. In works such as "Passage," by Philippe Bootz, the program guarantees that you will never see exactly the same scripton, no matter how many times you reread the poem.

The two main sources of mutability are defined by the programmer or the user. Programmed mutable e-texts have changes that result from authorial planning, whether it is to include random elements into the generation of scriptons, or whether these occur in a schedule, or through randomized animation. User-defined mutability results from the intersection of responsiveness and the programmed nature of the e-text. The difference between merely responsive e-texts and mutable responsive e-texts is that the changes in the text are at least partly dependent upon the reader/user's input. In a mutable e-poem such as "Passage" by Philippe Bootz, the reader's input during the second movement is essential to the changes that manifest themselves in the third movement of the poem. Different users, and repeated reading performances of the entire work by the same user, will necessarily produce different interactions, which will result in a newly configured third movement of the poem.

Mutability is necessarily a general category, but a significant one because it literalizes the textual instability present in all texts, whether in print or in electronic media. The changes take place as part of the production history of the material text that may or may not include interventions by the reader. Some change—however minuscule—is possible in any electronic text, as was discussed in the introductory chapter, but in mutable e-texts this happens to an even greater degree, and as part of the design of the poem.

AURAL TEXTS

Poets have used writing as a recording medium for centuries by translating the sounds of poetry into alphabetic scores for oral reconstruction—just as composers have written musical scores on sheets of paper for subsequent musical reinterpretation. In poetry, sounds and units of breath become space: lines, stanzas, punctuation, spaces between words, formatting, and other visual markers become part of what readers learn to interpret in order to come up with to provide an oral rendition. The use of writing, however, led many poets to explore the expressive potential of writing in and of itself, leading to the visual Concrete Poetry movement.

The rise of sound recording technologies allowed for poets to explore the aural element of language beyond the limitations of the writing and oral reconstruction model. These technologies are fairly new and have therefore accrued a smaller body of work—and market—than print. For the most part, sound recording technologies have been used to record poets reading their work: serving as an archive of authorial interpretations of the written poems. However, the Concrete Poetry movement also explored sound as a means in and of itself using the sounds of language beyond the traditional constraints, such as using words. Poets like Paul de Vree and Henri Chopin experimented with recording technologies to mix sounds, voices, and sound effects, creating sound poems that could only exist as recordings. This is yet another example of how production, storage and dissemination technologies have an impact on poetry, at times transforming it into something not witnessed before.

Computers have become increasingly apt for multimedia compositions, particularly since most come equipped with sound cards and speakers enabling writers to explore the potential of adding a sound component to their texts. Writers like Jim Andrews and Jörg Piringer take the exploration a step further by creating works of interactive music, such as "Nio" and "ABCDEFGHIJKLMNOPQRSTUVWXYZ," respectively.

So what are some possibilities for the use of sound in e-poetry? There are several different types of sound recordings possible for use with e-poems. Some kinetic works attach noises to the movements of the words on the screen. For instance, "Faith" by Robert Kendall has the word "logic" fall on and bounce off of the word "Faith," making a clinking sound when they make contact. This reinforces the illusion of solidity of the words—yet playing on their meanings at the same time.

"Faith" by Robert Kendall

Ambient sounds can also communicate volumes, such as establishing a situation or setting. Katharine Norman's award winning poem "Window" powerfully evokes a sense of place by providing year-round sound clips of natural and domestic sounds recorded from the liminal space of a window in an upstairs room of a house (see figure 10).

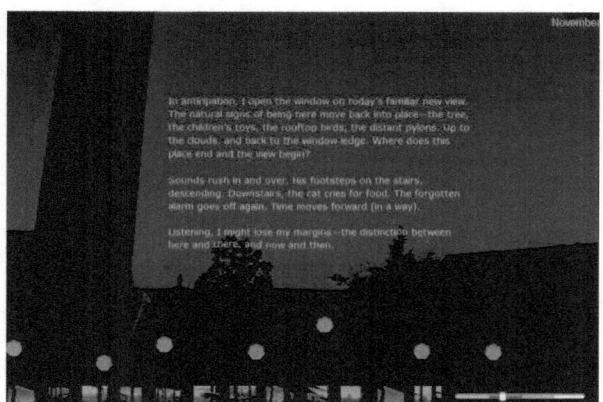

"Window" by Katharine Norman

Young Hae Chang Heavy Industries, an artistic duo based in South Korea, have become well-known for synchonizing poetic texts to jazz and other kinds of music. Examples abound of the use of music in works of electronic literature, though one might be hard-pressed to find more varied incorporations of music and audio than in Alan Bigelow's Webyarns, his collection of poetic stories for the Web. Sound is one of many media integrated in his work.

Readers need to become careful listeners when part of the text are presented aurally—at least if they want to get the whole text. David Knoebel makes clever use of overlaying verbal and visual text in "Thoughts Go," leading readers to decide what text they will devote their attention to since given the difficulty of simultaneously apprehending two different texts.

At times the audible text is the same as the readable component, adding information such as tone, volume, and paucity clearer. This can be seen quite dramatically in María Mencía's "Birds Singing Other Birds' Songs" in which voice recordings reading transcribed birdsongs accompany kinetic visual poems in the shape of flying birds.

"Birds Singing Other Birds' Songs" by Maria Mencía

I believe that the computer, and by extension poetry native to it, is a mostly visual medium that is slowly incorporating sound into its workings. Most navigation and interactivity, for instance, occurs through visual and not aural cues. I also believe that the use of aural elements figures prominently in the future of e-poetry, because the silence associated with reading is linked to print technologies. While it is true that texts speak when they are read (whether aloud or silently) on the page, it is thanks to screens and speakers that they have literally begun to dance and sing.

To conclude, it is important to pay attention to these diverse textual behaviors when reading electronic literature. I recommend considering the impact of a given behavior or group of behaviors in the text as part of a work's signifying strategies. For examples of textual behaviors integrated into analyses of works of e-poetry, read my research and visit my scholarly blogging project, I ♥ E-Poetry.

REFERENCES

Aarseth, Espen J. *Cybertext: perspectives on ergodic literature.* Johns Hopkins University Press, 1997.

Andrews, Jim. "Arteroids." *Vispo.com.* 2001-2004. URL: http://vispo.com/arteroids/

--. "Nio" *Electronic Literature Collection, Volume 1.* 2001. URL: http://collection.eliterature.org/1/works/andrews__nio.html

--. "Seattle Drift." *Vispo.com.* 1997. URL: http://vispo.com/animisms/SeattleDrift.html

"Behavior." *Merriam-Webster Online Dictionary.* 2013.

Bigelow, Alan. *Webyarns*. URL: http://www.webyarns.com
Bolter, Jay David and Richard Grusin, *Remediation: Understanding New Media*. Cambridge, MA: The MIT Press, 2000.
Bootz, Philippe. "Passage" *Alire* 11. 1998. CD-Rom.
--. "The Functional Point of View: New Artistic Forms for Programmed Literary Works," *Leonardo*, 32:4, 1999.
Campbell, Andy. "Dim O'Gauble." *Dreaming Methods*. 2007. URL: http://www.dreamingmethods.com/dimogauble/
Cayley, John. "Bass Resonance." *Electronic Book Review*. 11 May 2005.
Cubitt, Sean. *The Cinema Effect*. Cambridge, Mass: The MIT Press, 2004.
Flores, Leonardo. "A Shifting Electronic Text: Close Reading *White-Faced Bromeliads on 20 Hectares*" *Emerging Language Practices 2*. 2012. URL: http://epc.buffalo.edu/ezines/elp/02/Flores-Bromeliads.pdf
--. *I ♥ E-Poetry*. Blog. December 19, 2011 to present. URL: http://leonardoflores.net
--. "Typing the Dancing Signifier: Jim Andrews' (Vis) Poetics." Dissertation. University of Maryland. 2010.
Glazier. "White-Faced Bromeliads on 20 Hectares." *Electronic Literature Collection, Volume 1*. 1999. URL: http://collection.eliterature.org/1/works/glazier__white-faced_bromeliads_on_20_hectares.html
Hayles, N. Katherine. *How we became posthuman: Virtual bodies in cybernetics, literature, and informatics*. University of Chicago Press, 1999.
--. "Virtual Bodies and Flickering Signifiers," in Mirzoeff, Nicholas (ed. and introd.); The Visual Culture Reader. London, England; Routledge; 2002.
Kendall, Robert. "Faith." *Electronic Literature Collection, Volume 1*. 2002. URL: http://collection.eliterature.org/1/works/kendall__faith.html
Kirschenbaum, Matthew. "Machine Visions: Towards a Poetics of Artificial Intelligence" *Electronic Book Review* 6, Winter 97/98.
--. "Materiality and Matter and Stuff: What Electronic Texts Are Made Of." *Electronic Book Review* 12, Fall 2001.
Knoebel, David. "Thoughts Go." *Click Poetry*. 2001. URL: http://home.ptd.net/~clkpoet/thoughts/index.html
Manovich, Lev. *The language of new media*. MIT press, 2002.
Mencía, María. "Birds Singing Other Birds'Songs." *Electronic Literature Collection, Volume 1*. 2001. URL:

http://collection.eliterature.org/1/works/mencia__birds_singing_other_birds_songs.html

Michel K. and Dirk Vis. "Ah" *The Electronic Literature Collection, Volume 2.* 2008. URL: http://collection.eliterature.org/2/works/michel_ah.html

Nelson, Jason. "Birds Still Warm From Flying" *Secret Technology.* 2010. URL: http://www.secrettechnology.com/ausco/poecubic2.html

Norman, Katharine. "Window." *Novamara.* 2012. URL: http://www.novamara.com/window/

Piringer, Jörg. "abcdefghijklmnopqrstuvwxyz," iTunes Store. 2010. URL: http://joerg.piringer.net/index.php?href=abcdefg/abcdefg.xml

Queneau, Raymond, and François Le Lionnais. *Cent mille milliards de poèmes.* Gallimard, 1982.

Rosenblueth, Arturo, Norbert Wiener, and Julian Bigelow. "Behavior, purpose and teleology." *Philosophy of science* (1943): 18-24.

Saemmer, Alexandra. *Matières textuelles sur support numérique.* Publications de Université de Saint-Etienne, CIEREC 2007

Shillingsburg, Peter L. *Scholarly editing in the computer age: Theory and practice.* University of Michigan Press, 1996.

Soderman, Braxton and Roxanne Carter. "Larvatus Prodeo" *Persephassa.* 2006. URL: http://persephassa.com/etext/valence.html

Stefans, Brian Kim. "The Dreamlife of Letters." *Electronic Literature Collection, Volume 1.* 2000. URL:
http://collection.eliterature.org/1/works/stefans__the_dreamlife_of_letters.html

Strehovec, Janez. "The software word: digital poetry as new media-based language art." *Digital Creativity* 15.3 (2004): 143-158.

Strickland, Stephanie, Cynthia Lawson Jaramillo, and Paul Ryan. "Slipping Glimpse." Electronic Literature Collection, Volume 2. URL:
http://collection.eliterature.org/2/works/strickland_slippingglimpse.html

Uribe, Ana María. "Gimnasia 3," *Vispo.com*, 1997. URL:
http://www.vispo.com/uribe/gym3.html

Wikipedia contributors. "Control flow." *Wikipedia, The Free Encyclopedia.* Wikipedia, The Free Encyclopedia, 9 Dec. 2012. Web. 1 Feb. 2013.

Young-Hae Chang Heavy Industries. "Dakota," *Young-Hae Chang Heavy Industries*, 2001. URL: http://www.yhchang.com/DAKOTA.html

ABOUT THE AUTHOR

Leonardo Flores is Full Professor of English at the University of Puerto Rico: Mayagüez Campus and the Treasurer for the Electronic Literature Organization. In 2012-2013, he was Fulbright Scholar in Digital Culture at the University of Bergen in Norway. His research areas are electronic literature (especially poetry), and its preservation via criticism, documentation, and digital archives. He is the creator and publisher of a scholarly blogging project titled *I ♥ E-Poetry* (http://iloveepoetry.com) iand a co-editor for the *Electronic Literature Collection, Volume 3*. For more information on his current work, visit http://leonardoflores.net. Contact: HC 06 Box 59800, Mayagüez, PR 00680

CHAPTER 20

Cross-perceptual Metamorphosis: From Analogue Art to 3D e-Installation

Asunción López-Varela Azcárate

Digital technologies have enabled a greater interplay of perceptual modes and opened the way to the contemporary blending of artistic domains. The first part of this paper traces the roots of analogic patterns in inter-art comparisons in Western culture, a process once termed 'ekphrasis'. The development of technologies that enable the reproduction and preservation of information simultaneously in several formats –image, photography, moving pictures or cinematography, audio, video and so on- has been increased exponentially with the introduction of digitalization in the second half of the 20th century, and the discussion on ekphrasis has given way to a growing interest on the intermedial aspects of representation. Thus, the last part of the paper focuses on the possibilities open up by 3D and virtual reality (VR) technologies for the preservation, dissemination and production of media art. In particular, it focuses on a project called "e-Installation" described in Muñoz Morcillo et al. as "a virtualized media artwork that reproduces all synesthesia, interaction, and meaning levels of the artwork."(Morcillo, Faion, Zea, Hanebeck and Robertson-von Trotha 2014: 1)

The project e-Installation takes its name from the idea of the 'e-Book' as the electronic version of a book extrapolating this analogy to media art installations. For this purpose, relevant media art installations are being virtualized by means of advanced 3D modelling, virtual reality (VR) and telepresence technologies. Initiated and hosted by ZAK | Centre for Cultural and General Studies, and the Intelligent Sensor-Actuator Systems Laboratory at Karlsruhe Institute of Technology (KIT), this project allows the virtual re-enactment of works of media art that are no longer performable or exhibited, enabling a very high level of synesthetic immersion. The example of e-Installation helps to illustrate the transformation of the synesthetic aspects, already present in the analogic paradigm, and their new potentialities in digital and 3D formats.

As early as the 4th millennium BCE, writing systems like Mesopotamian cuneiforms and Egyptian hieroglyphs used as logograms (ideograms denoting an object pictorially), phonograms (representing sounds), and determinatives (providing clues to meaning) (Davies 1990, 102 – 105). Although writings and art forms of the ancient Near East are in no way homogeneous and cultural aspects civilizations vary from a demographic, political, social, and theological viewpoint, there seem to be common features which connect and distinguish the traditions of art archiving in spite of its multiple and varied ideologies. The Sumerian and later Akkadian, Babylonian, Assyrian, Hittite (Hurrian), and Ugaritic (Canaanite) cultures developed their own new and creative views, values, narratives and representations, and in doing so, old traditions were reintegrated into the new under the guidance analogic principles. It is possible to find consistency in cult practices, court ceremonies and rituals, cosmological concepts, and ideologies that emerge in all cultural representations such as their writings, sculptures and architecture. An in-depth study of semiotic patterns within artistic heritage, beyond the scope of this paper, would show the great concern with analogies in establishing connections between the world of humans and the greater cosmos. In early Greek thought, representational forms were already defined by means of analogy. Poetry was considered painting that speaks, and painting as silent poetry (Markiewicz 1987, 535; *The Republic of Plato* 1968, 289; Campbell 1991: 357, 497, 363). The combination of words was believed to follow bio-physical ordering principles. Thus, in the *Theaetetus* Socrates relates: "Methought that I too had a dream, and I heard in my dream that the primeval letters or elements out of which you and I and all other things are compounded, have no reason or explanation." (cited in Drucker 1995: 111) The Greek word for the letters of the alphabet *stoicheia* carries the meaning elements with all the cosmological and atomistic associations of that term. One of the first descriptions of the analogic relations between the 'elements' of the world [στοιχεῖα], letters, numbers, music and the harmony of the universe can be discerned in Plato's dialogue "Timaeus":

> It is necessary to consider, what was the nature of fire, water, air and the earth before the birth of heaven and what were they then. By now nobody explained their origin, but we call them elements and consider them to be elements [στοιχεῖα] of the Universe as if we knew what the fire was and what was the rest, but it seemed clear to each at least a little an intelligent man in mind that there is no ground to compare it with some type of syllables. (*Timaeus,* 531)

In the same paragraph, Plato goes on to describe the creation of the world as a recursive modelling of parts, following the Pythagorean tradition:

> First of all, he took away one part of the whole [1], and then he separated a second part which was double the first [2], and then he took away a third part which was half as much again as the second and three times as much as the first [3], and then he took a fourth part which was twice as much as the second [4], and a fifth part which was three times the third [9], and a sixth part which was eight times the first [8], and a seventh part which was twenty-seven times the first [27]. After this he filled up the double intervals [i.e. between 1, 2, 4, 8] and the triple [i.e. between 1, 3, 9, 27] cutting off yet other portions from the mixture and placing them in the intervals, so that in each interval there were two kinds of means, the one exceeding and exceeded by equal parts of its extremes [...] (*Timaeus*, 531)

In Book One of *De Rerum Natura* Lucretius also draws the analogy between atoms and letters to explain the idea of structure: "basic bodies take a certain structure, / And have defined positions, and exchange / Their blows in certain ways. The same bodies, / With only a slight change in their structure, / Are capable of forming wood or fire. / Like letters in the words for these same things, / Ignes and lignum: with slight transpositions, / They can be nominated 'flames' or 'beams'. ' Atoms then are to bodies what letters are to words: heterogeneous, deviant, and combinatory." (Rasula and McCaffery 1998: 532). These references illustrate how pattern repetitions gradually became assimilated as ordering principles in the cultural unconscious, forming part of languages and other forms of cultural representation - writing systems, geometry, algebra, and so on.

The concept of 'ekphrasis' was initially defined as a sort of modelling mechanism for drawing analogies between words and images, the first creating a vivid description and evocation as if placed before the listener's or the reader's inner eye. As I have explained elsewhere (López-Varela 2014: 105-131), in Western languages, this modelling principle followed alphabetic patterns, with correspondences between letters and numbers. For most authors, words were inferior to images in reproducing the mimetic faithfulness of representation (Krieger 1992: 14). Aristotle's *Poetics* draws attention to the use of analogy within the different arts, each varying in relation to the medium, subject (also term agent by some translators) and manner. The Greek philosopher develops the parallel between poetry and painting and claims that although the object of both arts is the imitation of human nature in action, their means for achieving this are different. Poetry uses language, rhythm and harmony, and painting uses colour and form. Aristotle explains genre division with regards to the subject/agent who performs the analogy or mimetic act (Aristotle 1954). This close relation between poetry and painting (or 'silent poetry') was captured more importantly in Horace's *Ars poetica* as "*ut pictura poesis*" (Markiewicz 1987: 535).

The prevalence of 'the word' was reinforced by the spread of Biblical traditions in the Western world. For example, the institutionalized forms of knowledge developed in the first European universities taught the Trivium (grammar, rhetoric, and dialectic), and the Quatrivium (arithmetic, geometry, astronomy and music) not including painting and sculpture, which were considered manual rather than intellectual. Not until the 19th-century, art began to be envisioned as a complex and plastic process of creativity that might involve inter-art forms. Until recently it has not been acknowledged that art itself, whether it is in the form of poetry, painting, sculpture, architecture or music, is a synesthetic experience, materialized in the form of analogies and metaphors that bridge the senses by means of emotional aesthetic correlations.

The idea of the complete work of art or *Gesamtkunstwerk*, used first by the German writer and philosopher K.F.E. Trahndorff (1827), was reformulated by Richard Wagner in accordance with his aesthetic ideals regarding opera as a fusion of music, poetry and painting. Under the influence of Théophile Gautier and Charles Baudelaire, who in his 1857 poem "Correspondances" introduced the notion that the senses can intermingle, a topic he further developed in *Artificial Paradises*, French Parnassian artists such as Théodore de Banville, Stéphane Mallarmé, or Paul Verlaine also produced inter-art contributions. In "Voyelles" (1871), Arthur Rimbaud drew synesthetic associations between letters and colors, although this may have been the result of drug experimentation (Baron-Cohen and Harrison 1997: 9; Wettlaufer 2003). In Great Britain, William Blake was one of the first to cultivate both the pictorial and the poetic, drawing aesthetic correspondences between the two in order to incorporate greater sensorial experiences. This trend continued in the Victorian period with authors such as Algernon Charles Swinburne, the pre-Raphaelite Dante Gabriel Rossetti and his sister Christina, or Mary Ann Evans, also known as George Eliot, who wrote many of the descriptions under the influence of John Ruskin's *Modern Painters* (1843).

The 20th-century showed a gradual re-evaluation of the visual arts with the development of technologies that enabled the cheaper reproduction of images – photography and moving pictures or cinematography. There innovations enabled a greater interplay of perceptual modes, enhancing diverse forms of emotional and aesthetic charge, alternating between showing (*mimesis*) and telling (*diegesis*), and enabling the projection of simultaneous occurrences in narrative, for instance, by borrowing techniques from montage in the visual arts and sculpture.

Many avant-garde experiments, such as those by Marcel Duchamp or Picabia, cultivated crossings not only between poetry and the visual arts but including other arts. The Futurists were open to new multi-sensory experiments, particularly the impact of typography, ink colours, typefaces, paper texture, bookbinding techniques, etc. They brought to the fore the material aspects of language by focusing on graphic coding, the acoustic as well as the visual aspects. Art begins to be contemplated as a process of expression and execution, freeing itself from analogic conceptualization, and figurative relations (Merleau-Ponty 1945: 21, 23 and 1964: 32).

In the second half of the century, graphic designers such as the Japanese Freeman Lan, the Dutch Maarten Evenhuis, the Finish Pirjo Paolo, or the Polish Wasilewski, Tandensz Piechura and Jacek Povemba have used the interplay between texts and images in order to manifest the plasticity of art. Another example is the changing role of images over the architecture of the buildings as another structural layer. Nowadays, digital media adds information data through screens able to read augmented reality. Objects, and not just buildings, can carry live visuals and information, including a history of the object in the form of a visual timeline. With the introduction of digital technologies and multimodal representations, the discussion on 'ekphrasis' has shifted toward the study of intermedial aspects and the perceptual and cognitive cross-sensory patterns that emerge with digitalization.

Cross-sensory patterns are present in digital representations because these direct our attention simultaneously to more perceptual modalities than their analogic counterparts. For example, while printed text and image were fixed, their screen digital versions can be easily relocated even in the most basic text programs. Copy-pasting and the use of Photoshop techniques are part of our everyday life. Other computer programs and software applications enable sophisticated forms of kinesis for letters and images used in contemporary forms of e-literature and online concrete poetry. As Lanfranco Aceti writes in the editorial to *Live Visuals*

> iPads and iPhones – followed by a generation of smarter and smarter devices – have brought a radical change in the way reality is experienced, captured, uploaded and shared. These processes allow

reality to be experienced with multiple added layers, allowing viewers to re-capture, re-upload and re-share, creating yet further layers over the previous layers that were already placed upon the 'original.' This layering process, this thickening of meanings, adding of interpretations, references and even errors [...] (Leonardo Electronic Almanac 2013: 8)

Correlations, analogies and mappings between the world of objects and their representations are becoming increasingly layered and cross-modal. This is particularly so in immersive virtual environments which display multi-sensory associations in order to better capture the user's attention and direct it in different ways. For example, some recent applications of Virtual Reality are used for pain relief and in order to direct attention away from the source of physical discomfort (Reif and Alhalabi; Gold, Belmont, Katharine, Thomas 2007: 536–544). Dutch neuroscientist Peter Meijer uses a system called vOICe that transcodes video from a small camera into synthetic audio in an attempt to use sound to provide visual information to those with little or no vision.[1] He explains that in this project they "are interested in forms of learned synesthesia (acquired synesthesia) that might result from machine-generated cross-modal mappings." (Meijer n.d.) Over time, blind users of vOICe seem to integrate image transcoded into sound, as functional vision. Their project performs a form of sensory substitution that operates by mapping an otherwise absent modality into an existing one; absent vision into existing hearing, in the case of the vOICe (Whitelaw 2006, 259–76). Another example is the Eyeborg, a device developed by Adam Montandan that incorporates the auditory and visual spectra. It makes it possible for people with color-blindness to hear colors (Montandon n.d.).

Neural plasticity is a topic that attracts much interest in neuroscience. It has become clear that multi-sensory processing is a widespread phenomenon in the human mind, and that it helps provide a unified experience of the position of our bodies in space. It does so by means of a combination of vision, touch, and proprioception, which yields such information as the position of the body in space, including muscular and weight sensations. Synesthesia (from the Greek σύν *syn* "together" and αἴσθησις *aisthēsis*, "sensation") has been defined as "stimulation in one sensory or cognitive stream leads to associated experiences in a second, unstimulated stream" (Hubbard 2007: 193) and characterized as a "startling sensory blending" (Cytowic 1996: 17). It is a remarkable experience of cross-sensory perception that brings to the fore neural plasticity. Synesthesia may arise not only on the basis of exteroceptive sensations (externally stimulated

---

[1] See http://www.seeingwithsound.com/

sensations such as hearing, sight, etc.). Interoceptive and proprioceptive (internally generated) sensations may also contribute. Furthermore, interoceptive sensations are unconscious and related to the most basic emotions of biological beings (fear, compassion, etc.). (Hochel, Milan, Martin, Gonzalez, Garcia, Tornay, & Vila. 2008: 703-723).

The idea that perception takes the form of mental representations is widely accepted. A perceptual state, such as hearing a sound, is caused by physical external or internal stimulation (via the mediation of non-sensory processing) and its content co-varies with changes in the environment and in the emotional state of the perceiving individual as well as the mental relations he or she stablish with previous similar situations. Richard Cytowic, one of the pioneers in the study of synesthesia, found that it is "involuntary but elicited," and that synesthetic perceptions are "durable and generic". He also mentioned that it aids in recollection by evoking a certain stimulus; "accompanied by a sense of certitude that he links to William James' description of religious ecstasy, and in particular with "knowledge that is experienced directly, an illumination that is accompanied by a feeling of certitude." (Cytowic 1989; Cytowic 1996: 23–31) Indeed synesthesia is related to good visual perception in photographic memory, and also to an exceptional capacity to create mental and emotional associations that help in retrieving a stimulus. Synesthetic associations are so vivid that they are visualized as existing outside the mind as projections. They even bear specific emotions and feelings of physical and mental comfort or discomfort. Hypermnesia (exceptionally increased capacity for remembering) and synesthesia are also mutually connected.

Neurological evidence supports this complex nature of cross-sensory connectivity (Bargary & Mitchell 2008: 335-342). Linguistic studies point in the same direction. For example, terms such as "bright" or "dark" are often thought in association to sounds "high" and "low", and to tactile experiences like "warm" and "cool", as well as colors such as "white" and "black". Furthermore, analogies between music melodies, rhythm, and mechanical motion occur in relation to audio proprioceptive synesthesia (Galeyev 1993: 76-78). Optophono synesthesia refers to visual experiences as a consequence of sound, and 'kinesichromia' refers to sensations of color associated to movement.

Some scholars argue that cross-sensory perception modes, such as synesthesia, are higher cognitive-linguistic phenomena that occur in brain regions endowed with multisensory neurons (Simner 2007: 23-29; Simner 2011). Additionally, in the case of local cross-activation, research shows that some senses are more integrated than others. For example, we commonly think of the gustative sense as a combination of taste, smell, and texture. And most people experience the mental pictures of sequences (numbers, letters, weekdays, months, etc.) in spatial configurations that move from the bottom upwards as numbers increase, and from right to left (small numbers are mentally placed on the left and large numbers on the right for right-handed people and the other way around for left-handed). Involuntary hand or eye movements evidence the mental location of these processes. The SNARC effect (numerical association of response codes, as this effect is called) takes place in the reverse direction in cultures who use writing systems from left-to-right (Eagleman 2009: 1268).

Dr. Ramachandran, Director of the Center for Brain and Cognition at the University of California, argues that synesthesia is much more common in artists, poets, and novelists, because of a potentially increased hyper-connectivity in their brains (Romano 2002). Besides, there seems to be evidence that some complex forms of synesthesia are not just biophysical and genetic, but that they can be learnt. For instance, Simon Baron-Cohen insists on the primacy of the limbic system, and thus of emotion, over more cortical or rational processes, and he mentions as evidence the Cross-Modal Transfer (CMT) hypothesis which posits that infants can recognize objects in more than one modality because of their ability to represent objects in imaginative abstract form (Baron-Cohen 1996; Ramachandran and Hubbard 2001: 3–34). The possibility of synesthesia being related to the mirror neurons present in motor areas of the brain and linked to the development of inter-subjectivity and empathy is an exciting area yet to be explored. Research also shows that the sharing of emotional patterns (inter-subjectivity) may be developed in simulated conditions such as storytelling in infancy (LópezVarela 2010: 125-147).

Studies on synesthesia connect research on neuroscience and Virtual Reality with philosophical questions related to aesthetics, the sublime experience of art and a desire for its hypothetical plasticity, evident in the first conceptions of *ekphrasis* presented at the beginning of this paper. However, the cross-activation model does not explain all forms of synesthesia. A second theory defends the hypothesis that some types of synesthesia may be attributed to "disinhibited feedback" from a "multisensory nexus", such as temporo-parietal-occipital junction. The main principle in disinhibited feedback is the idea that the information does not only travel from the primary sensory areas to association areas in the parietal lobe, but that it also travels in other directions, from "high ordered" cortical regions to basic sensory areas. This process might explain why the activation of visual cortical areas when listening to sound tones is more intense in synesthetes than in non-synesthetes (Mykus, 2013, 440).

Mitchell Whitelaw has documented the correspondence between research on synesthesia and the evolution of aesthetics from mysticism to contemporary avant-garde, and has provided some interesting examples of transcoded audiovisuals (Whitelaw 2004; Whitelaw 2006: 259–76). Whitelaw's main concern is if transcoded audiovisuals realize the synesthetic ideal or literalize analogic patterns. His examples of contemporary art show that cross-wiring from one sense to another, for example audio to vision, is automatic, literally hardwired, embodied in the analog electronics (Fischinger 1932; Fox 2005; Gadow 2005; Hodgin 2007).[2] However, Whitelaw also indicates that the mapping takes place in a different way; as a modulated construction depending on the cultural/technical artifact; almost as rhythmic and visual correlations between sound, form and movement that trigger a particular mental cross-sensory process. Unlike sensory substitution, which involves long-term integration and interaction by means of new channels, artificial synesthesia enhanced by transcoded audiovisuals, or by Virtual Reality, is bounded to specific aesthetic objects that cannot realize permanent perceptual transformations.

Whitelaw explains that "While synesthesia offers a neurological analogy for the generation (poetics) of fused AV, this correlated quality leads into the neuroscience of perception, and thus offers a way to frame these works from the other side, the side of reception (or aesthetics)." (Whitelaw 2006: 268) As an example, he mentions that in perception, initial attention is captured in the recognition of uncategorized objects within the perceptual field, and that only later, our cognitive apparatus 'binds' elements that detect correlations in the perceptual system. In other words, our brain fills in the missing details in the image of the Dalmatian dog, presented as unconnected undifferenciated dots in Whitelaw's example (McLaren 1940; see also McLaren 1971) He cites Ramachandran and Hirstein's work in suggesting that artists and designers "tease the system with as many of these 'potential object' clues as possible" because this search is a pleasurable activity (Whitelaw 2006, 269; Ramachandran and Hirstein 1999: 31).

If sensory substitution shows that these channels can be re-wired, studies of cross-modal perception indicate that they are barely even distinct, at least in the case of audiovisual representation. Whitelaw reviews a number of experiments that show the range of these mutual influences: how vision can alter the content and spatial location of perceived sound; and how sound can alter the perceived intensity and timing of visual stimuli. In particular, he discusses an experiment in

---

[2] For an extended description of contemporary works in audio-visual performance, Gibson 2013, 214-229, and Gibson, *Virtual DJ*.

which subjects were presented with two moving dots on intersecting paths (Sekuler, Sekuler and Lau, Renee 1997: 308). In one mode of perception the dots pass each other without touching; in the other they collide and bounce off each other. It was found that in the absence of sound the former interpretation was dominant. Adding a brief sound at the crossing point biased perception strongly towards collision. Whitelaw cites this example as a case of cross-modal binding where correlated stimuli in different modalities become fused into a coherent whole.

More importantly, Whitelaw notes that the sensory and affective textures of a media substrate, what he terms media infrastructures or inframedia, below or within the mainline of electronic media, are critical for perception; even more so than content or the technological artifact in itself (Whitelaw 2001, 51). The fusion of perceptual modes in digitalization occurs in a concrete space, characterized by a particular surface, depth, etc., and time. Thus,

> Instead of mapping signal anthropomorphically on to perceptual "inputs," these works show us where signal and affect meet or overlap, as well as where they diverge; they show us signal passing into, out of and through perception. These works also direct us to the map – the abstract space of possible transformations between signals. Thus, the domain of transformation is also inframedial, a key structure in digital media forms and cultures. (Whitelaw 2006, 273)

He goes on to add that "in most digital media objects, the map is inextricable from the residue or artifact it shapes. We perceive only the output – the image, sound or form – in which the input and its transformations are collapsed" so that the digital work 'feels' outside any kind of fixed mapping. Whitelaw situates the map as the space of correlation, where "the feeling of noesis or revelation common to both synesthesia and cross-modal binding, could be described as the affect of the map." (Whitelaw 2006: 273-4)

Somatotopy is a one-to-one correspondence of an area of the body to a specific position on the brain. Wilder Penfield's sensory homunculus, a non-uniform 2D map of this phenomenon, describes how sensory information from parts of the body - color, character visual processing, sound pitch and spatial tactile sensations - has an underlying structure that can be modeled by a spatial representation in the form of sense 2D maps corresponding to cortical sites in the brain.³ However, it is not clear how maps function in digital 3D (three dimensional) environments that, as Whitelaw indicates, might 'feel' outside any kind of fixed mapping.

Although 3D technologies existed in some form since the beginning of cinematography, the high cost of production and display of these films relegated them to special IMAX theatres that became more popular in the late 1980s. The standard for shooting live-action films in 3D involves using two cameras mounted so that their lenses are about as far apart from each other as the average pair of human eyes. Images are recorded from two perspectives which use parallax to provide the illusion of depth. This enhances the perception of depth, placing the viewer inside the art work instead of facing it as an external observer. The earliest method for presenting 3D was the use of anaglyph techniques, where two images are superimposed using two filters, read and cyan. Glasses with colored filters in each eye separate the images by cancelling the filter color. The first anaglyph movie was invented in 1915 by Edwin S Porter and these 3D movies became particularly popular after the 1950s and until the emergence of IMAX in the 1980s, when other polarization systems became available.

The project presented in this paper, e-Installation, is pioneer in the use of 3D modeling and telepresence technologies in archiving and presenting media art. e-Installation is oriented to offer a long-term solution for the archiving and virtual re-enactment of works of media art that are no longer performable or exhibited. In particular, space-based installation art, where three-dimensional perception is fundamental because these projects, presented in temporal exhibitions in museums or other centers⁴, are often designed to transform the perception of space and time by means of enhancing synesthetic qualities that help immerse the viewer in a broader multimodal sensory experience.

Installation art implies the dissolution between art and life, and presents the artwork as part of the sensory experience of life (Kaprow 2003: 6 and 12). Thus, its roots can be traced back to the *Gesamtkunstwerk* or total work of art, mentioned before. In its origins, the idea was inspired by the inclusion of three major art forms in classical Greek performances: painting, poetic writing and dance/music. Wagner's operas can be seen as a precursor of these complex forms,

---

³ Penfield's Illustration of a Homunculus - a somatotopic brain map is at http://www.intropsych.com/ch02_human_nervous_system/homunculus.html

⁴ Exhibition Lab at New York's American Museum of Natural History, the Mattress Factory <http://www.mattress.org/>, the Museum of Installation in London <http://www.artdesigncafe.com/Museum-of-Installation-Nico-de-Oliveira-Nicola-Oxley-2008> or, the Center for Art and Media Karlsruhe (ZKM) <http://on1.zkm.de/zkm/e/about>

for he created a web of leitmotifs associated with characters and recurring themes, many of them coming from the Germanic tradition and Arthurian legends. Stage architecture and ambience were manipulated in order to encourage a state of total artistic immersion in the audience. Installation art, which became widespread in 20th-century avant-gardes and in the work of artists such as Marcel Duchamp and his use of the readymade, Kurt Schwitters' *Merz* art, and the conceptual art of the 1960s, has a similar aim (for more information see Bishop 2005; Rosenthal 2003).

The ephemeral character of installation art makes its preservation difficult (Ferriani 2013). Many works require maintenance and take up exhibition space in museums and galleries. Thus, important pieces of cultural heritage are dismantled, temporality unavailable or no longer accessible to the public. Traditional audio-visual archiving methods such as photography, audio and video do not capture the multimodal immersive potential of most installations. Besides, nowadays many projects employ mobile connections, augmented reality, and online applications that would require and archiving method that relies on 3D modeling. The project "e-Installation", developed by Jesús Muñoz Morcillo, Florian Faion, Antonio Zea, Uwe D. Hanebeck and Caroline Y. Robertson-von Trotha allows the synesthetic documentation of media art via telepresence technologies that preserve all kinetic and sensorial experiences as well as the sense of spatial depth in 3D modeling.[5]

> e-Installation materializes the idea of synesthetic documentation in the form of photogrammetrically comprehended, 3D-modelled and programmed artwork, and a suitable telepresence-based visualization of the virtualized media artwork using, e.g., head-mounted displays (HMD), body tracking systems and haptic interfaces. It enables the virtualization of material parts of the installation, integrating all digital software components and audio-visual signals, as well as all kinetic and interaction patterns, in a consistently playable, dynamic, and interactive 3D model (Muñoz Morcillo *et al.* 2014, 4).

---

[5] e-Installation is an interdisciplinary project at the Karlsruhe Institute of Technology based on a perception-related documentation concept as formulated by art theorist Jesús Muñoz Morcillo in "Überlieferung von Medienkunst und digitale Nachlassverwaltung" in: Caroline Y. Robertson-von Trotha & Robert Hauser (Eds.): *Neues Erbe. Aspekte, Perspektiven und Konsequenzen der Digitalen Überlieferung*, KIT Scientific Publishing, 2011, S.127. The initiators and members of the project are: ZAK | Centre for Cultural and General Studies, and the Intelligent Sensor-Actuator Systems Laboratory (ISAS),

The cross-modal condition of synesthesia can be an asset when planning for complex user interaction in 3D space. Thus, in e-Installation there is no 'simulation' but "a realistic interaction with a 'living document' that re-enacts all features of the real artifact" (Muñoz Morcillo *et al*. 2014: 4). Another interesting project concerning the idea of virtual art as a 'living document' is Steve Gibson's *Virtual VJ*, where user's movements in 3D space activate artificial synesthesia of audio and visual stimuli and space becomes tangible. When light is instantiated in synch with sound and one enters a spatial zone one feels as if that zone has some kind of weight, presence or boundary, confirming the simulation of what Gibson terms 'optophonokinesia', the experience of sight and sound in relation to movement. For instance, in *Virtual VJ,* raising the hands will generally produce a rise in audio volume and an increase in image opacity. In this project, changes are logically mapped to movements so that results are predictable and repeatable, and users can gain a sense of control that they would not otherwise have in more 'randomly' mapped spatial environments.

To conclude this paper, I would like to point out that art installations can be contemplated as departures from traditional architecture and sculpture, which place their focus on fixed forms in a particular locations, disregarding any Platonic ideal form. Installations emphasize the plasticity of art and the total immersion in the art work, nowadays facilitated with web, digital, and mobile based applications where the user is not just immersed in the sensory experience but expected to take part in it. In this way, installations focus on the direct and individual experience of each participant entering the work, no longer an analogic mapped representation (Grau 2004).

e-Installation is a project aimed at the multisensory archiving of art objects and as the ultimate destination for documental support for such works. At the same time, e-Installation is also capable of capturing by means of tele-present synesthesia those spatiotemporal aspects that make audiences 'feel' art. The simulation enabled by e-Installation transcends the materiality of art. It moves beyond its analogue physical limitations in order to enact new experiences that speak about the blurring of boundaries, the flux of material elements and the intermedial (a termed coined by Dick Higgins within the Fluxus network) plasticity of art, something that many artists had been seeking for a long time.

Note: This research was supported by a grant from the Ministry of Education (Spain) for a research-stay at Harvard University. The author is indebted to the Harvard Institute of World Literature and its director, Prof. David Damrosch, for various forms of academic support. The author also would like to acknowledge Jesús Muñoz Morcillo, Florian Faion, Antonio Zea, Uwe D. Hanebeck, Caroline Y. Robertson-von Trotha for the use of photographs and information on their project.

REFERENCES

Aristotle. *Poetics*. Translated by I. Bywater. New York: Modern Library, 1954

Bargary, Gary & Mitchell, Kevin. "Synaesthesia and cortical connectivity." *Trends in Neuroscience* 31.7 (2008): 335-342.
<DOI 10.1016/j.tins.2008.03>

Baron-Cohen, Simon and John Harrison, eds. *Synaesthesia: Classic and Contemporary Essays*. Oxford: Blackwell Publishers, 1997.

Baron-Cohen, Simon. "Is There a Normal Phase of Synaesthesia in Development?" *Psyche* 2.27(1996)
<http://psyche.cs.monash.edu.au/v2/psyche-2-27-baron_cohen.html>

Bishop, Claire. *Installation Art a Critical History.* London: Tate, 2005.

Campbell, David. *Greek Lyric: Stesichorus, Ibycus, Simonides, and Others.* Vol. III. Harvard University Press: Loeb Classical Library, 1991.

Cytowic, Richard. *Synesthesia: A Union of the Senses.* New York: Springer Verlag, 1989.

Cytowic, Richard. 1996. "Synesthesia, Phenomenology and Neuropsychology: A Review of Current Knowledge." In *Synesthesia: Classic and Contemporary Readings* edited by John E. Harrison and Simon Baron-Cohen, 23-31. London: Blackwell. Originally published in Psyche 2.10 (1996) <http://www.theassc.org/files/assc/2346.pdf>

Drucker, Johanna. *The Alphabetic Labyrinth: Letters in History and Imagination.* London:Thames & Hudson Ltd, 1995.

Eagleman, David M. "The objectification of overlearned sequences: A new view of spatial sequence synesthesia." *Cortex* 45 (2009): 1266-1277, < www.elsevier.com/locate/cortex>

Ferriani, Barbara. *Ephemeral Monuments: History and Conservation of Installation Art.* Los Angeles: Getty Publications, 2013

Fischinger, Oskar. "Sounding Ornaments" *Deutsche Allgemeine Zeitung*, 1932 <http://www.oskarfischinger.org/Sounding.htm>

Fox, Robin. *Backscatter.* Videorecording. Melbourne: Synesthesia Records SYN012 DVD, 2005

Galeyev, B.M. *Man, Art and Technology: Problem of Synesthesia in Art* (in Russian). Russia: Kazan Univ. Publishers, 1987. Translated in *Leonardo Electronic Almanac* 26 (2013): 76-78.

Gadow, Andrew. *Techne.* DVD-R courtesy of the artist. Hodgin, Robert. 2007. "Trentemøller and Me."< http://www.flight404.com/blog/?p=52>

Gibson, Steven."Simulating Synesthesia in Spatially-Based Real-time Audio-Visual Performance". Leonardo Electronic Almanac 19.3(2013): 214-229 Leonardo, the International Society for the Arts, Sciences and Technology. Istanbul: Sabanci Universit.

Gibson, Steve. *Virtual DJ*, 2005-10. <http://www.telebody.ws/VirtualDJ>

Grau, Oliver. *Virtual Art, from Illusion to Immersion*, MIT Press, 2004.

Gold, Jeffrey I.; Belmont, Katharine A.; Thomas, David A. "The Neurobiology of Virtual Reality Pain Attenuation". *CyberPsychology & Behavior* 10.4 (2007): 536–544. <doi:10.1089/cpb.2007.9993>

Hubbard, EM. 'Neurophysiology of synesthesia', *Current Psychiatry Reports* 9.3 (2007): 193-199.
Kaprow, Allan. *Essays on the Blurring of Art and Life*. Edited by Jeff Kelley. Berkeley: University of California Press, 2003.
Krieger, Murray. *Ekphrasis: The Illusion of the Natural Sign*. Baltimore and London: Johns Hopkins University Press, 1992.
López-Varela Azcárate, Asunción. "Antiabecedarian Desires: Odd Narratology and Digital Textuality," edited by Carolina Fernández Castrillo, Special issue. *Icono 14*. 12.2 (2014): 29-55. <DOI 10.7195/ri14.v12i2.727>.
López-Varela Azcárate, Asunción. "Exploring Intercultural Relations from the Intersubjective Perspectives offered through Creative Art in Multimodal Formats (SIIM research program)." *Lexia 5-6* (2010): 125-147. Universitá degli studi di Torino Revista di Simiotica Centro Interdipartimentale di Ricerche sulla Comunicazione.
Markiewicz, Henryk. "Ut Pictura Poesis: A History of the Topos and the Problem," *New Literary History* 18.3 (1987): 535-558
Meijer, Peter. "Artificial Synesthesia for Synthetic Vision." <http://www.seeingwithsound.com/asynesth.htm>
Merleau-Ponty, Maurice. *Phénoménologie de la perception*, Paris: Les Éditions Gallimard, 1945.
Merleau-Ponty, Maurice. *L'oeil et l'esprit*, Paris: Les Éditions Gallimard, 1964.
Montandon, Adam. "Colourblind Eyeborg Colours to Sound" <http://www.adammontandon.com/neil-harbisson-the-cyborg/>
Muñoz Morcillo, Jesús."Überlieferung von Medienkunst und digitale Nachlassverwaltung". In *Neues Erbe. Aspekte, Perspektiven und Konsequenzen der digitalen Überlieferung*. Edited by Caroline Y. Robertson-von Trotha and Robert Hauser, Germany: KIT Scientific Publishing , 2014, 123-140.
Muñoz Morcillo, Jesús, Florian Faion, Antonio Zea, Uwe D. Hanebeck, Caroline Y. Robertson-von Trotha. 2014"e-Installation: Synesthetic Documentation of Media Art via Telepresence Technologies." *ZAK | Centre for Cultural and General Studies & Intelligent Sensor-Actuator System Laboratory (ISAS), Karlsruhe Institute of Technology (KIT)* <arXiv:1408.1362>
<http://arxiv-web3.library.cornell.edu/abs/1408.1362>

Mykus, Nina. "Approaches in synesthesia research: neurocognitive aspects and diagnostic criteria." *Interdisciplinary Description of Complex Systems* 11.4 (2013): 436-445.

Plato. *Timaeus*. <http://www.gutenberg.org/ebooks/1572>.

Plato. *The Republic*. Edition, translation and introduction by Allan Bloom. New York: Basic Books, 1968.

Ramachandran, Vilayanur S. and William Hirstein. "The Science of Art: A Neurolgical Theory of Aesthetic Experience." *Journal of Consciousness Studies* 6.6–7(1999): 15–51. <http://www.imprint.co.uk/jcs_6_6-7.html>

Ramachandran, Vilayanur S. and Edward. M. Hubbard. *Synaesthesia—A Window Into Perception, Thought and LanguageJournal of Consciousness Studies*, 8.12 (2001): 3–34.
<http://cbc.ucsd.edu/pdf/Synaesthesia%20-%20JCS.pdf>

Rasula, Jeff and Steve McCaffery. *Imagining Language*. MIT Press, 1998.

Rosenthal, Mark. *Understanding Installation Art: From Duchamp to Holzer*. Munich: Prestel Verlag, 2003.

Sekuler, Robert, Allison B. Sekuler, and Lau, Renee. "Sound Alters Visual Motion Perception." *Nature* 385 (1997): 308 <DOI 10.1038/385308a0> <http://www.nature.com/nature/journal/v385/n6614/pdf/385308a0.pdf>

Simner, Julia. "Beyond perception: Synaesthesia as a psycholinguistic phenomenon." *Trends in Cognitive Sciences*, 11.1 (2007): 23-29.

Simner, Julia. "Defining synaesthesia." *British Journal of Psychology*, 2011.
<DOI 10.1348/000712610X528305>

The International Society for the Arts, Sciences and Technology. Istanbul: Sabanci University *Leonardo Electronic Almanac* 19.3 (2013) <http://www.leoalmanac.org/>

Trahndorff, Karl Friedrich Eusebius. *Ästhetik oder Lehre von Weltanschauung und Kunst*. Berlin: Maurer, 1827.

Wettlaufer, Alexandra. *In the Mind's Eye: The Visual Impulse in Diderot, Baudelaire and Ruskin*. Amsterdam: Rodopi, 2003.

Whitelaw, Michael.. "Synesthesia and Cross Modality in Contemporary Audiovisuals," *Senses & Society* 3.3 (2006): 259–76

Whitelaw, Mitchell. *Metacreation: Art and Artificial Life*. MIT Press, 2004.

Whitelaw, Mitchell.. "Inframedia Audio." *Artlink* 21.3 (2001): 49–52

About the Author

López-Varela Azcárate López-Varela is professor at Facultad Filología, Universidad Complutense de Madrid since 1994. She holds a PhD Anglo-American Culture and Literary Studies. Her research interests are Comparative Literature, World Literature, Cultural Studies and Intermedial Semiotics. In 2007 he created the research program Studies on Intermediality and Intercultural Mediation SIIM.

López-Varela has been visiting scholar at Brown University (2010) and Harvard University (2013) and visiting professor at Delhi University (2011), Beijng Language and Culture University (every year since 2012) and Kazakh National University, Almaty (every year since 2013). She is a member of Hermeneia Research Group at Universitat de Barcelona Mitocriticism Research Group at Complutense Madrid and Semiótica Comunicación y Cultura

A proactive member of the profession, López-Varela is in the Executive Committee of the Association of Alumni of the Real Colegio Complutense in Harvard University, and in the European Network of Comparative Literary Studies (*ex officio*). She is also external evaluator for the EU Educational, Audiovisual & Culture Executive Agency EACEA the European Union Research Program Horizon 2020 , the postgraduate programs of Dublin City University and collaborates as advisor with the Department of Romance Studies Harvard University.

Lopez-Varela is keen in giving international visibility to researh by colleagues and younger peers, and editorial activities are a clear sign in this direction. She is Editor International Journal of the Humanities SJR Rank Associate International Editor Journal Comparative Literature and Aesthetics Editorial Board Member and Scientific advisor of journals such as: de Signis Journal of the Federación Latinoamericana de Semiótica, Cultura International Journal of Philosophy of Culture and Axiology, Southern Semiotic Review, HyperCultura, "Studii şi cercetări ştiinţifice Seria filologie at University Vasile Alecsandri, and the Cypriot Journal of Educational Sciences CJES at the World Education Center. Between 2008 and 2013, she was review-editor of ClCWeb Journal of Comparative Literature and Culture. She also collaborates with other publishing houses such as Aracne editrice S.r.l., and MacMillan.

www.ingramcontent.com/pod-product-compliance
Lightning Source LLC
Chambersburg PA
CBHW020537300426
44111CB00008B/704